Martin Erdmann

THE TRIUMPH OF PROGRESSIVISM

A Religious Quest for an Ideal Society

Volume 5
Abridged by Beate Gsell
Translated by Hannah M. Munday

VOX MEDIA

Verax Vox Media
780 Morning St. • Worthington, OH 43085 • United States of America
VeraxVoxMedia.com

The Triumph of Progressivism
Vol. 5: A Religious Quest for an Ideal Society

Copyright ©: 2021 by Martin Erdmann
Hardcover ISBN: 978-1-7347541-7-9
Paperback ISBN: 978-1-7347541-5-5
Date of Publication: January 2021
Cover image: Estelle Chérie Erdmann
Cover design: John Battenfield

Dedication

This book is dedicated to all the friends who have supported me in many different ways throughout the project. Without their help, this substantial work would not have been possible. I extend my special thanks to the following people: Beate Gsell, who produced an excellent abridgement of the three German volumes; Hannah M. Munday, who adeptly and diligently translated the abridged German manuscript into English; Jörg Schwagmeier, who formatted the texts for publication; and my wife Joy and children Estelle and Johannes, as well as my mother Alide Erdmann, sister Beate Gsell, and brother-in-law Felix Gsell, whose love and encouragement constantly motivated me to finish this project well. The glory for all that I do belongs to God alone, as revealed to us through His Son, Jesus Christ.

Revelation 19:6-9,11-16 (King James Version)
And I heard as it were the voice of a great multitude, and as the voice of many waters, and as the voice of mighty thunderings, saying, Alleluia: for the Lord God omnipotent reigneth. Let us be glad and rejoice, and give honour to him: for the marriage of the Lamb is come, and his wife hath made herself ready. And to her was granted that she should be arrayed in fine linen, clean and white: for the fine linen is the righteousness of saints. And he saith unto me, Write, Blessed are they which are called unto the marriage supper of the Lamb. And he saith unto me, These are the true sayings of God.

And I saw heaven opened, and behold a white horse; and he that sat upon him was called Faithful and True, and in righteousness he doth judge and make war. His eyes were as a flame of fire, and on his head were many crowns; and he had a name written, that no man knew, but he himself. And he was clothed with a vesture dipped in blood: and his name is called The Word of God. And the armies which were in heaven followed him upon white horses, clothed in fine linen, white and clean. And out of his mouth goeth a sharp sword, that with it he should smite the nations: and he shall rule them with a rod of iron: and he treadeth the winepress of the fierceness and wrath of Almighty God. And he hath on his vesture and on his thigh a name written, King Of Kings, And Lord Of Lords..

Author

Dr. Martin Erdmann studied theology at Columbia International University, SC (Master of Divinity), the University of Basel, Switzerland and the University of Aberdeen, Scotland (Master of Theology). In 1999, he was awarded a doctoral degree in Modern Church History at Brunel University London, England. The senate of the Károli Gáspár University, Budapest, Hungary, conferred on him a Habilitation degree (Dr. habil.) in Systematic Theology in 2017. In 1996, he founded Online Communication Systems, Inc. in Columbus, Ohio. For four years he headed up the New Testament department of the Staatsunabhängige Theologische Hochschule Basel (State-independent Theological Seminary), Switzerland. In his position as Senior Scientist at the University Hospital in Basel, he was involved in researching the ethical implications of Nanotechnology for five years. From 2003 to 2010 he was Assistant Professor of Biblical Studies (distance education) at Patrick Henry College, Purcellville, VA. Since 2003 he has directed the Verax Institute (Christian apologetics).

Dr. Erdmann is married to Joy and has two children, Estelle Chérie and Johannes Luc.

Foreword

Faster, higher stronger – the motto of the Olympic Games now applies to the whole world. Whoever wants to achieve anything does so by progress. Progress has brought humanity to accomplish great things while simultaneously driving it into the abyss. The young generation is now rebelling against this, seeking to turn the tide at "five minutes to twelve" with waves of protest around the world. As the latest machines are given human features and voices through Artificial Intelligence, an ominous feeling comes over us all. "Where is this leading to?" we ask.

Where does the quest for progress come from in the first place? This is an equally important question. Dr. Martin Erdmann draws a trajectory from the beginning of the idea of progress, through its entanglement with religious zeal, to its development into a civil religion in politics and economics. The author has chosen to examine Progressivism largely through the example of the U.S.A., since its 500-year history offers a prime demonstration of the trajectory – while also making repeated references to the situation in Europe. He shows the reader how the Bible views man's ambitions to perfect his own nature and to shape society according to his ideals. The Christian, under the authority of God, realizes that history is underpinned by a divine plan. This good plan is recorded in the Bible and brings comfort and confidence to those who believe in God.

The author, who holds a doctorate in church history and systematic theology, provides an overview of how Progressivism emerged from Greek philosophy and how it has developed practically since the seventeenth century. In order to discern deviations from the biblical message, the author dedicates an entire chapter to presenting the Gospel from the perspective of the Reformers. This concise summary is a treasure in its own right.

The theologian explains how American Progressivism was inspired by the doctrine of Postmillennialism, which teaches that there will be no literal thousand-year reign, but rather a period of global reformation before the return of Christ. The author shows how Americans have pursued human perfection and elevated themselves above other peoples, such as Indians and slaves, in order to build a totalitarian society. The road to the "kingdom of God on earth" led directly to war. Dr. Martin Erdmann explains in detail how the well-known evangelist Charles G. Finney beguiled the Christian population, and given the great impact Finney had on Evangelicalism, it is troubling to realize that this branch of Christianity has been influenced by mystical and esoteric beliefs while supposedly presenting the biblical Gospel.

Progressivism was the driving force behind American Imperialism. The First World War seemed to put a damper on belief in progress: instead of the promised heaven on earth, vast areas of the world lay in ruins and millions of people lost their lives. But here Progressivism showed its true colors. This ultimate anti-Christian religion refuses to tolerate a life guided by biblical principles such as charity, peace, and the worship of God. It seizes state power and claims for itself the honor and devotion that religion gives to God. Dr.

Martin Erdmann offers a multifaceted portrayal of this so-called civil religion which has been spread throughout the globe by aggressive American Imperialism. Since belief in progress is based on European philosophies and ideologies, Europeans are also well acquainted with it without realizing that it is founded on Progressivism. It has infiltrated Christian congregations in various forms, including that of the "Social Gospel." Believing that they are doing something good, churches act as the extended arm of an anti-Christian religion which misleads them with its Christian vocabulary.

The author's goal is therefore to inform readers of the origin, nature, and consequences of Progressivism. He reveals the true motives and aims of those in power, who either deceive people with fine promises or – if people are unwilling to obey them – use violence. American governments have pretended to apply the "gospel of social benefit" in many countries, while in reality instigating or interfering with one catastrophic war after another. Their eventual aim is to introduce a centrally governed world order. The word "triumph" in the title is to be understood in this respect; those in power seem to be achieving their goal. However, it carries a degree of irony and could be placed in inverted commas, since the author knows who the ultimate Victor is.

This book is a summary of the three-volume work *The Triumph of Progressivism*. It is an exciting historical book with well-researched facts and a comprehensive presentation of developments in church history and world politics, conveyed in a clear and fluent literary style. Anyone who wishes to examine the subject more closely and is conversant with the German language can consult the three volumes, which also contain many explanations of terms. This could lead to a revival among Christian congregations, turning them again to the heart of the Gospel. Just as in the days of the Reformation.

Beate Gsell
Journalist

Table of Contents

Dedication III

Author V

Foreword VII

Mysticism as the basis of American Postmillennialism (Chs. 1-4) 1

1 The continuous development of civilization 2
1.1 Metaphysical model of the idea of progress 2
1.2 Secularized model of the idea of progress 5
1.3 Conflicting views on the idea of progress 8
1.4 Ideological reversal of the idea of progress 11
2 The Gospel of the Reformation 12
2.1 Authoritative self-revelation of the sovereign God 13
2.2 Full reliance on God's work of salvation 14
2.3 Theological controversies over the Gospel 20
2.4 A strict distinction between two kingdoms 24
2.5 Liberal foundations of the modern world 26
3 The esoteric conception of an earthly paradise 28
3.1 The natural philosophy of Renaissance Neoplatonism 29
3.2 Mysterious immersion in the life cycles of creation 30
3.3 Mystical drive for human deification 32
3.4 Magical manipulation of natural processes 33
3.5 Rediscovery of ancient theology 35
3.6 Proclamation of a universal reformation 38
3.7 Attempt to reverse the Fall 41
3.8 Pansophic coherence of truth 46
3.9 A grand vision for a new era 50
3.10 A turn to the mystery of Irrationalism 54
3.11 Pursuit of absolute perfection 56
4 Prophetic vision of a hopeful future 59
4.1 Millennialist vision of a perfect society 61
4.2 Prevalence of Puritan Postmillennialism 67
4.3 The theosophical basis of "Pennsylvania religion" 68
4.4 Refining the human character 71
4.5 Kindling religious enthusiasm 74
4.6 Anthropocentric approach of the New Theology 75

Postmillennialism as the inspiration for American Progressivism (Chs. 5-9) 77

5 The urge for revolution in an enlightened age 78
5.1 Questionable business relations among the wealthy elite 78
5.2 Lucrative enterprises of the "Boston Brahmins" 83

5.3   Secrets of the American elite 88
5.4   Differing beliefs among American Freemasons 92
5.5   Ideological foundations of the American Revolution 99
5.6   Religious orientation of Enlightenment philosophy 104
5.7   The purported ideal of religious tolerance 107
5.8   Deistic origins of the Declaration of Independence 111
5.9   Influence of Freemasonry on the American Revolution 114
5.10 Mercantilist bias of the American System 119
5.11 Victory in the American-Tripolitan Wars 125

6 The quest for human perfection 126
6.1   Religious character of the democratic state 127
6.2   Central tenets of Romantic Democracy 132
6.3   Unitarian ideal of a Christian nation 138
6.4   Idealistic essence of Transcendentalism 141
6.5   Transcendentalist attack on Christianity 143

7 Ideals of America's new age 147
7.1   Revolutionary effects of religious Patriotism 147
7.2   Propagation of a rationalistic doctrine of self-redemption 152
7.3   The sociopolitical impact of Postmillennialism 157
7.4   Pelagian undertones of the revival movement 163
7.5   Enthusiastic expressions of New Protestantism 169

8 The development of authoritarian Progressivism 176
8.1   Fateful development of the American Federation 177
8.2   Subsidization of special interest groups 183
8.3   Aggression provoked by a national religious cult 185
8.4   Full implementation of political patronage 187
8.5   Cultural development of a fanatical Nationalism 188
8.6   Violence caused by a policy of genocide 190
8.7   Hegemony of consolidated state power 193
8.8   Reinforced monopolization of economic systems 195

9 Religious essence of Progressivism 201
9.1   Evolutionary interpretations of social change 201
9.2   Impact of faith in science 205
9.3   Socio-economic reforms in the Progressive Era 206
9.4   Totalitarian principles of a collective social order 207
9.5   Universal indwelling of God in society 210
9.6   Gradual formation of an idealized world federation 211

Progressivism as the driving force of American Imperialism (Chs. 10-15) 221

10 Implementing a progressive social order 222
10.1 Conceptual metamorphosis of eschatological expectations 222
10.2 The Golden Age of the future 223
10.3 Religious significance of the new pedagogy 229
10.4 Technocratic reform of society 232
10.5 Sociopolitical development of Democracy 233

10.6   Collective ideology of Reform Darwinism 235
10.7   Monopolistic synchronization of the national economy 237
11   America's military attacks as a world power 239
11.1   Fateful consequences of a territorial expansion policy 239
11.2   Role of a redeemer nation in world politics 243
11.3   Global manifesto of "Manifest Destiny" 246
11.4   Progressives' authoritarian mentality of reform 250
12   The era of American Imperialism 253
12.1   Political power behind the throne 254
12.2   Complete rejection of a peace policy 258
12.3   The great Crusade for Justice 263
12.4   Violation of American civil rights 266
12.5   Enforcing an interventionist foreign policy 268
12.6   Variable success of a global revolution 271
13   The ideological battle against Militarism 275
13.1   Grave shortcomings of modern Democracy 276
13.2   Blame for the outbreak of the First World War 283
13.3   Exposing the lies of war propaganda 291
13.4   Relentless propagation of a world federation for peace 297
13.5   Corruption among the war profiteers 303
14   The age of American global dominance 307
14.1   Pacifist spirit of Continental Americanism 307
14.2   Social Democratic character of Progressivism 316
14.3   Consolidation of State Monopoly Capitalism 318
14.4   The dilemma of escalating Militarism 321
14.5   Tragic consequences of American diplomacy 325
15   Postscript 330
15.1   Beginnings of a progressive society 331
15.2   Development of a progressive world order 337
15.3   Realization of a progressive world order 343

A personal note to my readers 352

Bibliography 353

Index 407

Volume 1

Mysticism as the basis of American Postmillennialism (Chs. 1-4)

1 The continuous development of civilization 2
2 The Gospel of the Reformation 12
3 The esoteric conception of an earthly paradise 28
4 Prophetic vision of a hopeful future 59

1 The continuous development of civilization

Progressivism has developed exclusively in the Western world. It consists of a belief that humanity has been advancing constantly from past to present, and that this process will continue for the foreseeable future. However, it is impossible to identify anything as progress – as improvement in living conditions – without knowing its long-term consequences.

1.1 Metaphysical model of the idea of progress

(The origin of the idea of progress)
The English historian John B. Bury (1861-1927) believed that the idea of progress emerged in the late sixteenth century, as Humanism caused the Christian world view to decline in influence.[1] A true understanding of Progressivism requires closer examination of its origin and development. Its image has been distorted by the bias of academic historiography against Christianity, which has become increasingly evident since the late nineteenth century. This ideology of continual social advance and human improvement essentially constitutes a religion in its own right, which, despite often bearing the name of Christianity, is in resolute opposition to biblical beliefs.

Unlike Bury, twentieth-century historians such as W. K. C. Guthrie[2] (1957), Ludwig Edelstein[3] (1967), Eric R. Dodds[4] (1973), Moses I. Findley[5] (1977) and Robert A. Nisbet[6] (1980) believed that the idea of progress originated among the ancient Greeks. In the eighth century B.C., the philosopher Hesiod looked back on a past Golden Age as a reference point for his considerations. He was convinced that society was deteriorating but continued to believe that goodness existed in the midst of evil. His Prometheus legend was taken up in the fifth century by the playwright Aeschylus, who conveyed hope in man's ability to live a good life through his own efforts.

---

[1] John Bagnell Bury, *The Idea of Progress: An Inquiry into Its Origin and Growth* (London: Macmillan, 1920); https://archive.org/details/b29981311

[2] W. K. C. Guthrie, *In the Beginning: Some Greek views on the origins of life and the early state of man* (Ithaca, NY: Cornell University Press, [1957] 1965); https://archive.org/details/inbeginningsomeg00guth_0/page/n5

[3] Ludwig Edelstein, *The Idea of Progress in Classical Antiquity* (Baltimore, MD: Johns Hopkins Press, 1967); https://archive.org/details/ideaofprogressin00edel/page/n5

[4] Eric Robertson Dodds, *The Ancient Concept of Progress and Other Essays on Greek Literature and Belief* (Oxford: Clarendon Press, [1973] 1974); https://archive.org/details/ancientconceptof0000dodd/page/n5

[5] Moses I. Finley, "Progress in Historiography," *Dædalus*, vol. 106, no. 3, Discoveries and Interpretations: Studies in Contemporary Scholarship, vol. 1 (Summer, 1977), 125-142; https://www.jstor.org/stable/20024497

[6] Robert Alexander Nisbet, *History of the Idea of Progress* (New York City, NY: Basic Books, 1980); https://archive.org/details/historyofideaofp0000nisb/page/n5

Plato (428/427-348/347 B.C.) also stated that good is constantly mixed with evil in the world. Progressives often go astray by seeing only good in technological advance, failing to consider the evils that accompany it. The humanistic Credo, "man is the measure of all things," highlights a fundamental aspect of Progressivism which was already present in ancient times: the idea that man is capable of greatly improving his living conditions through his own endeavors. Plato discerned a deterioration in social structure through successive forms of government. The Greeks believed that history is pervaded by recurring cycles which develop either for better or for worse. According to the Greeks' concept of destiny, the universe has a fixed order, and man should not penetrate the divine realm by striving for progress. Aristotle (384-322 B.C.) had no conception of the idea of progress, but rather spoke about the wickedness of human nature.[7] Seneca, a Roman statesman and philosopher (c.1-65 A.D.), believed that every improvement in art and invention encouraged the decline of civilization by promoting the pursuit of luxury and indulgence in vices. Lucretius (99/94 B.C. – 55/53 B.C.) was first to use the term "progress," referring among other things to the pleasures of life, the use of fire, the discovery of precious metals, the fortification of cities, and the application of the law.[8] His concept of progress lacked a key aspect of its modern version: its automatically fulfilled historical necessity. (Progress, defined as the gradual improvement of human morality and living conditions, was eventually regarded as a historical necessity, and as such would occur automatically as a law of history.) Bury therefore concluded correctly that the idea of progress played almost no role at all in ancient Greek and Roman civilization.

The idea of progress developed among the Church Fathers in the first centuries after Christ. According to Augustine (354-430), the goal of the entire course of history was to secure the bliss of the elect in a future world. The idea that man would make continuous earthly advances in morality and cultural achievements was far from his mind. He categorized world history into seven stages of development, with the final stage – the age of bliss and peace on earth – being yet to come. Augustine's conception of the structure of progress was based on the Christian doctrine of the omnipotence of God. He criticized the pursuit of imperial power, taking Rome as an example. Many believed that Rome had been chosen by Jupiter to establish a universal, eternal kingdom of peace, law, and justice. The Church Fathers described this as "imperial idolatry." However, subsequent civilizations throughout the world believed similarly that by expanding their power they were obeying a divine call or destiny. Imperialism prevailed everywhere at one time or another, regardless of country, religion, or culture. Superpowers strove to

---

[7] Aristotle, *Politics*, tr. Benjamin Jowett (Oxford: Oxford University Press, 1885) vol. 2: 5; https://archive.org/details/politicsaristot09arisgoog/page/n198

[8] Lucretius, *De Rerum Natura*, H. A. J. Munro, ed. (London: Novi Eboraci Apud Harperos fratres 1883) book 5, II. 1452-1453; https://archive.org/details/dli.bengal.10689.17921/page/n261

extend their political, military, and economic spheres of influence ever further, for example in Confucian China, Hellenistic Greece, Augustan Rome, Ottoman Turkey, Romanov Russia, Napoleonic France, Victorian Britain, and Wilsonian America.

Some elements of Augustine's teachings were secularized in the late eighteenth century as follows: the idea that world history can be divided into defined eras; the doctrine of historical necessity, which became the most important concept for scientific historians and social evolutionists after being released from any relationship to the divine; and the alluring vision of a future world in which people would be freed from the trials and tribulations of life, and dwell in an earthly paradise for the first time since the Fall.

Joachim de Fiore, who lived in the second half of the twelfth century, had a great influence on explorers and philosophers of the Renaissance.[9] He saw human history as an advancement through three stages: first came the Age of the Father, or of the law, followed by the Age of the Son, or of the Gospel, and lastly the Age of the Spirit, still in the future, when man would be set free from his physical, fleshly desires and be surrounded by contemplative peace and sensual bliss. Joachim believed that the appearance of the third age would be preceded by a period of destruction and conflict. According to this bizarre notion, man could hasten the arrival of the Age of the Spirit by beginning the work of destruction himself using fire and sword.

One of Joachim's most influential followers was the Dominican scholar Campanella. In 1602, Campanella described a secular utopia in which all people would be ruled by reason and science and live in a socialist community of goods.[10] The elevation of Ancient Greece and Rome to a position of unattainable excellence prevented any potential idea of progress from emerging, as it later did among Enlightenment philosophers.

John B. Bury listed three prerequisites for grasping the idea of progress. First, a linear view of history had to replace the cyclic conception of the late Greek and Roman eras. This task was in line with the Hebrew and Christian understanding of history – which held that the significance of historical events emerged over a long period of time. The second prerequisite was willingness to rely on facts of nature more than on classical authors. A third factor – also resulting from the Renaissance – was the secularization of reasoning, which ultimately allowed man the freedom to break away from the Christian view of history. Marveling at the abundance of new discoveries, people in the sixteenth century began to rebel tentatively and cautiously against the tyranny of the ancient world. Nicolaus Copernicus (1473-1543) undermined the authority of the Ptolemaic worldview. Jean Bodin

---

[9] Marjorie Reeves, *The Influence of Prophecy in the Late Middle Ages* (New York City, NY: Oxford University Press, [1969] 2000); Melvin J. Lasky, *Utopia and Revolution* (London: Macmillan and Company, 1977) 19; https://archive.org/details/utopiarevolution00lask/page/18

[10] Tommaso Campanella, *La città del Sole* (Roma: Newton & Compton [1995] 2018; edizione digitale); https://archive.org/details/CampanellaTommaso.LaCittaDelSole2018/page/n1

(1529/1530-1596) rejected the classical teaching of degeneration, which was based on a primeval Golden Age of virtue and bliss.[11] He believed that there had been a gradual advance from times when men lived like wild animals to the dawn of sixteenth-century European social structure. Francis Bacon (1561-1626) saw the remarkable inventions of gunpowder, printing, the compass, and the discovery of foreign lands as proof of the great speed at which knowledge was advancing. Although Bodin and Bacon had come close to the idea of progress, they still had too high a regard for classical knowledge; furthermore, they believed in the doctrine of divine providence and its constant intervention in human affairs, which opposed the idea that man could continually improve human living conditions on his own terms. René Descartes (1596-1650) asserted the immutability of the laws of nature and the supremacy of reason. In so doing, he undermined the authority of the tradition and doctrine of providence, which until this point had been held in high regard.

According to the historian Robert A. Nisbet, seventeenth-century Puritans added a further dimension to the idea of progress by believing that they were advancing toward a perfect earthly society which would materialize in the distant future.[12] Fontenelle (1657-1757), a contemporary of Boyle, Newton, and Leibnitz, saw an enormous increase in the value placed on science during his lifetime. Theology was forced to concede more and more of its authority to science. Fontenelle looked ahead to the future as well as back to the past, consequently presenting a more comprehensive view of intellectual progress. Scientific achievements played a key role in the overall development of the idea of progress.

1.2 Secularized model of the idea of progress

A view of human history from the perspective of Progressivism – defined by John B. Bury as the positive development of a civilization from past to present to future – highlights its fundamental rejection of traditional authority, especially the revelation of God in the Bible. It maintains that the universe is governed by absolute, immutable laws which can be discovered and applied to improve man's existence on earth. If informed about the laws that determine social processes, the individual can take the course of history into his own hands. The social philosopher Charles Irénée Castel de Saint-Pierre, known as Abbé de Saint-Pierre, captivated the wealthy Parisian elite with this emerging Western idea which became a lasting phenomenon in consequence. It developed into a philosophy with great positive potential, as well as

---

[11] Jean Bodin, *Methodus ad facilem historiarum cognitionem* (Paris: Martin Juven, 1566; Jaccobum Stoer, 1610); https://archive.org/details/bub_gb_CfOYnGbhNSAC; English: *Method for the easy comprehension of History*, tr. Beatrice Reynolds (New York City, NY: Columbia University Press, 1945).

[12] Nisbet, *History of the Idea of Progress*, 124.

negative. Saint-Pierre suggested that a political academy should be founded in France which would plan and effect the holistic development of society. Scientific research was already producing so many results that this seemed to be a logical conclusion. The emerging idea of progress, although focused initially on the expansion of knowledge, caused much excitement as people considered the endless possibilities of reshaping the world around them.

The first full statement of the idea of progress was probably a paper by Jacques Turgot (1727-1781) entitled "Discours sur les progrès successifs de l'esprit humain"[13] (Philosophical Review of the Successive Advances of the Human Mind), presented at the University of Paris in 1750. The French Enlightenment philosopher observed progress not only in the arts and sciences, but also in all other cultural achievements, including manners, morals, institutions, codes of law, and the economy. The writers of the best-known early encyclopedia (1751-1765) believed that destroying existing institutions which had supposedly caused much injustice would provide the solution to social problems. The particular method of destruction was considered irrelevant. This shows how Enlightenment philosophers had secularized Christian teachings on the millennial reign (Rev. 20:1-6[14]) and introduced their own utopian ideas. Constant expansion of rational knowledge was seen as the key to success, and people believed that persistence in the task would bring about the necessary social reforms.

In 1793, amid the Reign of Terror of the French Revolution, an important work[15] was written by the Freemason Marquis de Condorcet, a disciple of Turgot. His mysterious death on March 27, 1794, shortly after he was imprisoned, sharply contradicted his optimistic belief in the unlimited potential for the improvement of human nature. By the end of the eighteenth

---

[13] Anne Robert Jacques Turgot, baron de l'Aulne, "Discours sur les progrès successifs de l'esprit humain," in Gustave Schelle, ed., *Oeuvres de Turgot* (Paris: Librairie Felix Alcan, 1913-1923) vol. 1: 214-238; https://www.institutcoppet.org/turgot-discours-sur-les-progres-successifs-de-lesprit-humain-1750/

[14] King James Version: 1 And I saw an angel come down from heaven, having the key of the bottomless pit and a great chain in his hand. 2 And he laid hold on the dragon, that old serpent, which is the Devil, and Satan, and bound him a thousand years, 3 and cast him into the bottomless pit, and shut him up, and set a seal upon him, that he should deceive the nations no more, till the thousand years should be fulfilled: and after that he must be loosed a little season. 4 And I saw thrones, and they sat upon them, and judgment was given unto them: and I saw the souls of them that were beheaded for the witness of Jesus, and for the word of God, and which had not worshipped the beast, neither his image, neither had received his mark upon their foreheads, or in their hands; and they lived and reigned with Christ a thousand years. 5 But the rest of the dead lived not again until the thousand years were finished. This is the first resurrection. 6 Blessed and holy is he that hath part in the first resurrection: on such the second death hath no power, but they shall be priests of God and of Christ, and shall reign with him a thousand years.

[15] Marie Jean Antoine Nicolas Caritat, Marquis de Condorcet, *Esquisse d'un tableau historique des progrès de l'esprit humain* (chez Agasse, 1793); *Outlines of an historical view of the progress of the human mind, being a posthumous work of the late M. de Condorcet* (Philadelphia, PA: M. Carey, 1796); http://oll.libertyfund.org/titles/condorcet-outlines-of-an-historical-view-of-the-progress-of-the-human-mind

century, man's aspiration for self-improvement had become an all-consuming desire. Enablement of this goal was now considered the primary purpose of science, with medicine in particular expected to contribute to the extension of life. Most champions of progress believed that the development of the human spirit would be brought to fulfillment if man were set free from the burdens of ignorance, superstition, and tyranny. The emergence of a philosophical period during a primitive stage of general ignorance would initiate the history of human salvation.

A connection was also made between modern scientific methods and ancient mythology. The physician Erasmus Darwin (1731-1802), grandfather of Charles Darwin, wrote poetry that contained esoteric ideas.[16] Erasmus combined mythology with Naturalism and came to be regarded as a great prophet of progress. His ideal worldview consisted of both the further development of nature and pagan myths which he believed would reveal dimensions otherwise inaccessible to the human mind. The myth of eternal restoration, for example, revealed a point of contact with ancient scientific speculations. In the late nineteenth century, the conception of the idea of progress began to change from that of the Renaissance. Progress was understood to render human development not only possible, but inevitable. The idea of progress as salvation demanded a new form of religion, and the idea of recovering paradise spread widely during the nineteenth century. The biblical view of the thousand-year reign was significantly modified by even orthodox theologians. Divine providence gradually came to be understood as merely the impersonal workings of natural laws in the world, rather than as a process of God's direct intervention in the course of history.

In his philosophy of Positivism, Auguste Comte (1798-1857) defined the famous three stages of development in the evolution of intelligence. He thereby drew indirectly on the original Joachimite theory of the three ages of human history (the Age of the Father [Old Testament], the Son [New Testament until 1260], and the Holy Spirit), suggesting this to be the reason why progress had become a lasting phenomenon. Despite the disillusionment caused by the violence of the French Revolution, Progressivism was not exposed as being groundless; only the enthusiasm around it was diminished. The primary challenge was to develop a social science that would work in tandem with natural scientific discoveries, thus providing a theorization of the development of progress. The new science of sociology emerged soon after. The idea of progress remained a strong force through unprecedented scientific and technological development, the Industrial Revolution, overseas expansion, and burgeoning prosperity. Progressivism was so broadly established by the nineteenth century that it was no longer questioned by the general public.

---

[16] Erasmus Darwin, *The Temple of Nature, or, The Origin of Society* (London: Johnson, 1803; New York City, NY: Garland Pub., 1978); https://archive.org/details/templenatureoro02darw-goog/page/n6

1.3 Conflicting views on the idea of progress

(Development of the idea of progress from firm belief, to rejection, to revival) Many Americans were influenced by the attitudes of conservative Anglicans, believing in consequence that the economy and the social sector would be improved if citizens sought to shape their own future. They prioritized the maintenance of individual autonomy above all else. This conception of cultural advance conflicted with attitudes in continental Europe, which sought to effect progress by destroying traditional relationships. Americans wanted to improve their situation by increasing their prosperity. The American continent had an abundance of valuable raw materials which could be used in industrial development to attain higher standards of living.[17] No one felt a need for revolutionary change since immigrants had already experienced the same process in their native countries. The distinct character of their new national life engendered deep Patriotism, which was considered the driving force of progress. The history of America seemed to offer unmistakable evidence for continual advance and for the inevitable improvement of life on earth.

The nineteenth century was by and large an era of peace, bringing only limited, short-lived warfare while humanitarian objectives were implemented throughout the Western world. Cautious belief in the possibility of progress developed into firm persuasion of its inevitability. The triumph of industrial Capitalism served as an object lesson that demonstrated the merits of progress. Machines were regarded as engines of Democracy[18] and emblems of advance. Apart from during some periods of economic depression, Americans were presented with golden opportunities to climb the social ladder, and many took advantage of them.

For the average nineteenth-century American, Progressivism was an absolute, unquestionable law of history. The ideological basis of the concept was a belief in the rationality and goodness of mankind, as well as in the continual improvement of living conditions.[19] This reached a climax when the period from 1896 to 1921 was named "Progressivism." The idea of progress was accepted on the basis of the country's vast size, rich natural resources, political freedom, general education system, and limitless possibilities for the common man to improve his social status. Americans

---

[17] Merle E. Curti, *The Growth of American Thought* (New York City, NY: Harper & Brothers Publishers, [1943] 1951); https://archive.org/details/in.ernet.dli.2015.206048

[18] Roger Burlingame, *Engines of Democracy: Inventions and Society in America* (New York City, NY: Charles Scribner's Sons, 1940; New York City, NY: Arno Press, 1976); https://archive.org/details/in.ernet.dli.2015.228946

[19] Curti, *The Growth of American Thought*; https://archive.org/details/in.ernet.dli.2015.190916; Merle E. Curti, *The Roots of American Loyalty* (New York City, NY: Russell & Russell [1946] 1967); Alice Felt Tyler, *Freedom's Ferment: Phases of American Social History to 1860* (Minneapolis, MN: University of Minnesota Press 1944); https://archive.org/details/freedomsfermentp00tyle

were confident in their "Manifest Destiny," and in the meantime, a firm sense of optimism was also spreading through English society.

The World's Fair, hosted in London in 1851 and Paris in 1900, proved that great material progress was underway and seemed to provide reassurance that peace would continue to reign among Western nations. However, criticism of the unhealthy atmosphere at the court of Kaiser Wilhelm II and of the façade of false optimism put up by Chancellor Bernhard von Bülow provoked unrest among Germans. Despite their enormous industrial and commercial expansion, they began to feel that they were surrounded by enemies. Belief in the idea of progress lost momentum in Germany as Militarism increased under Kaiser Wilhelm II, the educational system began to deteriorate, and Friedrich Nietzsche introduced his philosophy of Nihilism.

Little by little, ideas of Progressivism based on Enlightenment philosophy decreased in prominence until they were largely abandoned for new religious concepts. As a result, progressives frequently borrowed terms from popular Darwinian and pragmatist jargon. They also referred to traditional teachings of political ideology, with no concern for how confusing their portrayals of socialist Progressivism, Classical Liberalism, or patriotic Conservatism might be to others. They may have been unaware of how inconsistent their statements were. Eighteenth-century rational belief in human goodness and in the existence of a universal moral order was joined by nineteenth-century Romantic belief in the excellence of human emotion. The goal of the Social Gospel movement was to improve life to such an extent that the world would eventually reach a state of paradise. Advocates of religious Progressivism were convinced that man could so improve himself as to lead global society toward a collectivist utopia. These ideas conflict with Christian doctrines concerning the sinfulness of human nature and the exclusive indwelling of the Holy Spirit in the hearts of born-again believers.

The colorful robes of Progressivism were spun from a great variety of threads which together constituted the nineteenth-century humanistic belief in progress. They included science and technology, Unitarianism and Transcendentalism, Social Darwinism, Liberalism, and Pragmatism.

Around the turn of the twentieth century, the great escalation of industrialization and urbanization brought radical changes to many people's circumstances. The simplicity of rural and provincial life which had been conducive to Progressivism gradually vanished, with naive belief in the inevitability of progress dissolving into virtually nothing. Americans rejected their blind faith in the positive workings of divine providence, and the First World War may thus be considered symbolically as the launch of an entirely new outlook on life. As a result of the catastrophic impact of the war, the grueling post-war years of unemployment and economic depression, and the League of Nations' promise to maintain world peace, initial thoughts of progress temporarily disintegrated in the Western Hemisphere. For a time, the traditional belief in future human perfection was lost amid the dark reality of appalling, inhuman aggression. The attitude of the contemporary generation was one of cynicism, selfishness, and meaninglessness. Like

President T. Woodrow Wilson (ΦBK),[20] progressive reformers hoped that the horrors of the World War would themselves lead to the abolition of war as a means of destruction in international relations. Americans still held on to their belief in the possibility of progress, but confidence in better living conditions and the identification of this idea with a moral regeneration of the entire population retreated ever further into the background. Progressives complained that everything in America and Europe revolved around the question of how to gain power, the intention being to acquire immense wealth by systematically pillaging the state. Idealism was dashed to pieces on the rocks of reality. People came to understand that far from becoming virtuous, man had become egotistic, irrational, and absurd without even realizing it. Civilized culture had allowed him to become unrestrained. Within the brief period from 1914 to 1920, many influential thinkers of the progressive movement lost their following.

During the post-war years, men who had authoritatively shaped public opinion before the war were neither able to understand the new generation, nor to reach it with their socialist ideals. An entirely new world emerged in which social change was swift and revolutionary. The idea that the object and purpose of history was to improve human life forever had been dealt a crushing blow by Fascist and Nazi success in Italy, Spain, and Germany, as well as by the hideous atrocities of World War Two. There were clear signs that even the highly revered, culturally rich Western civilization was in decline.

During the twentieth century, the literary genre of dystopia (fictional, futuristic narratives with negative endings) enjoyed immense popularity. For example, George Orwell published his book *Nineteen Eighty-Four*[21] in 1949, portraying the horrors of an imagined surveillance state in the year 1984. In the narrative, the will of the rebellious Winston is completely defeated by the totalitarian party. The ideal of perfection was similarly rejected by other contemporary writers.

Classical utopias, such as Plato's *Republic*, criticized contemporary societies by comparing them to a theoretical ideal society. Modern dystopias criticize existing nightmarish societies by claiming that they are the inevitable results of current social trends. These literary works are fundamentally no different in content to classical utopias: at their core, they are simply variations of the Platonic utopia. The ideal of a perfect society still influences modern thought. Aldous Huxley's *Brave New World* is primarily about cheerful acceptance of personal obligations and joyful welcoming of an inevitable fate of oppression and exploitation. Within such a cunningly devised Totalitarianism, all people are free to express their opinions since no one will contradict the group consensus.

---

[20] Member of the Phi Beta Kappa Society, Wesleyan University, 1898

[21] George Orwell, *Nineteen Eighty-Four* (London: Secker & Warburg, 1949); https://archive.org/details/NineteenEightyFour1984ByGeorgeOrwell/page/n1

1.4 Ideological reversal of the idea of progress

Philosophers such as Plato, Aristotle, and Seneca recorded their thoughts on human development over several generations. Christian theologians believed that human progress was determined by God and linked historical events with salvation history. The focus of this historical interpretation was not obscure events of the past, but rather the spiritual development of mankind. Enlightenment philosophers, on the other hand, believed that human progress was determined not by the grace of God, but by natural causes. Furthermore, the course of progress was no longer revealed to man by God, but by nature alone. Although some philosophers still believed in the existence of a God, they saw Him merely as a distant Creator who ceased to intervene in human affairs after creating the universe and setting it in motion. Progress was no longer seen in terms of man's spiritual development, but rather the development of his relationship to external nature and its causes.

By the nineteenth century, the idea of progress had become an integral part of the universally popular Progressivism, from which any idea of relationship to the divine had disappeared altogether. Progress was seen as an essential historical phenomenon which could only be understood through reason. Western civilization was compared with its own past, as well as with other civilizations, in order to evaluate the progress of human development. However, a turning point was reached when the cataclysmic events of the First World War showed that progress was not a historical necessity.

Progress, in the sense of development toward a perfect society, can be said to exist only in Christian salvation history[22]: all things will be perfect in the new Jerusalem, for there will be no more sin. A state of perfection will never exist in secular history because of man's sinfulness. Despite this, however, the idea of progress remained a powerful intellectual force which relied on the spectacular achievements of Western civilization.

The conceptual change in the idea of progress triggered a crisis in modern society. It became increasingly clear that there were inconsistencies in the hopes raised by the idea of progress, which released centrifugal forces that destroyed the very elements that constitute a well-functioning society. Among these forces were egotistic and hedonistic influences. Once the religious dimension of human existence was banished from Western minds, they could understand progress only in temporal and material terms. The attempts of a progressive elite to determine the course of history led only to war, revolution, and criminality among other devastating consequences.

Plato was the first political Monist[23] of the Western world, with Thomas Hobbes and Jean-Jacques Rousseau following him as modern representatives

---

[22] Robert Alexander Nisbet, *The Social Philosophers: Community and Conflict in Western Thought* (New York City, NY: Washington Square Press, 1982) 221ff.; https://archive.org/details/socialphilosophe00nisb/page/220/

[23] Robert Alexander Nisbet, *The Quest For Community: A Study in the Ethics of Order and Freedom* (New York City, NY: Oxford University Press, 1953; San Francisco, CA: Institute for

of the tradition. They defined the true nature of the state as one of neither power nor oppression, but of justice, freedom, and peace which benefits the individual. Whereas Hobbes was content for individuals to shape their own lives as they wished within the state, Rousseau was the first modern philosopher to see the state as a means of resolving conflicts not only among institutions, but also within the individual person. He considered the state to be absolute, indivisible, and all-powerful, and believed that a civil religion would be able to settle all social and individual disputes. The origin of this new ideology, which had only the interests of the state in mind, was Rousseau's idea of general will (Fr. volonté générale). It was first implemented during the French Revolution and held that individuals were not to serve the purposes of local groups or traditional communities, but of the state. The individual citizen could supposedly live a free life only under the direct supervision and guidance of the state, despite its common arbitrary bureaucracy.

The same illusion of state sovereignty as a political ideal has captured the imaginations of American progressives since the mid- nineteenth century. Advocates of the American welfare state, which began with the state education system introduced in Massachusetts, stubbornly insist that the state is the only institution that guarantees well-being. However, loyalty to the state proved to be a curse. Since the end of the Second World War, the general sense of belonging to the state has broken down in Western civilization.

The idea of progress is a vital component of the war ideology used by the state to justify the centralization of its power to the disadvantage of traditional communities such as families, churches, and societies. The state's territory and totalitarian authority have grown most during times of war. War evokes an incomparable sense of community among citizens.[24] Over time, the state developed from an exclusive military alliance into an institutional power that controlled almost every aspect of human life.

2 The Gospel of the Reformation

God reveals Himself in the Holy Scriptures, which are the source of supreme authority. This was the fundamental belief of the Reformation. Biblical doctrines are accordingly definitive for the Christian and should never be placed on a par with human opinion. They were given to man by God through infallible prophetic and apostolic writings, thereby establishing a framework for all earthly events, including those of the Christian life.

Contemporary Studies, 1990) 115; https://archive.org/details/RobertNisbetTheQuestFor-Community/page/n137

[24] Nisbet, *History of the Idea of Progress*, 309.

2.1 Authoritative self-revelation of the sovereign God

Martin Luther recognized that God's Word is eternal in both duration and validity: "Heaven and earth shall pass away, but my words shall not pass away" (Matt. 24:35 KJV). During the Middle Ages, the Latin translation of the Bible could only be accessed by a few monks, scholars, and high-ranking officials in the Roman Catholic Church, and not by the common people. One of Luther's greatest realizations, which had a great impact on his thoughts and actions, was that God gave His Word to man in a Book which He desired him to read and follow. For this to be possible, the Holy Scriptures needed to be translated into individual languages. God conveyed His eternal mind exclusively through human means of communication – as a great Poet, creative Narrator, and Master of verse. The heavenly message was delivered in a way that could be understood by all who desired it. God is always willing to speak to men and thereby draw them to Himself. Salvation is found only in Him – through faith in Jesus Christ alone, the Word of God Incarnate.

Luther taught that Christians are bound by complete obedience to the Scriptures. They are thus released from any human authority that seeks to take the place of God's Word, be it Pope, church council, or ruler. The Roman Catholic Church accused Luther of heresy and threatened him with papal excommunication. The Church falsely claimed to be the only institution through which salvation could be attained. Furthermore, it claimed that the Pope was the sole interpreter of the Holy Scriptures, who alone could render them valuable and effective. Strengthened by the knowledge that all things are governed by the sovereign hand of God, Luther set fire to the Papal Bull of Excommunication in 1520. He was more concerned with making the Word of God accessible to the common people than he was with the affairs of his own life. He would soon receive the death sentence as the Pope sought to carry out his threats.

Luther referred to the Holy Scriptures as the external Word in order to emphasize that it is objective, fixed, and immutable. It stands beyond our subjective sensitivities and is thus unaffected by our wandering and wavering thoughts and feelings. Luther's great esteem for the Book of Books encouraged reverence of the Holy Spirit as one of the divine Persons of the Trinity: a Person who could be known and loved. Only by reading the Scriptures did Luther come to realize the importance of the outpouring of the Spirit – the One who ensures that the true meaning of Scripture can be discerned and believed. The written Word of God also exalts the Word Incarnate, Jesus Christ. Without it, Christ would be left to the arbitrary whims and fancies of the human mind.

People's general understanding of the Son of God had been distorted by all kinds of myths since late antiquity. During the Middle Ages, it was shrouded by philosophical speculation and pagan superstition. This perilous situation improved only gradually during the Renaissance, chiefly through the 1516 publication of the Greek New Testament in Basel. After years of inner strife with his sinfulness and sense of being forsaken by God, the conscience of a humble Augustinian monk was suddenly enlightened by the bright beam of the Pauline doctrine of justification. He realized that only through faith in Christ and His substitutionary atonement on the cross, on which the Son of God endured the awful punishment of His people, could a person be saved from the burning wrath of God and from certain condemnation.

Luther possessed a weapon which enabled him to stop the corrupt selling of the Word of God in the markets of Saxony and other regions. With the whip of the external Word, he cast out the moneychangers – the Dominican indulgence sellers – from their tables. The Word of God was in constant danger of being altered at will by Catholic priests, since almost no one was able to check whether they were faithful in their duties. Even if they were, very few of their listeners could speak Latin, the exclusive language of the Mass.

According to Luther, only the Bible could reveal the almost indescribable glory of the Word Incarnate. Christ would never appear in any questionable form of ecstatic rapture. The apostles understood the necessity of recording the New Testament in the common business language of the day, Koine Greek, in order to ensure its preservation. If the Word were merely recited from memory – as was customary in the secret rituals of ancient mystery cults – the church would come to possess a collection of nonsensical, distorted interpretations of biblical doctrines which would plunge people into great spiritual darkness.

2.2 Full reliance on God's work of salvation

The Reformation began with Luther's troubled conscience. He found himself in the depths of despair as he saw no way for sinners to escape God's retributive justice. The teaching which he had received until this point can be summarized by a common proverb of the day: "Strive to live justly, and God will help you." Luther did all he could to keep this principle, but nothing eased his seared conscience. However, his blinding despair was suddenly lifted on his discovery of a new doctrine. He read in the Scriptures that the sinner is saved by the infinite grace of God alone, by which everything necessary for salvation is accomplished, and that nothing more is required of the sinner in order to be saved. The consequences of Luther's dramatic conversion triggered the forces which shaped the modern world from the Middle Ages onward. The key element which changed the world, discovered in the Augustinian monastery in Wittenberg, was the doctrine of justification by faith alone: "The just shall live by faith" (Rom. 1:17). From the minute that Luther grasped the doctrine of justification, the central doctrine of the divine Gospel, he ceased to look for any other truth – for he had found it.

The humanist Erasmus of Rotterdam was highly suspicious of any claims that the truth could be known with unquestionable certainty. Erasmus counted Pope Leo X among his most important friends. The Pope had absolved him from the vows that he had taken as an Augustinian monk, and afterwards supported his favorite's humanistic studies. No one came close to Erasmus in mastery of the classical languages. No one was so knowledgeable in the writings of the Greek philosophers and Church Fathers. No one came close to having such ready access to the Pope, to cardinals, and to kings. To a vigilant Christian concerned about the grave shortcomings of contemporary Christendom, no one seemed better suited than Erasmus to reform the Roman Catholic Church from its corruption, worldliness, and policies that were aimed at exorbitant financial gain and ruthless power.

Erasmus made a significant contribution to the Reformation. He placed Humanism at the service of religion and sought to purge medieval scholarship of theologians' questionable ideas.[25] He also sought to do everything he could to promote practical Christian devotion. When the first edition of the Greek New Testament was published by Fröbe in Basel, critically prepared and annotated by Erasmus, many people believed that a great reformation of church doctrine and practice had begun. Another remarkable feat was the production of a Latin translation of the New Testament. However, Erasmus's writings and Bible version were banned at the Council of Trent (1545-1563), and believers were forbidden to read them. His edition of the New Testament would nevertheless provide the foundation for the majority of modern, vernacular translations produced between the sixteenth and nineteenth centuries.

Erasmus consistently highlighted the contemporary relevance of scriptural words in his Bible commentaries. One of the main concerns of humanists was to give all social classes the opportunity to read the Scriptures for themselves and to encourage their duty to do so. The Bible therefore needed to be translated into many languages. In contrast to the monastic ideal of mystical contemplation and to the ceremony of Catholic worship, Erasmus emphasized the practical side of religion and its ethics. He strongly discouraged subjective speculations on religious realities. His most notable contribution to the Reformation was probably his sharp criticism of the corruptions in the Roman Catholic Church, the impact of which can be compared to a spiritual volcanic eruption. The Pope's suggestion that Erasmus lead bishops in reforming the Church from the inside therefore seems highly ironic. The one condition was that Erasmus take a peaceful approach. His goal was to abolish clerical corruption, promote reading of the Holy Scriptures, encourage the preaching of divine truths, and call for holy living. However, this never happened. The countercurrents were too strong for radical reform to be carried out within the Church. Luther was uncompromising in pointing out the real reasons: financial greed, desire for pleasure, and obsession with power. Erasmus's reform efforts had no long-term success because the real cause of church corruption was not identified at its deepest level. It was rooted in the entire theology of the Roman Catholic

---

[25] Robert Blackley Drummond, *Erasmus: His Life and Character as shown in his correspondence and works* (London: Smith, Elder & Co., 1873).

Church, which had been constructed over the centuries to gain political power over the contemporary Western world. There could be no effective reform without a return to the Gospel of the New Testament. What was needed was a fresh declaration of unconditional salvation in Jesus Christ and its reception through faith. Nothing else could breathe new spiritual life into European Christianity. However, Erasmus wanted to reform the wickedness around him without the Christian doctrine of salvation, which alone could have brought about the desired changes. What Erasmus regarded as Christianity was not true New Testament Christianity. It was a pseudo-Christian faith which lacked the essential elements of its genuine counterpart, for it did not have Jesus Christ at its innermost core.

It is therefore unsurprising that Erasmus distanced himself from the Reformation. He most likely felt a sense of inner satisfaction on hearing of Luther's indignation at the sale of indulgences. At the same time, he feared that Luther would face bitter consequences if his temper continued to get the better of him. In a letter written to the German Reformer in 1519, he urged him to restrain his zeal. In a moment of benevolence, he advised that Luther be treated leniently. Later, however, when the Roman Curia's feelings were increasingly heated by Luther's antics, the Dutch scholar became openly hostile. In order to contradict Luther directly, Erasmus wrote a book in 1524 which later became known under the title *On the Freedom of the Will*[26]. The reasons why Erasmus kept his distance from the Reformation were never a great mystery. His ultimate priority was always his pursuit and achievement of his own ambitions, so that making common cause with Luther seemed counterproductive. Furthermore, as a leading humanist of his time, he felt obligated to promote literary scholarship and saw the commotion caused by Luther as a threat to this matter. The two men were also divided when it came to theology. While Luther preached justification by faith, Erasmus promoted a different understanding of salvation which emphasized man's duty to imitate Christ's example of moral excellence.

The Reformation brought tremendous upheaval as a whole system of theology was displaced by another. One system was dominated by fear of death and Hell; the other was perceived as the wellspring of God-given life. The Reformation awakened not only the forces of life, but also living, biblical Christianity itself. The Reformation quickly spread among the exploited and oppressed people of Germany. As a result of Luther's theses, posted on October 31, 1517, and of the publication of writings by other Reformers, Pope Leo X issued a bull of excommunication which forced Luther to choose between rejecting his heretical teaching, which ran contrary to church doctrine, or being excommunicated from the Roman Catholic Church. Luther reiterated again and again that man can never attain salvation through his works and that the soul must rely on the grace of God alone. Rome taught very artfully that man could achieve eternal salvation through his own deeds.

---

[26] Desiderius Erasmus, *De libero arbitrio Diatribe sive collatio* (Basel: Ioannem Frobenium, 1524) 1-195.

It was ultimately not Luther and his writings that Rome condemned and rejected, but rather the cross of Christ and the Gospel which meant everything to him.

In his book *On the Freedom of the Will*, Erasmus wrote that the Holy Scriptures contain secrets which God has not revealed to man. He taught that authoritative, infallible knowledge cannot exist, for God has determined nothing by absolute, divine decree. Erasmus approached the subject of free will from a moral, pragmatic, and human perspective. He was not concerned with accepting what the Bible actually teaches, but rather with defending what he considered correct on the basis of Thomistic scholarship – namely the validity of the free will. He thought that he discerned an innate force in man which could act against God and believed that man could contribute an essential part to his own salvation. Erasmus took a middle ground: on the one hand, he stood apart from Pelagius who believed that man could be saved entirely of his own accord, and on the other hand, he distanced himself from the Reformers who proclaimed that man is saved by God's grace alone. Erasmus is therefore referred to as a Semi-Pelagian, and the doctrine of righteousness by works spread widely during his time.

In response to Erasmus's book *On the Freedom of the Will*, Luther wrote a treatise in 1525 entitled *On the Bondage of the Will*[27]. The German Reformer largely considers the subject of human will from an ethical standpoint, rather than a psychological one. He convincingly presents the biblical teaching on the complete inability of the natural man to do anything good before God. Few people accept this teaching against free will, for it insists that without the grace of God, the sinner can do nothing of merit in God's sight. When Erasmus employed the term "free will," he did not have its common understanding in mind. He did not intend to show that man should live responsibly, but that man can be completely autonomous from God. This is a radical understanding of the term. The theological debate gives rise to the question of whether God or man has final authority over the other. Can man maintain a certain degree of autonomy from God, or is man one of God's creatures, entirely under His control? For Luther, rejection of free will was the basis of the biblical doctrine of grace. Unless a person is aware of being helplessly under the enslaving power of sin, it is, according to Luther, impossible for him to understand any aspect of the Gospel whatsoever.

The humanist Erasmus presented his readers with a sophisticated Agnosticism. In the name of peace and harmony, he sought to take an attitude of indifference toward divine law in order to retain the ethical principles of human autonomy. Catholic modernist theologians, who since the twentieth century have sought to establish connections with contemporary scientific and philosophical knowledge, have firmly supported the idea that man is autonomous, independent from God. Although the evangelical church was

---

[27] Martin Luther, *The Bondage of the Will: A New Translation of De Servo Arbitrio (1525), Martin Luther's Reply to Erasmus of Rotterdam*, J. I. Packer and O. R. Johnston, trans. (Old Tappan, NJ: Fleming H. Revell Co., 1957).

initially well-advised to follow Luther's example, it must itself accept responsibility for the way that Modernism has, in retrospect, so quickly breached and influenced its course.

Martin Luther abandoned the monastic ideal of achieving sinlessness by his own efforts with a sense of relief. Unlike Augustine, he was not dismayed by his persisting human weaknesses. He believed that such sins do not prevent holiness as long as the sinner trusts in God alone and is repentant. The matter of free will was no academic issue for Luther; he knew that the salvation of precious souls was at stake. This explains his willingness to present his argument against free will so determinedly, thus underlining his conviction that this is the very essence of Christian faith. The confidence with which the German Reformer confronted his learned opponent is astonishing. He not only presented his arguments against free will through detailed consideration of the Scriptures, but also with the necessary assurance that this was sufficiently convincing. He commended Erasmus's great scholarship and cultivated manner but held nothing back in valiantly resisting his opponent whenever he questioned and altered the Word of God.

Luther battled on several fronts: he not only rejected the Pelagian view (which holds that there is no original sin, and, therefore, that man is not depraved and can be perfected *in and of himself*), but also the Semi-Pelagian compromise (that *God will bring the essential human nature to perfection with man's consent*). Augustine had already argued similarly, but Luther went a step further by contradicting the popular belief of the Roman Catholic theologian Erasmus – that man has a free will which, with or without God's help, enables him to choose goodness. Luther rejected the idea of a psychological mechanism available inherently to man which could enable him to change his own sinful nature in an instant. He did not deny this hesitantly or reluctantly but with immense relief. He argued that in trying to achieve his own salvation, he had never been sure of having done everything within his power despite his tremendous efforts. Free will, Luther declared, is a term which can rightly be applied to God alone. Man's attempt to consider himself "free" is therefore only another way of seeking to consider himself godlike. The truth is that he is utterly helpless in matters of spiritual welfare. Luther's greatest concern was to spread the Augustinian doctrine of grace, which teaches that an individual cannot save himself through his own efforts but must, through faith, trust completely and only in the divine grace of God's work of salvation on the cross. The Reformer's emphasis on divine grace and its implied rejection of human agency in attaining salvation opposed the tenets of the later belief in progress. Representatives of Progressivism believed that the goals of the independent human will would secure the hope of a better life in this world.

Martin Luther cast a harsh light on the theory of perfection held by the Roman Catholic and Greek Orthodox Churches, convinced that it falsified the biblical doctrine of salvation. How could such a doctrine have arisen? The Catholic humanist Erasmus was influenced strongly by Greek philosophy. Like all other Reformers, Martin Luther firmly rejected any idea of justification before God based on human effort by pointing to divine grace alone; furthermore, he denied the idea of a "state of earthly perfection" which dispensed with dependence on God's unmerited favor. The Genevan Reformer John Calvin stated that it is more fitting to refer to acts such as adultery, fornication, theft, hatred, murder, and drunkenness as the "fruits of sin" than it is to call them "sins." Taking the opposite position, according to Calvin, robs God of his rights and encourages man's self-conceit.

Calvin believed that man still retains something of God's image, however distorted it may be. Man still has abilities in "earthly things" – in government affairs, domestic matters, mechanical skills, and the liberal arts – and is not entirely without "some general precepts of honesty and civil order." In Luther's terms, man belongs to the earthly as well as to the heavenly kingdom and is able to develop his reason and purpose to a high level. Only when it comes to spiritual matters is reason "blinder than moles," as described by Calvin, or "the devil's whore," as Luther put it. Reason does undoubtedly retain certain abilities even in religious matters; Calvin said that by considering nature and human history, it is able to discern the goodness, foresight, and justice of God. However, the fact remains that man is so corrupt that without the help of the Holy Spirit he is "altogether stupid and blind." At best, reason can achieve a very general recognition of the existence and goodness of God, and acquire a certain ability to "act righteously" when judging external actions. In spiritual terms, all human works are under the judgment of God, however they may appear on the outside. Only the Christian, born again through the Holy Spirit, is enabled to perform good works to the glory of God.

The Reformers focused on Paul's declaration that the sinner is entirely helpless in his sins and is saved by the free, unconditional, and irresistible grace of God. The sovereignty of divine grace is also expressed in the doctrine of monergistic regeneration, which states that faith in Christ for justification is itself the free gift of a sovereign God. God awakens the individual from being dead in his sins through His life-giving Spirit, and leads Him to faith. He then justifies the repentant sinner for the sake of Jesus Christ. In summary, God is the giver of faith as well as of justification. Monergism (Gr. "working alone") is the view that God alone effects our salvation. This view is held primarily by Calvinists and Reformed denominations, and is closely connected with the doctrines of grace. In contrast, Synergism (Gr. "working together") is the view that God works with us to bring about our salvation. While Monergism is associated closely with John Calvin, Synergism is connected to Jacobus Arminius, whose views shaped much of the modern evangelical landscape. Calvin and Arminius did not introduce these ideas themselves, but have become the best-known representatives of Calvinism and Arminianism.

2.3 Theological controversies over the Gospel

The Frenchman Peter Baro (Baron), a theologian at the University of Cambridge, caused a commotion in 1579 when he suggested that God had predestinated all men to eternal life. Taking the description of Nineveh in the book of Jonah as an example, he argued that the prerequisites for salvation are faith and obedience.[28] William Barrett put forward the same teaching in 1595. It was refuted by the Anglican Church in the nine Lambeth Articles, but a strong anti-Calvinist movement soon arose within the Church which was based on Baro and Barrett's theology. The natural theology of the Cambridge Platonists received wide support because of its emphasis on morality. After the Restoration of the Stuart monarchy, Calvinism was considered a strange teaching held by only a handful of Nonconformists, with most theologians in the state church being influential Arminians. This tragic situation led to the rejection of the doctrine of justification. Reformation theology had upheld the righteousness of Christ as the basis of justification; the Anglican Church now replaced this with the idea that Christ's personal righteousness afforded every individual the potential to attain his own salvation. Faith was no longer understood as the means of justification, but rather as its prerequisite. Man therefore had a moral obligation to exercise faith as an act of obedience. This Semipelagian doctrine of salvation and election was taught by Jakob Hermandzoon, a minister in Amsterdam who called himself Jacobus Arminius. He preached it until his death in 1609, and it subsequently came to be known by his name.

The theological disputes between Jacobus Arminius (1560-1609) and Petrus Plancius (1552-1622), both Dutchmen, infuriated many Protestant theologians in the religious debates of the seventeenth and eighteenth centuries. After Arminius died in 1609, his followers soon formed a movement and earned the disfavor of the Reformed by publishing their "Five Articles of Remonstrance" in opposition to the Calvinistic doctrine of salvation. In response, Reformed theologians drew up the "Five Points of Calvinism" at the 1619 Synod of Dort, summarizing their view of the Christian doctrine of salvation.

The fundamental difference between Calvinism and Arminianism does *not* lie in the following points, as some believe:

- Arminians follow the Scriptures, while Calvinists are bound by their logic.
- Arminianism emphasizes Christ's free offer of the Gospel, which has no place in Calvinism.
- Arminianism connects faith and obedience as a means of grace to attain eternal life, which is rejected by Calvinism.

---

[28] Philip Schaff, *Creeds of Christendom: with a history and critical notes*, 3 vols. (New York City, NY: Harper [1919] 1931) vol. 1: 659.

- Arminianism emphasizes human responsibility before God and consequent commitment to holy living, whereas Calvinism teaches nothing of the kind.
- Arminians recognize only the love of God, while Calvinists invoke His authority.

The difference is that Calvinism recognizes a dimension of God's saving love that is entirely overlooked by Arminianism. For the Calvinist, everything revolves around the acknowledgement of God's sovereignty. God alone decides which sinners will be saved. And God alone leads the elect sinner to faith and upholds him in faith until the end. These Calvinistic teachings are categorically rejected by Arminianism.

The Reformers' doctrine of justification can be summarized as follows. On the one hand, every person will one day appear before the judgment seat of God and give an account of himself as a sinner in nature and in deed. Man has refused to live in accordance with the law of God, and can therefore only expect God's wrath and condemnation. But on the other hand, God's verdict in pardoning the guilty sinner is justification, by which He accepts him as just and appoints him as His son and heir. The sole source of justification is God's grace, not the efforts and initiatives of man. The sole basis of justification is the vicarious righteousness and shed blood of Jesus Christ, not man's own merits. Neither is anything contributed by the so-called surplus merits of the saints, the purchase of indulgences, or a multitude of Masses; nor do the torments of the medieval concept of Purgatory have any meaning. In reality, they do not exist. Justification is not a divine payment for some human achievement, but the gift of God, received through the mediation of Jesus Christ. The sole means of accepting justification here and now is faith. Christ's substitutionary atonement through the shedding of His blood for the remission of sins enables a righteous God to forgive every past, present, and future sin of the believer. The fruit of faith – the proof of its authenticity and, consequently, the evidence that a person's Christian confession is genuine – is a life of repentance and good works.

The Roman Catholic Council of Trent (1545-1563) rejected the Reformation understanding of the doctrine of justification, defining it dogmatically as a renewal of the inward man. It stated that God views the individual as just because He truly has made him inwardly just. The individual can therefore no longer be punished for sin. Sanctification, beginning with new birth, was declared the basis of justification. The bishops and cardinals assembled in Trent cursed anyone who upheld the Reformed doctrine of justification. Reformed theologians turned to Calvin's exposition of the doctrine of justification (*Institutes* III, 11.23) in their response to and rejection of the Roman Catholic doctrine of salvation as laid out at Trent. The single basis of justification is not the *imparted righteousness of God*, but the *imputed righteousness of Christ*.

Reformed theologians branded Arminians as crypto-Catholics (crypto = hidden): those who are no longer Catholics, but who still hold the same beliefs because they see faith itself as the true righteousness required for salvation. As a result, *faith* is counted to believers for righteousness, because righteousness is manifested in acts of faith themselves and not in reliance on Jesus's vicarious atonement. The Reformed accused Catholics and Arminians of advocating human pride by believing that the foundations of justification are found within believers themselves, and of robbing God's Son of the glory due to Him alone.

Why did Arminians accept the Catholic doctrine of justification which the Protestants opposed so strongly? They were driven to this conclusion by their logic, since they denied that salvation is entirely the work of God. They rejected the doctrine of an eternal decree which God accomplished in salvation history by effectually calling the individual and sovereignly preserving the believer. The essence of this decree lies in the gracious, unconditional offer of salvation.

The Arminian doctrine of justification consists of five denials which arise from its principal denial of salvation as the work of God alone:

1) Man's act of faith is not the gift of God in its entirety.
2) In God's plan, there is no direct relationship between the reception of salvation through Christ's obedience on the cross and the application of salvation by the Holy Spirit. Arminians believe that Jesus's atonement made it possible for all men to be saved without exception, but also that it does not necessarily guarantee the salvation of any one person. As a result, the idea that Christ's death was a substitutionary atonement has to be abandoned.
3) The Covenant of Grace is not a relationship initiated unconditionally by God Himself through the effectual call. Arminianism sees the Covenant of Grace as a new law which offers instant forgiveness on the condition of instant faith, as well as future salvation on the condition of ongoing faith.
4) Faith is not a matter of knowledge which relies on what has been accomplished by another. The Arminian alternative centers on the idea that faith causes man to make a decision. From the seventeenth century, many Pietists followed this Arminian concept as if it were a fundamental principle of the Protestant faith.
5) The basis of justification is not Christ's imputed righteousness, but faith itself. Arminius cited Romans 4:3, 5, and 9, in which Abraham's faith is counted to him for righteousness.

However, the Apostle Paul insisted that the Christian's righteousness is the gift of God (Romans 5:15-17). He emphasized that the sinner is justified by faith in the blood of Christ regardless of his own works (Ephesians 2:8-9): "For by grace are ye saved through faith; and that not of yourselves: it is the gift of God, 9) not of works, lest any man should boast." These statements alone make Arminius's interpretation impossible. The Arminian doctrine of justification is ultimately underpinned by a veiled form of righteousness by works. In principle, therefore, it accords with the doctrine of justification taught by the Roman Catholic Church for almost five hundred years since the Council of Trent. This doctrine necessarily led to a new legalism, the key idea of which is a call for constant moral self-improvement in order to secure future salvation by the individual's own efforts.

Following the Synod of Dort (1618-1619), Arminians were forced into exile until 1626, when they were allowed to return to their churches and open a theological seminary in Amsterdam. Three theologians, Episcopius, Curcellaeus (Courcelles), and Limborch, occupied successive positions of leadership in the seminary and became well known as influential Arminians, earning a reputation which endures to the present day. They sought to promote a theology which was characterized by an ever-changing Liberalism. This resulted in the rapid deterioration of Dutch Arminianism into a dogmatic Moralism that hardly differed from Socinianism, which teaches that the resurrected Jesus Christ could not be both man and God.

There are two strands of Arminianism: Remonstrants and Wesleyans (which includes the Methodist Church). Remonstrants claim that sin has weakened man morally and spiritually but has not ruined him completely; despite the damage of sinful tendencies, man retains an innate ability to live justly. Wesleyans, following Jacobus Arminius, believe that man lost his ability to accept the divine offer of salvation at the Fall, but that this will be restored to all men by the grace of God.

Remonstrants sought to improve man's fallen nature, to downplay the significance of sin, and to portray Christianity as a religion of moral living. Expressed in New Testament terms, they favored a Judaistic "Christianity" of strict adherence to the law – as does Catholicism. This was another Gospel, cursed twice by the Apostle Paul in the Epistle to the Galatians. As demonstrated by the century following the Synod of Dort, this path led to Deism, which taught that salvation is earned through moral living without the grace of God. Wesleyans, on the other hand, opposed Deism by clearly addressing the problem of sin so that God's grace would appear greater still. But did they truly represent the Reformation doctrine of justification?

The origins of Wesleyan Methodism – the oldest form of eighteenth-century English Pietism – can also be traced back to Pietist influences, although Pietism had a lesser role in its subsequent development. Pietism introduced the idea that methods discovered and applied by man guarantee a more spiritual life than do the means of grace. Although Wesley claimed to preach Calvin's doctrine of justification, he refused to speak of Christ's imputed righteousness as the basis of justification. He ignored the differences between Calvinistic and Arminian teaching, and had no clear conception of how Christ's obedience and man's faith were related with respect to the doctrine of justification. Wesley consequently adopted the views of Jacobus Arminius. In 1879, the Methodists conceded that Arminianism and Calvinism are indeed irreconcilable. The Arminians admitted to the Calvinists that their teaching has no logical place for a doctrine of original sin and substitutionary atonement. Methodists thus began to teach that man is not by nature under the wrath of God, and that Christ did not bear the punishment of sin as substitute for the elect.[29]

In the all-decisive matter of the biblical view of justification, it is vital to follow the Reformation teaching of Jesus's substitutionary atonement on the cross. Within the humanistic system of Arminianism, logic plays a relentless game with the teachings of Christianity. Its highest principle is freedom, and it consequently presents the doctrine of atonement as temporary, universal, and conditional. With respect to Christ's atonement, Wesleyans teach that salvation is possible for man, but that there is no way of guaranteeing that any one person will be saved. They believe that salvation depends entirely on fulfillment of the conditions of true collaboration between God and man.

2.4 A strict distinction between two kingdoms

Martin Luther was principally a church reformer and not, like Thomas Hobbes or Jean-Jacques Rousseau, a political agitator or philosopher. At thirty-four years of age, he began breaking new ground through his intensive studies of the Pauline epistles, which soon resulted in his initiation of the Reformation. He focused primarily on revising Catholic theology and church policy on the basis of the Holy Scriptures. His religious views were therefore key in shaping his political principles, which were never more than a secondary concern throughout his life. However, Luther can still be characterized, at least to some extent, as a political theologian who vehemently opposed the deplorable sale of indulgences, through which the Roman Catholic Church made vast sums of money to accommodate the inordinate extravagance of the Roman Curia. Luther fully rejected the Church's claims regarding the sacraments and publicly declared that priests had neither the right nor the authority to forgive man's sins. He confidently stated the doctrine of universal priesthood – that there is no fundamental difference between the clergy and the layperson. He challenged the Catholic doctrine of "Two Swords," which claims that the Pope is the source of all authority in both temporal and spiritual matters. He combatted this with the biblical teaching that governing authorities receive their secular power from God. Only the ministerial duties of the church are spiritual in nature, and by fulfilling the commandment of love, they have a bearing on man's physical life as well as his inner life.

Believing that man is depraved by nature and stands before God as a sinner, Luther defined his political principles and issued three works in 1520. In 1523, he published a text entitled *Secular Authority: to what extent it should be obeyed* in response to his excommunication and the imperial ban, which forbade the printing and sale of his writings. In addition to being outlawed,

---

[29] John Miley, *The Atonement in Christ* (New York City, NY: Eaton & Mains; Cincinnati, OH: Jennings & Graham, [1879] 1907); https://archive.org/details/atonementinchris00mile/page/n7

Luther also suffered considerable financial loss. However, he refused to be affected by his adverse circumstances and pressed on with his writing undeterred. He dedicated his *Secular Authority* to Duke Johann I of Saxony, who desired to know the extent to which his secular power was consistent with the Christian faith. Luther pointed to Romans 13 and I Peter 2:13-14 – verses which can provide a basis for the exercise of civil government authority. His explanations appear to contradict biblical passages such as Matthew 5:38-41, 44, Romans 12:19, and I Peter 3:9, which seem to forbid Christians from wielding the sword even in civil government. In order to prevent this misunderstanding and propose a solution, Luther divided mankind into two categories: the kingdom of Christ and the kingdom of the world. The kingdom of Christ consists of true Christians who are under the authority of the Messiah, "taught, ruled, and upheld" by the Gospel. Luther believed that Christians do not need to be ruled by a secular, sword-bearing government, for the Holy Spirit causes them to love their neighbors and seek justice. The law was rather given by God for the sake of the wicked (I Tim. 1:9) – to prevent man from stubbornly living in intentional sin. Furthermore, Luther believed that the law teaches man to recognize the absolute necessity of grace for deliverance from the enslaving, devastating power of sin. The secular kingdom contains those who neither are Christians nor behave like them, despite often pretending to be believers. They are therefore governed by civil law and authority and, according to Luther, the law of the Gospel should not be applied to the secular kingdom. His idea cannot be interpreted to mean that the Christian kingdom opposes the secular. Neither did he think that a united Christian kingdom would one day be established in the world. The German Reformer divided all people into specific spheres of authority so that Christians would be governed by the Word of God and non-Christians by lawgivers appointed by God. Neither kingdom is licensed to control the other. The Church should not look to secular government as the ultimate basis of authority; neither should secular governments usurp spiritual authority within Christianity.

Luther never desired to imitate a radical sociopolitical revolution. He believed that if people had a right understanding of God's love, they would perform good works spontaneously and voluntarily out of gratitude. He rejected the idea that social change could be brought about merely through human effort. Reform could only take place if the human heart were wholly transformed by the Word of God and the work of the Holy Spirit. The vital means of effecting this change was the preaching of the Gospel. Every person – whether Pope, cleric, prince, or beggar – had the same need for grace. Luther's teaching was a spiritual attack on the principle of hierarchy; he never intended to undermine the very foundations of medieval society. When peasants defied royal and ecclesiastical authorities with a bloodthirsty revolt in 1525, he condemned the use of arms and violence to confront social injustice. The force with which he resisted the Peasants' Revolt provided a model for the call for peace in society and politics into the twenty-first century.

If all men were in equal need of grace, any special spiritual disciplines such as monastic life were rendered meaningless. As a result, monastic orders were dissolved in Lutheran areas. The use of church estate for other – often secular – purposes had far-reaching political consequences: the distribution of monastic land facilitated social and political change. Contrary to Luther's own expectations, the political power of sovereign rulers was decisive in determining the "eternal salvation" of their subjects, at least in terms of whether they would be Catholic, Lutheran, or Reformed. Secular authorities increased enormously in their significance for many people as they regulated virtually all areas of physical and religious life.

Unlike the Greco-Roman world, the Post-Reformation world welcomed social reform. Institutions that had enjoyed unassailable dominance for centuries were no longer immune to the corrosive influences of revolutionary change. Church structure was also subjected to thorough revision as the concept of the hierarchical state church was consciously abandoned. It gradually became clear that state and church authorities were no longer in a position to claim divine rights.[30]

2.5 Liberal foundations of the modern world

John Calvin achieved great things as a writer. However, he also stood up practically for the concerns of the Reformation. Driven by a burning desire to put biblical principles into practice, Calvin engaged in a storm of religious, political, and personal disputes. He demonstrated astonishing perseverance and determination despite numerous setbacks, never abandoning his vision nor ever being satisfied with half measures. People today are sadly unaware of his tremendous achievements beyond his theological work – in society and in politics. Calvin transformed the politics of not just one city, but of all European nations and ultimately the whole world without this ever being his aim. He was concerned first and foremost with contemporary problems in theology and the church.

The Reformation was politically a lost cause surrounded by overpowering enemies. However, Calvin's combined spiritual-moral strength was of such force and magnitude that it helped the Reformation to victory, saving it from obliteration and thereby preserving Europe from downfall. The force of the Reformation which he sparked in French-speaking Switzerland has been felt throughout the world down to the present day. Tragically, he is the last person considered when the benefits of liberal social structure are discussed. On arriving in Geneva, Calvin immediately realized that although the Gospel was being preached, the church was still far from resembling the biblical ideal. In his opinion, a true church was marked not only by declaration of the Gospel, but also by following it intentionally and faithfully. He saw his

---

[30] Martin Walzer, *The Revolution of the Saints: A Study in the Origins of Radical Politics* (New York City, NY: Atheneum Publishers, 1968).

primary role as a Reformer as urging the evangelical church to conform to what, according to the Scriptures, it should look like in the eyes of the world. He wanted to achieve this ambitious goal through neither the Sunday sermon, nor teaching, nor an appeal for morality, but through church discipline. It is perhaps surprising that the church has only just begun to align itself with biblical standards for the structure of church services and to be mindful of moral purity in the lives of its members when Calvin insisted on consistent discipline in Geneva more than four centuries ago.

The proper conduct of worship services, especially in terms of who was and was not permitted to participate in the Lord's Supper, was a central matter in church discipline. Calvin placed great importance on the purity of the church, and subsequent Reformed theologians and ministers similarly emphasized church discipline as a vital mark of the true Church. Calvin wanted to ensure that those who claimed to be Christians were indeed true believers. What he never foresaw was the impact that application of this principle would have on areas other than the church. We have church discipline to thank for a free church in a free country, for Calvin released the church from the political clutches of the state. God never appointed national governments to control the internal affairs of the church and have supreme authority in matters of the Christian faith; rather, the rule of His church belongs to King Jesus. The fact that Calvin restricted this claim of power deliberately and exclusively to the Church is particularly important in our day. Postmillennialists are unjustified in referring to Calvin's alleged influence on Genevan government in order to support their own claim to power in world politics. Calvin did not spark the censorship of private and public morals in Geneva. This censorship – which was often illiberal, overstated, and tyrannical – was practiced in all European cities with similar systems. It was part of the regular population control carried out by local law enforcement officers. The only valid argument for Calvin's role in the censorship is that he sought to use his spiritual influence for the good of the city's inhabitants. He was anxious to bring order to the arbitrary application of civil law, which was certainly a necessary and positive task. He never held a public office nor exercised political power in Geneva, and was not even granted citizenship until the end of his life. As with so much of the prejudice against Calvin's work, the accusation that he acted dictatorially is not founded on historical truth but on malicious interpretation of contemporary customs which Calvin neither provoked nor endorsed. Historical knowledge of his exceptional work is often completely lacking, or if known remains in silence. It is fair to say that every Swiss person, and indeed innumerable people around the world, benefit directly and personally from Calvin's work.

Calvin stated the essence of his view on church discipline in the first edition of his *Institutes*, published in the spring of 1536. When he arrived in Geneva the following year, he lost no time in putting it into practice. In 1537, he presented the city council with a document signed by all Genevan ministers which summarized the new understanding of church discipline. The key element of its constituent principles was not punishment but liberty. Three points were proposed. First, it was necessary to see which of the city's inhabitants desired to be members of the church of Jesus Christ, and to prepare a confession of faith for this purpose. Second, children needed be instructed in the doctrines of faith. And third, certain individuals who had a good reputation among the believers, who were blameless, and who had a steady mind should be appointed as overseers. These would be instructed to monitor the behavior of church members, to advise and admonish them, and to draw the minister's attention to any stubborn individuals. If the latter proved incorrigible, they would be suspended from the fellowship. Their excommunication would be indicated by prohibition from participating in the Lord's Supper, and their names were also to be given to the other believers in order for them to cease fellowship. Through this structure of church discipline Calvin founded the Protestant Church.[31] He did not want to interfere with the official regulations of civil rule; the authorities would still carry out government tasks as before within their own sphere of power. But the Church needed to be exempted in order to govern its own affairs.

The Genevan city council did not grant Calvin his requests in 1537 – yet he was constantly willing to endure suffering and inconvenience in defending and enforcing his principle. This was especially evident in 1538, when the failure of his proposal to introduce church discipline led to his exile. His petition was still denied when he returned to Geneva in 1541, but he continued to fight without wavering. Only in 1555 – fourteen years after his return and eighteen years after commencing his *Institutes* – did the Genevan city council grant the Church its spiritual liberties. Every Protestant church that can freely perform the duties of a church of Christ owes this to Calvin's tireless appeal for church discipline. The principle of liberty, first applied in the Church, gradually infiltrated many other areas of community and led to the formation of institutions which brought about a social, economic, and political Liberalism in the best sense of the word – in the biblical sense. The foundation of our modern world was laid by Calvin. We should be constantly aware that our civil rights are owed to the implementation of church discipline during the Reformation.

3 The esoteric conception of an earthly paradise

For hundreds of years, theologians tried to protect the Christian faith from the virulent elements of Paganism which emerged in the public sphere. They were successful to an extent, but were unable to get rid of secret societies. At the heart of pagan philosophy was the idea that nature could provide sufficient explanation for the existence of man and the universe. The Christian doctrine of Creation was rejected above all, and mystics dedicated themselves

---

[31] John Calvin, *Institutio* (1559), IV, 12-21.

to searching for cosmic unity. There is fundamentally only one esoteric tradition which is manifested in countless legends, myths, and philosophies. "Black magic" has been practiced systematically throughout the ages and across the world.

3.1 The natural philosophy of Renaissance Neoplatonism

(Renaissance scholars entangled in Esotericism)
Progressive historians dedicated themselves to studying the Renaissance because they saw in it the first signs of future developments. Renaissance scholars are said to have wanted to revive classical philosophy, science, and literature, and to cast off the intellectual chains of the monastic and superstitious Middle Ages. However, this representation is misleading: Renaissance men were often involved in astrology, magic, and alchemy, with Neoplatonism and Hermeticism playing a vital role. Neoplatonism was presented in such a way as to gain wide approval and has consequently influenced intellectual history down to the present day in the form of Esotericism. It teaches that divine nature is immanent in matter, and that the microcosm of humanity and the macrocosm of the universe are interconnected.[32]

Renaissance esotericists wanted to reunite Christian denominations under one doctrine in order to end the religious wars. To this end, they proposed the so-called "ancient theology" which God supposedly gave to Moses on Mount Sinai. Although Christian in name, it was pagan in origin.[33] Magic was at the heart of the scientific tradition of the European Renaissance, laying the foundation for the later development of Skepticism and encouraging the emergence of new religions.

Renaissance scholars were interested in natural philosophy. Desiring to revolutionize science, they questioned all traditional knowledge[34] and thereby created a link between rationalistic science and irrational Pantheism. Like Gnosticism, Neoplatonism holds that the human soul is spirit held captive by matter. Ancient religions or mystery cults, such as those of Hermes Trismegistus[35], Zoroaster, and Orpheus, taught that the material universe is

---

[32] Keith Thomas, *Religion and the Decline of Magic: Studies in popular beliefs in sixteenth- and seventeenth-century* (London: Weidenfeld and Nicolson, 1971; London: Folio Society, 2012) 165-166; https://archive.org/details/ReligionAndTheDeclineOfMagicStudiesInPopular-BeliefsInSixteenthAndSeventeenthCenturyEngland/page/n165.

[33] Frances Amelia Yates, *Giordano Bruno and the Hermetic Tradition* (London: Routledge, [1964] 2015) passim.

[34] Hugh J. Kearney, *Science and Change: 1500-1700* (New York City, NY: McGraw-Hill, 1971) 48; https://archive.org/details/sciencechange15000kear

[35] Lyndy Abraham, *A Dictionary of Alchemical Imagery* (Cambridge: Cambridge University Press, 2001) 100-101; Johannes Fabricius, *Alchemy: The Medieval Alchemists and Their Royal Art* (Cockeysville, MD: Diamond Books, 1994) 214, 225; Charles Nicholl, *The Chemical Theatre* (London: Routledge & Kegan Paul, 1980; New York City, NY: Akadine Press, 1997) 49;

animated by a divine soul.[36] They claimed that there is no divine person, only a divine force immanent in all things, and that the planets and stars are living beings filled with divine spirit.[37] In contrast, Christian doctrine emphasizes the unity of man as body and soul, offers eternal salvation to every individual, and teaches that the material world is essentially good.

Renaissance scholars turned to the sources of ancient Mysticism in order to access the world of magic. They used obscure symbols in order to protect their findings from rivals, with scholarship consequently becoming a secret enterprise which was only of use to the elite. Pythagoreanism gave rise to a belief that the deep secrets of the universe could be revealed through numbers.[38] Neoplatonist philosophers hoped to gain greater personal power by studying the occult and used manipulation to find sources of supernatural strength.[39] They believed that the human spirit could communicate with invisible forces, but only in order to bring them in line with its own will. The Renaissance man saw himself as a new god in the making. The Renaissance, the Enlightenment, the Romantic era, and every other movement of modernity are united by a common feature. Each in its own characteristic way staged a powerful protest against Christianity.[40]

3.2 Mysterious immersion in the life cycles of creation

The word "Hermeticism" comes from the mythical figure Hermes Trismegistus.[41] Hermeticism replaces systematic explanation of rational principles with mystical immersion in the life cycles of the universe. Despite the obvious antitheses, it does agree with at least two Christian doctrines: that 1) the Almighty God prevails over chaos, and 2) carnal pleasure can be an "error of love."[42] In every other respect, however, it promotes the anti-

---

Charles John Samuel Thompson, *The Lure and Romance of Alchemy* (London: G. G. Harrap, 1932; Detroit, MI: Gale Research Co., 1974) 31; https://archive.org/details/b3032015x/page/30

[36] Daniel Pickering Walker, *Spiritual and Demonic Magic from Ficino to Campanella* (London: Warburg Institute, University of London, 1958) passim.

[37] Kearney, *Science and Change: 1500-1700*, 100.

[38] Ibid.

[39] Walker, *Spiritual and Demonic Magic from Ficino to Campanella*, passim.

[40] Giorgio de Santillana, ed., in Introduction to *The Age of Adventure* (Indianapolis, IN: Houghton Mifflin Company & New American Library of World Literature, Inc., 1956; New York City, NY: George Barzieller, 1957) 29; https://archive.org/details/ageofadventurere-00desa/page/28

[41] Antoine Faivre, *The Eternal Hermes* (Grand Rapids, MI: Phanes, 1995); Antoine Faivre, *Access to Western Esotericism* (Albany, NY: State University of New York Press, 1994); Antoine Faivre, J. Needleman, eds., *Modern Esoteric Spirituality* (New York City, NY: Crossroad, 1992); Antoine Faivre, Rolf Christian Zimmermann, eds., *Epochen der Naturmystik: Hermetische Tradition im wissenschaftlichen Fortschritt* (Berlin: Erich Schmidt, 1979).

[42] J. Everard, *The Divine Pymander of Hermes Mercurius Trismegistus* (London: G. Redway,

Christian "chaos syndrome." The Hermetic God is both male and female. Hermeticism teaches that man separates himself from God by desiring to serve only himself, and that by leaving his original circle of living, he seeks to understand the force controlling the fire. The Seven Governors of the world turn to him in love and grant him a share in divine nature. In contrast to Christianity, which teaches that the world is approaching inevitable destruction, Hermeticism posits the idea of "Eternal Restoration." It holds that the ongoing transformation of all things should effect a continuous process of purification.

According to Hermetic theory, the divine stoops down to Earth and participates in its affairs, appearing as laborers, artists, and sculptors. Hermetic ideas were embraced by English writers such as Edmund Spenser[43] and William Shakespeare[44]. Man is understood to ascend the same ladder by which God descends to him. The earth dweller is seen as a mortal God, while the Father of All is viewed as an immortal man.

Such a union between God and man is irreconcilable with the Christian faith because of the separation of God, man, and nature. Hermeticism called magicians to surmount mortality and transience through divine strength. The Renaissance brought a great increase in the glorification of man, which was based on ideas of ontological commonality with the divine.

The works of Giovanni Pico della Mirandola (1463-1494) and Henry Vaughan (1621/1622-1695) contain alchemical speculations which cite Hermeticism as their source. Other eminent writers such as Bernadus Silvestris (1085-1160/1178), Giordano Bruno[45] (1548-1600), John Milton (1608-1674), William Blake[46] (1757-1827), Jakob Böhme (1575-1624), and Friedrich Nietzsche (1844-1900) took up ideas such as the cyclic renovation of the world, the predominance of chaos and darkness, the connection between God and man, and the eternal persistence of both order and confusion.

1884) 13; https://archive.org/details/b2487839x/page/12

[43] Edmund Spenser (1552?-1599), *The Complete Poetical Works: The Faerie Queene*, Book VII. Two Cantos of Mutabilitie, Canto VI, 14-17, R. E. Neil Dodge, ed. (Boston & New York City, NY: Houghton Mifflin Co., [1590] 1908): "[…] But chiefely Mercury, that next doth raigne / Ran forth in haste, unto the king of gods to plaine. […]"; https://www.bartleby.com/br/153.html

[44] Betty Jo Teeter Dobbs, *The Janus Face of Genius* (Cambridge: Cambridge University Press, 1991) 274-275.

[45] Giordano Bruno, *Spaccio de la bestia trionfante* (1584).

[46] William Blake, "The Tyger" (1794), in *Songs of Experience* (Mineola, NY: Dover Publications, [1794] 1984): "[…] In what distant deeps or skies / Burnt the fire of thine eyes? ..[…] what shoulder, & what art, / Could twist the sinews of thy heart? A terrible God, yet human; a powerful God, yet a workman. […]"

3.3 Mystical drive for human deification

(Attaining immortality through the philosopher's stone)
Alchemy is the process of converting base metals into noble metals. Its origins are found in the myths of Mesopotamian metalworkers (c.1200 B.C.).[47] According to Hermetic legend, the founder of alchemy and writer of the alchemical text *Tabula Smaragdina*[48], Hermes Trismegistus, introduced the secret of transmutation to Egyptians in 2500 B.C. People came to believe that the Egyptians' wealth was gained through their use of alchemy. The "royal art" spread from Egypt to Greece and the Middle East, with Middle Eastern cultures mixing Gnostic thought with the art of alchemy and Arabs becoming patrons of the Hermetic scholarship which they received from the Greeks. Europeans discovered alchemical writings during the medieval crusades, and many soon began chemical experiments in the hope of turning lead into gold. In the Middle Ages, some alchemists encrypted their procedures through allegory, while others who were connected to the church pointed to the relationship between the regenerating properties of the philosopher's stone (lapis philosophorum) and Jesus Christ.[49]

The idea that the alchemist wanted to turn lead into gold using the philosopher's stone is a common legend. Crucially, however, alchemists were motivated by a belief that the stone would bring them immortality, of which gold was considered a symbol.[50] The themes of death and reincarnation are therefore frequently addressed in alchemical literature.[51] Striving for human deification, man placed himself on a par with God as a creator.[52] However, the secrets of conversion were known only to the initiated. Frequent mixing of chemical elements was believed to lead to a transformation in which the alchemist himself was also changed. Furthermore, the philosopher's stone

---

[47] Mircea Eliade, *The Forge and the Crucible: The Origins and Structures of Alchemy* (New York City, NY: Harper & Row, [1956] 1971) 19-26; https://archive.org/details/forgecrucible00eliarich/page/18

[48] Lyndy Abraham, *A Dictionary of Alchemical Imagery* (Cambridge: Cambridge University Press, 2001) 100-101; Johannes Fabricius, *Alchemy: The Medieval Alchemists and Their Royal Art* (Cockeysville, MD: Diamond Books, 1994) 214, 225; Charles Nicholl, *The Chemical Theatre* (London: Routledge & Kegan Paul, 1980; New York City, NY: Akadine Press, 1997) 49; Charles John Samuel Thompson, *The Lure and Romance of Alchemy* (London: G. G. Harrap, 1932; Detroit, MI: Gale Research Co., 1974) 31; https://archive.org/details/b3032015x/page/30

[49] Henry Carrington Bolton, "The Literature of Alchemy," republished in *The Pharmaceutical Review*, vol. XIX, nos. 4, 5 (1901); John Read & Frederick Henry Sawyer, *Prelude to Chemistry* (New York City, NY: The Macmillan Company, 1937); H. M. E. De Jong, *Michael Maier's Atalanta Fugiens* (Lake Worth, FL: Nicolas-Hays, 1969) 21-39. Michael Maiers *Atalanta Fugiens* wurde zuerst 1617 in Oppenheim veröffentlich. Stanton J. Linden, *Darke Hieroglyphicks* (Lexington, KY: University Press of Kentucky, 2015) 6-36.

[50] Eliade, *The Forge and the Crucible*, 151; https://archive.org/details/forgecrucible00eliarich/page/150

[51] Ibid., 155, 161; https://archive.org/details/forgecrucible00eliarich/page/154

[52] Ibid., 170; https://archive.org/details/forgecrucible00eliarich/page/170

was ascribed miraculous healing powers.[53] Esotericists believed that there was unity of being in both matter and spirit, and magicians therefore tried to reconvert all existing elements into one material and reconcile all opposing elements.

Esotericism holds that the lower and upper worlds are united by a hidden line of connection. This knowledge gives the magician access to the secret power centers of the universe, and he is thus supposedly capable of altering fate by skillfully manipulating the celestial bodies. The aim of magic is to rule nature, man, and spirit. The improvement of the imperfect world is referred to as a second creation. Alchemistic mythology equates the philosopher's stone with God's perfect knowledge; gold is symbolic of light, which ultimately comes from God. The philosopher's stone would supposedly reconcile all conflicts. Both before and during the Renaissance, paintings were used to translate philosophical and theological language into esoteric symbols. Talismans were produced which would supposedly bring about the desired changes in the upper and lower worlds if, like the statues of Hermes, they were appropriately used.

The alchemical conception of man and the idea of transformation have inevitable social implications. The alchemist sees himself as the first man of a new race, the present-day representative of a new ethnic group. This is an elitist view of social reformation. During the Enlightenment, practitioners of alchemy were closely connected with revolutionary agitators. The Mysticism of the Renaissance, which often took the form of alchemy, eventually led to the surge of political Radicalism demonstrated in the French Revolution.[54]

3.4 Magical manipulation of natural processes

The influence of Hellenistic Mysticism is manifested in Judaism as well as in other high religions. Kabbalists take up Neoplatonic speculations about God – "the One" – in order to recast Him as a distant, impersonal figure whose primary function is to be the fullness of being. Jewish Mysticism has a low opinion of the material world, the human body, and historical chronology. Kabbalah[55] reverses the relationship between Creator and creation, seeking to put God at man's disposal with divine power serving human purposes.[56] It teaches that mankind has a duty to save the universe, a task that includes

---

[53] Cit. in ibid., 167; https://archive.org/details/forgecrucible00eliarich/page/166

[54] Margaret C. Jacob, *The Radical Enlightenment: Pantheists, Freemasons and Republicans* (London: George Allen & Unwin, 1981).

[55] Heinrich Elijah Benedikt, *Die Kabbala als jüdisch-christlicher Einweihungsweg* (Freiburg: Hermann Bauer, 1985; München: Ansata Verlag, 2004); Johann Maier, *Die Kabbalah. Einführung – Klassische Texte – Erläuterungen* (München: Verlag C.H. Beck, 1995).

[56] Shlomo Giora Shoham, *Bridges to Nothingness: Gnosis, Kabala, Existentialism, and the Transcendental Predicament of Man* (London: Associated University Presses, 1994) 111.

perfecting a defective God who is wholly dependent on man for his salvation.[57] This great commission can supposedly only be accomplished by a Kabbalist as a partner of God.

Kabbalah even suggests that man can destroy God and create a replacement.[58] This is seen as desirable, since the God of the Old Testament, a Creator responsible for the physical existence of man, is considered blind, arrogant, and merciless.[59] Mystical experience of God takes precedence over understanding the divine revelation recorded in the Pentateuch. Kabbalah received great interest in Christian circles during the Renaissance and had a lasting influence on European intellectual history. The royal advisor John Dee probably received a substantial salary from William Cecil (Lord Burleigh) (1520/1521-1598) and later from Queen Elizabeth I as a reward for his occult knowledge. Cecil believed that Kabbalah had an enormous influence on new scientific developments and hoped that it would prove useful to the secret service. In the 1590s, Shakespeare addressed the cultural revolutions provoked by Dee in his plays, highlighting both positive and negative results.

Dee saw himself as a "Christian" Kabbalist. On the one hand, "Christian Kabbalah" asserted itself as a potential worldwide reform movement and was taken up throughout Europe as well as in Elizabethan England, consequently becoming responsible for the almost complete loss of the influence of medieval scholasticism on scholarly thinking.[60] On the other hand, "Christian Kabbalah" presupposes that there is good, or "white," magic. One method of magically manipulating natural processes, known as "Gematria," consists of learning the numerical significances of Hebrew words since every letter of the Hebrew alphabet holds a numerical value. Dee also strove to discover the names of angels through Kabbalah, so that like God he could command these supernatural beings to perform miraculous tasks.

In a meeting held in November 1577 between Queen Elizabeth I and her advisors, John Dee presented his imperialist plans for North America. This was the first demonstrable endorsement of the establishment of a British Empire, which was supposedly intended to spread the Protestant faith. The emerging empire formed political preconditions for the introduction of a new world order, based on the dark fantasies of a Kabbalist who had devoted himself wholly to the study of books on magic. Dee initiated a process of development founded on the close relationship between Messianic politics, high finance, and magic. The British Empire was to resemble the Holy Roman Empire of the German nation in order to take its place. According to Dee, the downfall of the Habsburg Empire had already been declared by the stars.

---

[57] Ibid., 110-111.

[58] Ibid., 112.

[59] Ibid., 97.

[60] Ibid., 79; https://archive.org/details/YatesFrancesTheOccultPhilosophyInTheElizabethanAgeRoutledge/page/n91

Dee's mission to Prague in 1583 was his most important service to Queen and country. William Cecil intended to isolate Philip II of Spain politically and at the same time thwart the plans of the Jesuits and Habsburgs, who were bent on taking control of England. He therefore ordered Dee to go undercover as a spy and become a trusted advisor to the Habsburg Catholic Emperor Rudolf II. Elizabeth sided with her warmongering advisors who wanted to take up arms against the Catholics in the Low Countries, thus attacking the Habsburgs where they seemed to be most weak. However, the military campaign of 1586 ended in England's defeat. After a six-year stay in Prague, Dee realized in 1589 that his mission to the continent had failed. On his return journey, he met the physician and renowned hermeticist Dr. Henricus Khunrath[61], who reported Dee's Kabbalism to members of esoteric circles in the German lands.[62] The significance of this meeting is that through it Dee sowed the seeds of the later Rosicrucian movement.[63] This outlasted Rudolf's reign, continuing to exist as a secret society for many years after. Both Freemasonry and the Royal Society were influenced by Rosicrucianism. After Elizabeth's reign, Dee fell from favor on account of his sorcery and was exiled from the royal court.[64]

3.5 Rediscovery of ancient theology

Twenty years after the death of John Dee, Francis Bacon took Dee's vision a step further in his utopian novel *New Atlantis*[65]. Bacon was careful not to say that he had been inspired by Dee's Esotericism, although it was not difficult to see that this is what he was doing. Like his contemporary Shakespeare, Bacon was unquestionably one of the great intellectual giants of sixteenth-century England. In accordance with esoteric "ancient theology" ("prisca theologia"[66]), he believed in the possibility for man to regain his lost status as an earthly god. With nature fully under his control, man could restore society to a state of perfection. Bacon and other early modern scholars believed that

---

[61] Frances Amelia Yates, *The Rosicrucian Enlightenment* (London and Boston: Routledge & Kegan Paul, 1972) 38.

[62] Henricus Khunrath, *Amphitheatrum Sapientiae Aeternae, Solius, Verae, Christiano-Kabalisticum, Divino-Magicum, Physico-Chymicum, Tertriunum-Catholicon* (Hamburg, 1595; Magdeburg 1608, 1609; Frankfurt 1653).

[63] Yates, *The Rosicrucian Enlightenment*, 38.

[64] Ibid., 188.

[65] Francis Bacon, *New Atlantis* (London: J. Crooke, 1627); http://archive.org/details/fnewatlantis00baco; republication: Francis Bacon, *Advancement of Learning and The New Atlantis* (Oxford: Oxford University Press, 1913); https://archive.org/details/advancementnewat00bacouoft/page/236

[66] Marsilio Ficino (1433-1499) was the first who used the term "prisca theologia". Christopher S. Celenza, "Marsilio Ficino," in Edward N. Zalta, ed., *The Stanford Encyclopedia of Philosophy*, Summer 2015 Edition (Stanford, CA: Stanford University Press, 2015); http://plato.stanford.edu/archives/sum2015/entries/ficino/

science offered inexhaustible knowledge about the secrets of the universe, and consequently saw it as a new form of salvation. Bacon led the rejection of traditional scholarship and the radical reformation of the foundations of philosophical and scientific research more than any other seventeenth-century philosopher. He not only encouraged an inductive approach to research (working from the specific to the general), but also sought to establish a society which would focus on increasing scientific knowledge – a goal that was later taken up in earnest by the Royal Society. Bacon also encouraged international scientific collaboration. He believed that almost all traditional knowledge was at best untrustworthy and at worst entirely false, since there had been no adequate research methods in the past. He proposed a new method consisting of empirical observation, experimental replication, and functional manipulation of natural processes. Despite the fact that Bacon never conducted any experiments himself and therefore made no significant contribution to science, few philosophers have demonstrated greater eloquence in scientific matters. He considered science a redemptive gospel and saw scientists as elected prophets and priests, provided that they worked within the framework of his empirical method.

Bacon was certain that a utopian social structure would be developed in the future, having complete confidence in the vast potential of science for achieving humanity's goals in seeking perfection. He refuted the ancient belief that anyone who wanted to transcend the limitations of human nature would meet with condemnation in consequence, and that the idea of assuming divine nature was a sacrilegious act that could not remain unpunished. According to Bacon, man should intentionally seek to transcend anything that restrains his personal development. He would thereby symbolically enter the higher realm – the realm of divine nature. Adam sinned in desiring the knowledge of good and evil, but this was entirely separate from the knowledge which God desired to give man so that he could govern the world. Natural science therefore had nothing to do with the original sin of eating from the tree of the knowledge of good and evil. On the contrary, this sin could only be redressed if nature were subjected to the rule of the human intellect. To that end, Bacon called for old truths to be replaced by the new. Doing away with traditional knowledge was the only way by which knowledge could be raised to a new level. Bacon stated paradoxically that rediscovering "ancient theology" was vital to gaining new knowledge. He thus made it clear, despite all assertions to the contrary, that he was indeed influenced by a tradition of knowledge acquisition that stretched far back into the past, even though it stood in opposition to other ancient traditions of truth-seeking.

The effort to make Bacon a patriarch of natural science, and by extension a herald of the secularization of Western culture, required an interpretation of his works which downplayed the importance of the religious language found on so many of their pages. However, such language is so obvious that it cannot be overlooked. His writings show that he turned to the religious tradition of Hermeticism. In taking up the theory of pre-Adamism, he highlighted a reinterpretation of the biblical narrative which closely paralleled the creation myth of the *Corpus Hermeticum*. Bacon asserted that it was man's prerogative to govern the world as the pinnacle of God's creation. In order to do so, however, man required a knowledge comparable with the omniscience of God, which he could obtain only through Hermeticism and Kabbalah. Bacon was interested in a mythological Solomon who, as the most erudite of all magicians, knew every secret of nature. He encouraged King James I to present himself as a new King Solomon, and James's consequent identification with the illustrious son of David indicated his firm belief that he was following a divine call to build a new Jerusalem. However, he could only justly fulfil this calling if he possessed the new knowledge offered to him so eagerly by Bacon. Building the New Jerusalem with the holy temple at its center would only be possible if it were based on the esoteric "prisca theologia." In this way, England could overcome the spell of ignorance that had been cast over Europe. The ideal conditions required to restore the perfection that had existed before man lost his perfect knowledge were thus clearly presented. Only in this way could man get rid of the sinfulness of limited knowledge.

The British Imperialism inspired by Dee's Cabbalism fell out of royal favor when James I ascended the throne of England. Elizabeth I had encouraged the Protestant faith, but anyone now desiring to pursue it had to do so secretly while unsupported at court. Imperialists were forced to form a secret society, identifying themselves from this point as Rosicrucians[67] and shortly after as Freemasons. Bacon's *New Atlantis* marked the beginning of a long tradition in Western literature in which science and technology are viewed as salvation. His book became highly popular as both English and American Puritans implemented its ideas during the seventeenth century, living in expectation of a Golden Age – the millennial reign. The fact that Bacon's religious views were completely different from those of Christianity – even in complete opposition to them – was disregarded. Divine revelation lost its primacy as the basis of natural philosophy, thus conceding its leading role in conveying infallible knowledge of the natural world. It was replaced by the discernment of autonomous human reason. The doctrine of natural law, conceived by Zeno of Citium who founded the Stoic school of philosophy, was developed further and promoted as an ethical foundation.

Bacon lived during a time that was virtually dictated by the symbols of Hermeticism and Kabbalah. Even if he had intended to resist their influence, he would only have had partial success. He saw science as the instrument of religious reformation. Although he argued that divine revelation was futile, historians have convincingly indicated a Millennialist dimension to his thinking which was based on the book of Revelation. His decision to use the term "Instauration"[68] (restoration) so prominently can only be properly

---

[67] Yates, *The Rosicrucian Enlightenment*, 128.

[68] Francis Bacon, *The Great Instauration* (1620), trans. by R. L. Ellis & J. Spedding, ed. by J. M. Robertson, *The Philosophical Works of Francis Bacon* (London: Routledge, 1905); https://archive.org/details/philosophicalwo00robegoog/page/n262; The cover images is missing in

understood in the context of his age. At the time, Puritans were seeking to initiate a reform movement aimed at fundamental social transformation. They were able to achieve this in part during the English Civil War (1642-1649) and the Interregnum (1649-1660), although the concrete effects were of relatively short duration despite being dramatic during the time of the Republic and the Protectorate.

3.6 Proclamation of a universal reformation

(The Rosicrucian idea of spiritual and political world reform)
The origins and ideas of Rosicrucianism resulted from discontentment among noblemen and scholars, who were dissatisfied with how the Reformation had developed after Martin Luther. Many people resented the social upheaval caused by the Lutheran Reformation and were consequently hostile to the new social order.

The legend of Christian Rosenkreutz was well known from 1610. Rosencreutz had intended to share the knowledge that he had gained in the Near East and Africa with European scholars but met with general disinterest. In his disappointment, he established a fraternity to preserve his knowledge for posterity. Its members spread across the European continent so that they could reveal their secret knowledge when the right time came. The 1614 pamphlet *Fama Fraternitatis, or a Discovery of the Fraternity of the Most Laudable Order of the Rose Cross*[69] made an appeal to the European upper class for a society based on Christian charity – one which would initiate a second global Reformation and completely transform science, religion, culture, and society. The *Confessio Fraternitatis*[70], published by the Order of the Rose Cross in 1615, rejected the papacy. In the 1616 novelistic allegory *Chymical Wedding of Christian Rosenkreutz*[71], the Lutheran theologian Johann Valentin Andreae (1586-1654) described the initiation of Christian Rosencreutz. Andreae contributed substantially to the developing legend of the secret Rosicrucian Order, with the faculty of theology at the University of Tübingen playing a key role in shaping his thinking.

---

this edition.

[69] Johann Valentin Andreae, *Fama fraternitatis, oder, Entdeckung der Brüderschafft des löblichen Ordens dess Rosen Creutzes: beneben der Confession, oder, Bekantnus derselben Fraternitet, an alle Gelehrte und Häupter in Europa geschrieben: auch etlichen Responsionen von Haselmeyern und anderen gelehrten Leuten auff die Famam gestellet* (Dantzigk: Andream Hünefeldt, 1615); https://archive.org/details/famafraternitati00andr/page/n6

[70] The full Latin and German titles were: 1) *Confessio Fraternitatis R. C. Ad Eruditos Europae*; 2) *Confession oder Bekandnuß der Societet und Brüderschaft R. C. an die Gelehrten Europae.*

[71] Johann Valentin Andreae, *Die Chymische Hochzeit des Christian Rosencreutz*, gedeutet und kommentiert von Bastiaan Baan (Strassburg: Lazari Zetzners s. Erben, 1616; Stuttgart: Verlag Urachhaus, 2001); https://archive.org/details/chymischehochzei00rose/page/n4

In order to understand the origins of the *Fama* and *Confessio*, it is important to realize that people at the time had a great desire for reformation. Since Luther's day, they had turned increasingly against the clergy. They had sought to form an alternative association to the Catholic *Societas Jesu*, the Jesuit Order, which was pushing for the Counter Reformation. The Rosicrucian manifestos were heard all around Europe as their supporters sought to realize their ecumenical vision of a "Second Reformation," encouraging all Christian denominations to unite under their leadership for this purpose.[72]

Every attempt made by Rosicrucians and Pansophists to unify Christian denominations resulted in failure, as influential orthodox Lutherans stubbornly refused to comply with the Roman Catholic Church even with symbolic gestures. Many people eventually saw the Rose Cross as symbolic of a third denomination.[73] Johann Valentin Andreae established a "Christian" society called the *Societas Christiana*, which was a forerunner of London's Royal Society as a scientific academy. Nevertheless, the Royal Society never claimed to initiate, let alone drive forward, the general reformation of the world. Its activities were strictly limited to the organized and institutionalized exchange of scientific knowledge.

Over the following centuries, the Rosicrucian idea of spiritual and political world reform had a lasting influence on the history of European Mysticism and spirituality. Many mystics dreamed of being accepted into the fraternity, hoping to receive its important secrets. Endless speculations over the Rosicrucians' secret knowledge were made in the growing Furor caused by the esoteric movement. Rosicrucians considered their greatest practical secrets to lie in the esoteric teachings of alchemy and astrology. Believing themselves to be the rightful heirs of Brahminic and Egyptian wisdom, they sought to perfect the human spirit in accordance with Hermetic instructions by drawing on the symbolic perfection of metals.[74]

Shaped by Christianity, Western culture has always objected to chaos and mystery. In viewing chaos as an evil force, the Christian faith takes an opposite position to that of Hermeticism. The Bible clearly teaches that God created an ordered universe out of nothing. The fallen world is headed toward final destruction, and man is at enmity with himself, his environment, and the eternal God from whom he is separated. Although artistic talents enable man to play God and imitate divine creation on a small scale, they give him no right to do so.

---

[72] Will-Erich Peuckert, *Die Rosenkreutzer: Zur Geschichte einer Reformation* (Jena: E. Diederichs, 1928); G. Krüger, *Die Rosenkreuzer: Ein Rückblick* (Berlin: Verlag von Alfred Unger, 1932); H. Schick, *Das ältere Rosenkreuzertum* (Berlin: Nordland Verlag, 1942); Wilhelm Maurer, *Aufklärung, Idealismus und Restauration*, 2 vols. (Gießen: A. Töpelmann, 1930) vol. 1: 107ff.

[73] Peuckert, *Die Rosenkreutzer*, 168.

[74] Claus Priester, "Alchemie und Vernunft: Die rosenkreuzerische und hermetische Bewegung in der Zeit der Spätaufklärung," in Monika Neugebauer-Wölk, ed., *Aufklärung und Esoterik* (Hamburg: Felix Meiner Verlag, 2016) 305-334.

Under the Habsburg Emperor Rudolf II (1552-1612), Prague became an oasis for Jewish and Christian Kabbalists as well as a center for the Counter-Reformation. Ferdinand of Styria, a devout Catholic, succeeded Rudolf as king of Bohemia. His desire for a Counter-Reformation led to the Hussite Wars: the reformative, or rather revolutionary, movements in fifteenth-century Bohemia which were sparked after the theologian and Reformer Jan Hus was burned at the stake in 1415. In a heated exchange, representatives of the Protestant states threw the royal governors Jaroslav Borzita of Martinice and William Slavata, as well as the secretary of the chancery, Philipp Fabricius, out of the window of the castle in Prague. This incident became known as the Second Defenestration of Prague, and led to the outbreak of the Thirty Years' War. It resulted immediately in Ferdinand being ousted from the Bohemian monarchy. From then on, Ferdinand rebelled openly against the Habsburg Empire and tried to gain military support from Protestant princes. The Hussites crowned the Elector Palatine, Frederick V (1596-1632), as King of Bohemia. In the Battle of the White Mountain, King Frederick was defeated outside Prague by the Duke of Bavaria on November 8, 1620. Catholic troops also destroyed his castle in Heidelberg. As the awful tragedy of the Thirty Years' War unfolded, the people of Europe became disillusioned and lost faith in the second Reformation promised by the Rosicrucian pamphlets. The idea of leading a dark world to enlightenment may have been desirable, but the harsh, unpoetic reality was the destruction of vast areas of Germany through the turmoil of war.

The abatement of the Furor brought the Rosicrucian Enlightenment to an inglorious end, until it was taken up once again in the eighteenth century by the Order of the Gold and Rosy Cross. This was a form of "Christian" Mysticism that promoted the teaching of the ascent of the soul to God. Its preoccupation with the "unio mystica" formed a connection between Rosicrucians of the eighteenth century and of the Enlightenment. Despite their rationalistic worldview, the adepts of the Order never refrained from declaring the possibility of union with God. Yet only esotericists could understand the secrets of the universe.[75] From there, only one step was necessary for Christ, who had laid down His life on the cross and risen from the grave on the third day, to be recognized as the center of the world – a view that was also held by Pietists. Science therefore gained a religious significance as the salvation of the world, as claimed by Gnosticism.[76] Rosicrucians believed that they had been predestined to receive supernatural powers. Although seemingly pointing toward Christianity, these ideas nonetheless took on mystical meanings through their background in alchemical Esotericism.

---

[75] Maurer, *Aufklärung, Idealismus und Restauration*, vol. 1: 104.

[76] Ibid., 109.

3.7 Attempt to reverse the Fall

During the seventeenth century, an informal circle of scholars sought to redress man's broken relationship with God. Their overriding aim was to restore the perfection that man had possessed in Paradise, but which he had lost by his own fault. This effort reveals the true motivation behind Progressivism.

After Catholic mercenaries devastated the Palatinate at the beginning of the Thirty Years' War, Samuel Hartlib and Johannes Duraeus[77] (John Dury) emigrated to England where they were soon at the center of a movement of educational and social reform. Hartlib's plan was to disseminate and apply scientific discoveries for the benefit of humanity. He formed a circle of prominent contemporary scholars with close international connections.[78] An informal association was set up during the 1630s which lasted around thirty years. Robert Boyle, a member of the Hartlib Circle[79], renamed it the "Invisible College," from which the Royal Society would later emerge. A true entrepreneur in the scientific field, Hartlib raised funds for research, published books, and promoted new technologies.[80] The emergence of an international circle of scholars was a result of the spread of Pansophism in Western society. Pansophism was a religious-philosophical movement of the sixteenth to eighteenth centuries which aimed to unite all sciences in universal scholarship and peace. New scientific research tools such as the telescope and microscope promised to provide the perfect sensory perception enjoyed by Adam in the Garden of Eden. Europeans were convinced that history did not just consist of the periodic rise and fall of social developments, but also that constant development could be achieved by making and implementing new discoveries.

The four Old Testament accounts of the Garden of Eden, Noah's Ark, the Tower of Babel, and Solomon's Temple motivated scholars to determine the ideal conditions for human cohabitation. However, interpretations of these accounts were often based on a mystical worldview – largely influenced by Neoplatonic, Hermetic, and Kabbalistic ideas – rather than the biblical view. A syncretic assortment of opinions emerged, superficially seeming to express

---

[77] Joseph Minton Batten, *John Dury, Advocate of Christian Reunion* (Chicago, IL: Chicago University Press, 1944).

[78] Gillian Darley, *John Evelyn: Living for ingenuity* (New Haven, CT: Yale University Press, 2006) 146; Blanche Henrey, *British Botanical and Horticultural Literature Before 1800*, 3 vols. (London: Oxford University Press, [1975] 1999) vol. 1: 169; Samuel Hartlib, *The Reformed Commonwealth of Bees: Presented in Severall Letters and Observations to Samuel Hartlib* (London: Printed for Giles Calvert, 1655); https://archive.org/details/reformedcommon-w00hartgoog/page/n7

[79] Ronald Sterne Wilkinson, "The Hartlib Papers and Seventeenth-Century Chemistry," Part 1, *Ambix* 15.1 (February, 1968), 61; https://www.tandfonline.com/doi/abs/10.1179/amb.1968.15.1.54

[80] Michal Rozbicki, "Between East-Central Europe and Britain: Reformation and Science as Vehicles of Intellectual Communication in the Mid-Seventeenth Century," *East European Quarterly*, XXX:4 (January, 1997), 401-416.

Christian truths, but on closer examination conforming to a concept completely opposed to the Gospel and exhibiting strong similarities to ancient Gnosticism. Old Testament narratives were generally thought to teach man how to combine knowledge with religiosity and wisdom in order to improve his condition. Making habitable the environment cursed by God required concentration on the intelligence available to man. Using technology, man could ingeniously construct machines that would advance common welfare. Nevertheless, man needed to beware of moral failure, which would impede the success of technological achievement.

Scholars in the early modern period believed that lost Paradise could be regained through a revival of knowledge. Only in this way could man's former perfection be restored.[81] The goal could be attained not only through spirituality, but also through practical steps such as planting fruit trees in imitation of Adam and Eve's faithful cultivation of the Garden of Eden.[82] The Garden's optimistic message was reinforced by the account of Noah's Ark, which intimated that Noah regained power over nature once the innocent part of Creation had been saved from destruction. The story of the Ark was seen as a power demonstration of the possibility of fully recovering human dominion over nature, once possessed in Paradise but lost through the Fall. Extensive and diverse collections of natural objects –thousands of insects, for example – came to represent "new Arks" which broadened the horizons of knowledge. Early modern scholars believed that newly acquired knowledge of nature could be recorded in encyclopedias and preserved for posterity. Man's wildest dreams therefore began to be fulfilled through the introduction of new teaching and learning methods, as well as through the establishment of new institutions for education and research.

Many scientists recognized the warning posed by the account of the Tower of Babel. Technology allowed man to rise above the physical limitations of his fallen state to a certain extent, but doing so through any act of rebellion against God was forbidden. Scholars dedicated to this academic challenge became absorbed with the formation a new natural philosophy. They imagined themselves to be the true offspring of Adam and Noah, who had also supposedly tried to devise a philosophy of nature. The consequences of the curse of Babel – the confusion of tongues – would be resolved when humanity's division into different language groups was reversed by a single language. Early modern scholars labored arduously on this project, communicating easily with one another in Latin. This aroused linguistic and ethnographic interest and encouraged general research into the natural

---

[81] Everett Gordon Alderfer, *The Ephrata Commune: An Early American Counterculture* (Pittsburgh, PA: University of Pittsburgh Press, 1985) 35, 107ff. (chap. IX, Recovery of Eden); s. also: Julius F. Sachse, *The German Sectarians of Pennsylvania, 1708-1742 (1742-1800): A critical and legendary history of the Ephrata Cloister and the Dunkers*, 2 vols. (Philadelphia, PA: Printed for the author by P. C. Stockhausen, 1899-1900) vol. 1: 73; https://archive.org/details/germansectarian00sachgoog/page/n122

[82] Samuel Hartlib, ed., *A Designe for Plentie by an Universall Planting of Fruit-Trees: Tendred by Some Wel-Wishers to the Publick* (London: Printed for Richard Wodenothe, 1652).

world. Although the original language had been lost after Adam and Eve were banished from the Garden of Eden, even before the Tower of Babel, its essence could be recovered through the formulation of a philosophical language.

Jan Amos Komenský[83] (1592-1670), better known by his Latin name "Comenius," published his book *Janua Linguarum Reserata*[84] (The Door of Languages Unlocked) in 1631. It became one of the most successful textbooks of the seventeenth century. The original idea behind the publication was to ground students in the Latin and English languages. Over time, an encyclopedia was created containing many pages of practical advice about everyday affairs and the natural world. Hartlib was impressed by Comenius's promotion of Pansophism and immediately began publishing numerous texts by the Bohemian bishop. His writings had a clear philosophical concern with the reconciliation of sensory perception, reason, and the Bible. Comenius was among the many Protestants who were forced to leave their homeland in 1628, during the Thirty Years' War. After a stay in Poland, he was persuaded by Hartlib to relocate to England in the autumn of 1641 – a time at which a peaceful reformation of church and state still seemed possible. In England, Comenius wrote a book exploring how a universal institution could develop theology and pedagogy in order to advance human welfare.[85] The ultimate goal, to which Comenius had dedicated his whole life, was to overcome the confusion of languages with which God had cursed humanity at Babel. He wanted to introduce a universal language which would convey the light of reason. In 1642, Samuel Hartlib published a book by Comenius containing ideas for a radical educational reform, and during the same year, Comenius was asked to implement educational reforms in Sweden.

The negative consequences associated with the Tower of Babel were balanced out by a positive view of the Temple: a building that typified God's plan for His people more than any other. The architectural skill demonstrated in the building of the Temple was considered a pinnacle of human achievement, while the inspired blueprint was understood to reflect principles of divine geometry. Christian scholars in the early modern era emphasized the importance of retracing the standardized units of measurement in order

---

[83] *Johann Amos Comenius, sein Leben und seine Schriften* (Leipzig: J. Klinkhardt, 1892); Jan Amos, Comenius Robert Fitzgibbon Young, John N. Libbey, ed., *Comenius in England; the visit of Jan Amos Komenský (Comenius), the Czech philosopher and educationist, to London in 1641-1642; its bearing on the origins of the Royal society, on the development of the encyclopaedia, and on plans for the higher education of the Indians of. New England and Virginia* (Oxford: Oxford University Press, 1932; New York City, NY: Arno Press, 1971).

[84] Jan Amos Comenius, *Janua Linguarum Reserata, cum Græca versione Theodori Simonii Holsati, innumeris in locis emendata à Stephano Curcellæo qui etiam Gallicam novam adjunxit* (Amsterdam: apud Danielem Elzevirium, [1631] 1665); https://archive.org/details/bub_gb_ZxePqt-fKFQC/page/n4

[85] Jan Amos Comenius, *Via Lucis, vestigata et vestiganda* (London: 1641/42; first published in 1668); English translation: John Amos Comenius, *The Way of Light*, trans. E. T. Campagnac (London: The University Press of Liverpool; Hodder & Stoughton, 1938) 8.

to determine their original values. As the restoration of a universal language could assist recovery of the knowledge of the world inhabited by Adam and Noah, so the use of universal measurements would facilitate man's control of nature. This gave rise to emphasis on the importance of a social order based on well-defined principles. The extraordinary mathematical versatility underlying the units of measurement evidenced profound human understanding, which assured man of his spiritual uprightness before God. This Pelagian idea clearly indicates how far early modern scholars had departed from the biblical doctrines of grace. They could hardly have been more opposed to the Apostle Paul's statement that man cannot obtain salvation by any means other than faith in Jesus Christ.

One reason for early modern scholars' fascination with Solomon's Temple was their conviction that God's nature can be seen only indirectly in His Creation. Algebra and geometry became the focus of attention as the best means for a rational understanding of reality. Squares became particularly significant in the endeavor to fathom the hidden nature of God.[86] Divine glory was supposedly manifested in a specific configuration of forms and figures. The structure of the Temple was treated like a talisman through which man's desires could be fulfilled. Its importance as a meeting place to worship the Creator in ritual services paled into the background. The Temple, built for the glory of God, was viewed as the ultimate example of the acquisition and application of the knowledge of nature. Contemporary scholars desired not only to understand the natural world, including humanity, but also to control it. The masterly construction of the Temple, which had been enabled by cooperation among so many individuals, inspired the establishment of new institutions dedicated to natural philosophy and experimentation.

The religion of geometry has its roots in antiquity,[87] with the Creator God equated with the architect of the universe. The idea of architects as magicians can be traced back to Plato. The Athenian philosopher's most famous work, *The Republic*, presents geometry as fundamental to establishing a politically centralized social system in which philosopher kings control the affairs of their subjects. Over many centuries, the religion of geometry spread through Judaism, Islam, Neoplatonism, and Hermeticism. During the Middle Ages, it became increasingly like an occult doctrine known only to an elite fraternity. It spread with particular success among members of the Stonemasons' Guild, unbeknown to anyone outside, giving rise to the beginnings of the later "speculative" Freemasonry.

The Hartlib documents show that members interested in alchemy focused their research exclusively on the application of this esoteric art to medicine and other fields. Alchemy was a common pastime and is an ideology

---

[86] Michael Baigent & Richard Leigh, *The Temple and the Lodge: The strange and fascinating history of the Knights Templar and the Freemasons* (New York City, NY: Arcade Publishers, 2011) 138; J. E. McGuire & P. M. Rattansi, "Newton and the Pipes of Pan," *Notes and Records of the Royal Society of London*, XXI (1966), 108-143.

[87] Baigent & Leigh, *Temple and Lodge*, 132.

in its own right. Science and technology that are underpinned by Rationalist principles work on the assumption that subject is separate from object. The scientist analyzes the individual components of his object of experiment with the intention of manipulating them to produce his desired outcome. Alchemy is based on a completely different assumption: the inseparability of subject and object is one of its most important principles. Even the production of an elixir of youth, which alchemical teachings promise will grant man immortality, can only be considered as a union or transcendence of subject and object. This union can be initiated by chemical processes in the laboratory, which then develop into spiritual enlightenment in the mind of the alchemist. Only in its early stages is the elixir of youth a physical substance, before becoming a spiritual experience of great significance. This is what alchemists claim, at least. The ideology of alchemy was primarily a kind of "scientific method" which did not explore the world for better understanding of it, but in order to change its fundamental essence.

The Hartlib Circle included eminent individuals with a keen interest in the spiritual side of alchemy. Many of them even practiced it themselves. Scientists such as Roger Bacon, Isaac Newton, and Gottfried Wilhelm Leibniz were members of various secret societies as well as enthusiastic, practicing esotericists. A publication on Newton's interest in Occultism[88] caused a great stir as modern science was forced to admit that the father of modern physics had held mystical beliefs which had undoubtedly influenced his scientific thought. The study of alchemy, magic, and Paracelsianism became a popular pastime among the upper classes,[89] and it is therefore unsurprising that the American members of the Hartlib Circle showed great interest in alchemy. The first governor of Connecticut, John Winthrop, Jr. (1606-1676), was the son of the founder of the Massachusetts Bay Colony. Winthrop began building an extraordinary library in England before leaving for America in 1631 to help his father manage the colony. He swiftly became known in America as a collector of alchemical books.[90] Winthrop's test tubes were borrowed by colonists who, following alchemical teaching, sought to attain immortality by mixing different chemicals.[91] Paradoxically, many people were charged with witchcraft during Winthrop's time in office, although "only" two women and one man lost their lives at the stake. Winthrop gave George Starkey (1627-1665) and Jonathan Brewster (1593-1659) thorough training in the art of alchemy. A widely read treatise on alchemy, written either by Winthrop, Jr.,

---

[88] Michael White, *Isaac Newton: The Last Sorcerer* (Reading, MA: Perseus Books, 1999).

[89] Jon Butler, *Awash in a Sea of Faith: Christianizing the American People* (Cambridge, MA: Harvard University Press, 1990; Ann Arbor, MI: University of Michigan Library, Scholarly Publishing Office, 1992).

[90] D. Michael Quinn, *Early Mormonism and the Magic World View* (Salt Lake City, UT: Signature books, 1998) 10.

[91] Ronald Sterne Wilkinson, "The Alchemical Library of John Winthrop, Jr., 1606-1676," *Ambix* 11.1 (February, 1963), 33-51; https://www.tandfonline.com/doi/pdf/10.1179/amb.1963.11.1.33

or by Starkey, had an enormous influence on English-speaking society in the seventeenth and eighteenth centuries. Starkey, Brewster, and Winthrop were only the most famous of contemporary alchemists in colonial America; there were many others who were similar interested in discovering the philosopher's stone.

Both the common people and the elitist upper classes believed in the existence of supernatural forces. Esotericism seeks to understand the interaction of cosmic powers and to use them for its own purposes. It extends the capabilities of man's five senses to a sixth area: a spiritual "technology" which works like a machine through the finely balanced powers of meditation and ritual. So-called "Christian Kabbalah" fuses mystical elements from Judaism, Islam, and Christianity which are said to constitute the common basis of all three religions. It was introduced to America at the time of the first settlers. The well-known German mystic Johannes Kelpius settled with a group of Pietists by the Wissahickon Creek in Philadelphia, where they practiced astrology, magic, and alchemy. An offshoot of the Kelpius Group formed the Ephrata Community, which was involved above all in studying Rosicrucian thought.

3.8 Pansophic coherence of truth

(The Pansophic era: global unification of science and religion)
Alchemy inspired two esoteric traditions which emerged in England and on the continent during the seventeenth century. These were Pansophism (Gr. "all-knowing"; a religious-philosophical movement which sought to condense all knowledge and establish a worldwide kingdom of peaceable scholarship) and Theosophy (Gr. "divine wisdom"; a religious doctrine whereby higher insight into the meaning of all things can only be gained through a mystical view of God). Pansophism draws on sources of magic, alchemy, Kabbalah, and herbal medicine. By studying nature, it evokes much earlier pagan traditions in ancient Egypt and Persia and distinguishes itself within Esotericism from the still older Theosophy. The Pansophic movement originated at the beginning of the seventeenth century and incorporated key elements of Greek philosophy. It held that divine ideas emanate from a single, invisible source and gradually take on material form in time and space, thus becoming visible and vivid representations of the divine spirit. Once the divine goal is reached, the diverse array of visible manifestations is brought into the original perfection of divine unity from which each originally proceeded.

Pansophism was heralded on the continent by the works and publications of Johann Heinrich Alsted[92] (1588-1638) and his student Jan Amos Comenius[93] (1592-1670). In 1630, Alsted compiled an encyclopedia[94] which was thought to contain everything that a seventeenth-century scholar could possibly know. Alsted taught at the Calvinistic seminary (theological academy) in Herborn and was generally considered an orthodox Calvinist. However, he was also a keen alchemist, Kabbalist, and Neoplatonist.[95] He saw the encyclopedia as a convenient means of achieving his real goal: the recovery of the image of God in man. He did not attribute any part of this process to the grace of God, believing that it was solely dependent on human effort and ingenuity. Alsted, a Calvinistic theologian, held a doctrine of salvation that was entirely different from – even diametrically opposed to – the teachings of Calvin. This affirms the departure of Germany's preeminent Christians from biblical statements of faith, as they masked Renaissance Neoplatonism with Christian terminology. Alchemy played a significant role in Alsted's thinking, since he was convinced by the writings of Giordano Bruno that the philosopher's stone could reverse the degeneration of human nature. The Reformation of the previous century provided a model of sociopolitical regeneration, and rulers of the German states came to see alchemy as a new type of warfare through which to expand their territory.[96]

Before the negative consequences of the Thirty Years' War were felt in Herborn, Alsted put forward an Augustinian Amillennialism in his eschatological teachings. It is important to note that he altered his view on

---

[92] Howard Hotson, *Johann Heinrich Alsted 1588-1638: Between Renaissance, Reformation, and Universal Reform* (New York City, NY: Clarendon Press, 2000); Howard Hotson, *Paradise postponed: Johann Heinrich Alsted and the birth of Calvinist millenarianism* (Dordrecht: Kluwer, 2000); Percival Richard Cole, *Neglected Educator: Johann Heinrich Alsted* (Sydney: William Applegate Gullick, 1910); Friedrich Adolf Max Lippert, *Johann Heinrich Alsteds Pädagogisch-Didaktische Reform: Bestrebungen und ihr Einfluss auf Johann Amos Comenius* (Meissen: C. E. Klinkicht & Sohn, 1898); Herman Pixberg, *Der Deutsche Calvinismus und Die Pädagogik* (Gladbeck: Martin-Heilman Verlag, 1952); Jürgen Klein & Johannes Kramer, eds., *Johann Heinrich Alsted, Herborns calvinistische Theologie und Wissenschaft im Spiegel der englischen Kulturreform des frühen 17. Jahrhunderts: Studien zu englisch-deutschen Geistesbeziehungen der frühen Neuzeit* (Frankfurt am Main: Lang, 1988).

[93] Jan Amos Comenius, *A Reformation of Schools: Designed in two excellent treatises, the first whereof summarily sheweth, the great necessity of a generall reformation of common learning* (London: Printed for Michael Sparke, 1642) 24: "And Praised be thou, O Lord, forever, which dost likewise give us thy works and word for a pattern, whereby to erect this Pansophy, or temple of Wisdom: that as thy word and works are true and lively representations of thee: so this, which we are about, may prove a true, and lively image of thy word and works."

[94] Johannem Henricum Alstedium, *Scientiarum omnium encyclopaedia Omnia Praeceptorum, Regularum, Et Commentariorum serie perpetuâ contexta, insertis passim Tabulis, Compendiis, Lemmatibus marginalibus, Lexicis, Controversiis, Figuris, Florilegiis, Locis communibus, & Indicibus. Complectens huius Operis Partem Tertiam* (Herbornae Nassoviorum: Corvinus Erben, 1630; Stuttgart: Frommann-Holzboog, 1989-1990); https://archive.org/details/bub_gb_02hEAAAAcAAJ

[95] Hotson, *Johann Heinrich Asted*, 224.

[96] Ibid., 104.

the millennial reign in a book published in 1627.[97] Referring to Daniel 12:11-12, he stated that the Millennium would begin in the year 1694. The daily sacrifice in Jerusalem had been taken away in the year 69 B.C. Alsted first added 1290 years to this date (believing each prophetic day to equate to one year) before adding another 1335 years. This meant that the Millennium would end in the year 2694. Subtracting one thousand years from this date gave the year 1694. Alsted's interpretation of the millennial reign caused Christian eschatology to take a fateful turn. Hermetical ideas entered Protestant teaching on the Millennium, reinterpreting it in terms of what would later emerge as Postmillennialism. Puritans in England, the Netherlands, and America were especially influenced by this teaching, having uncritically and keenly accepted the Mysticism spread by Francis Bacon in the form of scientific Empiricism. Leading Puritans such as John Milton lost their way in the darkness of Esotericism, laying the foundations of Puritan Occultism.[98] The occultists Pico della Mirandola, Johannes Reuchlin, Francesco Giorgi, Henry Cornelius Agrippa, and John Dee practiced a form of Occultism that combined Jewish, Islamic, and "Christian" Mysticism, and influenced the thinking of many Puritans such as John Milton and William Ames under the name "Christian Kabbalah." Johann Heinrich Alsted, William Ames, and Jan Amos Comenius dedicated themselves to synthesizing esoteric and Christian truth.[99] Alsted's encyclopedia strongly influenced William Ames's work *Technometria*; the English Puritan and the Herborn theologian probably met in 1618 at the Synod of Dort – a crucial event in church history. Publications by both theologians came to occupy a prominent place among the literature of many Puritans.

Alsted influenced the development of Pansophism most directly through his tuition of Jan Amos Comenius. Comenius saw his primary task as writing books which he hoped would radically change the education system. Over the following years, he became one of the most important theorists of a scientific pedagogy. Comenius's thinking is clearly aligned with the ideals of early English Freemasonry. He visited England, then a hotbed of Pansophism, from 1641 to 1642. In order to realize his Pansophic vision, he sought to found a college in which scholars from around the world could meet to

---

[97] Johann Heinrich Alsted, *The Beloved City: or, the saints reign on earth a thousand yeares: asserted, and illustrated from LXV. places of Holy Scripture; besides the judgement of holy learned men, both at home and abroad; and also reason it selfe. Likewise XXXV. objections against this truth are here answered. Written in Latine by Ioan. Henr. Alstedius, professor of the University at Herborne. Faithfully Englished; with some occasionall notes; and the judgement herein not onely of Tycho Brahe, and Carolus Gallus; but also some of our owne famous divines* (London: [publisher not identified], 1643).

[98] Francis Amelia Yates, *The Occult Philosophy in the Elizabethan Age* (London: Routledge, Kegan Paul, [1979] 2001) chap. 17: "The Occult Philosophy and Puritanism: John Milton"; https://archive.org/details/YatesFrancesTheOccultPhilosophyInTheElizabethanAgeRoutledge/page/n233

[99] Perry Miller, *The New England Mind: The Seventeenth Century* (Cambridge, MA: Harvard University Press, [1939] 1954) 96; https://archive.org/details/in.ernet.dli.2015.188454/page/n109

investigate and integrate any fields of knowledge. His stay in London allowed him to engage closely with Samuel Hartlib and to record the knowledge which he acquired. In 1639, Hartlib published Comenius's *Pansophiae Prodromus* in London. The work argued that a Pansophic reform of philosophy and education could only occur through harmonization of the three "books of revelation": the Holy Scriptures, nature, and reason.

The key element of the Hartlib Circle's intellectual activity was a desire to combine Empiricism (knowledge gained through scientific experience) and Rationalism at least partially with theosophical and millennialist speculation. The scholars' common goal was to stand up to the widespread Skepticism of their time. Most members of the Hartlib Circle resided in Protestant countries such as England, Holland, and Germany, where they lived in burning anticipation of the imminent coming of the Millennium. Despite the many negative consequences of their work, their consideration of the eschatological events prophesied in the Bible did positively support the fight against Skepticism. Anyone who took biblical Eschatology at face value could claim to possess certain knowledge of the future. Others believed that they found intellectual assurance in the Theosophy of Jakob Böhme, who had apparently discovered a direct path into the presence of God. Henry More developed a rational metaphysics, dealing with the ultimate foundations and relationships of being which underlie the sensually experienced natural world. It ultimately became completely severed from Christian scriptural prophecy. Lady Anne Conway (1631-1679) embraced the central tenets of Neoplatonism as rediscovered and reconfigured by Henry More, who gave her private tuition while he lectured at the University of Cambridge. Lady Conway was arguably the most astute metaphysician in England at that time. Her monistic Vitalism taught that all events are determined by an infinitely perfect deity who is a purely spiritual being. According to this theory, Jesus Christ mediated between the human soul and the divine spirit, His task being to unite them. Lady Conway's greatest influence was on the philosophy of Gottfried Wilhelm Leibniz (1646-1716), who derived his system of metaphysics from her thinking.

In the early 1640s, radical Separatists and Puritan Reformers looked forward to the coming Millennium. They believed that the world first needed to be reformed according to the scientific principles laid out by Francis Bacon and Jan Amos Comenius. Many Puritans had high expectations during the first years of the English Revolution (1642-1649), having developed a strong interest in the occult sciences as the key to mastering nature.[100] From the mid-1640s to the restoration of the Stuart monarchy, England was swept by one wave of social Radicalism after another. Such social upheaval caused by religious and political conflict was unprecedented in Britain.[101] The

---

[100] P. M. Rattansi, "Social Interpretation of Science in the Seventeenth Century," in Peter Mathias, ed., *Science and Society 1600-1900* (Cambridge: Cambridge University Press, 1972) 1-32.

[101] Christopher Hill, *World Upside Down* (London: Temple Smith, 1972); https://archive.

seventeenth-century Pansophists made a final effort to unite European culture on the basis of a common religion without any sectarian conflicts. Among the Lutheran Pansophists, Christ internalized as the Book of Conscience became a third way of understanding God's works, open alongside the Book of Scripture and the Book of Nature.

Although Gottfried Wilhelm Leibniz publicly rejected Comenius's Pansophism, he developed a view similar to its idea of a universal republic. As a Kabbalist, Leibniz displayed the same utopian spirit as Pansophists before him, becoming the most ambitious proponent of scientific and religious unification of his age.[102] Comenius and other Pansophists considered scientific experiments to be unnecessary; Pansophism was ultimately nothing more than a utopian fantasy. With its Hermetical beliefs, it was treated with suspicion in respected circles and therefore largely continued to be practiced in secret. Members of the Rosicrucian fraternity shared common ideas and objectives with the proponents of Pansophism, including attempts to unify the church, the project of initiating a universal language, the devising of peace plans for Europe, and strategies for global promotion of an esoteric "Christianity."

3.9 A grand vision for a new era

The key tenets of Theosophy consist of the following four points: 1) Wisdom (Sophia) is at the center of all considerations, 2) the fulfillment of deep desires occurs through contact with supernatural spirits, 3) great knowledge is acquired through the study of nature, and 4) religious insights into world affairs are gained through spiritual mentors.

There are clear parallels between modern Theosophy and ancient Gnosticism. Clement of Alexandria (150-215 A.D.), one of the first scholars of the early church, claimed that the church had a true Gnosis (knowledge) rather than a falsified one.[103] Seventeenth-century theosophists often harked back to Clement since they believed similarly in the existence of a Christian Gnosis. They held this Gnosis in high regard, even placing it on a par with the apostolic teachings of the New Testament. They also referred back to Pseudo-Dionysius the Areopagite (6th century A.D.) who distinguished between positive and negative statements ("via positiva" and "via negativa") about the nature of God. He taught that both "paths" would assist the individual in his

---

org/details/TheWorldTurnedUpsideDownRadicalIdeasDuringTheEnglishRevolution; s. also: Peter Burke, *Popular Culture in Early Modern Europe* (London: Temple Smith, 1978) 188-189.

[102] Allison P. Coudert, "Leibniz, Locke, Newton and the Kabbalah," in Joseph Dan, ed., *The Christian Kabbalah* (Cambridge, MA: Houghton Library of the Harvard College Library, 1997) 149-179; s. also: Allison P. Coudert, *Leibniz and the Kabbalah* (Dortrecht: Springer Science & Business Media, 1995); http://archive.org/details/coudert

[103] *Ante-Nicene Fathers* (Grand Rapids, MI: Eerdmans, 1990) vol. 2: 538; Clemens von Alexandrien, *Stromata*, VII.x.

contemplation (meditation) of the divine nature, and that this would enable a mystical union between the human soul and spiritual reality: an entrance into the "darkness of God."[104] Everything visible to the eye can give insights into the divine realm, yet God cannot be grasped conceptually. A turn to the positive or negative paths as a prerequisite of mystical knowledge of God became a distinguishing mark of Theosophy.

Modern Theosophy began with the dissemination of philosophical works by Jakob Böhme (1575-1624), a shoemaker from Görlitz. Its name stems from the Greek word "theosophia" (divine wisdom). In contrast to Christian theology, it is not concerned with inferential or rational knowledge of God, but rather with the experiential "Gnosis" of a supernatural reality imbued with the Spirit of God. Böhme's followers claimed that this Theosophy had been influenced by the writings of the secret Rosicrucian fraternity. However, it is questionable whether such a fraternity even existed at the time, or whether Christian Rosenkreutz and his Order were merely a fictitious invention by Johann Valentin Andreae. Just as Rosicrucianism merged various mystical trends which had circulated in the West since ancient times, Theosophy also brought together esoteric movements which had swept across the European continent since the Middle Ages.[105]

Jakob Böhme claimed to be self-taught, having grappled long and hard with the vast literature of Esotericism. He did not believe in the thousand-year reign as prophesied in the book of Revelation. In Böhme's opinion, the future Golden Age would bring a recovery of original paradise.[106] Jesus Christ would appear as light incarnate and destroy the principle of darkness forever. Possession of this mystical knowledge would deliver man from imprisonment in his earthly being – in evil substance. Böhme's writings display elements of Paracelsian Spagyric.[107] Throughout his life he faced repression from the Electorate of Saxony, which distrusted him thoroughly. The Görlitz shoemaker could never allay suspicion that he had released heretical teachings into the world. Nonetheless, many considered him to be a God-fearing man, and he maintained a strong allegiance to the Lutheran Church. His books were distributed widely in Separatist Pietist circles, but many Christians within the established Church were also exposed to his Theosophy. Philipp Jacob Spener saw that Böhme had erred in many areas, but nonetheless did not believe that he deserved condemnation.[108] In the context of its predominantly Protestant

---

[104] Dionysius the Areopagite, *The Complete Works* (New York City, NY: Paulist Press, 1987) "Celestial Hierarchies," 140c, 151.

[105] Will-Erich Peuckert, *Pansophie: Ein Versuch zur Geschichte der weißen und schwarzen Magie*, 3 vols. (Stuttgart: Kohlhammer, 1936; expanded edition: Berlin: E. Schmidt, 1956-1973).

[106] Nils Brorson Thune, *The Behmenists and the Philadelphians: A contribution to the study of English mysticism in the 17th and 18th centuries* (Uppsala: Almqvist & Wiksell, 1948) 31-32.

[107] Ibid., 28.

[108] Johannes Wallman, *Philip Jakob Spener und die Anfänge des Pietismus* (Tübingen: Mohr Siebeck, 1970) 323.

environment, Böhme's Theosophy was distinguished by its synthesis of almost every major esoteric trend in Europe. In this form, it could easily be made accessible to colonists in North America. The German Pietists who settled there in the early eighteenth century, mainly in Pennsylvania, became known for their theosophical communities, the most famous being the Ephrata Community in Lancaster County.

England's first theosophical circle was formed in the 1620s. Members of the later circle of Dr. John Pordage and Jane Ward Leade called themselves the Philadelphians in reference to Revelation 3:7-11, and the term was also adopted by other theosophical societies on the continent. They saw it as a highly appropriate name for them given the text's mention of steadfast perseverance in the midst of temptation. Many European and English emigrants had been introduced to Jakob Böhme's Theosophy and made their way directly to Philadelphia, Pennsylvania, when they arrived in North America. One of their reasons for leaving their homeland was a desire to settle in a country where they would not have to face constant religious persecution. Jane W. Leade was one of the most influential interpreters of Böhme's Theosophy in England during the second half of the seventeenth century.[109] The literature of the Philadelphia Society described a future period in which a divine order would be established, first in England and later throughout the world. Leade was God's "chosen vessel" for bringing the dawn of the new era to pass. Jakob Böhme saw no need to express his spiritual ideas (which were nothing more than human speculations on the invisible spiritual realm and the end of the world) in terms that could be universally understood. His books, which appeared first in German and then in other languages, challenged readers to interpret their contents correctly; however, grasping the meaning of his whimsical spiritual fantasies was an almost impossible task for English-speaking Böhmists. As one of the first interpreters of Böhme's work in England, Pordage sought to make sense of his theosophical writings and rewrite them more simply in his own books. His publications never saw great popularity, but Pordage nonetheless succeeded in conveying Böhme's ideas to Jane W. Leade in understandable language, thus introducing her to the secrets of Theosophy. Leade simultaneously became interested in Paracelsian alchemy.[110] She set out to write spiritual books for the common people – the only way to make German Theosophy accessible to the public in England.[111] Leade went far beyond Böhme's and Pordage's imaginative ideas in her concepts of the theosophical Virgin-Wisdom and of universal rest-oration. Whereas Böhme had identified the Virgin-Wisdom ("Sophia") with

---

[109] Julie Hirst, *Jane Leade: Biography of a Seventeenth-Century Mystic* (Aldershot, Hampshire: Ashgate, 2006) 89.

[110] Joanne Sperle, *God's Healing Angel: A Biography of Jane Ward Lead* (Ann Arbor, MI: University of Michigan Press, 1985) 8; Paula McDowell, *The Women of Grub Street: Press, Politics, and Gender in the London Literary Marketplace 1678-1730* (Oxford: Clarendon Press, 1998) 168.

[111] Thune, *The Behmenists and the Philadelphians*, 17.

the self-humiliation of Christ, Leade saw her as an entirely distinct divine figure, even seeming to award her the status of a fourth person of the Godhead.

Leade put forward an eccentric reinterpretation of the Christian faith. The older she became, the further she turned from a Reformational understanding of Christianity. Her affinity with Kabbalah (Jewish occult doctrine and Mysticism) became increasingly evident in her writings, consistent with her position as a visionary mystic who held Theosophy in the highest regard.[112] The existence of the society hung in the balance from 1692 to 1694, when its membership began steadily and inexplicably to decrease.[113] However, a Brandenburg-Prussian statesman provided the means to publish Leade's books. Her translated works were distributed widely in Germany and the Netherlands in 1694 and 1695, causing a great stir in theosophical circles. Books containing her millennialist, ecumenical, and universalistic ideas dealt in particular with changes in English politics and religion in the late seventeenth century and called urgently for restoration of order in church and state. Although these works were published after the Glorious Revolution (1688-1689), it must be remembered that the author was elderly by this time and had lived through the turmoil of the Civil War, the Interregnum, and the Restoration of the Stuart monarchy. Her life had been shaped by these radical changes in English government. The theosophical perspective of Leade's detailed assessment of this dramatic period of history provided a very different view of the situation than would have been given by a purely factual interpretation of historical events.

The central idea of Leade's teaching was that of universal restoration, which promised that Creation would be returned to its original state of paradise. The awful fate of eternal damnation would be escaped not only by all men, but also by demons and even Lucifer.[114] Leade and her followers believed that Christ could not return until the Church was united in an ecumenical network. In order to achieve this unification, she conveyed her urgent message to the six Protestant churches in England, none of which were holy enough in the sight of Christ for an "eternal Church" to be established on His return.[115] Only the seventh church, the Philadelphian, would be "a virgin church that was still to be born into the world." It would

---

[112] Daniel Pickering Walker, *The Decline of Hell: Seventeenth-Century Discussions of Eternal Torment* (Chicago, IL: University of Chicago Press, 1964) 225.

[113] Paula McDowell, "Enlightenment Enthusiasms and the Spectacular Failure of the Philadelphian Society," *Eighteenth-Century Studies* 35.4 (2002), 516; Thune, *The Behmenists and the Philadelphians*, 90-91; McDowell, *Women of Grub Street*, 172-173.

[114] Hirst, *Jane Leade*, 117.

[115] Jane Leade, *A Message to the Philadelphian Society*, [...] *together with a call to the several gathered Churches among Protestants in this nation of England* (A further Manifestation, [...] being a second message to the Philadelphian Society, etc. – The Messenger [...] or a third message to the Philadelphian Society), vol. 2: *A Message to the Philadelphian Society*, [...] *together with a call to the several gathered Churches among Protestants in this nation of England* (London: Printed for the Booksellers of London and Westminster, 1696) 8-9.

come into existence if Leade united with God through the Virgin-Wisdom. Furthermore, the spread of her ecumenical vision through her books would play a vital role in the unification of churches, which would take place through the formation of an "invisible" church within all other established churches. Only then could the final state order be restored, and enduring peace and unity be maintained. Jane W. Leade expected all sinful signs of disunity and disorder within the Philadelphia Society to be removed through a process of spiritual cleansing (burning) in order to bring about the state of perfection.[116] These ideas stemmed from a Kabbalist[117] and alchemical worldview, rather than from Neoplatonism.

3.10 A turn to the mystery of Irrationalism

(Connecting Pietism to Catholic mystics, esotericists, Freemasons, and philosophers)
Pietism[118] was initially known as "practical piety," appearing first in England and Scotland, and shortly after in Holland and Germany. German Pietism was one of many religious movements that swept through Western and Central Europe during the seventeenth century. It considered the Reformation to be incomplete and in need of a successful conclusion. Pietists particularly criticized Reformation theology of underemphasizing the new birth as a guarantor of Spirit-filled Christian life. They believed that people needed to strive for a higher level of morality and religion. For the Pietists, religion did not consist merely in agreement with Christian doctrine and in government of the Church according to Scriptural principles; they also stressed the necessity of inward, spiritual communion with Christ. An active, practical Christian piety could be achieved through Asceticism, catechesis, and religious exercise in public meetings. Pietists therefore emphasized the need to deny the sinful nature ("mortification of the flesh") and to receive biblical teaching in small groups. Philipp Jacob Spener (1635-1705), the founding father of German Pietism, urged Lutherans to put his programmatic work *Pia Desideria*[119] (1675) into practice. In his treatise, Spener complained that Orthodox Lutheran theologians had presented the doctrine of justification by faith as though mere agreement with it was the key to salvation. He rejected traditional Lutheran teaching on the end times, and took utmost care that the *collegia pietatis*, as he named the small-group meetings, did not become an "ecclesiola" or "little church" within the wider church. However, anxious

---

[116] Ibid., 38-39.

[117] Walker, *The Decline of Hell*, 225.

[118] Fred Ernst Stoeffler, *The Rise of Evangelical Pietism* (Leiden, Boston, Köln: Brill, 1965); Martin Greschat, ed., *Zur Neueren Pietismusforschung* (Darmstadt: Wissenschaftliche Buchgesellschaft [Abt. Verl.], 1977).

[119] Paul Grunberg, *Philip Jacob Spener*, 3 vols. (Göttingen: Vandenhoeck & Ruprecht 1893-1906; republication: Erich Beyreuther, ed., Hildesheim: Olms, 1988).

church ministers saw this model of church reform as a daring attempt to cause division.[120] Spener called on Christians to create a "New World," and taught that they could hasten its onset through dedication to church reform. He fought against the secularization of the Lutheran Church and turned against Orthodoxy, which had proved powerless amidst the immorality and awful social conditions that followed the Thirty Years' War.[121]

The Mysticism of Jakob Böhme and his spiritual offspring played an extremely important role in the thinking of many Pietists. Böhme shaped German Pietism more than anyone before or after him by calling for the formation of a spiritual elite. The success of Pietism was limited to the extent of its visibility in the Church. The movement failed above all to understand the biblical structure of full independence from the state church. The latter, with its close connections to the authorities, was unwilling to allow the formation of Christian fellowships outside of its control. The compromise of an *ecclesiola in ecclesia* (a little church within the church) proved to be a tragic mistake. On the one hand, Pietism gradually accepted the strict Orthodox Lutheran doctrine; on the other hand, its roots absorbed essential spiritual nutrients from the ground of Jakob Böhme's Mysticism.

The ecclesiastical problems which Spener wanted to solve had originated in a state church that was not structured on scriptural principles. What German Lutherans needed more than Spener's pious religious practices was church reform based on biblical guidelines. Internal corruption has been a constant problem in state churches since the time of Emperor Theodosius I (347-395). When those in power have supreme authority over church affairs, the spiritual direction of the congregation loses its vitality.

Böhme's Mysticism consisted of a combination of ideas from spiritual and philosophical sources such as Kabbalah, alchemy, and Renaissance Platonism. The publication of his books gained him influence across national borders. There was very little difference between Pietist contemplation (meditation) and Quietism, the Catholic approach to spiritual peace of mind. Pietism brought popularity to "Mysticism of the ground of one's soul," which involved an irrepressible desire for direct union with God.[122] The more that radical Pietists turned to Mysticism, the more Individualism became apparent and weakened the desire for organization in congregations, which had been the initial intention and practice. Some of the key characteristics of Pietism reveal parallels with Freemasonry.[123]

---

[120] Philipp Jacob Spener, *Pia Desideria*, in Kurt Aland, *Kleine Texte für Vorlesungen und Übungen*, vol. 170 (Berlin: A. Marcus und E. Weber's Verlag, 1940) 80.

[121] Sinclair B. Ferguson, David F. Wright, James I. Packer, eds., "Pietism," in *The New Dictionary of Theology* (Downers Grove, IL: IVP Academic, [1988] 2008) 516.

[122] W. Struck, *Der Einfluss Jakob Boehmes auf die englische Literatur des 17. Jahrhunderts* (Berlin: Junker und Dünnhaupt, 1936) 50ff.

[123] Eugen Lennhof, Oskar Posner, Dieter A. Binder, eds., *Internationales Freimaurer-Lexikon* (Wien: Amalthea-Verlag; Graz: Akademische Druck- und Verlagsanstalt, 1965; München: Herbig, 2015) 701ff., 818ff.

Quietism was developed by Catholic Mysticism and is still practiced in other religions today. The French mystic Peter Poiret (1646-1719) saw the mystical idea of solidarity as a means of fusing old and new forms of Christian and esoteric spirituality. He believed that Catholicism and Protestantism needed to be united in brotherly love, which would enable the majority of secret societies to join the church. Poiret made a great effort to promote this early form of Ecumenism to the public. The immediate effect of Quietism on French secret societies was high-degree Freemasonry. Pietist groups in Germany felt a connection with the Quietist legacy of François Fénelon and Madame Guyon. Quietists sought to find God within their own souls and to lose themselves in Him. Gerhard Tersteegen (1697-1769) was also involved in this movement. Quietists had connections with illuminists, esotericists, Freemasons, and German Romantic philosophers. As a mediator between secret societies and Pietism, Johann Kasper Lavater (1741-1801) was influenced by the occult ideas of both movements.

3.11 Pursuit of absolute perfection

Natural man has always been in danger of yielding to the temptation of claiming ability to become equal with God. The serpent said to the woman: "Ye shall be as gods, knowing good and evil." "Christian" Mysticism promised to satisfy man's irrepressible desire for a union of his nature with the nature of God. The term "Theosis" literally means "deification," "becoming God," or, as some prefer, "participation in God." It is a spiritual view which asserts man's potential to attain perfection in this life through progressive deification until he reaches complete union with Christ. There are two different perspectives within the doctrine of Theosis. The union model teaches that mankind will become divine in a literal sense: the difference between Creator and creation will be fully abolished, and men will become gods and goddesses, perfect sons and daughters in the family of God. The correspondence model takes the metaphorical view that God's image will be restored in man, but that man will nevertheless retain his status as creature. He will assume certain divine characteristics, but will never properly become a divine being. This process can be likened to a mirror which offers a perfect reflection, but which objectively is and remains a mirror.

The idea of man's divine nature has been expressed in numerous ways throughout the ages and originated in the ancient world. In his *Theaetetus*, Plato defined Theosis as "a greatest possible God-likeness." The viability of this view was debated within the Platonic tradition for centuries without yielding any definitive conclusion. During the first centuries after Christ, the Christian Church Fathers adopted the Greek idea of Theosis in their theology, in the sense of a deification conferred by the grace of God. According to this view, a Christian could partake in the divine nature if this heavenly gift was bestowed on him. Writing toward the end of the second century, Irenaeus, Bishop of Lyon (120-202) expressed the doctrine of Theosis as follows: "The

Word was made flesh, so that flesh may be made God."[124] According to the "Christian" Platonist Origen (182-254), the goal of the Christian life is an internalized (contemplative) consideration of God. Through direct observation of the divine nature, man is himself deified. Human deification is made possible by the incarnation of God in Jesus Christ. Origen's view of salvation is characterized by the Platonic idea of progressive unification with God.[125] He believed that the soul will be brought gradually to perfection until the essential differences between God and man are reconciled and time ceases to exist.[126] According to Hilary of Poitiers (c.310-368), the main purpose of Christ's life on earth was the deification of man.[127] The fourth-century Christian apologist Athanasius (293-373) wrote: "Christ became man so that we could be made God."[128]

Although the doctrine of Theosis originated in the period before the Council of Nicaea (325 A.D.), it cannot be dismissed as an antiquated historical curiosity. The idea of deification, which implies that the human being is able to participate directly in the life of God, was surprisingly common during the Christian era. Although the doctrine of Theosis is one of the greatest heresies, it survived the struggle of Orthodoxy against Heterodoxy in the fourth and fifth centuries and played a key role in contemporary Christological debates. In accordance with biblical teaching, the Greek Church Fathers insisted that Christ was God. However, in conflict with Christian doctrine they concluded that Christ, as the Son of God, had imparted divine life to mankind. Maximus the Confessor interpreted the doctrine of deification similarly in the seventh century, believing that man could assume the form of God and consequently display certain divine qualities such as compassion and selflessness. Hundreds of years later, Meister Eckhart (1260-1328) claimed in an almost pantheistic manner that believers have a genuine possession of divine nature.[129]

The doctrine of Theosis is little known among Western Christians. However, it is one of the most important teachings in the theology of the Greek Orthodox Church. In a revealing book on Eastern Christianity, Daniel Clendenin claims that it would be no exaggeration to view the deification of man as "the central theme, the principal goal, the fundamental purpose, or the primary religious ideal of [Greek] Orthodoxy."[130]

---

[124] Irenaeus, *Adversus haereses*, V. (Cantabrigiae: Typis academicis, 1857) foreword, col. 1035; https://catalog.hathitrust.org/Record/009025834; s. also: Ibid., 3.10.2.

[125] Origines, *On Prayer*, xxxvii.13.

[126] Origines, *Contra Celsum*, 3.28.

[127] Hilarius von Poitiers, *On the Trinity*, 9.4-5, NPNF, 2d Series 9.156.

[128] Athanasius, *On the Incarnation of the Word*, book IV. Par. 65, NPNF, 2d Series.

[129] W. Corduan, "A Hair's Breadth From Pantheism: Meister Eckhart's God-Centered Spirituality," *Journal of the Evangelical Theological Society* 37/2 (1994), 269-271.

[130] Daniel B. Clendenin, *Eastern Orthodox Christianity: A Western Perspective* (Carlisle, Cumbria, UK: Paternoster; Grand Rapids, MI: Baker, [1994] 2004) 120; s. also: Daniel B. Clen-

It is commonly known that John Wesley (1703-1791) combined Anglican practice with the style of worship of the Bohemian Brethren. However, very few are aware that the founder of the Methodist Church drew on resources by the Church Fathers in forming his doctrine of salvation. It is particularly important to note that almost all the works of the Church Fathers, especially those of Clement and Origen of Alexandria, make explicit reference to the doctrine of Theosis. In the *Stromateis*, Clement describes Theosis from a perspective based on the *Corpus Hermeticum*; in the language of the Alexandrians' "gnostic" viewpoint, the soul ascends to God through knowledge and wisdom obtained through meditation.[131] John Wesley extracted quotes from the *Stromateis* and adapted them to his theology. According to Clement (150-215), a person passes from Paganism to Christianity when he turns to faith. From here he rises to God by means of Gnosis (knowledge), which is necessary in order to see God face to face. After this the process of deification commences: "Being baptized we are illuminated; illuminated, we are made sons (i.e. heirs); being made heirs, we obtain perfection; being made perfect, we are made immortal; as the Scriptures say, 'Ye are gods.'"[132]

John Wesley wanted to restore both church and society in England. He idealized and sought to emulate the culture of Christian antiquity, in this respect resembling contemporary humanist philosophers who drew on classical antiquity as a cultural model for the secular Enlightenment. The latter had already become a source of religious contention in Britain by the mid-seventeenth century. The Methodist Church in Great Britain adopted certain elements of the Theosis doctrine, which contained Eastern as well as Western ideas.

John Wesley's brother Charles also had an endless longing for the life of God in his soul. His hymns present poetic descriptions of the doctrine of Theosis: the Son of God, Jesus Christ, took on human flesh in His incarnation, enabling the transformation of man into a divine being through the indwelling life of God.[133] The poet Ann Griffiths (1776-1805) spoke of the union of human nature with the divine. She believed that man does not lose his human nature, but that it becomes united with the divine without the two becoming one. She emphasized both the divinity of man and the humanity of God. More names can be added besides those of Wesley and Griffiths as proponents of the Theosis doctrine, including Henry Scougal, William Williams, Richard Hooker, Lancelot Andrewes, and Edward Bouverie Pusey. These men

---

denin, "Partakers of Divinity: The Orthodox Doctrine of Theosis," *Journal of the Evangelical Theological Society* 37/3 (1994), 365-379.

[131] Clemens von Alexandria, *Stroemateis* IV, 4, p. 9, col. 253.

[132] Clemens, *Stromateis*, chap. 6.

[133] Arthur M. Allchin, *Participation in God: A Forgotten Strand in Anglican Tradition* (London: Darton, Longman and Todd, 1988) 26-27, 32-33.

presented the doctrines of the Trinity, the incarnation of Jesus Christ, and the deification of man as being inextricably entwined.[134]

Given John Wesley's great admiration for the speculative Mysticism of the early Greek Church Fathers, it is unsurprising that the rediscovery of their theology several centuries later led to a spiritual and institutional outbreak of traditional English religion. The theological essence of Wesleyan Methodism is Sinless Perfectionism, which strongly influenced the later Holiness movement. John Wesley's doctrine of perfection was founded on the tradition of Anglican and Catholic Mysticism, which upheld not only the possibility of sinless perfection, but also the doctrine of deification as its most important component. John Wesley described Jakob Böhme's writings as "the most sublime nonsense." Not all Pietist movements were so bold in exposing themselves to the Mysticism of Böhme and his spiritual offspring, but Theosophism nonetheless entered Methodism through the back door. Although the Philadelphia Society no longer existed by the time of the Wesley brothers, it continued to influence the English religious scene through the numerous writings of its former leaders.

John Wesley first preached the duty of perfection in a sermon given in Oxford in 1733, defining it as the commandment of sanctification.[135] Having to admit his ultimate inability to fulfill this ideal caused him great vexation. He could not deny the fact that sin remained in his life. When asked whether he himself was sinless, he answered that despite great efforts, he had never managed to climb to the highest rung of perfection. He later corrected his view and said that Christians will never be free of ignorance, error, temptation, and infirmity in this life, but that they nonetheless have a duty to pursue perfection.[136]

4 Prophetic vision of a hopeful future

Many treatises have been produced on the various Christian doctrines of the end times, but most theologians agree on only a few points. They agree that the Millennium (the thousand-year reign) will be an extended period of peace and world restoration, and that Christ will return at a certain point in time to govern the world. They also agree that God will judge the heathen in the last days, and that the world will eventually be destroyed. However, there is much disagreement over the order in which these events will unfold. There are three main teachings, as follows:

---

[134] Ibid., 38-39, 44-46.

[135] John Wesley, *A Plain Account of Christian Perfection* (London: J. Paramore, 1728) in *The Works of John Wesley*, vol. 11: 158-250.

[136] Ibid., vol. 11: 178ff.

Premillennialism teaches that Christ will return at the beginning of the Millennium to establish his earthly kingdom, which will last exactly one thousand years. His return will be followed by an almost complete destruction of the world. Only after His reign in Jerusalem will the yet unfulfilled heavenly conditions prophesied in the Old Testament be realized on earth.

Postmillennialism teaches that Christ will return during or after a long, unspecified period of global restoration. There will be increasing world peace among nations, which will enjoy an almost perfect society even before Christ returns. Those who have been born again by God's Spirit, and more importantly the Christianized nations, will enter the kingdom of God unharmed. Unbelievers, on the other hand, will face God's judgment at the end of time.

Amillennialism teaches that there will be no literal Millennium. The new covenant era is understood to be the decisive period in salvation history, with many of God's promises to Old Testament Israel fulfilled figuratively in the Christian church. Christ's return and the subsequent Day of Judgment will be immediately followed by the destruction and recreation of the earth, and by eternity in the heavenly Jerusalem.

Postmillennialism was one of the most significant legacies of sixteenth-century radical reformers, as well as of seventeenth-century Pansophic Millennialists who strove for a world united in scholarship and peace. Over time, this eschatological doctrine led to the mixing of secular and sacred history. Its proponents were primarily concerned with the great project of perfecting man and his surrounding world, their single-minded aim being to realize the kingdom of God on earth by following religious rules and making use of technological achievements. Justice, peace, and love would ultimately reign over all. They also believed that man possessed the disposition and ingenuity required to create heaven on earth, with no need for Christ's immediate presence as ruler of the world. The utopian enthusiasm that developed from Puritan Postmillennialism yielded much fruit in the fight for freedom of the American Revolution, which was followed by success in the War of Independence and the abolition of slavery. From the start of the First Great Awakening (1739-1743) in the U.S.A., spiritual awakening and political reform took place hand in hand, stimulating each other with ever-increasing intensity.

Postmillennialism was the generally accepted eschatological doctrine among American Protestants during the first three quarters of the nineteenth century. Although Premillennialism never lacked supporters, it had almost no influence on society. A new dispensational doctrine was introduced by the Englishman John Nelson Darby (1800-1882), a leading theologian of the Plymouth Brethren. However, some Premillennialists disagree with aspects of Darby's theology and hold beliefs that relate directly to the Premillennialism of the Apostolic and Post-Apostolic Ages. These refer to their eschatological position as historical Premillennialism.

Although Premillennialism spread gradually through influential churches and seminaries, largely in the form of Dispensationalism, it was not until the end of the nineteenth century that it challenged the dominance of Postmillennialism across wide stretches of the American ecclesiastical landscape.

4.1 Millennialist vision of a perfect society

The "thousand-year reign" was a complex and much debated subject in sixteenth- and seventeenth-century England. Some writers took a radical, populist direction, some speculated on the year of Christ's return, and others described a utopian Jerusalem. The Pope was frequently portrayed as the Antichrist, the conversion of the Jews was seen as a sign of Christ's imminent return, and some writers formed ideas based on astrology.

Thomas Brightman[137] (1562-1607) had a strong influence on the Puritans. His commentary on the book of Revelation[138] is one of the classic English works on Millennialism. He suggests a historical periodization that is supposedly based on biblical prophecy, teaching that the letters to the seven churches of Asia Minor in the second and third chapters of Revelation symbolize different eras of church history. He believed, for example, that the letter to the church in Sardis was a prophecy about the Lutheran church, and that the letter to the church in Philadelphia concerned the Calvinist church. The letter to the church in Laodicea was prophetic of the Church of England, which was neither hot nor cold. The six trumpets in chapter 8 pointed to the increased political power of the Ottoman Turks in 1300. Taking one prophetic day as equal to a literal year, Brightman interpreted Revelation 9:15 as a prophecy that the Turks' power would last until the year 1696. His interpretation of chapter 20 shows particularly clearly that he understood the thousand years mentioned in verse 2 as a literal millennium that had begun with the rule of Constantine in 306 and lasted until approximately 1300. The second thousand-year period (verse 5) had begun at the end of the first in the year 1300, and would therefore last until the year 2300. Brightman believed

---

[137] "Brightman, Thomas," in Sir Stephen Leslie, *Dictionary of National Biography* (London: Smith, Elder & Co. 1885-1900) vol. 6: 339; https://archive.org/details/dictionaryofnati06ste-puoft/page/338

[138] Thomas Brightman, *A Revelation of the Revelation that is, The Revelation of St. John opened clearly with a logicall Resolution and Exposition. Wherein The Sence is cleared, out of the scripture, the euent also thinges foretold is Discussed out of the Church-Historyes* (Amsterdam: [publisher not identified], 1615; Amsterdam: Printed by Thomas Stafford, [1644] 1664); s. also: Katherine R. Firth, *The Apocalyptic Tradition in Reformation Britain, 1520-1645* (Oxford: Oxford University Press, [1978] 1979) 166; C. A. Patrides & Joseph Anthony Wittreich, eds., *The Apocalyse in English Renaissance Thought and Literature* (Manchester: Manchester University Press, 1984); B. S. Capp, *The Fifth-Monarchy Men: A Study in Seventeenth-Century English Millennarianism* (London: Faber, 1972); Rob Iliffe, "'Making a Shew': Apocalyptic Hermeneutics and the Sociology of Christian Idolatry in the work of Isaac Newton and Henry More," in James E. Force & Richard H. Popkin, eds., *The Books of Nature and Scripture* (Berlin: Springer Science & Business Media, 1994) 55-88; Louise Fargo Brown, *The Political Activities of the Baptists and the Fifth-Monarchy Men* (New York City, NY: B. Franklin, [1911] 1964).

that the influence of biblical truth would grow throughout the world during this second Millennium. He expected the papacy and its power over Europe to collapse, after which the conversion of the Jews would take place.[139] The Ottoman Empire (Gog and Magog) would also fall. Despite the poor quality of Brightman's interpretation, his commentary spread widely and influenced the development of Postmillennialism. Later theologians continued to expand his ideas. Along with Joseph Mede, Thomas Brightman was the most important "revisionist" of conventional Anglican eschatology, which was then based primarily on John Foxe's (1517-1587) belief that the English were God's chosen people.

Joseph Mede[140] (1586-1638) revolutionized the interpretation of New Testament eschatological writings through the publication of his commentary on the book of Revelation. He was awarded a professorship by the regents of Christ's College, Cambridge, in recognition of the profound intellect of their former student and fellow. Many eminent figures such as Henry More, Isaac Barrow (Newton's teacher), and John Morton considered themselves fortunate to have been taught by him. After overcoming his early Skepticism[141], he became a shrewd logician, intelligent philosopher, instructive mathematician, excellent anatomist, great philologist, linguist, and historian. A particularly productive area of his research was astrology.[142] He eventually surmounted the last remnants of his Skepticism when he delved into exegesis of the book of Revelation.

In his *Clavis Apocalyptica* (The Key of the Revelation), published in 1627, Joseph Mede (1586-1638) introduced the general public to the belief that the Millennial Reign would be an era of unrestrained human bliss. Although Mede's new teaching on Millennialism was based on a literal thousand-year reign, it rejected the idea that Jesus Christ would exercise earthly power as the returning King of kings. The origins of Postmillennialism can therefore be traced back not only to Alsted's eschatological view, but also to Mede's interpretation of Revelation 20, which focused more on the Rosicrucian call for general reformation than on a literal interpretation of the passages in Revelation that concern the Millennium.

Joseph Mede's book *Clavis Apocalyptica*[143] remains an important part of the interpretative arsenal of Christian Millennialists today. Mede's particular

---

[139] Brightman, *A Revelation of the Revelation*, 643.

[140] Also: Joseph Meade, Joseph Mead

[141] John Worthington, "The Life of the Reverend and most learned Joseph Mede," in John Worthington, ed., *The Works of the Pious and Profoundly-Learned Joseph Mede, B.D., sometime fellow of Christ's Colledge in Cambridge* (London: Printed by James Flesher for Richard Royston, 1664) iii.

[142] Ibid., iii-iv.

[143] Joseph Mede, *Clavis Apocalyptica* [...] *una cum commentario in Apocalypsin: quibus accessit hac tertia editione conjectura de Gogo et Magogo, ab eodem autore* (Cantabrigiae: R. Daniel, 1627); *The Key to Revelation, searched and demonstrated out of the Natural and proper Characters of the Vision*, trans. by Richard More (London: By J. L. for Phil. Stephens, 1643); R.

achievement was in devising a seemingly plausible yet imaginative timetable of concrete dates for the future fulfillment of prophecies in the books of Daniel and Revelation. Although some of his predictions proved incorrect, his former student John Worthington regarded Mede's work as a "faultless key" (clavis non errans) in comparison to other interpretations.[144] Mede stayed in contact with numerous members of the Hartlib Circle and other intellectuals in England and Holland for many years. He sought to use his extensive correspondence to win an increasing number of scholars at home and abroad to his eschatological view.

Among these scholars was the Scot Johannes Duraeus (John Dury, 1595/96-1680). After completing his theological studies, he served as a Reformed minister in Cologne and in Elbing, near Danzig. Jan Amos Comenius, Samuel Hartlib, and Johann Valentin Andreae visited and spent time with him in Elbing. Duraeus later became personal chaplain to Princess Mary, later Mary II, Queen of England (1662-1694, daughter of King James II and wife of William III of Orange). He participated in the spreading of millennialist ideas throughout the Protestant world, and consequently had a degree of influence on contemporary politics. He spent almost fifty years seeking to unite Protestant churches in Europe and North America, believing this to be the only way to create the conditions required for the return of Jesus Christ. He also engaged in missions to convert the Jews and to develop science still further. Every step toward the fulfillment of these causes was believed to reduce the time remaining before the dawn of the Millennium. Duraeus returned to his former workplace in London during the English Revolution (1642-1649) in order to take every opportunity to implement secular educational reform and Christian religious practice. By founding the "Invisible College," he continued to influence subsequent generations of scholars even after his death, with many of them later becoming members of the Royal Society.[145]

The Puritan theologian Dr. William Twisse (1578[?]-1648) believed that Mede's system of biblical interpretation was infallible.[146] Twisse studied theology in Oxford and became a prominent Puritan of his day. From 1640, he played a significant role in the religious disputes which had a direct impact

---

Bransby Cooper, *A translation of Mede's Clavis apocalyptica* (London: Printed for J. G. & F. Rivington, 1833); https://archive.org/details/atranslationmed00medegoog/page/n5; s. also: Jeffrey K. Jue, *Heaven Upon Earth. Joseph Mede (1586-1638) and the Legacy of Millenarianism* (Dortrecht: Springer, 2006).

[144] Worthington, "The Life of the Reverend and most learned Joseph Mede," in John Worthington, ed., *The Works of the Pious and Profoundly-Learned Joseph Mede, B.D.*, xii-xiii.

[145] J. Minton Batten, *John Dury: Advocate of Christian Reunion* (Chicago, IL: The University of Chicago Press, 1944).

[146] William Twisse, *The doubting conscience resolved. In answer to a (pretended) perplexing question, &c. Wherein is evidently proved, that the holy Scriptures (not the pope) is the foundation whereupon the Church is built. Or, That a Christian may be infallibly certain of his faith and religion by Holy Scriptures* (London: Printed for Thomas Matthews at the sign of the Cock in St Pauls Church-yard, 1652).

on English politics. Twisse was apparently the first person to realize that Mede had made a monumental discovery. According to the Puritan theologian, Mede had insisted that the events prophesied in the books of Daniel and Revelation would come to pass during the present era, meaning that the beginning of the Millennium was supposedly imminent. When Mede died in 1638, Twisse published some of his works which had previously been circulated as manuscripts. In 1643, the Committee of the House of Commons issued a decree ordering the English translation and publication of *Clavis Apocalyptica*. Twisse interpreted Daniel 12:4 ("[…] many shall run to and fro, and knowledge shall be increased." KJV) in accordance with Mede's work: people would have access to all regions of the world through seafaring and trade, with knowledge increasing enormously at the same time. Any vigilant observer would be able to discern the occurrence of these events in the present day. The Roman Catholic Church had long condemned belief in Christ's thousand-year reign on earth as a pernicious heresy; however, since the kingdom of the Antichrist (understood as the power of the Roman Catholic Church) was approaching its end[147], the literal interpretation of Jesus's earthly rule could now be taken up in good faith. Through the enlightenment of the Holy Spirit, people would recognize the true beliefs that were available to them.[148] Only in this way could Skepticism be overcome. All doubts would be dispelled through infallible knowledge of biblical doctrine.

The Cambridge Platonist Henry More (1614-1687) suggested that God's method in saving mankind was a gradual, general deliverance which would take place through several successive eras. Some saw a positive work of God in the emergence of a period of general enlightenment; knowledge was not only increasing in matters of theology, but also in the theoretical understanding and practical application of science.

During the seventeenth century, England played an important role in the development of sophisticated tools for achieving spiritual goals. It was by no means uncommon for scientists to deal with doctrines of salvation and the end times, as people were convinced that science was the ideal means of attaining human salvation. Scientists were believed to have a special relationship to God and were therefore considered "Priests of Nature." Foreign discoveries encouraged European hopes for a Pansophic society which would subsume the whole of humanity. A key precondition would be the turning of Christians, Pagans, Jews, and Muslims to Hermeticism, which was portrayed as being in accordance with the promise of a New Jerusalem in the book of

---

[147] Twisses Preface in Joseph Mede, *Apostacy of the Latter Times. In which, (according to Divine Prediction) the World Should Wonder After the Beast, the Mysterie of Iniquity Should So Far Prevaile Over the Mysterie of Godlinesse, Whorish Babylon Over the Virgin-Church of Christ, […] Revived in the Latter Times Amongst Christians, […] &c. […]* (London: Printed by L. N. for Samuel Man dwelling at the signe of the Swan in Pauls Church-yard, 1644) A2v; https://archive.org/details/bub_gb_OzFzA_zHnpQC/page/n1; In a letter of 11 November 1629 Mede had told Twisse that the people would not be allowed to talk about the millennium, as long as the Antichrist held on to power.

[148] Twisse, *The Doubting Conscience Resolved*, 105.

Revelation. A New Atlantis (Francis Bacon), a Christianopolis (Johann Valentin Andreae), or a City of the Sun (Tommaso Campanella[149]) would then be created. The more knowledge of the real world was acquired, the closer the union of "Christian" nations would come to perfection. Detached from the fiction, utopia developed into a manifesto. The religious schisms and their polarizing political effects, the fanaticism of the Reformation, and the drive for a Counter-Reformation threatened Europe with terrible wars of extermination.

The Puritans were also convinced that the end of the world was imminent. Their attempts to gain new knowledge of the earth and to improve human technology were an endeavor to bring about the millennial conditions prophesied by John in the book of Revelation. Technology was important in regaining control over the natural world as described in the book of Genesis, which had been governed by Adam and Eve before the Fall but lost thereafter.[150] Progress was seen as a true utopia – "a heavenly city of virtuosi" – in which man's achievements in developing civilization would become ever better and more comprehensive.

The English pastor John Archer published his book *The Personall Reigne of Christ Upon Earth*[151] in 1642, and it soon became a manifesto of the "Fifth Monarchy Men." Archer believed that Christ would rule the earth on His return. With reference to Daniel 2:31-46, he saw Nebuchadnezzar's vision of the statue as relating to four earthly kingdoms.[152] He believed that the final kingdom consisted of the Roman Empire and the monarchies that still existed in 1642, which would give way to the Fifth Monarchy – the kingdom of Christ.

Archer said that the papacy would fall in the year 1666, that great numbers of Jews would convert to Christianity in 1656, and that the Millennium would commence in 1700. Many people were persuaded by the idea of the Fifth Monarchy during the 1650s. Oliver Cromwell had great difficulty keeping them under control, since many of them objected to human government and declared undivided loyalty to the Fifth Monarchy, which they believed to be imminent. The Puritan theologian John Owen wrote to English churches, warning them against the wild conjectures of the "Fifth Monarchy" movement.

Jan Amos Comenius was a convinced Millennialist. In a manuscript sent to Hartlib and Duraeus, he stated that the events prophesied in Revelation would commence in the year 1655, culminating in the emergence of the

---

[149] Real name: Giovanni Domenico; born on 5 September 1568 in Stilo, Calabria; died on 21 May 1639 in Paris.

[150] Charles Webster, *The Great Instauration: Science, Medicine And Reform, 1626-1660* (London: Duckworth, 1975; Bern: Peter Lang, 2002) 506-507.

[151] John Archer, *The Personall Reigne of Christ Upon Earth: in a treatise wherein is fully and largely laid open and proved that Jesus Christ together with the saints shall visibly possesse a monarchiall state and kingdome in this world* [...] (London: Printed by Benjamin Allen, 1642).

[152] Ibid., 2.

thousand-year reign. The Bohemian bishop firmly believed that all Christians needed to prepare for these eschatological events.[153] In this respect he was in full agreement with Hartlib and Duraeus. In 1641, he published a document which promised global peace during the thousand-year reign and affirmed the legitimacy of seeking help from secular powers in the effort to bring about the new era. In order to be prepared, the English education system needed to be reformed and peaceful relationships between individual churches needed to be encouraged.[154] While Comenius devoted himself primarily to reforming the European education system, Hartlib was to set up an academy in London of which Comenius would be principal. Furthermore, Hartlib was to persuade scientists of the importance of cooperation, this being the only way to attain comprehensive knowledge. Johannes Duraeus's (John Dury's) main task was to unite all Protestant churches within a single organization, as well as to ensure the conversion of the Jews to Christianity.

In order to promote Pansophism as a teaching method, Comenius designed a reform of the educational system which could not have been more revolutionary. He began writing a series of textbooks for cross-cultural use in multiple languages. By 1650, approximately half of all textbooks used in European and American colleges and universities were authored by Comenius. His pedagogical innovations earned him a reputation as father of the modern education system. Never a man of modest ambitions, Comenius's utopian vision included a universal language, worldwide evangelization, global government, and church reunification. His ultimate goal was no less than a pancultural Christian reformation of world civilization.

As news of the Puritan revolution spread across the continent, it was listened to carefully by remaining Rosicrucians who had persevered in the background. Some of these esotericists considered emigrating to England. Among them was Samuel Hartlib, born in Elbing, Königlich-Preußen, in 1600. He and his followers wanted to create a Christian society and welfare state in connection with a radical reformation in sociopolitical and economic relations.[155] However, any sense that a new era was dawning soon became lost in the turmoil of the English Civil War (1642-1649).

---

[153] Webster, *The Great Instauration*, 48-51; s. also: Johann Amos Comenius, Robert Fitzgibbon Young, John N. Libbey, ed., *Comenius in England: The visit of Jan Amos Komenský (Comenius), the Czech philosopher and educationist, to London in 1641-1642; its bearing on the origins of the Royal Society, on the development of the encyclopædia, and on plans for the higher education of the Indians of New England and Virginia, as described in contemporary documents* (Oxford: Oxford University Press, H. Milford, 1932).

[154] George H. Turnbull, *Hartlib, Dury, and Comenius: Gleanings from Hartlib's Papers* (London: University Press of Liverpool and Hodder & Stoughton, 1947; London: Hodder and Stoughton, 1968) 358.

[155] Hugh Redward Trevor-Roper, "Three Foreigners and the Philosophy of the English Revolution," *Encounter. Literature, Arts, Politics* 14 (1960), 3-20 in Hugh R. Trevor-Roper, *The Crisis of the Seventeenth Century: Religion, the Reformation and Social Change* (Indianapolis, IN: Liberty Fund, 2001) 219-272; https://oll.libertyfund.org/titles/roper-the-crisis-of-the-seventeenth-century

After the Puritans lost their political power, King Charles II turned his attention to science which had notoriously stemmed from, and been subsequently influenced by, John Dee's "Christian" Cabbalism. Freemasons founded the "Invisible College," from which the Royal Society – a British academic society for the encouragement of scientific development – was formed in 1662. Scientists of the Royal Society continued to meet in Masonic lodges.

From 1740, the Royal Society sought to discourage religious enthusiasm, doing so primarily by spreading a new conception of God. One hundred years earlier, Cromwell had believed that he was following a divine command in launching a military campaign against the Catholic Irish. However, the main characteristic of the modern God was found in the order and harmony of His created universe, whose galactic cycles He had now left to be governed by the laws of nature. The Royal Society said that in their efforts to create a perfect society, Christian, mystical, and Liberal groups (such as the Puritans, Quakers, Ranters, Diggers, and Fifth Monarchy Men) had instead produced chaos in the lands formerly ruled by King Charles I. Thomas Hobbes and his followers argued that motion is inherent in matter itself, and that there is consequently no need to believe that a divine providence governs the universe and determines all things according to the will of God.[156]

The Royal Society opposed the idea that the universe requires a determining power in order to maintain order and harmony – a power that Newton referred to as "gravity." The word was originally used to indicate an attribute of God, but Newton applied it to matter. There could have been no better term for the new capitalist society and its theologically liberal episcopate. Anglican clerics hoped that King Charles II would support this "external power," and that he would curb religious enthusiasm on the one hand and atheistic materialism on the other.

4.2 Prevalence of Puritan Postmillennialism

(Puritans consider themselves God's chosen people)
Regardless of their theological position, Protestants had no doubt that God had charged them in His Providence with settling the New World.[157] The Puritan Calvinists who had been persecuted in England went on to establish Postmillennialism as the predominant eschatological doctrine of the English colonies in North America.[158] Considering themselves a people made holy by

---

[156] Thomas Hobbes, *Leviathan, or The Matter, Forme, & Power, of a Common-Wealth Ecclesiasticall and Civill* (London: Printed for Andrew Crooke, 1651); https://archive.org/details/leviathan00hobbgoog/page/n11; Thomas Hobbes, *Leviathan*, J. C. A. Gaskin, ed. (Oxford: Oxford University Press, [1651] 2009).

[157] Sacvan Bercovitch, *The American Jeremiad* (Madison, WI: The University of Wisconsin Press, 1978) 8-9.

[158] Iain H. Murray, *The Puritan Hope* (London: Banner of Truth, 1971).

God and anticipating great blessing, they set out on a mission to build a new city of Jerusalem. This would be a visible sign of the goodness of God, which already granted them temporal blessings in this life. Protection, peace, purity, prosperity, and ultimately eternal reward would come in good time. They believed that the Spirit of Christ would soon be poured out on the whole world, and that God would then establish His universal rule. Over time, this Postmillennial view became a central theme of American history. Americans felt themselves called to go into all the world to build God's kingdom, and to spread their social model and system of government to all other countries of the earth.[159]

4.3 The theosophical basis of "Pennsylvania religion"

Johannes Kelpius (1670-1708) was the leader of a group of German emigrants who embraced the influence of Theosophy. Theosophy teaches that deeper insight into the meaning of all things can only be obtained through a mystical view of God. On their way to the U.S.A. in 1694, the group made a detour to England in order to meet the Philadelphians in London, especially Jane W. Leade. Kelpius's notes contain numerous astrological symbols, implying that the group relied on the stars for direction[160], and his most important instrument was a telescope. Kelpius was eagerly awaiting the coming of Jesus Christ.

After studying at the University of Helmstadt, Kelpius made his name as an astrologer, alchemist, and theosophist, and gained a reputation for his vast knowledge of the various esoteric doctrines. He and his group seem to have committed themselves to pursuing the Rosicrucian vision of a perfect society. However, the year 1694 came and went with no sign of the Millennium. The disappointment hit Kelpius hard[161]: he had emigrated from Germany to Pennsylvania in order to experience Christ's arrival on the continent, as prophesied by his predecessor Johann Jacob Zimmermann. Kelpius often withdrew to a cave[162] to practice his alchemy.[163] His group had built a large

---

[159] Alan Heimert, *Religion and the American Mind from the Great Awakening to the Revolution* (Cambridge, MA: Harvard University Press, 1966); https://archive.org/details/religion-american00heim; Ernest Lee Tuveson, *Redeemer Nation: The Idea of America's Millennial Role* (Chicago, IL: University of Chicago Press, 1968); https://archive.org/details/redeemernation00erne

[160] Julius Friedrich Sachse, trans., "The Diarium of Magister Johannes Kelpius," in *The Pennsylvania-German Society, Proceedings and Addresses* (Lancaster, PA: 1917) vol. 25: 31; https://archive.org/details/diamagiste00kelp/page/30

[161] Johannes Kelpius, "Brief an Heinrich Johann Deichmann [Engl. spelling: "Heinrich John Deichman"], 24. Februar 1697," in "The Diarium of Magister Johannes Kelpius," ed. and trans. by Julius Friedrich Sachse, *Pennsylvania German Society, Proceedings and Addresses*, 30; https://archive.org/details/diamagiste00kelp/page/30

[162] Cave of Kelpius; https://www.atlasobscura.com/places/cave-of-kelpius

[163] J. McArthur Jr., "The Enigma of Kelpius' Cave," *Germantown Crier* 3 (Summer, 1983),

hall to live in together, and they treated their possessions as common property. They lived in celibacy, prayed and fasted, spent time in solitary meditation, and observed celestial signs in the night sky. Although Kabbalah and astrology are rarely thought of as elements of American popular religion, they played a crucial role in shaping American society.[164] Hermetic insights were central to the theological understanding and practical spirituality of many men and women in early modern Europe, and European settlers brought these views and practices to the New World.[165] Lutherans, Separatist Pietists, and Quakers were united by their interest in the hermetic tradition despite their differences in doctrine, theology, and church politics. The study of Kabbalah was more than an academic interest for them. It kindled their desire for a Christianity that was no longer divided into sects that followed their own creeds, and encouraged their hope that the Millennium would soon commence. However, after Kelpius's death in 1708, virtually the entire party scattered in all directions. The majority married, and some were ordained as Lutheran ministers.

Taken alone, Kelpius's story seems obscure. It can be better understood within its wider context: a combining of Christian views with Egyptian and Jewish Mysticism. Christian Knorr von Rosenroth (1636-1689) was probably the most important influence behind the esoteric thinking that inspired Johannes Kelpius. Knorr von Rosenroth was a Lutheran minister, academic, poet, writer, and evangelical hymnwriter from Bavaria and was widely respected as a Kabbalah scholar. He had close connections with the Pansophic-Kabbalist group that met at the court of Duke Christian August of Palatinate-Sulzbach, and was also at the center of a network of reformers who saw the incorporation of Kabbalah into the Christian faith as a prerequisite for social reformation in seventeenth-century Europe.[166] They also accepted the reincarnation theory developed in the post-Renaissance period by Jewish Kabbalist Isaac Luria, who claimed that the essence of God's nature is goodness and love, and that every person will eventually be saved through repeated reincarnation. This teaching was used to resolve the problem of reconciling the attributes of a loving God with those of one who would take vengeance.

Among the numerous spiritual groups in Pennsylvania at that time were the Kelpius Society, the "Woman in the Wilderness," the Anabaptists, and the Labadist colony.[167] The Kelpius Society and the Labadist colony were

---

54-56.

[164] Jon Butler, "Magic, Astrology, and the Early American Religious Heritage," *American Historian Review*, 84, no. 2 (April, 1979), 317-446.

[165] Keith Thomas, "An Anthropology of Religion and Magic, II," *Journal of Interdisciplinary History*, 6, no. 1 (Summer, 1975), 91-109.

[166] Allison Coudert, "A Quaker-Kabbalist Controversy: George Fox's Reaction to Francis Mercury van Helmont," *Journal of the Warburg and Cortauld Institutes*, 39 (1976), 172-178.

[167] "The Labadists of Bohemia Manor," Maryland Historical Society, http://www.mdhs.org/labadists-bohemia-manor

characterized by celibacy and asceticism. They tried to achieve perfection by leading contemplative lives, this being the principal message taught by Jean de Labadie (1610-1674). However, when their leader died, the community once again disbanded. "Pennsylvania religion" was often ridiculed by American colonists: their religious enthusiasm produced some strange effects, and the communities provided places of refuge in which theosophists could practice their bizarre rituals. One example is the career of Matthias Bauman, an uneducated laborer from the Rhineland. During a period of serious illness, Bauman had a vision of paradise. Believing that he had been spiritually enlightened, Bauman travelled to Pennsylvania in 1719 and immediately began to tell its inhabitants that they could lead entirely sinless lives if they allowed themselves to be filled with the Spirit of God. In this sinless state they would no longer need the Bible; neither would they need to be part of a church. It would no longer be necessary to live under social constraints as they would live in innocence, just as Adam had in the Garden of Eden before the Fall.[168] Bauman's followers called themselves the "Newborns" and scattered far and wide after their leader died in 1727.

Johann Conrad Beissel's (1690-1768) Ephrata Community[169] should be considered in the context of the contemporary spiritual atmosphere in Pennsylvania. This almost monastic community made a significant contribution to the development of America's colonial history. The wide range of esoteric traditions practiced by its members, including alchemy, astrology, and magic, can be collectively termed "Theosophy." This created another variation of "Christian" Mysticism in its own right. Dealing with Theosophy is very different from dealing with other esoteric traditions. For example, the Ephrata Community saw engagement with magic as a sacred activity that was integral to their theosophical worldview. Magic was only used properly when it served a spiritual purpose, such as the protection of its members and the community buildings. In order to increase the power of their magic formulae, they performed lengthy rituals on certain days of the week and on nights when the moon was waning.[170] Alchemy also played an important role in Theosophy alongside astrology and magic. Terms such as the "philosopher's stone" were used in direct relation to the idea of spiritual

---

[168] Everett Gordon Alderfer, *The Ephrata Commune: An Early American Counterculture* (Pittsburgh, PA: University of Pittsburgh Press, 1985) 35, 107ff. (chap. IX, Recovery of Eden); s. also: Julius Friedrich Sachse, *The German Sectarians of Pennsylvania, 1708-1742 (1742-1800): A critical and legendary history of the Ephrata Cloister and the Dunkers*, 2 vols. (Philadelphia, PA: Printed for the author by P. C. Stockhausen, 1899-1900) vol. 1: 73; https://archive.org/details/germansectarian00sachgoog/page/n122

[169] Oswald Seidensticker, *Ephrata: Eine amerikanische Klostergeschichte* (Cincinnati, OH: Druck von Mecklenborg & Rosenthal, 1883); https://archive.org/details/ephrataeineameri-00seid/page/n6; s. also: F. Reichmann, E. E. Doll, "Ephrata, as seen by contemporaries," in *Pennsylvanian German Folklore Society*, vol. 17 (Allentown, PA, 1953); Martin Lohmann, *Die Bedeutung der deutschen Ansiedlungen in Pennsylvanien* (Stuttgart: Ausland & Heimat, 1923).

[170] Julius Friedrich Sachse, *The German Pietists of Provincial Pennsylvania for the Chapter* (Philadephia, PA: Printed for the Author, 1895) vol. 1: 152, 37, 39, 77, 120, 148, 247, 387; https://archive.org/details/germanpietistsof00sach/page/37

transformation, and the discovery of an elixir of life was among practicing alchemists' primary goals.[171] The Ephrata Community's engagement with these esoteric traditions and their spiritual interpretation of aspects of daily life, such as their mystical interpretation of Sabbath day observance, distinguished them from other communities such as the Moravian Church of Count Nikolaus von Zinzendorf. Zinzendorf initially wanted to establish a relationship with the Ephrata Community; however, there was no further contact between the two communities after rumors spread that the Ephrata Community was the "instrument of the devil."[172] The spiritual origins of the Ephrata Community lie in Jakob Böhme's Theosophy, with Johann Conrad Beissel becoming one of the first American authors to write and publish books on the tradition. According to Beissel, the Sabbath symbolizes certain numerical and cosmological mysteries that prefigure the end times and signify an "Eternal Sabbath."[173] Members of the Ephrata Community embraced an esoteric Millennialism and influenced the evolution of many American colonists' religious views. Beissel's successor, Peter Müller (1710-1796), was particularly adept at maintaining personal relationships with powerful individuals such as Benjamin Franklin and George Washington. One of his foremost concerns was for freedom of religion. The guarantee of religious freedom and the separation of church and state later became two of the most important aspects of the American Constitution.

Philadelphia, Pennsylvania was the first capital city of the newly founded United States – not only because of its geographical proximity to the Ephrata Community, but also because of its spiritual orientation. Benjamin Franklin's inclination for esoteric spirituality was demonstrably influenced by the publications which his printing business produced for the Ephrata Community. He tirelessly supported the principle that no religious community should be privileged by the state – which was one of Theosophy's highest concerns. Following Johann Georg Gichtel, theosophists in Germany, France, the Netherlands, England, and North America stood up for the equality of all religions and refrained from establishing their own religious communities. The only group of theosophists to give themselves a name was Jane W. Leade's Philadelphia Society in England. Other theosophists deplored the fact that this was possible in the first place, fearing that written teaching would replace direct contact with spiritual powers.

4.4 Refining the human character

(Rejection of the Reformation and Puritanism during the Enlightenment)

---

[171] Sachse, *German Sectarians of Pennsylvania, 1708-1742*, vol. 1: 112, 207; https://archive.org/details/germansectarian00sachgoog/page/n174

[172] Alderfer, *Ephrata Commune*, 78ff.

[173] Johann Konrad Beissel, *Das Büchlein vom Sabbath* (Philadelphia, PA: Bradford, 1728).

The group of seventeenth-century thinkers known as the Cambridge Platonists[174] came from a Puritan background but largely rejected its influence. These English scholars were opposed to Puritan Calvinism on the one hand, and on the other hand to Thomas Hobbes's Materialism which offered a God-less explanation of the world and its processes. In general, they opposed dominant attitudes of their day by advocating tolerance in an age of polarization. The name "Cambridge Platonists" is somewhat misleading, since they drew on other Classical philosophers besides Plato such as Plutarch, Cicero, and Seneca. However, they were most sympathetic to the work of Plotinus (205-270 B.C.), the founder of Neoplatonism. Six hundred years after Plato, this Alexandrian scholar had developed his predecessor's philosophy into a system of thought which taught that God could be found in the human psyche. He believed that there was an essential identity between human reason and "Nous," the all-controlling spirit of the universe.[175] The "Platonism" so greatly valued in Cambridge was a Mysticism derived from Plotinus, primarily consisting of a natural spirituality which deified the soul. The English philosophers strove to reach perfection by means of the human intellect and pursued communion with the incomprehensible through the path of knowledge. These Panentheists combined Christianity with the philosophical ideal of the ancient Greeks.

Henry More was one of Joseph Mede's most notable students. He began studying at the University of Cambridge on December 31, 1631, and remained there for the rest of his life as one of the most influential scholars of his time. After four years of study, he admitted that all philosophizing amounted to nothing but Skepticism. In a shattered state of mind, he asked whether "progress in knowledge truly constitutes man's highest bliss, or whether there may be a still greater and happier way."[176] He subsequently applied himself to intensive study of Platonic, hermetic, and mystical works, through which he came to understand that purification of the soul must precede the inspiration of God – the attainment of comprehensive knowledge. He thus decided to devote himself to daily meditative exercises and came out of his deep depression. The mystical knowledge which he now systematically acquired

---

[174] Rosalie Colie, *Light and Enlightenment: A Study of the Cambridge Platonists and the Dutch Arminians* (New York City, NY: Cambridge University Press, 1957); James D. Roberts, *From Puritanism to Platonism in Seventeenth Century England* (Dordrecht: Springer Netherlands, 1968); Gerald R. Cragg, *From Puritanism to the Age of Reason* (Cambridge: Cambridge University Press, [1950] 2008); Frederick J. Powicke, *The Cambridge Platonists* (London: J. M. Dent and Sons, 1926).

[175] William Ralph Inge, *The Philosophy of Plotinus*, 2 vols. (New York City, NY: Longmans, Green and Co., [1918] 1948) vol. 1: https://archive.org/details/in.ernet.dli.2015.209465/page/n7; vol. 2: https://archive.org/details/in.ernet.dli.2015.219392/page/n5; Emile Brehier, *The Philosophy of Plotinus* (Chicago, IL: University of Chicago Press, 1958). Inge translated "Nous" as "Spirit"; Brehier as "Intelligence".

[176] John Worthington, "The Life of the Reverend and most learned Joseph Mede," in John Worthington, ed., *The Works of the Pious and Profoundly-Learned Joseph Mede, B.D., sometime fellow of Christ's Colledge in Cambridge* (London: Printed by James Flesher for Richard Royston, 1664) 12.

instructed him to surrender his self-will, and thus accept unquestioningly what God in His sovereignty had allegedly determined for him. He submitted entirely to the divine will which supposedly gave him a new life – a type of new birth – thus gaining "a greater assurance than ever [he] could have expected." Unable to explain exactly what had happened to him, he stated simply that he was "got into a most joyous and lucid state of mind." Sensing the work of a vital spiritual force within him, he immediately began to create a theoretical basis for the philosophy which went down in the annals of history as Cambridge Platonism. He set out its precise, certain principles in a way that would be understood and accepted by his contemporaries. In 1656, More felt a responsibility to examine the many religious currents which had appeared throughout the country. He was justifiably concerned about the willingness of many English and Dutch scholars to embrace Jakob Böhme's Mysticism.[177] More believed that inspiration (spiritual enlightenment) and enthusiasm (ecstasy) were antitheses.[178] Without inspiration from God, the individual would fall into enthusiasm which would eventually lead to Atheism. The Cambridge Platonist John Smith (1616-1652) explained that the pseudo-prophetic spirit is found only in the powers of imagination and the faculties inferior to reason, whereas the true prophetic spirit is inherent in the rational faculties and emotions. It is recognized by the mind as a part of its own self. The role of the prophetic spirit is to carry out the crucial task of enlightening the mind.

As the result of personal and professional relationships between the Cambridge Platonists and Puritans in national government, the Puritans came to embrace pagan concepts. The spirituality of the Cambridge scholars had an even greater effect on the Puritans in New England as theologians overcame their doubts about incorporating Greek philosophy into their Christian doctrine. Henry More's *Enchiridion Ethicum*[179] (1666) became the authoritative textbook for moral philosophy at Harvard College, marking a turning point in the reorientation of New England Puritans' philosophy in the 1680s. The book, which placed a particularly strong emphasis on Neoplatonism, was later even included on the compulsory reading list at Yale College.

A distinct vein of Neoplatonism ran through the religious thinking of New England scholars both before and especially after the War of Independence (1775-1783), originating in the writings of the Cambridge

---

[177] Henry More, *Philosophia Teutonicae Censura* (London: 1679), in Henrici Mori, *Opera omnia, tum quae latine, tum quae anglice scripta sunt, nunc vero latinitate donata* [...] *impensis* [...] *Johannis Cockshuti,* [...] (Londini: Sumptibus J. Martyn et G. Kettilby, 1679) vol. 1: 529-561; http://www.cambridge-platonism.divinity.cam.ac.uk/view/texts/diplomatic/More1679A

[178] Henry More, *Enthusiasmus Triumphatus: or a Brief Discourse of the Nature, Causes, Kinds and Cures of Enthusiasm*, in Henry More, *A Collection of Several Philosophical Writings of Dr. Henry More* (London: Printed by James Flesher for William Morden Book-seller in Cambridge, 1662) Sec. II, 2.

[179] Henry More, *Enchiridion Ethicum* (London: Benjamin Tooke, 1666); https://archive.org/details/enchiridionethic00more/page/n7

Platonists. This was evident in the theology of Jonathan Edwards[180] (1703-1758) and the New Divinity theologians who came directly after him, particularly Samuel Hopkins (1721-1803). They believed that all created beings emanate directly from the divine, and that there is therefore no difference between Creator and creation. Liberal theologians also accepted the doctrine of Panentheism which was spread by the Neoplatonic tradition. When the Enlightenment finally reached America, these ideas fell on fertile ground and were eagerly received. It was believed that truth could be illuminated by reason in all areas of knowledge. In consequence, both Reformation heritage and Puritanism were rejected in theology, politics, the economy, and the social sector.

4.5 Kindling religious enthusiasm

(Combining the millennial reign with politics)
Dismayed by the spiritual decline in New England, some Calvinistic ministers confronted the Nominalism and Skepticism of their day and preached the beliefs of the Reformation. The First Great Awakening (1739-1743) and Second Great Awakening (1790-1850) had an impact on the religious disposition of the whole nation that has endured to the present day. The First Great Awakening already caused divided opinions between those holding to the Reformational doctrine of grace (conversion as the work of God) and those teaching subjective conversion (conversion as the work of man). Mass conversions were seen as preludes to the millennial reign. The influential theologian Jonathan Edwards (1703-1758) reinterpreted the Millennium[181] and taught that the fall of the Antichrist, the Pope, would be followed by a Golden Age. Edwards used language that corresponded almost word for word with what is written about the Antichrist in Revelation 13, forcing his interpretation of the passage to fit his Postmillennial views. Those who accepted this teaching denounced slavery as a heinous crime that would delay the coming of the great day, calling instead for selfless charity. After Edwards' death, Postmillennialism and politics became connected even more strongly. The ultimate goal was no longer to convert all nations to Christianity, but to glorify America as the new land of liberty.[182]

---

[180] Jonathan Edwards, "Concerning the End for Which God Created the World," in Paul Ramsey, ed., *The Works of Jonathan Edwards*, vol. 8, Ethical Writings (New Haven, CT: Yale University Press, 1989).

[181] Stephen J. Stein, "A Notebook on the Apocalypse by Jonathan Edwards," *William and Mary Quarterly* (Ser. 3) 29 (1972), 623-634.

[182] Ernest Lee Tuveson, *Redeemer Nation: The Idea of America's Millennial Role* (Chicago, IL: University of Chicago, 1968); https://archive.org/details/redeemernation00erne

4.6 Anthropocentric approach of the New Theology

(Adapting theology to the spirit of modernity)
Jonathan Edwards's followers desired to uphold traditional beliefs; however, they presented them in new forms and thereby also altered their substance. They took an uncritical approach to Humanism and drifted ever further away from Calvinism. Their new teaching became known as the "New England Theology" or the "New Divinity." It rejected the doctrines of original sin and Christ's atonement, focusing no longer on the sinner in need of salvation but rather on moral living, which was believed to be possible without the new birth. It was eventually even claimed that man is capable of saving himself. The Second Great Awakening (1790-1850) was characterized by emotional excess and schisms within the church. Calvinistic doctrine was replaced by the "New England Theology" in ministerial training: Calvinistic views of God and man seemed outdated in discourses shaped by Enlightenment teachings on inalienable rights, Kantian ethics, and democratic freedom. In seeking to adapt Calvinism to the spirit of the age, fundamental doctrines such as original sin, the new birth, and the bondage of the will were discarded. Idealistic teaching rose to prominence under the influence of Nathaniel W. Taylor (1786-1858), president of Yale College. In stark contrast to biblical teachings on sin, Taylor emphasized the pursuit of happiness and the belief that man can overcome his sinful inclinations with nothing more than his willpower. Through the theologians of Yale College and the well-known evangelist Charles G. Finney (1792-1875), the New Divinity teaching became widely accepted[183], culminating in the Protestant Liberalism of the late nineteenth century.

---

[183] Whitney R. Cross, *The Burned-Over District: The Social and Intellectual History of Enthusiastic Religion in Western New York, 1800-1850* (New York City, NY: Harper Torchbooks, 1950) 160; https://archive.org/details/burnedoverdistri00cros/page/160

Volume 2

Postmillennialism as the inspiration for American Progressivism (Chs. 5-9)

5 The urge for revolution in an enlightened age 78
6 The quest for human perfection 126
7 Ideals of America's new age 147
8 The development of authoritarian Progressivism 176
9 Religious essence of Progressivism 201

5 The urge for revolution in an enlightened age

In the early seventeenth century, Puritans who had migrated to the U.S.A. desired to establish the kingdom of God in America. Utopian enthusiasm developed from the remnants of Puritan Postmillennialism, erupting in the struggle for freedom that led to the American Revolution.[1] After the successful outcome of the War of Independence, many ideologues hoped to see the ideals of the new era brought to fulfilment: free thinking, natural rights, charity, and progress. Instead, utopians were forced to accept the ratification of a conservative constitution in 1787 by the Philadelphia Convention, maintaining the long classical tradition of Western civilization. In their indignation, they dreamed of the revolutionary potential demonstrated by France. However, many Americans still held onto their idealistic hopes for a nation in quest of a Golden Age.

5.1 Questionable business relations among the wealthy elite

Europe was in a permanent state of war throughout many decades of the seventeenth century. Fearing for their lives, followers of various religious groups embarked on the dangerous voyage across the Atlantic, seeking refuge from the executioner in America. Some still argued over matters of faith even in their new homeland. Only the American Freemasons managed to bridge the gaping void between the different religious beliefs. The lodges' values of tolerance, impartiality, and fraternity gave them an enormous force of attraction in the midst of an intolerant world.

Pirates went a step further. The strong sense of cooperation required to capture valuable treasure created a unique sense of camaraderie. The key change that they wanted to make to the social fabric was the introduction of a pure Democracy. Their kingdom of Libertalia could have been considered an ideal society had its immense wealth not been based on stolen goods. The colony, founded in Madagascar, gave every pirate a say in local government. Rights of ownership were strictly preserved, and every individual contributed to the maintenance of law and order. Invalids and the elderly were supported by a common fund, and violent crime was rare. There were of course exceptional circumstances: relationships among the pirates were still affected by human weaknesses.

A symbiotic relationship was cultivated over many years between leading families of the American colonies and the pirates which they frequently supplied with ship and crew. Many of the financiers who became rich through pirates' looted treasure were influential politicians, and many

---

[1] Nathan O. Hatch, *The Sacred Cause of Liberty: Republican Thought and the Millennium in Revolutionary New England* (New Haven, CT: Yale University Press, 1977); https://archive.org/details/sacredcauseoflib00hatcrich

converted their growing fortunes into political and economic power. In order to trade with the rest of society, pirates needed to be connected to secret societies. This was the only way for them to build business relations with people who were willing to pay large sums of money for stolen goods. Codes of honor were used to prevent pirates from betraying one another to the authorities, and they maintained close links with government officials who provided them with accommodation, legal protection, and markets for their stolen goods. Pirate captains gave regular reports to the powerful patrons who made the trade possible. Masonic lodges provided meeting places where personal relationships could be formed and strengthened. Governors, mayors, and judges licensed the pirates' raids at sea and invested in ship and crew. Close-knit fraternities that fought for the interests of their members were marked by many years of underground activity, having effective communications channels that traversed national borders and language barriers. Among the important services offered to their members were provision of accommodation, negotiation of employment, production of food, and distribution of clothing. Pirates' most urgent need was for guaranteed personal protection, especially when it came to evading justice with as little punishment as possible. The only international fraternity that could meet all these demands was Freemasonry.

Disreputable businesses followed the same model of secrecy: piracy was not the only criminal enterprise on the oceans. The eighteenth century saw particular growth of smuggling as a global business, despite being illegal in many places. Seaports from Salem (Massachusetts) and Newport (Rhode Island) to Hamilton (Bermuda) and Kingston (Jamaica) enabled pirates to sell their spoils, becoming home to many smugglers who knew exactly where to exchange their contraband without attracting too much attention. Bermuda became a stronghold of Freemasonry. The customs house looked more like a Masonic temple than a government building.

The British military appointed Benjamin Fletcher to the strategically important office of governor of New York. From 1692 onward, he developed a keen ability to convert his political power into cash. Generous sponsors could expect Governor Fletcher to give them the most profitable areas of land.[2] Fletcher received huge sums of money as bribes from piracy. In 1696, the first set of trade laws and customs regulations was issued in England, which severely restricted the colonies' business opportunities. Braver souls who were unafraid of risking their lives blatantly disregarded the customs duties, enabling them to acquire immense fortunes. This led to the shameful tradition of the wealthy being exempt from submitting to any laws.

Two of the most notorious pirates were Thomas Tew and William Kidd. Spurred on by endless greed, Tew obtained letters of marque from governors, made them rich, and in doing so also made enormous amounts of money for himself. William Kidd's strategy for gaining wealth was ingenious, if

---

[2] Clare Brandt, *An American Aristocracy: The Livingstons* (New York City, NY: Doubleday, 1986) 38.

dangerous and illegal. Neither he nor his business partner gave any place to moral considerations in their actions. From Kidd's perspective, he was not pursuing a career as an outlaw but as a land speculator, constantly buying land in New York. This required an almost endless stream of financial capital, and the only way for Kidd to obtain a smooth cash flow was by raiding the high seas. As a sign of his feigned high-mindedness, he helped finance the building of Trinity Church. Only a few days after the second husband of Sarah Bradley Cox Oort died, Kidd married his wealthy widow and moved into her grand house on Wall Street. From this time on, he insisted on being addressed as a "gentleman."[3] A few years later, he was hanged. At the same time, piracy against English shipping in the British Empire was growing at a dangerous rate. The Asian countries which traded with England complained bitterly about the American pirates who were damaging their business, putting the blame on the king of England.

The clergyman Nicholas van Rensselaer owned one of the largest estates in the New York colony. He entrusted its management to Robert Livingston, a Scotsman who had immigrated to New York.[4] A born businessman, Livingston took advantage of his ability to communicate relatively well in the Iroquois language in order to negotiate good business deals with the Indians. After Rensselaer died, Livingston did not wait long before taking possession of his estate. All he had to do was marry his widow, Alida. The rumor soon spread that the wealthy clergyman, who died in 1678 at forty-two years old, might have been poisoned.[5] The Freemason Robert Livingston, who like George Washington was the son of an alcoholic and defrocked clergyman, acquired the second largest landed property in New York State during his lifetime. He became infamous for his lack of moral principles. Governor Fletcher was occasionally forced to indict pirates or smugglers; had he not done so, his political enemies would have discovered his tricks much sooner. In 1694, he seized a pirate ship on its way back to New York after a successful raid in the Caribbean. One of the shipowners was Robert Livingston, at that time the richest man in New York. Livingston had to raise a large sum of money in order to regain possession of the ship. He did not forget his humiliation by Governor Fletcher, and from that time on did all he could to drive Fletcher out of office. With the help of two business partners, his plan succeeded four years later.

---

[3] Robert C. Ritchie, *Captain Kidd and the War Against the Pirates* (Cambridge, MA: Harvard University Press, 1986) 36.

[4] Brandt, *An American Aristocracy*, 21.

[5] Stephen Birmingham, *America's Secret Aristocracy: The Families that Built the United State* (Boston, MA: Little, Brown and Company, 1987) 33-34.

During his time as Grand Master of Holland Lodge No. 8[6], F. & A. M.[7], Robert Livingston founded ten other lodges. However, Holland Lodge remained the most influential. It provided a meeting place for the old guard of New York's wealthy society, who had full control over the whole body of Free and Accepted Masons in America. Robert Livingston's grandson, Robert R. Livingston (1746-1813), was a key figure in politics and Freemasonry in New York State from 1784 to 1801. He showed remarkable sagacity in carrying out his duties as Grand Master of the Grand Lodge of New York and as a member of Holland Lodge No. 8, F. & A. M. On April 30, 1789, he swore in the first president of the United States, George Washington. Robert R. Livingston was shrewd enough to keep his political views to himself during wartime, and was thus able to side with the victorious patriots when the right moment came. In the background, he played his aces in favor of the Tories, without revealing his preference for the autocratic rule of the English Crown over any other form of government. Always seeking to increase his own power, he sought to use his children's and relatives' dynastic marriages to expand his sphere of influence.

In 1801, President Thomas Jefferson sent Robert R. Livingston and James Monroe (ΦBK)[8] to Paris in order to negotiate the price of the Louisiana Purchase with the French government. When Napoleon made Livingston and Monroe an offer of 15 million U.S. dollars for the entire area of Louisiana in 1803, they saw the relatively low offer price as a unique opportunity and agreed to it without consulting Jefferson. At the time, Louisiana stretched from the Gulf of Mexico to the southern border of Rupert's Land, and from Mississippi to the Rocky Mountains. Livingston wanted to take full credit for the diplomatic coup; however, the scam was exposed, and he failed to gain any political capital. A few weeks after the Louisiana Purchase was officially settled, the new Governor William C. C. Claiborne arrived in New Orleans. Businessmen in New Orleans noted with concern that the market for Barataria had become highly competitive. They put pressure on Louisiana's new rulers to seize the Laffite brothers, Jean and Pierre. They ruled the nearby Barataria like a kingdom, with many similarities to the pirate kingdom of Libertalia in Madagascar. The Laffite brothers' reputation as notorious pirates had spread from the Indian Ocean to the Caribbean Sea over the previous years. However, Governor Claiborne dropped the charges against Pierre Laffite when he realized that the combined forces of the Freemasons were against him.

Jean and Pierre Laffite were French noblemen and did not recoil from any danger. In order to invest and profit from their wealth, they bought an extensive piece of land in the then French colony of Louisiana, near the city

---

[6] *Bicentennial Commemorative Volume of Holland Lodge No. 8* (New York City, NY: Published by the Lodge, 1988); current address: 71 West 23rd Street, Suite 701 New York, New York 10010; https://www.hollandlodgeno8.org

[7] Free and Accepted Masons

[8] Member of the Phi Beta Kappa Society, College of William and Mary, 1776

of New Orleans. This was the origin of the kingdom of Barataria.[9] Jean Laffite had to leave Barataria around 1820 in order to escape imprisonment. After a period of hiding[10], he was hired by a group of Philadelphia bankers as one of their chief couriers. The French writers Georges and Germaine Blond first drew attention to the remarkable fact that the Freemason Karl Marx was a friend of the pirate Jean Laffite in their *Histoire de la filibuste*. Lafitte financed the printing of the Communist Party's manifesto,[11] which interestingly favors neither the bourgeoisie nor the working class. It outlines a plan for the seizure of power by an elitist clique, which becomes clear on realizing the identity of Marx's financially powerful patrons who Jean Laffite worked for. It is also worth mentioning that Karl Marx took the content of the Communist manifesto from another work: it plagiarizes the text *Principes du Socialisme: Manifeste de la Democratie au Dixneuviéme Siecle* published by the French socialist Victor Considérant in 1843.[12] Considérant worked in close collaboration with Charles Fourier, a strong critic of early Capitalism.

John Jacob Astor (1763-1848) was one of the most unscrupulous businessmen of the early American Republic. In 1784, he arrived completely penniless in the United States from the Electoral Palatinate. His ancestors were Waldensian refugees from the Italian Savoy who had settled south of Heidelberg. The fortunes which Astor left to his descendants came from his enormous estate. He was also involved in the fur trade. His strategy not only involved depriving his Indian hunters of their wages, which were well deserved for their arduous labor in the almost impassable wilderness, but also removing them completely. In his eyes, the best means of doing this was the high percentage liquor which he sold at exorbitant prices – more than twenty times the cost of production. His agents sometimes mixed the watered-down liquor with red pepper and tobacco to create a poisonous concoction. Some politicians in Washington, D.C., were impressed by Astor's effectiveness in getting rid of unwanted Indians and gave him public funds to subsidize the purchase of large quantities of the harmful rum. Many Indians fell into alcohol addiction and were driven to an early grave.[13] Astor's inability to feign respectability appearance did not prevent him from rising to New York's upper class. His marriage to Sarah Todd, a relative of the wealthy Breevort family, was a brilliant move. It was probably through this family connection that he was soon offered membership of New York's most

---

[9] David Leon Chandler, *The Jefferson Conspiracies* (New York City, NY: William Morrow and Company, 1994) 151.

[10] http://www.britannica.com/biography/Jean-Laffite

[11] Georges & Germaine Blond, *Histoire de la filibuste* (Paris: Stock, 1969; Geneve: Editions Famot, 1974) 78.

[12] W. Tcherkesoff, *Page of Socialist History* (New York City, NY: C. B. Cooper, 1902) chap. 10: "The Origin of the 'Manifesto of the Communist Party,'" 55-66.

[13] Gustavus Myers, *History of the great American Fortunes*, 3 vols. (Chicago, IL: C. H. Kerr, 1907-1917) vol. 1: 110; https://archive.org/details/historyofgreatam01myer/page/110

prestigious Masonic Lodge, Holland Lodge No. 8. F. & A. M.[14] John Jacob Astor artfully established lucrative business relations with wealthy Freemasons[15] and consequently made a fortune. Bribes were abundant in Masonic circles, since their oath of secrecy offered protection from the law. The American Fur Company expanded enormously in 1794 when Astor began to hire numerous white trappers and agents, and sent them to the far corners of the American continent. He instructed them to take furs from every Indian they met. Should the Indians resist them, they would merely have to fire a well-aimed shot.

Astor invested much of his income from the fur and opium trades in land, the value of which soared as the exponentially growing population of New York required large areas to build. The profit margin on beaver fur sold in London increased sixfold.[16] Astor's exasperation at having to pay excessive amounts of money to American and English shipping companies in order to transport the furs across the Atlantic encouraged him to acquire his own fleet. On their return voyages from England, his ships were packed with products manufactured specifically for the American market.[17] Astor later became America's richest opium runner. The opium trade began when the East India Company licensed him to smuggle drugs into inland China as well as to sell furs.

In 1825, Astor bought up large areas of land that had originally belonged to the U.S. government. Poor farmers had previously received permission from the state to cultivate the land as tenants. When it passed into Astor's hands, he ordered their eviction. Seven hundred families lost their livelihoods, virtually overnight. Astor was able to make a far greater profit by using the land to build than by collecting the low rent. In order to increase his land in New York City, he bought up the mortgages of many Irish immigrants in 1826 and then drove them out of their homes.

5.2 Lucrative enterprises of the "Boston Brahmins"

The luxurious lifestyle of the English nobility was quickly adopted by wealthy, upper-class Puritans in New England, New Jersey, and Pennsylvania – Anglican dissenters who resisted subordination to the established church and were consequently forced to leave their homeland. The irony of this

---

[14] *Bicentennial Commemorative Volume of Holland Lodge No. 8* (New York City, NY: Published by the Lodge, 1988).

[15] Axel Madsen, *John Jacob Astor: America's First Millionaire* (New York City, NY: John Wiley, 2001) 32.

[16] Edward Robb Ellis, *The Epic of New York City* (New York City, NY: Kondansha, 1997) 177; https://archive.org/details/epicofnewyorkci000elli/page/176

[17] Ibid.

situation was that Puritans in England strongly resented the wealth flaunted by the aristocracy.[18]

Shortly after arriving in America, the Puritans became caught up in the lucrative slave trade. They imitated the business methods of their ancestors, who, as merchants in Plymouth, England, had been engaged in the slave trade since 1570. Soon after moving to the American continent, many settlers bought their own slaves in order to cope with the arduous job of cultivating the hitherto untouched land. How they were able to reconcile this inhuman enterprise with their profession of Christian faith will never find a satisfactory explanation. Over the following 246 years from 1619 to 1865, in which slavery was legal in America, New England merchants earned more from this despicable trade than any elsewhere in the country, with the exception of a few southern landowners. A small number of northeastern Yankees first expressed their aversion to the inhumanity of the slavery in the South during the last thirty years of this period, following the abolition of slavery in the British Empire in 1834. Slavery was not restricted to black people in Virginia. There were four distinct classes distinguished by their socio-political positions: a small number of wealthy plantation owners, a larger number of free white people who owned small areas of land, a similar number of white people who earned their living as contracted laborers under hard working conditions, and, finally, a large number of slaves. Many slaves were better off than contracted workers despite their terrible circumstances. The most valuable agricultural product at the time was dried tobacco leaves, which became a commodity currency that could be exchanged for any other product or service.

The royal houses of Europe profited from the trade of black slaves by giving licenses to influential merchants. The latter, as courtiers, obtained privileges and advantages in business relations. Licenses were granted to those who agreed to share their profits with the rulers of their countries. The trade triangle prospered for around two hundred years from around 1630 to 1830, bringing in huge sums of money despite relying on economic Imperialism abroad, which had negative effects on national politics. Slaves traded in Africa for rum were sold to plantation owners in the West Indies – a group of islands in the Atlantic Ocean, off the coast of Central and South America. They were forced to work on the sugar plantations in order to provide raw material for rum production. The molasses required to produce a high-percentage liquor were one of the most sought-after commodities of the time. Tradesmen who became rich through these products never paused to consider the great suffering that excessive alcohol consumption was causing in many parts of Africa.

Seaports were ideal bases for Freemasons. From Newport on Rhode Island to Charleston in South Carolina, membership of Masonic lodges was essential for obtaining loans to purchase and transport slaves, and to insure

---

[18] Myers, *History of the great American Fortunes*, vol. 1: 23-27; https://archive.org/details/historyofgreatam01myer/page/n31

ships and cargo. Another reason for slave traders' involvement in Freemasonry was its secret network of business relations. Freemasons wanted to maintain English Mercantilism: an economic policy that promoted foreign trade and the export industry in order to strengthen financial capacity and state authority. The slave trade could therefore be carried out unobstructed. Slavery was abolished seventy-eight years after the adoption of the American Federal Constitution. Washington and Jefferson, along with most members of Congress and the Senate, were also wealthy slave owners, sometimes taking the whip in their own hands to remind their slaves who was boss.

The vast fortunes of Boston's longstanding families were gained almost entirely through the "rum and niggers" business. Slave traders worked shrewdly to gain influence in the presidential elections. If they were unsuccessful in bringing their favored candidate into power, they resorted to other means of securing their economic interests. Two vice presidents, both of whom had campaigned for the continuation of slavery, moved into the White House after Presidents Harrison and Taylor died in office under mysterious circumstances. The inhuman slave market disappeared in the northern metropolises at the beginning of the nineteenth century as wealthy tradesmen in New York, Philadelphia, and Boston no longer saw economic advantage in exploiting slave labor. In the South, by contrast, slaves' market value increased constantly due to the area's large, labor-intensive agricultural economy. The trade of human beings was not abolished until the War of Secession ended in 1865.

Harvard University, one of America's oldest and most prestigious universities, came under the leadership of a group of conspirators known as the "Essex Junto." "Essex" referred to the county of Essex in Massachusetts, north of Boston. The group aimed to separate the most important northern states from the rest of the United States if the federal government opposed its business interests, which were closely linked to those of the British Empire. They wanted to divide the Union in order to reintegrate the weakened states into the British Empire.[19] However, their various attempts to do so through trade, presidential election, sabotage, and propaganda came to nothing.

Boston's most distinguished families became known as the "Boston Brahmins." Their ancestry can be traced back to the Puritans who founded the Massachusetts colony, and they formed a new kind of aristocracy in New England. Among them was the Lowell family. After the judge John Lowell (1743-1802) was elected to the board of governors of Harvard College, the educational institution was largely financed out of his own pocket. His generosity earned him the right to direct the college for mutual advantage. From this time until 1943, with the exception of one short period, the board consisted exclusively of members of the Lowell family. Leading families did everything in their power to secure their social status, since this was the only means by which they could multiply their wealth. It became customary for

---

[19] Henry Adams, *Documents Relating to New England Federalism: 1800-1815* (Boston, MA: Little, Brown, 1877) 346-391; https://archive.org/details/cu31924074296942/page/n365

the children of rich families to intermarry. Much of their money was gained through piracy and the West Indian slave trade. The cotton picked by slaves on the southern plantations was used by the British textile industry to make cheap clothes, which found their biggest market in India. The Indians largely paid with opium, which the British sold for large profits in the Chinese drug trade. At the center of the whole business was Thomas Handasyd Perkins (1764-1854). The Boston-based company J. & T. H. Perkins Co. took almost complete control of the slave trade with the Caribbean islands. After the slave revolt in Santo Domingo, it traded only with Europe and China, which proved to be far more profitable. The story of how New England's aristocratic families accumulated such wealth began in 1787, when the British Secretary of State, Henry Dundas, devised a plan to expand Britain's opium trade in China. Most of the British merchant navy's "tea clippers" occasionally transported opium from the poppy fields of Bengal to drug addicts in China, returning to London laden with silver and tea. Importing opium to mainland China was illegal. J. & T. H. Perkins Co., together with other companies in Massachusetts, operated a drug cartel.

Six generations of export trade with China commenced in 1784, one year after the American War of Independence ended with a peace treaty between the United States and England. The United States demanded almost the same privileges that the British Empire had forced illegally from the Ching Dynasty. Established Boston families earned a reputation as patrons of the general public, and their vast fortunes are still known today as the "rum and nigger" assets. The port of Canton (Guangzhou) served as an entry point and storage location for imported goods.[20] Thomas H. Perkins's nephew, John Perkins Cushing, lived in the Chinese city of Canton in order to head up the company's overseas business. Meanwhile, his respected relatives, such as Francis Cabot Lowell, established themselves in the cotton manufacturing town of Lowell, Massachusetts, using the great profits from the China business. Their Waltham textile factory processed cotton from the southern states, and its commercial success exceeded their wildest expectations. Thomas H. Perkins also managed the publishing house D. Appleton & Company for several years, but remained the most influential ship owner and manufacturer of his time in Boston. From 1816, the Perkins company operated an illegal drug trafficking of Turkish opium to China. Other Boston families had similar dreams of gaining immeasurable wealth.

Thomas H. Perkins's nephew, John Perkins Cushing (1787-1862), became the most influential foreigner in Canton during the 1820s. The Boston business in China was initially based on fur and silver, and later on opium. Cushing's successor, John Murray Forbes, acquired a large fortune over the years. One of the people who profited most from his legendary generosity was the transcendentalist Ralph Waldo Emerson (ΦBK)[21].

---

[20] Russell B Adams Jr., *The Boston Money Tree* (New York City, NY: Crowell, 1977); https://archive.org/details/bostonmoneytree00adam

[21] Member of the Phi Beta Kappa Society, Harvard College, 1828

Transcendentalism could not have spread as widely as it did without financial grants from the Forbes family assets, which were gained initially through the slave trade and later through the drug trade in China.

Responsibility for financing the China trade belonged almost entirely to the Baring Bank in England. Even after Alexander Hamilton founded the Bank of the United States to provide domestic industry with the necessary financial resources, American foreign trade still required loans issued in British pounds. Like the British, Americans smuggled opium over the Chinese border, bribed imperial officers, and amassed vast fortunes by selling drugs, ruining the health and economy of a whole generation of Chinese citizens as a result. Their immense profits were only gained because they identified themselves with the financial interests of the British Empire.[22] The fortunes of families such as the Perkins, Cabots, Forbes, and Higginsons were based on close business and family connections among the upper class in Salem, Massachusetts.

In 1836, the Chinese government banned the opium trade under threat of severe penalties. Three years later, the First Opium War broke out between China and Great Britain. Thomas H. Perkins welcomed the Chinese government's efforts to restrict opium trade, knowing that dealers who were less willing to take risks would withdraw from the business in order to avoid the harsh punishments. It was a perceptive, yet daring idea, and soon paid off financially. J. & T. H. Perkins was then able to take over a dominant share of the market. For years afterwards, the companies Perkins and Bryant & Sturgis – often known as the Boston corporations – had a near monopoly on the import of Turkish opium into China. William Sturgis was Perkins's nephew. The end of the First Opium War and the defeat of the Chinese by the British opened up new opportunities for the drug trade. Under the 1842 Treaty of Nanking, the Chinese government had to open the ports of Amoy, Foochow, Ningpo, and Shanghai for trade with Western companies. The island of Hong Kong came under British rule in 1844. Immediately after, Jardine Matheson and other British trading companies established their headquarters in Hong Kong, which became the center of the opium trade during the 1840s and 1850s. Indian opium was brought into Hong Kong's harbor, from where it was shipped to other Chinese ports. The valuable goods received in exchange were transported back to Hong Kong via the same routes.

The wealthy upper class in Essex County, Massachusetts, was characterized by the cult of irrationality and a preference for an anti-industrialized society that idealized Feudalism in both culture and politics. Among them was George Peabody, founder of the bank George Peabody & Co. which was first registered in England and later operated in America. Through loans granted by the Brown Brothers and Nathan Mayer Rothschild, Peabody was able to realize his dream of becoming a banker in 1835. Nineteen years later, Junius S. Morgan joined him as a partner. One of their specialist

---

[22] Adams, *The Boston Money Tree*, 106-111, 125-131; https://archive.org/details/bostonmo-neytree00adam/page/106

financial services was dealing with the foreign exchange trading and shares of American corporations. When Peabody died, the bank fell into the hands of the Morgan family. Junius S. Morgan's son, John Pierpont, relocated to America and a few years later renamed the bank J. P. Morgan & Co.

The profits made from the slave and drug trades, arms smuggling, and piracy served as startup capital for some of the country's most important banks. The first insurance companies in New England formed contracts with the shipowners who transported opium and slaves across the oceans. The extensive railroad network built to connect the East and West Coasts in the nineteenth century was largely financed by money made through illegal drug trafficking. The earliest investments in the telecommunications industry were funded by one of the largest fortunes made through opium. American presidents received immense assets from their relatives which they had obtained through piracy. The elite universities of Harvard, Yale, Columbia, Brown, and Princeton were financed with generous endowments from aristocratic New York and New England families which had made their fortunes through illegal drug smuggling. These same men built railroads and textile factories, invested in banks and insurance companies, and kept their family assets in good order for several generations. Besides Roosevelt and Grant, other presidents such as Taft (ΦBK[23], Skull & Bones, Linonian Society) and Coolidge (ΦBK)[24] belonged to the wealthy upper class which originally earned its wealth through trade with China.

5.3 Secrets of the American elite

As the Chinese opium trade expanded in the 1830s, the most important shipping company fell into the hands of Samuel Russell. Russell and Company, founded in 1823, became the key agent in the drug business, buying opium from Smyrna, Turkey and shipping it to China. Two of Russell's partners were Cleve Green and Abiel Abbot Low, who had invested large sums in his entrepreneurial project in the Far East. Green later become a patron of Princeton University and Low of Columbia University.[25] When the Cushings left China, the Forbes family took over trade relations with the general public, much of which had fallen into opium addiction. In order to outmatch their formidable competitors, they had to smuggle far greater quantities of contraband into the country without being discovered by Chinese government officials. Like the Gardiners and other tradesmen involved in illegal drug trafficking, they invested the money that they gained through selling opium in local estates and industries. Joseph Coolidge (1798-1879) and other

---

[23] Member of the Phi Beta Kappa Society, Yale University, 1878

[24] Honorary member of Phi Beta Kappa Society

[25] Peter Ward Fay, *The Opium War 1840-1842* (Chapel Hill, NC: University of North Carolina Press, 1995) 140.

members of the Sturgis family also invested in the Russell company. The Hathaway, Forbes, and Perkins families combined their respective business interests to form one partnership: Russell, Sturgis & Company. The families were also closely connected through marriage. Russell, Sturgis & Company's primary agent in Canton was Warren Delano, Jr. (1809-1898), grandfather of the future president Franklin D. Roosevelt. The Delanos were one of the most distinguished families in nineteenth-century America. In order to form still more lucrative trade relations in China, Delano, Jr., decided to become a partner with Russell, Sturgis & Company. He demonstrated his elevated social status by purchasing a large manor house in Macao and invested much of his wealth in land and real estate in New York City, as well as in coal and copper mines in Pennsylvania and Tennessee.

In August 1857, the insurance company Ohio Life Insurance and Trust declared bankruptcy. The resulting financial crisis brought many banks to ruin. Over the following months, five thousand companies were forced to cease business, tens of thousands of employees lost their jobs and houses, and many people starved and froze in the streets of cities on the Atlantic Coast and in the Mideast. Although Warren Delano had lost almost his entire fortune in the stock market crash, he remained for some time in Algonac, his luxurious manor in Balmville, NY. He eventually had no choice but to resume drug trafficking in order to finance his opulent lifestyle. In seeking to recover his former wealth, he not only smuggled opium into China, but from 1859 also sold it to drug addicts in America. The two prominent branches of the Roosevelt family who had settled in Hyde Park and Oyster Bay, New York, similarly amassed huge fortunes by trading opium in China. During a cabinet meeting in 1933, President Franklin D. Roosevelt proudly expressed his strong sympathies for the Far East, since both his paternal and maternal ancestors had obtained their wealth through the Chinese opium trade. He deliberately overlooked the fact that the sale of harmful drugs in the Chinese Empire during both opium wars had been carried out by armed force, since the emperor and his government had placed a strict ban on the consumption of opiates.

Through their generous grants, the Russells gained great influence over Yale College in New Haven, CT, and the family has maintained a close relationship with the elite university to the present day. Samuel Russell's cousin, William Huntington Russell (1809-1885), and Alfonso Taft (1810-1891) founded the student society Skull & Bones at Yale College in 1832. In 1858, Russell registered the society as a corporation in Connecticut under the name "Russell Trust Association." Its headquarters have shared the address of the investment bank Brown Brothers Harriman in New York City ever since. It has also been partly financed by this bank. Skull & Bones is the oldest and most prestigious of Yale's seven secret societies, which recruit young men for careers in civil service, law, public finance, and other areas that influence and control American society. Other universities, such as Harvard, Princeton, and Cornell, also have their own exclusive secret societies. The two best known at Harvard University are the Porcellian Club and the Fly Club. Skull

& Bones has an intake of only fifteen new members each year, most of whom are the sons of prominent upper-class families such as the Harrimans, Bushes, Kerrys, Tafts, Whitneys, Bundys, Weyerhaeusers, Pinchots, Goodyears, Sloanes, Phelpses, Pillsburys, Kelloggs, Vanderbilts, and Lovetts. Since the year it was founded, Skull & Bones has taken in around 2500 members. The "Bonesmen" believe that they are God's elect, chosen to govern North America. The relatively small membership emphasizes the extraordinary concentration of power that lies in their hands.

It is worth considering the circumstances that led to the founding of Skull & Bones. In 1832, leaders of the Phi Beta Kappa fraternity decided to renounce its status as a secret society and become an open honor society. This prompted William H. Russell, Alphonso Taft, and thirteen other Phi Beta Kappa members to form the exclusive order of Skull & Bones at Yale College.

The fraternities FHC and PDA were founded in 1750 and 1773 respectively at the College of William and Mary in Williamsburg, VA. Both organizations were distinguished by their exclusivity. Only specially selected students could become members, and they had to swear to silence on the initiation rites and other secrets. However, their regular meetings often degenerated into rowdy drinking sprees. The ruinous state of the existing fraternities was a thorn in the flesh for five students who consequently founded the Phi Beta Kappa Society, which was abbreviated to the Greek letters ΦβΚ. It would later become the most important of its kind in America, and its key would become one of the most coveted symbols of academic excellence. It stands to reason that its founders formed the secret society in order to give members freedom to discuss any theme, whether controversial or conventional, without restriction. The Phi Beta Kappa Society was influenced by Freemasonry from the outset. By the 1750s, there was already a Masonic lodge in Williamsburg, VA, which received an official foundation charter from the Grand Lodge in England in 1773. Thomas Smith belonged to the Williamsburg Lodge before joining John Heath as one of the five founders of the Phi Beta Kappa Society. Another nine members of the secret society became Freemasons the following year, and twelve of the original members of the Williamsburg lodge eventually joined. It is therefore no mistake to believe that the founding members adopted the following ideas from Freemasonry: an oath of secrecy, symbols, a special handshake, a Greek motto, carefully devised rules, and a complex initiation ritual. The young students' confidence in the longevity of the society and its future achievements is evidenced by the foundation charters given to other affiliated societies, known as Alpha, at various renowned educational establishments. In its early years, the society awarded graduate memberships to men from previous years. From 1790, the Phi Beta Kappa Society at Yale College began to confer honorary memberships on prominent individuals.

Three important changes took place during the first century of the Phi Beta Kappa Society's existence. As a result of the hatred toward Freemasonry in the 1820s, Alpha of Massachusetts (Harvard College) revoked its members' pledge to secrecy in 1831. The Harvard Phi Beta Kappa Society was subsequently spared further public criticism for its Masonic rites. Most of the other affiliated societies still maintained the formal demand to secrecy for many more years. The last secret rites were abolished in 1883. The Phi Beta Kappa Society was originally a union of likeminded students with a similar basis and orientation to many other literature and debating societies; however, with time the nature of the society changed into that of an honor society which disclosed all secrets and encouraged students to maximize their potential in their liberal arts studies. A second change took place when women were admitted to membership. The third change was the founding of the umbrella organization "United Chapters" (a union of local Phi Beta Kappa branches).

Prominent members of the honor society in America included influential individuals in politics, law, the business world, and the entertainment industry. Seventeen United States presidents belonged to the Phi Beta Kappa Society, including John Quincy Adams, James Monroe, T. Woodrow Wilson, Theodore and Franklin D. Roosevelt, Calvin Coolidge, Harry S. Truman, Dwight Eisenhower, Jimmy Carter, George H. W. Bush, and Bill Clinton. Among its members were ten judges from the Supreme Court of Justice and 136 Nobel Prize winners. The almost countless names of other members also included William T. Sherman, John C. Calhoun, Caleb Cushing, Ralph Waldo Emerson, Nathaniel Hawthorne, Walter Lippmann, and John Dewey. John D. Rockefeller, Jr., the son of the wealthiest man in America, was initiated in the honor society at Brown University in 1897 and eventually took on the role of ΦBK Senator (a member of the executive board). When bodies of the Phi Beta Kappa Society began to be formed outside of educational institutes to improve the fulfilment of the society's aims, the name of the honor society was changed back from "United Chapters" to the "Phi Beta Kappa Society." One of the Phi Beta Kappa Society's primary concerns was to spread the idea of progress. One example is a speech[26] given in 1848 by Charles Sumner, a Senator from Massachusetts, for which he received extremely positive feedback.[27] Sumner saw the idea of progress as a logical explanation of the course of history and a decisive factor in the nineteenth-century reform movements. Sumner found it unlikely that man could achieve a state of perfection.[28] However, he did believe that man was capable of reaching a permanent state of higher development. The law of progress was realized

---

[26] Charles Sumner, *The Works of Charles Sumner* (Boston, MA: Lee and Shepard, 1870) vol. 2: 89-138; https://archive.org/details/workscharlessum31sumngoog/page/n98

[27] Charles Sumner, Edward Lillie Pierce, *Memoir and Letters of Charles Sumner* (Boston, MA: Roberts Brothers, 1877-1893) vol. 3: 30-32; https://archive.org/details/memoirandletter-14sumngoog/page/n48; s. also: John Weiss, *Life and Correspondence of Theodore Parker, minister of the Twenty-eighth Congregational Society, Boston* (New York City, NY: D. Appleton, 1864) vol. 1: 316; https://archive.org/details/lifeandcorrespo05unkngoog/page/n338; Octavius Brooks Frothingham, *George Ripley* (Boston, MA: Houghton, Mifflin and Company, 1883) 214-215; https://archive.org/details/georgeripley00frotgoog/page/n228

[28] Sumner, *The Works of Charles Sumner*, vol. 2: 115; https://archive.org/details/workscharlessum31sumngoog/page/n124

very slowly, but nonetheless provided great inspiration that could bring consolation in hard times. Confidence in the progress of the human race was to be held constantly in all subjection to God.[29]

5.4 Differing beliefs among American Freemasons

One clear fact of American history is that Freemasonry has had a strong and consistent influence on politics and the economy.[30] America's intellectual life has always been a strange mixture of religious enthusiasm and Messianic politics. By 1730, New England, Pennsylvania, and Georgia were centers for the spread of Masonic teachings, and lodges were established widely over the following decade.[31] Freemasons were leading figures among many cities' economic and social elite. Some Protestants even believed that Freemasonry would replace Christianity and create a sense of unity, and for this reason joined the fraternity.[32]

Religious freedom was severely restricted in early eighteenth-century Europe. Men who hoped for a better future joined the Freemasons, wanting to create a universal fraternity with God as its Father, and emigrated to America in search of religious freedom.[33] Many Freemasons acquired considerable wealth as the colonies began to prosper, believing the Masonic principle that a virtuous life evokes the goodwill of the Creator. Many Freemasons tend to identify Freemasonry with Americanism and are convinced that the most important events in American history can be traced back to the initiatives of the secret societies. Their ideal system of government, as eventually formulated in the 1788 Constitution of the United States, was a fulfillment of the ideas of leading Freemasons among America's Founding Fathers.[34]

Freemasonry began during the Middle Ages as one of many craft guilds that wanted to preserve their secrets. Stonemasons had been interested in spiritual enlightenment since the remote past, when they had close contact with Islamic, Jewish, and "Christian" mystics, largely in Spain and Provence.

---

[29] Ibid., vol. 2: 137; https://archive.org/details/workscharlessum31sumngoog/page/n146

[30] "Freemasonry," by William James Hughan, in *Encyclopaedia Britannica*, 11th edition (Cambridge: Cambridge University Press, 1910–1911) vol. 11: 78-85; https://archive.org/details/in.ernet.dli.2015.83467/page/n87

[31] Bernard Fay, *Revolution and Freemasonry* (Boston, MA: Little, Brown & Co., 1935) 230, 234. English translation of the French original *La franc maçonerie et la révolution intellectuelle du XVIIIe siècle* (Paris: Cluny, 1935).

[32] Anson Phelps Stokes, *Church and State in the United States*, 2 vols. (New York City, NY: Harper and Brothers, 1950) vol. 1: 245; https://archive.org/details/churchandstatein-012700mbp/page/n315

[33] Ibid., 4-5.

[34] Philip A. Roth, *Masonry in the Formation of Our Government (1761-1799)* (Milwaukee, WI: Masonic Service Bureau, 1917) 15.

The first Masonic manuscripts, the *Old Charges*, show the guild's connections with ancient mythology, from which they derived their moral doctrine. Over time, a religious fraternity formed out of the original society of operative stonemasons and pursued interests aside from the art of a practical craft. A former craft guild thus became an institution that resembled a church, its chief goal being to advance a new religion.[35] Speculative Freemasonry drew especially on the esoteric teachings of antiquity, the Middle Ages, and the early modern age.

Modern English Freemasonry was officially initiated when four London lodges were joined on June 24, 1717 – St. John's Day. Together they formed the Grand Lodge of England, renewing the ideals of the English Masonic Lodge which sought to honor God as the great architect of the universe. From this time onward, Freemasonry became a hotspot for intellectuals, politicians, and artists. The ultimate goal of the secret society was to achieve an ethnic and religious reorientation in their own lives and in society at large. With its mystical undercurrent and medieval roots, Freemasonry proved particularly fascinating to the lower nobility.

Rosicrucian ideas also played an important role in conveying hermetic beliefs which had spread through the West since the Renaissance. The ultimate objective was a general reformation of the whole world, based on principles from various Eastern and Western esoteric traditions. According to the *Fama* and *Confessio Fraternitatis*, texts published in 1614 and 1615, the Rosicrucian Order was an association of scholars charged with sharing their discoveries, healing the sick at no charge, and heralding the Age of Science which would bring a great increase in the knowledge of nature.[36] The Rosicrucian vision, as described by the *Fama* and *Confessio*, was to create a peaceful and universal culture based on the mystical teachings of Kabbalah and alchemy. Furthermore, Rosicrucians turned to the study of nature as manifested in the microcosm (man)[37] and the macrocosm (the universe). The Rosicrucian Furor lasted only a few years: in 1623 there was a noticeable change in general sentiment toward Rosicrucianism, with particularly strong opposition coming from France. However, the theosophical ideas of Rosicrucianism were still preserved in Western cultural circles, although often only within secret societies.

The spread of Hermeticism and the constitution of the Masonic Lodge system were directly linked in early seventeenth-century Scotland. The styles and methods of architecture developed by the Roman Vitruvius in the first century B.C. were seen as essential not only to the education of an architect[38],

---

[35] Lewis Mumford, *The Condition of Man* (London: Secker & Warburg, 1944) 312: "For a time, Masonry became a rival to that other universal institution, the Roman Catholic Church."

[36] Frances A. Yates, *The Rosicrucian Enlightenment* (London: Routledge and Kegan Paul, 1972) 67-70.

[37] Ibid., 238.

[38] Douglas Knoop & G. P. Jones, *The Genesis of Freemasonry* (Manchester: Manchester University Press, 1949) 63.

but also to the development of a man. Thus the two most important elements of Masonic thought were formed in the seventeenth century: 1) the palpable world of Vitruvian architecture[39], and 2) the mystical world of hermetic philosophy. Both elements arose from Hermeticism, which was passed on from Rosicrucianism to Freemasonry. The latter drew its membership from the bourgeoisie and aristocracy. From the eighteenth century, it was particularly fixated on building "Solomon's Temple" – which referred to man's relationship with moral perfection. There were many different incentives for becoming a Freemason. Some members enjoyed the social life in the lodge, while others felt most at home among enlightened individuals.[40] Many liked to be informed about the latest political, economic, and cultural ideas. Others wanted to acquire secret, mysterious knowledge.[41] One of the strongest motives was the desire for further training in the art of architecture.[42] Freemasons generally show indifference toward national politics in order to emphasize their principle of personal autonomy, which should not be influenced by everyday political opinion. Nevertheless, eighteenth-century English Freemasons sought to follow the principles of constitutional monarchy as laid down in the 1689 Bill of Rights, which for the most part corresponded with the Masonic values of equality and fraternity.[43]

Modern Freemasons were intent on carrying out social reforms and made great efforts to spread and implement their ethical ideals among the general public. They particularly wanted to abolish the privileges held by the nobility and clergy in order to lay a foundation for true unanimity and solidarity among all people. Social and political institutions also needed to be changed radically in order to bring the blatant corruption under control. In the late eighteenth century, belief in the continuous development of civilization, which centered around a sense of social duty, prepared the ground for democratic revolutions in Europe. This was the only way for Freemasons to succeed in guiding society as a whole along the path of virtue.

---

[39] Marcus Vitruvius Pollio, *Zehn Bücher über Architektur*; übersetzt und erläutert von Jakob Prestel (Baden-Baden: Verlag Heitz GMBH, 1959).

[40] Norman Mackenzie, *Secret Societies* (London: Aldus Books, 1967) 162.

[41] John Morris Roberts, *The Mythology of Secret Societies* (London: Watkins Publishing, 2008) 25-27.

[42] William Auld, *The Free Masons pocket companion: containing the origin, progress and present state of that antient fraternity, the institution of the Grand Lodge of Scotland, lists of the Grand Masters and other officers of the Grand Lodges of Scotland and England, their customs, charges, constitutions, orders and regulations: for the instruction and conduct of the brethren: to which is added, by way of an appendix, act of the Associate Synod against the Free Masons, with an impartial examination of that act* [...] (Edinburgh: Printed by Ruddiman, Auld, and Company; and sold by William Auld [...], 1761).

[43] "On the design of Masonry. Delivered in the Union Lodge, Exeter, n. 370, 1770," in George Oliver, *The golden Remains of the early masonic Writers* (London: Richard Spencer, 1847) vol. 1: 187-199; https://archive.org/details/OliverGTheGoldenRemainsOfTheEarlyMasonicWritersVolI1847/page/n201

The leader of the Masonic Renaissance – which consisted of far more than a return to ancient cults – was the French Huguenot John Theophilus Desaguliers (1683-1744), a close friend of Isaac Newton. His greatest achievement was without doubt his reform of English Freemasonry. In 1719, he was rewarded for his self-sacrificial dedication with the title of Grand Master of England's newly founded lodge. He obtained remarkable recognition for the young organization, which until this point had had little social influence. Although the book *Old Charges* was primarily written by James Anderson, much of it was based on Desaguliers's ideas. It was first printed and published in 1723 and contained the basic constitution of the newly formed English Freemasonry.[44] The deist-rationalist orientation of its authors is unmistakable. As the new "church" of the London lodge had been founded with the aim of moral, social, and religious reform, this constitution provided it with a historical foundation.[45] Of far greater importance, however, is the second part of the book – "The Charges of a Free Mason" – the Magna Carta, as it were, of Freemasonry.[46]

The core of Masonic religion consisted of commitment to an all-powerful creator and observance of the moral law which he had established as the supreme duty of man. Many of the secret society's documents called the brothers to lead lives of virtue in the name of (i.e. in honor of) this highest being. Although Freemasonry encouraged a general religiosity, individual members were allowed to imagine the creator as they liked. The only thing forbidden was Atheism. The doors of the lodge were thus open to anyone who wanted to believe in a supernatural deity without having to adhere to a specific religious denomination or follow a particular creed. An increasing number of men turned to Freemasonry in the mid-seventeenth century as a result of their aversion to the religious conflicts in England. Membership of a fraternity that allowed them to be theists without having to define their beliefs more explicitly was very attractive to them, having turned their backs on all dogmatic religions, especially Christianity. The earliest expression of their religious confession, found in Anderson's *Old Charges*, leaves no doubt as to the authors' sources: Enlightenment Humanism on the one hand, and "Christian" Mysticism on the other. Freemasonry, therefore, is ultimately nothing other than a bold experiment to unite the rational and irrational elements of Humanism and Mysticism into a single religion. The underlying intention was to bring the various components of both religions into harmony on a higher moral level than was previously possible. There were probably very few individuals in England who had a clear vision for this high goal, and an even smaller number of brothers who adhered steadfastly to the moral principles of Freemasonry. They were exempt from the accusation of being

---

[44] James Anderson, *The Constitutions of the Free-Masons* (London: William Hunter, for John Senex, and John Hooke, 1723); https://archive.org/details/constitutionsoff00andeuoft/page/n11

[45] Ibid., 50; https://archive.org/details/constitutionsoff00andeuoft/page/50

[46] Ibid., 54; https://archive.org/details/constitutionsoff00andeuoft/page/54

merely a place for frivolous entertainment, which was true for many other men's clubs – although the fact does remain that Freemasonry degenerated to the status of a social institution. However, its moral principles remained unharmed by the dead weight of Opportunism (willingness to conform to a current situation out of expediency) which every religious denomination must contend with. These principles are the main means of gauging the meanings of early English Freemasonry, with the same criteria also applied to the various later Masonic associations.

Since the English Grand Lodge was founded in the early eighteenth century, Freemasonry has had an exoteric form of appearance which addresses the public and makes out that everyone is welcome and can understand the aims of the organization. At the same time, it has had an esoteric form known only to insiders, which carefully guards its secrets. The Scotsman Andrew Michael Ramsay (1686-1743) excelled in configuring esoteric rituals within the high degrees of Freemasonry. He called on all scholars and artists within the fraternity to contribute their collective knowledge for the compilation of a universal encyclopedia of liberal arts and applied sciences.[47] This endeavor placed an emphasis on Rationalism as a definitive philosophical foundation; however, it gave no place to theology or politics. In contrast, Rosicrucianism had a considerable impact on the socio-political sphere. Its writings focused on the transformation of society and realization of a utopia – a goal that played an important part in the development of modern Freemasonry. The Rosicrucian, theosophical, and Pansophic movements had carefully planned structures of organization (unlike other esoteric movements that emphasized individualism). Hierarchy among members thus became essential to Freemasonry, despite protests to the contrary. Freemasonry became widespread and was influenced directly by Rosicrucianism, adopting its esoteric cosmology among other things.[48]

Since the beginning of the nineteenth century, there has been continuous conflict between followers of Jean-Baptiste Willermoz (1730-1824), who favored an esoteric high-grade Freemasonry (understandable only to insiders), and members of the English Grand Lodge, who upheld the ideal of an exoteric Freemasonry (aimed at outsiders). Willermoz's Scottish Rite consists not merely of the three degrees of apprentice, journeyman, and master, but of thirty-three different degrees. These two opposing forms of Freemasonry had a strong influence on America's political development.[49]

American Freemasonry underwent great changes in the mid-eighteenth century, particularly through a weakening of its original ideals. While

---

[47] Marsha Keith Schuchard, *Freemasonry, Secret Societies, and the Continuity of the Occult Traditions in English Literature* (Austin, TX: University of Texas, 1991) 191.

[48] Antoine Faivre, *Access to Western Esotericism* (Albany, NY: State University of New York Press, 1994) 79.

[49] Margaret C. Jacob, *Living the Enlightenment: Freemasonry and Politics in eighteenth-century Europe* (New York City, NY: Oxford University Press, 1991) 72.

freedom was still upheld as an inviolable human right, the principle of equality was replaced with a new class system.

English and American lodges divided, encouraging the separation of the American colonies from England. American Freemasons wanted to present their ideals as prominently as possible. The esoteric symbols of the guild appeared everywhere, such as on the signs of taverns and the facades of government buildings. Even the Great Seal of the United States consists of the secret fraternity's symbols, including the all-seeing eye and the unfinished pyramid. Over several decades there was a battle between two groups: the "Ancients" and the "Moderns."[50] These names referred not to their dates of establishment, but mainly to the class differences of their respective members and their attitudes toward the English Whig Party. The longest fight took place in South Carolina, where there was no united lodge until 1814. The "ancient" faction's key to success was their open door to citizens outside the upper class of society. Over time, they were joined by more and more members of the working class. On the other hand, individuals from the economically weak sector of the population were rarely admitted to the elitist Masonic lodges of the "Moderns," who were anxious to maintain their genteel image. They felt most comfortable in the exclusive company of those who shared their higher status. A self-assured group of wealthy businessmen formed within these lodges, concerned primarily with increasing their riches and prosperity. This development constituted a rejection of the original ideals of Freemasonry.[51] A social and institutional change took place within the secret society which became particularly clear when Benjamin Franklin died.[52] While Freemasons ignored the death of Franklin, who had belonged to the "Moderns," extravagant ceremonies were held on the death of George Washington, an "ancient" brother.[53]

Democratization went further than the doors of the lodge. Its traditional structure, shaped by English colonial administration and claiming unlimited power, collided with a growing desire for self-determination among the general public. The eventual revolutionary crisis caused by this conflict was the logical consequence of the hardened position on both sides of the conflict.

Freemasonry has presented itself since time immemorial as a guardian of ancient wisdom. Public statements emphasized humanistic values which, it was claimed, had universal validity. Identification with existing systems of

---

[50] Colin F. W. Dyer, *William Preston and His Work* (Shepperton, Middlesex: Lewis Masonic, 1987) 39-41.

[51] Steven C. Bullock, *The Ancient and Honorable Society: Freemasonry in America, 1730-1830* (Providence, RI: Brown University, 1986) 127-146.

[52] Grand Lodge of Pennsylvania, *Proceedings of the right Worshipful Grand Lodge of [...] Pennsylvania [...] Bicentenary of the birth of [...] Benjamin Franklin [...]* (Philadelphia, PA: Grand Lodge F. & A.M. Penn., 1906) 167-169.

[53] Norris S. Barratt, Julius F. Sachse, *Freemasonry in Pennsylvania, 1727-1907, as shown by records of Lodge No. 2. F. and A. M. of Philadelphia, from the year A.L. 5757, A.D. 1757*, 3 vols. (Philadelphia, PA: Grand Lodge F. & A.M. Penn., 1908-1910) vol. 2: 167, 252-256, 258-270.

belief was deliberately avoided. Shortly before the Revolution, however, this attitude changed, and religious themes were addressed for a better understanding and realization of Freemasonry's deepest secrets. After the American rebels won the War of Independence, they founded a new republic using a wide range of Masonic symbols for self-representation. In the period that followed the Revolution, as American Christians increasingly accepted the humanistic values upheld by Freemasonry, the fraternity seized the chance to adopt a Christian outlook. In place of universal teachings about humanity, Freemasons now began to state that religion was the "foundation stone" of the fraternity. It was crucial for them to have influence over Christian churches. Through emphatic commitment to Christianity, they defused the pointed arguments from their opposition within local churches.

The abolition of the established state church and spread of deistic thinking seemed to encourage the denial of Christianity in the late eighteenth century. To avoid any suspicion, Freemasonry rejected Deism and Skepticism.[54] From this time on, most lodge brothers ceased to spread the anti-religious principles of Rationalism and joined the chorus of Presbyterians who awaited the start of the thousand-year reign.[55] They believed that Freemasonry was on the brink of an age of prosperity, and that this would bring indescribable joy to all inhabitants of the earth.[56] Their rituals now consisted of a combination of Christian and pagan elements. American Freemasonry claimed to be a religion that was closely related to Christianity, deliberately disregarding the original rule in its constitution which prohibited any involvement in religious matters. In 1829, Freemasons in Maryland built a hall for brothers to meet and for Christians from all churches to hold public services.[57] It accommodated Baptists, Episcopalians, Reformed Methodists, and "New

---

[54] Henry F. May, *The End of American Innocence: A Study of the First Years of Our Own Time, 1912-1917* (New York City, NY: Alfred A. Knopf, 1959) 253-277; https://archive.org/details/endofamericaninn027203mbp/page/n275; Jon Butler, *Awash in a Sea of Faith: Christianizing the American People* (Cambridge, MA: Harvard University Press, 1990; Ann Arbor, MI: University of Michigan Library, Scholarly Publishing Office, 1992) 218-220; https://archive.org/details/isbn_9780674056008/page/218

[55] Salem Town, A *System of Speculative Masonry* (Salem, NY: H. Dodd and Co., 1822) 163-164; https://archive.org/details/A_System_Of_Speculative_Masonry_-_S_Town/page/n163

[56] Ibid., 163.

[57] Charles Albert Snodgrass, *The History of Freemasonry in Tennessee, 1789-1943: Its founders, its pioneer lodges and chapters, Grand lodge and Grand chapter, the Cryptic rite, the Templars, the Order of high priesthood and the ancient and accepted Scottish rite, with a foreword of its lineage and the ancient history and traditions* (Nashville, TN: Ambrose Printing Co., sold by Masonic History Agency, Chattanooga, TN, 1944) 75.

School" Presbyterians.[58] Ministers from all churches were able to join the fraternity free of charge.[59]

New or adapted rituals were formed in America which explicitly prescribed prayer and Bible reading. The fraternity's new image emphasized its identification with world religions in general, and in particular with Christianity. Freemasonry continued to uphold the universal validity of humanistic values, and non-Christians could therefore be admitted to lodges without problems. However, American lodge brothers often referred to themselves even in public ceremonies as "Christian Freemasons."[60]

5.5 Ideological foundations of the American Revolution

Calvinistic covenant theology defended the four key spheres of relationship and threatened divine penalties if they were disregarded. First and foremost was the relationship between God and man. This gave rise to man's binding affiliation to the church, which in turn regulated the cohabitation of man and wife and designated their position in society. In 1690, the first of two significant phases in the transformation of the Western worldview began to take place. The idea of a covenant made before God was eclipsed in social thinking by the idea of a social contract (1690 to 1890), until this new concept itself largely gave way to a collective Despotism (1890 to the present day). One ardent supporter of covenant-based political theory was Johannes Althusius[61] (1563-1638). His fiercest opponent was Hugo Grotius, an Arminian theorist of natural law (1583-1645). [62] English and Scottish Presbyterians sympathized with Althusius's theory; however, they were forced to admit the failure of their poorly conceived social revolution following Oliver Cromwell's untimely death on September 3, 1658, and the forced abdication of his son, Richard, on May 15, 1659. Presbyterians were

---

[58] Edward Thomas Schultz, *History of Freemasonry in Maryland: of all the rites introduced into Maryland, from the earliest time [1783] to the present [...]*, 3 vols. (Baltimore, MD: J. H. Medairy, 1884-1887) vol. 2: 585.

[59] Albert Gallatin Mackey, *History of Freemasonry in South Carolina: from its origin in the year 1736 to the present time; written at the request of the Grand Lodge of ancient Freemasons of South Carolina* (Columbia, SC: South Carolinian Steam Power Press, 1861) 198-199; https://archive.org/details/historyoffreemas00mack/page/198; Joseph Howell Hough, William Silas Whitehead, *Origins of Masonry in the State of New Jersey, and the Entire Proceedings of the Grand Lodge, from its First Organization, Trenton, NJ: A.L. 5786* (Trenton, NJ: J. H. Hough, 1870) 238.

[60] "Rule for the Guidance of Christian Freemasons," in Thomas Smith Webb, *The Freemason's Monitor, or, Illustrations of Masonry* (Salem, MA: Flagg and Gould, Printers, 1818) 249-251; https://archive.org/details/freemasonsmonit02webbgoog/page/n260

[61] Johannes Althusius, *Politica*, trans. by Frederick S. Carney (Indianapolis, IN: Liberty Fund, [1964] 1995). This is the abridged version of his book *Politica methodice digesta* (1614).

[62] Gary North, *Cross Fingers: How the Liberals captured the Presbyterian Church* (Tyler, TX: Institute for Christian Economics, 1996) xlvii-xlviii.

consequently marginalized in English society for two generations. As they became more acutely aware of their political insignificance and were increasingly repressed by their opponents, the call of the North American wild sounded more urgently than ever. Many of them followed the Pilgrim Fathers to the New World.

As philosophical ideas spread, the social contract was awarded the same legitimacy as had been previously given to the concept of the covenant. With the general dwindling of religious life, colonists became increasingly disillusioned with the idea that God kept a watchful eye over the lawfulness of civil affairs and intervened correctively where necessary. Many people gradually came to adopt a secular worldview which appeared in two principal forms in the contemporary Christian Occident. On the one hand, John Locke's Whiggism was spread through England and America in his *Second Treatise on Government* (1690). Adam Smith's ideas of free market economy, mainly laid out in his work *Wealth of Nations* (1776), found support as they fell on fertile ground in the political realm. On the other hand, a variation of Whiggism formed on the continent which grew more or less into its antithesis, originating in Rousseau's *Social Contract*[63] (1762). From 1790 onward, the social contract was employed in various ideological forms in French, English, and American national law.

The idea of liberal social order was by no means the invention of seventeenth- and eighteenth-century philosophy. The European doctrine of liberty had its roots in Christianity, and the fundamental components of English Constitutionalism and common law were embedded deeply in the structures of Feudalism. These seeds of liberty were nourished by the theological ferment of the Reformation. The same social order that enabled the development of Reformational beliefs, including the sociopolitical significance of the doctrine of the Trinity, also ensured a balanced relationship between liberty and order. Wherever the monistic principle of humanistic philosophy prevailed (the idea that all earthly events and phenomena can be traced back to one fundamental principle), there eventually arose a totalitarian domination, oppression, and exploitation of the vast majority for the exclusive benefit of an infinitesimal minority. The theological basis of the idea of freedom had been stable for centuries; however, it was unable to resist erosion by the incessant waves of humanistic attacks in the modern era, which was influenced strongly by Enlightenment philosophy. The consequences of secular resistance to the biblical teaching of liberty became more and more apparent throughout the nineteenth century, entering increasingly into public consciousness.

Three concepts were fundamental to the development of the Enlightenment in Europe and its introduction in America: 1) The inherent

---

[63] Jean-Jacques Rousseau, *Du contrat social ou Principes du droit politique* (Amsterdam: Chez. Marc Michel Rey, 1762); Jean-Jacques Rousseau, *The Social Contract Or Principles Of Political Right* (London: George Allen And Unwin Limited, 1948; Harmondsworth: Penguin, 1968); https://archive.org/details/socialcontract00rous

integrity of human nature, 2) the potential perfection of human character, and 3) the inevitable progress of human culture. At that time, however, the idea of progress did not yet have the revolutionary significance that it would later be given by Karl Marx. It rather referred to the anticipated historical development of a humanity striving for perfection. The influence of Enlightenment philosophy soon became apparent in colonial life, leading to a conception of the American dream that was completely different to that of the Puritan forefathers. The new philosophy drew directly on Renaissance Neoplatonism, presenting a sensual attitude toward life and a desire for freedom from any external forces. Authoritative religious and political demands were rejected altogether. The political expression of the new Individualism avowed man's independent reason and intrinsic goodness. The idea that unaided human reason could discern truth in every field of knowledge was contrary to the Christian necessity of divine revelation, which lays claim to exclusive truth. Enlightenment philosophers therefore rejected the legacy of the Reformation which had been valued by the Puritans as their greatest possession.

The Renaissance gave rise to the concept of the autonomous individual, or "masterless man." The idea of the supreme value of the individual, and of all individuals universally, was a Christian notion that stemmed from the belief that all people are created by God and are equal before Him.[64] When the Reformation began to see the church in a biblical way – as a gathering of believers centered on the things of God – responsibility for the salvation of souls took on a very personal and individual tone.[65] As people gradually turned from a theistic to a deistic conception of God, still regarding Him as Creator but no longer as ruler of the universe, the individual was attributed greater freedom of will and wider freedom of movement. The knowledge of nature afforded by modern science led many to believe erroneously that man could dispense with the idea of God through a more comprehensive use of scientific methodology. The rising merchant class began to consider the inalienable rights to which the individual is entitled by virtue of his humanity. They discussed the rights of property obtained through their own work, the inviolability of the human constitution, rights of freedom of speech and fair trial, freedom from arbitrary arrest and cruel punishment, rights of initiative and assembly, and religious freedom. They insisted on being given a greater part in the formation and implementation of national politics. Furthermore, they opposed birth into aristocracy from an innate sense of principle. The ultimate goal of Liberalism, the embodiment of the new Individualism, was individual freedom.

---

[64] Reinhold Niebuhr, *Nature and Destiny of Man* (New York City, NY: Charles Scribner's Sons, 1941) vol. 1: 64; https://archive.org/details/in.ernet.dli.2015.90216/page/n77

[65] A. D. Lindsay, "Individualism," in Edwin R. A. Seligman, ed., *Encylopaedia of the Social Sciences*, 8 vols. (New York City, NY: The Macmillian Co., 1932) vol. 7: 673; https://archive.org/details/in.ernet.dli.2015.460531/page/n695

Liberalism tried to strike a compromise between two antithetical principles. On the one hand, it insisted on the absolute value of human personality and the autonomy of human reason and individual will. On the other hand, it highlighted the existence of a universal, rational, and eternal law to which the individual will of man must be subordinated. Liberalism appealed to the Christian conscience in an effort to find middle ground between these conflicting principles. However, the liberals' "Christian" conscience, which had detached itself both from the tutelage of the Church and from divine revelation in the late eighteenth century, soon deteriorated into mere sentimentality. The individual will of man was therefore no longer restricted by any absolute ethical principles. As one Christian doctrine after another was rejected, the "religion of justification by faith" turned swiftly into a "religion of justification by self-esteem."[66]

In this way, Enlightenment Rationalism was able to invade the fortress of Puritan Calvinism and establish itself inside it. Educated individuals in New England, Pennsylvania, and the southern colonies, especially Virginia, rejected Christianity in favor of either Deism (the idea that God created the world but had no further influence on it) or Unitarianism (rejection of the doctrine of the Trinity and the divinity of Jesus Christ). Transcendentalism (the combined influences of English Romanticism, Mysticism, and Indian philosophies) and Social Darwinism (in which social inequalities are justified as natural occurrences) were later established as other alternatives. The gradual decline of Calvinism gave rise to an ethos among colonists which was entirely different to the Puritanism which predominated in the seventeenth century. The new attitude was marked by unlimited confidence in the ability of human reason to grasp all truths necessary to shape earthly existence in a positive way. Belief in a blissful eternity in heaven was maintained, but drastic changes to Christian beliefs were otherwise readily accepted. Biblical truths only retained their validity if they were consistent with the absolute principles of human reason. Christian doctrine was forced to conform to the growing pool of scientific knowledge. This scientifically-qualified school of thought excluded any possibility of miracles, since they contradicted the asserted inviolability of natural laws. No place was given to central teachings of the Christian faith such as Christ's substitutionary work of redemption, which is directly related to His death on the cross and His resurrection. The doctrines of the Trinity and of justification were similarly dismissed along with the other great teachings of Reformation Christianity. Man's chief duty – to glorify God as his Creator and Savior – thus lost its significance.

Locke sought to establish natural rights as the basis for liberty, but this ultimately proved to be entirely incapable of preserving civil freedom. The assertion of property as a natural right in the eighteenth century led logically to the denial of this right. By referring to Locke's Epistemology, Marx turned

---

[66] Hoxie Neale Fairchild, *Religious Trends in English Poetry* (New York City, NY: Columbia University Press, [1942] 1964) vol. 2: 372-373; https://archive.org/details/religioustrendsi-02fair/page/372

the English empiricist's liberal philosophy on its head. The natural consequence of Classical Liberalism was therefore Communism. Locke's concept of natural rights had already been applied decades before in the radicalization of politics during the French Revolution, as radicals seized the property of the conservatives who resisted their frantic efforts to introduce a new social order. The rationale of the French Declaration of the Rights of Man contains the seed of three revolutions: liberal, democratic, and socialist. Without an "a priori" recognition of his duty toward God, man does not truly know whether he has any rights at all. He consequently lacks an effective means of defense against the attacks of radical philosophers such as Auguste Comte and Karl Marx. John Locke's Empiricism, which teaches that knowledge is gained solely through sensory experience and observation, was a key influence on the emergence of modern Democracy. All historians agree that its impact on the thinking of American revolutionaries cannot be overestimated. Locke's view of human nature and the process of obtaining knowledge were entirely contrary to biblical teaching. He gave no place to the Calvinistic doctrine of total depravity, although he was careful not to appear openly opposed to Christianity. Locke's political principles broke away categorically from the biblical principles of God-ordained government, both in their origins and in their implications. Governments would be legitimated by the agreement of their citizens to accept the terms of the social contract as the basis of the state. Citizens would have the natural right to rebel against their rulers should the latter fail to meet the conditions of the contract. The sovereignty of God was replaced by the sovereignty of the people, and the government's duty to act according to the law of God lost its significance. Submission to the power of a personal God whose eternal counsel determined the temporal destiny of all men was exchanged for surrender to impersonal, arbitrary fate.

Locke's philosophy provided American colonists with a model for interpreting the British Constitution as best suited their subversive intentions. Furthermore, it provided them with apparently compelling arguments to justify their separation from their motherland. Without drawing on Locke, Thomas Jefferson could not have written the Declaration of Independence as he eventually did. The American Revolution was a direct result of the wide dissemination of Enlightenment writings, with the works of John Locke prominent among them. Many people considered revolution against the English authorities to be inevitable after 1770. Colonists believed that this was justified if the government no longer fulfilled the obligations stipulated by the social contract, instead violating the rights of its subjects through acts of tyranny. However, this is not the whole story. Locke was widely approved by colonists for two reasons. On the one hand, his philosophy was rooted in Deism; on the other hand, it was based on natural law. The Classical Liberalism which was accepted by many Americans rested on the same pillars. The more Deism spread, the more closely Classical Liberalism followed on its heels.[67]

---

[67] Joseph Blau, *Men and Movements in American Philosophy* (New York City, NY: Prentice-

It is a known fact that Jonathan Edwards, evangelist of the First Awakening, read Locke's *Essay Concerning Human Understanding* as a thirteen-year-old at Yale College in 1717. Jonathan Edwards is sometimes considered the last great Puritan, but this view arises from a misjudgment of his theology. The theological construct presented by the pastor from Stockbridge, Massachusetts, was essentially an ethical Dualism.[68] In seeking to reconcile Locke's Empiricism with Christian theology, Edwards made compromises with Enlightenment philosophy that had far-reaching consequences, effecting permanent change to the entire structure of Puritanism. Furthermore, Edwards imported a metaphysical Idealism into the teaching of Calvinistic Puritanism, insisting that objects have no inherent existence and that being is only a mental reality. Edwards sowed the seeds of a fruit that was later instrumental in the rejection of Calvinism in New England. Over time, the breach in the doctrinal dam made by Edwards and others became so wide that it eventually could not hold back the torrents of Arminianism (the rejection of John Calvin's doctrine of predestination and advocacy of the freedom of man's will from God) and Arianism (the teaching that Christ is not consubstantial [of the same nature] with God, but only of "like" essence or being with Him), which then poured out over the entire church of the American colonies. Edwards took the first steps toward the teaching that man is sovereign in all earthly matters. By awarding a significant place in religion to Locke's Empiricism as well as to Neoplatonic Rationalism and metaphysical Idealism, despite the fact that these philosophical positions were mutually exclusive and contrary to Calvinistic theology, he initiated the spread of a democratic attitude in Christian fellowships. The momentous consequence was that from this time on, the supreme authority in church and society was no longer the will of God but the majority decision of the people. This was ultimately instrumental in Americans' complete turn to Deism and Unitarianism.

5.6 Religious orientation of Enlightenment philosophy

During the Age of Enlightenment, natural religion provided an escape route from the destructive forces and chaos of Nihilism. Nihilism advocated the complete renunciation of all ideals, standards, and values after the Christian religion had been largely rejected. Man became the sole object of his own worship, and the biblical description of the Holy Spirit as Comforter was applied to a type of "noble man." Carl L. Becker believed that eighteenth-

---

Hall, 1952) 10-11.

[68] Jonathan Edwards, *The Nature of True Virtue* (1749), in Paul Ramsey, ed., *Ethical Writings* (WJE Online vol. 8): "Concerning the Secondary and Inferior Kind of Beauty" (chap. 3), "Of Natural Conscience and the Moral Sense" (chap. 5), and "In What Respects Virtue or Moral Good Is Founded in Sentiment; and How Far It Is Founded in the Reason and Nature of Things" (chap. 8); http://edwards.yale.edu/archive?path=aHR0cDovL2Vkd2FyZHMueWFsZS5lZHUvY2dpLWJpbi9uZXdwaGlsby9nZXRvYmplY3QucGw/Yy43OjYud2plbw==

century Enlightenment philosophers had demonstrated a religious orientation, and in line with this theory, it is no exaggeration to say that they had founded a new faith. Every time that they spoke disparagingly of religion and the *Ancien Régime* (a period of French Absolutism preceding the revolution of 1789), they made a mockery of anything that they disliked. They firmly believed that religion – or superstition and ignorance, as they called it – was a major stumbling block that needed to be removed in order for humanity as a whole to attain perfection. A new aspect of great historical significance came into play: the factor of disillusionment. Disillusionment had never been an issue during the Middle Ages, when eternity had been man's ultimate goal and the gauge of his significance. However, when human hopes and dreams for temporal "projects" are brought low, disillusionment becomes an immense historical factor. In light of the unfulfilled hopes of the past, human beings ask legitimately whether there is any hope at all. What is the point of making great sacrifices if they never see the success that they anticipated?

In *The Heavenly City of the Eighteenth-Century Philosophers*[69] (1932), Carl Becker wrote that philosophers will never find a way to fulfil their humanistic dreams that will exceed the thrill experienced by Christians through the thought of a blissful eternity.[70] French Enlightenment philosophers dismissed the concept of a heavenly afterlife as a delusion. Becker believed that the idea of a transcendental heaven had been replaced by the idea of a perfected humanity on earth. The biblical doctrines of providence and atonement had to make way for the collective cultural aspirations of man himself. Final judgment by God had been replaced by the ruling of history. Philosophers became enslaved to the vision of a perfect humanity, most of them remaining unaware of its religious foundations. It is surprising to learn from Becker that while religion was despised by the foremost representatives of the Enlightenment – such as Montesquieu, Voltaire, Rousseau, Diderot, d'Holbach, and Condorcet – they nonetheless subtly retained many aspects of the Christian past in their philosophy. For example, they rejected the authority of the Church and the Bible, yet placed naïve faith in the authority of nature and reason. They denied that miracles could ever take place, yet believed that the human race could reach perfection. The writings of eighteenth-century Enlightenment philosophers mutated Christianity's promise of heaven into a hope of utopia in this world. All of a sudden, man was required to build his own paradise.

In his analysis of the close spiritual-historical relationship between Enlightenment philosophy and Catholic theology during the Middle Ages, Becker notes that the eighteenth-century enthusiasm for realizing projects and promoting "progress" was underpinned by the "Christian ideal of service,

---

[69] Carl L. Becker, *The Heavenly City of the Eighteenth-Century Philosophers* (New Haven, CT: Yale University Press, 1932); https://archive.org/details/heavenlycityofei00beck

[70] Ibid., 129; https://archive.org/details/heavenlycityofei00beck/page/128

the humanitarian impulse to set things right."[71] His appraisal of the eighteenth century thus contrasts sharply with the modern conception of the Enlightenment as an integral part of the modern worldview and is instantly provocative to the reader. Becker takes the almost scandalous view that the Enlightenment belief in progress was closer to the spirit of the Middle Ages than it is to that of the present day.[72] In 1956, eleven years after Becker's death, historians worked together to reevaluate his book.[73] Peter Gay, a recognized authority on Enlightenment history, was highly critical of the volume and wanted to refute the idea that the Enlightenment philosophers had been religious. Once again, Becker's intentions had been entirely misunderstood.[74] He had never claimed that the philosophers, with their faith in progress, had been "Christians" in any sense of the word. He had, however, emphasized that they could be described as "true believers" in their enthusiasm for a secular alternative to the Christian faith. This was expressed clearly in Becker's explanation of the main articles of faith of the Enlightenment religion: 1) Man is not born evil, 2) the meaning of life is life itself: earthly existence requires a willingness to live a good life on earth rather than to hope for a life of bliss in the next world, 3) guided by the light of reason and experience alone, man is capable of attaining a perfect life on earth, and 4) the chief and most important prerequisite for a good life on earth is the liberation of human thought from the chains of ignorance and superstition, and of the body from the arbitrary suppression of social authorities.[75]

Becker never swore allegiance to the Enlightenment philosophy that inspired the eighteenth century, and which has continued to be promoted widely to the present day. Having long abandoned the social and political optimism of Enlightenment faith in progress, his observations arose from a deep skepticism of the validity of its principles.[76] He believed that they stemmed from philosophers' delusion that man's evil inclinations would disappear along with traditional structures. He was deeply disillusioned with the idea that history would develop in a positive way. The promising dream of the Enlightenment dissolved to nothing in his mind and was replaced by

---

[71] Ibid., 40-41; https://archive.org/details/heavenlycityofei00beck/page/40

[72] Ibid., 29-30; https://archive.org/details/heavenlycityofei00beck/page/28

[73] Raymond O. Rockwood, ed., *Carl Becker's Heavenly City revisited: Studies resulting from a symposium held at Colgate University, Hamilton, New York, October 13, 1956, as a phase of the sixth annual meeting of the New York State Association of European Historians* (Ithaca, NY: Cornell University Press: Ithaca, 1958; Hamden, CT: Archon Books, 1968); https://archive. org/details/carlbeckersheave0000rock/page/n5

[74] Louis Gottschalk, a participant at the symposium, exposed Gays misunderstanding; s. ibid., 89-95.

[75] Becker, *The Heavenly City of the Eighteenth-Century Philosophers*, 102-103; https:// archive.org/details/heavenlycityofei00beck/page/102

[76] Leo Gershoy in Rockwood, ed., *Carl Becker's Heavenly City revisited,* 197; https://archive. org/details/carlbeckersheave0000rock/page/196

an all-destroying cynicism.[77] Gay was concerned that Becker's quasi-nihilistic interpretation of history would undermine progressive Liberalism. He mainly criticized Becker because he had a certain measure of personal enthusiasm for the Enlightenment ideal – which he was unwilling to give up.

5.7 The purported ideal of religious tolerance

The two most well-known Freemasons and Enlightenment philosophers among the Founding Fathers of the United States were George Washington (1732-1799) and Benjamin Franklin (1706-1790). Together with other Founding Fathers, they promoted the religious focus of Enlightenment philosophy and encouraged others to do likewise. In accordance with Masonic principles, George Washington was fully convinced that man is good at the core of his being. He therefore believed it necessary to grant civil liberties in society, since they were conducive to moral living and would engender peaceful coexistence within a democratic confederation. From this perspective, it is clear that the cause of American Liberalism had a thoroughly religious significance for Washington. Furthermore, he believed that a supernatural power was at work in all elements that ensure progress in society – a virtuous force which promotes human prosperity. He often used religious terms in his public speeches and personal correspondence, but his vague expressions do not indicate any specific religion.[78] As a lifelong member of the Episcopal Church, Washington valued the Christian promotion of morality and peace, and loathed disputes over religious matters on account of the consequent disunity.[79] To the onlooker, he thus appeared to uphold the values of tolerance and human sympathy.[80] At the time, Freemasonry was characterized by a liberal attitude towards those who were of a different mind.

Even if this accommodating outlook was widely praised, one important aspect must not be overlooked. The apostles of tolerance were filled with the anticlerical spirit of the Enlightenment and had no intention of approaching all religions with the same open-hearted mindset. Washington knew exactly what he was doing when he ordered a strict separation of church and state. In doing so, he joined a number of leading American Freemasons who were vehemently opposed to the desire of many Christians to give the Church a preeminent position in the American republic, as had largely been the case during the colonial period. Efforts to uphold the traditional model of an established church which had been promoted by Puritanism for over a

---

[77] Becker, *The Heavenly City of the Eighteenth-Century Philosophers*, 158; https://archive.org/details/heavenlycityofei00beck/page/158

[78] Paul F. Boller, Jr., *George Washington and Religion* (Dallas, TX: Southern Methodist University Press, 1963) 75, 93, 108, 120-121.

[79] John C. Fitzpatrick, ed., *The Writings of George Washington*, 39 vols. (Washington, D.C., 1931-1844) vol. 29: 259, cit. in Paul F. Boller, Jr., *George Washington and Religion*, 120-121.

[80] Boller, Jr., *George Washington and Religion*, 167-168, 179-180.

century would prove to be a futile endeavor. In the following early days of Washington's presidency, he did pay lip service to maintaining the ideal of religious tolerance; however, behind the scenes he sought an uncompromising secularization of society. He saw this as the only means of allowing the liberal principles of the Lodge to have full effect. He thus followed confidently in the footsteps of the French Freemasons, wanting the rule of religion and revelation to be replaced with the dominance of science and reason. By propagating his anti-Christian stance, Washington gained the support of two other Founding Fathers who strongly advocated the cessation of church influence on the state: the two Virginian lawyers and later U.S. Presidents Thomas Jefferson and James Madison.

The deist Thomas Paine, one of Benjamin Franklin's closest friends, spoke in favor of the advancement of natural religion in his well-known book *The Age of Reason*. The book expressed his hope that "Christian superstition" would be overcome by human reason. In an essay on the origins of Freemasonry[81], he claimed that the order was in possession of divine revelation. However, its doctrine was not derived from the Bible; Paine suggested that the origins of Masonic teachings lay in the historical records of ancient religions, most likely in the beliefs of the Druids – priests of the sun. The image of the sun is displayed on the walls of many lodges and is the central symbol on the Masonic apron. There was even a sun depicted on the back of the chair on which George Washington sat during the three-month Constitutional Convention.[82]

Benjamin Franklin became a Freemason in Philadelphia in either 1730 or the following year.[83] His admittance to Freemasonry may indicate that he had a mystical, passionate, and personal change of heart without feeling the need to turn to Christianity.[84] Furthermore, the Lodge enabled him to come into personal contact with financiers, businessmen, and politicians in Philadelphia and other metropolises in colonial America. Around this time, he developed a close friendship with Thomas Paine who shared his opinions on many issues.[85] Acquaintances with respected individuals in high society elevated his own status as a publisher, and he went on to hold several offices in the Freemasonry of Pennsylvania.[86] He was a member of the American

---

[81] Thomas Paine, "Origins of Freemasonry," in Philip S. Foner, ed., *Complete Writings of Thomas Paine*, 2 vols. (New York City, NY: Citadel Press, 1945) vol. 2: 829-841.

[82] The Rising Sun Armchair, Independence Hall Association; https://www.ushistory.org/more/sun.htm

[83] J. Hugo Tatsch, *Freemasonry in the Thirteen Colonies* (New York City, NY: Macoy Publishing and Masonic Supply Company, 1929) 21; https://archive.org/details/freemasonryinthi-00tats/page/20

[84] Ibid., 21-22; https://archive.org/details/freemasonryinthi00tats/page/20

[85] Fay, *Revolution and Freemasonry*, 164.

[86] Julius Friedrich Sachse, *Benjamin Franklin as a Freemason; compiled at the request of the right worshipful grand master of Pennsylvania and read at the bi-centenary of the birth of Benjamin Franklin before the right worshipful grand lodge of Pennsylvania, free and accepted masons,*

Philosophical Society and consequently brought it under the influence of the Grand Lodge of Pennsylvania. Over time, a close association developed between the two societies, which explains why most of the American Philosophical Society's members were Freemasons. Franklin is said with some justification to have done more for the spread of Freemasonry in America than anyone else at the time. Over the years, he came to own a number of newspapers which were known in America's English colonies for conveying a Masonic perspective on current affairs.[87] Franklin knew that his commercial success in publishing was directly related to his membership of the Masonic lodge St. John's No. 1. He certainly held the philanthropic ambitions of Freemasonry in high regard, took great interest in ancient legends and architectural symbols, and encouraged their deistic teachings and universalistic ethics. Furthermore, he saw Freemasonry and the Junto and Leather-Apron Clubs (which he founded himself) as humanitarian unions located in the colonies' urban centers and believed that they provided the population with valuable moral education.[88] Franklin wrote deistic essays in which he described man as a mechanical part of a far greater machine. For some time he considered himself an atheist; however, he revised his negative outlook on religion on returning from a visit to London. In the period that followed, his fanciful beliefs consisted of his conception of a multiplicity of gods. Franklin joined a number of different churches during his lifetime, and his credo came to be formed of inconsistent elements which he drew from a variety of Christian confessions.[89]

Franklin's conduct was sometimes quite unusual, and he found it impossible to restrain his hedonistic and blasphemous tendencies. He associated with various disreputable characters from among the English nobility, such as the founder of the Hell Fire Club, Sir Francis Dashwood, 11th Baron le Despencer (1708-1781). Franklin and Lord Dashwood amused themselves by writing a parody of the Anglican Book of Common Prayer. In their irreverence, both individuals saw their actions as an obscene joke, thinking that they had "improved" the church service in making it resemble a wild orgy.[90]

March seventh, nineteen hundred and six (Philadelphia, PA: The New Era Printing Company, 1906) 48-49; https://archive.org/details/benjaminfranklin00sach/page/48

[87] Charles W. Meister, *The Founding Fathers* (Jefferson, NC: McFarland and Co., 1987) 147, 233; Bernard Fay, *Franklin: The Apostle of Modern Times* (Boston, MA: Little, Brown, and Co., 1929) 485.

[88] Ronald W. Clark, *Benjamin Franklin: A Biography* (New York City, NY: Random House, 1983) 51-53; H. T. C. De LaFontaine, "Benjamin Franklin," *Ars Quatuor Coronatorum*, XLI (1929), 3-27.

[89] Charles Francis Adams, ed., *The Works of John Adams: Second President of the United States* (Boston, MA: Little, Brown, 1851) vol. 1 (Life of the Author) 661, cit. in Alfred Owen Aldridge, *Benjamin Franklin and Nature's God* (Durham, NC: Duke University Press, 1967) 8.

[90] Aldridge, *Benjamin Franklin and Nature's God*, 173.

The revolutionary creed that was conceived and implemented in America was immediately adopted by the French bourgeoisie and lower nobility. This was largely due to the fact that Benjamin Franklin was responsible for its conveyance while staying in Paris from 1776 to 1785. Franklin was regarded as a representative of the democratic ideal of a new humanity that was freed from the restraints of privilege and tradition.[91] Furthermore, Franklin is known to have accepted no laws other than those of nature and reason.[92] He was certainly one of the most influential individuals to adopt the rationalist spirit of the late eighteenth century.[93] As American ambassador to the French court, he participated actively in the events of the Parisian lodge Les Neuf Soeurs (The Nine Sisters), which was named after the ancient Muses of Greek mythology. During the American Revolution, Parisian Freemasonry had established the organizational stability that it needed in order to identify fully with the ideals of the Enlightenment. As French Freemasonry became an increasingly important cultural institution, it gathered a growing number of members from the upper classes.[94] One of the highlights in the early history of Les Neuf Soeurs Lodge was the admission of François Marie Arouet (1694-1778), known as Voltaire, to membership. Franklin congratulated Voltaire on his decision before embracing him. No other gesture could have demonstrated more perfectly the close relationship between American and French Freemasonry.[95] An official speech was given which made special mention of Voltaire's achievements in widely disseminating the ideals of Enlightenment philosophy. This highlighted the fact that the humanistic principles of the Enlightenment were entirely consistent with the teachings of Freemasonry. The philosopher, who was known for his unparalleled blasphemy, died around seven weeks later.

Benjamin Franklin was Grand Master of the lodge from 1779 to 1780, taking on both its privileges and duties. During this period, two important meetings took place in which the assembled Freemasons decided to do as much as possible to support the American Revolution. This decision was of great historical significance because it went against the Masonic tradition of avoiding discussion of religious or political issues within the lodge. Franklin consequently had a lasting impact on French Freemasonry, especially in terms of the political engagement of its members. The French Revolution

---

[91] Margaret C. Jacob, *Living the Enlightenment: Freemasonry and Politics in 18th Century Europe* (New York City, NY: Oxford University Press, 1991) 172.

[92] Ibid.

[93] Paul Elmer More, *Benjamin Franklin* (Boston, MA; New York City, NY: Houghton, Mifflin and company, 1900) 114ff.; https://archive.org/details/benjaminfranklin01more/page/114

[94] Pierre Chevallier, *Histoire de la Franc-Maconnerie Francaise: La Maconnerie: Ecole de L'Egalité, 1725-1799* (Paris: Fayard, [1974] 2002) 172-177; Gaston Martin, *La Franc-Maconnerie Francaise et La Preparation de la Revolution* (Paris: Les Presses universitaires de France, 1926; Paris: Champion, Slatkine, 1989) 17-28.

[95] Carl Van Doren, *Benjamin Franklin* (New York City, NY: The Viking Press, 1961) 606; https://archive.org/details/in.ernet.dli.2015.182793/page/n627

could never have been carried out without the preparations and actions of the Grand Lodge Grand Orient de France as the governing body of French Freemasonry. The same can be said with respect to the American Revolution, which would never have been successful without extensive assistance from the French Freemasons, especially King Louis XVI.[96] By making use of his various Masonic connections, Franklin managed to convince the French to enter the war with England on the side of the American rebels. Most of his connections in Europe were wealthy slave traders, often Huguenots, who made use of the network of lodges in the countries to which their ships sailed. This enabled the transportation of much needed supplies and armaments from the Netherlands to America.

5.8 Deistic origins of the Declaration of Independence

Deism, which teaches that theological statements are legitimized not by the authority of revelation but by rational arguments, had a revolutionary influence on the political, social, and economic life of colonial America during the eighteenth century.[97] It provided the philosophical basis that inspired the American Revolution and simultaneously produced a new theological view that supported the revolutionary propaganda. Separation from England would not have been possible had not a revolt against the Puritan worldview taken place in the colonies beforehand. The fight against the Absolutism of the King of England was a side effect of the fight against the sovereignty of the Puritan God.[98] Convinced that the obligations imposed by Christianity were no longer necessary, Deists claimed that man's happiness could be best increased through exclusive use of reason. Brotherly love would promote the interests of society, for the individual would treat his neighbor with respect and protect his rights. Opponents argued that sinful man relies on an external force in order to be capable of living in an agreeable way.

---

[96] Richard William Weisberger, *The Cultural and Organization Function of Speculative Freemasonry During the Enlightenment: A study of the craft in London, Paris, Prague, and Vienna* (Ann Arbor, MI: University Microfilms International, 1980) 138-139.

[97] Adam Storey Farrar, *A critical History of Free Thought in reference to the Christian Religion: Eight lectures preached before the University of Oxford, in the year M. DCCC. LXII* [...] (London: John Murray, 1862; New York City, NY: D. Appleton and Co., 1863) 118ff.; https://archive.org/details/acriticalhistor01farrgoog/page/n168; Alfred William Benn, *History of English Rationalism in the Nineteenth Century* (New York City, NY: Longman, Green, and Co., 1906) vol. 1: 177ff.; https://archive.org/details/in.ernet.dli.2015.41772/page/n205; Alexander Pope, "Essay on man," Mark Pattison, ed. (Oxford: The Clarendon Press, 1871) 58-59; https://archive.org/details/popeessayonmane00popegoog/page/n66; John Bagnell Bury, *A History of Freedom of Thought* (New York City, NY: H. Holt and company, 1913) 137-138; https://archive.org/details/ahistoryfreedom01burygoog/page/n140; John Herman Randall, *Making of the Modern Mind* (Indianapolis, IN: Houghton Mifflin, 1940) 285; https://archive.org/details/in.ernet.dli.2015.1227/page/n299

[98] Richard Mosier, *The American Temper* (Berkeley, CA: University of California Press, 1952) 70.

Whenever the Christian religion is rejected as a guarantor of moral conduct, chaos will ensue.

Throughout the eighteenth century, and particularly during its second half, an increasingly extreme form of Deism spread among the American population. The influence of French culture in the American colonies had prepared the ground for the spread of freethinking. Contemporary political sentiment was wholly consistent with the religious philosophy of Deism, which insisted on liberation from the rule of a God who was deliberately and disdainfully presented as being tyrannical and arbitrary. In full awareness that each step towards independence effected a radical break with a past built on Christian principles, revolutionary colonists strove to introduce a new social order despite the resulting deaths of many soldiers. However, they failed to consider the conceptual inconsistency of Locke's philosophy, which in time had fatal consequences. Although they escaped the power of the English Parliament after a successful revolution, American patriots introduced a new political system which in the long run amounted to Totalitarianism. Locke's teaching on human rights did not provide an adequate basis on which to keep the ever-increasing power of the American president under control.

The reputations of the scientist Isaac Newton and the political philosopher John Locke were key to the acceptance of the Enlightenment in the American colonies.[99] In contrast to an apparently mythological Christianity, Rationality was attractive in its mechanistic ideas about natural processes and a liberty-oriented system of government. The promises of materialistic Newtonism, which subordinated idealistic considerations to the acquisition of wealth, seemed greater than the promise of a Christian heaven in the next world. Pastors were also open to Enlightenment ideas and placed the human mind and divine revelation on a par as sources of human knowledge.[100] The generations following the original Puritans distanced themselves increasingly from the theology of their forefathers, until they gradually adopted the imperialist essence of modern American foreign politics. The explosive mixture of biblical prophecy and political self-determination led to the outbreak of the American Revolution (1775-1783), in which the British colonies in America broke away from their motherland. Republican social order was distorted completely through the incorporation of millennial expectations: the Republican Party changed its goal and concentrated on geographical expansion. This strategy also diverted attention away from intra-party conflicts.

Economic, political, and constitutional forces played an important role in provoking the American Revolution. After the military conflict ceased,

---

[99] C. Gregg Singer, *A theological Interpretation of American History* (Philadelphia, PA: Presbyterian and Reformed Publishing Co., 1964) passim.

[100] Merle Eugene Curti, *The Growth of American Thought* (New York City, NY: Harper & Brothers Publishers, [1943] 1951) 108; https://archive.org/details/in.ernet.dli.2015.544082/page/n127

Enlightenment philosophy had a significant influence on the democratic revolution of social affairs. Taking up arms was a necessary evil used to begin a social revolution that extended beyond the military conflict, with the aim of restructuring American society according to the principles of democratic philosophy.

Many American revolutionaries were inspired by Enlightenment philosophy, and this had a direct impact on their theological understanding. They were largely unaware that separating biblical moral teaching from divine revelation was tantamount to fully rejecting it. The doctrine of divine goodness was one of the most important of its time, since it gave rise to the universalistic principle that all men are able to attain eternal salvation. The doctrine of universal reconciliation was a logical result of the liberal premise that man is both good and capable of improvement by nature. Unitarianism spread, rejecting the doctrine of the Trinity and of the divinity of Jesus Christ. After 1740, the educated upper class in most American colonies converted almost unanimously to Unitarianism. Leading politicians in the newly founded nation were either Deists or Unitarians. Most of the signatories of the Declaration of Independence and participants in the Continental Congress of 1776 were influenced by the Enlightenment, the majority being Deists. Many were also Freemasons.[101] Theological Radicalism, which at its core was no different to religious Humanism, was seen as a contraposition to Puritan Calvinism. The democratic philosophy derived from it was a secularized caricature of the Christian worldview.

The demand for political separation from the British Empire was aimed at realizing the philosophical principles of the Enlightenment in a new society. Revolutionaries held back in their attacks on the church but were hostile toward Christian doctrine and praxis. Thomas Jefferson (1743-1826) was the guiding theorist and driving motivator behind the American Revolution. Not only did he adhere to deistic Unitarianism as the truest expression of his own religion, but it also served as a point of reference in the formation of his political and social philosophy. This is reflected directly in the Declaration of Independence. The result was a full Radicalism based on John Locke's Liberalism and Thomas Paine's Deism. The fact that contemporary Christians were willing to sign the Declaration of Independence should not cause its fundamentally un-Christian character to be overlooked. Jefferson was a Deist who rejected divine providence, the divinity of Jesus Christ and thus the Trinity, and the inspiration of the Bible; he believed that God does not reveal Himself in the Bible, but in nature. He believed that the revolution which he had supported would bring about the eighteenth-century philosophers' celestial city in America. He was convinced that man could achieve this monumental task without the help of God or the church. The idea that Jeffersonian Democracy is based on Christian principles and reflects the

---

[101] Philip A. Roth, *Freemasonry and the Causes That Led to the American Revolution* (Whitefish, MT: Kessinger Publishing, [1927] 2010) 43-45.

social consequences of the Gospel is one of the most deep-seated misconceptions among contemporary Christians in America.

Jefferson promoted the democratic philosophy most clearly in the Declaration of Independence, which was to be the foundation of the new America. He hoped that it would come into effect after the war with England, which was a prerequisite for the realization of the Declaration. Jefferson's Democracy was based on rejection of the sovereignty of God. The Christian doctrines of original sin, reconciliation, and the new birth were replaced with the concept of man's inherent goodness and progressive perfection. The Christian teachings of repentance and conversion had completely lost their meaning in the improvement of man's living conditions.

The Declaration of Independence was signed on July 4. Among its signatories were up to forty-one Freemasons, although not all of them declared themselves as such. They swore to promote the Rosicrucian ideals of Cosmopolitanism, united science, and universal religion in the newly dawning era. In Europe, the Declaration of Independence was seen as a document which proclaimed Freemasonic principles. Freemasons considered July 4 a holy day, and it became established as a national holiday in the United States.[102]

5.9 Influence of Freemasonry on the American Revolution

Over the hundred years beginning in 1660, Great Britain issued a series of laws which limited the trade of consumer goods in the American colonies. The first product on which trade tariffs were placed was tobacco. The next was the molasses produced from cane sugar on the Caribbean islands. The king of England showed no remorse at imposing high taxes on prospering American merchants for the sake of filling his own coffers. Traders in the newly founded colonies saw no option but to circumvent the laws that were hindering their business by smuggling. The necessity of foreign trade was deeply ingrained in New Englanders' minds, and they consequently saw smuggling as a necessary addition to their business, forced on them by the British government. English customs officers who dared board ships to examine their cargo were often treated very badly. England's insistence on taking military action where necessary to enforce the laws against piracy and smuggling led directly to the American Revolution (1775-1783). A traders' network based on mutual trust was essential if products were to be manufactured and business was to be conducted at all. Freemasonry was at the heart of the network. The rebels who reacted against English rule in the American Revolution were recruited from it, and most of them were Freemasons working as pirates, smugglers, and slave dealers. Pirate ships often functioned as Masonic lodges at sea.

---

[102] David Ovason, *The Secret Architecture of Our Nation's Capital* (New York City, NY: Harper Collins, 1999) 142-149.

John Hancock (1737-1793) was a Freemason who belonged to an elite as well as a working class lodge. He placed great importance on the ideal of freedom and was also concerned with the promotion of local industry. The ships owned by his uncle, Thomas Hancock, transported food products to Newfoundland, exchanged them for whale oil, and then sailed to England to sell their expensive cargo at a good profit. Hancock's wealth grew far more quickly than that of competitors who were pursuing the same business strategy. He lived in a large house, wore expensive clothes, and bought a small fleet of merchant ships. The secret to his considerable revenue was that he imported tea from the Caribbean island of Sint Eustatius to America. His ships would leave the Dutch harbor of Sint Eustatius loaded with legal products and return with contraband – an illegal business which had to be conducted in complete secrecy. On hearing word that a European conflict, the Seven Years War (1756-1763), would soon spread to the American colonies, Hancock saw his chance to make money by selling arms.[103] When the anticipated war actually came to pass, the poorly equipped British troops turned to Hancock's firm to buy ammunition. When he died in 1764, his heir, John Hancock, became America's richest businessman overnight.

Among the smuggled goods transported by Hancock's ships was tea. Prospering trade relations with China and the popularity of the exotic drink in England led to a huge increase in imports. The settlers drank an average of six million pounds of tea per year, around a sixth of which was brought to America illegally by Hancock's ships in 1773. There was scarcely a more lucrative business in America at the time, its only requirement being knowledge of how to circumvent the restrictive British trading laws without being caught. The British East India Company (BEIC) had a monopoly on the global tea trade. One of its investors was the governor of Massachusetts, Thomas Hutchinson, whose entire fortune consisted of shares in the company.[104] Furthermore, his salary was proportional to the amount of customs duty that he collected by taxing imported tea. After the Bank of England, the British East India Company (BEIC) was the largest financial institute in Great Britain. However, it stood in danger of bankruptcy, not yet having the enormous income that it would later gain through importing opium into China. The company charged three shillings for each pound of tea, whereas the Dutch East India Company charged only two. The British government contained many BEIC shareholders and prohibited its subjects, including American settlers, from buying tea from any company other than the monopolizing BEIC. The only significant consequence of this was a marked rise in profits for New England's smugglers. This angered the Governor of Massachusetts, for whom the situation was a distinct

---

[103] Herbert Allen, *John Hancock: Patriot in Purple* (New York City, NY: Macmillan, 1948; New York City, NY: The Beechhurst Press, 1953) 61-69; https://archive.org/details/johnhancockpatri0000alla/page/60

[104] A. J. Langguth, *Patriots: The Men Who Started the American Revolution* (New York City, NY: Simon & Schuster, 1988) 179.

disadvantage. The American Revolution began when Hancock's ship *Liberty* was taken into custody by Thomas Hutchinson in order to inspect and confiscate its cargo.

The plans and schemes made against the British Empire during the American Revolution were largely the work of secret societies. The Saint Andrew Lodge[105], founded in Boston on January 1, 1756, became the center of the movement. The Masonic meetings in which the first steps of the Revolution were planned took place in the tavern "The Green Dragon, or the Arms of Freemasonry." America's first revolutionary act was the Boston Tea Party, in which three ships – the *Dartmouth*, *Eleanor*, and *Beaver* – were seized by rebels dressed as Indians who threw their cargoes of British East India Company tea into the sea. 340 chests were destroyed. The news of the daring venture spread like wildfire through the colonies, and thus began the War of Independence.

Three societies – the Caucus Club, the Loyall Nine, and the Sons of Liberty – united together with the aim of providing lines of communication between the rebels and coordinating their military action. They first formed the Committees of Correspondence before creating the Continental Congress and setting up militia units. These treacherous initiatives had to be carried out in secret. Many of the conspirators largely kept quiet because they had taken blood oaths in Masonic lodges. George Washington became a Freemason on November 4, 1752, and as commander-in-chief of the Continental Army encouraged his soldiers to do likewise. Only those willing to take up membership of a military lodge were raised to the rank of officer.[106]

In the American War of Independence (1775-1783), all the aces were held by the British. They had all the advantages imaginable: a superior land army, an additional contingent of 9000 Hessian soldiers, a large fleet of ships, sufficient supplies, and enough funds to purchase more. The rebellious Americans had inferior military power, no navy, insufficient supplies, and initially very few means to buy more. The majority of people in the eastern area of Long Island remained loyal to the king and supplied the British army with sufficient provisions, including large quantities of beef. New Jersey stood almost unanimously with the English crown and provided the royal military units with food. Meanwhile, Washington's troops on the other side of the Delaware River in Pennsylvania went hungry. The loyal Scottish Tories in the South sided with the British – a fact which greatly demoralized the American rebels. The grim situation became worse still as the inexperienced Continental Army, led by Commander-in-Chief George Washington, suffered one defeat after another. They had to retreat further and further as the British troops marched on. Half of the Continental Army died in combat, while much of the other half was dying of hunger and disease. Many of the American soldiers deserted when the opportunity arose. George Washington could easily have

---

[105] The Lodge of Saint Andrew, 186 Tremont Street Boston, MA 02111-1095; http://massfreemasonry.org/

[106] Fay, *Revolution and Freemasonry*, 150.

provided his hungry soldiers with the much-needed supplies from his own pocket as they faced the freezing elements in the hard winter of 1777-1778; instead, however, he sent one petition after another to Congress demanding higher pay for himself.[107] Landowners in North and South Carolina had close business relations with the English Tories and opposed the rebels for nothing but commercial motives, even though some of them secretly wanted a Republican social order. There was nothing to suggest any possibility of the rebels winning the War of Independence – and yet they achieved a resounding victory.

What tipped the scales was a strategically important coup staged by a handful of men, many of whom were members of Masonic lodges. As heroically as they may have acted, it should be remembered that they did so illegally. Their boldness and audacity made possible the great victory at Yorktown. A further factor was the allocation of substantial bribes, which was not uncommon in wartime during this period. Of great historical significance, although usually kept quiet, is the background to the covert conspiracies led by Benjamin Franklin and his fellow Freemasons. During his second stay in England from 1757 to 1762, Franklin spent some time at West Wycombe Park, Buckinghamshire, the estate of Sir Francis Dashwood. As already mentioned, Dashwood had founded the Hell Fire Club to which Franklin also belonged. Its members met regularly for orgies at Medmenham Abbey. The American ambassador took the opportunity to speak to his brothers John Stuart, John Wilkes, John Montagu, and other prominent members of the Whig Party about the storm clouds gathering over the Thirteen Colonies, and together they forged a plan for a successful revolution.[108] When Franklin arrived in France in 1776, the leading French Freemasons Sieur Montaudoin (Nantes) and Dr. Jacques Barbeu-Dubourg (Paris) introduced him to the secret world of seafaring smugglers and slave traders. Nantes was the second largest port in France at the time and was heavily involved in the trade triangle of molasses, rum, and slaves. Franklin's contact with the traders in Nantes proved extremely advantageous to the cause of the American Revolution; it provided the only way to organize the transportation of ammunition and other armaments across the Atlantic. Barbeu-Dubourg purchased the necessary weapons, ammunition, and supplies which were sent to America on Montaudoin's ships. Around ninety percent of the gunpowder required by Washington's army came from France. News that the French were doing thriving business with the colonial rebels spread through the Masonic underground. Many Dutch and Spanish merchants as well as pirates offered to sell their captured goods to the Americans. The climax of

---

[107] Washington Irving, *Life of George Washington* (New York City, NY: Putnam, 1865) 307, 315-323, 357; https://archive.org/details/lifeofgeorgewas03irvi/page/n417; Douglas Southall Freeman, *George Washington: A biography*, 7 vols. (New York City, NY: Charles Scribner's Sons, 1948) vol. 5: 4-14; https://archive.org/details/georgewashington0005free/page/4

[108] Michael Howard, *The Occult Conspiracy: Secret Societies, Their Influence and Power in World History* (Rochester, VT: Destiny Books, 1989) 80.

these secret schemes was the arrival of French troops led by high-ranking Freemasons. Influential lodge brothers in the American colonies and in France had worked extremely hard to win over the Bourbon King Louis XVI, himself a Freemason, to the side of the American revolutionaries in early 1778. In July of the same year, the French monarch declared war on England.

In a sense, it is understandable that Benjamin Franklin turned to Freemasons, occultists, slave traders, and smugglers to obtain sufficient support for the rebels battling in the Thirteen Colonies. Political idealists such as Samuel Adams and Patrick Henry were prepared to risk their lives in order to gain independence for their country, while many settlers who sided with the rebels acted out of pure selfishness. When war broke out with England, American traders took the opportunity to make their fortunes. The sale of weapons and supplies imported from overseas became a lucrative business which formed the basis of the fortunes of cunning profiteers such as Robert R. Livingston, Elbridge Gerry, Stephen Girard, and Benjamin Harrison.[109] In order to coordinate the acquisition of war material, Benjamin Franklin turned to the Secret Committee. Its members, all wealthy traders, shamelessly exploited their powerful positions to increase their own wealth.[110] In July 1780, when the troops of the insurgent settlers were so decimated that immediate defeat was anticipated, seven cargo vessels brought the French army to the shores of Rhode Island, bringing with them ample weapons, supplies, and financial resources. The final attack on the British military could never have been carried out without the active assistance of European allies. The thousand-man German auxiliary corps fought with the American rebels, particularly in the Battle of Yorktown, and contributed significantly to their victory. Lauzun's legion included soldiers from Sweden, Italy, Germany, Poland, and Russia, speaking eight different languages between them. All of them were adventurers who had signed up voluntarily for military service. One reason for the defeat of the British army was that Admiral Rodney was bribed by the French and failed to fulfil his duty. There is no doubt that the outcome of the American War of Independence was decided by bribes.

Financial and military support from France, Spain, and Holland enabled the colonies to gain their independence from the British Empire in the first place. If this fact is left aside in assessment of the American Revolution, one thing becomes particularly clear. The English Whigs were not displeased by the Americans' rebellion against Tory rule, since they were determined to establish a member of their own party in the office of Lord Chancellor. They were more concerned with gaining political influence through the prestige and power of this position than they were with keeping hold of distant colonies. The defeat of the English mercenary army at Yorktown, Virginia in 1781 worked to their advantage, since it destroyed the power of the Tories for a whole decade. The most capable British commander in the war was General

---

[109] Helen Augur, *The Secret War of Independence* (Boston, MA: Little, Brown, and Co., 1955) 70-71.

[110] Ibid., 37.

William Howe. His political sympathies lay with the Whigs, not the Tories, and he secretly made his military decisions in line with his favored policies. This is the only explanation for Howe's strategic mistakes which enabled the Americans to gain the upper hand on the battleground in what was an almost hopeless situation. The London Whigs considered the loss of the American colonies in the late eighteenth century to be of relatively low importance compared with the West Indian sugar plantations. The islands' production of molasses was far more economically valuable for the Whigs than was the entire income from trade with the colonies.

The influence of Freemasonry on the young American republic was most evident in its political administration. The establishment of government bodies at district, state, and federal levels reflected the structural organization of the Masonic Federation which was led by the grand lodges. Shortly after the Thirteen Colonies became constituted as the United States, grand lodges were established in every state. The turbulent years of the War of Independence were followed by a period of political consolidation, which was temporarily suspended when a Freemason was sworn in as president on April 30, 1789. George Washington took the oath of office on the Bible of St. John's Lodge, standing before the Grand Master of New York State, Robert R.. Livingston. The influence of Freemasonry on the political development of the new nation is evident from the building plans for the capital city, which were based on the geometric principles of the secret society. The official opening of the city followed the protocol of a Masonic ceremony and was conducted by high-ranking government officials wearing Masonic aprons. The importance of Freemasonry in the founding of the United States cannot be overstated. The lodge brothers were largely responsible for the spiritual conceptualization of civil rights, the rule of law, and Democracy.

5.10 Mercantilist bias of the American System

(The American System favors the elite at the expense of the general public) International trade boomed between 1450 and 1750 with the development of new technologies, especially in shipping. The enormous expansion of trade across continents also encouraged international division of labor through the specialization of specific working processes, enabling competitors to achieve cost benefits.[111] Wherever countries were given free rein to conduct business as they liked, it was reflected by an enormous increase in world trade. However, ruling powers resented the prosperity in Europe's commercial centers, feeling it to threaten their privileged positions. In order to counteract their increasing loss of power, they opposed free trade. Their preferred system of trade restrictions and other state economic interventions became known as "Mercantilism," which peaked in Europe during the seventeenth and

---

[111] Nathan Rosenberg & L. E. Birdzell, Jr., *How the West Grew Rich* (New York City, NY: BasicBooks, 1986) 71-112.

eighteenth centuries. During the eighteenth and nineteenth centuries, liberals waged an ideological war against the propagandists of Mercantilism and recorded some landmark victories for the free market economy. In 1776, the Scottish moral and Enlightenment philosopher Adam Smith attacked Mercantilism more than other economist of his time. Smith knew that Mercantilism was a statist system based on fallacious economic principles to justify the expansion of imperial power. He established free trade on a basis of moral and economic arguments taken from his teaching of "natural justice." He enforced this principle by giving smugglers the right to bring contraband into the country in order to bypass mercantilist trade restrictions.[112]

Colonists were shrewd tradesmen and knew how to conduct business with both the French and the English, who were enemies at the time. The military conflict between them reached a climax in 1763 when France was forced to admit defeat and largely lost its political influence in the American colonies as a result. Greed among American colonists was fomented by lucrative trade with the victorious English and grew almost out of control. From that time onward, America was unmistakably politically ruled by the rich (Plutocracy). To concede willingly to the restrictive trade terms demanded by English imperialists therefore seemed completely illogical. Colonists soon realized that the English had not stationed enough troops in America to enforce the mercantilist laws issued during the seventeenth century. After the first Treaty of Paris between England and France came into effect in 1763, the London Parliament was forced to supplement its desolate state finances with additional revenue from the colonies. The old economic laws, which had been created for exploitation, were reapplied with the required severity.

Closer consideration of the development of the War of Independence shows that it was a rebellion among English subjects who no longer wanted to submit to their own government. The conflict was a dispute between two groups of rich landowners who, as wealthy colonists, wanted to expand their territory. However, this would only be possible if they held the reins of political power. Englishmen who owned large plantations and vast areas of land knew that they could only exploit colonists economically if they also had administrative power over America. Another reason why the ringleaders of the American colonists, later called patriots, decided to risk military conflict with the powerful British Empire was London's mercantilist tax policy. It is revealing to examine why no significant damage was done to the unofficial yet dominant system of Plutocracy in America, even though the balance of power had changed radically (at least on the surface) when the British Empire lost its American colonies. Reactionary statesmen with legitimate hopes of joining the wealthy upper classes ensured that America, which had gained independence from England, was not too distant from the British Empire either politically or financially. One of the most important sources of revenue

---

[112] Adam Smith, *An Inquiry into the Nature and Causes of the Wealth of Nations* (New York City, NY: Oxford University Press, 1976) 898.

at that time was the ownership of large estates, on which the vast fortunes of many American families were founded. Four of the early presidents – Washington, Jefferson, Madison, and Monroe – became the most prominent landowners not only in their home state of Virginia, but also in most other states. When George Washington died in 1799, he was the richest man in the United States. Most of the Founding Fathers were involved in dubious methods of moneymaking. This can be seen by their cautious push for a centralized regime in 1789 – the only way by which they could make excessive profits from their speculative investments in government bonds and estates. When necessary, however, they did not hold back from using the military to add force to their demands when threatened with violence. The costs arising from these questionable ploys were borne exclusively by the general public. After the War of Independence ended, a modified version of English customary law was taken as the authoritative legal basis of the United States, solely because it was best suited to many of the economic interests of the Founding Fathers. Patriots motivated by freedom, such as Patrick Henry and Thomas Jefferson, largely failed to stand up to the power of plutocrats such as Franklin, Washington, Adam, Hancock, and Madison in their fight against the hated justice system. In order to conceal their greedy actions, the leading Founding Fathers hired professional historians to portray their motives as an outflow of pure philanthropy. This situation remains unchanged to the present day, except that methods used to suppress truth about past events have become far more violent. A whole spectrum of malicious tactics is employed against historians who seek to set the record straight, including defamation of character, discrimination, and murder, as well as financial discrimination and prosecution.

The mid-eighteenth century witnessed a struggle for power between two economic systems. Thomas Jefferson (1743-1826), the main author of the Declaration of Independence, wanted to protect the freedom gained from being destroyed by state Paternalism. His opponent was America's first secretary of the treasury, Alexander Hamilton (1755-1804), who fought against Liberalism.[113] Hamilton wanted to encourage foreign trade and domestic industry in order to strengthen financial capacity and government power.[114] To this end, he introduced the corrupt system of British Mercantilism into the newly founded United States. He called for protective tariffs, an increase in national debt, higher taxes, and the establishment of a central bank that was not under political control. Hamilton euphemistically called this the "American System" and purported that Americans would profit from it. In reality, however, it only had benefits for certain stakeholders.

According to conventional historiography, the Constitution drafted by the Founding Fathers was rooted in a unique combination of historical, theological, philosophical, and political ideas about humanity and society.

---

[113] Thomas DiLorenzo, *Hamilton's Curse* (Danvers, MA: Crown Forum, 2009) 14.

[114] Clinton Rossiter, *Alexander Hamilton and the Constitution* (New York City, NY: Harcourt, Brace & World, 1964); https://archive.org/details/alexanderhamilto00ross.

The Founding Fathers' political understanding was allegedly based more on the old social structures of democratic city states than on the innovations of the radical Enlightenment. They relied on the trustworthy guidance of Classicism and Christianity to establish the ideal social order and apparently had no intention of transforming the world into heaven on earth. The distinctive features of the U.S. Constitution, as drawn up by the Founding Fathers in 1787, have been deeply embedded in Americans' collective conscience for centuries. They appear again and again in the writings of acclaimed historians such as George W. Carey[115], promoting a view that contains a grain of truth, but which ultimately serves only to reinforce a historical myth. This myth expresses virtually the opposite of what the Founding Fathers wanted when they met in Philadelphia for the Constitutional Convention. The general public was strictly excluded from the convention, and participating delegates were sworn to self-imposed secrecy. The conventional description and explanation of the key considerations in the formulation and ratification of the U.S. Constitution are summarized exemplarily by George W. Carey, who stated that it reflects, at least in part, an "old constitutional morality." According to Carey, the Founding Fathers defended the four fundamental principles of America's political system: Republicanism, division of powers, Federalism, and a minimal government apparatus.[116] Members of the Constitution committee believed that centralization of power would be dangerous and would undoubtedly be abused. At the same time, they retained the Enlightenment's optimistic idea that man is capable of achieving a higher degree of self-mastery through reason. The Founding Fathers were afraid of frequent, radical reforms that promised to simplify the system of government but which ultimately destabilized politics. They therefore hindered major changes to the system of government which could be implemented far too easily. According to Carey, complexity and slowness are sometimes good and necessary.

This traditional portrayal of the factors which led to the Constitutional Convention and the monumental consequences that followed disguises the real motives behind the Founding Fathers' secret decision to reject the Articles of Confederation. The Articles had granted national sovereignty to each of the original states in favor of a completely different Constitution – in their eyes a necessary move. On May 25, 1787, a group of fifty-five men gathered in Philadelphia to draw up a new U.S. Constitution. The official reason given for the convention was a desire to revise the already existing Constitution – the Articles of Confederation. Some state governments had authorized their delegates to work solely on this task. They were explicitly forbidden to draw up a new Constitution. In order to ensure that the general public did not discover the real reason for the convention, the delegates took an oath never to tell outsiders about the negotiations. No reports from

---

[115] George W. Carey, *In Defense of the Constitution*, revised and expanded edition (Indianapolis, IN: Liberty Fund, 1995); https://oll.libertyfund.org/titles/678

[116] Ibid., 4, 16.

participants appeared until 1836, the year in which James Madison – the last of them to survive – passed away. The decision for the new Constitution to come immediately into effect when ratified by nine state governments was a direct contradiction to the regulations of the Articles of Confederation. It is thus beyond doubt that this group of conspirators devised a political conspiracy, aiming to stage a secret coup. The existing 1781 Constitution, the Articles of Confederation, needed to be abolished since it left the regulation of U.S. financial affairs to the thirteen states. It seemed unlikely that the wealthy upper class in late eighteenth-century America could successfully maintain political control over the administration of each state.[117]

The Founding Father Robert Morris and his supporters, all of whom were "Federalists," aimed to impose nothing other than British Mercantilism on the newly formed American confederation – shortly after a rebellion had been fought to abolish the system. The first Secretary of the Treasury, Alexander Hamilton, spent the rest of his life advocating excessive public debt and exorbitant public spending.

During the War of Independence, the provisional government intentionally spread the rumor that the war bonds owned by many citizens would lose all value. When the government still had not paid its debts around ten years later, upper-class agents offered five percent of the war bonds' nominal value to anyone who wanted to divest them. This dubious offer was made under false pretenses; however, it was largely accepted despite the fact that it also meant accepting enormous losses. The rich, who had bought almost all the government bonds issued during the War of Independence for next to nothing, demanded that the government repay them the nominal value with interest, thereby making an enormous profit. The borrowed money which the government repaid to the rich amounted to a colossal 75 million U.S. dollars.

With the help of the Constitution, which was effective from 1788, the coalition of affluent individuals successfully took the reins of power for their own best interests and established a stronger centralized state. Only a few years after the Constitution had been ratified, Hamilton quelled a revolt in Pennsylvania which broke out because of the excessive taxes demanded. Northern upper-class merchants and southern plantation owners stated that the decentralized politics initiated by Thomas Jefferson were responsible for the general unrest in some states. Jefferson opposed Hamilton in order to preserve the liberty of the people. He wanted to prevent statesmen from accruing a permanent national debt, believing that it would be the height of immorality for a generation to leave behind immense debts on account of its unbridled consumption.

There were at least two tasks for the new Constitution to fulfill: it needed to authorize the federal government to pay off the national debt in full, and it

---

[117] Charles Austin Beard, *An Economic Interpretation of the Constitution of the United States* (New York City, NY: Macmillan, 1913; New York City, NY: Simon and Schuster, 2012); https://archive.org/details/in.ernet.dli.2015.59388/page/n6

needed to raise a powerful army. This was the only way for the delegates to multiply their wealth. The Virginia delegate, James Madison, drew up the seven articles of the draft Constitution. He took most of the articles from the book *The Spirit of Law* (French: *De l'esprit des lois,* originally spelled *De l'esprit des loix*[118]), published by Montesquieu in Geneva in 1748.

The "Federalists," who would be better termed Nationalists, wanted first and foremost to take executive and judicial control of the federal state and central government. As the wealthy minority, they feared the destitute majority of the population. They therefore turned their attention to the nation's political and economic affairs in order to exploit them for their own advantage, making use of the opportunities offered by the Constitutional Convention to achieve their purposes. This could only have led to a coup, which they saw as the single means of minimizing the democratic rights of the population. The chief motive behind the new Constitution was to stage a counter-revolution against the influence of Classical Liberalism, which had arisen during the American Revolution. The "Federalists," including Robert Morris, Alexander Hamilton, and George Washington, gave the impression that they were striving for a federal state in which individual states would have a large degree of autonomy. In reality, however, they were seeking to prevent decentralization. They therefore opposed the strengthening of the rights of individual states against federal government power. They planned to implement the principles of state-imposed trade regulations, aimed against a free market economy, under the guise of Democracy. They saw this to be the only means of favoring their own economic interests at the disadvantage of the general population. The so-called "Anti-Federalists" criticized the centralization of political power at federal level. When the Constitution was ratified in 1788 – in many respects an ingeniously engineered drama of tyrannical deceit – the "Federalists" had the upper hand. The "Anti-Federalists'" worst fears were realized when an at least theoretically viable Totalitarianism was introduced, which developed over time into a comprehensive centralization of government power in the hands of the wealthy upper class. As a result, American state and economic philosophy changed gradually from a policy guided by democratic principles and liberal trade relations into repressive tyranny.

After Thomas Jefferson was sworn in as the third president of the U.S.A. (1801-1809), he was drawn to the economic principles of the French physician and economist François Quesnay (1694-1774) and his many followers. These believed that value is derived solely from nature, and therefore that land is the only source of a country's wealth. A surplus can only be achieved through agriculture, forestry, mining, and fishing – a teaching known as physiocracy. It encourages free enterprise to be brought to its full potential. There would be little to criticize in Quesnay's economic policy had it been maintained with high moral standards and not, as during the French Revolution,

---

[118] Charles de Secondat, Baron de Montesquieu, *De l'esprit des loix* (Geneve: Chez Barrillot & Fils, 1748).

accompanied by an almost unimaginable amount of pillage and murder. The American president was also aware of the advantages of a capitalist economic policy. Unfortunately, even he failed to maintain the moral standards required to ensure that physiocracy was implemented in the way intended by its French initiator.

It is regrettable that the principles of the free market economy have never been fully applied anywhere, not even in England or the United States. Self-interested exporters, manufacturers, and militarists relied as much as possible on state power to enact measures that would generate high profits, using armed force where necessary. Their aim was to occupy foreign property and penetrate the international markets. Growth in prestige and political importance were welcome by-products. The realization of imperialist objectives was considered essential for the protection of national prosperity.

5.11 Victory in the American-Tripolitan Wars

The American-Tripolitan War of 1801 to 1805, also known as the First Barbary War, was the young United States' first military conflict.[119] A second war against the Islamic powers of North Africa took place in 1815. Although President Thomas Jefferson sought peace, trade, and friendship with all nations and wanted to avoid forming close alliances, he asked for assistance in dealing with the Barbary States when he was inaugurated in 1801. The Barbary Coast consisted of states charged with barbarism from the sixteenth to the early nineteenth century, including the Sultanate of Morocco and the Ottoman regency in Algiers, Tunis, and Tripoli. Their main sources of revenue were privateering and the kidnapping, slave trade, and extortion that accompanied it. Many merchant vessels were captured, their crews detained in miserable prisons for over a decade, and up to one million dollars demanded for their release. As American Ambassador to France and Secretary of State, President Jefferson spent around twenty years trying to reach agreements and pacts with the Barbary pirates in order to end their piracy and demands for tribute money from the trading nations of the Mediterranean. The corsairs (pirates of the Barbary Coast) had long ago convinced Europe's seafaring powers that paying ransom and tribute was cheaper than going to war. America also paid tribute money. Wide appeals were made to persuade the government to put a stop to the raids. The corsairs cited the forty-seventh Surah of the Koran as explanation for their actions: "Whenever you meet those who disbelieve, strike their necks until you have overcome them, then bind them as prisoners. Later either release them or hold them for ransom until the war is over."[120]

---

[119] Joseph Wheelan, *Jefferson's War: America's first War on Terror 1801-1805* (New York City, NY: Carroll & Graf Publishers, 2003) 41; https://archive.org/details/jeffersonswarame-0000whee/page/n5

[120] Cit. in ibid., 41; https://archive.org/details/jeffersonswarame0000whee/page/40

As the high sums demanded were unavailable, America was forced to loan money from Dutch bankers. Jefferson believed that paying tribute to the corsairs would encourage further attacks and drag the country into a financial abyss. When he became president in 1800, the ransom and tribute demanded by the Barbary states amounted to around twenty per cent of the government's annual income. Tired of paying high tributes which still failed to prevent the numerous raids, Congress decided in 1794 to create a navy.

When Jefferson refused to pay a tribute of 225,000 dollars to the Pasha of Tripoli in 1801, the Pasha declared war on America. When a cruiser from Tripoli attacked an American ship, the aggressors surrendered to the better equipped Americans after only a short battle. The corsairs' ship was captured and released shortly after in line with military regulations. In 1802, Jefferson extended America's naval presence in the region. In August and September 1804, the Americans repeatedly attacked Tripoli's naval vessels in the Mediterranean, and the city's high fortifications were also bombed by the American frigate *Constitution*. The climax of the Americans' punitive expedition was the explosion of the fireship *Intrepid* in Tripoli Harbor. Around the same time, the Americans attacked Tripoli on land. On July 4, 1805, Pasha Yusuf signed a peace treaty with the United States after hearing of the conquest of Derna.

However, this agreement had virtually no effect on treaties with the other Barbary States, to which excessive tributes still had to be paid. When the Algerian flagship *Mashuda* was seized in 1815, the defeated Algerians were willing to sign a humbling treaty that included the following terms: cessation of all tribute payments, reimbursement of all captured merchandise to its American owners, liberation of all Christian slaves, considerate treatment of all prisoners of war, and payment of 10,000 U.S. dollars for the release of a Muslim businessman who was being held hostage. The United States thus achieved a victorious ending to the American-Tripolitan wars. However, the final chapter of the piracy of the Barbary States did not take place until 1830, when France sent invasion forces to North Africa to set up a permanent government.

6 The quest for human perfection

In the 1830s, the young generation of American Unitarians (who reject the doctrine of the Trinity and the divinity of Jesus Christ) distanced themselves from the old guard of their preachers who taught that God had created the world but thereafter had no further influence on it (i.e. Deism). The young people joined a movement that aimed to radicalize not only theology but the entirety of American society according to the principles of what was later termed Reform Darwinism (collective or totalitarian Darwinism – a complete rejection of individualistic Social Darwinism). Among there causes were the liberation of slaves, women's rights, abstinence from alcohol, and moral reform. The many reform movements were initiated to counteract dissatisfaction with existing circumstances. Members of religious and academic circles wanted to enable a more humane existence for the many victims of social hardship.[121] In hope of bringing about the millennial reign promised in the Bible, political and social changes were made which resembled anything but an earthly paradise.

Traditional Calvinism was rejected, and the conscious dismissal of Reformation beliefs triggered a change that encouraged the rise of highly diverse spiritual movements. Liberal Unitarianism began to spread. Furthermore, the intellectual climate of the time was governed by English Romanticism (a countermovement to the rational and scientific worldview and to bourgeois lifestyle) and by monistic ideas (i.e. that there is only one basic principle in contrast to the God-man distinction of Dualism). The outbreak of German Idealism (the idea that the physical world exists merely as an object in the consciousness) produced not only Transcendentalism (a mystical philosophy that rejects all authority outside of the individual consciousness), but also Democratism. The common ground lay in the doctrine of human perfection. Progressiveness was understood as a gradually increasing likeness of the human spirit to the pure World Soul.

6.1 Religious character of the democratic state

The secular version of liberty is demonstrated most clearly in Rousseau's theory of the social contract.[122] The Genevan philosopher unequivocally emphasized the development of a Democracy that was based entirely on the attainment of liberty in the state. At the same time, however, his works also showed signs of autocratic Totalitarianism – or at least of democratic Absolutism. Rousseau's introduction of the idea of general will (French: Volonté Générale) was not only a significant departure from Locke's political ideas, but also an important step toward democratic Despotism. The liberty which the Swiss Romantic encouraged his contemporaries to embrace was a completely distorted caricature of the scriptural doctrine of the liberation of man from the dominion of sin, in which man recognizes his responsibility toward the sovereign ruler of heaven and earth in every area of life. Jean-Jacques Rousseau (1712-1778) proposed a more revolutionary theory of sovereignty than any other political scientist. Jean Bodin (1529-1596) defined the state's role as that of a referee arbitrating between two competing groups.

---

[121] Alice Felt Tyler, *Freedom's Ferment: Phases of American Social History to 1860* (Minneapolis, MN: University of Minnesota Press, 1944; New York City, NY: Harper & Row, 1962).

[122] Jean-Jacques Rousseau, *Du contrat social ou Principes du droit politique* (Amsterdam: Marc Michel Rey, 1762). English translation: Jean-Jacques Rousseau, *The Social Contract Or Principles Of Political Right* (London: George Allen And Unwin Limited, 1948; Harmondsworth: Penguin, 1968); https://archive.org/details/socialcontract00rous

In the eyes of Thomas Hobbes (1588-1679), the primary task of the state was to provide a political sphere that enabled individuals to be freed from the constraints of class and religion. Furthermore, he saw the state as key to the formation of a moral consciousness based on individual virtue. Rousseau viewed the state as the greatest manifestation of morality in society. For Rousseau, liberty, morality, and society do not exist outside of the state; state and people are a fundamentally indivisible entity. The result is the combination of radical Individualism with uncompromising Totalitarianism. Rousseau's ideas, no matter how inconsistent they might at first appear, constitute one of the most logical systems of thought in the history of political theory. His passionate defense of the individual stemmed from his resistance to the concrete structuring of society and the demands of civic duties. Rousseau saw the true attainment of liberty in what most people consider to be the worst form of slavery: he saw the power structure of the state as an appropriate means of forcing the individual to be "free." What Rousseau calls liberty is essentially little more than an unquestioning willingness to do what the supposedly omniscient state has ordered as civic duty. It is an interaction of cultural diversity and civil liberties through enforced equality of living conditions for all people. Other intellectuals idealized a similar system in the interests of justice or stability, but Rousseau was first to give it the significance of liberty. It is this that truly distinguishes his theory of sovereignty. Rousseau was the first modern philosopher to recognize the state as a means of resolving conflicts not only among institutions, but also within the individual. The state offered man the possibility of release from religious disputes and from the deceitful hypocrisies of traditional society. Rousseau thus portrays a spiritual haven, formerly provided in Europe by the church. Neither the ideal state structure of his philosophy nor the tremendous influence of his political vision on the following eras can be appreciated without considering the moral and social conditions which he took as his point of departure. He referred to this point as "uncertainty." Like Plato, he recognized that the structure of the absolute state provided the perfect conditions for mediating between liberty and order.

The effect that Jean-Jacques Rousseau's philosophy had on his generation cannot be emphasized too strongly. The elderly Voltaire was dismayed when he realized its impact and enraged at the sheer audacity of the lunatic and charlatan who had betrayed Enlightenment philosophy. Rousseau had shattered the forces of progress. The younger generation, searching for inspiration and direction, had turned from Voltaire to Rousseau. As the spiritual father of the Romantic era, they saw him as the embodiment of the spirit of revolutionary Idealism which would subsequently be manifested not only in Liberalism, but also in Socialism and Anarchism.

From 1749 onward, Rousseau rose as prophet of a new message of salvation, having previously failed to find success as a writer. He had come to believe that the true cause of all evil and misconduct was the injustice and corruption of Christian civilization. Neither sin nor the ignorance of man were to blame. All would work for man's best interests if he followed the divinely-inspired instincts of his own heart. From this point on, Rousseau upheld Romantic Democracy as the highest ideal attainable. He believed that the kingdom of God on earth was constituted by community as a whole and that social justice needed to be instated as the theme and aim of a new way of life. Rousseau saw this not only as the highest principle of a political system, but also as the sacred foundation of a general religious attitude. The revolution that he envisaged was neither political nor economic in nature, but religious. He criticized every part of the prevalent inequality and injustice of the existing social order. Rousseau never considered himself a socialist, despite seeing nothing good in the ideals of capitalist economy. He greatly admired the Republican freedom of Swiss society, which was founded on the principles of Protestantism. Yet he reviled the spirit of bourgeois Individualism more than anyone before and few after him. Rousseau sought to reinterpret Liberalism in terms of religious categories, becoming the founder and prophet of a new faith – the religion of Democracy – and drawing up a new creed.

Contrary to Christian doctrine, Jean-Jacques Rousseau claimed that man is not ruled by the innate depravity of original sin, but is virtuous by nature. The ruin of his virtue is the fault of modern society. The means of turning the situation from bad to good is therefore not confession of wrongdoing in order to avert God's wrath, but rather intellectual education and political reform. Of least help of all, according to Rousseau, is new life through faith in Christ's atoning sacrifice on the cross. The way to happiness is obstructed not by human sin, but by blatant ignorance and hostile environment. For man to find his destiny, he must discover and live according to natural law. Interestingly enough, Enlightenment philosophers such as Voltaire and Johann Gottfried Herder believed that natural law would demand the same ethical behavior as had been cultivated for centuries by the Christian tradition. The Golden Rule was understood as a principle of proper lifestyle that was prescribed by nature.

Combined faith in human virtue and science produced the idea of progress: a secularized version of the Christian doctrine of providence which became the dominant principle of the Age of Enlightenment. Science had finally provided man with the appropriate means of empowerment to perfect human nature and establish a perfect society on earth. In the America of the Founding Fathers as well as in Europe, many people's minds climbed to dizzying heights in their optimism about the future. Confidence in the never-ending effectiveness of progress was the greatest legacy left by the Age of Enlightenment to the nineteenth century.

In 1755, Jean-Jacques Rousseau published a treatise on the origin and foundations of human inequality.[123] Man had climbed step by step from his original, natural position to ever higher spheres of social development. The areas of cultural development that Rousseau particularly emphasized were

---

[123] Jean-Jacques Rousseau, *Discours sur l'origine et les fondements de l'inégalité parmi les hommes* (Amsterdam: Marc Michel Rey, 1755).

mores, the arts, languages, and the sciences. The final stage would be the happiest and most stable era of all. Rousseau's highest goal was to create a political state as quickly as possible in which general will would have full effect.

As conservatives and liberals realized by the early nineteenth century, Rousseau was the real founder of the new Egalitarianism (social equality) that characterizes the centralized national state. Modern political thinking is pervaded by Rousseau's ideological construct more than by any other. No other political scientist can claim remotely so justifiably to be the original source of the social Subjectivism which determines the consciousness of so many people in the West. The characteristic elements of Rousseau's thinking took shape in the worship of the ego and served as the essential inspiration for various schools of thought in education, psychology, literature, philosophy, and the social sciences. The Genevan philosopher's ultimate object of interest was not the emancipated individual within a provisional social order, but the power of the lawmaker over the rest of the population. The vision of religious Democracy projected by his philosophy can be seen in countless theoretical constructs that deal with the natures of humanity and the state. It is empowered by its unique combination of Individualism and Collectivism, leading people to believe that general will is capable of freeing the "ego" from the constraints of society. General will was to be based on the will of the people, who had made it their sacred duty to ensure the freedom of every citizen. Firstly, however, they needed to be purged of every corrupting prejudice inherent in the traditional social order. Nevertheless, the true hallmark of Rousseau's political society is not freedom but equality. This is a form of equality that only exists when every other form of social relationship that could compete with general will has disappeared entirely. The overarching aim of the Swiss visionary's political philosophy was the equality of every individual human being. Only when this was accomplished could the cause of freedom be inserted in the scale of values. It must be remembered that the liberal social order envisaged by Rousseau was completely different to those conceived by John Locke and David Hume. For Rousseau, there was no freedom outside of a fully synchronized political society. The lawmaker needed to exercise a great amount of power to ensure that all citizens stood on equal ground. No person was to differ in the slightest from his fellow man. This could only be achieved if all economic processes were managed by a coordinating body, which would provide a foundation for equality. Equality was to govern relations not only within the economy, but also within the cultural, social, educational, and psychological spheres.

According to Rousseau, inequality had resulted from the establishment of private ownership and the development of technology. The use of tools used primarily in agriculture had been an enormous step backwards to an earlier era. The real reason given by Rousseau for his negative evaluation of both elements was the opportunity that they offered for people to exploit one another. The Swiss visionary gave a detailed explanation of how the degeneration of mankind could be stopped and replaced with continual progress. This could only take place through complete willingness to submit to the dictates of general will. The latter upheld social equality as the highest principle of a perfect society. The idea of equality needed to be applied not only to politics, but also to marriage, family life, and education. Rousseau sided with the individual, the poor, and the common people, opposing society, the rich, and the privileged classes.

Rousseau must be seen as one of the chief prophets of progress, for he contextualized the injustices of the present within a process of development which would fulfil the promise of a coming golden age.[124] He considered nothing to be more important than the ultimate realization of the religious cult of Democracy. Man therefore needed to make a physical effort to achieve the predetermined goal of a perfect society. Many years later, Marx used the same approach to show his party members that he followed in Rousseau's line of tradition. Jean-Jacques Rousseau's political ideas found a hearing in the enlightened circles of the late eighteenth century.

The practical consequences of the ideology of the social contract became most evident when it came to religion. Rousseau knew that a socially independent church would restrict the effectiveness of general will, as would all forms of loyalty to any institution but the state. However, suppression of religious inclinations was impossible: as soon as a society was formed, people depended on a religion that would provide them with a sense of spiritual community. No nation had ever managed to dispense of all religions.[125] However, the religion that citizens venerated needed to identify fully with the values of national life – otherwise it would generate disunity and be harmful to general will. It wasn't enough for religion to produce good people; it also had to produce good citizens. The primary purpose of religion was to serve the social and political aims of the government, above all by promoting the fundamental unity of the state. Christianity can never be the optimal state religion, for it is fixated entirely on the spiritual and preoccupied exclusively with the heavenly; this world is not the Christian's home. In Rousseau's eyes, the greatest virtues of Christianity were evil through and through.[126] He believed that Christian indifference to secular law and national values would destroy the unity essential to the state. The spirit of servility embodied by Christianity would prevent the development of any truly belligerent spirit.[127] Christianity needed to be replaced by another religion on account of its Pacifism, belittlement of the state, and focus on the person rather than the citizen. Its replacement needed to embody the patriotic spirit that the state so

---

[124] Arthur O. Lovejoy, "The Supposed Primitivism of Rousseau's 'Discourse on Inequality,'" *Modern Philology* 21, no. 2 (1923), 165-186; republished in Arthur O. Lovejoy, *Essays in the History of Ideas* (Baltimore, MD: Johns Hopkins Press, 1948) 14-37; https://archive.org/details/essaysinhistoryo00love/page/14

[125] Rousseau, *The Social Contract Or Principles Of Political Right*, book 4, chap. 8, 220-229; https://archive.org/details/in.ernet.dli.2015.203938/page/n233

[126] Ibid., 226; https://archive.org/details/in.ernet.dli.2015.203938/page/n239

[127] Ibid., 225-226; https://archive.org/details/in.ernet.dli.2015.203938/page/n237

urgently required. The ruling sovereign needed to introduce a civil religion and delineate its articles of faith. Although people could not be forced into believing in civil religion, it could banish unbelievers from the state or even punish them by death.[128]

Other religions would be allowed to exist alongside civil religion, provided that they did not obstruct the development of civilization. The sovereign would have the authority to decide whether or not they presented an obstacle. All religions that tolerated others beside themselves would also be tolerated, so long as their teachings contained nothing that opposed the duties of the citizen.[129] Rousseau criticized Christianity for supposedly being incompatible with good citizenship. The Swiss ideologue was never truly serious about maintaining the principle of tolerance when it came to Christians. The articles of faith of civil religion, as stipulated by the sovereign, would serve the primary purpose of cementing the demands of the social contract so firmly that none would dare overstep the line. Rousseau saw the values of Christianity as incompatible with those of the state. He favored a political religion that was fundamentally indistinguishable from state law. Like his ideological predecessor Thomas Hobbes, he understood sin to be the violation of civil law and nothing else. This fact betokens the true nature of civil religion. Its key characteristics, as propounded by Rousseau, are an attitude of respect for the ruling sovereign, loyalty to the state, and renunciation of all personal interests that are contrary to the authority of state law. The symbol of the fatherland is the highest that exists; religion and Patriotism are two sides of the same coin.

6.2 Central tenets of Romantic Democracy

President Andrew Jackson (1767-1845), for a time the Grand Master of the Grand Lodge of Tennessee[130], introduced a new form of Democracy after his election in 1829. It displayed more internal contradictions than there had been in the Republic under previous presidents. The Democratic Party placed the ordinary American citizen, the "man on the street," at the center of the political scene. Since the 1830s, the term "Democracy" has held two different but related meanings for Americans: a Republican and a Romantic meaning. Republican Democracy consists of hotly contested election campaigns, ideological conflicts between parties, and regular trips to the ballot box. On the whole, the outcome depends on which of the various candidates for a political office wins the favor of the majority of voters. Martin Van Buren was the leading ideologist of the Democratic Party which elected Andrew Jackson as

---

[128] Ibid., 227-228; https://archive.org/details/in.ernet.dli.2015.203938/page/n239

[129] Ibid., 229; https://archive.org/details/in.ernet.dli.2015.203938/page/n241

[130] Eugen Lennhoff, Oskar Posner, Dieter A. Binder, eds., *Internationales Freimaurer-Lexikon* (Wien: Amalthea-Verlag; Graz: Akademische Druck- und Verlagsanstalt, 1965; München: Herbig, 2015) 431.

president. He was an experienced politician who personified Republicanism itself and was unaware that in promoting Jackson he assisted a man who would betray his principles after winning the election. By contrast, Romantic Democracy consists of diverse ideas that have come to form an ideological belief with the authority of a state religion – although it is rarely perceived as such. Some of its ideas are as old as Ancient Greece; others are as young as the American nation. However, their combination represents something new in America's political landscape. The assortment of contradictory ideals, all of which stem from different philosophies, is what characterizes America's democratic belief to the present day. The key to understanding the Jacksonian era is the religion of Romantic Democracy: a belief that has become increasingly prevalent in the United States since the mid-nineteenth century. Under President Jackson, Romantic Democracy became the most important religious conviction in America.

During the Progressive Era (1896-1921), Romantic Democracy finally gained uncontested supremacy in all key areas of society, and has maintained it ever more comprehensively and extensively to the present day. Modern Democracy is first and foremost a humanistic religion and has immense power and influence precisely because it is generally portrayed as religiously neutral. It could scarcely have a more ingenious disguise to protect it from its rival faith, Christianity. Under a feigned ideal of secularization that is based on Rousseau's philosophy of equality, it promotes religious values that are the antitheses of biblical doctrine. In the nineteenth century, Rousseau's principle of general will shaped a society that directly contradicted the principles of the original American republic. The radical change in the system of government could not have been more significant. Yet most Americans barely noticed the change or failed to perceive it at all: the Republican government remained unaltered in its outer appearance, retaining elements such as the party system, the presidential elections, and the House of Representatives.

During and after Andrew Jackson's presidency, some aspects of American Romantic Democracy came to differ radically from those of Republican Democracy. The key principle of the new form was a law that allegedly underpinned all standards and institutions of American society. So long as a person complied with its ethical standards, they had the chance to live a good, productive life. Any society that adhered to this principle would be founded on a stable system that would enable the maintenance of law and justice. This idea of universal law permeated American thinking from the mid-nineteenth century. It had two points of origin: the natural law described by Plato in ancient Athens and the moral law that has formed part of Jewish tradition since Moses, later assumed in Christian doctrine in a form revised by Jesus Christ. Natural law would supposedly motivate human beings to practice justice.[131] During the Age of Enlightenment, the Platonic idea of

---

[131] Clinton Rossiter, *Seedtime of the Republic: The origin of the American tradition of political liberty* (New York City, NY: Harcourt, Brace, 1953) chap. 13: 362ff.; https://archive.org/details/seedtimeofrepubl0000ross/page/362

natural law was altered in the philosophy of John Locke, who proceeded from the idea that the Creator of the universe had imbued nature with traces of His intelligence and sense of justice, and that these were discoverable by human reason.[132] Thomas Jefferson intentionally included Locke's idea in the Declaration of Independence, knowing that many colonists were in agreement with it at the time. However, Jefferson's wording of the theory of natural law differed in one respect from Locke's philosophy. John Locke affirmed the individual's natural rights to life, liberty, and property. By "property" he referred to items such as clothing, housing, and the tools which make human life possible. Jefferson, however, replaced this term with "the pursuit of happiness." The political changes that took place from 1776 almost completely abolished the remaining elements of Feudalism in the former colonies. An open class system developed in American cities which contrasted strongly with Europe's rigid social hierarchies. Rather than being trapped in the strict confines of a lower class, as was the case for people in the Old World, citizens of the New World could climb to new social heights on account of virtue and skill.

The second half of the doctrine of universal law concerned theology. The traditional presentation of divine law consisted of the Ten Commandments and the law of love added in the New Testament. Almost all Americans believed that the prerequisite for a moral life was a Christian attitude, which in turn was based on belief in good works. The intellectual offspring of the Enlightenment saw the natural law taught by John Locke and his interpreters as the embodiment of the moral law. Under Romantic Democracy, the principle of individual freedom came to be considered as an absolute value. Throughout the rest of the nineteenth century it was seen to contradict Rousseau's ideas; however, since the twentieth century it has been brought increasingly into alignment with them. The importance of the liberal attitude for Americans in the early nineteenth century is demonstrated by success in giving the vote to all white men from 1815. Universal suffrage gave the levers of government to these free citizens – but women and people of other skin colors were excluded. Responsible citizens behaved according to the universal principle of freedom under the law. They largely balanced the rights and duties of civil liberty in a way that was beneficial to social welfare.

The concept of human virtue led to an optimistic view of the future. Civilized mankind was supposedly on its way to a better world where the principle of individual freedom would be paramount. This principle would enable the individual to be released gradually from the Paternalism of the state, although this would require willingness to keep the moral law more consistently. The corresponding evangelical teaching was the abolition of Old Testament law, which restricted the Christian's freedom of action. Believers would be able to resist sinful tendencies through the Holy Spirit, with the help of the conscience – man's innate ethical compass which determines his moral conduct.

---

[132] Johnson and Graham's Lessee v. William M'Intosh, Wheaton, 543, 572

A further hallmark of Romantic Democracy was the principle of America's worldwide mission. A flourishing culture in which anyone willing to work could enjoy material prosperity would inspire the world to strive for ideal living conditions. The idea of progress expressed by early European and American philosophers corresponded perfectly with Americans' belief that God had determined the United States to set an example to the rest of the world by establishing democratic government. The principle of freedom needed to be spread around the world from one nation to the next. American Democracy would bring true life to all oppressed and impoverished people across the globe. Belief in progress would convince all Americans that Democracy would have the final victory over all other systems of government.[133]

The vision of a world reformed by Democracy was the secular counterpart to the postmillennial expectation of a future heaven on earth. The religious and secular visions of a golden future were not only similar in their concept of an ideal world that would be the grand finale to human history, but were also nurtured by the same hopes. The increase in humanitarian aid was seen as a welcome harbinger of the coming new age. The future appearance of the New Jerusalem was expected without question due to the resounding triumph of Romantic Democracy in America.

From 1815 onward, the growing belief in progress took on a patriotic tone. Many nationalists in both North and South America were filled with confidence in a glorious future. Some Spanish colonies in South America followed the United States' example in taking up arms against the European colonial lords. Revolutionaries took the establishment of people's republics in countries such as Columbia (1821), Venezuela (1821), and Bolivia (1825) as confirmation that the great bloodshed of the struggles for freedom had not been in vain. In comparison with the aristocracy of the European monarchs, who had defeated Emperor Napoleon's military regime, the virtually unlimited possibilities for acquiring wealth in the New World were seen as a clear sign of unrelenting progress. People believed that the United States would soon become a major world power and that many other nations would be inspired to embrace Democracy. A fatalistic attitude spread through government circles, which even considered adopting an aggressive war policy in order to fulfil America's global mission.[134] The United States' economic interests would ultimately lead to the building of an overseas empire under the American flag. An aggressive foreign policy would be beneficial to America's exporting corporations, which hoped to profit from trade concessions exacted from foreign governments at gunpoint by U.S. marines.[135]

---

[133] George Bancroft, *History of the United States from the Discovery of the Continent* (Boston, MA: Little & Brown and Company, 1834-1874; vol. 4: 1863; 7th edition) vol. 4: 5-6; https://archive.org/details/HistoryOfTheUnitedStatesFromTheDiscoveryOfTheAmericanContinent-Vol04GBancroft1863/page/n23

[134] William Henry Seward, *Cong. Globe, 33 Cong., 1 Sess., Senate (June 29, 1954)* (Washington, D.C.: U.S. Govt. Printing Office, 1954) 1566.

[135] Matthew C. Perry, "Remarks of Commodore Perry upon the Expediency of Extending

Disguising their aims in smooth rhetoric, the Americans tried to justify taking military action in order to find new markets, their only true goal being to promote their own economic interests at the expense of other countries. They pointed out the ways in which the spread of Christianity, Democracy, and freedom would supposedly benefit other countries. The eventual effects of progress were also used as a means of making America's imperialist plans appeal to other nations. Believing that the United States was heading for a glorious future, the "man on the street" felt a great sense of inner satisfaction at having contributed an important part to the fulfilment of this vision. The task of each individual was to be faithful in his civic duties.

Nationalism emerged within this historical context as a clear manifestation of Jean-Jacques Rousseau's Romantic Democracy. The nineteenth century brought the first indications that the worship of the state in the West would pose an immense challenge to traditional Christianity. However, it was not until the twentieth and twenty-first centuries that religious worship of the democratic administrative state in different countries became the most hostile rival to Christian worship of the Creator.

After the panic of 1837, frontier settlers' economic problems became far worse still. The annexation of Oregon and Texas thus seemed to offer an opportunity for the impoverished rural population to acquire land. Anyone who took on the hard labor of farming had the chance to find new sources of income. The prospect of an enormous increase in territory under the American flag inspired great Patriotism among the population. The growing number of U.S. citizens who liked the idea of living in a country of unrestricted possibilities was a receptive audience for the warmongering propaganda of the "yellow press". Romantic Democracy had produced the phenomenon of mass media, which was capable of manipulating public opinion to bring it in line with an aggressive foreign policy. As initiator of this new form of Democracy, which was celebrated widely as a type of state religion, Andrew Jackson enjoyed his role as a hero and personified the imperialist spirit of Manifest Destiny more than any other American president before him.

Perhaps the most significant aspect of Romantic Democracy was its radical rejection of Calvinistic beliefs. By the mid-nineteenth century, New Englanders viewed Calvinism as a fossilized relic from a bygone era. They saw it as a theology that no longer had any relevance to the Romantic spirit of the times. The idea of the hero became the highest ideal of the Romantic age. Despite the apparent parallels, the irreconcilable contradictions between democratic religion and Reformation Christianity led to an attack on every doctrine of the Calvinistic understanding of salvation during the nineteenth century. The redemptive work of Jesus Christ was seen merely as an outstanding example of noble self-sacrifice for the good of others, as was obvious to anyone who examined the exceptional character of the carpenter from Nazareth. The doctrine of election, which offers the prospect of heaven

---

Further Encouragement to American Commerce in the East," *Narrative of the Expedition* [...] *to the Cian Seas and Japan* (House Ex. Doc. no. 97, 33 Cong., 2 Sess., II, 177-178).

to only a few saints, was viewed as a futile attempt by a primitive age to explain the reward of those who took religion seriously. The new idea was that all men belong to the great number of the elect on account of their common propensity for self-confidence in life. No one was destined to the awful fate of eternal damnation.

The intention behind the criticism of Calvinism was to destroy the conception of man as God's slave – as a creature that must subject himself unconditionally to the absolute will of God. This objectionable doctrine could not be maintained, for it revealed the offensive nature of Christianity as a feudalistic religion. The Democrats felt that Calvinism denied man his most outstanding characteristic: his self-determining willpower. The most prominent symbol of Romantic Democracy – the granting of voting rights to every free man – was celebrated as humanity's greatest achievement. Average citizens who performed their civic duties as Democrats were not sinners worthy of damnation but guarantors of continual progress. People argued that the individual would be plunged into utter despair if told that he could not save himself from the plight of his own sinfulness. The teaching that man in his evil nature must rely entirely on the grace of God for salvation had become so offensive that it received virtually no support among America's population. Ralph Waldo Emerson said repeatedly that Romantic religion emphasized human virtue, whereas Calvinism emphasized human wickedness. Nothing was more ridiculous than believing that man could no longer live virtuously because of his sinfulness. Romantic Democracy's criticism of the Christian faith was not primarily focused on the doctrine of the sovereignty of God, but rather on the doctrine of man's depravity. The latter was firmly rejected, for the idea of man's permanent inclination to wickedness was incompatible with the idea of increasing human perfection. Furthermore, it was seen as absurd to believe that the precise workings of all historical events are predetermined by divine providence. The idea of an inevitable course of history put man into a stiff corset from which he could not free himself. The prophets of Romantic Democracy stressed the intelligence and honesty of the average citizen, and declared good works to be the foundation and premise of material prosperity. Every person had a duty to believe in themselves and to realize that they were fully capable of following good intentions with good deeds. The divine being was thus none other than man himself.[136] The sovereign power of the Calvinistic God, as proclaimed by Reformed Christians, needed to be discarded as a false teaching before the idea of the divinity of the American citizen could shine in full glory.[137]

---

[136] William Ellery Channing, "Likeness to God," in William Ellery Channing, *The Works of William E. Channing, D.D* (Boston, MA: James Munroe, 1846) vol. 3: 233; https://archive.org/details/worksofwilliamec03inchan/page/232

[137] Ibid., vol. 3: 235; https://archive.org/details/worksofwilliamec03inchan/page/234

6.3 Unitarian ideal of a Christian nation

(Uniting the human and divine spirits)
Many parallels can be found between seventeenth-century Neoplatonism (the belief that the divine is imminent in the material) in Cambridge, England, and nineteenth-century Unitarianism (the rejection of the Trinity and the divinity of Christ) in New England. Their supporters redefined Christianity as an ethical Humanism, although they retained a distinction from atheistic freethinking. Like the Cambridge Platonists, Unitarians upheld tolerance and peace as their highest principles. This worked to their advantage; being seen to promote high moral standards, they were joined by individuals who would have dismissed more radical means of spiritual influence.

Unitarians rejected an authority superior to human reason which could have given them definite, indisputable insights into material and spiritual reality. The goal of communion between the human and divine spirits seemed to be within reach as Neoplatonism was merged with the Christian concept of a God who condescends to humanity. Renaissance humanistic Liberalism, the Enlightenment, and nineteenth-century Rationalism made union between man and the World Soul seem still more easily attainable. A significant development was the publication in 1757 of a book by Samuel Webster, a Harvard-trained preacher, who sought to refute the doctrine of original sin.[138] Jesus Christ was to be honored as a great moral philosopher, but not as the God-Man. Mutual concern for acknowledging the reality of spirit and matter was the reason why the New England Unitarians were drawn to the Cambridge Platonists two hundred years later. At the same time, they also maintained that the spirit is of greater importance than matter. Both groups believed spirit to be the active energy in the universe, and matter to be the passive.

The Unitarian scholar Abiel Abbot Livermore reinterpreted Neoplatonism by combining ancient philosophy with Renaissance Humanism and nineteenth-century humanitarianism in his Postmillennial views. He denounced all forms of slavery and racial oppression as irreconcilable with his spiritual vision of a united humanity.

The Unitarian preacher Orville Dewey (1794-1882; ΦΒΚ[139]) combined Cambridge Platonism with Immanuel Kant's Idealism. He taught that man cannot be certain whether his inner voice is truly the "divine mind" or whether it is only his imagination of it. Either way, man has a duty to pursue the "Highest Good" to the greatest extent possible.

In the years following the American War of Secession (1861-1865), Platonism played a key role in the complex web of Transcendentalist (based

---

[138] Samuel Webster, *A Winter-Evening's Conversation upon the Doctrine of Original Sin* (Boston, MA: Green and Russell, 1757).

[139] Honorary member of the Phi Beta Kappa Society

on German Idealism, a fusion of influences from English Romanticism, mystical ideas, and Indian philosophies) and Christian ideas in scholarly works. Edmund H. Sears wrote the most influential of all Unitarian works on the Neoplatonic natural religion of the soul. He wanted to introduce the contemporary generation of religious liberals to the moral foundations of Christianity which were in line with Neoplatonism. The most critical aspect of Platonism entered Unitarianism through the work of Andrew Preston Peabody, professor of Christian ethics at Harvard University, who taught that divine ideas were the ultimate cause of all material phenomena.

Unitarians believed that the human mind was capable of fully comprehending the goodness of God. Unlike Calvinists, they believed that an essential identity was shared between human reason and the eternal spirit. These ideas were most central to the disagreements between Unitarians and Calvinists. According to Unitarianism, if man truly possesses the "lamp from the Lord" – the "psyche" in the sense of spirit, mind, and reason – and allows it to guide him, he cannot be totally depraved in his nature. The Calvinistic doctrine of divine predestination of the elect for salvation seems arbitrary and immoral to the human sense of justice, and must therefore be false. Passages of Scripture that portray God's wrath and judgment must be interpreted figuratively or analyzed critically in order to arrive at an alternative conclusion.

A further example of Unitarian theology is demonstrated in a sermon preached by James Walker in 1820. He quoted the Cambridge Platonists Henry More and John Smith to support his claim that man has a certain knowledge of the characteristics of the perfect God. Walker's search for an "authentic Mysticism" – one originating in true communion between the soul and its Creator – anticipates the essential reason why Unitarianism later developed into Transcendentalism.

The seventeenth-century Cambridge Platonists encouraged religious practice because they saw it as the only means of helping the individual to maintain harmony between the different faculties of the mind, especially in ruling the conscience and the emotions. Surprisingly few American Unitarians believed otherwise during the nineteenth century. They referred to the proper use of the mental faculties as cultivation of Christian character.[140] Character was perfected through a spirit of devotion; as the Cambridge Platonists had suggested earlier, "The mind is made whole through religion."[141] In stark contrast to Calvinism, classical Unitarianism considered neither grace nor salvation to be supernatural, denying the biblical teaching that they are given exclusively by a sovereign God to those whom He predestinated.

---

[140] Orville Dewey, *The Works of the Rev. Orville Dewey, D.D.* (London: Simms & McIntyre, 1844) 176; https://archive.org/details/worksorvilledew03dewegoog/page/n194

[141] Benjamin Whichcote, "Sermon on Philippians 4:8," in Gerald R. Cragg, ed., *The Cambridge Platonists* (New York City, NY: Oxford University Press, 1968) 68; s. also: Orville Dewey, *Works of Learned Benjamin Whichcote* (Aberdeen: Alexander Thomson, 1751).

In its own way, classical Unitarianism expressed the continual pursuit for Christian Perfectionism[142]: the pursuit of perfection (Lat. "perfectio") and complete freedom from sin, and the belief that this can be achieved either in whole or in part. Unitarians distinguished themselves from Reformed Postmillennialists by promoting a secularized version of the kingdom of God. They wanted to use the education system that was being developed in the nineteenth century in order to pursue their goal of a socialistic utopia.[143]

The Unitarians were joined by a large number of Congregationalists who left their churches during a period of revivalist preaching. Such churches prioritized the autonomy of the individual congregation, rather than being governed by any national committee or order of bishops. Between 1790 and 1850, the so-called Second Great Awakening swept through the United States. Many well-to-do, supposedly upright citizens were offended at being labelled Hell-deserving sinners and subsequently joined the Unitarians. In addition to the New England Congregationalists, the Unitarians recruited followers from the many cult members who had been marginalized within the established Church during the First Great Awakening. The corporate advance of the Unitarian Universalists was particularly noticeable in New England Congregationalism. The stream of conflicting opinions needed to be stopped, and in the face of the widespread heresies, the theologians of Yale College were compelled to take the lead in defending the Christian faith.

The Unitarians' demand for the liberation of slaves corresponded perfectly with the northern Presbyterians' ideal of a Christian nation, the Presbyterian Church having developed out of Calvinism. The Unitarians spearheaded the ideological campaign against slavery, but were less involved in the political agitation for its abolition.[144] Rebellious students from Lane Theological Seminary, who had left their conservative college when forbidden any expression on the subject of slavery, were subsequently admitted to Oberlin College in Ohio, founded in 1833. Oberlin College not only made a public stand against slavery, but also promoted the doctrine of sinless perfection, the Anti-Saloon League, new dietary theories, and other contemporary issues of social reform. The first appointment of a woman to the ministry can also be traced back to Oberlin College and the Holiness Movement. The principal of Oberlin College from 1851 to 1866 was the well-known evangelist Charles G. Finney (1792-1875), who was then an ardent supporter of Perfectionism and Postmillennialism. He impressed on Christians that they had a twofold responsibility – for their own salvation and for the social reformation of the nation as a whole.

---

[142] Robert Leet Patterson, *The Philosophy of William Ellery Channing* (New York City, NY: Bookman Associates, 1952) 64; https://archive.org/details/philosophyofwill00patt/page/64

[143] Ellwood P. Cubberley, *Public Education in the United States* (Boston, MA: Houghton Mifflin, [1919] 1947) 226; https://archive.org/details/in.ernet.dli.2015.203405/page/n261

[144] Bertram Wyatt-Brown, *Lewis Tappan and the Evangelical War Against Slavery* (Cleveland, OH: Case Western Reserve University, 1969); https://archive.org/details/lewistappanevang0000wyat/page/n7

6.4 Idealistic essence of Transcendentalism

(Man glorified by the new religion of Transcendentalism)
The apparently abstract and dispassionate nature of Rationalism was unattractive to anyone searching for a defined and emotional philosophy. This desire was not fulfilled by rationalistic Deism, but by mystical Transcendentalism. New followers of Transcendentalism abandoned their former Unitarianism: the radical theology of Ralph Waldo Emerson (1803-1882) and his group proved to be a more attractive system of religion than Unitarianism for many people, since it stimulated the emotions as well as the mind. Pantheistic tone (the idea that the divine is immanent in all things) of Transcendentalism was attractive to anyone who had lost interest in the "absent" God of Deism. Many Americans were disillusioned with the rationalistic character of German natural religion, which was void of any emotional warmth and passion.

Understanding Transcendentalism requires consideration of its European background. Intellectual revolution had been in full swing since 1800, and German Idealism had spread far beyond the borders of its country of origin. According to this philosophy, the world and existence are governed by idea, spirit, reason, and consciousness, which are physically manifest as matter. German Idealism became the predominant philosophy in both Europe and America, and the Romantic movement particularly attracted the attention of the English and Germans. Having begun with the work of Immanuel Kant, German Idealism reached its climax in the philosophy of Hegel, which provoked a profound revolution in all areas of human thought.

The generations following the Puritans distanced themselves increasingly from the theology of their forefathers. During the nineteenth century, a mystical undercurrent ran through both church and state in America, allowing the ideas of German Idealism to thrive. The theology and philosophy professor Georg Wilhelm Friedrich Hegel (1770-1831) disputed the Christian concept of man's separation from God. He was influenced by the mystic Jakob Böhme, who in turn was influenced by Neoplatonism. In the spirit of the German Romantic movement, Hegel pursued the goal of unifying man and God, virtually identifying man with divine reality as if the nature of one flows freely into that of the other.[145] Hegel did not believe in a supernatural God. Contrary to the teaching that the Son of God became man, Hegel believed that Jesus Christ was a perfect man who became God. He saw no difference between the human and divine natures.[146] According to Hegel, the man-God was unaware of his divine nature at the beginning of history, but over time came to a full knowledge and realization of it.

Hegelian philosophy appears frequently in the writings of the English Romantics and is also noticeable in the works of contemporary American

---

[145] Robert C. Tucker, *Philosophy and Myth in Karl Marx* (Cambridge: Cambridge University Press, 1961) 39.

[146] Ibid., 41.

Transcendentalists such as Whitman, Thoreau, and Emerson. American Transcendentalism is a two-fold construct: it is a product of the intellectual milieu that dominated America at the beginning of the nineteenth century, and it is a reproduction of the philosophical and religious countercurrent that was sweeping through Europe. Transcendentalism rejected the Unitarianism of the earlier generation and did not return to Christian orthodoxy. Through Hegelianism, it distanced itself much further from Calvinism than Deism ever had done despite its humanistic elements. Deism maintained that God had created the world but then had no further influence on it.

The acclaimed historian George Bancroft (ΦBK[147], Porcellian Club) promoted German Idealism among the American population, combining it with national politics. Supporters of the Republican Party believed that America had been appointed to save the world. Evangelicals wrongly believed that the United States was under God's special providence as a "Christian" nation and felt called to bring the paradisaical Millennium to pass. German Idealism rapidly infiltrated American universities. Fundamentalism was gradually adapted to rationalist theology, which eventually evolved into the Protestant Liberalism of the late nineteenth century. Theological seminaries began to incorporate biblical criticism in order to conform to scientific progress and the modern worldview, anxious not to lose all respect in a world that placed its faith in science.

The fear provoked by Transcendentalism among its liberal and conservative opponents was by no means unfounded, for its beliefs were in sympathy with various radical movements which had arisen during Jackson's era (1829-1837). Due to its extensive relationships with Jackson's administration, the movement was able to exert a strong influence on the country's political and social development.

A proper evaluation of American Democracy is only possible if the influence of transcendental thinking is taken into account. The processes of democratic reform would never have gained momentum had they not been driven and guided by Transcendentalism. The general transcendentalist views of God and man and their mutual relationship fitted perfectly with Andrew Jackson's contemporary political framework. Jacksonian Democracy placed the average American, the man in the street, at the center of its vision. It took Transcendentalism as a philosophical basis in order to generate new political, economic, and social relations in the United States. Transcendentalists promoted Hegelianism (German Idealism) and became influential opinion makers in America. As a result of their passionate campaigns, Hegel's idea that freedom can exist only within absolute state control took on great significance in American society. The many reform movements initiated in the years from 1830 to 1870 can also be traced back to the influence of this philosophy. Transcendentalists revived the tradition of the Cambridge Platonists – the deification of the human soul.

---

[147] Member of the Phi Beta Kappa Society, Harvard College, 1819

The novel aspect of Transcendentalism was its rejection of all authority beside that of the individual. Transcendentalism took two elements from the Anglo-American Neoplatonic tradition: an entirely new approach to the human being and also to nature. The individual supposedly discovers the divine "I am" in the depths of his own thoughts. Transcendentalism is primarily a religious philosophy: it was a revolt against the rationalistic Enlightenment of the eighteenth century, against the unending enthusiasm over the many applications of scientific methods, against Deism (the teaching of the withdrawal of God after Creation), Calvinism (the sovereign rule of God over all things), and Sensualism (the attribution of all knowledge to sensory perception). Its objective was to free man from the slavery of reason and nature. Returning to Christian teaching on true knowledge (Epistemology) and ultimate reality (Metaphysics) was out of the question: Transcendentalists strongly opposed them. Deism, with its separation of God and man, was therefore replaced by Pantheistic Metaphysics, which united God and man, as well as God and nature, into a single entity. Emerson believed that every human being is indwelt by a universal spirit of God. Man is therefore above all the incarnation of this spirit. Human knowledge lacks a logical or rational basis, however, and must rely on intuition alone in order to know God.

Transcendental Mysticism opposed Christian doctrine on almost every front.[148] It categorically rejected the church as an institution, seeing the individual as the ultimate authority on what was true or false in religion. It taught that if man looked within himself, he would see the image of God. The natural result of this mentality was religious Subjectivism, which would eventually lead to doctrinal and moral anarchy.

6.5 Transcendentalist attack on Christianity

(Cooperation between God and man to effect social progress)
Rebellion against Christianity enabled Transcendentalists to come much closer to their desired goal of a new system of religion than the Deists and Unitarians had dared.[149] They claimed that Christianity was not the pinnacle of religion, but only an interim stage in the development of man's religious knowledge. Nothing that Jesus Christ either said or did had eternal validity. The highest authority in the realm of religion could be found only in human experience, within man himself, not in any divine revelation outside of the human spirit.[150] This spiritual philosophy is a religion that deifies man[151]; the

---

[148] C. Gregg Singer, *A theological Interpretation of American History* (Philadelphia, PA: Presbyterian and Reformed Publishing Co., 1964) passim.

[149] Ibid.

[150] George Ripley, *Discourses on Philosophy of Religion*, cit. in Percy Miller, ed., *The Transcendentalists: An Anthology* (Cambridge, MA: Harvard University Press, [1950] 2001) 133.

[151] William Ellery Channing, "Likeness to God. Discourse at the Ordination of Rev. F. A. Farley, Providence, Rhode Island, 1828," in *The Complete Works of W. E. Channing, D. D.*

core of Transcendentalism is nothing but pure Humanism. God is understood to have no independent existence outside of human awareness.[152] The transcendentalist conception of the human condition, drawn from Pantheism, led inevitably to the doctrine of the absolute sovereignty of man, whose most prominent characteristics are seen to be goodness and virtue. Man is therefore capable of improving himself continually until he arrives at perfection. His temporary imperfection is neither the result of the Fall nor the effect of original sin, but is due solely to the fact that man has not yet undergone all the stages of development necessary to reach a state of perfection. Anyone with this bright vision and optimism knew and knows no boundaries. Human nature is something truly magnificent on account of the divine spark in man's soul. Transcendentalism was ultimately aimed at the glorification of man.

Transcendentalists exalted the individual and disregarded existing social institutions. For the writer and philosopher Henry David Thoreau (1817-1862), church and state regulations were no longer valid. Many Transcendentalists' expectations seemed entirely paradoxical and less consistent than those of Thoreau. They trusted the state to support them in a radical and comprehensive reformation of American society – yet the state repressed human liberty more than any other institution. Regardless of this fact, Transcendentalists saw it as the only means by which their wildest dreams could come true.

Transcendentalism was never a formally organized movement, although Frederic Hedge, Ralph Waldo Emerson (ΦBK)[153], and George Ripley (ΦBK)[154] founded the Transcendental Club in Boston in 1836 so that they could spread their philosophy more easily. Although Transcendentalism advocated Democracy for the common man and promoted a supposedly idyllic life between the borders of "civilization" and "wilderness," it never managed to win over much of the general public that it claimed to represent. On the contrary, transcendentalist philosophy attracted many intellectuals in New England, which is surprising given the tone of irrationality that pervaded Transcendentalism.

The rise of Transcendentalism was a frontal assault on every form of Christianity. It was most hostile of all to Calvinism, which made a particularly strong defense of the sovereignty of God. Emerson's philosophy was concerned not only with vehement resistance to Christianity, but also with altering the Christian faith so that it complied as much as possible with idealistic philosophy. Although relatively few of its supporters wanted a radical interpretation of metaphysical reality, transcendental philosophy appealed to a large number of people with diverse interests. Its success can be

---

(London: George Routledge, 1870) vol. 4: 230-239.

[152] Cit. in Miller, ed., *The Transcendentalists: An Anthology*, 23; https://archive.org/details/isbn_9781567312157

[153] Member of the Phi Beta Kappa Society, Harvard College, 1828

[154] Member of the Phi Beta Kappa Society, Harvard College, 1823

attributed to the fact that it conformed perfectly to democratic lifestyle during the time of President Andrew Jackson (1829-1837). It played an important role in the social ascent of the "man in the street" and caused tremendous upheaval in diverse areas of society, particularly in Christian circles. It had an enduring influence on the "democratization of American Christianity,"[155] which replaced Calvinistic teaching on the sovereign grace of God and the total depravity of man with a view that emphasized God's love rather than his justice and holiness. This view taught that man was not wholly corrupt and could cooperate with God at least partially in attaining his own salvation. However, the most important millennialist task seemed to be the building of God's kingdom on earth. Man allegedly possessed the abilities needed to fulfill his duty of creating a perfect society. In this way, a school of thought known as "New England Theology" formed among independent Congregational churches. It became known as mediating theology, upholding the majority of Christian doctrines but, like Transcendentalism, rejecting the substitutionary atonement of Jesus Christ, the bondage of the will of man, and justification by faith.

The Revivalist Charles G. Finney was particularly open to transcendentalist influence. This deviation from biblical teaching resulted from the way that Methodist and Baptist Churches and the Disciples of Christ opened themselves up to the democratic trend even before Transcendentalism was fully established. These churches opened the floodgates of their doctrine of salvation to Arminianism – the belief, as discussed before, that man can turn to God by his own will because of the cooperative grace of God. Arminianism is a variant of Catholic Semipelagianism, a teaching which arose in the fifth century A.D. Unlike Pelagius, Semipelagianism maintained the doctrine of original sin, but unlike Augustine and in agreement with Pelagius, it taught that the individual was free to decide his own beliefs and upheld the possibility of salvation for all men. Churches who adopted this position were therefore liable to making further deviations from Reformation Christianity.

The revolutionary character of transcendentalist philosophy found a fitting sphere of activity in the reforms of the Jacksonian era. Among the concerns of these reforms were slavery and civil rights, education and law enforcement, gender relationships, and the upbringing of children. The preservation of peace was another important matter, although there was a tendency to resort to warmongering if it seemed to offer a better opportunity for social reform. A traditional lifestyle shaped by Christian principles needed to be prevented at all costs. Democratic philosophy was used to deify the seemingly average citizen. Although Transcendentalists had a positive view of Anarchism, they did not hold back from exploiting the government to achieve their aims. They would be satisfied with nothing less than a complete transformation of every single area of society. Despite their compromise with

---

[155] Nathan O. Hatch, *The Democratization of American Christianity* (New Haven, CT: Yale University Press, 1989).

state-controlled interventions, they sought the pursuit of individual freedom above all else.

The life-long goal of Ralph Waldo Emerson, the transcendentalists' leading figure, was the spiritual renewal of the whole world. One object of his campaigns was the dissemination of Fourier's utopia. The most popular socialist in America was François Charles Fourier (although he had never set foot in the U.S.A.), and many distinguished citizens in New England and New York were devoted followers of Fourierism. Government officials and army officers took part in the efforts to implement utopian plans. As is usually the case among utopian thinkers, Fourier's wild imagination was mixed with ice-cold calculations of how he could benefit personally from the spread and practice of his philosophy. His fanciful scheme for a new society bore unmistakable signs of insanity. He believed that harmonious coexistence would be achieved where the human passions were given free reign. Any restrictions on lifestyle were unsupported by the French visionary's unstable thinking, which was inspired above all by Jean-Jacques Rousseau.

Albert Brisbane brought Charles Fourier's philosophy to America, spreading it far and wide through itinerant preaching. In 1839, he founded the Fourierist Society in New York. The aim of Brisbane's Fourierism was to bring about progress through social reform.[156]

The transcendentalist ideology implies that progress is inherent in nature. Man, a natural reformer, has a duty to accelerate progress and is able to direct its course through his intelligence. Transcendentalism therefore categorically rejects the Christian belief that the only viable basis for human progress is found in the justification and salvation presented in the Bible. Transcendentalism appeared optimistic in its ardent refutation of the biblical doctrine of sin and its claim that man possesses an inherent goodness. It taught that character could only be corrupted if society and its institutions were too strongly embraced, and that evil in the world would eventually be conquered. Transcendentalists could only come to these conclusions because they did not define the existence of evil in the biblical way, but saw it as a lack of proper understanding. The never-ending pursuit of complete social transformation was not aimed at improving man's situation, but rather at the next step: the personal fulfilment of the reformers. Their highest goal was the recognition of man's status as an integral part of divine reality. Under the inspiration of this philosophy, every social problem could be tackled with the expectation that the spiritually "enlightened" would eventually eradicate everything that was objectionable in American society.[157] Public campaigns were initiated for matters including world peace, women's rights, and

---

[156] Albert Brisbane, *Social Destiny of Man: or Association and reorganization of industry* (Philadelphia, PA: C. F. Stollmeyer, 1840) 92, 95, 199-200; https://archive.org/details/socialde-stinyma00brisgoog/page/n114

[157] William Henry Channing, "Manifesto," *The Western Messenger*, VIII, 108, cit. in Perry Miller, *The American Transcendentalists, their Prose and Poetry* (Garden City, NY: Doubleday, 1957) 430.

prohibition of alcohol production and distribution. The struggle to abolish slavery was given the most attention of all. These campaigns won many evangelicals to the transcendentalist cause, since they believed that God and man needed to cooperate in a mutually supportive partnership in order to effect social progress. The most important condition that enabled cooperation between Transcendentalists and Christians in almost every reform initiative was their common belief in Postmillennialism – the idea that the thousand-year reign would be established before the Second Coming of Jesus Christ.

7 Ideals of America's new age

In the decades following the War of Independence, the vision of a future thousand-year reign was more popular in the U.S.A. than in any other country.[158] Evangelicals across the land were gripped by the vision of a true Christian society that would eventually spread throughout the world.[159] They were convinced that God would gradually build His kingdom of peace and prosperity, and made great efforts to hasten its arrival. Most of the leading Postmillennialists were rationalists who lived in great anticipation of the coming of an immutable society. Despite its underlying paradoxes, their mindset can be partly understood when one considers that their expectations were focused on a future age of paradise. The well-known evangelist and later president of Oberlin College, Charles G. Finney, embraced Scottish Rationalism in the form of Thomas Reid's "Common Sense" philosophy and frequently drew on the symbols and expressions of Postmillennialism.

7.1 Revolutionary effects of religious Patriotism

After the successful end to the War of Independence in 1783, a second revolution began to gather pace before the eyes of the American public. In the late eighteenth century, people became increasingly aware of the immense implications of the founding of the United States of America. Although many Congregationalists and Presbyterians regarded the transformation of the former Thirteen Colonies from constitutional monarchy to democratic social order as a result of anti-Christian godlessness, the majority of the American

---

[158] James W. Davidson, *The Logic and Millennial Thought: Eighteenth Century New England* (New Haven, CT: Yale University Press, 1977); https://archive.org/details/logicofmillennia-0000davi/page/n5; s. also: Robert T. Handy, *A Christian America: Protestant Hopes and Historical Realities* (London: Oxford University Press, 1971); https://archive.org/details/christianamerica0000hand

[159] Ernest R. Sandeen, *The Roots of Fundamentalism: British and American Millenarianism, 1800-1930* (Chicago, IL: University of Chicago Press, 1970) 42-55, 284-289; https://archive.org/details/rootsoffundament0000sand/page/42

population viewed it in a completely different light. In their eyes, the establishment of Republican Democracy as the basis of a new system of government was the best way to initiate an economic upswing.

Alexander Campbell, founder of Bethany College (the training center of the Christian Church, Disciples of Christ), stressed the need for Christians to undergo a process of enlightenment which would play a vital role in bringing the millennium to pass.[160] The new system of government would be instituted through a second revolution. This system would preserve the external form of the republic, but in essence would be radically opposed to it. President Andrew Jackson (1829-1837) had the means to bring about the long-awaited democratic social order as set forth in Rousseau's work *The Social Contract, or Principles of Political Rights*[161] (1762). The idea that America would herald and announce the onset of the millennium[162] was based not only on willing rejection of an apparently outdated Calvinism, but also on the spread of a patriotic national cult. The unique significance of this development stemmed from an understanding of the ideals of civil and religious freedom – central values of the anti-Christian Enlightenment – as the main prophetic signs of the times. Democracy would be the key precursor of the coming millennium. Monarchy and aristocracy needed to be destroyed across the globe through a political revolution. Slowly but surely, American Nationalism began to take on a concrete form.[163]

The assertion of Rousseau's Romantic Democracy as a sacred cause becomes even more significant in light of contemporary events in France and England. In both countries, Liberals made aggressive attacks on Christianity in the name of reason, provoking retaliation from Christians who were skeptical about the celebrated human rights. Those in England and France who upheld Anglican and Catholic values could never support the introduction of a democratic order. In their eyes, it signified godlessness. However, the situation was different in America. Educated citizens saw the formation of a democratic social order as a crucial step toward the thousand-year reign. The Second Great Awakening (1790-1850) was driven by the hope of revivalists, pastors, and theologians that their manifold efforts to spread New Protestantism would help to establish the kingdom of God on earth.

Contemporary historians examine this subject in seeking to understand why the development of the American republic is widely identified with

---

[160] Robert Frederick West, *Alexander Campbell and Natural Religion* (New Haven, CT: Yale University Press, 1948) 168; https://archive.org/details/in.ernet.dli.2015.177842/page/n185; original source: *The Christian Baptist*, vol. 5: 251-252.

[161] Jean-Jacques Rousseau, *Du contrat social ou Principes du droit politique* (Amsterdam: Chez. Marc Michel Rey, 1762); Jean-Jacques Rousseau, *The Social Contract Or Principles Of Political Right* (London: George Allen And Unwin Limited, 1948; Harmondsworth: Penguin, 1968); https://archive.org/details/socialcontract00rous

[162] West, *Alexander Campbell and Natural Religion*, 4; https://archive.org/details/in.ernet.dli.2015.177842/page/n21

[163] Abel M. Sargent, "The Halcyon Itinerary, and True Millennium Messenger" (Marietta, OH: S. Fairlamb; August, 1807), 9.

Christian salvation history. They detect a confluence of two streams of thought which had a lasting influence on the psyche of the American population: an amalgamation of secular Nationalism and pseudo-Christian Postmillennialism.[164] Infused with the religious ideals of the new republic, postmillennial expectation came to form the most important component of nineteenth-century evangelical religiosity, which historians described as the religion of the republic or the American civil religion.[165] Historians agree that from 1830 onward, New Protestantism (New Divinity) reconciled the desired outcome of national determination with the religious concept of a people chosen by God, the nation therefore emerging gradually as the primary agent in God's working of history.[166] There was but a small step between this exaggerated Patriotism and a portrayal of the United States as the world's leading nation for all time.

The multidimensional framework of American civil religion was built on the shaky foundation of congregations split across many different denominations. This contributed significantly to the shift from the biblical understanding of the church as a community of the redeemed to the mystical conception of a nation specially privileged by God, set apart from all other countries as a result of its unique placement. The people as a whole were understood to constitute the "soul of a church"[167]: no single denomination could claim any longer to have sole possession of the truth. As many religious institutions began to reduce their specific beliefs to a common denominator, the American public was encouraged to search for common identity.[168] The ideal means of promoting a sense of commonality among U.S. citizens was glorification of the nation, which was seen as the highest of all values. In the early years of the new republic, rigid denominational boundaries and creeds began to dissolve – and historians consider this the decisive factor in the rise of civil religion. The spread of religious Pluralism forced Presbyterians to

---

[164] Ernest L. Tuveson, *Redeemer Nation: The Idea of America's Millennial Role* (Chicago, IL: University of Chicago, 1968); https://archive.org/details/redeemernation00erne; s. also: Martin E. Marty, *Righteous Empire: The Protestant Experience in American* (New York City, NY: Dial Press, 1970); https://archive.org/details/righteousempirep00mart/page/n7; Robert T. Handy, *A Christian America: Protestant Hopes and Historical Realities* (New York City, NY: Oxford University Press, [1971] 1984); https://archive.org/details/christianamerica00robe/page/n5; Ernest Sandeen, *The Roots of Fundamentalism: British and American Millenarianism, 1800-1930* (Chicago: University of Chicago Press, [1970] 2008); https://archive.org/details/rootsoffundament0000sand/page/n5

[165] Robert M. Bellah, "Civil Religion in America," *Daedalus* 96 (1967), 1-21; Russell E. Richey & Donald G. Jones, *American Civil Religion* (New York City, NY: Harper & Row Publishers, 1974); Henry Warner Bowden, "A Historian's Response to the Concept of American Civil Religion," *Journal of Church and State* 17 (1975), 495-505.

[166] John E. Smylie, "National Ethos and the Church," *Theology Today*, vol. XX, no. 3 (October 1, 1963), 314; https://journals.sagepub.com/doi/abs/10.1177/004057366302000301

[167] Sidney E. Mead, "The Nation with a Soul of a Church," *Church History* 36 (1967), 262; s. also: Sidney E. Mead, *The Lively Experiment: The Shaping of Christianity in America* (New York City, NY: Harper & Row Publishers, [1963] 1987) 62-66.

[168] Mead, "The Nation with a Soul of a Church," 273.

realize, at least to some extent, the ideal of a more inclusive "Christian" community which embraced all people through numerous outreach campaigns.

The contemporary intellectual climate in America was shaped by German Idealism as well as by English Romanticism. Georg Wilhelm Friedrich Hegel stated that the individual was capable of claiming divinity. It was therefore only logical that Calvinism was categorically rejected. The American citizen could grow ever more virtuous on his own terms; he even had a duty to maintain a continual quest for perfection. Since the biblical understanding of Christianity had largely lost its significance and influence in American society, the idea of personal autonomy (free will) prevailed everywhere under the banner of New Protestantism. Puritan Calvinism was replaced by New Divinity, also known as "New Haven Theology" or "Taylorism." Although church historians categorized this theology as moderate Calvinism, closer examination soon reveals that the new teaching bore the hallmarks of an old heresy. It was essentially a radical rejection of the theological system that stands behind the name "John Calvin." Yale College was responsible for spreading New Divinity in the plausible guise of a theology which, in the words of the historian Stephen E. Berk, was an adjustment of "Calvinism to prevailing conditions"[169] of unbelief.

Out of genuine concern for the spiritual welfare of Yale students, most of whom had turned to Deism (the belief that theological statements are legitimized through reason alone, not by the authority of revelation), President Timothy Dwight (1752-1817) began to emphasize the role of man's free will in attaining salvation. Dwight encouraged his students to accept the false teaching of Semipelagianism (a fifth-century doctrine which opposed Pelagius by upholding the teaching of original sin, but which agreed with Pelagius's teaching of free will in believing and upheld the possibility of salvation for all people). Dwight dismissed the doctrine of original sin as an untenable Calvinist theory. Adam's personal guilt, accounted to him by God because of his sin in the Garden of Eden, was never passed down to his descendants.[170] Every individual was responsible for his own sins alone, not for the disobedience of Adam. Dwight promoted the doctrine of "divine constitution," which maintains that sin influences man but is not automatically attributed to him. Man had inherited a tendency to sin from Adam, but it was not inevitable that he would actually sin.[171] Since man's guilt was caused by

---

[169] Stephen E. Berk, *Calvinism Versus Democracy: Timothy Dwight and the origins of American evangelical orthodoxy* (New York City, NY: Archon Books, 1971) 74; https://archive.org/details/calvinismversusd00berk/page/74

[170] Timothy Dwight, "Sermon XXXII: Human Depravity; Derived from Adam," in *Theology: Explained and defended, in a series of sermons*, 4 vols. (New Haven, CT: S. Converse, 1825) vol. 1: 477-488; https://archive.org/details/theologyexplain13dwiggoog/page/n486

[171] Ibid., vol. 1: 479; https://archive.org/details/theologyexplain13dwiggoog/page/n488; s. also: Samuel J. Baird, *A History of the New School* (Philadelphia, PA: Claxton, Remsen & Haffelfinger, 1868) 218; https://archive.org/details/historyofnewscho00bair/page/218

his will, not by his nature, Christ's death had yielded virtue but had not atoned for man's blame before God.[172]

Dwight's successor as president of Yale College was Nathaniel William Taylor (1786-1858). Taylor was widely known for having initiated the New Haven Theology (Taylorism; New Divinity). This teaching sought to 1) refute Unitarianism, 2) combat Old School Presbyterianism, and 3) support the revivalist movement. Taylor claimed that human will had never been tainted by Adam's sin.[173] Man, who had absolute freedom of will, was thus permanently able to decide either for God or against Him. Sin proceeded from unjust actions, not from a depraved nature that every sinner had borne since birth. Taylor was an open advocate of pure Pelagianism. He believed that the doctrine of the bondage of the will would halt the course of Revivalism and offend the average citizen in democratic, freedom-loving America.[174] The gradual modification of Calvinism, which amounted to its radical rejection, can be summarized as follows: Jonathan Edwards, the evangelist of the First Great Awakening, claimed that man had inherited a sinful nature and was capable of nothing but sin; Dwight believed that human nature was only partially corrupt; Taylor now taught that man was capable of committing no sin at all.[175] New Haven Theology prepared the ground in which America's theological Liberalism (Progressivism) took root in the form of the Social Gospel. Many of the 768 graduates who enrolled onto the Yale president's theology courses became leaders in the great rise of liberal thinking.[176] However, the strongest driving force behind the nineteenth-century revivalist movement was the New Divinity: Finney was "Taylor's true successor."[177]

Many Americans were delighted by the idea of living however they wished. President Andrew Jackson stated exuberantly that man was even capable of divinity.[178] He wanted to maintain institutional improvement until

---

[172] John Hannah, "The Doctrine of Original Sin in Postrevolutionary America," *Bibliotheca Sacra* 134 (July-September, 1977), 247.

[173] Nathaniel W. Taylor, "Concio ad Clerum: A Sermon Delivered in the Chapel of Yale College, September 10, 1828." S. also: Baird, *A History of the New School*, 191-192; https://archive.org/details/historyofnewscho00bair/page/190; Frank Hugh Foster, *A Genetic History of New England Theology* (Chicago, IL: University of Chicago Press, 1907) 370; https://archive.org/details/genetichistoryof00fost_0/page/370; Sydney Eckman Ahlstrom, ed., *Theology in America: The Major Protestant Voices from Puritanism to Neo-Orthodoxy* (Indianapolis, IN: Bobbs-Merrill, 1967) 215.

[174] Ahlstrom, ed., *Theology in America*, 212.

[175] Sidney E. Mead, *Nathaniel William Taylor, 1786-1858: A Connecticut Liberal* (Chicago, IL: University of Chicago Press, 1942) 189.

[176] Ibid., 163.

[177] Foster, *A Genetic History of New England Theology*, 453; https://archive.org/details/genetichistoryof00fost_0/page/452

[178] Cit. in Alice Felt Tyler, *Freedom's Ferment: Phases of American Social History from the Colonial Period to the Outbreak of the Civil War* (Minneapolis, MN: University of Minnesota Press, 1944; New York City, NY: Harper & Row, 1962) 22; https://archive.org/details/freedomsferment0000unse_j5b9/page/22; s. also: Dixon Wecter, *The Saga of American Society: A*

Democracy reached such a degree of perfection that the voice of the people could be heard as the voice of God.[179] The New Divinity agreed with Jacksonian Democracy on many points. Romantic belief in the supreme value of the individual came to permeate theology and politics: man was understood to be called to determine his own path, which refuted the Puritan view of man's moral depravity and total dependence on a sovereign God.[180] Finney contributed more than any of his contemporaries to the placement of the "divine individual" at the center of the American state religion introduced by Andrew Jackson, in full awareness of its significance. As a result, Progressivism became a force of supreme importance in the period that followed.[181]

7.2 Propagation of a rationalistic doctrine of self-redemption

In the decades surrounding the turn of the nineteenth century, a theological change took place in America with enormous impact. As paradoxical as it might sound, the First Great Awakening (1739-1743) paved the way for the spread of deistic Enlightenment philosophy in the United States. Following the publication of Thomas Paine's book *The Age of Reason* in 1794, many Americans came to understand the terms "Deism" and "Democracy" as signifying one and the same thing.[182] Their hopes for the future revolved entirely around the introduction of a Republican Democracy. The influence of Calvinism had already declined before the American Revolution, as the doctrine of the predetermination of all events (Determinism) which permeated Jonathan Edwards's teaching was regarded increasingly as theologically untenable and morally objectionable. The idea that God had arbitrarily elected some for salvation and left others to a permanent state of sin had long seemed abhorrent to Americans' acute sense of justice. Counter-reactions were inevitable not only on the rural fringes of society, but also in the higher classes of the urban population. The most significant counter-

---

Record of Social Aspiration, 1607-1937 (New York City, NY: Charles Scribner's Sons, 1937) 100; https://archive.org/details/in.ernet.dli.2015.75585/page/n133.

[179] Tyler, *Freedom's Ferment*, 22; https://archive.org/details/freedomsferment0000unse_j5b9/page/22

[180] William Gerald McLoughlin, Jr., *Modern Revivalism: Charles Grandison Finney to Billy Graham* (New York City, NY: Ronald Press Co., 1959) 21; https://archive.org/details/modern-revivalism0000mclo/page/20: "The second generation, to which Finney belonged, attained manhood in a more settled, prosperous, and confident atmosphere than their parents had faced. Their faith in man's ability to solve life's problems by himself, and their growing optimism about the future, made the pessimistic religion which their parents had found strangely satisfying seem singularly unattractive and unreasonable."

[181] Tyler, *Freedom's Ferment*, 22; https://archive.org/details/freedomsferment0000unse_j5b9/page/22

[182] James K. Hopkins, *Woman to deliver her People: Joanna Southcott and English Millenarianism in an Era of Revolution* (Austin, TX: University Of Texas Press, 2010) passim.

reactions were the Enlightenment, Unitarianism, and Transcendentalism. However, none of these intellectual currents found universal acceptance, as they were opposed by a trinitarian Evangelicalism which was becoming increasingly prominent in the northern states in the early nineteenth century. It was given impetus by two characteristics in particular: advocacy of free will and representation of pietistic beliefs.

Although most history books portray the Second Great Awakening (1790-1850) as an insignificant episode in the United States' social development, it is true to say that it shaped national character more than anything else at the time. It helped the young nation discover its value as a unified community.[183] According to the historian Percy Miller, America was led out of the eighteenth century by neither Jefferson, Madison, nor Monroe, but by Charles G. Finney[184] – the man who embodied the purpose and philosophy of the awakening. News of a rapidly spreading revival was heard everywhere. Many people were gripped by the sensationalism and driven to evangelistic meetings. Emotionally touched by the message they heard, they took their seats on the "anxious benches" and subsequently declared themselves to have been converted. Influential pastors were primarily concerned about protecting the federal unity of the state from the centrifugal forces of skeptical Rationalism and social anarchy. They sought a solution which would not only promote solidarity among Christians, but also ensure national cohesion, and believed that the best means of achieving this was a widespread, effective revivalist movement.[185] The main idea expounded at public meetings was the need for an enthusiastic Patriotism. In contrast to pastors of the previous era, who had steered clear of anti-Christian philosophies, New Protestants aligned themselves with prevalent social sentiments and adapted their message to the spirit of the age. They placed particular importance on two ideas: Romantic optimism and national Idealism. Most pastors fully assented to the national creed and compared the kingdom of God to the American nation. They were unconcerned by the fact that the entire creed was centered around a secular principle. Civil religion merged almost completely with the prevailing Democratism, and nothing was seen to be of greater value than the cult of progress.[186]

Evangelicalism adapted easily to the new nation's democratic position. New Protestants were particularly keen to base their theology on the political

---

[183] Perry Miller, *The Life of the Mind in America: From the Revolution to the Civil War* (New York City, NY: Harcourt, Brace & World, 1965) 71; https://archive.org/details/lifeofmindinamer00mill/page/70; s. also: Ibid., 56; https://archive.org/details/lifeofmindinamer00mill/page/56

[184] Ibid., 9; https://archive.org/details/lifeofmindinamer00mill/page/8

[185] Ibid., 71; https://archive.org/details/lifeofmindinamer00mill/page/70

[186] James F. Maclear, "The Republic and the Millennium," in Elwyn Allen Smith, ed., *The Religion of the Republic* (Philadelphia, PA: Fortress Press, 1971) 196; s. also: George M. Marsden, *The Evangelical. Mind and the New School Presbyterian Experience* (New Haven, CT: Yale University Press, 1970) 239; John R. Bodo, *The Protestant Clergy and Public Issues, 1812-1848* (Princeton, NJ: Princeton University Press, 1956) 251.

principles of Andrew Jackson's Romantic Democracy. A mindset of political and social equality spread through the American population, constantly boasting of its autonomy. Its form of expression was without doubt the revival movement. Revival campaigns were first and foremost a community experience effected by their typical format. Speakers told the crowds that each individual had to lay aside their personal wishes and submit themselves unreservedly to the will of their fellow citizens as a whole.[187] True revival was expected to result in a society that behaved as it ought. The reference to Rousseau's idea of "general will" was unmistakable. The rationalist and mystical movements which broke away from Calvinism and overwhelmed the country before the American War of Secession (1861-1865) led to the formation of a political alliance which had previously been considered impossible. During the course of this intellectual-historical development, Calvinism came to a temporary low point in American society and was replaced by the increasing dominance of Arminianism – the teaching that man has a free will and, with the help of God's quickening grace, can make his own decision to turn to God and follow Jesus Christ.[188]

The popularity of Evangelicalism is evidenced most clearly in the phenomenal success of the revival movement.[189] One reason why Evangelicalism became so eminent was that it shrewdly portrayed itself as a serious representation of Christianity. Finney's treatise *Lectures on Revival* is today considered a key work in America's intellectual history.[190] Evangelicals viewed Christian conversion as an act of the will which was subordinate to the dictates of reason without being influenced by the emotions. They put forward philosophical arguments to defend free will against Calvinistic belief in predestination. Jonathan Edwards had proclaimed this to be the only biblical position; however, according to the New Protestants he was gravely mistaken. This widespread evangelical belief took on the significance and influence of a state religion, characterized by a united, pietist-perfectionist nation, social reforms, missionary zeal, and imperialist Expansionism.[191] Although Evangelicalism rose like a mythological phoenix from the ashes of Puritanism, it initially only stood alongside Methodism but eventually merged with it. The united forces of the rapidly growing New Protestantism generated the Holiness movement in the second half of the nineteenth

---

[187] Miller, *The Life of the Mind in America*, 34-35; https://archive.org/details/lifeofmindinamer00mill/page/34

[188] James H. Moorhead, "The Millennium and the Media," in Leonard I. Sweet, ed., *Communication and Change in American Religious History* (Grand Rapids, MI: William B. Eerdmans, 1993) 216-221.

[189] Miller, *The Life of the Mind in America,* 14; https://archive.org/details/lifeofmindinamer00mill/page/14

[190] Ibid., 9; https://archive.org/details/lifeofmindinamer00mill/page/8

[191] William Gerald McLoughlin, *The American Evangelicals, 1800-1900* (New York City, NY: Harper Torchbooks, 1968) 1.

century, which was eventually established as a denomination in the Pentecostal church.

Many colleges were founded during the first forty years of the nineteenth century in order to meet the growing need for pastors. From then on, evangelical scholars largely exerted their influence in universities. During the nineteenth century, the American college system organized all knowledge, including facts about man, society, and the universe, into one comprehensive system in order to bring secular knowledge and Christian principles into relationship.[192] The best example was the secular defense of freedom, which corresponded to the evangelical emphasis on spiritual renewal. The new educational institutions endorsed the New Protestantism which emphasized man's freedom of will and quest for perfection, and the new generation of pastors consequently took an anti-Calvinistic stance which sooner or later approximated to a liberal position. In most older colleges, professors of philosophy came to the forefront of institutional power, many of them becoming presidents of the establishments.[193] The salient feature of their theology was a radical rejection of Calvinism, which they made out to be scriptural. In their eyes, no teaching was more important than that of the free will. Since it was impossible for them to prove pure Pelagianism from the Bible, they based their arguments on the Scottish Philosophy of Common Sense taught by Thomas Reid and his followers: the idea that what can be recognized by Common Sense equates to reality.[194] Professors of philosophy initiated various reform movements with the intent of radically changing society. They needed to create a clear framework so that a comprehensive revolution could take place in politics, society, and religion. The best way to create the conditions necessary for social change was to support the evangelical revival movement. Oberlin College was one of the key institutions to pursue this strategy under the leadership of Asa Mahan and Charles G. Finney. Finney had already been influencing the evangelistic campaigns for some time by surreptitiously spreading the Philosophy of Common Sense.

Scottish Realism became bound up with the Arminian theology of Evangelicalism. Only in this light is it possible to understand the true significance of the Second Great Awakening (1790-1850), which served the purpose of widely and effectively spreading Romantic Democracy – an anti-Christian state religion. Asa Mahan was successively or simultaneously principal of Oberlin College (1835-1850), Cleveland University (1850-1872), and Adrian College (1859-1873), as well as professor of mental and moral philosophy at each institution. After turning to New Protestantism, he

---

[192] Donald Harvey Meyer, *The Instructed Conscience: The shaping of the American national ethic* (Philadelphia, PA: University of Pennsylvania Press, [1972] 2016) 4; https://archive.org/details/instructedconsci00dona/page/4

[193] Edward H. Madden, *Civil Disobedience and Moral Law in Nineteenth Century America* (Seattle, WA: University of Washington Press, 1968) 5.

[194] Baruch Brodys Introduction of the M.I.T. edition of Thomas Reids *Essays on the Intellectual Powers of Man* (Cambridge, MA: The M.I.T. Press, 1969).

engaged actively in organizing evangelization campaigns. He enjoyed nothing more than generating "revivals" through Finney's methods of evangelization.[195] He underwent the monumental transition from a Calvinistic to an Arminian position in the course of his own theological development. Following his own intuition, Mahan saw clearly that compliance with God's commands to mankind must be central to the Christian's life.[196] The two main dogmas to which he gave most attention until his death were the doctrines of absolute freedom of the will[197] and entire sanctification[198]. He believed that if a man can turn to the grace of God by his own decision, it must also be possible for him to live a sinless life. Having been born to Calvinist parents, he was initially incredulous when first introduced to the idea that man could reach a state of moral and spiritual perfection in this life. However, his troubled conscience was calmed by Jesus's command for the Christian to be perfect. Although this command is scriptural, Mahan arrived at a false conclusion in believing that man can live sinlessly by his own efforts. He also rejected the biblical doctrine of justification, which states that the perfect righteousness of Christ will be attributed to believers.[199] Both Mahan and the revivalist preacher and theologian Charles G. Finney held the same erroneous view that man is able by nature to fulfil any righteous act demanded by God.

Evangelicalism met with wide approval among Americans in the following period, as philosophy professors and theologians deliberately identified it with the Philosophy of Common Sense and as it was spread by revivalist preachers through evangelization campaigns. In order to realize this two-track program, the idea of man's free will had to be emphasized as strongly as possible. All of America's educational institutions were committed to implementing the program, being united by their adherence to Arminianism. Finney integrated fundamental elements of Thomas Reid's rationalistic philosophy and Francis Bacon's empirical scientific methods in his perfectionist teaching of self-redemption.[200] He derived his system of logic from the principles of geometry: just as there are certain axioms (basic principles) in geometry that do not need to be proved, but are considered

---

[195] Aaron Merritt Hills, *Life of Charles G. Finney* (Cincinnati, OH: God's Revivalist, 1902) 231.

[196] Asa Mahan, *Autobiography: Intellectual, Moral and Spiritual* (London: J. Woolner, 1882) 50-51, 357, 375, passim; https://archive.org/details/autobiographyin00mahagoog/page/n65

[197] Ibid., 208; https://archive.org/details/autobiographyin00mahagoog/page/n223

[198] Ibid., 321, passim; https://archive.org/details/autobiographyin00mahagoog/page/n337

[199] Ibid., 292-294, passim; https://archive.org/details/autobiographyin00mahagoog/page/n309

[200] John Leroy Gresham, *Charles G. Finney's Doctrine of the Baptism of the Holy Spirit* (Peabody, MA: Hendrickson, 1987) 5; s. also: David C. Weddle, *The Law as Gospel: Revival and Reform in the Theology of Charles G. Finney* (Metuchen, NJ: Scarecrow, 1985) 2-3; Mark Noll, ed., *The Princeton Theology 1812-1921* (Grand Rapids, MI: Baker, 1983) 35; William Gerald McLoughlin, *Modern Revivalism: Charles Grandison Finney to Billy Graham* (New Haven, CT: Yale University Press, [1984] 1994) 69; https://archive.org/details/modernrevivalism00mclo/page/69

self-evident, so also in moral philosophy.[201] Finney was interested in the Common Sense Method because of its applicability to moral philosophy, theology, and ethics. He saw its usefulness for understanding the psychological, philosophical, theological, ethical, and practical facts which constitute the natural law which supposedly governs the relationship between God and man. Through numerous large-scale revival campaigns, Finney introduced his listeners to Scottish Realism and English Baconism. He was particularly adept at wording his message of self and world improvement in a way that was received with enthusiasm by contemporary audiences in North America. The Philosophy of Common Sense invariably resulted in some kind of natural theology. National wellbeing was seen to depend on the extent of genuine piety among citizens[202], while the true purpose of evangelization was supposedly the salvation of souls from a meaningless existence rather than eternal life in heaven. Nothing was of greater importance to the principal proponents of the New Divinity – Nathaniel W. Taylor, Asa Mahan, and Charles G. Finney.[203]

7.3 The sociopolitical impact of Postmillennialism

Charles Grandison Finney (1792-1875), a nominal Presbyterian and for some time a Freemason, converted to the New Protestantism of Yale theologian Nathaniel W. Taylor in 1821, when he was twenty-nine years old.[204] From then on, Finney was a dedicated preacher of the New Divinity. His life was a perfect demonstration of the ideals of Protestant Postmillennialism, which urged all Christians to unite in the supposedly admirable task of building God's kingdom on earth. In his character, Finney was the epitome of a typical

---

[201] Thomas Reid, *Essays on the Intellectual Powers of Man, to which are added, An essay on quantity, and An analysis of Aristotle's logic* (London: Thomas Tegg, [1785] 1827) 69-70; https://archive.org/details/cu31924029079759/page/n87; s. also: Theodore Dwight Bozeman, *Protestants in an Age of Science: The Baconian ideal and antebellum American religious thought* (Chapel Hill, NC: University of North Carolina Press, 2012) 14.

[202] Bozeman, *Protestants in an Age of Science*, 61-62.

[203] Douglas A. Sweeney, *Nathaniel Taylor, New Haven Theology, and the Legacy of Jonathan Edwards* (New York City, NY: Oxford University Press, 2003) 62.

[204] James Harris Fairchild, *Reminiscences of Rev. Charles G. Finney: Speeches and Sketches at the Gathering of His Friends and Pupils, in Oberlin, July 28, 1876, Together With President Fairchild's Memorial Sermon, Delivered Before the Graduating Classes, July 30, 1876* (Oberlin, OH: E. J. Goodrich, 1876) 49; https://archive.org/details/reminiscencesofr00fair/page/48; s. also: George Frederick Wright, *Charles Grandison Finney* (Boston, MA: Houghton Mifflin Co., 1891) 179; https://archive.org/details/charlesgrandison00wrig/page/178; Sidney E. Mead, *Nathaniel William Taylor, 1786-1858: A Connecticut Liberal* (Chicago, IL: University of Chicago Press, 1942) 167; https://archive.org/details/nathanielwilliam00mead/page/166; William Gerald McLoughlin, *Modern Revivalism: Charles Grandison Finney to Billy Graham* (New York City, NY: Ronald Press Co., 1959; New Haven, CT: Yale University Press, [1984] 1994) 45-47; https://archive.org/details/modernrevivalism00mclo/page/45; David L. Hollon, "Love as Holiness: An Examination of Charles G. Finney's Theology of Sanctification, 1830-1860," (Ph.D. diss., Southern Baptist Theological Seminary, 1984) 50-52.

Yankee. He worked harder than anyone to facilitate the acceptance of New Protestantism in America. However, from the perspective of Reformation Christianity, his emergence into the public spotlight had only negative consequences.

As a young man, Charles began attending Calvinistic Congregationalist services in Warren, Connecticut, at the invitation of his uncle with whom he lived for four years. However, he was greatly offended by their insistence on the sovereignty and grace of God. When he returned home, he lost interest in Christianity but joined the Freemasons[205] from 1816 to 1824 in order to satisfy his need for religiosity. After finishing his law studies, Charles G. Finney worked as a clerk in the office of Judge Benjamin Wright in Adams, New York.[206] While walking in the woods one day in 1821, he had a mystical experience in which his mind was suddenly taken over by an overwhelming vision. For an hour he was under the spell of a spiritual force which put him into a kind of trance. The emotional intensity of the experience was so strong that he ascribed his success as a preacher to this "baptism of the Holy Spirit" for the rest of his life.

Finney was denied a place to study theology at a renowned Presbyterian seminary and reacted adversely to the theological schooling that he received instead from Pastor George W. Gale. He was concerned only with pragmatic implementation of theological concepts in order to "Christianize" more of the population, believing that he was called first and foremost to establish a new religious community. The "revival movement," which was led largely by Finney, eventually resulted in entire areas of western New York being "scorched" with the fire of revival, consequently becoming known as the "Burned-Over District."[207]

After his ordination in 1824, Finney commenced a preaching career which gained him the title of "father of the modern revival movement." His religious understanding was clearly founded on legal principles. As an evangelist, his manner of speaking resembled that of a defense lawyer seeking to convince the jury of his client's innocence in the courtroom. The budding revivalist followed his inner voice and began organizing public evangelization meetings in the northern areas of New York State. They saw immediate success. Finney was convinced that the best approach to evangelization was a practical one that aimed to elicit affirmative responses from the audience through fiery preaching and additional resources. He consequently rejected Calvinistic theology and its emphasis on the sovereign work of God in the

---

[205] A photo of Charles G. Finney as a freemason: https://dirvinish.files.wordpress.com/2013/03/finney-charles-05.jpg

[206] Sydney Eckman Ahlstrom, "Theology in America: A Historical Survey," in James W. Smith & A. Leland Jamison, ed., *Religion in American Life* (Princeton, NJ: Princeton University Press, 1961) vol. 1: 251-271.

[207] Whitney R. Cross, *The Burned-Over District: The Social and Intellectual History of Enthusiastic Religion in Western New York, 1800-1850* (New York City, NY: Harper Torchbooks, 1965); https://archive.org/details/burnedoverdistri00cros/page/n5

lives of the elect. Finney followed the example of many ministers in New England who were well aware of the dangers of excessive Emotionalism, but who were unable to resist stirring up the emotions of their listeners.

Since Finney rejected the traditional view of revival as supernatural intervention by God[208], it was up to revivalists to incite spiritual enthusiasm by their own skill. Regular spiritual activities in local churches, such as preaching and prayer, were considered insufficient to sustain interest over extended periods of time. Churches therefore made use of travelling revivalists who could conduct emotionally charged evangelistic meetings. The sole aim of such meetings was to arouse mystical ecstasy among those present, stirring up their emotions so that their behavior could be manipulated. Finney tried to use gestures and expressions that would produce optimum emotional responses, and many Methodists consequently imitated the approach of their role model and mentor.[209] The new methods introduced by Finney (the "New Measures") were characterized by a direct, confrontational manner of preaching. The most important aspect was the so-called "protracted meeting" – an evangelistic event typically held each evening for several weeks. The most well-known feature of these events was the "anxious seat" at the very front of the tent. People willing to convert would sit on the bench and publicly express what was on their minds. This method eventually led to the altar call (an invitation to conversion), which was directed at anyone who "wanted to decide for Jesus."

Finney sent colleagues ahead to drum up interest before arriving at any venue. His mission could only be guaranteed success through mass attendance at his meetings. He copied the tactics of travelling circuses, similarly making use of a large tent. Before any campaign, Finney found out about notorious villains in the area and prayed for their wayward souls at the meetings. If any of them turned up at the tent, he would invite them to stand up and declare their penitence before all present. The dramatic effect left people spellbound. Finney would then pray for local pastors who wanted to put an end to what they considered "godless events" and who were dismissive of the revivalist movement in general. Through his provocative choice of words, Finney suggested that they were even still in need of spiritual conversion.

Revivalists became increasingly involved in healing the sick. Prayer over invalids was rarely made through belief in supernatural intervention, but through faith in the effects of natural healing powers. Travelling preachers focused on improving the theatrics of their preaching style, often in ways that were unseemly.[210] Power of persuasion was seen as the vital key to successful evangelization and social reform. Finney's preaching was based on the principle that all men were responsible for their own salvation, which would take place at an emotionally charged moment of new birth. He taught that the

---

[208] Ibid., 199; https://archive.org/details/burnedoverdistri00cros/page/198

[209] Ibid., 175; https://archive.org/details/burnedoverdistri00cros/page/174

[210] Ibid.

gates of Heaven stood open to all, and that every person therefore needed to win as many souls to the Gospel as possible. People's efforts to bring others to salvation sprang from deep fear of not otherwise escaping Hell themselves. However, every Christian was faced with the fact that they could never do enough to prevent others from sinning. As a result, people came to believe that ultimately only the state was capable of stamping out sinful tendencies and establishing a New Jerusalem on earth.

Finney's revival campaigns sowed seeds of discord wherever their influence was felt. This is ironic considering that the primary criticism levelled at Calvinistic ministers who upheld the creeds was that they provoked disputes. In reality, the fanaticism surrounding the revival movement caused trouble far more quickly than did the much-criticized Calvinism. Before the War of Secession began in 1861, it was considered improper and undignified for women to speak in public; however, revivalists and cult leaders granted women greater personal involvement. Presbyterian church leaders of the New School, and even some of the Old, were increasingly supportive of the new methods. Outward success was interpreted as evidence of divine blessing.

What was missing at these meetings was systematic teaching in Christian doctrine and continuous exposition from the books of the Bible. The artificial enthusiasm could not be maintained at the same intensity over a long period of time. People influenced by this type of spirituality either remained caught up in a pseudo-Christianity that deviated from biblical teaching or turned to an anti-Christian spirituality[211] in order to experience fresh surges of emotion.[212] Yankees wanting emotionally charged experiences joined the Social Gospel movement, adopted the historical-critical method of Bible study, and encouraged the reform initiatives of Progressivism.[213] This eventually led to the emergence of a vast number of cults with wildly different religious views, including the Shakers[214], Mormons[215], Adventists[216], Spiritists[217], and Perfectionists[218] among other utopian societies[219]. Finney's revival campaigns, which supposedly aimed to lead many people to the Christian faith, led to a total destruction of Christianity in western New York State which eventually spread to many other parts of the world. The Burned-Over District should be a constant reminder of what can happen if the

---

[211] Ibid., 184; https://archive.org/details/burnedoverdistri00cros/page/184

[212] Ibid., 257, 284; https://archive.org/details/burnedoverdistri00cros/page/256

[213] Ibid., 278; https://archive.org/details/burnedoverdistri00cros/page/278

[214] Ibid., 30-32; https://archive.org/details/burnedoverdistri00cros/page/30

[215] Ibid., 114, 138-150; https://archive.org/details/burnedoverdistri00cros/page/114

[216] Ibid., 287-321; https://archive.org/details/burnedoverdistri00cros/page/286

[217] Ibid. 30-32; https://archive.org/details/burnedoverdistri0000unse/page/30

[218] Ibid., 238-252; https://archive.org/details/burnedoverdistri00cros/page/238

[219] Ibid., 322-340; https://archive.org/details/burnedoverdistri00cros/page/322

authority of God's Word is rejected in favor of a never-ending search for rousing emotional experiences.

Like many revivalists, Charles G. Finney took the Postmillennial position on the thousand-year reign. The expectation of a gradually dawning millennium was based on the idea that man was in a continual process of advance, in accordance with the popular idea of progress. Radical social reform was high on Finney's list of priorities. He interpreted the few Bible passages that mention the thousand-year reign according to his own preconceived views. He took single verses out of context and paid no attention to their precise wording, while continuing to insist that biblical revelation was his final authority. The evangelical movement eagerly looked forward to having boundless opportunities to spread Christianity – as they understood it – throughout the entire land. Although Oberlin College's definition of the millennium did not state that conditions on earth would become those of utopia, it nonetheless reflected a hope that the world would continue to get gradually better and better. Oberlin's professors and students were excited by the prospect of a world in which politics, society, and private life would be filled with the Spirit of God, in which peace would reign among people who knew and obeyed the truth, and in which most of the earth's population would live holy, devout lives. They were confident that the objectives of social reform would succeed wherever it was implemented.

The millennialist view became a guiding principle which steered all philosophical, dogmatic, and reformist efforts in a certain direction. Postmillennialism took on a life of its own as the shared hope of a whole society. Since it never had a clear conceptual definition, it was able to reinvent itself over and over again and thus maintain its preeminence for another six decades. Studying the revivalist movement of the 1830s is key to understanding the origin and consequences of the civil religion of New Protestantism, which came to shape American political thought. Finney believed that the millennium would dawn as soon as adherents to the New Divinity multiplied through evangelization campaigns and consequently engaged in comprehensive social reforms. He imagined the thousand-year reign as an age of humanitarian work. Like movers and shakers supercharging their activities with moral laws, people could hasten the arrival of the kingdom of God through active philanthropy. Only stubborn selfishness could stand in the way. Motivated by Enlightenment belief in progress, particularly in terms of improved social order, Finney encouraged his contemporaries to apply themselves to the moral challenges present in American society. He saw the value of mass meetings not only for spreading New Protestantism but also for increased social action. His eight-year campaign (1824-1832) for a "sanctified" social order represented the peak of the popularity of Postmillennialism in America. Spurred on by Finney's optimism, many U.S. citizens supported charities working for the abolition of slavery and the introduction of prohibition (laws against the consumption of alcohol) among other causes. In the years between his first revival campaign in Evans Mills, New York (1824) and his call to the pastorate of Chatham Street Chapel in New York

City (1832) – the period during which he was most active as an evangelist – Finney succeeded in motivating thousands of New Yorkers to participate in revival campaigns and social reforms. Finney believed that he could draw a line of connection between evangelization and social reform based on an unbiblical interpretation of Revelation 20:4-6. Evangelists saw America as the future center of a universe governed by God. The entire American population would willingly submit to divine authority as obedient subjects. They would be led by the light of the "eternal law of charity". Finney stated that Christians had a responsibility to scale the walls of Satan's fortress and cleanse society from its sins. Corruption and deception would be defeated, business practices would be reformed, and slavery would be abolished. With his typical optimism, Finney prophesied that these glorious conditions would soon be achieved. The millennium would appear soon after, if Christians were of one mind and were united in taking the necessary steps for global social reformation.[220]

In contrast to the Calvinistic teaching that man is incapable of saving himself, Finney came to believe that man can indeed effect his own salvation with or without the help of God. It was therefore only logical that many of his followers took part in various social reforms in order to fulfil the duties assigned to them. Most popular of all was participation in the charitable organizations which were springing up in every corner.[221] Finney spread a millennialist ideology which helped unite the work of existing charities in a comprehensive campaign for social action.[222]

One cause overarched all other activities: the need for all Christians to hasten the arrival of the kingdom of God on earth. To this end, many New Protestants joined charities which were originally founded to support those afflicted with illnesses or other forms of suffering.[223] This elicited a great upswing for the reform movement inspired by Finney's preaching. People now also worked for the rights of slaves, gave women new opportunities for political and social agendas, promoted abstinence from alcohol, offered further education, improved the care of injured or crippled stagecoach drivers, and put pressure on politicians to ban the delivery of mail on Sundays.

---

[220] Charles G. Finney, *Lectures on Revivals of Religion*, 2nd ed. (New York City, NY: Fleming H. Revell Co., [1835] 1868) 290; https://archive.org/details/lecturesonreviva00finn/page/290

[221] Lefferts A. Loetscher, "The Problem of Christian Unity in Early 19th Century America," *Church History* 32 (March, 1963), 3-16.

[222] Finney, *Lectures on Revivals of Religion*, 289-290 https://archive.org/details/lectureson-reviva00finn/page/288

[223] William F. Peck, *History of Rochester and Monroe County, New York* (New York City, NY: The Pioneer Publishing Company, 1908) 212-217; https://archive.org/details/bub_gb_IvssAAAAYAAJ/page/n201

7.4 Pelagian undertones of the revival movement

(Revivalists preach a doctrine of self-redemption)

When Charles G. Finney was appointed professor of theology at Oberlin College in 1835, he was already well-known for his revival campaigns and his teaching of New School Presbyterianism. He immediately began to write up his theology lectures on paper with the help of other professors at Oberlin. His resulting textbook, *Lectures on Systematic Theology*[224], has remained in print to the present day and conveys the essence of his doctrine through its call for moral reformation. Finney taught that the fundamental aspect of Christianity was a continual quest for moral improvement, echoing the Anglo-Saxon Masonic motto of "making good men better."[225] Charles Hodge, professor of theology at Princeton Theological Seminary and one of the foremost representatives of the Old School, criticized Finney's central idea that moral obligation and free will are fundamental to the Christian life. Hodge regarded his New Divinity as an entirely errant conception of the Christian faith.[226] Finney was seeking to remodel the New Divinity as a variant of Deism, so that it would be taken seriously by the enlightened age. Although historians classified Finney as an important figure[227], this does not necessarily mean that he had their admiration. They merely noted that his great intellect enabled him to make an extraordinary social impact. However, a considerable number agree with the church historian John H. Gerstner who described Finney as "the greatest enemy to Evangelicalism of the nineteenth

---

[224] Charles G. Finney, *Lectures on Systematic Theology* (New York City, NY: George H. Doran, 1878; 2nd edition) xii; https://archive.org/details/cu31924010376030/page/n21

[225] "How Freemasonry Makes Men (& Society) Better: Making good men better is to extract the essence of the Masonic experience. The ritual and ceremony serve to convey and teach certain moral lessons and elevate the individuals to a position higher than themselves. The lessons are things you have likely already heard or have learned in a moral society. [...] We have met numerous men who have truly touched our hearts in many ways. We have learned through their example to be more compassionate, more understanding, more forgiving, more sincere, and above all, more loving. [...] Masonry strives to teach its members that it would be great if we could convey this message throughout the whole world in ways we would have never thought possible. [...] We are also taught to have benevolent goodwill toward, or love, for humanity and be lenient in our judgment of others. This Most Benevolent Brotherhood Has Men of Good Character." https://masonicfind.com/how-did-the-freemasons-contribute-to-society

[226] Charles Hodge, "Finney's Lectures on Theology," *Biblical Repertory and Princeton Review*, XIX (April, 1847), 237-277; s. also: George Frederick Wright, *Charles Grandison Finney* (Boston, MA: Houghton Mifflin Co., 1891) 208-209; https://archive.org/details/charlesgrandison00wrig/page/208

[227] Sydney Eckman Ahlstrom, *A Religious History of the American People* (New Haven, CT: Yale University Press, 1972; Garden City, NY: Image Books, 1975) vol. 1: 558; https://archive.org/details/religioushistory01ahls/page/558; s. also: Richard Hofstadter, *Anti-Intellectualism in American Life* (New York City, NY: Alfred A. Knopf, [1962] 1966) 92; https://archive.org/details/richard-hofstadter-anti-intellectualism-in-american-life-vintage-1966/page/91; Frank Hugh Foster, *A Genetic History of New England Theology* (Chicago, IL: University of Chicago Press, 1907) 453; https://archive.org/details/genetichistoryof00fost_0/page/452

century."[228] There are only two conflicting views on Finney's theology: it is either regarded as wholly consistent with biblical truth, or it is labelled as a rigid, prescriptive moral system from which God can be entirely excluded without any substantial change to its essence.[229] What follows is an explanation of why only one of these perspectives reflects the truth of the matter.

The theology which Charles G. Finney presented to countless people in the Northeastern United States stemmed from the late eighteenth-century teaching of the New Divinity.[230] The latter was a modified form of the New England Theology taught originally by Jonathan Edwards. After Finney decided to take up a career as a preacher, he commenced intensive theological studies under the guidance of Pastor George W. Gale. He rejected the Calvinistic doctrines of Old School Presbyterianism held by Gale from the outset, relying primarily on the inspiration of his own reason which, he believed, revealed to him the true meaning of biblical doctrines.[231] He was far more convinced by Pelagian belief in self-redemption[232] than by the Reformation teaching of salvation by the grace of God. According to Pelagianism, human nature is uncorrupted by original sin; since it was created by God, it must be good. Finney often spoke of an ultimate "intelligence" (or "mind," "law," or "principle") that underlies the universe, to which even God Himself has to submit. He had an almost psychotic hatred of Calvinism[233]

---

[228] John Henry Gerstner, "Theological Boundaries: The Reformed Perspective," in David F. Wells, John Woodbridge, eds., *The Evangelicals: What They Believe, Who They are, Where They are Changing* (Grand Rapids, MI: Baker, 1977) 27.

[229] Benjamin B. Warfield, *Perfectionism* (New York City, NY: Oxford University Press, 1931; Grand Rapids, MI: Baker, [1932] 2003) vol. 2: 193; s. also: Hodge, "Finney's Lectures on Theology," *The Biblical Repertory and Princeton Review*, XIX, 237-277; John D. Hannah, "The Doctrine of Original Sin in Postrevolutionary America," *Bibliotheca Sacra* 134:535 (July, 1977), *238-256.*

[230] Whitney R. Cross, *The Burned-Over District: The Social and Intellectual History of Enthusiastic Religion in Western New York, 1800-1850* (New York City, NY: Harper Torchbooks, [1950] 1965) 160; https://archive.org/details/burnedoverdistri00cros/page/160.

[231] Charles G. Finney, *Memoirs of Rev. Charles G. Finney* (New York City, NY: A. S. Barnes & Company, 1876) 54; https://archive.org/details/memoirsofrevchar1876finn/page/54: "Now I could not deny that there was a good deal of force in this; but still I found myself utterly unable to accept those doctrines as mere dogmas, I could not do it. I could not be honest in doing it; I could not respect myself in doing it. Often when I left Mr. Gale, I would go to my room and spend a long time on my knees over my Bible. [...] I had no where [sic.] to go but directly to the Bible, and to the philosophy or workings of my own mind, as revealed in consciousness."

[232] Benjamin B. Warfield, *Princeton Theological Review*, XIX (January, 1921), 17: "Finney's thought was not merely into the general mold of Pelagianism, but into the special mold of the particular mode of stating Pelagianism which had been worked out by N. W. Taylor."

[233] Finney, *Memoirs of Rev. Charles G. Finney*, 7, 59, 368-369; https://archive.org/details/memoirsofrevchar1876finn/page/6: "As soon as I learned what were the unambiguous teachings of the confession of faith [Westminster Confession] upon these points, I did not hesitate on all suitable occasions to declare my dissent from them. I repudiated and exposed them. Wherever I found that any class of persons were hidden behind these dogmas, I did not hesitate to demolish them, to the best of my ability." (p. 59)

since it supposedly led to a fatalistic outlook on life. Calvinism taught that man was incapable of doing anything himself except waiting for God to save him – but even this would never happen were it contrary to divine will. No one could know whether they were among the elect in whom alone the Holy Spirit would effect the work of salvation. Finney never came to realize that this view of Calvinism was a distorted caricature of what was really taught by the Genevan reformer.

As a young theology student in Adams, New York, Finney embraced "Taylorism" (New Divinity) as soon as he was introduced to it.[234] Gale sought to explain the articles of the Westminster Confession to his protégé, but fought a losing battle against the influence of the New Divinity. In his few months of formal theological studies, Finney flatly refused to read the Presbyterian statement of faith.[235] His consequent lack of reference to the Bible is particularly evident in the *Lectures on Systematic Theology*, in which many of his statements have no biblical foundation or reasoning. His theology was derived from philosophical principles rather than the Holy Scriptures. In the forward to his theological book, he wrote the following: "What I have said on 'Moral Law' and on the 'Foundations of Moral Obligation' is the key to the whole subject."[236] He spent a long time seeking to establish the extent to which man is capable of keeping God's commandments on his own terms, and his eventual answer essentially came to form the basis of his entire theology. Reformed theology maintains that man is incapable of obeying God by his own efforts. Finney argued that if that were the case, man could not be blamed for what he was incapable of doing. He was convinced that the linchpin of his theological beliefs was the sinner's guilt before God, precisely because man sins willingly despite supposedly being able to obey God at all times.

The doctrine of the moral government of God became a central part of Finney's theology, as he insisted that this Arminian conception of the atonement was the truth. The main idea was that God had divided the world into two categories: the physical and the moral. God's moral government was primarily concerned with man's inner motivations, as the Almighty used His own will to influence the "minds of intelligent creatures."[237] The latter would then live in a way that glorified Him to the highest degree. God was perfectly justified in condemning sinners as the just ruler of a moral system of government, but He was also able to forgive sinners instantly if they turned to Him. He was certainly no hard-hearted, uncompromising tyrant who had

---

[234] Frank Hugh Foster, *A Genetic History of New England Theology* (Chicago, IL: University of Chicago Press, 1907) 453, 457; https://archive.org/details/genetichistoryof00fost_0/page/452

[235] Finney, *Memoirs of Rev. Charles G. Finney*, 60; https://archive.org/details/memoirsofrev-char1876finn/page/60

[236] Finney, *Lectures on Systematic Theology* (New York City, NY: George H. Doran, 1878; 2nd edition) xi; https://archive.org/details/cu31924010376030/page/n19

[237] Charles G. Finney, *Sermons on Important Subjects* (New York City, NY: John S. Taylor, 1836) 67; https://archive.org/details/sermonsonimporta00finn/page/66

chosen to save some and condemn others to a lost eternity. Anyone who deliberately broke God's law was fully responsible for his own lost condition.[238] Conversely, all people had a responsibility to live uprightly in order to be saved. Every other aspect of Finney's theology proceeded from this basic premise that man was able to make his own decision on whether or not to live uprightly. All sin was to be regarded as a criminal offence, and men were culpable on the basis of their own sin, not because they had inherited that of Adam. Every individual was therefore tasked with doing something to overcome his personal sin.

In a classic reinterpretation of the Reformed position, Finney completely rejected the Christian doctrine of Christ's vicarious atonement. True to the teaching of the New Divinity, he replaced it with the French philosopher Peter Abaelard's theory of moral influence and the Dutch scholar Hugo Grotius's idea of the wise government of God.[239] It should be noted once again that according to Finney, the purpose of the atonement could not be the salvation of sinners from the wrath of God. In Jesus's death, God had ultimately provided an example of His retributive justice. The sight of the execution of an innocent man ought to compel sinners to suppress their selfish deeds. Christ's work was categorized as pure moral activity. He could not have died for the sins of others: His death brought no atonement, but was ultimately a statement of His willingness to obey God. His acceptance by God was based on the fact that He kept the law perfectly throughout His sinless life. For a guiltless person to have died for a sinner would have been legally impossible and unjust.[240] The idea of a vicarious atonement was therefore regarded as the product of theological error and needed to be firmly rejected. Finney's theology demanded moral improvement. Salvation was received on the condition of perfect obedience and on the basis of the mercy of God.[241]

In his revival campaigns, Finney taught that sinners needed to experience the new birth through a decision of the will before they left the tent or church building.[242] In contrast to preachers of the First Great Awakening who recognized that the new birth and revival were "supernatural works of God," Finney taught that human action was decisive in the creation of spiritual life.[243]

---

[238] Charles G. Finney, *Sermons on Gospel Themes* (Oberlin, OH: E. J. Goodrich; New York City, NY: Dodd, Mead and Company, 1876) 194; https://archive.org/details/sermonsongospel-00finngoog/page/n208

[239] Charles G. Finney, *Lectures on Systematic Theology* (Boston, MA: Crocker & Brewster, 1846) 403; https://archive.org/details/lecturesonsyste00finngoog/page/n426

[240] Finney, *Lectures on Systematic Theology* (New York City, NY: George H. Doran, 1878; 2nd edition) 281; https://archive.org/details/cu31924010376030/page/n313

[241] Finney, *Lectures on Systematic Theology* (Boston, MA: Crocker & Brewster, 1846) 398; https://archive.org/details/lecturesonsyste00finngoog/page/n422

[242] Wright, *Charles Grandison Finney*, 232-233; s. also: Finney, *Lectures on Systematic Theology* (New York City, NY: George H. Doran, 1878; 2nd edition) 586; https://archive.org/details/cu31924010376030/page/n619

[243] Ted A. Smith, *The New Measures: A Theological History of Democratic Practice*

He became known as one of the most ardent advocates of free will.[244] For God to require man to do something that he was unable to do, threatening him with eternal death despite knowing his incapability, would be "endless tyranny."[245] So bold a belief would be blasphemy. True conversion was a turn from selfish, sinful interests to complete dedication to God's will. Finney claimed that man was capable of contributing to his own salvation, and that the evangelist's task was to convince listeners to act on their conviction when called to conversion.[246] All who genuinely sought salvation would be saved, whether or not it had been divinely predestinated.

By emphasizing that man could play a part in even his own salvation, Finney raised the question of what role was played by the Holy Spirit. Calvinists believed that man, being spiritually dead, was unable to do anything until given spiritual life by the Holy Spirit through the new birth. They accused Finney and other evangelists of entirely overlooking the work of God in the conversion of the soul.[247] By contrast, Finney believed that the role of the Holy Spirit was to convince people that they would make the right decision.[248] However, the sinner might resist the voice of the Holy Spirit, in which case, his mind needed to be influenced externally to make the right decision.[249] The fastest way to achieve this was for the decision to be made while in a trance-like state induced by the preacher. There were numerous ways in which preachers could produce a suitable emotional atmosphere, not least through enthusiastic preaching that created mass hysteria.

A position based on the ability of the sinner could lead to nothing but the questionable idea of human self-improvement. Finney's teachings on the nature of humanity lacked thorough biblical exegesis. They also betrayed a tenuous understanding of the history of theology. In his unparalleled sense of self-importance, he proved that he was influenced by the contemporary spirit of Pragmatism. His writings reveal unmistakable undertones of Humanism beneath their veil of Christianity. Finney easily convinced his audience that the humanistic principles which he propagated were essentially Christian, while simultaneously counteracting the biblical truth that the entire man – thoughts, feelings, and will – is dominated by sin because of the Fall. According to the biblical perspective, man is incapable of understanding the

---

(Cambridge: Cambridge University Press, 2007) 114.

[244] Albert Temple Swing, *Bibliotheca Sacra*, LVII (190), 466-467.

[245] Finney, *Sermons on Gospel Themes*, 74; https://archive.org/details/sermonsongospel-00finngoog/page/n88

[246] Perry Miller, *The Life of the Mind in America: From the Revolution to the Civil War* (New York City, NY: Harcourt, Brace & World, 1965) 33; https://archive.org/details/lifeofmindi-namer00mill/page/32

[247] Benjamin B. Warfield, *Princeton Theological Review*, XIX (July, 1921), 482.

[248] Finney, *Sermons on Important Subjects*, 22; https://archive.org/details/sermonsonim-porta00finn/page/22

[249] Ibid., 20; https://archive.org/details/sermonsonimporta00finn/page/20

message of the Gospel: he is spiritually helpless and lost, and can only understand God's message of salvation if enabled to do so by the Holy Spirit (1 Cor. 2:14). However, Finney taught that man is able to attain the absolute perfection demanded by God through his own efforts. It may indeed be tempting to think that God could not require us to do anything that we are incapable of doing. However, this contradicts Paul's statement that the law only shows us that we are lost because we are incapable of living according to God's will.

Finney never accepted the Calvinistic doctrine of man's total depravity (or better, incapability). His entire system of theology revolved around the Pelagian idea of absolute free will. He accordingly viewed the classic doctrine of original sin as "unscriptural"[250] and wholly "nonsensical."[251] He explicitly denied that man has a sinful nature and completely reinterpreted Bible verses which clearly present the doctrine of original sin.[252] He said that Adam had led his descendants into sin by his poor example, logically concluding from this that Christ's redemption was based on his perfect example. Guilt and corruption were not intrinsic to human nature, but were consequences of man's decision to sin. Furthermore, Finney's rejection of the doctrine of original sin was also naturally accompanied by denial of a supernatural new birth.

Finney unashamedly rejected the doctrine of justification which was central to Martin Luther's doctrine of salvation, and which Luther had believed would determine whether the church would stand or fall.[253] He presented an undisguised doctrine of self-redemption and advocated an extreme form of justification by works. The Christian was only justified so long as he was obedient, and would be condemned if he disobeyed.[254] Without repentance, he could never be forgiven. The sinful Christian and the unconverted sinner were thus in the very same position.[255] Finney disregarded the Reformation's motto of "both just and sinner"[256] because it seemed obvious to him that no one could be a sinner and a saint at the same time.[257] All fresh sin required fresh justification. The requirement for salvation was absolute obedience.[258] Finney's message of salvation was pure law. He could

---

[250] Finney, *Lectures on Systematic Theology* (New York City, NY: George H. Doran, 1878; 2nd edition) 243; https://archive.org/details/cu31924010376030/page/n275

[251] Ibid.

[252] Ibid., 243-244.

[253] Lat.: Articulus stantis et (vel) cadentis ecclesiae.

[254] Finney, *Lectures on Systematic Theology* (Boston, MA: Crocker & Brewster, 1846) 167; https://archive.org/details/lecturesonsyste00finngoog/page/n192

[255] Ibid.

[256] Lat.: Simul iustus et peccator

[257] Finney, *Lectures on Systematic Theology* (New York City, NY: George H. Doran, 1878; 2nd edition) 123; https://archive.org/details/cu31924010376030/page/n155

[258] Ibid., 385; https://archive.org/details/cu31924010376030/page/n417

never accept the Gospel of the free, sovereign grace of God[259], and therefore preached only a social salvation in this world, based on a concept of moral perfection.[260]

7.5 Enthusiastic expressions of New Protestantism

Many spiritual elements of the American revival movement displayed characteristic traits of German Pietism. Liturgical services, Lutheran-Reformed confessions, and hierarchical church structures were regarded as unfortunate products of narrow-minded, uncompromising Formalism. The division of Christianity into denominations seemed outdated in a modern society striving for unity and democracy. When Charles G. Finney appeared on the scene, he initially seemed to bring these critical developments to a climax. His revival campaigns in Rochester, New York in 1826 and 1831 had the greatest impact of all. Churches were mistakenly led to believe that by discarding denominational distinctions they would finally overcome the divisions caused by denominational traditions and creeds. With their battle cry of "no creed but Christ," they took up arms against the supposed narrowmindedness of Calvinism. However, the results of their passionate campaigns were far less commendable than they have since been portrayed to be. Many churches were torn apart by internal conflicts under the influence of the spiritual enthusiasm. They split into all kinds of fanatical groups, with scarcely two of them upholding the same beliefs. Numerous religious cults and utopian societies sprang up in an area which rightly retains a stigma to the present day. Questionable views on spirituality were tolerated, if not welcomed, while popular social reforms were also put in motion.

At the center of the abiding influence of Finney and his followers is the idea that bizarre experiences of spiritual ecstasy are an essential element of true Christianity.[261] Revivalists taught that making a subjective decision of belief was an expression of free will. Their message of self-redemption (Pelagianism) resonated with an urge for self-development in the bourgeoisie, which was becoming increasingly aware of its self-worth. Many Free Will Baptists and Methodists regarded revival enthusiasm far more positively than did the liturgy-oriented Presbyterians, and consequently saw far greater numeric growth during the Second Great Awakening. They interpreted the Scriptures symbolically rather than being guided by the actual wording, as had been the traditional Reformed approach which also suited the poorly educated rural population.

---

[259] Ibid., 384; https://archive.org/details/cu31924010376030/page/n417

[260] Benjamin B. Warfield, *Perfectionism*, Ethelbert Dudley Warfield, ed. (New York City, NY: Oxford University Press, 1931; Grand Rapids, MI: Baker, [1932] 2003) vol. 2: 154.

[261] Whitney R. Cross, *The Burned-Over District: The Social and Intellectual History of Enthusiastic Religion in Western New York, 1800-1850* (New York City, NY: Harper Torch-books, [1950] 1965) 163, 183; https://archive.org/details/burnedoverdistri00cros/page/162

The central and western regions of New York State became known unofficially, but with good reason, as the "Burned-Over District". This name was less descriptive of a geographical area than of a religious reality.[262] The events that took place there in the first half of the nineteenth century had a strong, lasting impact not only on religion, but also on culture and politics. American Christianity underwent radical changes as the revival movement spread not only through America, but also throughout Europe and eventually the entire world during the nineteenth and twentieth centuries in the form of the Holiness movement and Pentecostalism. The experiential aspects of its irrational Emotionalism have led some Christian circles to seek enthusiastic manifestations in Christianity ever since.[263]

It gradually became clear that simply dismissing the hyper spirituality of the Second Great Awakening (1790-1850) as a passing craze was not an option. It stirred up a religiosity that affected the poorly educated rural population as well as the wealthy urban upper classes, who led the procession of the "reborn."[264] In the South it was manifested by an individualistic approach to the salvation of souls. Emphasis was placed on individual conversion to a popular form of national Christianity, which in Fundamentalist circles bore features of Arminianism and Dispensationalism. Little attention was paid to calls for social or political engagement. In the North, by contrast, and especially in Yankee areas, a completely different form of New Protestantism developed with an evangelical and Postmillennial outlook. In accordance with Charles G. Finney's doctrine of perfection, every Christian was urged to strive for others' salvation, the latter signifying a meaningful way of life in the here and now; furthermore, they were called to engage in social and political initiatives that went beyond supporting missionary work. Churches taught that Christians needed to work to establish the kingdom of God on earth and thus create a perfect society, first in their own country and then throughout the world. Sins such as slavery, alcohol consumption, Sabbath breaking, gambling, dancing, and irreligiousness needed to be eradicated so that Americans could be turned into saints. The nation was urged to prepare morally for the dawn of the thousand-year reign. Between 1800 and 1850, a diverse array of religious communities was formed in the Northeastern United States. The religiosity in the frontier areas was conducive to sects with millennialist and gnostic views.[265] Spiritualist mediums and visionaries were in abundance, and the area in and around Oneida County became justifiably known as the "psychic highway."[266] New York State was hit

---

[262] Ibid., ix; https://archive.org/details/burnedoverdistri00cros/page/n11

[263] Ibid., 10-11; https://archive.org/details/burnedoverdistri00cros/page/n27

[264] Ibid., 155; https://archive.org/details/burnedoverdistri00cros/page/154

[265] Ibid., 341ff.; https://archive.org/details/burnedoverdistri00cros/page/340

[266] Keith J. Hardman, *Charles Grandison Finney: Revivalist and Reformer* (Grand Rapids, MI: Baker and Syracuse University Press, 1987) 25.

with the devastating fire blight of frenetic religious zeal[267] even before Finney became known as a revivalist. The people could never have anticipated the far greater damage that the new revivalist campaigns would do to their collective consciousness.

From the beginning of the First Great Awakening in 1739, outbreaks of religious enthusiasm and political reforms went hand in hand with growing intensity. Even the wildest ideas for a collective economy were tolerated at very least. However, utopian reformers never succeeded in winning majority support for their experimental ideas for social togetherness. Toward the beginning of the nineteenth century, a few people took up the perfectionist ideas that were circulating in the American cultural landscape. Perfectionism signifies a religious attitude characterized by a pursuit of moral perfection and the belief that this can be achieved either partially or entirely. The social reform movements stemmed from a spiritual impulse reflected in the aim of many Christians to build the kingdom of God on earth.[268] They consequently founded rural, self-sufficient communities which functioned as independent micro territories, sealed off from the wider world for at least some time.

The United Society of Believers in Christ's Second Appearing was one of the most significant Yankee communes. Ann Lee (1736-1784), also known as Ann Elizabeth Lees, emigrated from England to New England with a group of followers in 1774 and settled in Niskayuna, Albany County, in New York State. They were nicknamed the "Shakers" because of their ecstatic dancing in religious services, which turned into uncontrollable shaking of their whole bodies. Another of their distinctive rituals was speaking in tongues. Lee pretended to be the reincarnation of Jesus Christ Himself, and if members did not fully bow to her spiritual authority, she accused them of fornication and bestiality. Years later, the sect moved to Ohio and Kentucky and formed a socialist community of property. New rules introduced by the religion prohibited members to marry and start families.

The theosophist Johann Georg Rapp (1757-1847), born in the German Duchy of Württemberg, established himself as a spiritual leader in the 1790s and rallied a small group of followers who called themselves Harmonists, or occasionally Rappites.[269] Rapp, who himself had fathered many children, forbade sexual intercourse among his followers as a sign of total submission. They willingly obeyed his command of celibacy, since he had promised them exclusive membership of a communist utopia on earth. Rapp derived this

---

[267] Charles G. Finney, *Memoirs of Rev. Charles G. Finney* (New York City, NY: A. S. Barnes & Company, 1876) 78; https://archive.org/details/memoirsofrevchar1876finn/page/78

[268] Timothy L. Smith, *Revivalism and Social Reform: American Protestantism on the Eve of the Civil War* (Nashville, TN: Abingdon, 1957); s. also: Stow Persons, "Christian Communitarianism in America," in Stow Persons & Donald Drew Egbert, eds., *Socialism and American Life* (Princeton, NJ: Princeton University Press, 1962) vol. 1: 127-151.

[269] Karl Arndt, "George Rapp's Harmony Society," in Donald E. Pitzer, ed., *America's Communal Utopias* (Chapel Hill, NC: University of North Carolina Press, 1997) 57-88; https://uncpress.org/book/9780807846094/americas-communal-utopias/

teaching from Jakob Böhme's belief[270] that man had been androgynous (having both male and female characteristics) in his original state. In order to preempt their banishment from Württemberg, Rapp and his followers emigrated to Harmony, Pennsylvania, in 1804. They were influenced heavily by contemporary esoteric teachings, especially Theosophy (the belief that divine wisdom can only be gained through the mystical view of God). Dominated by their consciousness of the end times, they believed that the thousand-year kingdom would emerge during their lifetime. Rapp gained a nation-wide reputation as a practicing alchemist.[271] He sought to find the "philosopher's stone," the key not only to turning base metals into gold, but also to enduring health and heavenly wisdom. The Harmonists welcomed Bernhard Müller from Germany after he claimed to be the promised Messiah and the embodiment of the "philosopher's stone."[272] The community dispersed in many directions in 1875, following Rapp's death. Several years later, half a million dollars' worth of gold was discovered in his house, which he had accumulated through his followers' flourishing trade and through land speculation. Perhaps the most well-known utopian socialist experiment was one conducted in New Harmony, Indiana by Robert Owen, whose primary goal was to abolish private property. Some of his followers coined the term "Socialism" and set up "Owen Clubs" in various parts of America. Apart from the Mormons who emigrated to Utah, no utopian community managed to maintain the ideals of their unconventional lifestyles for more than a few years. Degeneration of morals among their members was often followed immediately by economic ruin.

Oneida County in western New York had a particularly poor reputation by the end of the eighteenth century, having become known as the home of notorious necromancers. John Humphrey Noyes founded the socialist Oneida Community (a Perfectionist sect[273]) in September 1848. Most shocking of all was the Oneida members' practice of exchanging husbands and wives, following the example of their founder. Perfectionist churches, which were based on the doctrine of sinless existence on earth, taught that marriage would cease to exist in its outdated form and would soon be replaced by something new and "more sacred" – namely sexual intercourse at will with frequently changing partners.[274] The Oberlin professors Finney and Mahan

---

[270] S. also: Chap. 3.8 Pansophic coherence of truth; chap 3.9 Sublime vision of a new era; chap 3.10 Turning to the mystery of Irrationalism; chap 6.4 Idealistic foundations of Transcendentalism

[271] S. also: Chap. 3.3 The mystical incentive of human deification

[272] Arndt, "George Rapp's Harmony Society," 76.

[273] Cross, *Burned-Over District*, 333-334; https://archive.org/details/burnedoverdistri-00cros/page/332

[274] William Hepworth Dixon, *Spiritual Wives* (London: Hurst & Blackett, 1868) vol. 1: 81; https://archive.org/details/spiritualwives00dixogoog/page/n110

fiercely condemned the identification of their teaching of entire sanctification with this abhorrent form of "Perfectionism."[275]

After Finney became president of Oberlin College, northern Ohio in 1835, he considered his chief task to be the propagation of the doctrine of entire sanctification.[276] He had unlimited confidence in man's ability to lead a completely sinless life. He was thoroughly convinced that God required man to be perfect in every respect, but believed that justification before God was contingent on total obedience to divine law in everyday life[277] rather than on the imputation of Christ's perfect righteousness through faith, as taught by the Bible (Romans 3:21-26).[278] Finney was particularly successful in creating Perfectionist groups within various denominations, such as the Wesleyans (1843), the Oneida Community (John Humphrey Noyes's "sect of Perfectionists," 1848), and the Free Methodists (1860).[279] Many Perfectionists had originally belonged to the Methodist Church, and John Wesley's followers opposed Reformation theology by spreading the doctrine of entire sanctification. Jacobus Arminius (1560-1609) had already stated that those who were born again were capable of keeping God's commandments perfectly. However, it was John Wesley who laid out the doctrine in writing[280], with Christian Perfectionism consequently becoming the distinguishing feature of Methodist theology.[281] Many Christians were attracted to the idea that man could be freed from the power of sin in the midst of an evil world and could live in perfect accordance with God's law. Over time, many Methodists dispersed in different directions in search of new spiritual experiences. Their religious odysseys led many of them to live as they pleased.[282] As preachers continually stirred up the emotions of the crowds, many listeners were put into a trance-like state in which they were willingly convinced by any idea, no matter how bizarre.

---

[275] Robert Allerton Parker, *A Yankee Saint: John Humphrey Noyes and The Oneida Community* (New York City, NY: G. P. Putnam's sons, 1935) 102-103; https://archive.org/details/yankeesaintjohnh0000park/page/102; Finney, *Memoirs of Rev. Charles G. Finney*, 343, 345; https://archive.org/details/memoirsofrevchar1876finn/page/342

[276] Cross, *Burned-Over District*, 249; https://archive.org/details/burnedoverdistri00cros/page/248

[277] Finney, *Lectures on Systematic Theology* (New York City, NY: George H. Doran, 1878; 2nd edition) 391; https://archive.org/details/cu31924010376030/page/n423

[278] Ibid., 121; https://archive.org/details/cu31924010376030/page/n153

[279] John Leland Peters, *Christian Perfection and American Methodism* (Nashville, TN: Parthenon Press, 1956) passim; Merrill E. Gaddis, "Christian Perfectionism in America," (Ph.D. diss., University of Chicago, 1929) passim.

[280] S. also: Chap. 3.11 Pursuit of absolute perfection

[281] Frederick Platt, "Christian Perfectionism," in James Hastings, ed., *Encyclopaedia, of Religion and Ethics* (New York City, NY: Charles Scribner's Son, 1908) vol. 9: 732; https://archive.org/details/bub_gb_HT0TAAAAYAAJ/page/n751

[282] William Warren Sweet, *Religion in the Development of American Culture* (New York City, NY: Scribner, 1952) 282.

Given that the term "Perfectionism" was used by extremely diverse religious groups to signify their individual versions of the doctrine of perfection, it was impossible to be certain of what one or the other believed. Much confusion arose in Christian communities over the true meaning of the term. It was one thing to take it as a serious desire to live a holier life, and another thing altogether to suggest that such a doctrine could be abused to justify a corrupt lifestyle. Perfectionists have often said that their critics have not yet reached the degree of perfection required to understand their unorthodox way of life. Noyes deflected criticism of his wild behavior by pointing out that he was supposedly sinless. The supernatural experiences associated with the doctrine of perfection were regarded as extra-biblical "revelations" which New York mystics placed on a par with the Word of God. According to the Presbyterian theologian Benjamin B. Warfield, Finney denied that he agreed with this unchristian view, but it nonetheless went hand in hand with the demand for a sinless life.[283]

Finney was convinced that the practice of entire sanctification, which would supposedly draw out man's innate virtue, was as relevant to the times as were revival campaigns and social reforms. In his view, the Jacksonian era could not have provided better conditions for the synthesis of different religious traditions.[284] A fundamentally modified form of Puritanism gradually merged with Methodism, which had previously opened itself up to Herrnhut Pietism. The Quakers detected an essential correlation between this spiritual melting pot and their mystical beliefs. The similarities between their religious construct, which is comprised of a range of different concepts, and the Transcendentalism of Emerson and Thoreau should not be overlooked. Like the Transcendentalists, the Perfectionists were driven by an extreme Individualism which occasionally involved elements of Anarchism and immorality. The theology of Perfectionism permeated the complex social relations that formed in America from 1830 with the introduction of Romantic Democracy. The goal of entire sanctification became so closely entwined with the cause of religious Patriotism that it was hard to separate the one from the other. America's civil religion took on concrete form as the ultimate ideal of a freedom-loving national community.

Reformed theologians categorically denied the doctrine of entire sanctification. With reference to the Bible and the writings of Augustine, they taught that a state of sinlessness could never be attained in this life. At no point do the Holy Scriptures indicate such a possibility. On the contrary, many passages clearly convey the opposite – 1 John 1:8-10[285], for example.

---

[283] Benjamin B. Warfield, *Princeton Theological Review*, XIX (January, 1921), 48; s. also: Warfield, *Perfectionism*, vol. 2: 248-249.

[284] Smith, *Revivalism and Social Reform*, 108.

[285] King James Version: 8 If we say that we have no sin, we deceive ourselves, and the truth is not in us. 9 If we confess our sins, he is faithful and just to forgive us our sins, and to cleanse us from all unrighteousness. 10 If we say that we have not sinned, we make him a liar, and his word is not in us.

Surprisingly, even many New School Presbyterians refused to accept Oberlin College's teaching of entire sanctification, since it was incompatible with the Westminster Confession. Perfectionism was also rejected by many church leaders.[286]

A key feature of the version of New Protestantism taught by Charles G. Finney was its call for churches to strive not primarily for the eternal salvation of souls, but for the social and material interests of all mankind in the here and now. Concentration of state power was necessary for the legal elimination of sinful social structures, thus enabling the whole nation to enter the state of sanctification. Advocates of Revivalism gave particular support to political initiatives which aimed to stop the consumption of alcohol, curb the influence of Catholicism, and eradicate anarchistic sentiments in society. New Protestants agreed on the need to fight the growing influence of the Roman Catholic Church, which could be traced back to the rise in immigration from southern European and Slavic countries and especially from Ireland. Members of this religious community were controlled by the anti-Christian agents of the Pope and had been deprived of exercising their free will. Children from Catholic families needed to be wrested from the influence of their parents and their devotion to the reality of sin by being forced into daily attendance of public schools. The school system was considered the most important means of "Christianizing" society. When contemporary New England historians began propagating strongly biased accounts of the history of the Spanish Empire and the Dutch Republic, their sense of superiority spread quickly through the population which was influenced by English culture.

After Finney died in 1875, numerous Perfectionists felt compelled to make the Higher Life Movement known across borders to a new generation of Christians. They saw social reforms such as the liberation of slaves, joint education for girl and boys, Feminism, prohibition of making or selling alcohol, and racial equality as the key ethical issues. The first ordination of a woman to the ministry took place at Oberlin College. The remarkable career of the former slave and washerwoman Amanda Smith as a world-travelling evangelist was long seen to validate the controversial decision to grant teaching and leadership positions to women in the church. The Higher Life Movement had originally developed out of Methodism and Quakerism, and itself led to an abundance of subsidiary movements which preserved former issues or changed some points of doctrine and practice. It became a dominant influence in the dynamic "Christianization" of North America, enabled by preachers of the Second Great Awakening who readily accepted and spread the movement's doctrines and practices by advocating Perfectionism. A new drive for domestic evangelization and world mission resulted from the movement's continuous influence on almost all churches in North America.

---

[286] Charles G. Finney, *Lectures on Systematic Theology, embracing ability (natural, moral and gracious) repentance, impenitence, faith and unbelief* […] (Oberlin, OH: James M. Fitch, 1847) 183; https://archive.org/details/lecturesonsystem00finnrich/page/182

In the third quarter of the nineteenth century it took Europe by storm. The founding of the Salvation Army, based on the social-ethical initiatives of the Methodist preacher and Freemason[287] William Booth (1829-1912), was directly influenced by the Higher Life Movement. The equality of genders in its organizational roles revealed its persuasions. The Western Christian scene was dominated by Pentecostalism until Fundamentalism, still full of Higher Life theology, became an established New Protestant doctrine around 1920.

In the late nineteenth century, after many years of intensive but often ineffective social reform, New Protestants began to grasp what Finney had already told his followers years before: that only the state could establish the kingdom of God on earth. Government power needed to be harnessed to eradicate every possibility of sin and thus promote the earthly welfare of the individual. Although the list of sins to be combatted grew ever longer, the Perfectionists devoted themselves above all to suppressing the "Demon Rum". Political agitation against alcohol consumption eventually resulted in the passing of the National Prohibition Act in 1919. No one was allowed to do anything on Sundays except go to church. Organized citizen initiatives called for the passing of "blue laws" which also largely banned Sunday trading. The Higher Life Movement was concerned not only with sanctifying Christians' mentalities, but also with reforming society at large according to ethical standards that were considered to be Christian.

8 The development of authoritarian Progressivism

(The true background to the American War of Secession)

The American War of Secession (1861 to 1865) is an odd one out among the United States' major conflicts. Interpretations of other wars have always been subjected to various revisions. In the case of the War of Secession, however, agreement was quickly reached on a single version which was maintained as though set in stone. The decisive factor that led to the outbreak of this devasting war was said to be the hostility in the northern states toward the slavery in the southern states. The general consensus among historians seemed so unshakeable that none of them suspected that the conventional interpretation could ever be overthrown.

However, the tide also turned in this respect. American historians agree that both the North and South made grave mistakes that ultimately provoked the devastating War of Secession, which could have been prevented. It is also clear that the interests of other countries were not directly impacted by the conflict. Resentment of slavery in the northern states was only one of several issues used to conceal motives of far greater weight, and of questionable

---

[287] A picture of William Booth showing him to be a freemason: https://upload.wikimedia.org/wikipedia/commons/7/7c/General_William_Booth.jpg

morality. Economic considerations were among the chief reasons for the outbreak of the war; ideological differences were of lesser significance.

8.1 Fateful development of the American Federation

The circumstances resulting from material and cultural progress revived the time-honored idea that America occupied a special and unique position in the world. Americans were filled with a strong faith in the efficacy of their own physical and intellectual achievements and generalized their own experience in a universal theory of progress. The silent expectation was that the rest of the world must therefore accept a secondary status. From the American perspective, the older European civilizations were already in decline. Speaking confidently about their own future in this age of optimism, they highlighted the primary differences between the Old and New Worlds. Another reason for their excessive optimism was the awakened Nationalism which had gripped patriotic American souls after 1815. In the mid-nineteenth century, Americans' heightened self-perception began to change as they adopted the emerging vision of Young America, expressed in the idea of a gradually evolving utopia. They began to see the Republic's westward territorial expansion as a God-given mission. The idealistic idea of a unique American destiny was formed in the hope that U.S. Democracy would set an example to other nations and thus become, to the greatest extent possible, the global model of government. In church circles, the same belief produced a commitment to spreading Christianity throughout the world under the American banner. Thus arose an extraordinary ideological climate that enabled a widespread, uncritical acceptance of progressive ideals. While some understood progress as an inevitable law of destiny or divine providence, others considered it an aspirational goal that could be achieved through human genius and willpower. During the nation's years of territorial expansion, which took place largely at the expense of the Indians and Mexicans, Americans explained why God had chosen them to spread the ideals of Progressivism throughout the world: 1) to increase material wealth, 2) to carry out extensive territorial expansion, and 3) to implement technological innovations. The idea of progress had so engulfed the minds of many Americans that they were in danger of losing a clear vision of their real life situation. The propagated Progressivism was characterized by an uncritically accepted Idealism, reflected in political slogans such as the much used "Manifest Destiny." This euphemism meant nothing other than a ruthless realization of worldwide Imperialism.

The Young America movement, promoted by the politician, author, and journalist Edwin De Leon[288] (1818-1891), first entered the public sphere in

---

[288] Cyrus Adler & L. Hühner, "Leon, Edwin De," in Isidore Singer, et al., eds., *The Jewish Encyclopedia* (New York City, NY: Funk & Wagnalls, 1901-1906) vol. 8: 3; https://archive.org/details/cu31924091768253/page/n29

1845. The term Young America was a deliberate allusion to mid-nineteenth-century revolutionary movements in Europe, such as Young Germany, Young France, and Young England. Thomas Cooper, a British revolutionary who had moved to South Carolina, urged the southern states to secede from the northern states, making use of his influence as rector of South Carolina College and as the most well-known author in the South. In order to set the Young America movement in motion, De Leon formulated a tripartite program: 1) assumption of political power in wide areas of America, 2) expansion of the area of liberty, and 3) readiness to defend the country against all foreign enemies.[289] What De Leon understood by an expanding area of liberty was clear from his pithily stated intentions, which extended far beyond the political destiny envisioned for America: 1) conquering the Western Hemisphere with its Spanish colonies and independent nation states, 2) supporting the revolutionary activities of the Italian freedom fighter Giuseppe Mazzini in Europe, and 3) abolition of Feudalism throughout the world. Revolutionary uprisings in both the U.S.A. and Europe were to be supported and new governments were to be installed. What De Lion most wanted to achieve through the Young America movement was a separation of the southern states from the Union. He secretly hoped that war would create the chaos needed to bring Young America's ringleaders into political power. The Governor of Mississippi, John A. Quitman, was also involved in plans to divide the Union until he was legally removed from office. Zachary Taylor, president from 1849 until his sudden death in 1850, constantly had to fight off subversive maneuvers. After the untimely death of a second Whig president, the Democratic Senator Stephen Douglas from Illinois devised a new plan for the future of the southern states after its approval by Congress. It was widely known that he was sympathetic to the cause of Young America.

Gerrit Smith (1797-1874), who became one of the U.S.A.'s foremost property owners through land speculation, donated at least eight million U.S. dollars to professional agitators such as Giuseppe Mazzini, who organized revolutionary action in Europe and America. He gave particular support to William Lloyd Garrison's extreme hate campaign and to John Brown's violent raids. William Lloyd Garrison (1805-1879) from Newburyport, Massachusetts led the movement for the abolition of slavery while simultaneously playing an equally important role in the Young America movement. Garrison made a great effort to implement the strategy of the conspiracy group Essex Junto, namely the original goal of the northern Tory sympathizers to destroy the Union of the American Republic and thereby reintegrate the weakened United States into the British Empire. Garrison founded the newspaper *The Liberator* in 1831. Its superficial aim was to stir up both Northerners and Southerners against slavery. In order to increase the paper's readership as quickly as possible, Garrison gave away many free subscriptions, including to the newspapers that most strongly criticized his views. A heated debate thus arose between advocates and opponents of southern slavery, followed with

---

[289] Ibid., 26.

growing interest by the general public. Garrison's significance did not lie in incitement of northern sentiment against slavery as an inhuman institution, as was the case for many other conscience-stricken opinion makers in the North, but rather in the way that he stirred up hatred among the northern population against southern slave owners to the point of incandescence. His primary motive was not so much to abolish slavery as to create political tensions between the northern and southern states that would lead to an "irrepressible conflict." The real goal was a quick secession of the southern states from the Federation as a prerequisite for a Young America under British control.

This ruthless approach to dealing with a race viewed as inferior and open to exploitation by wealthy landowners did not originate in the heartless corruption of southern plantation owners and northern manufacturers. It was rather the unmistakable sign of a newly emerging Feudalism. The driving force behind this development was the same oligarchy (a small group of people with political control) as that present in Europe, which had for centuries held the Old World under the thumb of its tyrannical Paternalism. This group alone must be blamed for the introduction of black slavery to the New World, driven by sheer greed.

The Young America movement advocated the liberation of slaves as demanded by northern abolitionists. At the same time, however, it also supported the cause of the southern slave owners. How can this paradoxical behavior be understood? The only definite answer is found by pointing out the real aim of the movement: to divide the Federation of the United States. Only in this way could its Republican institutions be truly weakened. In order to achieve this goal, the hatred between North and South needed not only to be fired up, but to be brought to boiling point. The guiding principle for the resulting amoral acts was that the end would justify the means.

While the leader of the Northern Jurisdiction of the Scottish Rite of Freemasonry, the Swiss John James Joseph Gourgas, and his adjutant Killian Henry Van Rensselaer set up the Knights of the Golden Circle, which later formed the core of the Confederate Army on the Southern side, leaders of the Southern Jurisdiction recruited political leaders from the South. Shortly after, they implemented their plan to secede from the rest of the American republic. The man responsible for this project was Albert Pike, Caleb Cushing's protégé. Both men came from Newburyport, Massachusetts, and were lifelong friends. Caleb Cushing, a Freemason and Attorney General of the United States, encouraged Albert Pike to leave the North and establish himself as a political figure in the southern state of Arkansas. Pike soon became Arkansas's most influential advocate of secession. During the 1850s, he became a key organizer and leader of the American Party, or "Know-Nothings," a third party which particularly opposed the immigration policies of the established parties. In 1858, Pike and eleven of his political allies published a manifesto expressing their determination to work for the expulsion of free "negroes and mulattoes" (children of a black and a white parent) from the state of Arkansas. Albert Pike was deeply involved in

Esotericism and was appointed Sovereign Grand Commander of the Masonic Southern Jurisdiction of the Scottish Rite in 1859.[290] In order to understand Albert Pike's importance as agent provocateur (a person who incites another to commit an illegal act on behalf of the state), it is first important to take a closer look at Caleb Cushing's eventful career.

Caleb Cushing (ΦBK)[291] began his university studies at Harvard College during the British-American War of 1812. His father was a wealthy shipowner, and his cousin, John Perkins Cushing, had made a fortune through his career as an opium dealer in China. One of Caleb's closest friends was John Lowell's nephew. The Essex Junto soon recognized that Caleb Cushing, a member of St. John's Masonic Lodge in Newburyport, Massachusetts, was a man of wild ambition. After finishing his law studies and training briefly in a law firm, he was appointed professor of mathematics by the principal of Harvard College, John Thornton Kirkland (ΦBK)[292]. Over the summer of 1822, Caleb Cushing wrote leading articles for the Essex Junto's local paper, the *Newburyport Herald*. He took on the eighteen-year-old *Herald* reporter William Lloyd Garrison as his assistant, instructing him to write articles as provocative as his own. William Lloyd Garrison had adopted the Essex Junto's separatist views at a young age. The remarkable relationship that developed between Cushing and Garrison over the following period must be examined more closely in order to understand their underlying political goals.[293] Why did William Lloyd Garrison establish himself as leader of the most extreme and provocative elements of northern Abolitionism, while Caleb Cushing acted as the southern slave owners' principal strategist? Both had one overriding aim: to weaken the Federation of the American states by provoking conflict between opposing positions in order to reintegrate Young America into the British Empire.

Caleb Cushing's mentor was John Lowell, Jr., son of an entrepreneur and federal judge living in Boston, Massachusetts. Lowell charged Cushing with fully taking up the cause of the Essex Junto: the division of the American Republic. In 1826, Cushing was nominated as Essex County's candidate for the U.S. House of Representatives. He quickly developed a talent for disguising disreputable politics in eloquent words and had a good chance of success in becoming a member of Congress. In order to secure an even better position, he accused his main rival in the election campaign of having conducted shady business with the Essex Junto, although he resolutely upheld the interests of his mentor John Lowell, Jr. Cushing also had the support of his

---

[290] Ray Baker Harris & James David Carter, *History of the Supreme Council, 33e, Mother Council of the World, Ancient and Accepted Scottish Rite of Freemasonry, Southern Jurisdiction, U.S.A., 1801-1861* (Washington, D.C.: Supreme Council, 33e, 1964) 244.

[291] Member of the Phi Beta Kappa Society, Harvard College, 1817, Vice-President, 1826-1827

[292] Member of the Phi Beta Kappa Society, Harvard College, 1789

[293] John L. Thomas, *The Liberator: William Lloyd Garrison, a Biography* (Boston, MA: Little, Brown and Co., 1963) 37; https://archive.org/details/liberatorwilliam017641mbp/page/n47

protégé William Lloyd Garrison, to whom he had introduced the political philosophy of the Essex Junto. Cushing's political opponent accused him of working secretly with Garrison. The "left-wing" Garrison then tried hard to give the impression that he was in no way colluding with the "conservative" Cushing.[294] At one of Cushing's public election events, Garrison stormed through the audience shouting a tirade of abuse against the candidate, denouncing him loudly as a coward and a cheat.[295] On election day, however, Cushing's attempt to enter the field of national politics utterly failed. His opponent received the vast majority of votes.[296] Cushing went on to lose further elections until the Boston Brahmins, who were becoming influential in government circles, helped him through the door of the United States House of Representatives.

William Henry Harrison, a member of the Whig Party, took office as president on March 4, 1841. He died one month later. There is very little known about the cause of the president's death, but the event became one of the most important turning points in America's history, since the nation's economic and foreign policies were immediately turned upside down once Vice President John Tyler was sworn in as the new head of state. Within a short space of time, President Tyler made it clear that he did not intend to implement the political program of the Whig Party, of which he was nominally a member. With the exception of the Secretary of State, Daniel Webster, all cabinet members immediately resigned from office. None of them would do the least to support the president in disregarding the key principles of Whig policy. Webster's peculiar willingness to serve Cushing, and thereby go against the former President John Quincy Adams (ΦBK)[297] who had also applied for this prestigious and influential position, can be easily explained: Cushing had loaned Webster a large sum of money which would subsequently increase enormously from its original value. Webster repaid his debts to Cushing throughout his life in "another currency." Caleb Cushing now had enough power to influence the most important decisions in Congress. His aim was to increase John Tyler's presidential power. Tyler, originally from Virginia, could rely entirely on Cushing, the Whig politician from Massachusetts, although Cushing should have pursued the very opposite policy had the criteria of his party membership been conclusive. The president prevented the establishment of a publicly controlled central banking system.

Representatives of the Boston Brahmins in China, supervised and led by the American consul in Canton, Warren Delano, Jr., watched with great satisfaction as the British military invaded China and imposed a punishing

---

[294] Ibid., 52-53; https://archive.org/details/liberatorwilliam017641mbp/page/n63; Garrison's biographer, John L. Thomas, interpreted the hostile action of the publicist as though he were really at enmity with Cushing.

[295] Ibid., 53; https://archive.org/details/liberatorwilliam017641mbp/page/n63

[296] Ibid.

[297] Member of the Phi Beta Kappa Society, Harvard College, 1787

peace treaty on the emperor of Peking.[298] The aim of this treaty, drawn up by the British Charles Elliot, was the deliberate humiliation of the Chinese government which had dared to thwart England's commercial interests and to strike back militarily after being provoked to take up arms. Figuratively speaking, Elliot's head was adorned with the laurels of the successful Opium War when, as British ambassador, he arrived in the Republic of Texas which had recently seceded from Mexico and completed his scheming plan. This turned out to be an immense disaster for the United States. President Tyler appointed Caleb Cushing as America's first minister to the Chinese government. When Cushing arrived in China, he carried with him a letter written by Daniel Webster to the Chinese emperor outlining the demands that America would make on China. During his trip, Cushing was greeted with cannon shots by the British governors of Gibraltar, Malta, Egypt, and India and was treated to exquisite food and comfortable accommodation.[299] He was invited to visit the task forces and to participate in a tiger hunt. He was particularly impressed by the communications network that spanned the Empire from one end to the other. The emperor of the Qing dynasty had no interest in a peace treaty imposed by another Western nation which would only bring him humiliation. Cushing announced that he would mobilize the entire fleet of American warships in order to get his treaty with China. The Chinese emperor was left with no option but to sign the Treaty of Wanghia on July 3, 1844. Like the British peace treaty, the American trade agreement contained a clause stating that Cushing's relatives should not be harassed by Chinese officials in their distribution of opium. All Americans living in China were granted the right to break Chinese laws without punishment. This treaty not only added America to the list of countries that had conquered China, but also stipulated that any future concessions granted by China to either Great Britain or America must also be automatically granted to the other country.

During his stay in China, Cushing received the news that the Tyler administration was making serious moves to annex Texas. According to the official announcement, Mexico would consider any such action taken by the American government as an act of war. As mentioned earlier, the British chief representative, Charles Elliot, who had previously fought in the Chinese Opium War, had arrived in the Republic of Texas as ambassador. Before the Texas Revolution, this state had constituted a large part of Mexico. American historians claim that the Tyler administration was forced to annex the independent State of Texas in order to prevent British interference in the Republic. Great Britain made no secret of its attempt to try every means of incorporating Texas into its empire. As a result, abolitionists such as William Lloyd Garrison sought to dissolve the union of the northern American states.

---

[298] S. also: Jack Beeching, *The Chinese Opium War* (New York City, NY: Harcourt Brace Jovanovitch, 1975).

[299] Claude Moore Fuess, *The Life of Caleb Cushing* (New York City, NY: Harcourt, Brace and Co., 1923) 422; https://archive.org/details/lifeofcalebcushi0001fues/page/422

Texas was under no circumstances to be affiliated with the federal state. England gave Garrison political control of the Republic of Texas and allowed him to manage the policing of the North American continent so that slavery would be abolished in the South. In 1846, Caleb Cushing arrived in Mexico as American general in order to participate personally in the war for which he was to a large extent responsible. The armed conflict, which brought death and destruction through battle, lasted from April 1846 to February 1848. Despite the United States' triumphant victory in the conquest campaign against their southern neighbours, who didn't have sufficient means of defence against the invading armies, America had now taken a route of violence that ran straight to the disaster of the War of Secession (1861 to 1865). Adding the Republic of Texas to the United States as a slave state increased the southern states' power enormously. This was the only reason why the Confederate States could later wage a war against the northern states that lasted many years.

Under the leadership of Caleb Cushing, a political alliance formed within Washington politics during the mid-1840s which played a decisive role in turning public opinion against the federalist State Union. As an agent of the Essex Junto, Cushing was elected chairman of the 1860 Democratic National Convention held in Charleston, South Carolina, despite holding no official government office at the time. Delegates from the Gulf States left the convention under protest, allegedly disliking the content of the program. The deliberate incitement of a rebellious attitude was key to the individual southern states' decision to steer an opposite course to government policies, ultimately triggering the tense secession crisis and provoking a catastrophic war.

8.2 Subsidization of special interest groups

The Freemason Grand Master Henry Clay (1777-1852) from Kentucky was a cunning statist concerned only with national interests. He sustained a mercantilist economic policy which actively encouraged the export of manufactured goods and restrained their import, as well as advocating Protectionism and inflation. Above all, Clay wanted to expand the American empire. As a leading member of parliament, he drove the young U.S.A. to war with England in 1812 by invading areas of Canada on dubious grounds. The consequences were catastrophic: the British burned down the White House, the Library of Congress, and vast areas of Washington, D.C. The general public were burdened with an enormous national debt, which in retrospect was used as a pretext to centralize the Bank of the United States. The resulting economic destabilization had serious consequences. As the central figure in government, Clay worked for forty years to implement excessive protective tariffs. He fought for state subsidies for his favored groups and profited personally from the central bank. Clay's ingenuity and cunning methods were designed to gain political power. High customs revenues financially benefited northern politicians, who had only come to power because of their wealth, at the expense of the general public. The southern states were forced to pay the lion's share, since at the time they were receiving eighty per cent of all imports.

The Whig Party, which had inherited the political legacy of the Federalists, favored a dominating Plutocracy. Financiers and major capitalists were both the leading actors and the profiteers. The introduction of protective tariffs led to the repression of international competition, and American businesspeople consequently raised the price of their goods. Southern farming businesses suffered the most from this, since they were supplied by the northern states. Protectionism presented the strongest attack on American property rights of the first half of the nineteenth century. At the same time, the Whig Party endorsed excessive subsidies for the transport industry, known as "internal improvements" (domestic infrastructure subsidies), thus increasing the wealth of construction companies and winning their support as a result. The majority of projects were never finished and ended in financial disaster. Taxpayers were made to pay the consequent enormous debts accumulated by the government.

Abraham Lincoln (1809-1865) sustained the "American System" of his political mentor, Henry Clay.[300] In the 1830s, he invested twelve million U.S. dollars in an absurd employment scheme, earning the contempt of the general public. For the Whig Party, however, this was a political success, since the money could be paid out to wealthy businessmen. Already one of the most successful lawyers of his time, Lincoln had established close relationships with powerful special interest groups. During and after the American War of Secession (1861-1865), this policy of favoring the elite to gain power and wealth was pursued under the leadership of the Republican Party which succeeded the Whig Party. One of the Republican Party's most prominent representatives was Abraham Lincoln (1809-1865), who used his political influence as a member of Parliament for Illinois and later as president of the U.S.A. to strengthen the wealthy elite in the northern states. Although the American Constitution forbade favoritism, it was precisely this that bought him political success. The Republicans who followed the Whigs found Lincoln to be their strongest supporter for a transcontinental railroad subsidized by the state. In this way, Lincoln secured the assets of a dynasty of American families who were closely connected to the Republican Party, and in return secured their votes for his policies.[301]

After the Republicans came to power in 1861, the American financial sector urged the government to start a war because of the enormous increase in national debt that was expected. Lincoln and his party successfully

---

[300] Michael Fitzgibbon Holt, *The Rise and Fall of the American Whig Party* (Oxford: Oxford University Press, [1999] 2003) 288.

[301] Dee A. Brown, *Hear That Lonesome Whistle Blow: The Epic Story of the Transcontinental Railroads* (New York City, NY: Holt, Rinehart and Winston, 1977; New York City, NY: Owl Books, 2001) 49; https://archive.org/details/hearthatlonesome00brow/page/48

introduced conditions for a mercantilist trade policy. Lincoln supported protective tariffs throughout the entirety of his political career, and his arguments against free trade were so nonsensical that they would never have been taken seriously had they been put forward by anyone other than the American president. His ambitions would be realized during and after the American War of Secession (1861-1865).

There is an awareness within politics that there has never been a democratic government that has not been controlled primarily by political and economic interests. In a Democracy, the reins of power are seized by the majority which then suppresses the politically weaker groups. Financial exploitation goes hand in hand with political oppression. The more resources are controlled by the government, the more intensely lobbyists seek to obtain subsidies from the treasury for economic projects. Huge government spending is financed with the help of a central bank which can print banknotes in any quantity desired.[302] Furthermore, no one in possession of a banknote has the right to exchange it for silver or gold. Two social classes emerge, taxpayers and tax consumers, with the upper class often robbing the masses of its earnings through force and fraud. Throughout American history, the northern idea of Conservatism has served to protect the rich from the poor. Southern Conservatism was a different matter altogether, valuing the preservation of the wisdom and ideals of the past.

Since Lincoln's day, America has lived in bondage to State Monopoly Capitalism (Corporatism). The existing system is not characterized by free market economy, but by the state's subsidization of the wealthy upper class. The quickest way for a government to boost inflation is to allow banks to continue operating without paying their debts. It is hard to imagine a more cunning example of political corruption than the subsidization of rich party members at the expense of the general public, who are left to pay high protective tariffs in the form of rising prices.

8.3 Aggression provoked by a national religious cult

Among the Republicans were many individuals with Christian backgrounds who had joined the New School of moderate Calvinism with its strict rules and regulations. They had a tendency to exercise their authority over others. The so-called Yankees campaigned for the abolition of slavery, believing that southern slaveholders were preventing the realization of heavenly conditions on earth. In their eagerness to establish a utopian society, they did all they could to abolish by law any practices which they considered to be unacceptable. They were opposed by the Democrats, among them Catholics and High-Church Lutherans, whose ideology centered on the principle of liberty. The strong influence of Republicanism on Christian eschatological teaching

---

[302] Richard Henry Timberlake, *Monetary Policy in the United States: An intellectual and institutional history* (Chicago, IL: University of Chicago Press, 1993).

(Postmillennialism) eventually led to the Imperialism of modern American foreign policy.

The abolition of slavery provoked acts of war – on the one hand because Northerners believed that God had chosen them to rule America, and on the other hand because influential individuals had turned away from Christianity to a bizarre religion of violence. The mass murderer John Brown led the fight against the Southerners and presented his execution as martyrdom. He was supported by a group of wealthy and distinguished men known as the "Secret Six," whose concern for the life and welfare of black slaves was only skin deep.[303] Their true aim was to destroy southern culture and civilization. The Yankee pamphletists led a hate campaign against the whole southern population that lasted for decades. The glorification of violence, mass killings, and war in the name of religion put the northern population into a state of frenzy.

One ideologist of progress was Francis Lieber (1800-1872), a German-born lawyer, publicist, and philosopher of law and state. Through his role as legal advisor, he had gained influence in Lincoln's war department. His highest creed was his conviction that the value of the state infinitely surpasses that of the individual, and that the state is therefore worthy of every sacrifice – whether of life, wife, or child. Lieber saw the state as the sacred union through which the Creator brought mankind to civilization.[304] He attributed general prosperity to the spirit of enterprise and considered the proper use of private property to be key to the shaping of progress.[305] With his conservative mentality, Lieber suggested that progress was only possible within the existing institutions of the state. These would protect freedom so long as it was understood as a right as well as a duty. This protective function would be essential to modern civilization. Progress depended on the development of human individuality, which was bent on accumulating as much wealth as possible.[306] In acquiring property, man had adopted the standards of behavior required for the development of a righteous character. After countries had turned in the direction of civilized society, God had left them to their own fate.

The idea of progress was central to social reformers' scope of action. A conservative such as Francis Lieber had no difficulty in expressing belief in progress with as much certainty as a social reformer, despite having a different understanding of what belief in progress entailed. He saw history as moving unequivocally toward the goal of a commonwealth of nations which would

---

[303] Otto Scott, *The Secret Six: John Brown and the Abolitionist Movement* (New York City, NY: Mason & Lipscom Publishers, 1974); https://archive.org/details/secretsixjohnbro00scot

[304] C. B. Robson, "Francis Lieber's Theories of Society, Government, and Liberty," *Journal of Politics*, 4, 2 (May, 1942), 237.

[305] Francis Lieber, *Letters to a Gentleman in Germany: Written After a Trip from Philadelphia to Niagara* (Philadelphia, PA: Carey, Lea & Blanchard, 1834) 49, 286-288; https://archive.org/details/letterstogentlem00lieb/page/48

[306] Ibid., 41, 42; https://archive.org/details/essaysonpropert00pottgoog/page/n52

have a religious character.[307] However, this would not exist as a socialist collective as aimed for by the progressive social reformers. The right to private property and the associated preservation of the citizen's individuality would be maintained.

8.4 Full implementation of political patronage

The slave trade itself was not the problem: millions of Americans in both South and North had material interests in its continuation. The driving force behind the war was not moral aversion to slavery, but rather the economic repercussions of reliance on forced slave labor. Financiers on the Northeast Atlantic coast saw slaveholders as the chief obstacle to the introduction of a mercantilist economy in America. National political and economic giants in the northern states joined forces in the Republican Party, strengthening themselves in order to enforce their will against the continuation of slavery even if this were to cost countless lives. Disagreements began to reach the limits of human obstinacy and self-interest, and could not be overcome without strife. Northern industrialists, who had become the largest industrial conglomerates with the help of state subsidies, fought against the Southerners, who had no share in the favoritism. The northern Yankee areas planned how they could dominate the southern states both economically and politically. When the Southerners realized their imminent danger of subjection to northern dictatorship, they formed a separate confederacy.[308]

The idea of the universal American meant that only those who paid homage to the federal government in Washington were accepted as Americans. Southerners were accordingly considered foreigners.[309] When Lincoln became president in 1861, he falsely asserted that the Union had existed before the Declaration of Independence was signed. He therefore declared any move toward independence from the Union to be an act of

---

[307] Francis Lieber, "Nationalism and Internationalism," *Contributions to Political Science: Miscellaneous Writings* (Philadelphia, PA: J. B. Lippincott & Co., 1881) vol. 2: 239-242; https://archive.org/details/in.ernet.dli.2015.172534/page/n235 "And the decree which has gone forth that many leading nations shall flourish at one and the same time, plainly distinguished from one another, yet striving together, with one public opinion, under the protection of one law of nations, and in the bonds of one common moving civilization. [...] The civilized nations have come to constitute a community, and are daily forming more and more a commonwealth of nations, under the restraint and protection of the law of nations, which has begun to make its way even to countries not belonging to the Christian community, to which the law of nations had been confined."

[308] William Appleman Williams, *The Contours of American History* (New York City, NY: New Viewpoints, [1961] 1973) 250-255, 297-300; https://archive.org/details/contoursofameric007738mbp/page/n261

[309] Cit. in James H. Moorhead, "Between Progress and Apocalypse: A Reassessment of Millennialism in American Religious Thought, 1800-1880," *Journal of American History*, 71, 3 (December, 1984), 532.

sedition and rebellion.[310] In 1861, when import tariffs lay at 47 percent in the North and 12 percent in the South, northern businesspeople feared economic disaster. They were reluctant to lose taxable territory and were filled with an ideological Nationalism. When South Carolina was bombed in April 1861, four more southern states joined the confederacy. Awful atrocities were committed until 1865 in the name of religious politics. The myth that Abraham Lincoln saved the Union and the Constitution, with his generals bringing the southern states to their knees, has long since been proven unfounded. The Republicans had monopolized political power in order to revolutionize the North ideologically and conquer the South militarily. Lincoln was no charitable democrat; he was rather an avaricious lawyer and cunning party official who invariably put himself and his party first. Lincoln anticipated a swift end to the war – but this proved to be a gross misjudgment.

The American War of Secession prepared the way for a new industrial system. War profiteers acted like business magnates, gaining immense wealth through extravagant government contracts, and aristocrats leading the country's economic development took every opportunity to acquire further subsidies from the state. The Republicans changed the principles of free market economy into the contrary stipulations of mercantilist politics. The southern states' inability to maintain political independence encouraged the rise of a culture of fanatical Nationalism in America. The emancipation of slaves, which was carried out through a war of extermination, prepared Americans for a new form of theological and social Radicalism which emerged in the South under the term "Reconstruction" shortly after the peace agreement.

8.5 Cultural development of a fanatical Nationalism

Southern slavery was only one reason why the northern states agitated for war. Many economic reasons carried just as much weight. The northern states eventually attained their goal of centralizing political power in Washington, D.C., for which Lincoln accepted numerous deaths, devastation, and plundering of private property. His appeal for a change in thinking justified his acts and pacified his conscience, and he presented his rescue of the Union and the abolition of slavery as acts of heroism. In truth, however, Lincoln had abandoned moral principles and assumed the power of a dictator.[311] There followed mass arrests without judicial assessment, restraints to the freedom of the press, removal of members of the opposition, and electoral fraud,

---

[310] President Abraham Lincoln, "First Inaugural" March 4, 1861, in Roy P. Basler, ed., *The Collected Works of Abraham Lincoln* (New Brunswick, NJ: Rutgers University Press, 1953) 264-265; https://archive.org/details/collectedworksof015582mbp/page/n279

[311] Clinton I. Rossiter, *Constitutional Dictatorship: Crisis Government In The Modern Democracies* (Princeton, NJ: Princeton University 1948; New York City, NY: Harcourt, Brace & World, 1963) 224; https://archive.org/details/in.ernet.dli.2015.499346/page/n231

among other illegal dealings. The war accelerated the development of a civil religion in which the state was venerated above all else. This was accompanied by the institutionalization and glorification of the administration – a critical aspect of civil religion.[312] In the light of this glorification, the government could get away with anything both immediately and later on, including the extermination campaign against the Indians and the mass murder of 200,000 Filipinos who did not want to be part of the American empire, among other global conflicts. All this took place in the name of virtue, liberty, guaranteed Democracy for every nation, and national self-determination. The absurd theory of American Exceptionalism – better described as "moral Narcissism"[313] – also served to justify the nation's interference in Europe during the First and Second World Wars.[314] The "Treasury of Virtue"[315] claimed by Americans is cast in an unfavorable light when one considers that Lincoln continued to allow slavery in the northern states, that he was a staunch racist who wanted to deport colored people from the United States, and that the law continued to discriminate against colored people for another century.[316]

After the war ended in 1865, doubt arose as to whether the postmillennial anticipation of the end times was really correct, since instead of progressive change for the better, both Northerners and Southerners met with desolation and poverty.[317] Nonetheless, a secular version of Postmillennialism with a patriotic and sociopolitical drive developed among Protestants. Biblical expectations of the future were supplemented with Enlightenment ideals, particularly the idea of progress and the improvement of human institutions.[318] Christians were encouraged to engage in evangelization, Ecumenism, and charity in order to hasten the arrival of the thousand-year reign.[319]

---

[312] Harold Bloom, *The American Religion: The Emergence of the Post-Christian Nation* (New York City, NY: Simon & Schuster, 1992) passim.

[313] Robert Penn Warren, *The Legacy of the Civil War: Meditations on the centennial* (New York City, NY: Random House; Lincoln, NE: University of Nebraska Press, [1961] 2015) 71.

[314] Ibid.

[315] Ibid., 59-66.

[316] Ibid., 61.

[317] James Moorhead, *American Apocalypse: Yankee Protestants and the Civil War, 1860-1869* (New Haven, CT: Yale University, 1978) x.

[318] Ernest Lee Tuveson, *Redeemer Nation* (Chicago, IL: University of Chicago Press, 1968) 36-38; https://archive.org/details/redeemernation00erne/page/36; s. also: Donald W. Dayton, "Millennial Views and Social Reform," in *The Coming Kingdom*, 66, 132 and James McDermott, *One Holy and Happy Society: The Public Theology of Jonathan Edwards* (University Park, PA: Pennsylvania State University, 1992) 91-92.

[319] Samuel Simon Schmucker, *Elements of Popular Theology*, 4th ed.. (Baltimore, MD: T. Newton Kurtz, 1853) 289-298; https://archive.org/details/elementsofpopul00schm/page/288

8.6 Violence caused by a policy of genocide

(Avaricious theft of vast Indian territories)
The escalation of violence and systematic genocide of Plains Indians began during the American War of Secession (1861-1865).[320] General Sherman's urge to exterminate anyone who hindered the United States' transition into a global empire was consistent with his earlier attitude toward his role in the war. William Tecumseh Sherman (ΦBK)[321] followed in the tradition of Secretary of State Henry Clay (1777-1852), who years before had publicly declared the "final solution to the Indian problem." Clay regarded the Indians as "inferior" to the Anglo-Saxon race. When 100,000 Cherokees were forced to leave their homes during the winter, around a quarter of them died. This rampant racism was taken to the extreme when the U.S. government began to describe the Indians not only as subhuman, but also as wild animals.[322] In order to avoid interracial mixing, General Sherman began an "ethnic cleansing" of the country, aiming to exclude all possibility of peaceful relationships with Indian tribes.[323] The Indians realized that they had become the victims of a systematic extermination campaign, and over the following two decades retaliated against all barbarous acts committed against them with equal force.[324] As white men made large profits from massacring herds of buffalo, the Indians were deprived of their livelihood.[325] By 1890, an estimated 45,000 Indians had been killed, and survivors led a meagre existence in restricted, guarded reservations. The U.S. government had cultivated an environment of violence and death for almost thirty years.

Not all white people were involved in the campaign to exterminate the Indians. Many were in favor of maintaining peaceful trade and good relations, as had been the case until the mid-nineteenth century.[326] Indians had helped the English Pilgrim Fathers at the beginning of the seventeenth century, when they arrived virtually destitute on the East Coast of America. John Smith had married Pocahontas. John Ross, a white man of Scottish descent

---

[320] Thomas J. DiLorenzo, "The Culture of Violence in the American West: Myth versus Reality," *The Independent Review*, vol. 15, no. 2 (Fall, 2010), 227-239. Some of the following passages are based on information contained in this article.

[321] Member of the Phi Beta Kappa Society, Dartmouth College, 1866

[322] Robert V. Remini, *Henry Clay: Statesman for the Union* (New York City: W. W. Norton, 1991) 314

[323] Michael Fellman, *Citizen Sherman: A Life of William Tecumseh Sherman* (New York City, NY: Random House Publishing Group, 1995; Lawrence, KS: University Press of Kansas, 1997) 24; https://archive.org/details/citizenshermanli00fell/page/24

[324] Dee A. Brown, *Bury My Heart at Wounded Knee: An Indian History of the American West* (New York City, NY: Holt, 1970) 92; https://archive.org/details/burymyheartatwou00brow/page/92

[325] Ibid., 265; https://archive.org/details/burymyheartatwou00brow/page/264

[326] Jennifer Roback, "Exchange, Sovereignty, and Indian-Anglo Relations," in Terry Anderson, ed., *Property Rights and Indian Economies* (Savage, MD: Roman & Littlefield, 1992) 9.

with Cherokee blood in his veins, had been chief of the Cherokees in Tennessee and North Carolina. Peaceful alliance with the Indians was far more common than hostile confrontation during the first half of the nineteenth century. The Europeans generally acknowledged the Indians' rights to their land. As the settlers knew: trade is profitable, war is costly. Contrary to popular opinion, there was no continual conflict between European settlers and Indians.

The policy of genocide against the Plains Indians was not a matter of white people seizing land for free settlement. It rather originated with the decisions of a relatively small group of white men at the head of the Republican Party, who at that time held power over the country. These men utilized the most recent technologies for mass murder which had been developed during the War of Secession. Those who benefited most from this policy of genocide were the industrial tycoons in the Northeastern United States. A primary reason for the drastic change in the second half of the nineteenth century was the mentality of the standing army which replaced the local militia, the latter only having been called up in the event of conflict. Soldiers gained self-confidence from their domination of others and their personal gain from the war, despite its adverse impact on the general public. Land speculators and railroad operators relied on soldiers in order to avoid the repercussions of their greedy theft of vast Indian territories. They made use of a popular argument in order to validate their illegal territorial claims: the progress of civilization could only be guaranteed if the vast majority of the North American continent were put to its best use.[327] Furthermore, the Indians' rights of ownership allegedly extended only to the land which they already inhabited. The majority of white men saw no reason to stop this wicked theft, since many of them benefited from it themselves. The governor of the Indiana Territory asked rhetorically "whether one of the most exquisite parts of the world ought to be left in its natural state – the habitat of miserable savages – if the Creator intended it to nourish a large population and be the seat of civilization, science, and true religion?"[328]

However, closer consideration of the situation of the Cherokees and other civilized Indian tribes in western North Carolina and Georgia shows that their problem was largely caused by the suitability of their settlements to the white man's way of life. Their agriculture and large-scale cattle farming greatly increased the value of the land that they cultivated. The often impoverished settlers envied the Indians' prosperity.[329] The transfer of rights of land ownership from the natives to the American settlers was generally

---

[327] Albert Katz Weinberg, *Manifest Destiny: A study of nationalist expansionism in American history* (Baltimore, MD: The Johns Hopkins University Press, 1935) 73; https://archive.org/details/manifestdestinys0000wein/page/72

[328] Cit. in ibid., 79; https://archive.org/details/manifestdestinys0000wein/page/78

[329] Charles Francis Adams, ed., *Memoirs of John Quincy Adams: Comprising portions of his diary from 1795 to 1848* (Philadelphia, PA: Lippincott and Co., 1874-1877) vol. 6: 272; https://archive.org/details/memoirsjohnquin55adamgoog/page/n281

regulated by treaties, with the settlers usually paying an adequate price. Many immigrants came to own land in this way. However, politicians in Washington, D.C., often declared contracts with Indians to be invalid. In 1871, Congress passed a law which categorically prohibited any treaties with the Indians under threat of disciplinary action. The political establishment could not have made it more clear to the Indians that white men were not looking for peaceful relations. Politicians were concerned above all with the swiftest possible settlement of the continent, especially the sparsely populated regions of the western frontier.[330] Tribes were displaced from their original districts and allowed to settle temporarily in desolate areas away from where the white colonists lived. Indians were gradually imprisoned in reservations assigned to them under threat of arms, and were declared by law to be a foreign nation. In this way, criticism of the American genocide policy and oppression of the Indians coming from the European press could be mitigated; Indians were treated as foreign terrorists who posed a threat to the internal security of the United States.

Promotion of a culture of war and violence is one of the tragic outcomes of the military interventions of the American state. In 1865, General Sherman was ordered to initiate a twenty-five-year war against the Plains Indians. This was considered necessary to enable the state's indirect subsidization of the building of transcontinental railroads.[331] Enormous profits were gained not only by the railroad companies involved, but also by other businesspeople who had close relationships with politicians in Washington, D.C. Financial donations streamed into the coffers of the Republican Party. The chief engineer of the state-subsidized transcontinental railroads was the Freemason Grenville Dodge, whose task was to "clean up" the planned routes from the Indians living along them. Immediately after the war, Dodge proposed that the Indians be taken as slaves and forced to level the ground for the railways.[332] The government rejected Dodge's suggestion and instead resolved to kill as many Indians as possible. Sherman had already invested in railroad companies before the war and was an extremely shrewd political leader[333]; this characteristic was also shared by his brother, the Freemason John Sherman, as well as by the vice president of the Union Pacific Railroad, Thomas Clark Durant, and the engineer Grenville Dodge.

---

[330] Ibid.

[331] William T. Sherman, *Memoirs of General William T. Sherman*, 2nd ed. (New York City, NY: Appleton, 1889) vol. 2: 411; https://archive.org/details/memoirs02sher/page/410

[332] Dee A. Brown, *Hear That Lonesome Whistle Blow: The Epic Story of the Transcontinental Railroads* (New York City, NY: Holt, Rinehart and Winston, 1977; New York City, NY: Owl Books, 2001) 64; https://archive.org/details/hearthatlonesome00brow/page/64

[333] Sherman, *Memoirs of General William T. Sherman*, 775.

8.7 Hegemony of consolidated state power

(The North treats the defeated South like a colony)
The image of Abraham Lincoln as a Christian-like savior-president became a widespread myth. However, there is no evidence to support it. Documented instead are his manic depression, suicidal tendencies, and conceit.[334] Endless veneration of this man contributed unimaginably to the formation of historical myths. Innumerable justifications were invented to pardon every instance of objectionable behavior on his part. The myth is more astonishing still in light of the fact that Lincoln was the most hated of all American presidents during his lifetime.[335] However, his assassination on Good Friday 1865 turned him into a self-sacrificing hero, and he was awarded the halo of a savior[336] who had liberated slaves and saved the Union.

After Lincoln's death, the Republican Party strove for supremacy during the Reconstruction Era of 1865 to 1876 by consolidating state power. They received no noteworthy opposition in Congress. Members of the Republican Party promoted the economic interests of northern banks and corporations, and in return received financial support in order to conduct their election campaigns successfully. The ruling Republican Party implemented a policy of corruption, vengefulness, and destruction in the militarily occupied southern states. "Reconstruction" referred not to an economic rebuilding of the South, but to its political reconfiguration.[337] In reality, the War of Secession was a revolution that destroyed and replaced the Union.

Reconstruction[338] came to an end for different reasons and at different times in each state, allowing local politicians to regain control over state government. The war had led to a marked decline in Gross Domestic Product in every state. Influential northern politicians did not want to recover the demolished southern economy on any account. The northern elite were not entirely successful in their dubious project, since the American population clung on to a constitutional government. Whereas the government had originally been intended to preserve individual freedom, it was now interested

---

[334] Joshua Wolf Shenck, *Lincoln's Melancholy: How Depression Challenged a President and Fueled His Greatness* (Boston, MA: Houghton Mifflin, 2005).

[335] Larry Tagg, *The Unpopular Mr. Lincoln: America's Most Reviled President* (El Dorado Hills, CA: Savas Beatie, 2009).

[336] Allen C. Guelzo, *Abraham Lincoln: Redeemer President* (William B. Eerdmans Publishing Company, [1999] 2013).

[337] Claude G. Bowers, *The Tragic Era: The Revolution after Lincoln* (New York City, NY: Houghton-Mifflin, 1929); https://archive.org/details/in.ernet.dli.2015.2473/page/n7; William Archibald Dunning, *Reconstruction: Political and Economic, 1865-1877* (New York City, NY: Harper & Brothers, 1907); https://archive.org/details/bub_gb_XgIOAAAAIAAJ/page/n5; William Archibald Dunning, *Essays on the Civil War and Reconstruction and related Topics* (New York City, NY: Harper & Row, 1965); https://archive.org/details/essaysoncivilwa07dunngoog/page/n6

[338] Thomas J. DiLorenzo, "The Consolidation of State Power via Reconstruction, 1865-1890," *Journal of Libertarian Studies*, vol. 16, no. 2 (Spring, 2002), pp. 139–161.

only in building an empire. The strengthening of a central government in Washington, D.C., was pushed forward to this end, consequently undermining the Constitution. In the post-war period – a uniquely revolutionary era – democratic philosophy and Transcendentalism merged together in the thinking of Republican Party members to form a program of reconstruction. This was aimed at a fundamental reshaping of political realities in both South and North. Radical ideals in theology have radical effects on politics, the social sector, and the economy. Many of the missions projects undertaken by northern churches were nothing other than actions ordered by the government in order to democratize the hierarchical society of the South. The preaching of the Gospel of Jesus Christ was of no significance to this cause and was completely ignored. Inland mission societies enthusiastically ran programs that soon came to characterize the activism of the "Social Gospel" movement. The idea that human behavior is completely determined by sinful tendencies, as taught by Calvinism, lost all meaning. The theory of evolution commenced its conquest of all areas of culture, for which Transcendentalism had paved the way.

Empty promises, lies, fraud, corruption, military dictatorship, political disenfranchisement, exploitation, and violence on the part of the ruling Republican Party led to immeasurable profits for its members and supporters.[339] On the other hand, it led to loss of property, poverty, famine, and prostitution for exploited Southerners, as well as to national debt. Exploitation became so great that even elected representatives in the South pillaged their fellow citizens.[340] Laborers became demoralized, industry was paralyzed, and leading citizens left the South. The inflated southern state apparatus imposed by the North was filled with northerners seeking lucrative positions. Black people were promised land in exchange for their votes, but it was never given to them. In 1862, black people were banned from settling in Illinois. The South was forced to serve as only producer and exporter of raw materials, while economic control lay fully in the hands of northern capitalists. They struggled under an enormous tax charge, while money was given to former warlords and Yankee veterans. Profits from southern agriculture were used to finance industrialization in the North.

The presidency of Ulysses S. Grant (1869-1877) went down in history as a rule of scandal, lawlessness, and corruption. The economy ground to a halt. Railroad companies built unnecessary detours, since they received state funds by the mile. In order to gain still greater profits, construction companies used cheap materials and demanded the utmost from their workers, resulting in many accidents and deaths among both laborers and passengers. Poor management and corruption led to bankruptcies[341] and stock market crashes,

---

[339] E. Merton Coulter, *The South During Reconstruction* (Baton Rouge, LA: Louisiana State University Press, 1947) 148-149.

[340] Bowers, *The Tragic Era*, 363; https://archive.org/details/in.ernet.dli.2015.2473/page/n401

[341] Burton W. Folsom, Jr., "Entrepreneurs and the State," in *The Freeman* (Atlanta, GA:

which were followed by many years of economic depression. Fearing a socialist revolution, the ruling class of the wealthy eventually withdrew voting rights from laborers and immigrants, and implemented reforms to improve the management of railroad companies.

8.8 Reinforced monopolization of economic systems

("Robber barons" increase their profits during the Gilded Age)
After the war, an enormous economic upswing known as the "Gilded Age" took place in the northeastern and midwestern states. Christian influences declined and were replaced by increasingly materialistic values. American businessmen acted as "robber barons," gaining excessive profits through their corrupt business practices. In addition, companies were exploited through manipulation of stocks and shares, and powerful politicians showed remarkable audacity in illegal activities. The term "Gilded Age" (the period from the 1870s to around 1900) was coined by the famous writer and Freemason[342] Samuel Langhorne Clemens (ΦBK)[343], better known under his pseudonym Mark Twain. It was superficially a period of economic boom and technological progress; however, it was at the same time rife with poverty and corruption. A surprisingly high number of influential American captains of industry originated from the Yankee area of New England. The Republican Establishment devoted itself to realizing former Secretary of State Henry Clay's dream of state-subsidized industrialization. The state supported stock market speculation, and authorities encouraged corruption in the political party system. It was said that the state could not subsidize everything as if it were a fairy godmother: "Government funding benefits the largest investments"[344] was a slogan used by the most cunning business owners to favor their own financial affairs.

The Freemason[345] Commodore Vanderbilt (1794-1877) gained political power and used it to his own economic advantage. In order to increase his social status, he referred to himself as "Commodore" (shipmaster). His name went down in American history with the quote, "What do I care about law? Ain't I got the power?" In 1877, the year of his death, his assets amounted to

---

Foundation for Economic Education, April 1, 1988); https://fee.org/articles/entrepreneurs-and-the-state/; s. also: Burton W. Folsom, Jr., *Entrepreneurs versus the State* (Herndon, VA: Young America's Foundation, 1988).

[342] Member of the Polar Star Lodge No. 79 A.F.&A.M. in St. Louis

[343] Honorary member of the Phi Beta Kappa Society

[344] Vernon Louis Parrington, *Main Currents in American Thought: The Beginnings of Critical Realism in America, 1860-1920*, 3 vols. (New York City, NY: Harcourt, Brace & World, Inc., [1927] 1958) vol. 3: 21; https://archive.org/details/in.ernet.dli.2015.187865/page/n1013

[345] A stature of Cornelius Vanderbilt showing him to be a freemason: https://diannedurantewriter.com/wp-content/uploads/2018/04/25Vanderbilt_2sm.jpg

105 million U.S. dollars.[346] A worker's monthly salary was 30 dollars, while a skilled worker could earn around 100 dollars. Scarcely any agricultural businesses at the time were exempt from the burden of a high mortgage. Banks had an easy job exploiting debt-ridden farmers, often until they were forced to give up their businesses.

Inflation rose continually in the American economy, leading periodically to financial crisis and economic depression. The defeated South was largely defenseless against the exploitation of northern financiers. The Greenbacks, properly called United States Notes, were a fiat currency issued by the treasury of the northern states to cover the costs of the war. These were interest-free banknotes that promised U.S. dollars to their owners at a future date determined by Congress. The primary goal of the War of Secession, for which thousands of soldiers on both sides were sacrificed in vain on the battlefields, was, in the eyes of English and American financiers, to use the war debts to control the American banking system. Bankers accordingly demanded the right to issue bank notes in a new U.S. currency. The large banking houses in Philadelphia, New York, London, and Paris were reluctant to use the national currency since it prevented them from making profits. Their primary concern was therefore to exchange the "Greenback" currency for another covered by war bonds. If successful, they could acquire large quantities or resell them to wealthy customers for a profit. The government centralized the national banking system under the control of Jay Cooke and the bankers working alongside him in the East Coast metropolises and in London and Paris. Banks within the new system were authorized to issue loans proportional to their government bonds in order to increase the amount of money in circulation. Measures taken in 1836 to restrict inflationary financial policies were thus largely nullified. The new national banking system allowed only established banks to issue loans to business enterprises. Since Jay Cooke's bank maintained close contact with the Republican Party, Drexel, Morgan & Co. was left to cultivate a relationship with the Democratic Party. J. Pierpont Morgan knew that it was vital for an investment banker to know the leaders of at least one dominant party personally, and to cooperate with them in making laws that would benefit banking and industry. The powerful British investment bank N. M. Rothschild & Co. was also well represented in American politics by its agent, August Belmont, the long-time treasurer of the Democratic Party.

During the 1870s, J. Piermont Morgan founded his own elite organization which he called the Zodiac Club.[347] Membership of this private, secret club was restricted to "twelve Christian men of the Anglo-Saxon race."[348] According

---

[346] Gustavus Myers, *History of the Great American Fortunes*, 3 vols. (Chicago, IL: Charles H. Kerr & Company, 1907-1910) vol. 2: 96; https://archive.org/details/historygreatame03myer-goog/page/n100

[347] Stephen Birmingham, *America's Secret Aristocracy: The Families that Built the United State* (Boston, MA: Little, Brown and Company, 1987) 203-204, 208-209, 212; https://archive.org/details/americassecretar00birm/page/202

[348] Ibid.

to his biographer, Ron Chernow, Morgan was fascinated by Occultism.[349] In 1895, he founded his own bank in New York City which he named after himself. The network of banks with which J. P. Morgan & Co. conducted business included other financial institutions on the European continent, including the investment banks N. M. Rothschild & Co. in England and MM de Rothschild Frères in France. President and lawyer Grover Cleveland (president from 1884 to 1888 and from 1892 to 1896) was influenced directly by the Morgan bank almost throughout his life. A main client of his law firm in Buffalo, NY, was the New York Central Railroad company which was governed by J. Pierpont Morgan. Almost all members of Cleveland's cabinet remained within the Morgan ambit throughout their lives. During his second term in office, Richard Olney, a leading lawyer for Boston's financial elite, became a driving force in U.S. foreign policy. From 1891, Cleveland and Olney were on the board for the Morgan-controlled Boston and Maine Railroad.[350] There were many close friendships and family ties between members of government, firms, and banks.

Following the War of Secession, expansion of the rail network was prioritized above all other economic projects. The period from 1850 to 1900 was the age of the railroad, as America's economic and political developments were dominated by the transport industry more than almost any other enterprise before or after. Key to the success of railroad companies was their receipt of generous state subsidies on both national and state levels.[351] Railway promoters and land speculators, most of whom lived in New England, were anxious to obtain treasury funding and remove obstacles that stood in their way. The largest blockade to their plans was the refusal of the southern states to support a policy of favoritism (patronage), as advocated first by the Federalists, then by the Whigs, and finally by the Republicans. Land speculators tried to obtain the largest profits possible through the construction of railroads. Railway companies later sold much of the government-donated land to settlers arriving in the West for large sums of money. By the mid-nineteenth century, they had grown into America's dominant industrial conglomerates and constituted the country's most lucrative economic sector.[352] Their flow of investment money came from several sources: the growing number of commercial banks, a handful of private investment banks in America and Europe, and – the most important investors – informal

---

[349] Ron Chernow, *The House of Morgan: An American Banking Dynasty and the Rise of Modern Finance* (New York City, NY: Simon & Schuster, 1990) 51; https://archive.org/details/houseofmorganame00cher/page/50

[350] Gerald G. Eggert, *Richard Olney: Evolution of a statesman* (University Park: Pennsylvania State University Press, 1974) 33-34; https://archive.org/details/richardolneyevol0000egge/page/32

[351] Edward C. Kirkland, *A History of American Economic Life* (New York City, NY: F. S. Crofts & Co., 1933) 390.

[352] Alfred D. Chandler, Jr., ed., *The Railroads: The Nation's First Big Business* (New York City, NY: Harcourt, Brace & World, 1965) passim.; Alfred D. Chandler, Jr., *The Visible Hand: The managerial Revolution in American Business* (Cambridge, MA: Belknap, 1977) passim.

syndicates of wealthy financiers from the eastern metropolises (Boston, New York City, and Philadelphia), London, and Paris. One of the best-known of these investors' unions was the Forbes Group.

John Murray Forbes directed the Perkins Syndicate in Canton, China. After seven years in the Chinese harbor city, the twenty-four-year-old Forbes returned to America in 1837, subsequently becoming one of the most important financiers on the East Coast. The group of financiers around him, who had earned millions of dollars smuggling drugs into China, could at any time liquidate their money and buy up financially profitable companies. The most important members of the Forbes Group besides John Murray were the influential Boston Brahmin Robert B. Forbes (brother), Thomas H. Perkins (uncle), John P. Cushing (cousin), William Sturgis, and Charles E. Perkins. The Forbes Group investors took over several strategically important railroads. When several railroad companies went bankrupt in the economic depression of 1857, Forbes was issued a personal loan of 2 million U.S. dollars by Barings Bank in England and thus preserved its dominance in the national transport industry.

By the 1880s, the enormous overinvestment problem could no longer be concealed. America's transport system had penetrated sparsely populated areas without proper consideration of the economic issues that would jeopardize further expansion. A temporary solution to this problem was to allocate land for settlement in the western territories and states. The vicious cycle of bankruptcy, reorganization, debt reduction, and issue of shares created a depressive atmosphere among businessmen. Once enthusiastic financiers were now confronted with the harsh reality that their immense investments would yield only small returns at best.[353]

Subsidized railroad companies were the first large corporations to introduce a bureaucratic administrative structure, thus becoming pioneers in the management of other groups. The emergence of nationwide markets was only possible because transport companies took advantage of political privileges such as donations of land across the country, exclusive rights of use, exploitation of raw materials, state subsidies, advantageous licenses, legally protected patents, bank loans, and high protective tariffs. Competition was largely eradicated through the formation of cartels, and companies gained similar advantages from statutory regulations which prevented financially weak competitors from securing disproportionately large shares of the market. There were numerous connections between banks, investors, businesses, and politics; for example, the company J. M. Forbes & Co. invested in the American Bell Telephone Company founded by Alexander Graham Bell (ΦBK)[354]. Thomas Jefferson Coolidge (1831-1920) and his son Thomas Jefferson Coolidge, Jr., founded the United Fruit Company by using their family fortune to finance dishonest New Orleans businessmen in buying and

---

[353] Ray Ginger, *Age of Excess: The United States from 1877 to 1914* (Long Grove, IL: Waveland Press, 1965) passim.; https://archive.org/details/ageofexcessunite00ging

[354] Honorary member of the Phi Beta Kappa Society

managing plantations in tropical countries. Thomas J. Coolidge, Jr. (1863-1912), became president of the company, among whose shareholders were many influential New England families. T. Jefferson Coolidge's nephew, Archibald C. Coolidge (1866-1928), co-founded the Council of Foreign Relations. President Calvin Coolidge (ΦBK)[355] was one of his distant relations. In 1929, the Coolidges merged the Old Colony Trust Company, a subsidiary company of the United Fruit Company, with the First National Bank of Boston. The executive committees of the United Fruit Company and the First National Bank of Boston consisted of more or less the same individuals. In practice, the two companies were one and the same organization.

American financiers operated under systematic mismanagement for almost a century. Many of them were rogues driven by a consuming desire to obtain other people's money in whatever way necessary.[356] The financial Capitalism influenced by and dependent on the government had begun in Lowell and Boston in 1837, but J. Pierpont Morgan, Sr., had increased its commercial potential by controlling the buying and selling of bank and company shares. John D. Rockefeller, Sr. (1839-1937), was a pioneer of State Monopoly Capitalism (Corporatism) and consequently of the future American New Deal (economic and social reforms carried out between 1933 and 1938 under President Franklin D. Roosevelt, initiated as an answer to the global economic crisis). Formal Corporatism would not be effective until decades later.

As mass production of consumer goods that could not be sold profitably in America accelerated, many manufacturers were confronted with an almost unsolvable problem. Economists suggested two temporary solutions: 1) set up cartels to curb production, and 2) reconfigure working conditions. As new machinery was acquired, highly skilled workers were dismissed and replaced with unskilled, low-paid workers in order to keep the machines running. The largely unqualified laborers were entirely at the mercy of their employers and were given very few rights. Foreign markets were opened in an attempt to solve the problem of overproduction and to get rid of the many unsold products. Debates took place on whether overseas markets should be opened through military intervention, or whether there were peaceful alternatives. A definite answer to this question was still some years away. Industrialized countries were governed by a jurisdiction that favored an effective economic process; furthermore, the American government adopted universal, highly profitable economic norms that were applied to the whole country. Since 1865, Classical Liberalism in America had become an ideology that could be shaped at will and which no longer had any clear contours.[357] By

---

[355] Honorary member of the Phi Beta Kappa Society

[356] John T. Flynn, *Men of Wealth: The Story Of Twelve Significant Fortunes From The Renaissance To The Present Day* (New York City, NY: Simon and Schuster, 1941) passim.; https://mises.org/library/men-wealth-story-twelve-significant-fortunes-renaissance-present-day

[357] Frank Tariello, *The Reconstruction of American Political Ideology, 1865-1917* (Charlottesville, VA: University Press of Virginia, 1981).

opposing the way that civilization had developed since the mid-nineteenth century, Liberals allied themselves with Capitalists in order to defend the existing status quo. They pretended to warn against the Communism spreading through other countries. The Neoliberal reformers of the Gilded Age considered themselves to be above the dirty business of politics and hoped that bureaucracy would bring efficiency to the free market economy.

While American historians of the Gilded Age decried these abuses, historians after the Second World War glorified the large-scale industry and colossal administrative bodies of the time for their merits and virtues. At the beginning of the Cold War, it seemed wise to initiate extensive and costly economic projects led by large-scale industry.

A variety of different influences became evident as certain economic, social, and political problems emerged from America's rapid industrial growth. Foremost among them was the blatant corruption of the Gilded Age, which stemmed from the state subsidies granted for projects such as the construction of transatlantic railroads. This was made worse by widespread unrest among workers, urban poverty, economic concentration, and financial manipulation. During the final decade of the nineteenth century, leaders of large enterprises began to introduce a neo-mercantilist economic regulation in cooperation with the government, designed to eliminate competition and merge their companies within their various branches of industry, thus functioning as cartels. At the same time, some of the same captains of industry, temporarily in the service of the state, began to demand government support in order to encourage overseas economic expansion. The state claimed the right to control every aspect of American life, considering themselves authorized to dictate people's permitted alcohol consumption. This policy was governed by a symbiotic relationship between influential directors in industry and technocratic opinion makers in society. Together they sought to force the most important branches of the national economy into the monopolistic strictures of cartels through a planned economy. Liberal social critics warned against the concentration of power and wealth in the so-called "Money Trusts" – the syndicates of the financial and economic world. Populists and Progressives accused captains of industry of financial corruption and human exploitation, in doing so hitting the nail on the head. Many Congressmen were also business owners, such as Thomas C. Platt, a delegate of the Republican Party. In addition to his political duties, Platt was chief executive of the Tennessee Coal, Iron, and Railroad Company, which benefited from high protective tariffs and employed prisoners as free laborers.

9 Religious essence of Progressivism

During the central decades of the nineteenth century, secular themes came to the fore which created new emphases within Postmillennialism.[358] These were later of central importance to social action. People no longer looked to God for the formation of a new society, but rather to man.

9.1 Evolutionary interpretations of social change

(Society shaped by the relentless competition of Social Darwinism)
During the Age of Enlightenment of the eighteenth century, the West was inundated with treatises on the reality of technological development and cultural progress. Of particular note were the works of the French Enlightenment philosopher Anne Robert Jacques Turgot (1727-1781) and of Marquis de Condorcet (1743-1794). Along with Herder and Godwin, they began to secularize the doctrine of the Christian millennium in their conception of progress.[359] They spread the idea of a political utopia which would eventually emerge and create a state of heaven on earth. The authors admitted that this optimistic prediction was derived from the biblical prophecy of a thousand-year reign but otherwise developed along completely different lines. They also predicted the formation of a political union among European states. There was but a small step between this inventive conception of Progressivism and the panoramic views of social evolution presented by Auguste Comte, Karl Marx, and Herbert Spencer among other nineteenth-century thinkers.

Darwin, Spencer, and Comte largely used the terms "progress," "evolution," "growth," and "decent" synonymously. They were equally applicable to biology as they were to sociology. Darwin rarely used the word "evolution" in his writings in comparison with his frequent use of the terms "Developmentalism" and "progress." It should be noted that key theories of Developmentalism – such of those of Comte, Marx, and Spencer – were already commonly known before Darwin's work was published in 1859. Darwin's work thus presents a number of ideas which took on their conceptual meaning in light of social changes that occurred a century before the publication of *The Origin of Species* (1859). Closer examination of Darwin's

---

[358] William G. McLoughlin, "Pietism and the American Character," *American Quarterly*, 17 (Summer, 1965), 163-186; John L. Thomas, "Introduction," *Edward Bellamy, Looking Backward, 2000-1887* (Cambridge, MA: Harvard University Press, 1967) 1-88; Herbert G. Gutman, "Protestantism and the American Labor Movement: The Christian Spirit in the Gilded Age," *American Historical Review*, 72 (October, 1966), 74-101.

[359] S. also: Chap. 1.2 Secularized model of the idea of progress

theory of evolution reveals that he drew on several ideas which emerged from studies of the laws of human cohabitation long before the Darwinian era.[360]

In 1845, John Henry Newman published his monumental *Essay on the Development of Christian Doctrine*[361]. This book applied the idea of development to a specific topic more consistently than almost any other work of the nineteenth century. According to Newman, the simple homogeneity of the early Christian church had slowly developed into a powerful institution with great influence on national politics. The innate forces of Christianity had created an irrepressible urge to dominate the world both culturally and politically.

Through the publication of his *The Origin of Species* (1859) and *The Descent of Man* (1871), Charles Darwin contributed significantly to a new surge of popularity for the theory of evolution.[362] However, the theory of biological evolution was not an original product of his imagination. On the contrary, his evolutionary views drew on the speculative hypotheses of scholars such as Jean-Baptiste de Lamarck[363] (1744-1829), Sir Charles Lyell (1797-1875), and his grandfather Erasmus Darwin (1731-1802). His own momentous significance lay in his achievement of a new scientific status for the theory of evolution. The English naturalist thus initiated a revolution in biology and social science which had profound and widespread consequences on virtually every area of human knowledge. The humanities, philosophy, and even theology became permeated with the theory of evolution.

Darwin's theory of evolution became quickly accepted, for belief in the possibility of perfecting human nature was more appealing to many people than the idea that they were sinners in need of salvation, meriting nothing better than the wrath of God. According to Darwin, the process of bringing human nature to perfection takes place within inevitable progress, effected through the initiation and advance of reform movements such as the abolition of slavery. Auguste Comte's Positivism, Theodore Parker's Naturalism, and Charles Darwin's theory of evolution laid the foundation for a naturalistic interpretation of the universe which saw man as the culmination of the process of evolution. According to this natural philosophy, man could now be fully released from dependence on God and could take his fate into his own hands. Belief in man's inherent goodness and natural capacity for self-improvement arose from the optimistic notion that he has the appropriate means at his fingertips. The most important among these means were education and politics. New discoveries concerning natural processes were

---

[360] Charles Darwin, *The Origin of Species* (London: John Murray, 1859) 489-490; https://archive.org/details/in.ernet.dli.2015.222367/page/n501

[361] John Henry Newman, *An Essay on the Development of Christian Doctrine* (London: Longmans, Green, [1845] 1891); https://archive.org/details/AnEssayOnTheDevelopment1891

[362] C. Gregg Singer, *A theological Interpretation of American History* (Philadelphia, PA: Presbyterian and Reformed Publishing Co., 1964) passim.

[363] Jean-Baptiste Pierre Antoine de Monet, Chevalier de Lamarck.

given an air of infallibility. On the other hand, many people believed that theology had received a death blow from which it would never recover. To the extent that it was still regarded at all, the concept of sin took on an entirely different meaning for those who accepted the hypothesis of Darwinism as scientific truth. Sin was understood to be no more than ignorance of the true condition of human nature. At very best, it was viewed as a deficiency in adjusting to social environment.

In contrast, Christianity teaches that man's loss of his original physical and moral perfection was his own fault. Since his exile from the Garden of Eden, he has been in a deplorable state of physical decay and moral depravity. Man's life ends inevitably in death. However, the biblical doctrine of salvation was reformulated in accordance with the evolutionary hypothesis. The most urgent duty of the church was said to be participation in charitable causes. Social welfare charity was the only desirable way through which all men, not only Christians, could ultimately find "salvation" through self-fulfillment.

The publication of Charles Darwin's *The Origin of Species* (1859) gave enormous impetus to the idea of progress. His theory of the evolution of species through natural adaptation and selection was restricted exclusively to the field of biology. It did not involve any element of social progress. The philosophical movement of Social Darwinism which emerged in the second half of the nineteenth century was an attempt to apply Darwin's principles of "survival of the fittest" to political, economic, and social philosophy.[364] The ideology soon pervaded schools, universities, churches, businesses, and public authorities. Progressive social reformers claimed that man was not determined by his environment, but that man could change his environment through conscious and purposeful efforts. Social progress could be encouraged more effectively if both individual and economy were brought under collective control through appropriate planning.

Social Darwinism was perfectly suited to the scientific ethos of the Gilded Age, which held the study of nature in high regard. The promised land of the "saints" would be gradually transformed into a paradise of abundance and prosperity. During the second half of the 1870s, the doctrine of divine sovereignty was replaced with belief in natural destiny (Determinism), and the infallibility of the Holy Scriptures was forced to make way for the self-confident decrees of science. Social and natural scientists now constituted a new priesthood. Darwin and his followers promoted the experimental scientific method as the one legitimate approach to truth.

The worldview which emerged from Darwinism, characterized as "social," differed in many respects from the Enlightenment philosophy of Newton and Locke. However, it was equally strong in its opposition to the Christian faith. Any political, social, or economic philosophy that refers to

---

[364] Herbert Spencer, *Social Statics, or the Conditions Essential to Human Happiness Specified, and the First of Them Developed* (London: John Chapman, 1850; New York City, NY: D. Appleton and Company, 1871); https://archive.org/details/socialstaticsor00unkngoog/page/n6; s. also: "Progress: Its Law and Cause," in the *Westminster Review* (April, 1857).

natural laws as an absolute norm and immanent frame of reference is in direct conflict with Christianity. Faith in a personal Creator-God, as He is shown in the book of Genesis, excludes the idea that man is determined by impersonal laws in surrounding nature. Social Darwinism consciously and comprehensively rejected the Christian faith, replacing biblical theology with an utterly naturalistic philosophy. Calvinism was dismissed, since it supposedly sought to destroy human liberty and relied on a sovereign God who exercised absolute control over all human affairs. However, in denying man's moral responsibility before God, Social Darwinism dealt a fatal blow to every effort to promote freedom. The sovereignty of God, by which man is given liberty and responsibility, was rejected in favor of the rule of impersonal forces of nature, thus subjecting man's intentional behavior to pure whim.

Leading industrialists and financiers realized immediately that they could now appeal to a universally accepted – albeit questionable – scientific theory which declared their profit-seeking approach to be the ideal strategy for gaining great wealth.[365] The main parties felt no guilt for having committed what can only be described as highway robbery. They were even less aware that they had frequently committed criminal acts which went unpunished by the existing legal system, but which had nonetheless caused tremendous harm to the lives of the vast majority of wage earners who suffered ruthless exploitation. In many situations, major capitalists evaded justice simply by bribing judges and politicians. Even this corrupt behavior was not considered illegitimate, for it was an integral part of the prevailing economic philosophy. In this cold environment of relentless competition, the possibility of an ethics which would prevent this amoral conduct never came into the question. Expediency imposed itself as the final arbiter on what was right and what was wrong.

The second half of the nineteenth century witnessed the gradual emergence of an ideology from Protestant Postmillennialism. Postmillennialists had formerly pursued the goal of eradicating sin among the population, with the help of the government, in order to create a perfect society. In the parlance of the Social Gospel of the time, this society was referred to as the kingdom of God on Earth. However, the significance of the kingdom changed over time. Although its initial emphasis lay on religion, it shifted slowly but surely toward politics. The role of the state in planning and organizing a perfect social order became increasingly important. In the idealistic imagination of many Americans, the government became an institution of social salvation and assumed divine attributes as the perfect designer of a homogeneous organism of national unity. In the period that followed, the American Whigs, Know-Nothings, and Republicans began to include Progressivism in their manifestos with increasing consistency.

---

[365] Andrew Carnegie, "The Gospel of Wealth," *North American Review*, No. CCCXCI (June, 1889), 253-255; https://www.swarthmore.edu/SocSci/rbannis1/AIH19th/Carnegie.html; Henry Steele Commager, *The American Mind: An Interpretation of American Thought and Character since the 1880's* (New Haven, CT: Yale University Press, 1950) 209.

Social Darwinism inspired the greatest intellectual revolution to occur in American history: the emergence of a new worldview which presented an entirely new point of departure for understanding man's inner and outer worlds. Darwinism was not simply a new development in philosophy and theology. It was a revolution which not only dismissed Christian Theism and its implications from political, social, and economic thought, but also transformed the entire ideological structure in accordance with the framework of Darwinian Naturalism and scientific method. It taught that all moral concepts were in continuous development and were consequently only relative; they thus lost their status as authoritative guidelines in politics, the social sector, and the economy. The ethical foundation of the West consisted largely of the moral teachings of the Old and New Testaments, summarized by Jesus Christ in two main commandments: love God, and love your neighbor (Mark 12:28-31). Were Darwinism and Pragmatism to win this dispute with Christianity, every aspect of American life would be subjected to a revolution which would lead to a complete overthrow of constitutional state, free market economy, and social structure. In the social realm, this meant the reconfiguration of family, church, school, and the state itself as the executive institution in realizing God's will for human society – a society endowed by the Creator with certain privileges and responsibilities, ultimately responsible for the way in which it has dealt with them.

At the turn of the century, Social Darwinism was replaced with new discoveries in social theory. The idea of progress rose to be the most fundamental and influential idea of the time.

9.2 Impact of faith in science

(The spiritual attitude among the American public during the Progressive Era)

During the Progressive Era which commenced in the late nineteenth century, Puritan Calvinism was superseded in American Protestantism by liberal Christianity. The latter was better suited to the optimistic attitude shared by many people and offered greater insight into why external conditions had improved so dramatically within so little time. The Calvinist doctrine of total depravity lost all credibility in the eyes of many Americans, who were convinced by the humanistic terms of Social Darwinism. The belief that a heavenly kingdom on earth could be established by the grace of God alone was displaced by the idea that society could improve through science alone. Many Christians regarded science as the gracious providence of God. While "grace" originally signified the promise of eternal salvation in the world to come, its new interpretation signified better social conditions. The church eventually ceased to be the most important institution in establishing God's kingdom, and natural and human sciences were awarded Messianic significance.[366] Progressives were supported by liberal theologians who promoted a Social Gospel and a secularized kingdom, and equated the kingdom of God on earth with a program of political reform. Liberal theologians reinterpreted the Bible in an effort for Christianity to survive in the age of science. Darwin's theory of evolution was readily accepted, since people preferred to believe in human improvement than to see themselves as sinners in need of salvation.

American Evangelicalism split into three categories. The largest was conservative, appealed to the middle class, and gave no thought to the social hardship suffered by many Americans. The second category went by the name "New Theology" and advocated a historical-critical interpretation of the Bible, a progressive conception of history, and authoritative belief in science. The third category, known as "Higher Life Theology," believed in the imminent return of Christ and supported the urban revival movement, worldwide mission, and divine healing. Representatives of the "Higher Life Theology" were the strongest critics of social injustice. The evangelical movement underwent a fundamental change and later became divided: neo-evangelicals separated from fundamentalists, and modernists united in the World Council of Churches.

9.3 Socio-economic reforms in the Progressive Era

In the early nineteenth century, factory owners dealt ruthlessly with their employees, many of whom were forced to carry out strenuous labor.[367] Working conditions in farms and factories declined sharply when the War of Secession broke out in 1861. Desperate workers tried to get themselves heard through strikes, seeking to make the miserable conditions in the workplace more humane. The state militia in Pennsylvania and New York had their hands full trying to end workers' protests. Fatal shots were fired at laborers on many occasions[368], and employers strengthened their claims by complaining about the audacity shown by their workers in forming trade unions.[369] The only way out of the misery seemed to be migration westward to untouched land. This possibility was closed to many people, however, since they were unable to raise the necessary starting capital. Those who dared to take the arduous journey often had to abandon the idea of becoming independent farmers when they reached their destinations, instead hiring themselves out

---

[366] H. Richard Niebuhr, *The Kingdom of God in America* (Middletown, CT: Wesleyan University Press, [1937] 1988); https://archive.org/details/kingdomofgodinam0000nieb

[367] Myers, *History of the great American Fortunes*, vol. 2: 59; https://archive.org/details/historygreatamer02myer/page/n63

[368] Ibid., vol. 2: 64; https://archive.org/details/historygreatamer02myer/page/n67

[369] Ibid., vol. 2: 59, 61; https://archive.org/details/historygreatamer02myer/page/n63

as low-paid agricultural laborers. The best land already belonged to railroad companies and large-scale cattle breeders.[370]

By the end of the nineteenth century, the hardship and suffering in urban working-class districts could no longer be ignored. Unstable trading conditions and large numbers of immigrants led to high levels of unemployment, disease, and alcoholism. Social reformers called on the nation to address the situation and to seek a remedy. The positive view of the future among Progressives arose from liberal theology, which emphasized man's free will, favored modern culture, encouraged faith in science, and in general was highly optimistic about the future. The new democratic era introduced an altered understanding of God in accordance with humanistic principles: man was seen to be assisted by God, but was not required to submit to Him.

Considering the overall effect of the alliance between socialist Progressivism and liberal Christianity, it is clear that the most important doctrines of the Christian faith – the doctrines of Creation, the Fall, and salvation in Christ – were rejected in favor of the radical concept of an absolute state. Since the practical implementation of this concept was based on the theory of evolution[371], it led to a completely irrational image of the nature and purpose of human society. Leading economists of the time joined the chorus of clergymen who readily and routinely drew on evolutionary concepts – such as heredity, selection, the struggle for survival, and race – in promoting their religiously motivated projects of economic reform. Many evangelicals who had joined the Social Gospel movement adapted biblical teachings to evolutionary science.

9.4 Totalitarian principles of a collective social order

(The Social Gospel advocates a totalitarian social order under the auspices of Socialism)
Most of the liberal theologians and church officers who accepted the "new Gospel" believed that the Pauline Gospel was no longer applicable to modern-day problems, and that biblical morality had ceased to be an adequate answer to people's needs. In contrast, the Social Gospel seemed to offer a satisfactory solution to America's many social and political problems. Those who promoted the Social Gospel wanted to give their cause – the introduction of a new social order – the impetus that it needed to appeal to the general public. Transcendentalism inspired the rise of theological Liberalism, which characterized American theology during the first half of the twentieth century. The Social Gospel endorsed Darwinism in order to receive the intellectual support of a scientifically accredited hypothesis.

---

[370] Ibid., vol. 2: 76; https://archive.org/details/historygreatamer02myer/page/n79

[371] David N. Livingstone, *Darwin's Forgotten Defenders: The Encounter between Evangelical Theology and Evolutionary Thought* (Grand Rapids, MI: W. B. Eerdmans, 1984) 2.

The Industrial Revolution created the necessary economic and political framework for proponents of the Social Gospel to achieve their aims. After the American War of Secession (1861-1865), the northern economy experienced an enormous upswing. The social milieu could not keep pace with this rapid development, resulting inevitably in serious social problems. Employers were nonetheless reluctant to recognize their workers' plight. At the turn of the century, many liberal theologians and church officials turned to the Social Gospel, which advocated a "Christian" Socialism. The effects of the Social Gospel on American life were probably more significant than those of any other ideology. The Social Gospel movement gained wide respect, since it claimed to pursue a Christian social policy and constantly referred to the Bible in its public statements. Many Christians were initially unaware that the Social Gospel misinterpreted the traditional message of the Holy Scriptures. For some time, many Americans failed to recognize its shift in emphasis on important aspects of the Christian faith and its misappropriation of Christianity for purposes completely separate from it. Postmillennial Protestants quickly found favor with the economy-controlling political Paternalism (the state's assumption of a custodian role toward citizens) that was gaining acceptance. This gave them the opportunity to disparage demon rum, Sabbath breaking, dancing, and gambling, as well as other forms of entertainment, in public opinion. An attempt was made to declare rural Catholic schools illegal; the introduction of the public school system was seen as a clever way to turn Catholic children into Protestants. People believed that only the federal government could create a perfect economy. The government also seemed to be a suitable means of eradicating sin of every kind. The Republican Party won the full support of many Christians as it was portrayed as "the party of great moral ideas." Shareholders, managers, and employees of the large railroad companies naturally formed a pool of Republican voters, since many of them were deep in debt and in need of generous subsidies in order to stay in business. They were joined by the Pennsylvanian iron and steel industry, which was highly inefficient and unable to survive economically unless protected from import competition by high tariffs. Most northern industrialists were Postmillennialists who longed for the establishment of a perfect society in which the public treasury would provide financial support wherever it was needed. The fusion of religious and economic interests created a powerful force that brought political, economic, and church affairs into a close relationship. After 1900, the intertwining of science, business, and politics resulted in a financially strong syndicate which offered numerous possibilities for the manipulation of public opinion.

Interest groups which did not want to be subordinated to a Postmillennial Theocracy found a political home in the laissez-faire Democratic Party. Among them were Irish Catholics, German Lutherans, Dutch and Scottish Calvinists, secular freethinkers, Baptists, and Methodists. Their manifesto largely consisted of promotion of a free market economy at national level which would include free foreign trade and the use of hard currency.

In light of the hardship endured by so many people during the 1890s, the American Baptist theologian Walter Rauschenbusch (1861-1918) called Christian churches to action.[372] His message was in accordance with the progressive ideas of Henry Demarest Lloyd, who was the most well-known protagonist of the religion of progress at the time. Convinced that he was offering an ingenious solution to the crisis, Rauschenbusch asserted that progress was inevitable. The liberal theologian believed that man was free to shape his future at will – that he had the opportunity to decide the course of his own life – and that the laws of progress guaranteed the appearance of the heavenly Jerusalem on earth. Rauschenbusch adopted the "three-step" theory of social evolution formulated by James Mark Baldwin (1861-1934), another exponent of the religion of progress, which taught that the pre-capitalist order had vanished, that the capitalist order had reached a climax, and that the collective order had not yet come to maturity.[373] By understanding the details of social evolution through sociology, man himself could direct the course of progress in the desired direction, so that society could be fully integrated in a collective order.[374] Despite the obvious contradiction, Rauschenbusch seemed to have no difficulty in synthesizing social freedom and social inevitability in a system of thought which, he claimed, was derived from Christian ethics. In order to bring about the social millennium, man had to conform to the spiritual process of progress. Rauschenbusch urged people to search for a religion capable of doing the seemingly impossible – of realizing the utopian, but achievable, goals of a collective social order in which no one would oppose the total rule of the state for the good of the people. Walter Rauschenbusch can be regarded as the theological founder of the Social Gospel movement. In his first work, he appealed to Christian churches to realize their responsibility in the face of the social crisis.[375] In his second, he provided an outline for social action[376], and in his third, he put forward a new theology in justification of his appeals in his first two works. He emphasized the need for a Christian Socialism that would be a cure-all in the fight against social injustice. He advocated a totalitarian social order under the auspices of Socialism, which he equated with the true concerns of Christianity.[377]

---

[372] Walter Rauschenbusch, *Christianity And The Social Crisis* (New York City, NY: The Macmillan Company, 1907); https://archive.org/details/christianitysoci00rausiala/page/n5

[373] Walter Rauschenbusch, *Christianizing the Social Order* (New York City, NY: The Macmillan Company, 1912) 384; https://archive.org/details/christianizingso00raus/page/384

[374] Rauschenbusch, *Christianity And The Social Crisis*, 209; https://archive.org/details/christianitysoci00rausiala/page/208

[375] Ibid., 422; https://archive.org/details/christianitysoci00rausiala/page/422

[376] Rauschenbusch, *Christianizing the Social Order*, 458; https://archive.org/details/christianizingso00raus/page/458

[377] Walter Rauschenbusch, *Theology for the Social Gospel* (New York City, NY: The Macmillan Company, 1917) 3, 29; https://archive.org/details/theologyforsocia00raus/page/2

9.5 Universal indwelling of God in society

(The Gospel is replaced by charitable action – the Social Gospel)
During the central decades of the nineteenth century, Postmillennialism was the generally accepted doctrine among American Protestants.[378] The latter believed that biblical prophesies represented true future events.[379] Under the influence of the liberal "New England Theology" (New Haven Theology, New Divinity), many people believed that the impending thousand-year reign would involve a complete reformation of earthly conditions. Liberal theologians opened themselves up to new ideas which later took on concrete form in the Social Gospel. The focus was thus no longer on the Holy Spirit's work of conversion, but rather on the moral improvement of the individual. Natural and social sciences increased in influence, with technological progress emphasized most of all as the fulfillment of eschatological expectations. A utopian social order was equated with the kingdom of God on earth.[380] People believed that the return of Christ could be brought about through evangelization, and the call to conversion was conjoined with the call to social action. Lyman Beecher, for example, was particularly committed to domestic mission during the 1850s[381]; like many of his Masonic brothers and evangelical contemporaries, he saw this as the key to bringing Kingdom Theology into effect.[382] Beecher had turned away from Old School Calvinism and had adopted Nathaniel W. Taylor's New Haven Theology (New Divinity). He spoke out against Catholic immigrants, took up the cause of the liberation of slaves, and sought to provide theological substantiation for the idea of America's Manifest Destiny. The final years of his life were overshadowed by a charge of heresy brought against him in 1835, which preluded the Presbyterian schism that followed two years later.

Secular institutions were also used to hasten the dawn of the new era of peace and justice. As clerics were offered positions in society and politics by the government, they were able to exercise a greater influence. This

---

[378] "History of Opinions Respecting the Millennium," *American Theological Review* 1 (1859), 655.

[379] "The Fulfilment of Prophecy," *Princeton Review* 33 (1861), 84; s. also: Hollis Read, *The Coming Crisis of the World, or, The great battle and the golden age: the signs of the times indicating the approach of the great crisis and the duty of the church* (Columbus, OH: Follett, Foster, and Co., 1861); "The Millennium of Rev. XX," *Methodist Quarterly Review* 25 (1843), 83-110; Robert K. Whalen, "Millenarianism and Millennialism in America, 1790-1880" (Ph.D. diss., Stony Brook, NY: State University of New York, 1972).

[380] Raymond H. Merritt, *Engineering in American Society: 1850-1875* (Lexington, KY: University Press of Kentucky, 1969) 23-24,   52-58;   https://archive.org/details/lifeof-mindinamer00mill/page/22

[381] Lyman Beecher, *A Plea for the West* (Cincinnati, OH: Truman & Smith, 1835) 10; https://archive.org/details/apleaforwest02beecgoog/page/n16

[382] Barbara M. Cross, "Introduction," *The Autobiography of Lyman Beecher* (Cambridge, MA: Belknap Press of Harvard University Press, 1961) xi-xxvi; https://archive.org/details/johnharvardlibra0000barb/page/n15

strengthened the power of the church, just as the government intended. Art, science, politics, and the economy were to be utilized in establishing the kingdom of God. If all people were indwelt by God, the new age could begin. All technological innovations that could be used to spread Christianity were considered instruments of the kingdom.

Toward the end of the nineteenth century, the Social Gospel (charitable efforts in the spirit of Progressivism) replaced Postmillennialism and preached the message of Progressivism. "Salvation" was now understood as the complete transformation of the social order; it no longer concerned the saving of the individual soul. Biblical scholarship in the form of textual criticism was no longer intended for understanding of the Holy Scriptures as the revelation of God. The Scriptures were understood as a mere historical document, and apocalyptic writings in the Bible were no longer regarded as the literal fulfillment of prophesied events.[383] Christianity was simply an ethical religion. The return of Jesus Christ was interpreted as His continual presence in His Church.[384]

9.6 Gradual formation of an idealized world federation

During the nineteenth and twentieth centuries, the West was characterized by a deeply religious milieu. However, most people failed to recognize this, overlooking the religious significance of the social and economic forces that were driving the development of the modern world. The ways in which these forces relate to civil religion need closer examination, not least because of their revolutionary long-term consequences.[385] Advocates of the Romantic movement acted like religious prophets in their response to contemporary socio-political developments. They sought to develop spiritual teachings that would influence the human will and thereby bring about a changed attitude to life. They formed a new conception of human nature to replace lost faith in the existence of a supernatural God, offering two changed aspects of reality: an idealized "humanity" and "history." According to this new perspective, society was a concrete construction from which the individual derived his meaning. Both society and the individual were bound together in a historical

---

[383] Charles A. Briggs, *Messianic Prophecy: The prediction of the fulfillment of redemption through the Messiah; a critical study of the messianic passages of the Old Testament in the order of their development* (New York City, NY: Charles Scribner's Sons, 1891) 34-45; https://archive.org/details/MN41861ucmf_0/page/n55; William H. Ryder, "The Fulfillment of Prophecy," *Andover Review* 13 (1890), 21, 23-24; Kemper Fullerton, *Prophecy and Authority* (New York City, NY: Macmillan, 1919) 197, 199-200; https://archive.org/details/prophecyandauth00full-goog/page/n221; Andrew C. Zenos, "Apocalyptic Symbolism," *Homiletic Review* 65 (1913), 199.

[384] Israel Warren, *The Parousia* (Portland, OR: Hoyt, Fogg & Donham, 1879) 24; https://archive.org/details/parousiaacritic03warrgoog/page/n30

[385] Albert Salomon, "The Religion of Progress," in *Social Research*, vol. 13 (December, 1946), 441-462.

process of flux and change. The present community, with its errant traditions and institutions, was seen as a web of evils from which the individual must free himself in order to find salvation in true "society." This could only take place if the individual "I" was subjected to society as a whole, becoming lost among the population at large. Although "humanity" and "society" would change with the historical process, they would only do so in accordance with a fixed program and within the limitations of a predetermined plan of progress. The aim was to bring into being a perfect "society of complete cooperation and liberal fraternity."

Belief in progress was seen as necessary for the individual to be complete. It involved spiritual contemplation of the ongoing historical process and its gradual formation of an ideal society. A person could only be inspired and guided in mind and soul if he believed in a spiritual force that underlay progress. He was to fight against present anarchy as manifest in the widespread appearance of Individualism. The ultimate purpose of this fight was to establish the kingdom of God on earth, where individual and social whole would be united. Amid the social rubble and amid the thousands of isolated individuals, the laws of progress would create a new society of perfect, absolute harmony. The fully socialized humanity would be the site of the lost individual's salvation, and history would be its means. Followers of the religion of progress received the good news that they were free to shape the future as they wished, for their social reality was controlled not only by history, but also by natural laws. At the same time, however, they would have to submit to the inevitable course of events that was determined by absolute natural laws.

Between 1850 and 1920, social thinking in America went from having a theological basis to having a scientific focus. Progressives stated this to be an objective development effected by science, but allowed it to change with time. They thus rejected the permanent standard set out in the Bible, turning instead to Relativism by making their own subjective opinions the standard. From the 1890s, scholars of philosophy and social science turned away from traditional thought and began to develop a new perspective. One of their most important assumptions was that the individual can never be released from dependence on other people and that his innermost nature is one that is variable. They taught that social environment has a determining influence on every individual, and that society is a constantly changing product of history. Through this idea of continual change, the concept of a fixed reality disappeared and was replaced by the theory of Relativism. Evidence indicates clearly that the new social theories were found first and foremost in the works of European philosophers who had distinguished themselves specifically as prophets of the religion of progress. Furthermore, these theories bore similarity to fundamental ideas about the individual, society, and history that were expounded by progressive academics in the decades that followed. In the present day, they have an all-pervading influence and are seen as the core truth of human knowledge, needing no further revision. All other knowledge is thus required to conform to them.

During the 1870s and 1880s, the views of the progressive journalist Henry Demarest Lloyd (1847-1903) became gradually consolidated until he was convinced that the dawning age of industrialization would be defined by a new religion.[386] This filled him not with optimism, but rather with negative premonitions about America's future. Industrialization had destroyed inter-personal relationships within society. Uprooted individuals would now drift into the void before the crushing power of the new economic institutions. The traditions, morals, and social and political forms of the past were no longer relevant to the present, and could afford the individual neither security nor direction within the new world.

However, having attacked the evident evils of American society, Lloyd went on paradoxically to assess the situation as a positive stroke of fate. The imminent collapse of civilization filled his heart with joy, since for the first time in history, the two conditions required for the full salvation of mankind could be fulfilled. Firstly, the destructive power raging in society would obliterate the traditional institutions and outdated philosophies that were no longer appropriate to modern society. Only in this way could the conditions required for absolute freedom be created. This would secondly enable man to shape his future as seemed best to him, without being constrained by a past that had been misguided in so many respects. Lloyd declared triumphantly that man is "the creator and redeemer of himself and society."[387] No higher power could now command obedience to a system of law imposed on humanity. There would be no fixed rules that man must obey at all times, for sociology – the science of social interaction – is only "what we make of it."[388] There was no transcendental power that determined the fate of humanity; thus nobody would be obligated to worship a higher being. All creations were the product of man's own creativity, which he is capable of constantly improving. However, the ideal could never be produced through the work of man's hands, since it was already predefined, at least in theory, as a humanity solidarized in an ultimate federation that would serve the common good. Over time, the ideal would come ever closer to perfection in its concrete form until it arrived at a state of completion.[389]

Lloyd believed in two types of society. In the present society, the religion of progress appeared in many different guises, their central theme being the goal of a humanity united in a federation of states.[390] The second type of society, the ideal society, would be established on earth in the future through

---

[386] Henry Demarest Lloyd, "Transcript Notebook 10," (October, 1888), 42 (*Lloyd Papers*, Madison, Wisconsin).

[387] Henry Demarest Lloyd, *Man the Social Creator* (New York City, NY: Doubleday, Page & company, 1906) 3; https://archive.org/details/mansocialcreator00lloyrich/page/n15

[388] Henry Demarest Lloyd, "Transcript New Zealand Notebook" (1899) 1 (*Lloyd Papers*, Madison, Wisconsin).

[389] Ibid.

[390] Ibid.

human ingenuity. The religion of progress would give man all the power and inspiration needed to implement this plan. As yet there was no coordinated federation that could be seen as the perfect human achievement; however, with combined faith and action, the task would eventually be accomplished by the majority of the world's population.

Historical records describe the philosopher James Mark Baldwin (1861-1934) as a key pioneer in social psychology who rejected the seemingly outdated schools of thought that prescribed a fixed human nature and an "artificial, mechanistic society."[391] The latter concept originated with Rousseau, who taught that man needed to return from the artificial state to one that was natural. By a natural state, he meant one of equality – in other words, the totalitarian state. Baldwin placed the importance of the theory of evolution, the renewal of society, the social nature of the individual, and the historical context of the individual in relationship to society on an entirely new conceptual basis. He was an outstanding thinker and convinced his country-men of the scientific position of historical Relativism. Henry D. Lloyd recognized him as a masterly propagandist for the religion of Progressivism. The great importance of his cultural role lay not only in his status as one of the most innovative social scientists, but also in the way that he acted as a priest for what Lloyd regarded to be the one true religion. According to Baldwin, the present form of community was an imperfect expression of the coming "society." Every person was free to overcome the status assigned to him by the community, thus gradually transforming present living conditions into a perfect "society."

At the core of Baldwin's social psychology was his idea of a three-stage, absolute social process that operates outside of history.[392] The first stage describes man's dependence on biology. The second opens up the possibility of escaping the control of biological laws. The third highlights the ways that man behaves consciously toward other people which can be attributed to neither biological nor social heritage. This process posited a completely new conception of life which holds that society will progress no further once it has reached its preordained point of perfection. According to Baldwin, the very essence of human freedom lies in the fulfilment of a predetermined destiny. The incompatible elements of the present community (physical and real) and of spiritual "society" (intangible and unreal) produce a conceptual tension that can never be satisfactorily resolved. Despite claiming that he had created a rational system of thought that was based on reality, Baldwin, like Lloyd before him, entered the category of the irrational. Religious faith was needed to compensate for all the conceptual inconsistencies that had crept into Progressivism. Henry Lloyd's idealistic construct, which Baldwin had modified and recommended to his countrymen, was nothing but fantasy. Nevertheless, Baldwin insisted that social solidarity could be effected through

---

[391] Chap. 6.2 Central tenets of Romantic Democracy

[392] James Mark Baldwin, *The Individual and Society* (Boston, MA: R. G. Badger, 1911) 43, 46; https://archive.org/details/individualandso00baldgoog/page/n48

a cooperative federation. He portrayed this process as a thoroughly religious idea, teaching that it would be brought about by a spirit deep within man.

When the individual reached the third stage of social evolution, he would voluntarily comply with ethical laws that he would regard as best practice. This would succeed because all individuals would be inspired by the same religion. Only in this way could all people in society be subordinated to the same set of rules and display the same patterns of behavior. Such a masterstroke could be effected by no power in the universe other than the religion of humanity, which, under the name of "Progressivism," would fill citizens' hearts and minds within a cooperative federation. This idea was completely revolutionary and spread like wildfire through every aspect of man's social existence. Above all, it inspired the individual to strive for social utopia.[393] Baldwin related every key part of his philosophy of progress, including free will and social solidarity, to the religion of an ideal humanity. The religion-inspired efforts of the individual were needed to bring about an age of social solidarity.[394] The perfect world would follow a path determined by the relentless law of progress.[395]

An almost unperceived change took place in the meaning of the term Democracy. Originally – during the time of Republican Democracy – politicians really did fight to gain the favor of the voters. This system was replaced by Romantic Democracy, the later administrative state, which sought to preserve the external forms of Democracy such as the party system, parliament, and elections. However, the core of the system has changed entirely – or rather, the true totalitarian core of this form of Democracy has emerged in our time. This understanding can be traced back to Rousseau's version of Democracy as presented in his book *The Social Contract*. This totalitarian Democracy consists of diverse ideas which form part of an ideological belief with the authority of a state religion, although it is largely unperceived as such. In order to gain wide approval, the administrative state is described as "social" and "democratic." This does not refer to any one particular party, since all current parties are concerned with modern Democracy. All Western countries have introduced this type of Democracy, which is totalitarian in nature while pretending to be something entirely different.

Modern Democracy is an almost perfect realization of the "socialized humanity" prescribed by Henry D. Lloyd and James M. Baldwin's model of a spiritual "society." During the twentieth century, this "society" took on the

---

[393] James Mark Baldwin, *Genetic Theory of Reality: Being the outcome of genetic logic as issuing in the aesthetic theory of reality called pancalism; with an extended glossary of terms* (New York City, NY: G.P. Putnam's Sons, 1915) 114; https://archive.org/details/genetictheory-re00baldgoog/page/n140

[394] Ibid., 117; https://archive.org/details/genetictheoryre00baldgoog/page/n142

[395] James Mark Baldwin, *Social and Ethical Interpretations in Mental Development* (New York City, NY: Macmillan & Co., 1902) 173-174; https://archive.org/details/socialandethica-03baldgoog/page/n206

form of an administrative state. The American philosopher James Burnham (1905-1987) described the transition from Capitalism to the administrative state, which was as profound in global significance as the previous change from Feudalism to Capitalism.[396] The author used a new term, "Managerialism," to convey the revolution taking place in the business world – a dramatic change in business relations that was driven by managers. The new caste of managers would assume responsibility for most cultural forms, economic resources, and government bodies. It would replace both capitalists and workers in order to take complete charge of the whole population. The official elite would press for a thorough abolition of private property, social Individualism, and democratic Parliamentarianism. If successful in implementing these drastic measures, the value of the present capitalist system would lose all meaning. It was highly probable, according to Burnham, that the administrative state would be fully totalitarian in nature. The mass media would relentlessly convince the population that the new social order was Democracy at its highest level of development.

Burnham pointed out the traits shared by Soviet Communism, National Socialism, and the democratic welfare state. A new caste of bureaucrats in each of these regimes had usurped political power by cunningly manipulating popular rhetoric and social revolutionary slogans, using them shamelessly to their own advantage. The differentiation of these models of governance as either Capitalism or Socialism – according to the common, but often misleading understanding of these terms – provided a starting point for the new administrative state to cultivate its own image. It intended to follow neither the libertarian principles of free market economy, nor the collectivist guidelines of State Capitalism. Its true goal was to effect economic and social equality among the entire population.

The writers Adolf A. Berle and Gardiner C. Means indicated two important facts about the way the economy had developed since the late nineteenth century.[397] Whereas traditional enterprises had been headed by their owners, the owners of corporations were shareholders who placed their companies' operations in the hands of a group of managers. These managers no longer had to take protection of property rights into consideration when making decisions. For this reason, they made no effort to stop the government when it claimed a more significant role in the economy.

This explains why the immense growth of state government in the twentieth century was no accident. On the contrary, it was integral to the revolution taking place in the business world, as shown by Burnham. Managers' declining interest in property rights led to the gradual unification

---

[396] James Burnham, *The Managerial Revolution*: What Is Happening in the World (New York City, NY: John Day Company, 1941; Bloomington, IN: Indiana University Press, 1973); https://archive.org/details/in.ernet.dli.2015.46583

[397] Adolf Augustus Berle, Gardiner Coit Means, *The Modern Corporation and Private Property* (New York City, NY: The Macmillan Company, 1933); https://archive.org/details/in.ernet.dli.2015.216028/page/n5

of the economic and political systems.[398] Furthermore, the crisis within industrial Capitalism caused an enormous expansion of state powers which allowed the state to intervene directly in the economic structure. The state had growing responsibility for enabling the optimization of mass production and distribution of consumer goods in a global economy. The prerequisite for creating the administrative state would be – Burnham anticipated – the elevation of bureaucracy to the highest level of state power. Only through bureaucracy could a Technocracy be introduced that would benefit all parties involved and commit to effecting progress across all areas of society. The bicameral parliament would thus need to be replaced by an efficient government of experts. Although there are errors and exaggerations in Burnham's account of the managerial revolution, his predictions of political trends proved correct. George Orwell wrote two extensive essays about Burnham's political prognoses, not holding back on criticism in his detailed comments. Despite this, however, Orwell's novel *Nineteen Eighty-Four*[399] (1949) is undeniably a fictional projection of the administrative state that Burnham foresaw in the real world.

The form and practice of the administrative state are the result of the practical implementation of Progressivism. In all its political, economic, and cultural aspects, the administrative state represents the most pronounced form of a social order and government opposed to Reformation Christianity. Whether or not Christians actually realize that they are living under the dictates of a political system that almost entirely rejects their creed is of secondary importance. They are given no choice but to submit to the norm of a democratic understanding of reality – in the sense of Rousseau's Romantic Democracy – while being constantly persuaded that they live in a free state that guarantees the privilege of living out their faith as they see fit.[400]

To give but one example, it is constantly maintained that the periodic, standardized ritual of going to the polls is a Christian and civic duty. Simply voting for a particular party, political candidate, or popular initiative is perhaps the most characteristic operation of the religion of progress. In contemporary Western society, it is impossible for most people to conceive of the state-granted right to vote as anything but an absolute right, even if they choose not to exercise it or do so only occasionally. They do not understand that the religion of progress, in the form of modern Democracy, requires periodic legitimization by citizens in order to assert the all-pervasive influence of administrative government in society. This is no democratic process in the true sense of the word, if based on the historical definition of Republican Democracy as a matter of which political candidate gains the

---

[398] Ibid., 123ff.; https://archive.org/details/in.ernet.dli.2015.46583/page/n131

[399] George Orwell, *Nineteen Eighty Four* (London: Secker & Warburg, 1949).

[400] Jean-Jacques Rousseau, *Du contrat social ou Principes du droit politique* (Amsterdam: Chez. Marc Michel Rey, 1762); Jean-Jacques Rousseau, *The Social Contract Or Principles Of Political Right* (London: George Allen And Unwin Limited, 1948; Harmondsworth: Penguin, 1968); https://archive.org/details/socialcontract00rous

favor of the majority of voters. With the inequality between rich and poor becoming ever greater, this form of government will ultimately head toward total chaos, even if it affords a higher standard of living for some in the meantime. In its most basic sense, to cast a vote in an administrative state is to perform a religious act of enormous consequence. This ingeniously allows only one of two or three dominant parties to come to power, even though there are only negligible differences between the parties' political agendas.

The book *Tragedy and Hope* was published in 1966 by Carroll Quigley, a prominent historian at the School of Foreign Service, part of the renowned Georgetown University (Washington, D.C.). Quigley described the technocratic vision for the administrative state. The expert would replace the industrial manager in controlling the economic system, just as he would replace the democratic voter in governing the state. Economic Liberalism would be replaced by planning. In general, the citizen's independence and freedom of decision would be controlled within tightly limited alternatives: he would be given a number at birth which would be used to monitor his education, compulsory military or civil service, tax payments, healthcare and medical needs, and finally retirement and payment of death benefits.[401] The direct relationship of the average citizen to the government would cease, and the breach would be filled with intermediaries with private rather than public power. This situation would equate to a form of Neo-Feudalism.[402]

Such a system makes a great pretense of being religiously neutral. It thus convinces all religious adherents within the system that they can freely follow their various religions under protection of the state. In order to preserve this right, they are called on to defend the authority of modern Democracy against all extremist positions, which are often collectively termed "Fundamentalism." Many Christians are convinced by this argument, having been indoctrinated with it since childhood. They could not imagine living in another political system that does not guarantee basic human rights – which are supposedly based on a rational ascertainable law of nature. For this reason, a thorough, in-depth analysis of the religious components of modern Democracy is all the more urgent. Christians must be made aware of the fundamental differences between their biblical beliefs and the technocratic administrative state. On closer examination, it becomes clear that the conflicts between Reformation Christianity and religious Progressivism could not be more fundamental nor more diametrically opposed. The truth of this is shown simply by the fact that Democracy makes it increasingly difficult, if not impossible, to practice a consistent Christianity. Progressives who follow the deeply religious rule of law have long realized that their ultimate conception of the enemy is embodied in Christianity, which teaches the biblical doctrine that eternal salvation is found in none other than Jesus Christ, the Son of God (Acts 4:11-12). The sinner, a designation applicable to

---

[401] Carroll Quigley, *Tragedy and Hope: A History of the World in our Time* (New York City, NY: The Macmillan Company, 1966) 866.

[402] Ibid.

all people, can only find forgiveness and salvation from eternal damnation – from punishment "with everlasting destruction from the presence of the Lord, and from the glory of his power" (2 Thess. 1:9) – through faith in the full atonement of Jesus Christ on the cross. Western Christians thus have a duty to confront the religion of progress that forms the core of modern Democracy – a Democracy related directly to the establishment of an autocratically governed administrative state.

Volume 3

Progressivism as the driving force of American Imperialism (Chs. 10-15)

10 Implementing a progressive social order. 222
11 America's military attacks as a world power. 239
12 The era of American Imperialism 253
13 The ideological battle against Militarism. 275
14 The age of American global dominance. 307
15 Postscript. 331

10 Implementing a progressive social order

(Progressive social order realized through the work of theologians and philosophers)

The centralization of American state authority that followed the War of Secession motivated churches to seek greater unity, having become increasingly divided. This led to the founding of the Federal Council of Churches of Christ in America in 1908. The contemporary intellectual climate was shaped by German Idealism, along with English Romanticism. In particular, the young generation of clerics opened themselves up to new theological trends: to Monism and Pantheism.

10.1 Conceptual metamorphosis of eschatological expectations

(Secularization of Postmillennial teaching on the thousand-year reign)
Progressivism had an increasing influence on the minds of well-educated Americans. The rise of liberal theology resulted in a secularization of the religious worldview from 1880 onwards. Those who accepted the Postmillennial interpretation of the thousand-year reign also followed the Social Gospel and sought to Christianize society. They believed that paradisaical conditions could be hastened and that secular companies should be guided by Christian ethics. This evangelical approach, promoted by Washington Gladden[1] (1836-1918), was taken still further. The new birth was no longer deemed necessary for a change in moral compass. Science, telecommunications, and industry were regarded as social saviors alongside the Church. The theologian Josiah Strong (1847-1916) placed his trust in the transforming power of human institutions. He offered material support to the poverty-stricken working class in the hope of fostering a spirit of fraternity, and furthermore instructed them in Christian ethics. Whereas Christ had been seen formerly as the giver of grace and Lord of history, He was now assigned the role of moral teacher and example. New technologies were used to promote solidarity as steam power and electricity enabled fast trans-portation of goods, instant exchange of information, and mass consumption.[2]

A general change in thinking took place, with people feeling a duty to work for public welfare. Josiah Strong declared science to be God's "agent of providence" in His plan for the world's perfection. He considered it a further means of God's revelation, thereby contradicting the prior understanding of

---

[1] Washington Gladden, *Tools and the Man: Property and Industry under the Christian Law* (Boston, MA: Houghton Mifflin, 1893) 22; https://archive.org/details/toolsandmanprop01g-ladgoog/page/n34

[2] Ibid., 18, 20-23; https://archive.org/details/toolsandmanprop01gladgoog/page/n30; s. also: Washington Gladden, *Applied Christianity: Moral Aspects of Social Questions* (Boston, MA: Houghton Mifflin, 1886) 214; https://archive.org/details/appliedchristian00glad/page/214

separation between divine revelation and human knowledge.[3] On the contrary, man was to cooperate with God in perfecting humanity. The social reformer, labor arbitrator, and pastor Graham Taylor (1851-1938) saw churches' shift away from an emphasis on eternity as proof that the kingdom of God would come to pass.[4] The sociologist Albion W. Small (1854-1926) continued to hold religiosity as important for the proper application of new discoveries, referring to this as the "sanctification of the individual."[5]

10.2 The Golden Age of the future

From 1900 onward, the Social Gospel movement began to infiltrate established Protestant churches in the northern states. One of its key proponents was Shailer Mathews[6] (1863-1941). According to Mathews, the key feature of the modern age was its belief in the universal validity of science.[7] He sought to show that process philosophy and Progressivism were generally consistent and considered the modern era to be defined by total commitment to the reality of continual progress. Christian theology thus needed to undergo radical revision in order to be brought in line with process philosophy. The divine had to be presented as an immanent process – an indwelling of God in all things – rather than as a ruler at work outside of the world.[8] Fundamentalists, as conservative Christians in America were called at the time, expressed a contrary view. They stated that the salvation wrought on the cross at Golgotha was effectual because it implies the work of a true, sovereign God; without this, the Gospel has no significance. They quoted Psalm 115:3 – "But our God is in the heavens: he hath done whatsoever he hath pleased." Mathews strongly resisted this supposed delusion, and

---

[3] Josiah Strong, *The New Era or the Coming Kingdom* (New York City, NY: Baker & Taylor, 1893) 39, 117-31, 296-317, 342-363; s. also: Josiah Strong, *Twentieth Century City* (New York City, NY: Baker & Taylor, 1898) 117-122, 161; Josiah Strong, *Our World* (New York City, NY: Doubleday, Page, 1913) 14, 79-81; Dorothea A. Muller, "Josiah Strong and the Social Gospel: A Christian's Response to the Challenge of the City," *Journal of the Presbyterian Historical Society*, 34 (September, 1961), 150-174.

[4] Graham Taylor, *Religion in Social Action* (New York City, NY: Dodd, Mead, 1913) 104; s. also: Ibid., 100, 110-111, 224, 235-238; Allen F. Davis, *Spearheads for Reform: The Social Settlements and the Progressive Movement* (New York City, NY: Oxford University Press, 1967) 27-28, 170-171; Louise C. Wade, *Graham Taylor: Pioneer for Social Justice: 1851-1938* (Chicago, IL: University of Chicago Press, 1964) 161, 166-169.

[5] Gerald Birney Smith, *Social Idealism and the Changing Theology* (New York City, NY: Macmillan, 1913) 110, 113, 123, 145, 154; s. also: "Theological Thinking in America," in Gerald Birney Smith, ed., *Religious Thought in the Last Quarter-Century* (Chicago, IL: University of Chicago Press, 1927) 109; https://archive.org/details/religiousthought008528mbp/page/n119

[6] Gary North, *Cross Fingers: How the Liberals captured the Presbyterian Church* (Tyler, TX: Institute for Christian Economics, 1996) 70-75.

[7] Shailer Mathews, *The Gospel and the Modern Man* (New York City, NY: Macmillan, [1910] 1912) 36; https://archive.org/details/gospelandmodern00mathgoog/page/n54

[8] Ibid., 43; https://archive.org/details/gospelandmodern00mathgoog/page/n60

categorical denial of the sovereignty of God thus became the central tenet of religious Progressivism.[9] Progressivism fundamentally rejects the absolute distinction between Creator and creature which is presented in the Bible as one of the most important doctrines of Christianity.

In order to uphold the Bible as complete truth, science-based Darwinism has to be rejected. The teaching that God created the universe out of nothing (Genesis 1:1) is dismissed by Progressivism as an impossibility, since the biblical account of Creation negates the idea that the whole sphere of reality is in continual evolution. The reinterpretation of the individual days of Creation as periods of time spanning millions of years, as posited by the theory of evolution, represented the surrender of liberal theology to process philosophy. The idea of a sovereign, omnipotent, and personal Creator-God had no place in the humanistic thinking of this theology.

Historical criticism came to be seen as the only scientifically valid method of interpretation. This corresponded with the liberal-theological view of the Bible as a text composed of numerous fragments which is historically implausible on multiple accounts. The various subdisciplines of the historical-critical method gradually emerged, such as redaction, literary, form, and tradition criticism, and it was soon claimed to be the only means of true biblical interpretation.[10] The method was characterized by circular reasoning: a fixed result was assumed from the beginning, which was confirmed through application of secular literary analysis. Any arising contradictions that suggested the conclusion to be false were quickly silenced by stating that the method was based on scientific principles.[11] According to Mathews, the uneducated lacked a proper understanding of Christianity[12]; only a modernist was a true Christian. The true successor of the Church Fathers, whose theology aligned with biblical truth, was thus not the fundamentalist who defended the doctrine of inerrancy, but rather the modernist.[13] The historical-critical method asserted itself against the traditional grammatical-historical interpretation in a conflict that dragged on for decades. It seemed strange to fundamentalists that biblical texts were interpreted through a method that proceeded unquestionably from a humanistic worldview. They were unsurprised that this improper method produced so many contradictory results.

Fundamentalists put up a strong fight against the modernists, aware of their essential differences of opinion and fully convinced of their own beliefs. In retrospect, however, the whole affair was merely a mock fight since both parties took the New Divinity teaching (the denial of a distinction between

---

[9] Ibid.

[10] Shailer Mathews, *The Faith of Modernism* (New York City, NY: AMS Press, [1924] 1969) 38-39.

[11] Ibid., 43.

[12] Ibid., 46.

[13] Ibid., 46-47.

Creator and creature, the rejection of the doctrine of original sin and of the atoning sacrifice of Jesus Christ, and the belief that sinful tendencies can be overcome through willpower alone) as their starting point.[14] While Charles G. Finney's stringent Moralism paved the way for spiritual enthusiasm, Nathaniel W. Taylor's sophisticated Humanism was combined with liberal sentiments. Despite their apparent differences, it is clear that both schools of thought donned the Pelagian robe more or less consistently. There can be no doubt that this is true given that Finney denied the doctrines of the sovereignty of God, original sin, supernatural rebirth, the vicarious atonement of Jesus Christ, and justification by faith alone! In step with Taylor, he replaced these central Christian dogmas with an optimistic belief in human ability, in moral and social redemption – as in Abaelard and Grotius's theories of the atonement – and the idea of natural perfectionism. Taylor's New Divinity had paved the way for Finney's acceptance of New Protestantism.

It is therefore justifiable to say that Fundamentalism comes from the same source as Modernism, even though fundamentalists claim to have withstood the influences of theological Liberalism. Their respective conceptions of salvation display striking parallels. This remains true even though Fundamentalism affirms the indispensability of certain biblical teachings which have long been thrown overboard by Modernism. Nonetheless, it must be noted that the New Divinity doctrine had a more enduring influence on the image of Fundamentalism than it did on the image of Modernism.

By 1869, when the branches of the Old and New Schools had been reunited in Reformed churches, Taylor's New Divinity had already passed the peak of its popularity. Confessional Presbyterianism, as taught at the Union Theological Seminary in New York City, came to an end in 1890 when the Old School theologian William Greenough Thayer Shedd retired. The following year, the Union Theological Seminary appointed Charles Augustus Briggs as professor of Biblical Theology. In his inaugural speech, Briggs firmly stated his intention to base his own teaching on historical criticism of the Bible.

Led by idealistic ideas, evangelical Presbyterians initially and naively sided with the modernists, believing that this would prevent them from hindering a faster spread of Christianity. They thus joined the chorus of appeals for orthodox Presbyterians to adapt their supposedly outdated teachings to the scientific knowledge of the modern world. The kind of conformity to the spirit of the age that this required soon became clear.[15] Absurdly, however, it was deemed necessary to carry this through in order to

---

[14] Alternative terms for "New Divinity" are "New Haven-Theology" and "Taylorism": S. also: chap. 4.4 Refining the human character; chap. 4.6 Anthropocentric approaches of the New Theology

[15] W. Robert Godfrey, "Haven't We Seen The 'Megashift Before?'," in *Modern Reformation* (January-February, 1993), 14-18.

avoid losing all respect of a world which had given in increasingly to faith in science.

The principal of Princeton Theological Seminary and Presbyterian theologian Benjamin B. Warfield (1851-1921) was right in saying that Pelagianism is the religion of universal Paganism and thus the religion of natural man. He stated furthermore that these developments, which proceeded from Taylor's New Haven Theology and were propagated most successfully by Finney, constitute an inconsistent adaptation of Fundamentalism to the principles of natural (rationalist) theology which flourished within late nineteenth-century Protestant Liberalism.[16] In his struggle against Liberalism, J. Gresham Machen (ΦBK)[17] was eventually not only pushed to the side in his own Presbyterian church (Presbyterian Church U.S.A.), but also reduced to a marginal figure in the wider context of American Fundamentalism. He was committed to Old School Presbyterianism and had no desire to adopt Finney's perfectionistic position, which was rooted in his constant support of Pelagianism.

Progressive ministers such as Lyman Abbott, Washington Gladden, and George Herron could find nothing useful in the theology of the Genevan reformer John Calvin. They found liberal theology to be much more beneficial, especially in its conception of the fatherhood of God and the brotherhood of man. The religious Humanism that it expressed seemed to offer advantages that could be found nowhere else. Among its prime virtues are human sympathy, universality, and altruism. These values proved particularly beneficial in meeting the social and political challenges that America faced at the turn of the century. In the end, there seemed to be only one reasonable answer to the prevailing problems in society: the continual introduction and implementation of Progressivism.

The nineteenth century brought two of the most important conceptual innovations in America's dominant civil religion: 1) the idea of God as King gave way to that of God as Father, and 2) the understanding of salvation as the spiritual deliverance of the elect was replaced with concern for the political transformation of the world. America launched an initiative to introduce a democratic system – in the sense of Rousseau's Romantic Democracy – to all nations of the world as the optimum form of government.[18]

A radical change had taken place in the American Protestant eschatological view. Pastor Lyman Abbott (1835-1922), for example, claimed that the kingdom of God would gradually materialize through civilizational achievements in education, legislature, science, and the church.[19] Aligning

---

[16] Benjamin B. Warfield, *Selected Shorter Writings of Benjamin B. Warfield*, (Philipsburg, PA: Presbyterian and Reformed Publishing Co., [1970] 2011) vol. 1: 387.

[17] Member of the Phi Beta Kappa Society, Johns Hopkins University, 1901

[18] Lyman Abbott, *Reminiscence*, with an introduction by Ernest Hamlin Abbott (Boston, MA: Houghton Mifflin Co., [1915] 1923) xxx; https://archive.org/details/reminiscence-s0000unse/page/n35

[19] Lyman Abbott, *The Evolution of Christianity* (Boston, MA: Houghton Mifflin, 1892)

public opinion with the demands of a social order based on social justice would be particularly important in this process. Faith became based on history, evolution, and reason, while the Bible was given no consideration at all. God was said to be immanent in all progressive institutions. His plans were fully in line with the secular idea of progress. Abbott claimed to deal with true Christianity, but his agreement with German Idealism was clear.

Like many American students who studied at German universities, Richard T. Ely[20] (1854-1943), a descendent of the Puritans, soon developed an enthusiasm for the organic planned economy which German social doctrine, following Hegelian Idealism, recommended as the best economic system – a third way between Socialism and Capitalism. After completing his doctorate in Germany, he became the first lecturer in political economy at Johns Hopkins University, where he taught a number of gifted students who later became well-known economists, sociologists, and historians. In 1885, he founded the American Economic Association in order to solve the country's social problems through aspects of Christianity, politics, and science. Richard T. Ely and Josiah Strong founded the Institute of Christian Sociology shortly after, aiming to create an ideal society modelled on the kingdom of God. In 1892, Ely was appointed professor of economics and director of the newly founded School of Economics, Political Science, and History at the University of Wisconsin-Madison, and as such had great influence on the progressive government in Wisconsin. The key to Ely's social philosophy was his deification of the state. He taught that God uses the state more than any other institution in the execution of His plans[21], and that churches would play an important role in the fight against evil.[22] The primary concern of the church was not the salvation of souls for eternity, but rather the perfection of a socialist society in the present world. The Industrial Revolution, universities, and churches would enable social scientists and clerics to establish the New Jerusalem.[23] Ely believed that the state had more saving power than any other social institution, and that Christianity needed

182-186, 193, 199-200, 246, 254; https://archive.org/details/evolutionofchris01abbo/page/182; s. also: Ira V. Brown, *Lyman Abbott: Christian Evolutionist: A Study in Religious Liberalism* (Cambridge, MA: Harvard University Press, 1953) 100, 108-109.

[20] Benjamin G. Rader, *The Academic Mind and Reform: The Influence of Richard T. Ely on American Life* (Lexington, KY: University of Kentucky Press, 1966); https://archive.org/details/academicmindrefo0000rade

[21] Sidney Fine, *Laissez Faire Thought and the General-Welfare State: A Study of Conflict in American Thought, 1865-1901* (Ann Arbor, MI: University of Michigan Press, 1956) 180.

[22] Richard T. Ely, *The Social Aspects of Christianity and other Essays* (New York City, NY: Thomas Y. Crowell, 1889) 73: "[…] a never-ceasing attack on every wrong institution, until the earth becomes a new earth, and all its cities, cities of God." https://archive.org/details/socialaspectsofc00elyr/page/72; s. also: Richard T. Ely, *The Labor Movement in America* (New York City, NY: Thomas Y. Crowell & Co., 1886) 319-326; https://archive.org/details/cu31924002356172/page/n339

[23] Richard T. Ely, *The Coming City* (New York City, NY: Thomas Y. Crowell, 1902) 73; https://archive.org/details/comingcity00elygoog/page/n76

to realize humanistic ideals. Christian and secular organizations needed to merge in order to socialize the American population, as demanded by the Social Gospel. Although Ely believed that cities needed religious revival in order to remind citizens of their ethical duties, he dismissed the importance of the individual's eternal salvation as expressed traditionally by the Reformational doctrine of justification. Ely's religious ideas were completely divorced from Christian teaching.

The professor of philosophy John Dewey (1859-1952) believed that the gradual formation of a Christian social order was evident in the enormously growing influence of science, society, and the state. From 1900, John Dewey (ΦBK)[24] and many other intellectual pragmatists gradually turned away from religious Postmillennialism to secular Statism. Despite completely rejecting the Christian faith, Progressives retained their parents' missionary spirit and desire to lead mankind to a utopian future. The two most important means for world salvation were seen to be the spread of Progressivism and the establishment of Statism. Dewey hoped for Allied victory in the First World War, since Great Britain and its allies fought to "protect world liberties and the highest ideals of civilization." Progressives saw the War as their chance to transform society: America's participation in the First World War would open up inconceivable opportunities for social collectivization.

Dewey believed that the Millennium could now take place on account of the explosive increase in scientific knowledge. Science would remove every restriction that Christianity had imposed on mankind. As man was released from supernatural powers and interpersonal barriers, a harmonious brotherhood of unity and sympathy could emerge within Democracy, fulfilling what Christ had said about the kingdom of God.[25] The most important condition would be a complete dissolution of traditional Christianity. Truth would be found within every individual, not in a written text, and would therefore be accessible to everyone.[26] The mind of modern man would assume the role of divine revelation as the primary instrument in bringing the kingdom to pass. After 1900, Dewey stopped using Christian terminology but continued to present the secular version of Postmillennialism. His thinking remained shrouded by an aura of religion.

John R. Commons (1862-1945), an economist in the labor movement and an active lay preacher, also presented the secularized Postmillennialism.[27]

---

[24] Member of the Phi Beta Kappa Society, Vermont College, 1879

[25] John Blewett, S.J., "Democracy as Religion: Unity in Human Relations," in John Blewett, ed., *John Dewey: His Thought and Influence* (New York City, NY: Fordham University Press, 1960) 33; https://archive.org/details/johndeweyhisthou00blew/page/32; s. also: Ibid., 34-58; Jo Ann Boydston, et al., ed., *John Dewey: The Early Works, 1882-1989* (Carbondale, IL: Southern Illinois University Press, 1969-1971) vols. 2 & 3.

[26] Boydston, et al., ed., *John Dewey: The Early Works*, vol. 4: 5; s. also: John Dewey, "Reconstruction," *Monthly Bulletin of the Students' Christian Association of the University of Michigan*, 15 (June, 1894), 153.

[27] John R. Commons, *Social Reform and the Church* (New York City, NY: Thomas Y. Crowell, 1894); https://archive.org/details/socialreformchur00comm/page/n3

He taught that the state needed to instruct people in the art of love rather than abusing its position of power.[28] Commons believed that every social problem could be resolved through political action. He was primarily occupied with urban planning, desiring to turn the city into an earthly idyll ("Paradise").

Josiah Strong and other exponents of the Social Gospel were the most zealous figures in the urban reform movement. The Evangelical Alliance of the U.S.A. adopted Strong's plan for the moral reformation and socio-economic transformation of America's large cities in 1897. When the Evangelical Alliance withdrew from the endeavor one year later, Strong mobilized other interest groups so as not to impede the coming of the kingdom. One of these organizations was the Religious Citizenship League, founded in 1913 by Washington Gladden, Walter Rauschenbusch, Jane Addams (ΦΒΚ)[29], William Dwight Porter Bliss, and Josiah Strong. They used political power to achieve social justice and strove to attain more humane labor laws, nationwide abstinence, and better living conditions for the poor.[30] "Christian mission" was understood increasingly as social reformation; the latter was considered the true "salvation of the world."[31] People believed that the sacred and secular were ultimately indistinguishable – that they were in reality one and the same.

10.3 Religious significance of the new pedagogy

G. Stanley Hall (1844-1924) was one of the first innovators to drive the development of scientific psychology in America.[32] He saw himself as an "Übermensch" (a sort of Titan[33]) who had been given new life. He believed that like Jesus and Buddha before him, he had been appointed to preach a message of salvation.[34] He considered himself the prophet of a new age and a

---

[28] Ibid., 13-26, 39, 78, 83; https://archive.org/details/socialreformchur00comm/page/12; Fine, *Laissez Faire and the General Welfare State*, 170-171, 181-82.

[29] Member of the Phi Beta Kappa Society, Northwestern University, 1918

[30] "A New Step Forward: The Religious Citizenship League for Social Progress through Political Action," *The Gospel of the Kingdom* (January, 1914), 11-15. Similar organizations were: League for Social Service (1898); American Institute of Social Service (1902). Muller, "Josiah Strong and the Social Gospel: A Christian's Response to the Challenge of the City," 162-163.

[31] Albion W. Small, "The Churches and City Problems," in John Henry Barrows, ed., *The World's Parliament of Religions* (Chicago, IL: Parliament Publishing, 1893) vol. 2: 1080-1082; s. also: Albion W. Small, "Christianity and Industry," *American Journal of Sociology*, 25 (May, 1920), 673-694.

[32] Dorothy Ross, *G. Stanley Hall: The Psychologist as Prophet* (Chicago, IL: University of Chicago Press, 1972).

[33] In Greek mythology the Titans were the pre-Olympian gods.

[34] G. Stanley Hall, *Life and Confessions of a Psychologist* (New York City, NY: D. Appleton

new religion. The "New Psychology" would lead "Mansoul," the soul of mankind, to the next stage of evolution. Hall was a notorious blasphemer, and his life was characterized by scandal.[35] In his fanaticism, he altered the Christian view of man to such an extent that there was no longer any correlation between the biblical teaching and his own ideas. As the priestly prophet of a new liberation, he preached the "gospel" of a new psychology that was optimally suited to the contemporary cultural landscape. This was far more than a new way of viewing the clinical treatment of mental illness; it was a new religion that confronted and proposed solutions to the serious problems in American society, politics, and economics.

Like other leading persons in American education, Hall invested much time in developing an innovative university system at the end of the nineteenth century. With the help of wealthy sponsors, he founded the Clark University in 1889. This was the first university in America that specialized in scientific research. Willing acceptance of Darwinism not only altered the political philosophy behind the American Constitution, but also caused a radical reorientation in every aspect of American thought and behavior. A new worldview emerged in which all intellectual interests were made to conform to the principles of Darwinism. This resulted in an evolutionary understanding of the economy, education, social and natural sciences, and religious studies. The common denominator behind these conceptual changes was the rejection of the biblical doctrine of human nature. The new conception sparked a completely new way of thinking about history, politics, and literature. Man was said to be an absolute point of reference, and allusion to the idea of a supernatural God was disallowed. The Harvard philosopher and historian John Fiske nonetheless tried to maintain a theistic perspective, believing in an evolution that was initiated and directed by God. In retrospect, his adherence to a supernatural reality that determines current events was a pitiful attempt doomed to fail from the outset, because he did not follow the Word of God but based his considerations on the principles of evolution.

Charles Pierce, William James, and John Dewey (ΦBK)[36] laid out this new philosophy, which James termed "Pragmatism," in their extensive works. In his famous book *Principles of Psychology*[37], first published in 1890, James made Darwinian Naturalism the basis of understanding the human psyche. He believed that the human soul has no actual substance and is merely the activity of the mind. This idea remains the prominent mark of the radical conception of the human psyche to the present day. John Dewey applied James's Pragmatism to every area of educational science. His pedagogical principles were based on the tenets of his personal philosophy which he

---

and Co., 1923) 596; https://archive.org/details/55612090R.nlm.nih.gov/page/n623

[35] Lorine Pruette, *G. Stanley Hall* (New York City, NY: D. Appleton and Co., 1926) 199.

[36] Member of the Phi Beta Kappa Society, Vermont College, 1879

[37] William James, *Principles of Psychology* (New York City, NY: Henry Holt und Co., 1890); https://archive.org/details/in.ernet.dli.2015.462769/page/n3

called Instrumentalism: his belief that ideas become true when they are in use in society. Dewey saw the essence of Darwinism in the idea that all life must be considered a continual experiment that is never concluded until it inevitably arrives at death. He believed that nothing can be identified as objective, absolute truth, but only as justified assertion. Something can be considered true not only because it is part of human experience, but also because it has instrumental value.

Dewey believed that any miraculous occurrences that could not be explained by the regular functioning of natural laws never really happened at all. He wanted to plan and effect progress in society through experimental methods and thus became one of the most influential philosophers of Democracy in America. He used the education system to recast society in the spirit of Instrumentalism. The entire American education system therefore rested on the basis of evolutionary philosophy which Dewey had largely taken from Darwin. His pedagogical theories were first systematically applied in 1895 in the experimental school of the University of Chicago, and were soon known throughout the country.[38] However, his revolution to the education system would only come into full effect after 1920, once American public schools had appointed teachers trained in Dewey's pedagogical methodology who applied it with conviction.

According to Lester Frank Ward, another of the most influential theoreticians of mass education, formal education was "a systematic process to produce true persuasions." It should be controlled exclusively by the government to prevent it being affected by any undesired influences.[39] The ultimate goal of the state was completely different to that of parents, guardians, and students. Lester Frank Ward's ideas about a new education system gained influence through the varied work of his principal protégé, Albion W. Small, and his younger colleague, John Dewey. Dewey was against limiting the curriculum to subjects traditionally given high status, and advocated the introduction of craft, vocational, and technical subjects in order to deny students the possibility of an academic career. Only the children of the elite who were destined for leading positions in society along with a few talented students from the lower classes should graduate from Ivy League universities such as Harvard, Yale, and Columbia. John Dewey often used abstract terms such as "social reconstruction."[40] His intention in using these encrypted terms was to conceal the real thoughts behind them. He abused the education system for the systematic collectivization and stultification of the masses,

[38] Lawrence A. Cremin, *The Transformation of the Schools: Progressivism in American Education, 1876-1957* (New York City, NY: Random House, 1961) vii-ix.

[39] Lester Frank Ward, *Dynamic Sociology: Or Applied Social Science* (New York, City, NY: D. Appleton, [1883] 1897) vol.2: 548, 589-590; https://archive.org/details/dynamicsocio-log05wardgoog/page/n562; s. also: Stephen J. Sniegoski, "State Schools versus Parental Rights: The Legacy of Lester Frank Ward," *Journal of Social, Political and Economic Studies*, X (Summer, 1985), 215-227.

[40] Sidney Fine, *Laissez Faire and the General Welfare State: A Study of Conflict in American Thought, 1865-1901* (Ann Arbor, MI: The University of Michigan Press, 1956) 288.

who were controlled and exploited by a highly educated elite to which he himself belonged.

The extension of education to areas such as health, profession, family, and society offered the power-grasping administrative elite the opportunity to steer the socialization of the entire population in the direction they wanted through mass education. Their primary intention was to undermine the supremacy of traditional institutions and effect the utopian ideas of an administrative state by means of a therapeutic social technique. In 1917, mass education began to be fused with the mass state, which agreed to subsidize general education. All pupils and students were placed beneath the control of the state. The Department of Education mainly disseminated progressive ideology. The National Education Association centralized and standardized mass education to the greatest extent possible, using all of its political power exclusively to promote progressive objectives.

10.4 Technocratic reform of society

The increasing secularization of American society became evident as the works of man were accorded equal status with the works of God. Working from a Postmillennial basis, writers described a future socialist and technocratic society which they referred to as the "great awakening of the twentieth century" (Edward Bellamy). Leaders among the working class anticipated the arrival of the kingdom of God on earth and encouraged their followers to strive for economic improvement of their living conditions. Bellamy predicted the rise of a tightly regulated society in which a strong nation state would abolish the profit system through economic and scientific revolution and take control of every stage of production.[41] The writer and Freemason Ignatius Donnelly called Christian churches to unite so that worldwide social reform could take place.[42] Bellamy and Donnelly believed that a new era could only be brought about through a religious reformation of society. The socio-critical works and novels of the Englishman H. G. Wells were received enthusiastically in Great Britain and other Western countries, and left a lasting impression on politicians such as Winston Churchill. Wells's books had great influence on progressive readers in America, and even President T. Woodrow Wilson later approved their utopian suggestions for reforming world order.

Karl Marx and Friedrich Engels had hoped that the United States, as a young nation, would be receptive to Socialism. However, later Marxists turned away from this hope. During the Progressive Era, most American Socialists favored a moderate form of Marxism, although the Socialist Labor

---

[41] Edward Bellamy, *Looking Backward: 2000-1887* (Boston, MA: Ticknor & Co., 1888; Boston, MA: Houghton Mifflin, 1889).

[42] Ignatius Donnelly, *The Golden Bottle Or the Story of Ephraim Benezet of Kansas* (New York City, NY: Merrill, 1892); https://archive.org/details/cu31924021984400/page/n7

Party under Daniel De Leon continued to promote totalitarian Communism. De Leon cultivated a rigid and academic style of leadership, and therefore failed to gain much support for his cause. The Socialism spreading through America only began to influence Progressivism in July 1901, when socialist groups united to form the Socialist Party of America. The Social Democratic Party, formed in 1898, demanded that the property rights of the syndicates of large capitalist corporations and banks be transferred to the government. The Socialism pushed for by various parties was progressive, as well as Marxist, in its political orientation.

10.5 Sociopolitical development of Democracy

The Freemason[43] William Jennings Bryan (1860-1925) was one of the most important representatives of the Progressive Era.[44] His religious views were conservative, while his political and economic ideas were progressive. Many of his contemporaries criticized the well-known social reformer for regarding Christianity as his source of vital energy. However, Bryan saw no conflict between belief in biblical revelation and humanistic Progressivism.[45] He was essentially a religiously cloaked Humanist, which is why he was also able to be a Freemason. Bryan's university studies and Christian environment sharpened his awareness of the concerns of the poorer social classes. He was sympathetic to the Populists, who advocated stronger state intervention in economic activity. He championed Democracy and criticized Capitalism, pleading ahead of his time for the introduction of a state pension scheme and campaigning for social justice.[46] The goal behind this campaign, he claimed, was to prevent Socialism and protect property rights – objectives that seem entirely contradictory to the typical aims and effects of social justice. A further paradox was his purported concern for a controlled Individualism.

---

[43] Eugen Lennhoff, Oskar Posner, Dieter A. Binder, eds., *Internationales Freimaurer-Lexikon* (Wien: Amalthea-Verlag; Graz: Akademische Druck- und Verlagsanstalt, 1965; München: Herbig, 2015) 157.

[44] Paolo E. Coletta, *William Jennings Bryan: Political Evangelist, 1860-1908* (Lincoln, NE: University of Nebraska Press, 1964) vol. 1; https://archive.org/details/williamjenningsb00cole; s. also: Paul W. Glad, *The Trumpet Soundeth: William Jennings Bryan and His Democracy, 1896-1912* (Lincoln, NE: University of Nebraska Press, 1960); https://archive.org/details/trumpetsoundethw0000glad/page/n3; Lawrence W. Levine, *Defender of the Faith, William Jennings Bryan: The Last Decade, 1915-1925* (Cambridge, MA: Harvard University Press, 1965); https://archive.org/details/defenderoffaithw00levi

[45] H. Richard Niebuhr, *The Kingdom of God in America* (New York City, NY: Harper & Row Publishers, [1938] 1980) 160-162; https://archive.org/details/kingdomofgodinam0000nieb/page/160; s. also: Guy Franklin Hershberger, *The Way of the Cross in Human Relations* (Scottdale, PA: Herald Press, 1958; Eugene, OR: Wipf and Stock Publishers, 2001) 77 ff.

[46] *The Commoner* (December 9, 1904), 2-3.

He saw Democracy as having religious characteristics, since – like Christianity – it was based on a love for humanity.[47]

During the 1890s, the spiritual direction of America's urban population moved far away from its former position of Calvinistic Puritanism. The Social Gospel was portrayed as a panacea for all evil in society by liberal theologians and gained wide acceptance. Bryan counted among the most loyal followers of the Social Gospel movement out of political conviction, describing the Federal Council of Churches in 1919 as the "greatest religious organization in the U.S.A." Many American Christians failed to see the goal that underlay the founding of the Federal Council of Churches. They were persuaded into assisting the institutional unification of churches which held completely different theological positions, not realizing that they had been led astray under false pretenses. They engaged actively in projects that largely pursued the very opposite of Christianity's historical mission. The preaching of the Gospel, which emphasized the eternal salvation of the soul, was turned into a message of socialization that stressed the improvement of earthly living conditions. Motivated by the challenge of biblical unity, American Christians consented to an outward-looking show of church unity which often only feigned the appearance of a common spiritual basis. Leaders of the ecumenical movement condemned the division of churches as a cardinal sin.

William Jennings Bryan became a spokesman for "progressive social Christianity." Although he never used the term "Social Gospel" in his writings, he denoted the same thing through his phrase "applied Christianity." Bryan lost the presidential elections of 1896, 1900, and 1908, each time receiving a significantly lower share of the vote than his political opponents despite advocating the cause of the "common people" against the "Money Trust," the *de facto* monopoly of J. P. Morgan and New York's other most powerful bankers. There was a fundamental shift in the structure of the American political landscape from the end of the nineteenth century, particularly evident in the election year of 1896. Bryan's 1896 presidential campaign was a turning point in the history of the Democratic Party: it was due to his maneuvering that socialist Progressivism was embraced by President Jefferson's party, which was devoted to Classical Liberalism.

Bryan was responsible for the establishment of Progressivism in American society during the twentieth century. After the Freemason Franklin D. Roosevelt (ΦBK[48], Fly Club) was elected president in 1933, Progressivism merged with Populism at a national level.

---

[47] *The Commoner* (October 28, 1904).

[48] Honorary member of the Phi Beta Kappa Society

10.6 Collective ideology of Reform Darwinism

(Birth of the secular millennium: intelligent man controls the destiny of the world)

The negative impact of Darwinism became increasingly evident toward the end of the nineteenth century. It seemed that no one could evade the influence of the forces of nature; every human being was subject to the unpredictable fate of a cold universe with no personal God. Many people turned away from Herbert Spencer's Social Darwinism in an effort to avoid social chaos.[49] The promises made by the state were more enticing. The state was seen to have Messianic qualities – to guarantee meaningful existence, advanced comfort, and material success – which acted as a great boost to centralization.

The teachings of Charles Darwin and Sigmund Freud were revised in order to maintain the development of the forward-moving age. A counterreaction to Social Darwinism was posed by a collective Darwinism, known from 1952 as "Reform Darwinism." It was promoted by Lester Frank Ward[50] (1841-1913), who introduced Collectivism to America[51] and believed that Progressivism would provide the basis of an ideal social system. His basic premise was that nature, after a long period of development, had produced a man capable of planning who could change the world through reason. Passive surrender to the blind forces of nature would no longer be necessary. Because of his intelligence, man could not only control the process of evolution, but also accelerate it and steer it in the direction needed to achieve the desired social behavior.[52] Filled with optimism, social scientists worked hard to spread the theory of evolution under its new banner. From this time onward, they wanted to determine the process of evolution just as they wished. Progress therefore needed to be planned in detail.

Both Social and Reform Darwinism led to antisocial behavior. By applying Ward's method, Ward and other sociologists would be able to initiate a secular millennium in which they would be established as authoritarian technocrats. Ward believed that science was the only legitimate method of reforming society from the ground up. Sociology was already the dominant science by this time, and every evil in society was understood to stem from economic competition. Ward called for the introduction of a completely new

---

[49] Eric Frederick Goldman, *Rendezvous with Destiny: A history of modern American reform* (New York City, NY: Knopf, 1952; Chicago, IL: Ivan R. Dee, 2001); https://archive.org/details/rendezvouswithde00goldrich

[50] Samuel Chugerman, *Lester Frank Ward: The American Aristotle* (Durham, NC: Duke University Press, 1939); https://archive.org/details/lesterfwardameri0000chug/page/n7

[51] Lester Frank Ward, *Dynamic Sociology: Or Applied Social Science* (New York City, NY: D. Appleton, 1883) vol. 1: http://archive.org/details/dynamicsociolog07wardgoog; vol. 2: http://archive.org/details/dynamicsociolog05wardgoog

[52] Lester F. Ward, *The Psychic Factors of Civilization*, 2nd ed. (Boston, MA: Ginn & Company, [1893] 1906) 157; https://archive.org/details/in.ernet.dli.2015.90772/page/n181

economic system which he named "collective achievements." He insisted that group initiative, not the individual, was responsible for human happiness.

The vision of Progressivism was substantiated throughout the twentieth century. Its formation as an ideology was supported by Russian Communists, Italian Fascists, and German National Socialists. The vision of the French Revolution and its Napoleonic fulfillment – a social Rationalism planned by the state[53] – was consummated in Reform Darwinism.

In the field of politics, Ward sought to introduce an idealized Sociocracy which would replace the constitutional republic with a totalitarian system. Sociocracy is a form of government in which the reins of power are held by experts trained in the principles of Reform Darwinism – Ward's own principles. Legislative power would therefore not be held by an elected Congress, but rather by specially appointed sociologists who would seek to create an ideal society on the basis of their scientific principles. During the Progressive Era, America's political and economic life was governed by Sociology as represented by Ward. After the Second World War, the establishment of State Monopoly Capitalism (Corporatism) became the highest goal of Western state government, and has since been largely achieved.

In many people's eyes, Ward offered the only solution that would impede the rampant and unruly competition of the free market economy, or at least set it on an orderly course. The remedy was found in a collective state which controlled the principle means of production and transportation. What most people never understood, however, was that the collective state was nothing other than a totalitarian regime disguised with smooth rhetoric. The claim that the individual could only find true happiness in this collective state reflected Hegel's idea that man is nothing without the state. Americans preferred political centralization and economic collectivization to the principles of a decentralized and liberal social order.

The Transcendentalism at the basis of Hegelianism paved the way for the triumph of totalitarian Progressivism. Ward derived the idea of using public education to achieve his social goals from Karl Marx's *Communist Manifesto* (1848). In Ward's eyes, religion was the product of misguided delusion. He did not believe that any supernatural reality could explain the existence of all life; in his eyes, man was merely the product of evolutionary forces. He continually took an opposite standpoint to Christian ethics. He had a negative view of marriage and family[54] (in a Sociocracy they would no longer be necessary) and replaced biblical ethics with a naturalistic and hedonistic moral philosophy which taught that man was not wicked by nature.[55] Ward believed that Hedonism was the superior outlook on life.

---

[53] Friedrich A. Hayek, *The Counter-Revolution of Science: Studies in the Abuse of Reason* (Indianapolis, ID: Liberty Press, [1952] 1979); https://archive.org/details/counterrevolu-tio030197mbp/page/n6

[54] Lester Frank Ward, *Pure Sociology* (New York City, NY: The Macmillan Company, 1903) 353; https://archive.org/details/puresociologyat01wardgoog/page/n370

[55] Lester Frank Ward, *Glimpses of the Cosmos* (New York City, NY: G.P. Putnam's Sons,

Reform Darwinism was soon established in Sociology and Jurisprudence[56] at America's renowned universities, thereby initiating the gradual rejection of Christian legal doctrine.

10.7 Monopolistic synchronization of the national economy

There are two forms of management: bureaucratic management and profit-oriented enterprise. The free market economy offers ideal conditions for successful management since it protects private property, makes every profession accessible, encourages competition, and enables a profit and loss system to function effectively. The smooth running of the economy is ensured by giving consumers the power to decide which goods they want to purchase and which they do not. Commercial success is achieved by those who best satisfy the needs of their customers. Bureaucratic management makes use of an opposite principle. Civil servants rely on state power to claim tax from citizens without offering them anything in return. Politicians are obliged to distribute the taxes collected to various government departments. No consideration is given to consumers' needs in the distribution of assets.[57]

The American government has always played a role in capitalist society. Through subsidies, high protective tariffs, and gifts of land to railroad companies, the state intervened in the economy for the benefit of certain interest groups. The protective tariffs had already caused an unnatural concentration of industry in the northern states before the American War of Secession. The majority of progressive laws, allegedly passed to control the exploitative business practices of large companies, found wide approval among business owners themselves. There was nonetheless strong competition in various industry sectors at the turn of the century, including in the steel industry, telecommunications, oil production, and refining. Since cartel initiatives confronted so many obstacles between 1897 and 1901, monopolists tried every means of controlling the internal market, seeking to establish some degree of stability and predictability in the economy. Since increasing competition thwarted any private attempts at monopolization[58], corporate Neoliberals in large businesses sought to get federal laws passed in all branches of industry in order to curb what they saw as the adverse effects of open competition.

[1913] 1922) vol. 5: 275-276; https://archive.org/details/glimpsesofcosmos05wardiala/page/274

[56] Oliver Wendell Holmes, Jr., *The Common Law* (Boston, MA: Little, Brown and Company, [1881] 1923) 1-2; https://archive.org/details/commonlaw00holm/page/n17

[57] Ludwig von Mises, *Bureaucracy* (New Haven, CT: Yale University Press, 1944; Grove City, PA: Libertarian Press, 1996).

[58] Gabriel Morris Kolko, *The Triumph of Conservatism: A Reinterpretation of American History, 1900-1916* (New York City, NY: Quadrangle Books, 1963; New York City, NY: Free Press, 1977); https://archive.org/details/KolkoGabrielTheTriumphOfConservatism

All forms of state economic regulation have a dual effect: they penalize efficient producers and give monopolistic privileges to the inefficient. Since governments derive their power from interest groups already existing in the economy, they use them to contain innovation and limit competition from efficient companies. American Corporatism seeks to restrict the free market economy as far as possible.[59]

Early twentieth-century Progressivism was a political and social movement based on four pillars. The first pillar consisted of an ambitious group of technocratic and socialist intellectuals. The second pillar of Progressivism was formed by the political establishment. The third was constituted by a coalition of national interest groups led by industrial magnates. The fourth pillar was an intellectual movement that began in universities, involving lawyers, philosophers, economists, and historians.

Revolutionary socialists and wealthy capitalists surprisingly shook hands in implementing their various interests. On the one hand, technocratic and socialist intellectuals used newspaper articles, books, and speeches to spread their revolutionary ideas to the people living in America's slums who had been radicalized through economic upheaval and social uprooting. Many leading journalists and publicists saw an opportunity to side with the oppressed. They seized their chance to gain political influence by acting as the voice of the exploited masses, working with politicians in order to be heard. Socialism seemed to provide their best philosophical basis. On the other hand, Capitalist corporations such as the private investment bank J. P. Morgan & Co. also engaged in politics in order to promote a progressive form of government. Their aim was to secure the dominance of large-scale industry in both the national and international economy.

Progressives had faith in a powerful national state, believing that the government was the best institution to promote social welfare and counteract the Individualism of Classical Liberalism. They were convinced that intellectuals in government would steer social and economic progress in the right direction. They mistakenly believed that these experts were selfless and honest, and that technocrats' expertise would not only serve social welfare, but also use the most favorable methods to achieve their desired goals.

The American political economy as developed since the early twentieth century presents a system of State Monopoly Capitalism (Corporatism). The center of power consists of large corporations, trade union confederations, and bureaucracy. The government intervenes and performs its task of balancing the different interests of large trading blocs[60], while simultaneously ensuring that the power of its affiliated companies is not jeopardized by

---

[59] Jane Jacobs, *The Economy of Cities* (New York City, NY: Vintage, 1969) 247.

[60] Murray N. Rothbard, *Man, Economy and State* (Auburn, AL: Ludwig von Mises Institute, [1962] 2004) 591.

potential competition from below – from the trade unions. The basis of the welfare state thus consists of an economic cartel united by political decrees.[61]

11 America's military attacks as a world power

After the United States gained independence from the British Empire, the North American frontier was extended to the Pacific. Since the nation seemed to be safe from potential enemies because of its advantageous geographical situation, the influx of immigrants entering the country settled in the most fertile lands from the Atlantic to the Pacific. After the War of Secession (1861 to 1865), national unity could be restored.[62] While the southern states imagined an expansion of American territory, the northern Yankees envisioned a future in which their domain would be maximized to the extent of worldwide military domination.[63]

11.1 Fateful consequences of a territorial expansion policy

The Founding Fathers of the U.S.A. largely resisted the revolutionary spirit of the French Jacobins. However, they were aware that their independence from the British Empire, gained through military force, had a global significance that would define the late eighteenth century. Their aim was to form a new nation. Thomas Paine, one of the Founding Fathers, warned in 1792 against ignoring the economic dangers that come with controlling an Empire.[64] Had Americans taken Paine's advice, they would not only have avoided wars abroad, but would also have evaded the bureaucratization of their own country which developed in parallel with the expansion of the American Empire.

In his farewell address, President George Washington clearly defined the kind of foreign policy that he supported. His thinking was guided by the pacifist undertones of the Protestant Reformation and the Anglo-Scottish Enlightenment. As tempting as the idea of equaling the commercial power and global reach of the British Empire may have been, Washington's keen

---

[61] Murray N. Rothbard, *Power and Market* (Auburn, AL: Ludwig von Mises Institute, [1970] 2006) 29.

[62] Dwight G. Anderson, *Abraham Lincoln: The Quest for Immortality* (New York City, NY: Alfred A. Knopf, 1982) 245.

[63] Major L. Wilson, *Space, Time and Freedom: The Quest for Nationality and the Irrepressible Conflict, 1815-1861* (Westport, CN: Greenwood Press, 1974) 67-70.

[64] Thomas Paine, "The Rights of Man," in R. E. Roberts, ed., *Selected Writings of Thomas Paine* (New York City, NY: Everybody's Vacation Publishing Company, 1945) 328; https://archive.org/details/in.ernet.dli.2015.51957/page/n337

sense of what was possible prevailed in the question of how America ought to shape its relations with the European powers. Principles derived from biblical commands were crucial in shaping American foreign policy and remained effective for around 120 years. Preservation of national unity and civil freedom was considered the primary objective, and was understood only to be possible if America refrained from overexerting ideological and political influence overseas. Subsequent history shows that the cause of the nationalistic Founding Fathers was changed over time – and even transformed into its opposite.

America's military operation against Mexico from 1846 to 1848 was a conquest campaign which favored wealthy landowners in California, New Mexico, Arizona, and Texas. The conflict was over political control of vast areas of land taken forcibly from Mexico by the American government under President James Knox Polk, and was a key factor at the start of the subsequent War of Secession between the northern and southern states. President Lincoln first refused the southern states independence from the Union, and then dealt a fatal blow to decentralization so that the federal government could have full control over the most important affairs of the state. Moreover, the northern states' triumphant victory had monumental consequences for the whole world. Lincoln became absorbed with the idea of a Union which would bring salvation. The U.S.A. felt morally justified in becoming the world's lawgiver: the assumption that America's cause was the cause of humanity indirectly provided the rationale for the Americanization of the whole world.[65]

The present-day Lincoln cult has nothing to do with the real American Lincoln, who had real human weaknesses as well as virtues. The fabricated figure at the center of this political religion is an absolutist lawgiver in the Rousseauian sense: a demigod who time and again seeks to unite all nations of the world through warfare. America's political and economic expansion beyond its borders can be interpreted as a process of world redemption.[66] Fixation on the idea of an American mission to spread democratic principles produced a greater readiness to follow revolutionary movements and political changes in distant countries. The early nineteenth-century territorial expansion on the American continent was an advance into sparsely populated regions that were generally regarded as almost impenetrable wilderness. On the other hand, the occupation of areas settled by Indians from time immemorial indicated the purely imperialistic drive of the United States. In general, the aims and implementation of this Imperialism were never truly peaceful, even though they did not always involve sustained, bloody conflict. Despite the Mexican War and America's aggressive attempts to annex Cuba during the early 1850s, continental expansion and pursuit of the policy of "Manifest Destiny" were aimed at forming a nation state rather than building

---

[65] Dwight G. Anderson, *Abraham Lincoln: The Quest for Immortality* (New York City, NY: Alfred A. Knopf, 1982) 192, 210.

[66] Ibid., 225.

a global empire. America's continual continental expansion came to an end in 1853 after the purchase of a large area of Mexico, today located in southern Arizona and New Mexico. Russia wanted to dispose profitably of the impenetrable Alaska near the Arctic Circle, and the U.S.A. purchased the territory in 1867 in order to gain land connected to the North American continent.

The surrender of the southern states was followed by the failure of a planned invasion of Mexico in 1865.[67] In 1866, the U.S. government initiated a military expedition on specious grounds against formerly friendly powers such as the British Empire, invading Canadian territory. However, rational voices in American government circles stood up to the warmongers of the Grant administration in order to mitigate the crisis. Shortly after, the planned annexation of Santo Domingo came to a more or less peaceful end. Despite other serious incidents, Secretary of State Hamilton Fish used his diplomatic skill to avoid conflict between the United States and European powers in the Caribbean islands during the 1890s.

During the same period, America extended trade relations to the distant Samoan Islands but deliberately avoided their annexation. The latter only happened in 1898, when the United States sought to emulate the imperial powers of the time in acquiring overseas colonies. The Washington government's dealings in China were similar both before and after 1865. Each time that the British overcame Chinese resistance to the enforcement of special privileges due to their military superiority in the Opium Wars, Americans demanded equivalent rights but were granted them only partially.

The great turning point in American foreign policy came in the early 1890s, during the second Cleveland administration,[68] when the United States turned from a peaceful foreign policy to an aggressive policy of economic and political expansion abroad. At the center of the new foreign policy were America's leading bankers, who were eager to exploit the country's growing economic power to their own advantage. The main focus of aggressive expansion during the 1890s was Latin America, and the main enemy to be defeated was Great Britain which dominated foreign investment in this vast region. Richard Olney (1835-1917), Secretary of State from 1895 to 1897, wanted to introduce the United States to the idea of an imperialist policy. The traditional Isolationism recommended by George Washington in his farewell address was over. The time had now come for America to take a dominant position among the world's great powers. The country's commercial interests required larger markets for American products to be opened up in other countries, especially in Latin America. The banker J. Pierpont Morgan, who had maintained a close relationship with Olney for many years, swore him

---

[67] Archibald Dunning, *Reconstruction: Political and Economic, 1865-1877* (New York City, NY: Harper & Brothers, 1907) 153; https://archive.org/details/bub_gb_XgIOAAAAIAAJ/page/n173

[68] Allan Nevins, *Grover Cleveland: A Study in Courage* (New York City, NY: Scribner's, 1932; Dodd, Mead, 1962).

into this imperialist policy. In order to put their warmongering intentions into action, Cleveland and Olney continued their plans to mobilize the American military in order to rob Great Britain of its markets and trading bases in Latin America. In 1893, there were violent clashes between American troops and France in Santo Domingo, followed by military clashes with the British in Brazil and Nicaragua in 1894. However, the most serious crisis of the period took place between 1895 and 1896, when the American government almost waged war with Great Britain over a territorial dispute between Venezuela and British Guiana.

In 1895, the crisis between the U.S.A. and Great Britain over the border between independent Venezuela and the British crown colony of Guiana came to a head. The British made claims on the contested territory because of the discovery of gold. President Cleveland (ΦBK)[69] referred to the Monroe Doctrine and offered to act as mediator. President Monroe (ΦBK)[70] had laid the foundations of America's long-term foreign policy in 1823. He had stated that the European powers, the Old World, had no territorial claims on the New World, and had demanded the cessation of all colonization efforts. In line with the slogan "America of the Americans," the European powers were not to recolonize the now independent states of Latin America. The British made it plain that the Monroe Doctrine was merely a one-sided American declaration with no binding authority in international law. The American government rarely referred to the Monroe Doctrine – so rarely that it was virtually never mentioned before the 1895 border conflict between British Guiana and Venezuela provoked a serious crisis with England. Military conflict could easily have ensued, had the British not been diverted by fighting in South Africa. President Cleveland even responded to a conciliatory British gesture to settle the conflict by raising talk of an Anglo-American alliance. America and Britain subsequently commenced negotiations for a new Panama Canal Treaty. President Grover Cleveland prevented various imperialist attempts to annex Hawaii during his second term of office from 1893 to 1897. When Cuba – a country of constant unrest – was hit by another revolution in 1895, Cleveland pursued a moderate policy; with time, however, his peaceable attitude began to change. The U.S. government initially sought to protect the American-owned plantations in Cuba from the attacks of the revolutionaries, supporting Spain in order to avert the immediate danger. At the same time, the government put pressure on the colonial masters to grant Cuba a certain degree of autonomy and thus satisfy its desire for independence. This double-track diplomacy cast a long shadow on subsequent U.S. foreign policy. In the period that followed, America often acted as arbitrator in foreign military conflicts, presenting itself as an impartial "third power." It claimed to be interested solely in reconciling violent disputes in

---

[69] Honorary Member of the Phi Beta Kappa Society

[70] Member of the Phi Beta Kappa Society, College of William and Mary, 1776

underdeveloped countries; in reality, however, it shamelessly exploited tensions in the various nations to its own advantage.

In the autumn of 1895, Richard Olney realized that Spain would lose the fight against the Cuban revolutionaries. In light of the important trade relations between America and Cuba, which had been greatly promoted by the millionaire Edwin F. Atkins who owned sugar plantations in Cuba, the Cleveland administration made a radical turnaround in its political action on the Caribbean island. Among the factors that tipped the scales in the decision were Atkins's long, close friendship with the Olneys, who like him were from Boston, and Atkins's intention to further the interests of the bank J. P. Morgan & Co. as one of its partners. The American government began working in the background to bring about Cuban independence. The fact that such a deceitful approach would lead to war was apparently not worth consideration. The government embarked on a collision course with Spain in full awareness of the inevitable outcome. It was nonetheless three years before the Spanish-American War actually broke out. Edward F. Atkins worked hard to push through the war with the support of August Belmont, a representative of the European Rothschild banking dynasties in America. As Spain's long-standing financier, the House of Rothschild refused to grant any further loans to the collapsing imperial power. Instead it guaranteed loans to the revolutionaries and even undertook full responsibility for the rest of the unsigned bonds. The decisive imperialist influence in government circles came from the young undersecretary of the Navy, Theodore Roosevelt (ΦBK[71], Porcellian Club, Fly Club), and his powerful mentor, Senator Henry Cabot Lodge (ΦBK[72], Porcellian Club). However, it should not be forgotten that in its dealings with Cuba, the Cleveland-Olney regime took the first steps toward an overseas empire.

11.2 Role of a redeemer nation in world politics

At the turn of the twentieth century, a new attitude toward overseas colonial property became increasingly evident, making it clear to all that America was entering the chaotic interchange of power in global politics which for centuries had shaped the history of Europe. Since there was no longer a frontier in the West, Americans began to exploit freely the raw materials in their vast backcountry. Tensions arose between employers and employees, and an industrialized urban population began to form. The same process also took place in the countries of Western Europe.

Josiah Strong (1847-1916), a chief exponent of the Social Gospel, agreed with the historian Frederick Jackson Turner (1861-1932) that the 1890s were a decade of crisis – particularly in terms of the disappearance of the frontier

---

[71] Member of the Phi Beta Kappa Society, Harvard University, 1880

[72] Member of the Phi Beta Kappa Society, Harvard University, 1871

which was an event of enormous significance. Strong resolutely advocated the expansion of Christian mission with the aim of a Christianized world. In order to be able to achieve this goal, he addressed certain aspects of American society which had direct implications for a policy of imperialist expansion. Anticipating a statement made eight years later by Turner, Strong warned that the land available for settlement and cultivation was limited. Industry in the West was developing as railroads were extended, and Strong feared that countless complex problems would arise. He stated that the West needed to take swift precautions to prevent social breakdown.[73] He believed that America would become the right arm of God in the fight against the ignorance, oppression, and sin that prevailed in the world.[74] Strong thus highlighted the New Protestant belief that the United States would have a unique role in the world as the "redeemer nation"[75] appointed by God, and that the Anglo-Saxon race was destined to spread across the entire earth. This belief in a divine calling, as perceived by many Americans, was a compilation of different and sometimes conflicting ideas and impulses.[76] Strong was convinced that Democracy was the highest form of government; however, he also believed that it would become anarchistic unless guided by moral principles. Material progress would lose its expediency if it degenerated to unrestrained Materialism.[77]

During the 1890s, the United States' forced economic interpenetration of remote, sparsely populated regions of the world opened opportunities for annexation. A trade balance with other nations, developed to America's advantage, encouraged the export of manufactured goods.[78] The majority of the American public supported William McKinley's presidential campaign and voted for the Republicans in 1900. They were probably in agreement that

[73] Josiah Strong, *Our Country: Its Possible Future and Its Present Crisis* (New York City, NY: Baker & Taylor, 1885; Cambridge, MA: Harvard University Press, 1963) 153-158; https://archive.org/details/cu31924020347534/page/n167

[74] Ibid., 218; https://archive.org/details/cu31924020347534/page/n235; s. also: Conrad Cherry, ed., *God's new Israel: Religious Interpretations of American Destiny* (Englewood Cliffs, NJ: Prentice-Hall, 1971); Winthrop Still Hudson, ed., *Nationalism and Religion in American Concepts of American Identity and Mission* (Gloucester, MA: Smith, 1978).

[75] Ernest Lee Tuveson, *Redeemer Nation: The Idea of America's Millennial Role* (Chicago, IL: University of Chicago Press, 1968); https://archive.org/details/redeemernation00erne; James H. Moorhead, *American Apocalypse: Yankee Protestants and the Civil War, 1860-1869* (New Haven, CT: Yale University Press, 1978); https://archive.org/details/americanapocalyp-0000moor; s. also: Charles Royster, *The Destructive War: William Tecumseh Sherman, Stonewall Jackson, and the Americans* (New York City, NY: Alfred A. Knopf, 1991) chap. 6, "The Vicarious War".

[76] James H. Moorhead, "The American Israel: Protestant Tribalism and Universal Mission," in William R. Hutchinson & Hartmut Lehmann, eds., *Many Are Chosen: Divine Election and Western Nationalism* (Minneapolis, MN: Fortress Press, 1994) 145-166.

[77] Strong, *Our Country*, 138; https://archive.org/details/cu31924020347534/page/n153

[78] Albert J. Beveridge, "The March of the Flag," campaign speech on September 16, 1898 in Albert J. Beveridge, *The Meaning of the Times, and Other Speeches* (Indianapolis, IN: Bobbs-Merrill, 1908) 47-57; https://archive.org/details/meaningoftimesot00beve/page/46

overseas expansion was preferable to state economic regulation, as was common in Europe at the time. When the American government set up an administrative office for economic planning in the newly acquired colonies, they portrayed it as necessary in order to bear the burden placed on the white man.[79] Official announcements on the provision of humanitarian aid diverted attention from the true significance of the policy of expansion, the sole purpose of which was to open new markets for America's surplus industrial products. International protective tariffs were to be lowered in order to encourage the American export industry. Tariffs in the home market were raised in order to protect America's fledgling industrial sectors from foreign competition.

Contrary to expectations, many industrial magnates initially held back from declaring themselves in favor of American Imperialism. The strongest support for a forced colonial policy came at first from eloquent publicists and politicians, missionaries and naval officers, professors and moral philosophers. The ideology of the aggressive foreign policy consisted of a colorful mix of diverse philosophies. Imperialists expressed great affinity with Social Darwinism; however, they also advocated Anglo-Saxon racism, economic Determinism, and military Nationalism. Despite the general aversion to Colonialism among American politicians until 1898, the tide turned slowly but surely in favor of Imperialism. An easy victory over Spain, President McKinley's invocation of the white man's duty to fulfill the divine providence of "Manifest Destiny," and the patriotic appeals of men such as Theodore Roosevelt (ΦBK[80], Porcellian Club, Fly Club) who had recently returned from adventures in Cuba, were effective psychological stimulants. A militant foreign policy and economic upturn offered optimistic respite from the difficulties of class struggle and unrest among workers during the 1890s. Foreign trade, colonies, and war suddenly became attractive options for strengthening and increasing American prosperity.

Critics of the annexation policy were found in both the Democratic and Republican camps. The policy was also opposed by journalists and intellectuals such as Mark Twain (Samuel Langhorne Clemens; ΦBK[81]). However, the anti-imperialist movement was never well organized. It rejected Imperialism because it was contrary to the principles of the American system of government. Anti-imperialists thought that rejecting these principles for the ways of the Old World would destroy the republic. They discerned a direct relationship between the progressive and imperialist ideologies, and in this they were entirely correct. However, they were often stigmatized as unrealistic idealists who were unable to keep pace with twentieth-century world politics. A number of classical liberals and conservatives devoted particular attention

---

[79] Rudyard Kipling, "The White Man's Burden," in *McClure's Magazine* 12 (February, 1899).

[80] Member of the Phi Beta Kappa Society, Harvard University, 1880

[81] Honorary member of the Phi Beta Kappa Society (ΦBK)

to this phenomenon, having become suspicious of the trends of growing government power.

In 1898, the United States waged a blatant war of aggression against Spain over the island of Cuba, wanting to acquire and make a profit from overseas colonies. A canal was to be built between the Pacific and Atlantic Oceans in order to improve transport routes. In 1900, the U.S.A. and England agreed that third countries, particularly the countries of Latin America, should have no say in the construction and use of the canal. Furthermore, the U.S.A. would have the exclusive right of disposal in building it, while only England would be granted most-favored-nation status for its ships. President Roosevelt treated his Colombian negotiators with disrespect and was unwilling to pay the extremely low purchase price (the country of Panama did not yet exist). The U.S. government had no qualms about attacking a peaceable country in Latin America purely in order to gain a business advantage for the financiers of its own wealthy upper class. The risk of war was accepted in cold blood. The unavoidable conclusion is that Theodore Roosevelt, a racist convinced by English Social Darwinism, was fundamentally only interested in teaching those "contemptible little creatures," as he called them, a good lesson on how to behave properly in his presence. The expected conduct was no less than complete subservience. Displaying a humble demeanor toward American presidents became the iron rule for diplomats from every country that subsequently came under American domination. This aggressive, power-hungry foreign policy would remain unchanged for the next one hundred years.

11.3 Global manifesto of "Manifest Destiny"

In 1895, the United States was the most enviable nation in the world. It owned vast territories that were rich in valuable raw materials, and the prosperity of the growing American population was largely secure. Economic depressions were frequent, but America was able to bolster its reputation as the country of unlimited possibilities. No other country could keep pace with the relatively rapid economic expansion which had taken place in America during the eighteenth and nineteenth centuries. Against the backdrop of this favorable situation, some American politicians began to ask whether overseas colonies and an alliance with England were even necessary.

America's idea of national mission consisted of a mixture of Roman, Puritan, Enlightenment, Romantic, nationalist, progressive, and modern elements. However, it developed not only from America's history, theological roots, and political ideologies, but also from French and English Enlightenment radicals' expectations of a global "redemption."[82] The latter would supposedly be effected as the political principles of the newly founded confederation

---

[82] Jack P. Green, ed., *Colonies to Nation: A Documentary History of the American Revolution* (New York City, NY: W. W. Norton, 1975) 424.

spread through America. The redemption myth was woven from many strands, including the New England Puritans' sacred covenant, the Founding Fathers' conception of the unique nature of the new republic, and the millennialist fever among abolitionists (advocates of the abolition of slavery) both before and during the War of Secession (1861-1865). Historians have discerned a persistent, excessive self-confidence among Americans. America is thus more the realization of the "idea of a redeemer nation"[83] than it is a place or political community.[84]

T. Woodrow Wilson (1856-1924) was one of America's most important presidents. He not only inherited the American ideal of national mission and "Manifest Destiny," but also contributed to its subtle transformation. His deep sense of divine calling is generally attributed to his Puritan-Calvinist upbringing, but he also drew inspiration from revolutionary France, nineteenth-century Romantic Nationalism, Giuseppe Mazzini (an Italian nationalist, advocate of world unification, and Freemason), and the contemporary Social Gospel. He especially applied the teachings of the Social Gospel to the merging of the sacred and secular in the United States. Wilson changed America's relatively simple self-perception as a "New Garden of Eden" or "New Israel" into the Romantic and progressive ideal of a "Christ Nation," an image that was subsequently promoted widely by the Social Gospel movement.

By the beginning of the nineteenth century, the U.S. government was eager to seize property in the Western Hemisphere that was still attached to the former Spanish Empire. In the late eighteenth century, Thomas Jefferson, Founding Father and third president of the U.S.A., already stated his interest in incorporating Cuba in the American confederation. In the "Ostend Manifesto" of 1854, American diplomats in Europe made it clear that the United States would not tolerate European interference in the future if Cuba were forcibly wrested from Spain. From his influential position as chairman of the Democratic Party, August Belmont (1813-1890) supported the imperialist plans of the "Ostend" diplomacy. In 1896, the Republican William McKinley was elected president. He soon faced the critical situation of a third Cuban revolution against Spanish rule, which threw trade into chaos and threatened American investments in Cuba. It was both a problem and an opportunity at the same time. A successful war with Spain would give the United States the opportunity to take possession of the Spanish colonies in

---

[83] Ernest Lee Tuveson, *Redeemer Nation: The Idea of America's Millennial Role* (Chicago, IL: University of Chicago Press, 1968); https://archive.org/details/redeemernation00erne; James H. Moorhead, *American Apocalypse: Yankee Protestants and the Civil War, 1860-1869* (New Haven, CT: Yale University Press, 1978); https://archive.org/details/americanapocalyp-0000moor; s. also: Charles Royster, *The Destructive War: William Tecumseh Sherman, Stonewall Jackson, and the Americans* (New York City, NY: Alfred A. Knopf, 1991) chap. 6, "The Vicarious War".

[84] David W. Noble, *The Eternal Adam and the New World Garden: The Central Myth in the American Novel Since 1830* (New York City, NY: George Braziller, 1968); https://archive.org/details/eternaladamnewwo0000nobl

the Pacific Ocean, with the Philippine Islands being the most sought-after object of all. Militarily secured with fortifications, the Philippines would provide an ideal base for American shipping on long voyages to the East Asian markets. A naval base could also be set up in order to have the necessary troops at hand for the conquest of new colonies in Asia. Spanish troops in Cuba had their hands full in suppressing the uprising, forcing the civilian population into concentration camps. Cuban propagandists and the American media sensationalized the atrocities and even fabricated reports, causing an immense increase in newspaper sales. A public outcry put pressure on the administration in Washington to take up the cause of the Cuban freedom fighters. Spain could eventually do nothing but either give Cuba full independence or wage war with the United States – and early in April 1898, Spain finally gave Cuba its independence. However, before Madrid could fully implement this step, McKinley called on Congress to issue a declaration of war in full awareness that Spain was willing to accept America's political demands in order to evade bloody, costly, and futile military conflict with the United States.

The Spanish-American War lasted only 113 days and kindled immense Patriotism among many Americans.[85] Its victorious end was seen as a fate earned by bravery. However, complications arose relatively quickly which had far-reaching consequences in the long term, one tragic after-effect being the Philippine-American War (or the Philippine Insurrection, as President McKinley termed it). The outcome was by no means pleasant for either party, although America achieved a far better result in the short term, at least. The United States unconstitutionally annexed the Hawaiian Islands and occupied Guam and the Mariana Islands, which belonged to the Spanish Empire. The Spanish received the relatively small sum of twenty million U.S. dollars in exchange for their former colonies of Guam, the Mariana Islands, the Philippines, and Puerto Rico. Cuba was taken over as a protectorate of the United States. Thus the prototype of a particular form of Colonialism appeared for the first time – one limited to an informal, but nonetheless effective, control of overseas territories. The Cuban and Filipino freedom fighters were ultimately forced to submit to new colonial rulers who treated them as oppressively as the Spanish had done before. The only marginal change was the means of exploitation.

There was no compelling reason for the United States to declare war on Spain in 1898. The crux of the matter was that Spanish rulers in Cuba agreed to a truce that fully complied with America's demands. This took place two days before McKinley made his war speech on April 11, 1898, in the United States Capitol. He ignored the Spaniards' concessions and proceeded with his plan to get Congress to declare war with Spain. He had furtively set his sights on aims other than the preservation of peace.

---

[85] John T. Bethell, "'A Spendid Little War'. Harvard and the commencement of the new world order," *Harvard Magazine* (November, 1998); https://harvardmagazine.com/1998/11/war.html

English public opinion mainly interpreted the Spanish-American War and the Imperialism that followed as indicative of a rejection of the former policy of neutrality which Washington politicians had generally pursued throughout the nineteenth century. Edward Dicey, a prominent English publicist, wrote that America was seizing the opportunity to exert its vested right to world domination, which was the birthright of the Anglo-Saxon race. British imperialist circles celebrated the reelection of President McKinley in 1900 as a triumph of colonial politics, anticipating support for their own Imperialism. In order to justify the American expansion policy, the former populist senator from Kansas William A. Peffer went so far as to blame Filipino partisans for the bloodshed in their struggle against American imperialists.

Although the 1898 war with Spain was short-lived, the United States would never return to its traditional isolationist policy of over a century once the peace treaty was signed. The long suppression of the revolt in the Philippines, the development of new naval bases in the Pacific, and the permanent occupation of Cuba and other Caribbean islands required deployment of additional troops from the American military and navy. The government in Washington saw it as its duty to ensure the promotion of Militarism within its own country and to boost arms industry production. In 1898, the United States was transfigured from republic to empire. Imperial Democracy took on a new reality after the Spanish-American War, as the ultimate goal of unrestricted world domination was in sight. In an era of rapid development and monumental change, the United States' global interests knew no bounds. A radical change in American domestic and foreign policy took place between the war with Spain and the First World War. Progressivism and Imperialism thrived as mutually stimulating systems with political, economic, social, and religious components. For enthusiastic advocates of American overseas expansion, the United States' new imperial interest was an inevitable and desirable historical phenomenon.[86] However, for many others who were ideologically close to the Classical Liberalism of American Democracy, Imperialism not only represented an undue departure from the ideals of the former republic, but also a monstrous interference in the internal affairs of distant lands.

In the late 1890s, the United States' peaceable attitude toward the Far East began to change. While the American government was rapidly expanding its influence in the Pacific for economic and financial advantages, Washington noted that Russia, Germany, and France had also expanded their territory. Using their diplomatic skills, these three countries had managed to extract economic concessions from the corpse-like Chinese imperial dynasty. As the last nation to join the imperialist game in Asia (for the time being, at least), but unwilling to spend large amounts of money on stationary troops, the

---

[86] Jürgen Wagner, "Amerikas Mission: Liberaler Imperialismus und US-Außenpolitik," in *Wissenschaft und Frieden* (3/2003) 48-51; https://www.imi-online.de/download/IMI-Analyse-2003-025-AmerikasMission-Wagner.pdf

United States under the leadership of Richard Olney and his Republican contemporaries decided to ally with Great Britain in conquering and exploiting colonies. The two countries wanted Japan to act as a shock troop to drive back Russia and Germany from Asia. The geographically separated allies were keen to divide the lavish spoils between themselves. Historians referred euphemistically to this pure imperialist aggression as the "open door." After Britain was forced to leave politics and economic affairs in Latin America entirely in the hands of the United States, America was all too willing to help Great Britain in the Far East. A strong impulse to implement a more aggressive policy in the Far East stemmed from the desire to extract lucrative rail concessions from Asian countries. However, in two cases the American syndicate was blocked: the Chinese concessions were won by Russia and by a Belgian syndicate backed by France and Russia.

The time had come for the U.S.A. to take more effective measures and to pursue an aggressive policy in China in the name of American economic interests. America helped China drive Russian troops out of Manchuria. In 1904, President Theodore Roosevelt finally succeeded in inciting Japan to declare war on Russia. He willingly agreed to the Japanese occupation of Korea and Manchuria, secretly hoping that Japan would also promote America's economic interests in both countries. Theodore Roosevelt was a politician who, through family connections and friends, was under the full influence of J. P. Morgan & Co. from the outset of his career. Roosevelt married Alice Lee, daughter of George Cabot Lee, who came from one of the most prominent families in Boston. Roosevelt's relative Henry Cabot Lodge was Roosevelt's political mentor for many years.

As the Industrial Revolution developed in important countries of Western Europe, disagreement arose among them over the domination of markets in other continents. The old colonial empires, founded during the sixteenth and seventeenth centuries when Europe's political dominance first spread across the globe, gained additional importance in the exploitation and transportation of raw materials. The colonial population also constituted a mass of willing buyers of manufactured consumer goods. England, France, and later Germany continually sought more colonial property in the continents of Asia and Africa.

11.4 Progressives' authoritarian mentality of reform

A centralized conception of the state characterized European Social Democracy as well as the American reform movement, the latter following the European example more closely than previous reform movements in the United States. The socialist ideology held by the Progressive Robert M. La Follette, Sr., was aimed at national interests and resembled the social policies of Bismarck in Germany and of the English socialists (the Fabian Society). It also resembled the war policy of the European socialists and the English Prime Minister Lloyd George, who took over Great Britain's affairs of state in

1916. Conservatives in the U.S.A. criticized the non-liberal nature of these so-called reforms. They were especially against the complete transformation of the American republic into a Social Democracy, following the example of many European states. They discerned a close relationship between progressive and imperialist ideologies, opposed T. Roosevelt's sinister war policy, and accepted criticism for being out of step with the development of early twentieth-century world politics. The raging Nationalism of the nineteenth century gave way to "the age of national Imperialism."[87] An eyewitness stated that leaders in Washington had thoroughly adopted monarchist traditions and customs, because the former state, which had been based on Republican principles, had been transformed into a vast contiguous empire. The driving force behind this monumental change was the insatiable greed of the ruling upper class in America's northeastern metropolises.

Contemporary justifications for Imperialism were based on progressive ideology. Appeals for Americans to work altruistically for social justice in the lower classes could be easily turned into calls for participation in "missionary crusades" to seize colonial property, thus fulfilling the responsibility of bearing the "white man's burden." Popular newspapers of the early 1900s were full of articles extolling the merits of Imperialism. The reasons were not just profit-oriented, but were also based on the United States' idealistic aim to fulfil its highest calling – to spread Democracy throughout the world. The Freemason Theodore Roosevelt was the supreme representative of the Progressive Era. He improved the army many times over and pursued a warmongering foreign policy. He was thus particularly responsible for enforcing the progressive view that the state should control and regulate cartels rather than dissolve them.

The domestic reform program was known as "New Nationalism." Among its objectives were the expansion of foreign trade, the establishment of a strong army and navy, and the encouragement of conservation. Preserving natural habitats would guarantee national security, which was the top priority in the fight for world domination. Both government and industry benevolently took up the cause of the "Gospel of Efficiency" proclaimed by the conservation movement, implementing it as far as possible. Conservationists advocated an efficient approach to managing natural resources through state regulation and control.[88] They criticized unrestrained competition and economic development that was uncontrolled by the state. They wanted to concentrate economic power in the hands of a select few in order to encourage cooperation between entire branches of industry. Using technology to increase production and thereby develop better machinery was the great goal of the apostle of "habitat conservation," meaning that financially strong industries were given an enormous advantage over small businesses with insufficient capital.

---

[87] Paul S. Reinsch, *World Politics: The End of the Nineteenth Century* (New York City, NY: Macmillan, [1900] 1908); https://archive.org/details/in.ernet.dli.2015.23664/page/n4

[88] J. L. Bates, "Fulfilling American Democracy: The Conservation Movement, 1907 to 1921," *Mississippi Valley Historical Review*, XLIV (June, 1957), 31.

Environmentalists did not side with the people by opposing capitalists' mercenary interests. Had this been the case, there would have been no compelling reason for large industries to make "preservation of the environment" one of their foremost concerns. Medium-sized companies and private farms often showed the strongest opposition of all to environmentalists' ploys, feeling their existence to be under threat. Proposals made by the most prominent state environmentalist, Gifford Pinchot (Skull & Bones, 1889), aimed for a more efficient use of natural resources which would be exploited according to a carefully considered plan. The government declared environmental protection to be the highest priority for national security.[89] The real goal was not to preserve nature, but rather to implement a policy of nationalization. In retrospect, the American conservation movement can be seen to have almost single-handedly effected the monumental shift from nineteenth-century Individualism to twentieth-century Collectivism.

The ideology of conservation was among the Western elements that contributed to the gradual transformation of American society in the early twentieth century. The worthy ideal of bringing nature and humanity into harmony was steered in a new direction. Progressives were convinced that this ideal could be achieved through careful planning, and that the conservation movement was the first step in this direction.[90] During the Progressive Era (1896-1921), growing faith in the power of science and the efficacy of state regulation formed a common basis for diverse interest groups which wanted to create a perfect society in America. The propagation of Socialism was never very popular in the United States. Proponents in government wanted to bureaucratize society little by little, seeing this as an indirect way to realize socialist objectives. They believed it to be the only way to keep fooling Americans that they lived in a free country that uniquely upheld the principles of Classical Liberalism, while simultaneously working hard to introduce the conflicting principles of Socialism. In the 1930s, a large number of progressive opinion makers welcomed Franklin D. Roosevelt's New Deal as the ideal social order. In order to conceal this catastrophic state intervention in economic processes, the government publicly declared its sole interest to be the protection of important natural resources. When the emergency of economic depression gradually improved during the Second World War, New Deal planners thought about how to convert the drastic measures taken to revive the economy into a long-term reform program. Their idea was to place society in a socialist corset which would lead people to live in economically independent communities, almost enabling an agricultural harmony with the environment. One of the key proponents of social planning with respect to efficient application of natural laws was the

---

[89] Gifford Pinchot, *The Fight for Conservation* (New York City, NY: Doubleday, Page and Co., 1910) 4, 20; https://archive.org/details/fightforconserva00pinc/page/4

[90] *Proceedings of a Conference of Governors: In the White House, Washington, D.C., May 13-15, 1908* (Washington, D.C., Government Printing Office, 1909) vol. 1: 6ff; https://archive.org/details/proceedingsacon00unkngoog/page/n52

sociologist Lester Frank Ward (1841-1913). Ward was firmly against a free market economy but was also skeptical of Socialism, considering it to be an unscientific philosophy. He put all of his energy into spreading his own conception of Collectivism.[91] The reality of a totalitarian policy needed to remain hidden behind the façade of a democratic government – otherwise the general public would resist the sanctions placed on them.

Roosevelt's rearmament of the navy revealed a close connection between the progressive plan to control key aspects of American society and imperialist attempts to take overseas colonies that were rich in raw materials. Even Japan, a nation at the other end of the world, no longer dared to challenge the United States militarily with any hope of victory. The European superpowers were similarly in awe of America's phenomenal naval power.

Since an aggressive foreign policy meant that the cost of commercially exploiting foreign markets fell to taxpayers, the American government consequently needed to ensure the prosperity of its citizens. However, some of the key figures of the so-called "great power policy" were given the chance to gain exorbitant personal wealth. The most ardent supporters of a central banking system benefited from the enforced introduction of an American "Gold-Dollar" system in the Philippines, in which the American government abolished the existing silver standard. Filipinos had previously considered their currency of Spanish silver coins to be entirely adequate. The pressure placed by Washington on Mexico to adopt the "Gold-Dollar" system played a major role in the onset of the Mexican Revolution of 1911 to 1927.

Marxists mocked Capitalism for the problems of overproduction and insufficient domestic consumption. Vladimir Ilyich Lenin concluded that capitalist states would wage imperialist wars in order to correct these undesirable developments. The only right way out of the dilemma was supposedly a communist social order which would eradicate inequality. It therefore seems strange that Karl Marx endorsed Western Imperialism, since it would wrench nations from the grip of fanatical tyranny in order to place them into the hands first of Capitalism and then of Socialism.

12 The era of American Imperialism

American society underwent such profound changes during the First World War that one historian referred to them as the "revolution of state power."[92] Like other revolutions, this one was preceded by an intellectual change more radical than almost any other, due to the fact that Progressivism

---

[91] Lester Frank Ward, *The Psychic Factors of Civilization* (Boston, MA: Ginn and Co., [1893] 1906) 323, chap. 33, passim.; https://archive.org/details/in.ernet.dli.2015.90772/page/n347

[92] Bruce D. Porter, *War and the Rise of the State: The Military Foundations of Modern Politics* (New York City, NY: Free Press, [1994] 2002) 269.

had begun to dominate political discourse. Influential intellectuals put forward their progressive ideas based on humanist ideals such as the inevitable failings of laissez-faire (free market economy), the enormous growth of government power, the urgent need for economic planning, and the social value of Collectivism. Under the influence of left-wing Neoliberalism, the nation's political direction began slowly but surely to change. The War opened up unimagined opportunities for American Progressives to implement their radical program of social transformation, which would scarcely have been possible during peacetime.

12.1 Political power behind the throne

At all times and in many places, the course of history has been influenced by a handful of advisors who have shunned the spotlight in order to act almost completely invisibly behind the scenes. Today Edward Mandell House (1858-1938) is an almost completely forgotten man, but during the twentieth century he was one of the most important individuals in America. His personal strategy for progressing to the center of power was to put all his effort into helping other men attain prominent positions and to advise them once installed. His remarkable achievements in American domestic and foreign policy throughout his life were based on his innate talent for making friends and influencing others.[93] Wherever he turned, doors to the residences of well-known individuals flew open almost effortlessly. House and his wife consistently kept an open house and entertained the social elite. Having begun his career as a businessman in Texas, he became the leader of the Democratic Party in his home state and later gained a place on the Democrats' national committee. He made a decisive contribution to the election of four successive governors in Texas.

By 1911, House had spotted a rising star on the political skyline. He decided to lend his support to this man, who ran for the governorship of New Jersey in November 1910 despite having no political experience. House proved his political acumen when he recognized T. Woodrow Wilson (1856-1924) as a promising candidate for the highest position in America; in his eyes, Wilson was capable of delivering the American economy into the hands of leading bankers and entrepreneurs. The economic elite were most concerned with gaining maximum control over industry and trade, and they commissioned House to initiate the monopolization of the entire national economy and take it as far as possible. On March 4, 1913, T. Woodrow Wilson was inaugurated as the 28th president of the United States. He is generally portrayed in contemporary historical literature as a progressive idealist;

---

[93] Godfrey Hodgson, *Woodrow Wilson's Right Hand: The Life of Colonel Edward M. House* (New Haven, CT: Yale University Press, annotated edition, 2006) 9; https://archive.org/details/woodrowwilsonsri00hodg/page/8

however, he was a man hungry for power.[94] He pursued a foreign policy that interfered with the economy and aimed for political control over foreign territories, seeing this as the way to increase his own personal power[95] although he hypocritically denied this in public speeches. His real intentions were betrayed by various American military operations which he either supported or initiated himself. He saw the division of powers ensured by the Constitution as an obstacle to effective government.[96] His later reputation as an idealist was largely due to his repeated assertions of having a peace-loving nature. Contrary to the isolationist tone of his election slogan in the 1916 presidential campaign, which claimed that he would keep America out of the war in Europe, his greatest desire was to go down in history as a wartime president. On paper, Wilson ensured the territorial inviolability and political independence of America's southern neighbors who had joined the Pan-American Union; however, the United States' constant influence on political affairs in Mexico and other Latin American states clearly shows that he was lying.[97] Before America entered the European war, the worst instance of Wilson's military interference in other countries' affairs was the invasion of Mexico by the regular army. His attempt to manipulate the course of the country's raging civil war resulted in the fiascos of Tampico and Vera Cruz.[98]

Reconsidering the circumstances that led the American government to enter the First World War in league with the Allies highlights the critical significance of the friendship between Colonel Edward Mandell House and T. Woodrow Wilson. The two swiftly developed a close and successful cooperation. Wilson was taken up with the bizarre notion that House was his

---

[94] T. Woodrow Wilson, *Congressional Government: A Study in American Politics* (Gloucester, MA: Peter Smith, [1885] 1973) 22-23; https://archive.org/details/in.ernet.dli.2015.32003/page/n47

[95] Walter A. McDougall, *Promised Land, Crusader State: The American Encounter with the World since 1776* (Boston, MA: Houghton Mifflin, 1997) 126-128; https://archive.org/details/promisedlandcrus00mcdo/page/126: "Not surprisingly, Wilson embraced Progressive Imperialism. It suited his belief in the white man's calling and his notion of presidential government. So he cheered annexation of the Philippines and Puerto Rico – 'They are children and we are men in these deep matters of government and justice' – and the fact that foreign policy again dominated U.S. politics. Now there would be 'greatly increased power and opportunity for constructive statesmanship given the President.' A strong executive, he wrote, 'must utter every initial judgment, take every first step of action, supply the information upon which [the country] is to act, suggest and in large measure control its conduct.'" (p. 127)

[96] Wilson, *Congressional Government: A Study in American Politics*, 186-187; https://archive.org/details/in.ernet.dli.2015.32003/page/n209

[97] Arthur S. Link, *Woodrow Wilson and the Progressive Era, 1910-1917* (New York City, NY: Harper and Brothers, 1954) 92-106, 122-128; https://archive.org/details/woodrowwilsonand007665mbp/page/n117

[98] Burton J. Hendrick, *The Life and Letters of Walter H. Page* (Garden City, NY: Doubleday, Page & Co., 1923) 205; https://archive.org/details/lifeandlettersw00pagegoog/page/n232; s. also: Michael C. Meyer & William L. Sherman, *The Course of Mexican History*, 5. Edition (New York City, NY: Oxford University Press, 1995) 531-534; https://archive.org/details/courseofmexicanh00meye/page/530

"alter ego" – his second persona.[99] In his European travels from 1914, House held the distinguished position of being the American president's most important delegate. He had an enormous influence on almost every decision of the cabinet, not least on America's momentous declaration of war on the Central Powers of Europe. His broad network of connections with the richest and most powerful individuals in the Western world also played a vital role. House was regarded by contemporaries as an obscure, even mysterious figure. Despite never holding public office, he managed to become the second most important man in American government, influencing domestic and foreign policy almost until the end of Wilson's second term.

Wilson won the Democrats' presidential nomination on the 46th ballot, thanks to House's backstage agreement with party representatives. In his election campaign program known as "New Freedom," Wilson promised to fight ruthlessly against undue concentrations of power in politics and economics. As president, he did everything possible to achieve the very opposite. When the First World War broke out, Wilson implored his countrymen to remain neutral in word and in thought. However, his disingenuity in this appeal is revealed by the fact that all cabinet members were united in supporting the Allies from the outset. The one exception was William Jennings Bryan, the Secretary of State, who was constantly snubbed and ignored in official acts. The sympathy shown by American politicians and elite citizens toward the English empire appears irrational[100], but it was exploited to the point of exhaustion by British propaganda.

On August 5, 1914, the Royal Navy cut the transatlantic telegraph cable between the United States and Germany. All subsequent messages from Europe to America had to be transmitted via England. In the communications hub in London, numerous censors distorted messages in favor of their own government. In the end, British war propaganda developed into a gigantic machine unlike anything the world had seen before. In the meantime, Colonel House devised a way to take full advantage of America's imminent entry into the war by promoting the cause of democracy and "putting the world on the right track."[101] He showed the president his high calling, saying that "God had chosen Wilson to accomplish great things."[102] The trial would be hard, but

---

[99] Charles Seymour, *The Intimate Papers Of Colonel House*, 4 vols. (Boston, MA: The Houghton Mifflin Company, 1928) vol. 1: 6, 114; https://archive.org/details/in.ernet.dli.2015.173367/page/n31

[100] Charles Callan Tansill, *America Goes to War* (Gloucester, MA: Peter Smith, [1938] 1963) 26-28; s. also: Horace C. Peterson, *Propaganda for War: The Campaign against American Neutrality, 1914-1917* (Norman, OK: University of Oklahoma Press, 1939) 10: "The American aristocracy was distinctly anglophile."

[101] Charles Seymour, *The Intimate Papers Of Colonel House*, 4 vols. (Boston, MA: The Houghton Mifflin Company, 1926) vol. 1: 473; https://archive.org/details/in.ernet.dli.2015.173367/page/n495

[102] McDougall, *Promised Land, Crusader State*, 126; https://archive.org/details/promised-landcrus00mcdo/page/126

"no matter what sacrifices we make the end [would] justify them."[103] After this final battle with reactionary powers, the United States would join forces with other democracies to protect world peace and freedom of movement on land and sea forever.

As British politicians had planned and hoped, Germany was afflicted by a great famine. On January 31, 1917, the emperor's government declared that it would commence unrestrained U-boat warfare the following day. The United States immediately broke off diplomatic relations with Berlin. The president decided that American merchant ships should be armed and defended by the navy, which was therefore given protection of armaments and other war goods that neutral ships were banned from carrying. Public opinion began to change, giving Wilson the opportunity that he so desperately needed. The Zimmerman Telegram was an encrypted dispatch probably sent by Arthur Zimmermann, State Secretary for the Foreign Office in Berlin, to the German ambassador in Mexico via the German Embassy in Washington, D.C., on January 19, 1917.[104] It proposed a military alliance with Mexico in event of war with the United States. Mexico was promised territory in the American Southwest, including Texas. The telegram was passed on to the press. For the first time, Wilson received support and authorization from citizens to arm American merchant ships. In mid-March, a number of freighters were sunk on entering the declared U-boat zone. Without hesitation, the president summoned Congress for a special session on April 2.

T. Woodrow Wilson can be considered the anti-Washington for his declaration of war. In his final speech, George Washington had advised that America's great rule of conduct should be to establish commercial relations with other nations, but to have as little to do with them as possible in terms of political alliances. Wilson was also the anti-Quincy Adams. As author of the Monroe Doctrine, Adams had emphasized in a Congress speech[105] that America "would not cross the seas in search of monsters to destroy."[106] Were

---

[103] Seymour, *The Intimate Papers of Colonel House,* vol. 1: 473; https://archive.org/details/in.ernet.dli.2015.173367/page/n495

[104] Thomas Boghardt, "The Zimmermann Telegram: Diplomacy, Intelligence and the American Entry into World War I"; *Working Paper No. 6-04* (Georgetown University, November 2003).

[105] John Quincy Adams, *An Address Delivered at the request of a Committee of Citizens of Washington: On the Occasion of the Reading of the Declaration of Independence, on the Fourth of July, 1821* (Washington, D.C.: Davis and Force, 1821); https://archive.org/details/addressdelivered1821adam/page/n9

[106] Ibid., 29; https://archive.org/details/addressdelivered1821adam/page/28: "Wherever the standard of freedom and independence, has been or shall be unfurled, there will her heart, her benedictions and her prayers be. But she goes not abroad, in search of monsters to destroy. She is the well-wisher to the freedom and independence of all. She is the champion and vindicator only of her own. She will recommend the general cause by the countenance of her voice, and the benignant sympathy of her example. She well knows that by once enlisting under other banners than her own, were they even the banners of foreign independence, she would involve herself beyond the power of extrication, in all the wars of interest and intrigue, of individual

it to do so, its political principles would be fundamentally changed. The ultimate goal would no longer be the preservation of liberty, but rather the exercise of brute force. Furthermore, politics would lose control of its own destiny: it would no longer be mistress of its own spirit. In rejecting this tradition, Wilson advanced a new foreign policy for America – one that engaged in numerous political alliances with foreign powers in order to realize the war objectives of other nations.[107] Wilson sought to pave the way for an imperialist foreign policy. The Republican Robert M. La Follette Sr. took issue with the president in an impassioned speech delivered in the Senate, and the Democrat Claude Kitchin did similarly in the House of Representatives. However, their joint efforts were in vain.[108] There was almost an atmosphere of hysteria in the House of Representatives when both chambers consented to the declaration of war. The political guild and its allies in the press, universities, and churches eagerly expressed their agreement with the decision, and the general public joined in the same chorus of war hysteria. They had a highly unrealistic vision of the bitter consequences that would befall America were it to take up arms.[109]

The America of the Founding Fathers no longer existed. America's entry into the First World War marked a decisive turning point in U.S. history. Under the leadership of T. Woodrow Wilson, the United States developed into a centrally controlled government machinery. The American president demanded a totalitarian authority beyond the wildest dreams of Alexander Hamilton or Abraham Lincoln. No one in the previous century could have foreseen how comprehensively Wilson's increasingly clear imperial ambitions would be put into practice. The historical significance of his presidency cannot be overestimated.

12.2 Complete rejection of a peace policy

The political magazine *The New Republic* was founded in 1914 by an influential group of Progressives in order to spread their ideas. Analyzing the political

---

avarice, envy, and ambition, which assume the colors and usurp the standard of freedom. The fundamental maxims of her policy would insensibly change from liberty to force." S. also: Fred Kaplan, *John Quincy Adams: American Visionary* (New York City, NY: Harper, 2014) 87.

[107] Arthur S. Link, ed., *The Papers of Woodrow Wilson, January 24-April 6, 1917* (Princeton, NJ: Princeton University Press, 1983) vol. 41: 525-527.

[108] Robert M. La Follette Sr., "Speech on the Declaration of War against Germany," in Arthur A. Ekirch, Jr., ed., *Voices in Dissent: An Anthology of Individualist Thought in the United States* (New York City, NY: Citadel Press, 1964) 211-222; Alex Mathews Arnett, *Claude Kitchin and the Wilson War Policies* (Boston, MA: Little, Brown and Co., 1937; New York City, NY: Russell and Russell, 1971) 227-235; https://archive.org/details/in.ernet.dli.2015.74807/page/n257

[109] Otis L. Graham, Jr., *The Great Campaigns: Reform and War in America, 1900-1928* (Englewood Cliffs, NJ: Prentice-Hall, 1971; Malabar, FL: Robert E. Krieger, 1987) 89; https://archive.org/details/greatcampaignsre00otis/page/88

views of its editorial staff from 1914 to 1920 shows how the fundamental terms of Progressivism changed during those years, and how the editors reacted to new political situations. The chief editor of this influential weekly was the collectivist and New Nationalism theorist Herbert D. Croly[110]. Working alongside him were Walter E. Weyl[111], another theorist of Teddy Roosevelt's politics, and Walter Lippmann[112] (ΦBK)[113], the ambitious former leader of the Intercollegiate Socialist Society. This editorial line-up is a classic example of an alliance between industry, the financial world (epitomized by J. P. Morgan & Co.), and a growing crowd of progressive intellectuals. The primary goal of the editors was to convey their dynamic belief in progress to the new generation. They wanted rational, upstanding individuals to develop a social order among the middle class. However, this dream soon dissolved to nothing. The postwar years destroyed their vision of a better America, for the intellectual and emotional assumptions on which they based their hopes for the beginning of a progressive age proved to be too utopian.

Flashback: In the years around 1900, the rapid, irrepressible growth of industry had left a deep imprint on America's middle class. The main factor behind the emergence of the progressive movement had been the reaction of the middle class to the defiance of traditional American ideals as social classes diverged and power was polarized in the hands of industry and the trade union.[114] While most Americans had wanted to maintain traditional Individualism, Theodore Roosevelt had suggested in his New Nationalism program that the crisis should be surmounted by no longer granting individuals a significant sociopolitical role in society. Roosevelt's policy of New Nationalism[115] derived its motto from a book[116] written by Herbert D. Croly, the first chief editor of *The New Republic*. Croly had advocated a "national Democracy" in which the individual would be subordinated to a

---

[110] David W. Levy, "Herbert D. Croly," John Arthur Garraty, Mark Christopher Carnes, American Council of Learned Societies, *American National Biography* (New York City, NY: Oxford University Press, 1999) vol. 5: 757; https://archive.org/details/americannational05garr/page/756

[111] Charles Forcey, *The Crossroads of Liberalism: Croly, Weyl, Lippmann, and the Progressive Era, 1900-1925* (New York City, NY: Oxford University Press, 1961); David W. Levy. "Weyl, Walter Edward" in "American National Biography Online" (2000); https://doi.org/10.1093/anb/9780198606697.article.1400764

[112] David Weingart, *Walter Lippmann: A Study in personal Journalism* (New Brunswick, NJ: Rutgers University Press, 1949).

[113] Member of the Phi Beta Kappa Society, Hamilton College, 1903

[114] George E. Mowry, "The California Progressive and His Rationale," *Mississippi Valley Historical Review* (Cedar Rapids), XXXVI (September, 1949), 239-250.

[115] Henry Fowles Pringle, *Theodore Roosevelt: A Biography* (New York City, NY: Harcourt Brace, [1931] 1944; New York City, NY: Houghton Mifflin Harcourt, 2003) 380; https://archive.org/details/isbn_0156889439/page/380; *New Republic* (New York City), vol. 63 (July 16, 1930), 251.

[116] Herbert D. Croly, *The Promise of American Life* (New York City, NY: Macmillan, 1909); https://archive.org/details/promiseofamerica00crol/page/n5

national goal, with the state playing the central role in the organization of this process. Industrialization had provoked revolutionary changes that in one way or another affected every established institution.[117]

The nineteenth-century idea of progress – the belief that mankind has been in constant development up to the present day, and that this process will continue for the foreseeable future – took on completely new forms of expression from 1914. Croly and his colleagues' frequent allusions to the theory of evolution and their advocacy of Instrumentalism (the idea that scientific theories are merely tools) show that they saw the world as an ever-changing reality which can be shaped at will, subject to human control. They believed in the continual need for man to observe social change in his actions and conduct. Man had access to tools that could simplify the task of controlling the environment, the most important being science – natural and social, for example. In their idea of a "transcendent humanitarian goal," the editors meant nothing other than a mystically perfected Democracy.[118] At the heart of their philosophy was a religious belief in Democracy: a belief that it was developing through the gradual realization of its ideals of liberty, equality, and fraternity. The promise of a just social policy, as had emerged in American life, was needed to continue improving the social, moral, and economic welfare of all people.

The Progressivism of Herbert D. Croly had a thoroughly religious essence, bringing a kind of message of salvation to a suffering world. Like a prophet, Croly promised that progress would counteract the anarchy of the present. Amid social ruin and a multitude of isolated individuals, progress would create a new society – a society of perfect cooperation and absolute harmony. "Humanity" would therefore be the site for the salvation of lost individuals, and "history" would be the means of imparting it as the self-realization of the emerging absolute. The world would be thrown into a moral conflict requiring man to fight the evil of anarchy as manifested in negative Individualism. Man needed to strive to establish God's kingdom on earth, in which the individual would be united with the social whole. Those following the religion of humanity, the religion of progress, received the glad news that they were free to shape their own futures since social reality was now beyond the control of natural laws and history – beyond the institutions and traditions of the past. This self-determined future was inevitable, and its governing principles were absolute. Industrialization would make the country realize that Democracy could only be effected in America in a socialized form:

---

[117] Ibid., 139, 276; https://archive.org/details/promiseofamerica00crol/page/138

[118] Herbert D. Croly, *The Promise of American Life* (1909) and Herbert D. Croly, *Progressive Democracy* (New York City, NY: MacMillan, 1914); https://archive.org/details/progressivedemoc00crouoft/page/n5; Walter E. Weyl, *The New Democracy* (New York City, NY: Macmillan, 1912); https://archive.org/details/cu31924024912119/page/n7; Walter Lippmann, *A Preface to Politics* (New York City, NY: Mitchell Kennerley, 1913); https://archive.org/details/prefacetopolitic00lipp/page/n13; Walter Lippmann, *Drift and Mastery: An attempt to diagnose the current unrest* (New York City, NY: Mitchell Kennerley, 1914); https://archive.org/details/driftmasteryatte00lipp/page/n5

society needed to be conceptualized as a whole, rather than as a more or less random combination of individuals. The editors of *The New Republic* wanted to awaken America's middle class to a vision of Social Democracy.[119] They saw signs everywhere that this awakening was taking place. More and more people were coming to see the importance of aligning their own desires and ambitions with the needs of society. By advocating a "religion of Democracy," the editors sought to reconcile the continuous development of society with belief in progress that culminated in "spiritual rebirth,"[120] thereby distancing themselves from the fixed utopias of the past.

Of all the Progressives who pushed for America's participation in the First World War, none had greater intellectual influence than Herbert D. Croly. Croly was an enthusiastic supporter of the European idea of State Socialism and did his utmost to introduce it against the backdrop of American Nationalism.[121] This had a particularly strong impact on the democratic system. By following in the footsteps of European history, America inevitably adopted some aspects of European life, such as a certain level of militarization. With regard to the defense readiness now incorporated in the law, Croly openly admitted the likelihood that the army and navy would be used for aggressive rather than defensive purposes.[122]

In the pages of *The New Republic*, Croly constantly weighed up the pros and cons of the debate as to whether America should enter the war, seeking to combine the nation's Romantic Idealism with realistic Progressivism. In doing so, he alluded to foreign policy statements made by Wilson and Roosevelt. The same matter was pursued by the progressive teacher John Dewey (ΦBK)[123] during the war years. The magazine's editorials expressed their writers' joy at the opportunities offered by the war to "extend social control [...], subordinating the individual to the group and the group to society," and argued that "the war should be used as a pretext to transform the country."[124] The global military conflict thus presented a phenomenal opportunity to realize long-held ambitions to reconfigure American politics. In order to counteract what Dewey saw as Pacifists' detestable ideas and to surmount Americans' apathy toward participation in the war, a policy was required which would bring about a liberal world order. The war offered the potential for a progressive social revolution which would include the abolition

---

[119] Weyl, *New Democracy*, 162, 269.

[120] Ibid., 156-168; https://archive.org/details/cu31924024912119/page/n173

[121] Herbert D. Croly, "The Effect on American Institutions of a Powerful Military and Naval Establishment," *Annals of the American Academy of Political and Social Science*, vol. 66 (July, 1916), 157-172.

[122] Ibid.

[123] Member of the Phi Beta Kappa Society, Vermont College, 1879

[124] David M. Kennedy, *Over Here: The First World War and American Society* (New York City, NY: Oxford University Press, 1980) 39-40, 44, 246; https://archive.org/details/overhere-firstwor00kenn/page/38; s. also: Arthur A. Ekirch, *Decline of American Liberalism* (Oakland, CA: Independent Institute, [1972] 2009) 205.

of private ownership and the replacement of the free market economy with State Capitalism.[125] Man was allegedly only truly human if he viewed himself as part of society rather than as an individual. Society was only fully constituted through its existence within the state.

Progressives used the new, supposedly widespread awareness of national destiny to justify America's entry into the war. The war had solved the problem of a lack of ideological orientation. With comprehensive social control and detailed economic planning, America could attain its providence-determined fate of becoming master of its own destiny, thus making the whole world its own. The sense of community boosted by the war could act as a prelude not only to promote progress at home, but also to bring about a new international order. President Wilson shared his vision of a League of Nations in which all nations of the earth would unite in social and political solidarity. Although many Progressives were pacifists, many also began to see the war as the crown and climax of the social justice movement in America, despite all its horrors and hazards. Progressives welcomed the gradual decline of the American free market economy, evidenced as the state took over the most important economic sectors – agriculture and rail transport. They welcomed the introduction of improved working conditions and social housing, women's rights, social insurance schemes, employment for black people, and prohibition of alcohol. However, the Progressives deceived themselves.[126] The benefits gained for the working class and for black people were short-lived, since they largely resulted from an emergency situation rather from genuine desire for reform. By 1920, few of the social reforms introduced during the war were still in effect except for prohibition, restricted immigration, and racial hysteria. Economic regulation, which was particularly effective in setting production quotas and fixing prices, was based on an agreement with American industrialists in line with their economic interests, at the expense of small businesses. Manufacturers appealed to the patriotic spirit among their workers to subdue any discontentment in the production halls. Impeding the production of armaments in protest against poor working conditions would be unjustifiable in time of war. Workers were paid higher wages in return for their willingness to accept the restriction of their right to take industrial action.

---

[125] John Dewey, "On Understanding the Mind of Germany," *Atlantic Monthly*, vol. 117 (February, 1916), 251-262; "Force and Coercion," *International Journal of Ethics*, Vol 26 (April, 1916), 364; "Force. Violence and Law," *The New Republic* (New York City), vol. 5 (January 22, 1916), 296; "The Future of Pacifism," vol. 11 (July 28, 1917), 359; "What America Will Fight For," vol. 12 (August 18, 1917), 69; "Conscription of Thought," vol. 12 (September 1, 1917), 128-130; "What Are We Fighting For?," *Independent*, vol. 94 (June 22, 1918), 474ff. s. also: Joseph Ratner, ed., *Character and Events: Popular essays in social and political philosophy* (New York City, NY: Holt, 1929) vol. 2, book 4: 550; https://archive.org/details/charactersande-ve017917mbp/page/n125

[126] Allen F. Davis, "Welfare, Reform and World War I," *American Quarterly*, vol. 19 (Fall, 1967), 516-533.

Progressives strongly supported the effects of the war which were contrary to the liberal spirit.[127] At the end of the war, Croly expressed dissatisfaction with the severity of the Treaty of Versailles and consequently lost his influence on the Wilson administration. As a result, *The New Republic* lost its role as the voice of a "great political leader." During the late 1920s, Croly discovered what he believed to be another great national leader: the fascist Benito Mussolini. Croly's admiration for Mussolini in the last years of his life is unsurprising given his early education in the authoritarian ideas of Auguste Comte. Herbert Croly's father, David[128], had introduced Positivism to the United States. His ultimate goal had been to ensure that the government gained complete control over the lives of every citizen.

12.3 The great Crusade for Justice

Progressive Protestants welcomed the outbreak of the war as a chance to achieve their ambitious plans for the Social Gospel. Ever since the Puritan colonies were founded in New England, spiritual leaders had used a symbolic language derived from biblical prophecy. They explained the current political conflict through foretold events, thereby justifying their government's war aims. After the successful end of the late eighteenth-century American Revolution, Christian leaders who sympathized with the objectives of the Declaration of Independence conveyed the idea of an emerging thousand-year reign to the United States. The new nation would be the first to discard the burden of the past and establish a new order of the ages. As God's chosen people, Americans were destined to lead the world into an era of reason and virtue. The progressive "gospel" spread like wildfire once it began to be proclaimed by America's influential urban churches. Protestants viewed the First World War as a continuation of Abraham Lincoln's great Crusade for Justice against the southern states. The fight for freedom needed to be reinitiated, this time extending to every corner of the earth. Protestants gladly agreed with President T. Woodrow Wilson's declaration of America's duty to act sacrificially as the suffering servant of the world.

Wilson was a staunch Progressive. As one of the first political scientists, he welcomed America's ascent to world power since it enabled an aggressive foreign policy, thus giving greater authority to the presidency. At the same time, he was a liberal Presbyterian who saw Jesus Christ primarily as a social reformer who had commissioned His first disciples to establish heaven on earth. Wilson pleaded for war, stating that neutrality was now neither possible nor desirable when it came to world peace and freedom of the people.

---

[127] William E. Dodd, *Woodrow Wilson and His Work* (Garden City, NY: Doubleday Page, 1920) 177-178; https://archive.org/details/cu31924030937134/page/n191

[128] Muriel Shaver, "David Goodman Croly," in Allen Johnson, Dumas Malone & Harris E. Starr, ed., *Dictionary of American Biography*, 21 vols. (New York City: NY, Charles Scribner's Sons, 1943) vol. 4: 560; https://archive.org/details/dictionaryofamer04ilamer/page/560

Congress capitulated to the wishes of the White House in the war debate. The Senate declared itself in favor of the war on April 4 by a margin of 82 to 6, and the House of Representatives approved the declaration of war two days later with 373 representatives voting in favor, 50 against, and 9 abstaining. This result did not reflect the will of the people, who were highly reluctant to enter the war.

Once the war had begun, the rhetoric of progressive Protestants began to bear the marks of a heightened Idealism. America's participation in the war was said to be an act of service toward God which would help the world come closer to His will. The war had developed into a conflict between two camps: on the one hand were those seeking to enable the coming of God's kingdom, and on the other were those who opposed it.[129] A key term used by the ministry of propaganda to stress the religious character of the war was the idea of a crusade.[130] Progressive Christian leaders had been referring to their reform movement as a new crusade for years, and front-line soldiers were ready to confront the armies of the Antichrist[131] in order to save civilization, mankind, and Christianity. Nothing was seen to be more important than emerging victorious from the war, since it was believed that the idealistic crusade would lead to everlasting peace. Progressive Protestants not only referred to the United States as a just nation participating in a modern crusade to free the global "Holy Land," but also portrayed the war as a collective reenactment of the crucifixion of Jesus Christ at Golgotha.[132] Making the same analogy used by members of Congress when they approved America's entry into the war on Good Friday 1917, they presented the European conflict as a new atonement for the ultimate, collective salvation of mankind.[133] Progressive Protestants openly presented the United States as the modern Messiah, unafraid of making such a blasphemous identification.[134]

Herbert G. Wells, freethinker and prophet of evolution, gained great respect among progressive Protestants. Wells coined the phrase "the war to end war." He said that "the kingdom of God on earth is not a metaphor, not a mere spiritual state, not a dream, not an uncertain project; it is the thing

---

[129] Samuel McCrea Cavert. "The Missionary Enterprise as the moral equivalent to War," *Biblical World* 50 (December, 1917), 351-352.

[130] Randolph McKim, "God's Call to America," *For God and Country: or, the Christian pulpit in wartime addresses* (New York City, NY: E.P. Dutton, 1918) 116; https://archive.org/details/forgodcountry00mcki/page/116

[131] Ibid., 118; https://archive.org/details/forgodcountry00mcki/page/118

[132] Frank W. Gunsaulus, "The War and the America of Tomorrow," *Christian Century* 34, No. 43 (25 October 1917), 10-11.

[133] McKim, "God's Call to America," 121, 129; https://archive.org/details/forgodcountry00mcki/page/120

[134] Frederick Henry Lynch, *The Challenge: The Church and the New World Order* (New York City, NY: Fleming H. Revell company, 1916) 20; https://archive.org/details/challengechurch00lyncgoog/page/n25

before us, it is the close and inevitable destiny of mankind."[135] He understood "God's kingdom" to mean the socialist utopia of the Fabians which would be achieved through total war against evil throughout the earth. Progressive Protestants combined warmongering with the Social Gospel. One group paradoxically called themselves "militaristic pacifists," claiming that their ultimate goal was world peace. As massacre increased on the European battlefields, they opposed public proposals on how to bring the enmity to a reasonable end as quickly as possible. They said that the greatest need of the hour was not the restoration of peace, but the application of the Social Gospel throughout the world in its most radical form. A curtailed war would allow "unjust regimes" to persist and carry out their reactionary social policies. The diplomatic consequences of the progressive Social Gospel could not have been greater: they brought the heresy of a widespread American civil religion into full bloom. In its new form, American civil religion promoted the opposites of its original values. Instead of neutrality, reciprocity, peace, and trade with all nations, it encouraged a protracted war and as much bloodshed as possible. The Progressive Era turned all honorable moral principles of the past age on their head. The secular and religious elite believed that the government could be led by certified experts with centralized power who could create a perfect society both at home and abroad. Virtue, humility, and wisdom in relations with other powers would now be replaced by domination, fame, and pride.

The point at which one form of conduct was replaced by its antithesis can be precisely determined. In President William McKinley's second inaugural speech on March 4, 1901, he stated that the success of the United States in the Spanish-American War was the will of God. He went on to praise the annexation of colonies and the brutal suppression of the Philippine independence movement. The idea of America's unique role was rooted in conviction that God had created a truly free and democratic nation on earth. This led to a belief that it was in the best interests of all nations to imitate the U.S. political system as closely as possible. Although Wilson did not initiate America's belligerent policy, he did have sole responsibility for its consistent implementation on such a large scale. For the majority of politicians in England and on the continent, the purpose of war was to protect the political and economic interests of their respective countries and to eliminate competition with other great powers. T. Woodrow Wilson and Franklin D. Roosevelt felt that it was their duty to prove them wrong. Wilson outlined the Allies' war aims in his Fourteen Points on January 8, 1918, in a speech given to both houses of Congress, and Roosevelt named the "Four Freedoms" on January 6, 1941, in his State of the Union Address to Congress, which he then extended in the Atlantic Charter[136] of August 14, 1941.

---

[135] Herbert G. Wells, *God The Invisible King* (London: Cassell & Co., Ltd., 1917) 170; https://archive.org/details/in.ernet.dli.2015.218241/page/n171

[136] The Atlantic Charter: https://avalon.law.yale.edu/wwii/atlantic.asp

T. Woodrow Wilson was without doubt the trailblazing pioneer; Roosevelt merely followed in his predecessor's footsteps, lacking the versatile talents and rock-hard determination of the 28th president. If Wilson's leadership can be described as a pure tragedy, Roosevelt's policy can be characterized as a grotesque travesty. Wilson strove for the establishment of a League of Nations and stated that the entry of all nations into this embryonic "world government" would be the only way for all inhabitants of the earth to receive the almost divine blessings that America had in store for member states. Wilson could not conceive of a higher ideal for humanity. However, he died on February 3, 1924, in full knowledge that he had failed to bring America into the League of Nations. His life could not have come to a more tragic end. Roosevelt, who shared the same dream, largely fulfilled Josef Stalin's plans for gaining territory during the Second World War, believing mistakenly that this would convert the Russian dictator into an assured democrat. This was the travesty. The terrible consequences remain an indisputable reality in the Western world down to the present day.

12.4 Violation of American civil rights

The ratification of income tax collection in 1913 paved the way for a huge increase in taxation once America entered the war.[137] The lowest rate of taxes tripled from 2 to 6 percent, while the highest was raised from 13 to 77 percent. However, even this large tax revenue was insufficient to meet the costs of the war. With the help of the Federal Reserve System, America's central bank, the government conjured up banknotes and loans "out of thin air" in order to finance its staggering deficit which reached one billion U.S. dollars per month in 1918 – more than the government's entire annual budget before the war. Industry welcomed the government's many interventions in business procedures, since War Socialism afforded them exorbitant profits guaranteed by the state. The government placated workers by allowing them to form unions and negotiate wages. This strengthening of large unions' political power ultimately resulted from the suppression of the American branch of Industrial Workers of the World (IWW), which had dared to criticize America's entry into the war. Samuel Gompers, founder and for some time president of the American Federation of Labor (AFL), used questionable means to gain success in a relentless power struggle against the IWW, earning the praise and political support of President Woodrow Wilson as a result.[138]

---

[137] David M. Kennedy, *Over Here: The First World War and American Society* (New York City, NY: Oxford University Press, 1980) 112; https://archive.org/details/overherefirstwor-00kenn/page/112; s. also: Bruce D. Porter, *War and the Rise of the State: The Military Foundations of Modern Politics* (New York City, NY: Free Press, 1993) 270.

[138] Kennedy, *Over Here*, 253-258; https://archive.org/details/overherefirstwor00kenn/page/252

Civil liberties were severely curtailed during the war. The irony is that Wilson purported to have joined the European conflict in order to create conditions that would favor the introduction of worldwide Democracy. The term "Democracy" began to take on the exact meaning that it is given today: the right of a majority-elected government to deal with the life, liberty, and property of its citizens as it wishes. The Espionage Act of 1917 and the Sedition Act of the following year covered a far wider area of jurisdiction than was necessary for the punishment of spies. Their real objective was to influence and censor public opinion. The threatened penalties included an exorbitant fine and a prison sentence of up to twenty years. The nationwide campaign to suppress every dissenting movement among the people was boosted when George Creel became leader of the Committee on Public Information. This was the first government agency to deal exclusively with war propaganda. Every charge of high treason brought before the High Court Judges was given instant confirmation by the judges.

Public officials used numerous precedents which had arisen during the crisis of 1917 to 1918 in order to continue restricting civil rights long after the official cease-fire. The greatest violation of American civil rights was the introduction of universal military service.[139] Only a few people had signed up voluntarily, and Wilson wanted to ship a large army to France – otherwise he would lack justification for his supposedly Providence-determined place in the ranks of successful statesmen.[140] This could only take place if a large enough number of American soldiers died on the battlefields.

Wilson was unwilling to give up the increased state power once the war was over. He proposed the founding of a recruit school for all eighteen- and nineteen-year-old men. His goal was to equal the size of Great Britain's army and navy. In 1920, the United States was the only nation involved in the war that refused to grant a general amnesty to political prisoners. The country's most widely known political prisoner was the socialist leader Eugene V. Debs. In June 1918, Debs had criticized the American government for its questionable war policy at a meeting with his supporters in Canton, Ohio. There was neither call for violence nor outbreak of it. An official stenographer recorded the speech and sent it to the federal agency in Cleveland. Debs was

---

[139] H. L. Mencken, "Mr. Justice Holmes," in *A Mencken Chrestomathy* (New York City, NY: Vintage, [1949] 1982) 258-265.

[140] Horace Cornelius Peterson & Gilbert C. Fite, *Opponents of War, 1917-1918* (Seattle, WA: University of Washington Press, [1957] 1968) 22; s. also: *Kennedy, Over There, 94;* Robert Higgs, *Crisis and Leviathan: Critical Episodes in the Growth of American Government* (New York City, NY: Oxford University Press, 1987) 131-132; Robert Higgs, "War and Leviathan in Twentieth Century America: Conscription as the Keystone," in John V. Denson, ed., *The Costs of War: America's Pyrrhic Victories* (Piscataway Township, NJ: Transaction Publishers, 1997) 375-388; https://archive.org/details/CostsOfWarAmericasPyrrhicVictoriesJohnDenson/page/n393

charged with high treason and sentenced to ten years in a federal prison.[141] He was released in 1921 by President Warren Harding.[142]

12.5 Enforcing an interventionist foreign policy

Over the past two centuries, changes to America's political system have resulted largely from the challenges of preparing for and participating in war. One political system was replaced entirely by another without a conscious decision ever being made. No essential aspect of society still resembles the original conception of a decentralized republic. Accepting the harsh reality is too disturbing and upsetting for many people to admit to the Totalitarianism of the present. Glimpses into a dictatorial regime which has been in place for some time, but which pretends to be a constitutional Republican government and holds regular elections as a matter of form, are consciously suppressed in order to evade the unwelcome truth that personal sacrifice is needed to avert the worst case scenario. The turning point was heralded by three aggressive military expeditions in the late nineteenth century: the war against the once proud Spanish Empire, the campaign of conquest in the Philippines, and finally America's participation in the First World War. Taken together, these wars represent a profound break in American foreign policy.

The United States' decentralized government system, inherited from the Founding Fathers, relied on peace as a normative condition. This was the only way for division and concentration of power to be maintained in the individual states. Following the principle of separation of powers, the division of government bodies into judiciary, legislative, and executive served the purpose of mutual control. Until the end of the nineteenth century, America's leading politicians tried more or less consistently to shape their foreign policy in accordance with George Washington's farewell address. Progressives referred disparagingly to the neutral "America First" policy as "Isolationism." However, the modern American empire is no more than an egotistic, ostentatious state that continually seeks to expand its sphere of influence through armed force. As a result of the relationship between state apparatus and interest groups intent on exploiting productive societies for their economic interests, Imperialism appears in the unique posture of an epic resort to violence. The unrestrained exertion of state power in implementing a war policy concerned solely with its own territorial and commercial advantage remains completely undisguised.

Congress passed the National Defense Act before America's entry into the war. This gave President T. Woodrow Wilson the authority, either just before the declaration of war or immediately after, to place orders with private

---

[141] Ray Ginger & Mike Davis, *The Bending Cross: A Biography of Eugene Victor Debs* (New Brunswick, NJ: Rutgers University Press, 1949) 356-359, 362-376, 405-406; https://archive.org/details/bendingcrossbiog00gingrich/page/356

[142] Peterson & Fite, *Opponents of War*, 279.

companies which were given precedence over all other business contracts. If a producer refused to carry out the order and to accept the "reasonable price" set by the Minister of War, the government had the power to take immediate possession of the factory with no appropriate compensation. If the owner refused to comply with state orders, he would be declared guilty of crime. The principle of a constitutional society that ultimately derived all civil rights from the right to private ownership, this being its only way of maintaining freedom within a legal framework, was pushed aside and lost all meaning. After Wilson's declaration of war was ratified by Congress, the power of the state rose to dizzying heights. The president's willingness to throw traditional restrictions on government power nonchalantly overboard encouraged the enforcement of a socialist planned economy. The Lever Act alone gave the government in Washington, D.C., dictatorial power over the production and sale of all food and fuel in the United States.

The U.S.A. followed the example of the European nations that had introduced Collectivism, leading to an unprecedented transformation of America's economic system. The World War gave the country a great push in the direction of state-regulated Socialism. It was the first war in which the government called the expanding body of leftwing ideologues and experts into the civil service to retool the economy through a large-scale, coordinated plan to produce sufficient war material. Many of them belonged to the progressive elite. Nothing came close to the war in potential for enabling the state to make its mark and to limit the individual freedom of its citizens. This did not only occur during the military conflict itself, but endured as a permanent legacy. Wilson thereby created a precedent that served to inspire and guide the introduction of State Monopoly Capitalism (Corporatism) in the United States during the twentieth century. Closely following industrial requirements, the U.S. government had a unique opportunity to eliminate competition from efficient companies and to transform the free market system – which had proved extremely advantageous at the end of the nineteenth century – into its complete opposite. State regulations meant that individual companies in all sectors of industry could unite in cartels, thus reducing the rate of production and limiting the variety of products for the sake of higher prices. Industries producing war material profited most from the deluge of government orders, but other producers also benefited immensely from government spending. It seemed easier to secure the favor of the government than that of consumers.

Wartime Socialism brought the nascent corporate state to cast its shadow over the economy, eventually covering the whole of the twentieth century. After the First World War, Herbert C. Hoover, Gerard Swope, Henry I. Harriman, and other technocrats sought to realize the totalitarian and imperialist objectives of State Monopoly Capitalism (Corporatism) which later emerged in the New Deal. During the Second World War and the Cold War, the oligarchic power of the developing, closely cooperating union of state power and industry expanded enormously and was consolidated across many areas of the economy and people's lives. The reason given was the protection of essential national security interests. In addition to the term "Liberal Corporatism," the resulting economic and government system has also been referred to as Neo-Mercantilism, Interest Group Liberalism, Neo-Fascism, Cooperative Liberalism, Political Capitalism, Military State Capitalism, State Monopoly Capitalism, Technocracy, and Corporate Syndicate. Each of these terms expresses the formation of a conglomerate of large economic blocs that are integrated and coordinated by the state. War Socialism also counteracted discontentment among the working class, which was permanently smoldering underground and occasionally rose to the surface. The rebellious spirit among many laborers was appeased by the promise of better working conditions and higher wages under a state monopoly system. Under these circumstances, there was nothing to impede unreserved promotion of trade unionism. Even able trade union leaders were offered a minor role in designing the planned economy system.

In America, nationalists within the progressive movement gradually took the lead and successfully suppressed Pacifism among classical liberals. When conflict erupted in Europe, President Wilson immediately began to address social problems arising from the war. Progressives gradually began to identify with the ideals of Militarism and Nationalism, which were supported by former President Theodore Roosevelt more than by any other contemporary politician. Some National Socialists applauded the success of War Socialism in England and Germany, and Roosevelt and his progressive followers admired German military power. Wanting to mimic the achievements of English and German socialization in America, Roosevelt pointed out the necessity of combining social and industrial justice with preparation for military defense. He secretly hoped that the government in Washington would still side with the Allies in the War. Roosevelt pleaded for compulsory military service to be introduced as a "true democratic ideal," seeing the formation of an absolutist government in wartime as a sign of progress. Before the Progressive Party merged with the Republican Party in 1916, it adopted an agenda that advocated general conscription. The First World War represented a turning point in the development of American Social Democracy. Before the war broke out in Europe, progressives in the United States were full of optimism and self-confidence. One generation later, however, they were forced to respond to the atmosphere of disillusionment, uncertainty, and pessimism that pervaded the public. Rival socio-political systems advocating the introduction of Totalitarianism in the forms of Fascism, National Socialism, or Communism proved attractive to voters, finding great popularity among the economically exploited and socially oppressed population.

The First World War allowed the government to intensify its control over the general public, and this continued during the era of the New Deal and the Second World War. The economic regulation demanded by progressives at the turn of the century became a reality in 1917, following the introduction of the War Socialism in the economy. Reformers worked hard for a successful campaign in order to secure important government positions.

However, the negative consequences of a bureaucratic state apparatus became increasingly apparent. By promoting sacrificial duty and social justice, Progressives ultimately encouraged a world war as a means of disseminating the purported advantages of Social Democracy.

American progressives debated the advantages of a nation state in which the government was based on totalitarian principles. They turned a blind eye to the fact that their desired goals of social control and planned economy would be achieved through mass destruction of life and substance. The fact that this connection went largely undiscerned owed to the extremely positive light in which social reform was viewed. Although socialists often spoke out loudly in favor of Pacifism, they nevertheless looked back at wartime social experiments with admiration. The dark clouds of war gathered so menacingly over Europe and Asia in the late 1930s that President Franklin D. Roosevelt expected strong support from the progressives among his own party. The president wanted to prepare the country for military conflict – although he often stated the opposite in political speeches, purely out of political calculation. At his insistence, the purported merits of the New Deal were touted to the whole world. In his State of the Union Address to Congress in January 1944, the president outlined the details of a new civil rights deed (the Second Bill of Rights), under which the "basis of security and prosperity" could be established for all.

12.6 Variable success of a global revolution

T. Woodrow Wilson had vowed to rid the world of tyranny and Militarism once and for all, and believed that he had fought the last of all wars for human freedom.[143] At the 1918 Paris Peace Conference, he declared his monumental idea for a complete reimagination of the map of Europe. His political lodestar was the vision of a democratic social order which would be introduced by the future League of Nations in countries where it was not yet established. Wilson caused great excitement when he set foot on European soil. He was welcomed in Rome, for example, as the "God of peace," and in Milan as the "Savior of mankind."[144] As prophet of the religion of Progressivism, he believed that he would succeed in harmoniously integrating its multifaceted components, especially those which were incompatible, such as Puritan Postmillennialism, the rational Enlightenment, Hegelian dialectics, and Darwinian racism. However, when months of tough negotiations failed to produce a universally accepted peace treaty, even Wilson had to admit that his reputed diplomatic

---

[143] T. Woodrow Wilson, "Address to a Joint Session of Congress," 2 April 1917, in Arthur S. Link, et al., ed., *The Papers of Woodrow Wilson* (Princeton, NJ: Princeton University Press, 1966-1993) vol. 41: 527; subsequently abbreviated as *PWW*. Wilson, "Address to a Joint Session of Congress," 8 January 1918, *PWW*, vol. 45: 539.

[144] Thomas J. Knock, *To End All Wars: Woodrow Wilson and the Quest for a New World Order* (New York City, NY: Oxford University Press, 1992) 194-195.

skills had reached their limit. Very few people present at the Paris Peace Conference noticed how hard he was trying to promote a global revolution based on the myth of the United States as a "redeemer nation."[145] There was enormous discontinuity between Wilson's proposals for a new world order and the Founding Fathers' warnings against forming alliances with other countries.

The signing of the Treaty of Versailles on June 28, 1919, marked the end of the First World War in international law. At the same time, it represented the founding of the League of Nations. The German delegation was excluded from the peace talks; only at the very end could they send a written request for amendments to the terms. The treaty assigned all blame for the outbreak of the war to Germany and its allies, forcing them into cession of territory, disarmament, and payment of reparations to the victors. The German delegation reluctantly signed the treaty in the Hall of Mirrors in Versailles. It came into effect on January 10, 1920, after its ratification and the exchange of documents. However, Congress refused to ratify the Treaty of Versailles: two factions within the U.S. Senate led by Henry Cabot Lodge and William Borah prevented it from being signed by the required two-thirds majority on November 19, 1919, and March 19, 1920, respectively. The reason given was fear of losing national sovereignty by entering the League of Nations, which was linked to signing the peace treaty. The U.S.A. therefore did not become a member of the League, but settled a separate peace with Germany in 1921 through the Treaty of Berlin.

The end of the First World War marked the conclusion of the most important phase in the formation and dissemination of American Progressivism.[146] Knowledge of the negative repercussions of Progressivism, gathered by historians over many decades, remained completely closed to the majority of Americans during the 1920s. The world would later be taken over by a new variety of Progressivism. T. Woodrow Wilson determined the trajectory of American foreign policy development from the beginning of the twentieth century to the present day. Every subsequent president that has seen himself as promoting the ideal of an expansionary policy, proving this by following Wilson's directives. The American government has consistently pursued a policy of world domination in the name of national self-determination and collective security against aggression, manifested in its violent suppression of any rebellion against the status quo in any corner of the earth. The United States first tried to destroy the power of traditional

---

[145] Ernest Lee Tuveson, *Redeemer Nation: The Idea of America's Millennial Role* (Chicago, IL: University of Chicago Press, 1968); https://archive.org/details/redeemernation00erne; James H. Moorhead, *American Apocalypse: Yankee Protestants and the Civil War, 1860-1869* (New Haven, CT: Yale University Press, 1978); https://archive.org/details/americanapocalyp-0000moor; s. also: Charles Royster, *The Destructive War: William Tecumseh Sherman, Stonewall Jackson, and the Americans* (New York City, NY: Alfred A. Knopf, 1991) chap. 6, "The Vicarious War".

[146] Richard Hofstadter, *The Age of Reform: From Bryan to F. D. R.* (New York City, NY: Alfred A. Knopf, 1955) 273; https://archive.org/details/ageofreformfrom000hofs/page/272

monarchies and then to prevent the spread of Marxist regimes. In order to hinder other nations' drive for Imperialism, the United States portrayed itself as a law enforcement agency for the world. It ironically took on the very same role of aggressor that it condemned in others – one more cruel and greedy than any previous imperial power.[147] Maintaining military superiority over large parts of the world became a vital part of U.S. international politics; furthermore, the coercive use of America's currency to control the entire world economy proved to be an even more effective means of achieving the same goal. Over the course of time, a growing number of statesmen and businessmen realized that securing foreign markets was the best way to solve the country's outstanding economic problems.[148] Individuals with great political and economic influence who wanted to establish an American empire portrayed the program as a charitable project that would solve the supposedly typical problems of a market economy. Their program of domestic Corporatism (State Monopoly Capitalism) and overseas "Open Door Imperialism" took on the features of an ideology, suddenly appearing in every nook and cranny. It soon conformed so well to the country's general state of affairs that most commentators failed to see how greatly it was changing the country.

America's entry into the Second World War was the decisive step in the permanent militarization of the economy and society. The conversion of the economy to prioritize production of armaments during the war contributed significantly to the emergence of a military-industrial complex, which in turn created the conditions for the introduction of a mixed economy after the armistice. The monopolistic character of the emerging State Capitalism became increasingly clear, greatly increasing the power of the federal government and encouraging state authorities to cooperate with industry and trade unions. As a result, the president's almost arbitrary freedom of action expanded so greatly that it can only be compared to that of a tyrannical Far Eastern caliphate.

The Second World War turned out to be a veritable cornucopia for many Americans. The number of American soldiers killed in action was lower than the numbers of the other warring nations. Domestic industry produced enormous quantities of goods, guaranteeing high profits and numerous jobs. Standards of living improved among all social groups (with the exception of Americans with Japanese origins, who were detained in concentration camps). The Cornell historian Carl L. Becker nonetheless stated pessimistically: "We seem to live in a world in which the easiest and quickest

---

[147] Leonard P. Liggio, *Why the Futile Crusade?* (New York City, NY: Center for Libertarian Studies, 1978) 3.

[148] Henry A. Wallace, *New Frontiers* (New York City, NY: Reynal and Hitchcock, 1934); https://archive.org/details/newfrontiers0000wall/page/n5; s. dazu Charles A. Beard & George H. E. Smith, *The Open Door at Home: A Trial Philosophy of National Interest* (New York City, NY: Macmillan, 1934); Lawrence Dennis, *Is Capitalism Doomed?* (New York City, NY: Harper & Brothers, 1932); Lawrence Dennis, *The Coming American Fascism* (New York City, NY: Harper & Brothers, 1936); https://archive.org/details/TheComingAmericanFascism/page/n1

way to abolish [...] unemployment and want is to practice on a grand scale [...] war."[149] Becker's fears were realized in the outbreak of the Cold War, which followed hot on the heels of the Second World War. The United States resigned itself to maintaining a permanent war economy. The fact that this war economy was accompanied by the non-liberal and undemocratic aspects of a garrison state were glossed over by the reform rhetoric of the Fair Deal (Harry S. Truman), the New Frontier (John F. Kennedy), and the Great Society (Lyndon B. Johnson).[150]

Americans still prefer the political class to explain their wars as though they were a type of social reform. Staunch militarists such as Douglas MacArthur, John Foster Dulles (ΦBK)[151], and Barry Goldwater never really gained favor with the electorate. In the presidential election of 1964, Goldwater's advocacy of aggressive Militarism lost out to Johnson's promise of a welfare state. During his years in office, however, Johnson used the steadily increasing military budget as an effective means of strengthening the pillars of the planned economy that was developing in America. Industrial magnates and bankers in the Northeast did not panic at the radical rhetoric of the Great Society. Despite their traditional sympathy toward the Republicans, they helped the Democrats win an overwhelming victory in the 1964 elections. Wealthy citizens in America's metropolises knew that the war and welfare state would be of greater benefit to them than to members of the weaker social classes, most of which had to send soldiers to the front line. The voters who were especially deceived by Johnson's questionable campaign promises were the neoliberal academics, who realized too late that Johnson's admiration for Franklin D. Roosevelt's political methods involved unbridled lying. Roosevelt had promised strict neutrality toward the warring nations while secretly plotting to achieve the very opposite.[152] Americans see Jefferson's classical-liberal philosophy as something exotic which can no longer provide a sufficient answer to the problems of a complicated contemporary world.[153] Scores of progressives are thus turning to the militaristic welfare state which is assuming ever greater dimensions. It has been proven, however, that modern warfare only intensifies Nationalism and Statism. It therefore seems highly ironic that much-lauded social reforms end in the brutal reality of war and subsequent Totalitarianism.

---

[149] Carl L. Becker, *How New Will the Better World Be?* (New York City, NY: Alfred A. Knopf, 1944) 8.

[150] C. Wright Mills, *The New Men of Power* (New York City, NY: Harcourt, Brace, 1948) 248-249; https://archive.org/details/in.ernet.dli.2015.84792/page/n261; s. also: Walter J. Oakes, "Toward a Permanent War Economy?," *Politics*, vol. 1 (February, 1944), 11-17.

[151] Member of the Phi Beta Kappa Society, Princeton University, 1908

[152] Charles A. Beard, *President Roosevelt and the Coming of the War, 1941* (New Haven, CT: Yale University Press, 1948).

[153] William V. Shannon, "Mr. Jefferson's Return," *New York Times* (Sunday, 17 October 1971), Section 4, 3.

The almost unrestrained domination of the international scene not only by the U.S. government and military, but also by American banks and international corporations, became a reality on March 12, 1947. On that historic day, the American President Harry S. Truman[154] (ΦBK)[155] delivered a speech to Congress on the recently commenced Cold War between capitalist and communist power blocs.[156] America's military defeat in the Vietnam War, determined years before by the unfavorable course and outcome of the Korean War, made it clear that America's power over vast areas of the earth had passed its zenith and was approaching an inevitably bitter end. Every country that had yielded to the allure of Imperialism was eventually brought to the painful realization that it had taken a course which would ultimately lead to financial and political ruin. The United States has experienced this since the final decade of the twentieth century. Only when the elite group of financiers and investors loses its manipulation-based power will a degree of peace be restored between individual nations.

13 The ideological battle against Militarism

America's imperialist policy during the Progressive Era (1896-1921) can only be rightly judged in the mirror of time when the cause, course, and consequences of the First World War are given adequate consideration. T. Woodrow Wilson believed that the true reason for the awful bloodshed on the battlefields was the greed of one nation state trying to appropriate the wealth of another by force. As compelling as this argument may have seemed to him, it was nonetheless insufficient to explain the terrible events of another war among European states. His blanket statement was too far removed from the reality of a war fully determined by the latest technology to provide sufficient information about what really took place in and outside of the trenches. Unpleasant and troubling thoughts were simply blocked out. The U.S.A. and the victorious powers presented the matter unambiguously, clearly specifying the guilty parties.[157] When the United States entered the First World War, American and British historians were the main figures to put the

---

[154] Grand Master of the Grand Loge of Missouri, 33rd Degree Mason, Ancient and Accepted Scottish Rite of Freemasonry, S.J.; https://nmasonic.com/wiki/freemasonry/famous-free-masons/freemason-presidents/harry-s-truman/

[155] Honorary member of the Phi Beta Kappa Society

[156] Frank Denna Fleming, *The Cold War and Its Origins, 1917-1960* (Garden City, NY: Doubleday, 1961).

[157] Karl Dietrich Erdmann, "War Guilt 1914 Reconsidered: A Balance of New Research," in H. W. Koch, ed., *The Origins of the First World War: Great Power Rivalries and German War Aims*, 2nd ed. (London: Macmillan, 1984) 342; s. also: Alan Sharp, *The Versailles Settlement: Peacemaking in Paris, 1919* (New York City, NY: St. Martin's Press, 1991) 87.

exclusive blame for its outbreak on the German emperor. They placed themselves in the service of their governments and offered a one-sided interpretation of history. America's behavior was inconsistent. Its true motives for entering the war were covered up, and it was celebrated as assistant to the Allies and as victor.

13.1 Grave shortcomings of modern Democracy

The sociologist William Graham Sumner[158] (1840-1910) was an astute scholar who studied the history of the American republic in great depth and analyzed the shortcomings of modern Democracy.[159] He made precise predictions about the historical development of the twentieth and twenty-first centuries with astonishing foresight.[160] William Graham Sumner (Skull & Bones, 1863) praised modern Capitalism as an integrated system in which all economic actors work together to achieve things far greater than anything they could achieve alone. According to Sumner, its characteristic feature is the division of labor, which is improved through a constant process of classification and specialization of trades and professions, as well as through the emergence of new businesses and services. The system governs itself by aligning all economic processes to a self-generated protocol developed over hundreds of years. Sumner saw Capitalism as one of the greatest achievements of Western

---

[158] H. A. Scott Trask, "William Graham Sumner: Against Democracy, Plutocracy, and Imperialism," vol. 18, no. 4, *Journal of Libertarian Studies* (Fall, 2004), 1-27. Some of the following passages are based on information contained in this article.

[159] William Graham Sumner, *History of American Currency, with Chapters on the English Bank Restriction and Austrian Paper Money, to which is appended "The Bullion Report"* (New York City, NY: H. Holt, 1874); https://oll.libertyfund.org/titles/sumner-a-history-of-american-currency; *Lectures on the History of Protection in the United States: delivered before the International Free-Trade Alliance* (New York City, NY: Putnam's for the International Free Trade Alliance, 1877); *Andrew Jackson as a public man: What he was, what chances he had, and what he did with them* (Boston, MA: Houghton, Mifflin, 1882); https://archive.org/details/andrewjacksonas01sumngoog/page/n9; *Alexander Hamilton* (New York City, NY: Dodd, Mead, and Company, 1890); https://archive.org/details/alexanderhamilt01sumngoog/page/n9; *The Financier and Finances of the American Revolution*, 2 vols. (New York City, NY: Dodd, Mead, and Company, 1891) vol. 1: https://archive.org/details/financierfinance01sumnuoft/page/n6; vol. 2: https://archive.org/details/financierfinance01sumnuoft/page/n6; *Robert Morris* (New York City, NY: Dodd, Mead, and Company, 1892); https://archive.org/details/robertmorris00sumngoog/page/n9; *A history of banking in all the leading nations; comprising the United States; Great Britain; Germany; Austro-Hungary; France; Italy; Belgium; Spain; Switzerland; Portugal; Roumania; Russia; Holland; the Scandinavian nations; Canada; China; Japan* (New York City, NY: The Journal of Commerce and Commercial Bulletin, 1896) vol. 1: https://archive.org/details/cu31924092584196/page/n6; vol. 2: https://archive.org/details/cu31924092584204/page/n8; vol. 3: https://archive.org/details/cu31924092584212/page/n10; vol. 4: https://archive.org/details/cu31924092584220/page/n10

[160] William Graham Sumner, *What Social Classes Owe to Each Other* (New York City, NY: Harper & Brothers, [1883] 1920); https://archive.org/details/whatsocialclass00sumngoog/page/n7

civilization[161] which could only develop properly where certain conditions were in place: private property, honest conduct, voluntary contracts, unhindered trade, and unrestricted mobility. He believed that "Laissez-faire" (economic Liberalism) constituted the height of political wisdom,[162] and that the principles of the free market economy could be applied equally well to society.[163] Society did not depend on any economy-regulating state. Society needed neither care nor supervision.[164]

William Graham Sumner rejected the idea that human beings have natural rights. He firmly believed that John Locke's doctrine of natural rights could not be taken seriously[165], since nature awards no special privileges to man. The only things that all individuals could gain from nature were habitat, food, and raw materials which enabled his existence in the first place. Nonetheless, the struggle for survival was not an unequivocal right, but a crucial requirement. According to Sumner, if a person had natural rights, nothing stood in the way of the consequent socialist idea that he had a right to whatever he needed, and his demands could extend to whatever he desired.[166]

Sumner believed that the government had a vital duty to defend national borders. The public similarly required protection from theft, swindling, and exploitation. A police force and an army were necessary in order to ensure peace, justice, and safety.[167] According to Sumner, a government that claims first and foremost to serve the people can be judged by its ability to maintain a just, peaceful social order in which liberty is valued, private property is protected, and all citizens are granted equality before the law. A state that tries to improve on natural conditions by manipulating the interplay of natural rights for the advantage of some and disadvantage of others, or by compensating artificially for the natural inequality among people, violates the principle of justice. The Marxist bid for a social justice that expropriates the productive sector of society in order to subsidize the unproductive sector was the exact opposite to what Sumner held to be right.[168]

Sumner had no interest in systematically analyzing the problems of restricting and balancing political power. He saw the solution in the laws and

---

[161] Ibid., 56; https://archive.org/details/whatsocialclass00sumngoog/page/n66

[162] Ibid., 58; https://archive.org/details/whatsocialclass00sumngoog/page/n68

[163] Ibid., 103; https://archive.org/details/whatsocialclass00sumngoog/page/n112

[164] Ibid., 104; https://archive.org/details/whatsocialclass00sumngoog/page/n114

[165] Ibid., 116; https://archive.org/details/whatsocialclass00sumngoog/page/n126

[166] Ibid.; https://archive.org/details/whatsocialclass00sumngoog/page/n126

[167] William Graham Sumner, *Lectures on the History of Protection in the United States* (New York City, NY: G. P. Putnam's Sons, 1888) 13.

[168] William William Graham Sumner, "Theory and Practice of Elections, First Paper," in William Graham Sumner, *Essays of William Graham Sumner* (New Haven, CT: Yale University Press [1911] (1940) vol. 1: 263-265; William Graham Sumner, "Republican Government," in William Graham Sumner, *Essays of William Graham Sumner* (New Haven, CT: Yale University Press, [1911] 1940) vol. 2: 203; https://archive.org/details/in.ernet.dli.2015.46494/page/n213

customs that had been long upheld in society and which were anchored in certain institutions. Sumner saw Democracy as a theory which assumes that all men were equal, and that power and governance are vested lawfully in a majority of equal and undifferentiated entities.[169] He believed that the realization of democratic principles and the emergence of their true totalitarian core causes liberal social order to evaporate and eventually dissolve into nothing. He saw the crux of Democracy as the principle of absolute equality among all people. However, he believed it to be a deceitful ideology, a sham religion, and a superstition, since its two principles – human equality and social atomization – find neither correspondence nor confirmation in human nature and experience.[170] According to Sumner, inequality, social differentiation, and complexity have increased at every stage in the progress of civilization. The principle of "one person, one vote" is therefore unjust, for Democracy does not politically acknowledge the differences between individuals.

Most people believe that they live in a free country since political leaders are appointed by voting in public elections. Holding periodic elections is therefore essential to the continued existence of free institutions.[171] The argument for extending the vote to all adult men and women was based on the idea that it was necessary to ensure that legislation was drafted in the interests of all people, not just to the advantage of a few. In his historical studies, however, Sumner made it unmistakably clear that the universal right to vote had a completely different effect shortly after its introduction. In a diverse society that allows every adult to vote as he or she wishes, an organized minority always succeeds in achieving its own interests. The reason is simple: the masses cannot make a firm stand because they bring many different ideas and motives to the table of democratic opinion making. Many prefer to remain politically inactive. The wavering, inconsistent, and apathetic behavior of the population enables an elitist group to achieve their particular interests against the wishes of the overwhelming majority. The secret of this group's success is the concentrated, determined, goal-oriented approach to the cause on which its heart is set.[172]

According to Sumner, all the talk about the liberal advantages of a government based on democratic principles could not be more misleading. He stated that freedom can be measured only by the extent to which the freedom of every individual in society is defended.[173] There are no grounds to

[169] William Graham Sumner, *Andrew Jackson as a public man: What he was, what chances he had, and what he did with them* (Boston, MA: Houghton, Mifflin, 1884) 224; https://archive.org/details/andrewjackson00sumngoog/page/n236

[170] Ibid.

[171] Sumner, *What Social Classes Owe to Each Other*, 27-30; https://archive.org/details/whatsocialclass00sumngoog/page/n36

[172] Sumner, "Republican Government," in *Essays of William Graham Sumner*, vol. 2: 200; https://archive.org/details/in.ernet.dli.2015.46494/page/n209

[173] Sumner, *What Social Classes Owe to Each Other*, 27-30; https://archive.org/details/

think that a Democracy can be more congenial to liberty than a monarchy, aristocracy, or another form of moderate Absolutism. If Democracy is understood as a system of self-regulation in which the government carries out the wishes of the majority, it is vital that all citizens are homogeneous – otherwise Democracy deteriorates into a form of government in which one class is raised above one or several others. In a society comprised of different races, Democracy degenerates to nothing more than a power struggle between them. Sumner believed that even the best government poses a constant threat to liberal social order, individual rights, and private property. The history of the human race includes many instances in which certain people and classes have tried to take control of state power in order to satisfy their worldly needs at the expense of others. Sumner noted with deep regret that these "people and classes" have been all too successful in carrying out state-legalized robbery. The introduction of a Democracy would change nothing in this respect. If the vast majority of the population had political power in their hands, they would abuse it for their own benefit as far as they were able, just as other classes had done before them. Only laws and institutions would be able to hold them back.[174]

However, Sumner believed that the real danger to freedom in a Democracy does not come from the majority. The tyranny of an elitist group of powerful schemers poses a far greater threat to the population than do the decisions of a majority government.[175] True liberty depends on the moral character and good practices of the rulers who have power over the state. Freedom-loving citizens who insist on ruling their own affairs without the constant interference of the authorities are forced to impose their own restrictions on themselves. They must also be constantly on their guard against the gradual removal of their civil liberties. If they are simply too lazy to take the measures necessary to prevent the state from overstepping the boundaries of its power, a dictatorship emerges. This can develop within a Democracy, just as in other systems of government, without being noticed for a long time. Should this take place, the ballot boxes would still be opened to give the appearance of a Democracy, but the votes cast would go unheeded. The writers of the U.S. Constitution of 1788 deliberately geared it to their own advantage over the vast majority. They therefore strongly opposed the introduction of a constitution that would give the ultimate power of decision to the people or to the individual states. Governing authority needed to be centralized to a large extent in the federal government. Implementing this principle was of great importance but needed to be done in a way that kept the majority believing themselves to be the true sovereign of the state, even though this was not the case. To this day, most people in Western nations

whatsocialclass00sumngoog/page/n36

[174] Ibid., 28, 32; https://archive.org/details/whatsocialclass00sumngoog/page/n38

[175] Ibid., 94; https://archive.org/details/whatsocialclass00sumngoog/page/n104

remain completely unaware of the real balance of power within what they believe to be a democratic social order.[176]

Sumner's critique of Democracy can be summarized as follows. 1) Modern, industrialized, Western nation states were geographically too extensive, demographically too populated, and culturally too diverse to be democratic in anything more than name. 2) The large populations in Europe and America were incapable of self-government. 3) Democratic institutions and structures in the United States, such as parties, elections, and members of parliament, were controlled by plutocrats – politically shrewd bankers and wealthy entrepreneurs. The true form of government was Plutocracy. 4) American plutocrats were turning increasingly to Imperialism and introducing a domineering system of control over the population by means of an escalating Militarism.

The term "Plutocracy" is at the core of Sumner's social philosophy. He did not understand it as signifying the rule of wealth, for he advocated the transfer of greater power of disposition to the upper class. He rather understood it as a form of government in which only wealthy men had access to the reins of power in order to use political means to increase their own wealth. Sumner was convinced that there was no better form of government than Democracy to give politically experienced plutocrats the chance to get rich at the expense of the vast majority.[177] The fate of a society that seeks to implement the democratic principles of the rule of law falls inevitably into the hands of an elitist group of plutocrats who know exactly how to direct events in their favor by enforcing state regulations. In the period following the American War of Secession, the U.S. government approved huge subsidies for the railroad industry, a centralized national banking system, extremely high protective tariffs, and a huge national debt – all within the framework of a supposedly democratic government.

In reality, almost all areas of power lay in the hands of a relatively small group of radical Republicans for twelve years (1865 to 1877). These individuals operated a full patronage policy in favor of wealthy steel manufacturers and other industrialists and bankers, for the most part unhindered by their own party officials or politicians from other parties. Furthermore, they carried out their vengeful and greedy plans to exploit the impotent southern states.[178] In Europe, the nobility still had power to impose certain limitations on the exercise of power over wealth. In the United States, there were unfortunately no noblemen who could have played the necessary part of a political counterweight. A high dose of naivety clouded their critical thinking and kept them trapped in a serene world of fantasy.

---

[176] Sumner, *Andrew Jackson as a public man: What he was, what chances he had, and what he did with them*, 225-227; https://archive.org/details/andrewjackson00sumngoog/page/n236

[177] Ibid.

[178] Sumner, *What Social Classes Owe to Each Other*, 95; https://archive.org/details/whatsocialclass00sumngoog/page/n104

The American population was deaf to Sumner's warnings of the government's need for a wall of protection against plutocratic control. The reason for this, according to Sumner, was that Americans generally have an attitude of carefree self-complacency, believing themselves to be immune from the social and political evils that relentlessly plague the rest of mankind.[179] More than one hundred years later, Americans are still just as bewitched by this myth. It has fully captivated public sentiment, leading Americans to believe that they rule their country since they are able to go to the polls. The fact that well-paid lobbyists in industry have a far greater influence over the legislative process – because they are backed by financiers who fund politicians' expensive election campaigns – is hardly perceived as what it really is: a grand-scale bribery and corruption of the entire political establishment. Neither do the plutocrats have any qualms of conscience when it comes to cheating and lying.[180]

Sumner labelled the American government with the following three terms: Paternalism, Plutocracy, and Imperialism. He saw territorial expansion as a fallacy. The U.S.A. had defeated the Spanish Empire in 1898, and would itself soon experience the same fate.[181] Following the conquest of the Philippines, Sumner criticized Americans of asserting its claim to life, liberty, and the pursuit of happiness without granting the same to the Filipinos. The United States failed to safeguard the rights of its own people in their own country, yet wanted to introduce Western civilization to the Philippines.[182] Sumner's criticism proved true in the Philippines: idealistic intentions to civilize the allegedly inferior races led ultimately to their destruction. Ironically, the ruthless actions of the Spanish colonialists provided the moral justification for America's entry into war with Spain. An impartial discussion about the advantages and disadvantages of an imperialist policy was impossible, since public opinion was fully under the influence of the inflamed warmongering. In summary, true Patriotism had degenerated to a frenzied state of intoxication which made it impossible to understand the real situation. The true motive of the policy was the financial exploitation and political oppression of other nations.

The hardened fronts between the diametrically opposed ideologies of classical Liberalism and Progressivism never clashed more vehemently than over the question of Imperialism. The lifelong disputes between William Graham Sumner and Theodore Roosevelt over the Spanish-American War of

---

[179] Ibid., 90-93, 94-95; https://archive.org/details/whatsocialclass00sumngoog/page/n100

[180] Sumner, "Theory and Practice of Elections, First Paper," in Sumner, *Essays of William Graham Sumner*, vol. 1: 268.

[181] William Graham Sumner, "The Fallacy of Territorial Expansion" (1896), in William Graham Sumner, *War and Other Essays* (New Haven, CT: Yale University Press, 1911) 292; https://archive.org/details/cu31924020331637/page/n323

[182] William Graham Sumner, "The Conquest of the United States by Spain" (1898), in *Essays of William Graham Sumner*, 302, 309-310; https://archive.org/details/cu31924020331637/page/n333

1898 and other products of American Imperialism did not result from their different temperaments, but from diverging conceptions of the role of the state which were so fundamental that they could never be reconciled. Despite the lack of unanimity among progressives, the dominant wing of the movement advocated an interventionist and expansionist foreign policy. The leader of the Progressive Party, Theodore Roosevelt, was an exemplary imperialist: he pushed for war with Spain, violently took over the Colombian (later Panamanian) canal zone, extended the decrees of the Monroe Doctrine, and sent the U.S. navy around the world. The president disguised his advocacy of Imperialism with the soothing words of an international reformer. Like other colonial powers, America had a duty to conquer "barbarian races" in the name of peace and civilization, since "every expansion of a great civilized power means a victory for law, order, and righteousness."[183] A fundamental aspect of the military conflict was that domestic reforms began to gain pace. America's imperialist involvement in the affairs of other nations took place in a logical, three-step sequence: conquest, suppression, exploitation.

It was not unusual for progressives to derive something positive from Imperialism. In England, the Fabians defended Imperialism as an effective – perhaps even the most effective – method of carrying out "national reforms" and creating an "international civilization."[184] Progressives shared President Wilson's dream of a world in which Democracy could spread unhindered. If necessary, this goal could also be achieved through armed force and military occupation.[185] The historian William Leuchtenburg considered Progressivism and Imperialism as different forms of expression of the same political philosophy.[186] William Graham Sumner lamented the loss of freedom and individuality in America and criticized state economic intervention and Militarism in the strongest terms. Sumner was one of several vice presidents of the Anti-Imperialism League (AIL): an organization that resolutely opposed expansionist Nationalism and considered the free market economy to be the optimum economic system – as maintained by English liberals of the Manchester School. According to Sumner, Imperialism was only of economic advantage to a relatively small interest group, whereas the financial costs of the conquest campaigns had to be borne by all citizens of the imperialist state.

William Graham Sumner's warning that ultimately only Plutocracy would benefit immediately from domestic Militarism and overseas

---

[183] Theodore Roosevelt, "Expansion and Peace," *Independent*, vol. 51 (December 21, 1899), 3404, in William Harbaugh, ed., *Writings of Theodore Roosevelt* (Indianapolis, IN: Bobbs-Merrill, 1967) 32; https://archive.org/details/writingsoftheodo00roos/page/32

[184] Herbert D. Croly, *The Promise of American Life* (New York City, NY: Macmillan, 1909) 289; https://archive.org/details/promiseofamerica00crol/page/288

[185] Harbaugh, ed., *Writings of Theodore Roosevelt*, 77; https://archive.org/details/writingsoftheodo00roos/page/76

[186] William Leuchtenburg, "Progressivism and Imperialism," *Mississippi Valley Historical Review*, vol. 39 (December, 1952), 483-504.

Imperialism went largely unheeded during his lifetime. He nonetheless refused to be disheartened, noting that the rampant Militarism would largely consume the wealth of the population and deprive them of the ability to focus on the challenges of their own lives. Pursuit of military glory had already brought the former European Empire to its knees. The best starting point for civilizational improvement, including a higher level of education for the general public, was the pursuit of peaceful relations, free trade, low taxes, and the production of industrial goods. Sumner called for a subjection of nature to its own control and needs in place of mutual overspending in costly and futile wars. The renowned Yale sociologist retrospectively equated the year 1898, in which the Spanish-American War broke out, with the beginning of a new era in the history of the United States which brought profound political changes.

A logical consequence of the process described by Sumner is the growth of the national security state, which restricts civil liberties at home and abroad, intervenes in the democratic process, and distracts the public from increasing social problems. Furthermore, enormous sums of money are spent on maintaining national security which could be used for more meaningful purposes. The totalitarian principles of the welfare state are engrained so deeply in the minds of contemporary Americans that Sumner's ideas meet with the general misunderstanding that the state owes nothing "to anybody except peace, order, and the guarantee of rights."[187] But what advantage does the general population gain from a policy that wants to witness and pursue the exploitation of other nations, if necessary by means of ruthless military force? History has amply demonstrated that the bitter fruit of an uninhibited exercise of power by both totalitarian and democratic regimes is a tyrannical rule over large areas of the earth. Streams of blood and the rubble of cities destroyed by bombs are the tribute paid.[188] Such abominable behavior is the product of human nature, which is evil through and through.[189] This cruel course of history will continue throughout the twenty-first century in exactly the same way, if not with far worse consequences still, if we do not turn away decisively from belief in Progressivism and return to biblical Christianity.

13.2 Blame for the outbreak of the First World War

No war has been treated more tendentiously in the history books than the First World War. Neither has any other war been assessed more defectively in recent years. The Treaty of Versailles assigned sole blame for the outbreak of World War I to Germany and its allies; however, war documents published shortly after revealed the hidden truth that all participating nations were

---

[187] Cit. in Maurice Davie, *William Graham Sumner* (New York City, NY: Crowell, 1963) 42.

[188] Ibid.

[189] Ibid.

responsible. Nevertheless, the dominant view in academia and journalism since the 1960s has placed the blame exclusively on one side. According to this view, the conflict was triggered by the German government under the leadership of a malevolent, authoritarian emperor and his belligerent colleagues, leading to the loss of more than thirty million human lives and to indescribable devastation on the European continent. The rest of Europe was allegedly drawn into the conflict against its will, simply because the anti-democratic Prussian elite, encouraged by an ultra-nationalist population, wanted to implement a plan which they had been devising for decades – namely to extend their empire by force. This one-sided judgment of war responsibility was driven by personal, ethical, and ideological points of view. The historians behind it deliberately overlooked certain facts, ignoring the measures taken by other European countries to initiate the war. In order to support their historically questionable views, they unjustly slandered the Chancellor Theobald von Bethmann-Hollweg, who made great efforts to reconcile the differences between England and Germany three years before the war began. Furthermore, they deliberately misquoted key German figures in the conflict including the emperor and the highest ranking officer among his staff.

In recent years, such arguments have been ignored by First World War historians.[190] In 2013, the Cambridge University historian Christopher Clark published his work *The Sleepwalkers: How Europe Went to War in 1914*.[191] Clark writes that the major European powers marched like sleepwalkers into a war from which European civilization has never fully recovered: all of them acted carelessly. The war originated as a multi-faceted historical event. 1) Russia wanted to defeat Turkey and take control of the Dardanelles, a strait in the Mediterranean Sea that connects the Aegean Sea and the Sea of Marmara. 2) Great Britain was seeking to destroy the power of its chief economic rival, Germany, despite the risks involved. Germany was surrounded by hostile alliances so that a war of annihilation could be waged. 3) Serbia attempted to divide the Habsburg Empire. 4) France desperately wanted to take revenge on the Germans for their military success in the Franco-Prussian War and did all it could to fan the flames of war.

The dual monarchy of Austria-Hungary maintained a peace policy for almost fifty years. A change occurred after an attack in the Bosnian city of Sarajevo on July 28, 1914, in which Gavrilo Princip assassinated the heir to the Habsburg throne, Franz Ferdinand, and his wife. The following breakdown of diplomatic relations between European powers led to the outbreak of war, first contained within Europe but soon widening into a dreadful global

---

[190] Niall Ferguson, *The Pity of War: 1914-1918* (London: Penguin Books, 1999); https://archive.org/details/pityofwar00ferg; Sean McMeekin, *The Russian Origins of the First World War* (Cambridge, MA: Belknap Press of Harvard University Press, 2011); Konrad Canis, *Der Weg in den Abgrund: Deutsche Außenpolitik 1902-1914* (Paderborn: Verlag Ferdinand Schöningh [2011] 2013).

[191] Christopher Clark, *The Sleepwalkers: How Europe Went to War in 1914* (New York City, NY: HarperCollins, 2013) passim.

conflict. Allied war propaganda vilified the Austrian Emperor Franz Josef I (1830-1916) as the sole arsonist in the Balkans; however, historical facts disprove this portrayal.

In the years immediately before the First World War, England initiated conflicts in order to add more countries to their empire. In countries where they were unsuccessful, they caused as much damage as possible in order to eliminate them as political and economic rivals. Other countries such as Russia sided compliantly with England in its imperialist campaigns. In 1907, Iran suffered the division of its land into English and Russian spheres of influence after failing to deter its invaders from their avaricious plans, especially in terms of exploiting oil reserves.

The German Emperor Wilhelm II was strongly dissatisfied with the way that England, France, Russia, and America had expanded their colonial territories so enormously since he had come to power – but did not hold back from extending his own, more modest colonial heritage.

In the late nineteenth century, the government in Washington used its military presence in Cuba and Puerto Rico to place the islands' lucrative sugar plantations under its own protectorate. Deliberate conflict ensued, since these Central American territories officially belonged to the Spanish Crown.

France occupied Morocco in 1912 – a strange development given that eight states had previously pledged to protect the nation's sovereignty. 1912 also saw Egypt become part of the British Empire, a few years after the same fate had befallen Sudan, Burma, Tibet, Zanzibar, the Transvaal Province, and the Orange Free State. Many other countries were also forced to surrender to British military power around this time.

In the fateful years from 1904 to 1912, English diplomats forged secret alliances with France, Russia, and Belgium, through which they intended to surround and crush the German Empire from three sides. Nationalist and imperialist sentiment prevailed in the U.S.A., England, and France. In Germany, Militarism began in the army and spread quickly throughout society, even taking hold of the Social Democrats.[192] Bismarck secured the support of left-wing radicals by introducing State Socialism in the German Empire and implementing it consistently throughout the following period.

In England, an interest group formed among national social reformers and imperialist warmongers.[193] They wanted Britain's colonial policy to be encouraged through all possible means until a socialist world federation

---

[192] Franz Neumann, *Behemoth: The Structure and Practice of National Socialism* (London: Gollancz, 1942) 16, 22-23, 170-171; https://archive.org/details/in.ernet.dli.2015.190043/page/n11; s. also: Barbara W. Tuchman, *The Proud Tower: A Portrait of the World Before the War, 1890-1914* (New York City, NY: Macmillan, 1966) 416-417, 444; https://archive.org/details/isbn_0553130749/page/416; Fritz K. Ringer, *The Decline of the German Mandarins: The German Academic Community, 1890-1933* (Cambridge, MA: Harvard University Press, 1969) 134, 139-140; https://archive.org/details/declineofgerman00ring/page/134

[193] John Atkinson Hobson, *Imperialism: A Study* (London: James Nisbet & Co., 1902) 86; https://archive.org/details/imperialismastu00goog/page/n98

became a reality. In 1909, the liberals accepted – against their own political convictions – the increase in household budget taxes demanded by Chancellor of the Exchequer David Lloyd George, thereby triggering a process which would ultimately lead to national bankruptcy.[194] At the beginning of the twentieth century, Great Britain's financial resources were overwhelmed by enormous state expenditure for social reform and colonial expansion.[195]

The British Foreign Secretary Lord Edward Grey did everything within his power to isolate the Germans and their Austro-Hungarian allies, who were justifiably concerned at being encircled by their adversaries. Some skillful diplomatic maneuvers brought about the Triple Entente (a three-fold alliance between England, France, and Russia), through which the French and Russians surrounded the Central Powers as hostile enemies. In July 1914, leaders of the German Empire felt obligated to support their Austrian allies in a war with Serbia, which at the time was a Russian satellite state. It soon became clear that by participating in this conflict, Germany would have to confront the bitter reality of a two-front war with Russia and France. The German military fatalistically accepted the possibility that England would join the fight against Germany – which it then did. The British were more hostile toward the Germans than the Germans were toward the British. Foreign Secretary Lord Edward Grey rejected Chancellor Theobald von Bethmann-Hollweg's attempt to persuade his government not to form any military agreements with Germany's enemies. The historian Konrad Canis points out the following facts which are largely absent from other historical treatises.[196] 1) Germany's Second Reich had a predominantly passive foreign policy. This applied not only to Bismarck after the unification of Germany in 1871, but also to German foreign policy after 1902. 2) Britain pursued a course contrived for conflict, leading inevitably to war. It saw Germany as a newcomer in the acquisition of overseas colonies which had become a chief economic competitor. At the same time, Germany established itself as the dominant military power on the continent. Chancellor Theobald von Bethmann-Hollweg considered friendship with the English so valuable that he even put German interests at stake in order to gain it. 3) The imperial government and the majority of the German press did hope that Germany would become a world power, but were unwilling to dominate all other countries. Canis believes that Germany should have had a pacifying effect on

---

[194] Robert J. Scally, *The Politics of Social-Imperialism, 1900-1918* (Princeton, NJ: Princeton University Press, 1975) passim; https://archive.org/details/originsoflloydge0000scal

[195] Elie Halévy, *A History of the English People in the Nineteenth Century: Epilogue, 1895-1905* (New York City, NY: Harcourt, Brace, 1926) vol. 2: 4-21, 140-141; s. also: Elie Halévy, *The Rule of Democracy: 1905-1914* (New York City, NY: Peter Smith, 1952) vol. 2: 427; https://archive.org/details/in.ernet.dli.2015.264300/page/n65; Samuel J. Hurwitz, *State Intervention in Great Britain* (New York City, NY: Columbia University Press, 1949) chap. 1; Bernard Semmel, *Imperialism and Social Reform: English Social-Imperial Thought, 1895-1914* (Cambridge, MA: Harvard University Press, 1960).

[196] Konrad Canis, *Der Weg in den Abgrund: Deutsche Außenpolitik 1902-1914* (Paderborn: Verlag Ferdinand Schöningh [2011] 2013) passim.

Austria, even after Archduke Ferdinand and his wife were murdered by Serbian assassins. The Russian government pursued an aggressive policy of expansion which led to the outbreak of the First World War. The role played by America in these confused power-political maneuvers in Europe must also be considered: before the First World War, the United States was merely an English satellite state.

The crisis began on July 28, 1914, with the assassination of Franz Ferdinand, heir to the throne of the Austro-Hungarian Empire, and his wife Sophie. It took place in Sarajevo, the capital city of the province of Bosnia which was annexed to Austria. Franz Ferdinand and his wife became victims of attack not because they were enemies of Serbia, but because the Serbs wanted independence. Serbian politicians spoke of an inevitable fight with Austria for the sacred cause of a Greater Serbia – a unified Serbia and Bosnia. A terrorist group fought against the political elite of the Habsburg state. Serbian and Bosnian nationalists intent on separating from Austria were a small minority. Ironically, most of them feared that their nation would be dominated by other powers, such as Germany or Russia, if it were no longer under Austria's protectorate.

As a result of Russia's disastrous defeat in its war with Japan (1904 to 1905), the Tsar directed his plans for expansion toward the Balkans in the West. France supported Serbia as willingly as Russia did. In the 1880s, the German Chancellor Otto von Bismarck had negotiated a series of treaties with Russia and Austria that aimed at a political isolation of France, which was bent on revenge. When Bismarck was removed from office in 1890, the German government allowed the treaty with Russia to expire. Clark contradicts an older view of this event by claiming that the failure to renew the alliance with the Tsar did not result from the recklessness of the new Kaiser Wilhelm II, but rather from the decision of inexperienced diplomats in the Foreign Ministry. France, as yet without an ally, was keen to gain a powerful new state as a confederate. The French-Russian alliance was formed in 1894 and was still in existence in 1914. The French foreign minister brought together two nations that were already allied with France. England and Russia reached mutual agreement on their colonial disputes and signed the treaty for the Triple Entente in 1907. The German Empire was now opposed by three empires. When the key factors that ultimately led to the First World War are considered, the arms race between the German and British navies fades into the background, serving simply as justification for England's hostility toward its German rivals. London never took seriously Wilhelm II's self-representation as commander of a powerful navy. Great Britain was constantly aware that it was able to deploy more battleships than any other country in the world. In the period before the outbreak of the war, public opinion played scarcely any role in Western Democracy: the individual populations of the countries that later went to war were kept completely in the dark about the military preparations that were frantically being made behind the scenes.

The outbreak of the First World War plunged humanity into a monumental crisis. Highly advanced weapons were produced by the thriving economies of Western industrial nations and employed with dreadful consequences. The exercise of tyranny by single dictators which would become typical of the twentieth century began in September 1914. The American public believed that their presidents' policy of neutrality, promoted by the Founding Fathers, would spare them from the negative effects of the war. Pašić, Sazonov, Conrad, Poincaré, Moltke, Grey, and other European politicians were exactly the type of statesmen of which the Founding Fathers had warned over 100 years earlier. Americans' favorable geographical situation seemed to guarantee their exemption from the senseless massacre of the Old World.

Hostilities in the North Atlantic also began in 1914 when war broke out in Europe, and eventually provided the pretext for America's entry into the war in 1917. One of the most pressing issues was the implementation of international law regarding economic relations between neutral nations and warring parties.[197] In gross violation of international law, Great Britain took absolute control of neutral trade.[198] The First Lord of the English Admiralty, Winston Churchill, an ardent Freemason[199], explained these illegal measures by stating that starvation would force the Germans into submission.[200] In November 1914, the entire North Sea was declared a military zone by the British Admiralty. Mines could therefore be laid in the English Channel, and neutral ships would enter the zone at their own risk. Britain's action was a blatant violation of international law and effectively meant that American trade with Germany came to an abrupt end. At the same time, America told the Entente (an alliance formed in 1894, initially between France and Russia) that it was willing to supply the Allied Forces with food, raw materials, and armaments from its virtually inexhaustible economic arsenal. Financial as well as sentimental considerations were thus the reason why almost the entirety of American industry identified with the Allies' military goals and put all its effort into ensuring that the Axis powers (including Germany and Austria-Hungary) would lose the war. The private bank J. P. Morgan & Co., which had immediately agreed to taken on the procurement of Great Britain's supplies, passed on regular information about the Entente's finances to the Wilson administration. The *Wall Street Journal* and other elite American

---

[197] Charles Callan Tansill, *America Goes to War* (Gloucester, MA: Peter Smith, [1938] 1963) 148.

[198] Edwin Borchard & William Pooter Lage, *Neutrality for the United States* (New Haven, CT: Yale University Press, 1937) 61; s. also: Patrick Devlin, *Too Proud to Fight: Woodrow Wilson's Neutrality* (New York City, NY: Oxford University Press, 1975) 193, 195; https://archive.org/details/tooproudtofightw00devl/page/193

[199] On 24 May 1901 Winston Churchill became a member of the United Studholme Lodge No. 1591 in London. He also attended the sessions of the Rosemary Lodge No. 2851 in London.

[200] Horace Cornelius Peterson, *Propaganda for War: The Campaign against American Neutrality, 1914-1917* (Norman, OK: University of Oklahoma Press, 1939) 83.

communication channels seized every opportunity to side with the British until the U.S. itself eventually entered the European war.[201]

Wilson had led America on a collision course with Germany. On May 7, 1915, the most significant incident of the North Atlantic war occurred when a German U-boat sank the British ocean liner *Lusitania*. An immense number of lives were lost. Among the 1,201 passengers[202] who died in the tragedy were more than a hundred Americans[203]. An outcry of horror resounded among the American elite, echoed by the most influential presses on the East Coast.[204] At the same time, the British published the "Bryce Report" which contained horrific accounts of atrocities allegedly committed by German soldiers in Belgium. This was a work of pure Entente propaganda, but was not recognized as such by American public opinion.[205] Americans were appalled. The elite of the Republican Party demanded that President Wilson take tough, unrelenting action. The majority of Americans wanted to avoid war but had no spokesman among the leadership of either national party. Wilson's Secretary of State, William Jennings Bryan, tried to bring the president to his senses. He reminded Wilson that Emperor Wilhelm II had welcomed a compromise proposed by America to cease U-boat warfare on merchant ships if Great Britain would allow food to be transported to Germany.

T. Woodrow Wilson knew from his political calculations that he needed William J. Bryan's support for success in the 1916 presidential election. His closest advisor, Colonel Edward M. House, held the same opinion and encouraged his decision to keep Bryan as Secretary of State until his services were no longer required to ensure the president's reelection. The fact that Bryan was the only cabinet member who was sympathetic to German politics[206], even after the German Empire entered into war with the Allied Forces, was surprising. It was of little importance, however, since House managed almost all of the important foreign policy affairs assigned to him by

---

[201] Tansill, *America Goes to War*, 132-133: "The Wall Street Journal was never troubled by a policy of 'editorial neutrality,' and as the war progressed it lost no opportunity to condemn the Central Powers in the most unmeasured terms."

[202] Colin Simpson, *The Lusitania* (Upper Saddle River, NJ: Prentice Hall Press, 1972) 3; https://archive.org/details/lusitania00simp/page/n17

[203] Ibid., 180; https://archive.org/details/lusitania00simp/page/180; the precise number of American lives lost was 124.

[204] Thomas G. Paterson, ed., *Major Problems in American Foreign Policy: Documents and Essays,* vol. 2: *Since 1914* (Lexington, MA: D. C. Heath, 1978) 30-32; https://archive.org/details/majorproblemsina00pate_0

[205] John Morgan Read, *Atrocity Propaganda, 1914-1919* (New Haven, CT: Yale University Press, 1941) 201-208; Peterson, *Propaganda for War*, 51-70; Phillip Knightley, *The First Casualty: The War Correspondent as Hero and Myth-Maker from the Crimea to Iraq*, 3 ed. (Baltimore, MD: John Hopkins University Press, 2004) 83-84, 107; https://archive.org/details/firstcasualtyfr000knig

[206] William Jennings Bryan & Mary Baird Bryan, *The Memoirs of William Jennings Bryan* (Philadelphia, VA: John C. Winston, 1925) 397-399; Tansill, *America Goes to War,* 258-259.

Wilson. Bryan was deeply humiliated by the abuse of his person and his resulting reduction to insignificance. Convinced that he would be unable to stop Wilson from entering the war, Bryan resigned as Secretary of State in June 1915.

The Washington government's interest in the naval war was reignited when a German U-boat sank the *Sussex*, a French passenger ship displaying no identifying national flag, injuring several Americans. A strong protest from the American president forced the German government to sign the Sussex Pledge. The emperor wanted to prevent a breakdown of relations with the United States at all costs and promised that Germany would cease unwarned attacks on the enemy's merchant ships in the war zone. However, this concession was made on the conditional assumption that "the United States government would challenge the British authorities and insist that they observe international law."[207] The Germans received a harsh reply from Washington stating that their own responsibility was unconditional and in no way dependent on the conduct of other powers.[208] President Wilson did not want to acknowledge the connection between Britain's infractions and German U-boat warfare.[209] The American leadership was anything but neutral, and the American ambassador in London, Walter Hines Page, made a great effort to please the British.[210] As Britain increasingly violated America's neutral rights, diplomatic notes were exchanged only for the sake of appearances, with a view to the two nations fighting side by side in the future.[211]

While the Wilson administration called on the American public to maintain strict neutrality toward nations involved in the war, Secretary of State Robert Lansing put pressure on Denmark to sell the Virgin Islands to the United States in 1916. By that time, the First World War had already been underway in Europe for two years. If Germany were to think of occupying Denmark and fortifying the Danish Virgin Islands, it would have a base from which to attack the United States should it enter the war. Denmark was forced to sell the islands to America; otherwise they would have been simply taken away.[212]

By January 1917, European statesmen and generals on both sides of the war wanted to readvance their stalled armies. The cause of the Entente was all but lost. Nevertheless, the British used every type of weapon at their disposal,

---

[207] Tansill, *America Goes to War*, 511-515.

[208] Ibid.

[209] Borchard & Lage, *Neutrality for the United States*, 168.

[210] Edward Grey, Viscount Grey of Fallodon, *Twenty-Five Years, 1892-1916* (New York City, NY: Frederick A. Stokes, 1925) 101-102, 108-111; https://archive.org/details/in.ernet.dli.2015.505196/page/n119

[211] Robert Lansing, *War Memoirs* (Indianapolis, IN: Bobbs-Merrill, 1935) 127-128; https://archive.org/details/warmemoirsofrobe0000lans/page/126

[212] Albert Katz Weinberg, *Manifest Destiny: A study of nationalist expansionism in American history* (Chicago, IL: Quadrangle, [1935] 1963) 398-409; https://archive.org/details/manifest-destinys00wein/page/398

old and new, to steer the war in their favor. A still deadlier massacre ensued. At the same time, the English intensified their propaganda in America to ensure that the U.S.A. sided with the Allies on entering the war. The War Propaganda Bureau in London paid large sums to American newspapers so that they would take the right position on the "American question." Hired propagandists went on long lecture tours and spread the *Bryce Report*, which revealed the atrocities allegedly committed by the Germans in Belgium. One of the most barbaric methods employed to get out of a hopeless situation relatively unscathed was the British hunger blockade of German civilians.[213] From the end of 1914, the English prevented neutral states from supplying Germany with food and other consumer goods. The obvious solution to end the bloodshed was to abandon hostilities and discuss negotiations. However, no one was prepared even to consider this as an alternative. Some statesmen tried desperately to settle the conflict; however, every attempt failed because of the enormous debts amassed by all parties during the war. Someone had to lose the war and pay reparations so that the victors could pay their war bonds and bank loans. The winter of 1916-17 was one of the severest experienced by Europeans of that time. Germany's starving population endured tremendous suffering and deprivation. The end of the war could not be far off. The outcome of the most harrowing military conflict in history now lay entirely in the hands of T. Woodrow Wilson. His decision to enter the European war in April 1917 unnecessarily prolonged the massacre of entire armies, during which time the United States reached the peak of its imperial expansion. The American Expeditionary Forces created the conditions which led to the complete destruction of the Russian Tsarist empire in the Bolshevik Revolution and later brought Germany under Hitler's dictatorship through the Nazi takeover. T. Woodrow Wilson was particularly adept at putting on a moralistic appearance in order to justify his policy of military aggression and imperialist domination. His selfish ambition was to make all countries of the earth submit to the ideas and demands of the U.S.A.

13.3 Exposing the lies of war propaganda

When the United States officially joined the Allied Forces in April 1917, many leading historians laid aside their gowns and marched in uniform. The chief task of historiography was to convince the American population that their president had taken the right decision in entering the European and Far Eastern war. The history of the enemy nations therefore needed to be portrayed as a long tradition of treachery and deceit. By wrapping themselves in cloaks of Nationalism, scholars often lose sight of their declared goal of

---

[213] David A. Janicki, "The British Blockade During World War I: The Weapon of Deprivation," *Inquiries* Journal, vol. 6, no. 8 (Boston, MA: Northeastern University, 2014), 1-5; http://www.inquiriesjournal.com/articles/899/
the-british-blockade-during-world-war-i-the-weapon-of-deprivation

objectivity in reporting historical events, whether to the praise of their own country or disparagement of the enemy. At the order of the president, the Committee on Public Information was established under the leadership of George Creel. Creel appointed Guy Stanton Ford, a prominent historian from the University of Minnesota, to chair a group of historians tasked with producing literature that supported America's war involvement. Both organizations published a steady stream of books and articles that reinforced Americans' conviction that they were fighting a unique and just war.

The American historian and sociologist Harry Elmer Barnes (1889-1968) was a progressive reformer.[214] Firmly convinced that governments could improve society through informed application of the new social sciences, he developed the "New History"[215] (progressive historiography) in 1912 in conjunction with well-known historians such as James Harvey Robinson[216] (1863-1936) and Charles A. Beard (1874-1948). Historical scholarship, they claimed, involves more than the mere recording of facts. Knowledge must serve a purpose, and scholarship should be used to solve the problems of human life.[217] Virtually nobody proclaimed the gospel of historical relevance with greater zeal than Harry Elmer Barnes.[218] His personal engagement in popular social order reforms provides a perfect example of progressive belief. He always found time and opportunity to participate actively in public life when it involved fighting for world peace, endorsing economic regulation, revising the criminal justice system, or promoting the science of genetic improvement. His activism was driven by a desire to improve human living conditions through conscious social planning. He warned against the Globalism that would soon emerge and urged the government to initiate socialist domestic reforms. In the 1930s, he published a series of studies on American Imperialism[219] which revealed the economic roots of an "empire without colonies," as described by William Appleman

---

[214] Joseph R. Stromberg, "Harry Elmer Barnes, Progressive and Revisionist," in *Old Cause* (Sunnyvale, CA: Antiwar.com, February 7, 2000) passim.

[215] Harry E. Barnes, *The New History and the Social Studies* (New York City, NY: The Century Co., 1925); https://archive.org/details/in.ernet.dli.2015.221792/page/n5

[216] James H. Robinson, *The New History: Essays Illustrating the Modern Historical Outlook* (New York City, NY: The Macmillan Company, 1912); https://archive.org/details/newhistoryessays00robi/page/n7; s. also: James H. Robinson, "The New History" (Proceedings of the American Philosophical Society, vol. 50, May 1st, 1911), 179-190; https://archive.org/details/jstor-984033

[217] Howard Zinn, *Politics of History* (Boston, MA: Beacon Press, 1970; Urbana, IL: University of Illinois Press, 1990) 17; https://archive.org/details/politicsofhistor0000zinn/page/16; s. also: Ibid., 288-291; https://archive.org/details/politicsofhistor0000zinn/page/288

[218] Carl L. Becker, "Review of Barnes's *The New History and the Social Studies*," *Saturday Review of Literature*, II (August 15, 1925), 38.

[219] In 1928 Barnes published the following books: Melvin Moses Knight, *The Americans in Santo Domingo* (New York City, NY: Vanguard Press, 1928); L. H. Jenks, *Our Cuban Colony: A Study in Sugar* (New York City, NY: Vanguard Press, 1928); M. A. Marsh, *The Bankers in Bolivia: A Study in American Foreign Investment* (New York City, NY: Vanguard Press, 1928).

Williams. Like many young men of his time, he was an ardent champion of T. Woodrow Wilson's progressive policy. Together with his older colleagues at Columbia University, he encouraged America's entry into the European war long before April 1917. Despite his criticism of the harsh demands placed on Germany by the victorious powers in the Treaty of Versailles, he closed his essay "National Self-Determination and the Problems of the Small Nations" with the following words: "The war was produced primarily by that ultra-nationalistic and super-patriotic intoxication, which had most completely overcome the Central Powers; the Allies have carried on the war in part to bring about the emancipation of the hitherto repressed nations."[220] Only in the summer of 1920 did Barnes begin to have serious doubts about the conventional reports of the diplomatic causes that supposedly led to the outbreak of the war.

The Harvard historian Sidney B. Fay initiated the drive to reconsider the reasons for the beginning of the military conflict. Referring to the Austrian Red Book and the recently published Kautsky Documents which were kept in the German archives, he concluded in a 1920 article in the journal *American Historical Review* that the German chancellor, Theobald von Bethmann-Hollweg, and Kaiser Wilhelm II were not criminals who had plotted the World War, but fools who had tied a noose around their own necks. The other end of the rope, according to Fay, lay in the hands of a stupid and clumsy adventurer, Leopold von Berchtold, Foreign Minister of the Austro-Hungarian Empire. In his second article, Fay showed how the Germans had tried to persuade the Austrians to accept a peaceful solution to the conflict with Serbia. In the third, published in 1921, he made it clear that Russian militarists had imposed a general mobilization of the military on the Tsar, and that the German mobilization was a forced and necessary reaction to Russia's actions for the sake of defense against imminent attack. Having noted this, Harry Elmer Barnes received his first opportunity in 1921 to express publicly his revised opinion on the origins of the European war. Subsequent history books on the First World War more or less contained Fay's disclosures, but historians still maintained their conclusion that the Central Powers had been the warmongers. Barnes, who had spoken out against this view, met with strong reactions to his historical revisions to the causes of the war whenever he published articles and books on the subject. His skepticism about the official version of First World War history propagated by the Allies meant that his brilliant academic career was increasingly undermined. However, his interest in world peace outweighed any desire for personal fame and prosperity. He was an unwavering champion of the later disparaged revisionist historiography – a term that refers to every attempt to revise an inadequate or defective interpretation of history.

---

[220] Stephen P. Duggan, ed., *The League of Nations: The Principle and Practice* (Boston, MA: Atlantic Monthly Press, 1919) 182-183; https://archive.org/details/in.ernet.dli.2015.166339/page/n217

In *The Genesis of the World War*[221] (1926), Barnes argued that documents held in the archives of the chambers and foreign offices of various countries supported his theory that Serbia, Russia, and France were more responsible for the catastrophe of 1914 to 1918 than were Austria and Germany.[222] Neither Austria nor Germany had wanted the outbreak of a universal war, but had been dragged into the conflict when it was provoked by other governments. During the 1920s, Barnes published his controversial views amid a climate of skepticism about the questionable events of the war. In general, however, the American public reacted positively to his conclusions. Many Americans were deeply disappointed by Wilson's grand crusade and showed growing interest in understanding what had led to the catastrophe. Barnes also edited a series of books for publication on American Imperialism, largely in Latin America.

In the 1930s, Harry E. Barnes joined a coalition of academics and activists who were opposed to Roosevelt's New Deal. Like the journalists and historians John T. Flynn, Henry L. Mencken, Albert Jay Nock, and Charles A. Beard, Barnes was regarded as an enthusiastic advocate of progressive reforms until he refused to sign Franklin D. Roosevelt's militant foreign policy. For this unforgivable sin, the progressive thinker was banished to outer darkness.[223] In the eyes of his former colleagues, he seemed suddenly to have become a right-wing fanatic and to have completely lost his common sense. The doors of renowned publishing houses which before had gladly issued his books were now shut in his face overnight. In 1929, he lost his position as professor of sociology at Smith College.

After the United States entered the Second World War, Barnes turned to the urgent task of revising the traditional view of how this war had come about. He shed glaring light on the lies of the war propaganda so that the significance of the military conflict, especially for the future, could be better understood. This worst of all wars, he said, was the direct result of the madness displayed by the Allied statesmen – especially T. Woodrow Wilson and the British Prime Minister, David Lloyd George – at the peace negotiations in

---

[221] Harry Elmer Barnes, *The Genesis of the World War: An Introduction to the Problem of War Guilt* (New York City, NY: Alfred A. Knopf, [1926] 1927); https://archive.org/details/in.ernet.dli.2015.24788/page/n7

[222] Ibid., 313; https://archive.org/details/in.ernet.dli.2015.24788/page/n347

[223] The historian James J. Martin made the following comments in the introduction of the book *Barnes against the Blackout* (Costa Mesa, CA: Institute for Historical Review, 1991) xi: "As the Establishment born in 1945 gradually got hold of itself and created the Cold War monolith and homogenized politics related to foreign affairs ('Politics stops at the water's edge'), the implications of Revisionism (the Establishment's Old Hands all remembered the bottomless disaster that struck them from 1918 on) became so repellent to them that they gradually converted Revisionism into a generic term. This was the lot of Revisionism's exponents as well ('*the* Revisionists'), a large part of us eventually losing even our names, let alone our reputations, professional careers and livelihoods, our friends and our futures. All this is mentioned, by the way, in *no* sense as a *complaint*, but as a fact, and as something about which to be proud: Ezra Pound said it best and for everybody, whatever their intellectual persuasion, when he declared that if a person was unwilling to risk anything for his opinions, either his opinions were no good, or he was *no* good." Emphasis in the original

Paris in 1919. This led to an even worse continuation of the military conflicts of 1914 to 1918. The task before him was therefore to apply the findings and methods of Revisionism used to record the history of the First World War in his studies of the Second.[224] The events connected to Japan's attack on Pearl Harbor on December 7, 1941, were central to Barnes's corrected history of the war. He hoped that a population which understood the causes of past wars would, in time, come to realize what triggered potential military conflicts and render it ineffective. He wanted to prevent this war from becoming the ideological justification for all of the American Empire's future campaigns of conquest. If the War of Secession was already viewed by the northern states as a "Treasury of Virtue,"[225] the Second World War would be seen as a far greater variant of the same thing, and would thus be used to justify all of America's military attacks on foreign territories. The idea of the "Treasury of Virtue" was based on the false assumption that Lincoln had started the war primarily and purposely to liberate slaves.[226]

Although Roosevelt had been warned in good time of a Japanese attack on Pearl Harbor, he never informed his commanders in Hawaii. He was clearly looking for a pretext to enter the war. Without studying the literature of Revisionism, all that remains is the official account of the events that led to the war, in which America's enemies are portrayed as evil, fear-inducing criminals. Roosevelt led his country into war through deliberate deceit, yet his lies are considered mere trifles. Given the enormous benefits reaped by Americans through participation in the war, this should come as no surprise. Roosevelt's highly questionable conduct is justified ethically: the war was about fighting racism, destroying Fascism, and saving civilization. In the twentieth century, no one expected to hear truth from the mouths of politicians. Since 1945, wars have been fought in many countries under the pretext of military intervention for purely humanitarian reasons.[227] Barnes claimed in 1942 that the real reason for the outbreak of the Second World War was the failure of the Central Powers to open up foreign markets and acquire valuable raw materials.

---

[224] Harry E. Barnes, ed., *Perpetual War for Perpetual Peace: A critical examination of the foreign policy of Franklin Delano Roosevelt and its aftermath* (Caldwell, ID: The Caxton Printers, 1953; New York City, NY: Greenwood Press, Publishers, 1969); https://archive.org/details/PerpetualWarForPerpetualPeace1953/page/n2

[225] Robert Penn Warren, *The Legacy of the Civil War: Meditations on the centennial* (New York City, NY: Random House; Lincoln, NE: University of Nebraska Press, [1961] 2015) 59-66.

[226] Ibid.

[227] Harry E. Barnes, *Social Institutions in an Era of World Upheaval* (New York City, NY: Prentice-Hall, 1942) 347; https://archive.org/details/socialinstitutio033149mbp/page/n371; Lloyd C. Gardner, *Economic Aspects of New Deal Diplomacy* (Madison, WI: University of Wisconsin Press, 1964); https://archive.org/details/economicaspectso0000gard/page/n5; Robert Freeman Smith, "American Foreign Relations, 1920-1942," in Barton J. Bernstein, ed., *Towards a New Past: Dissenting Essays in American History* (New York City, NY: Pantheon Books, 1968) 202-231.

President Truman finally pronounced the official new direction of American politics in the 1947 "Truman Doctrine."[228] The goal was to stop the expansion of the Soviet Union and support governments in resisting Communism. This doctrine signaled the end of the American war coalition with the Soviet Union and marked the beginning of the Cold War. For Barnes, the origin of the Cold War lay in the triumph of financial Capitalism. In forming enormous holding companies and investment firms, managers became distanced from owners and were no longer willing to be told by them how to lead their corporations. The economic system became so confused that the economy could only be stimulated by sustained war preparations.[229] Barnes remarked disparagingly that American politics had become characterized by "emotional orgies" and "anarchy." None of the political leaders, regardless of which party they belonged to, would now engage in constructive debates with the general public. Power-hungry officeholders and bureaucrats at the top of the established parties were occupied around the clock in manipulating the press and the machinery of government for the safeguarding of their own interests.[230] The only way to accomplish this was by obliging voters' irrational wishes and promising them the earth.[231]

In 1940, the progressive Barnes advocated the introduction of a welfare state that incorporated all areas of society.[232] The implementation of this socialist objective required a nationalization of the banking system, the railroad societies, energy companies, and potentially also heavy industry. In 1942, Barnes commended Thorstein Veblen's theory that a group of competent engineers could easily meet the needs of the nation.[233] With regard to the revision of the electoral system, Barnes proposed that only the educated should be given the right to cast their vote. Only a cabinet government with all judicial, legislative, and executive powers should exercise authority in the state. Barnes demanded with conviction that new standards of behavior be introduced among the population. Criminal law required comprehensive

---

[228] Harry E. Barnes, "Shall the United States Become the New Byzantine Empire?," (publisher not identified, 1947).

[229] Press release, Oneida-Herkimer Bankers Association (September 21, 1947), in *Papers of Harry Elmer Barnes*, University of Wyoming.

[230] C. Wright Mills, *The New Men of Power* (New York City, NY: Harcourt, Brace, 1948); https://archive.org/details/in.ernet.dli.2015.84792/page/n6; C. Wright Mills, *The Power Elite* (New York City, NY: Oxford University Press, 1956); https://archive.org/details/c_wright_mills_the_power_elite

[231] C. Wright Mills, "Mass Society and Liberal Education," in Irving Louis Horowitz, ed., *Power, Politics, and People: The Collected Essays of C. Wright Mills* (New York City, NY: 1963) 357, 361; C. Wright Mills, *The Sociological Imagination* (Oxford: Oxford University Press, [1959] 2001) 191.

[232] Harry E. Barnes, "The Responsibility of Education to Society," *Scientific Monthly*, LI (1940), 253.

[233] Harry E. Barnes, *Social Institutions in an Era of World Upheaval* (New York City, NY: Prentice-Hall, 1942) 290; https://archive.org/details/socialinstitutio033149mbp/page/n315

revision. Euthanasia[234] and eugenics[235] could be used to the benefit of a privileged elite; the "ruling classes"[236] should not leave the growth of the population to the "biologically inferior"[237] classes. The purchase and consumption of drugs, such as cannabis, cocaine, and heroine, needed to be legalized.[238] Legal restrictions had lost authority in regulating pornography and prostitution.[239] Divorce law needed to be applied far more liberally.[240] Hugh Hefner praised Barnes as an early exponent of the Playboy philosophy after hearing the public reform proposals of one of America's most controversial progressives.[241]

13.4 Relentless propagation of a world federation for peace

Most Progressives were secularized Postmillennialists and were joined by many liberal Protestants. Very few continued to uphold the teachings of Premillennialism. Robert Elliott Speer (1867-1947), a leader of the Presbyterian Church and a Premillennialist, readily accepted the National Security League's assertion of the United States' fight for "Freedom For All Forever." He stated that the church needed to support "the great ideal ends which the president has stated,"[242] seeing the First World War as a prime opportunity to establish a world government characterized by justice, rights, and fraternity.[243] After the war, Speer joined the campaign for the League of Nations led by President Wilson.[244]

Politicians from the victorious powers entered the Paris Peace Conference expecting great things from other nations. John Foster Dulles

---

[234] Harry Elmer Barnes, *Society in Transition* (New York City, NY: Prentice-Hall, 1952) 270-273; https://archive.org/details/societyintransit0000barn/page/272

[235] Ibid., 76-86; https://archive.org/details/societyintransit0000barn/page/76

[236] Ibid., 279; https://archive.org/details/societyintransit0000barn/page/278

[237] Ibid., 802; https://archive.org/details/societyintransit0000barn/page/802

[238] Ibid., 828-836; https://archive.org/details/societyintransit0000barn/page/828

[239] Ibid., 795-810; https://archive.org/details/societyintransit0000barn/page/794

[240] Ibid., 284-315; https://archive.org/details/societyintransit0000barn/page/284

[241] Ray H. Abrams, "Harry Elmer Barnes as a Student of Social Problems," in Arthur Goddard, ed., *Harry Elmer Barnes, the learned Crusader: New History in Action* (Colorado Springs, CO: Ralph Myles, Publisher, 1968) 439.

[242] Robert E. Speer, *The Christian Man, the Church and the War* (New York City, NY: Macmillan, 1918) 51; https://archive.org/details/christianmanchu00speegoog/page/n56

[243] Ibid., 78, 93, 109; https://archive.org/details/newopportunityc00speegoog/page/n103

[244] Robert E. Speer, "From World War to World Brotherhood," *Federal Council Bulletin* II (June, 1919), 103; cit. in Robert T. Handy, *A Christian America: Protestant Hopes and Historical Realities* (London: Oxford University Press, [1971] 1984) 161; https://archive.org/details/christianamerica0000hand/page/160

(ΦBK)[245], who would soon become the key American figure behind the introduction of a new world order, saw Nationalism as an insurmountable obstacle to this plan. The solution to the problem was to dissolve national sovereignty and unite the world as a single nation, thus automatically removing the barriers created by national borders. A new world order would require the abolition of Nationalism in all countries and the establishment of a League of Nations to unite them in one world federation.[246] The United States' system of federal government would be put forward as the ideal model.[247]

However, this goal could not be achieved through politics alone; something more influential had to be brought into play. If the Protestant Church could be convinced that a new world order would establish the kingdom of God, thus ending war, poverty, and injustice, its officers would gladly collaborate with politicians in creating a universal federation of states – a united world empire. Dulles wanted to inspire the church to play an active role in building a global society. The American Federal Council of Churches immediately came on board when presented with this plan. However, just as national sovereignty posed an obstacle to a new world order, so an exclusive Christianity would prevent the coming of the kingdom of God. Dogmatic beliefs were incompatible with ecumenical unity and were thus pushed aside in favor of the Social Gospel. This was achieved by downplaying the importance of Christian doctrine and promoting the principles of Progressivism, thus consolidating the progressive ideal of churches' "Social Confession" of 1932 which declared the necessity of establishing the kingdom of God on earth. Little by little, the theological description of the kingdom converged with the political and social agenda of the new world order. Also crucial was the acknowledgement that the moral or natural law was evident in other religions and could be understood by all people, and that it was therefore a moral force that transcended any individual religion. The salvation from sin offered by the Christian doctrine of the atonement was replaced by the projected eradication of war, poverty, unemployment, and injustice – an overarching goal which needed to be embraced by all world religions. In this way, the liberal conception of the kingdom of God was formed between the world wars in accordance with the political drive for a new world order.

The pastor and theologian Harry Emerson Fosdick (1878-1969) enjoyed unrivaled popularity[248] with the American population during the first half of

---

[245] Member of the Phi Beta Kappa Society, Princeton University, 1908

[246] Martin Erdmann, *Ecumenical Quest for a World Federation: The Churches' Contribution to Marshal Public Support for World Order and Peace, 1919-1945* (Greenville, SC: Verax Vox Media, 2016) passim.

[247] Samuel Zane Batten, *The New World Order* (New York City, NY: American Baptist Publication Society, 1919) 4-5; https://archive.org/details/newworldorder00battgoog/page/n18

[248] Robert Moats Miller, *Harry Emerson Fosdick: Preacher, Pastor, Prophet* (New York: Oxford University Press, 1985): "Reported *Time*, Fosdick's voice 'was the best-known and

the twentieth century.[249] Fosdick's views influenced the theological and political convictions of innumerable Americans of his time.[250] A self-proclaimed "evangelical liberal," he sought to make liberal Christianity appealing to his contemporaries by using the jargon of Progressivism. As a student, he was already an ardent follower of the liberal theologian and prophet of Progressivism Walter Rauschenbusch. Fosdick believed that a pastor's primary task was to inspire his congregation to strive above all for social development. Unlike other theologians, Fosdick (ΦΒΚ)[251] proclaimed from pulpits across the land that the U.S. government had a duty to engage in warfare. Extreme Pacifism was unsustainable, no matter how Christian it might appear. The overall aim of creating a democratic world was not to avoid war, but to win it. The primary goal was to bring peace to all nations.

After the war, Fosdick declared that the Allied Forces had agreed to retaliate against the defeated enemy during the Versailles peace negotiations.[252] The chance to do something good had been thrown away. Fosdick urged American Christians to take on the task of national and international renewal. They needed to be persuaded that the United States would bring salvation and cause progress to triumph throughout the world. However, the new era of progress was under threat from an implacable enemy which every Christian had a duty to relinquish – namely reactionary thinking.[253] The rest of society had already accepted progress as a universal law. Progressive ministers urged Christians to adapt as much as possible to what was taking place in the world – a world that had been shattered by war – for true faith in progress had to be rooted and grounded in reality. The presence of evil needed to be dealt with in every area of society: the unhappy reality was a world tainted by personal and social sin.[254] The idea of progress would change every area of human thought, and the future realization of an ideal society needed to be reduced to what was humanly possible.[255]

According to Fosdick, the idea of progress in the modern world – a world deformed by the First World War – was based entirely on science. Controlled use of natural force and the "mental and moral processes within"[256]

---

most influential one in Protestantism during the '20s and '30s.'" https://b-ok.cc/book/1005300/81df78

[249] Halford R. Ryan, *Harry Emerson Fosdick: Persuasive Preacher* (New York, NY: Greenwood Press, 1989) 10.

[250] William B. Lawrence, *Sundays in New York: Pulpit Theology at the Crest of the Protestant Mainstream 1930-1955* (Lanham, MD: Scarecrow Press, Inc., 1996) 15.

[251] Member of the Phi Beta Kappa Society, Colgate University, 1900

[252] Harry Emerson Fosdick, *Christianity and Progress* (New York City, NY: Fleming H. Revell Co., 1922) 42, 43, 45, 106; https://archive.org/details/cu31924007757937/page/n47

[253] Ibid., 128, 132-133, 143, 165; https://archive.org/details/cu31924007757937/page/n133

[254] Ibid., 171, 175; https://archive.org/details/cu31924007757937/page/n175

[255] Ibid., 8; https://archive.org/details/cu31924007757937/page/n13

[256] Ibid., 41; https://archive.org/details/cu31924007757937/page/n45

provided a machinery which could enable the changes needed for humanity's glorious future. Fosdick referred to the Progressivism of H. G. Wells and commended it as a prime example of Christianity. The English writer, despite being a convinced atheist, derived his faith in progress from a conception of God that seemed reasonable to modern man. God had allegedly called mankind to join a progressive crusade.[257] In His hands, the church would be the primary instrument for the realization of a global federation – a kingdom of justice on earth.[258]

During the 1920s, Harry Emerson Fosdick's denial of key Christian doctrines was central to the debate between Fundamentalism and Modernism. Within the Protestant church, his message was either completely rejected or received with great enthusiasm.[259] On May 21, 1922, Fosdick preached the most important sermon of his career, entitled "Shall the Fundamentalists Win?"[260] On the basis of its social impact, it was probably the most important sermon of the twentieth century. Fosdick immediately took center stage in the conflict between liberal theology (advocacy of Progressivism using Christian terms but diametrically opposed to Reformation Christianity) and conservative theology. Furthermore, Fosdick rose to fame in North America overnight. Within a few weeks, the sermon had been circulated throughout liberal theological circles. The famous public relations expert Ivy Lee requested Fosdick's permission to spread it far and wide. Fosdick agreed after hearing that John D. Rockefeller, Jr. (ΦBK)[261] was highly enthusiastic about the sermon's message and had promised to cover the costs of its dissemination. 130,000 copies were immediately sent to American pastors and lay preachers.[262] The only change that Rockefeller made was to the title, which he rephrased as "The New Knowledge and the Christian Faith." The liberal theologian's battle call spread like wildfire under the term "New Knowledge." At the same time, the term "Fundamentalism" (introduced by the Baptist editor Curtis Lee Laws in 1920) began to assume the same negative connotations that it still retains today.

Fosdick's sermon contained liberal theological statements which directly contradicted the fundamental tenets of traditional Christianity. He launched a frontal attack on the Christian faith, seeking to deal it a death blow. He denied four key doctrines of Reformation Christianity: the inerrancy of the Bible, the virgin birth, the vicarious atonement, and the future return of Jesus Christ. According to Fosdick, true Christians do not uncritically accept

---

[257] Ibid., 42; https://archive.org/details/cu31924007757937/page/n47

[258] Ibid., 43-45; https://archive.org/details/cu31924007757937/page/n47

[259] E. Glenn Hinson, "Baptist Contributions to Liberalism," in *Baptist History and Heritage*, 35, no. 1 (Winter, 2000), 39-54.

[260] Harry Emerson Fosdick, "Shall the Fundamentalists Win?," *Christian Work* 102 (June 10, 1922), 716-722.

[261] Honorary member of the Phi Beta Kappa Society, 1897; ΦBK-Senators

[262] Miller, *Harry Emerson Fosdick*, 116; https://b-ok.cc/book/1005300/81df78

everything the Bible says, but rely instead on their good common sense. Fosdick knew very well that the doctrine of the virgin birth, which he ridiculed particularly strongly[263], was one of the most important teachings in the Bible. Were it not a historical event, there could be no eternal salvation in Jesus Christ. Only a God-man untainted by original sin could atone for the sins of believers on the cross, bringing them salvation through the sacrifice of His own life. Contrary to this view, Fosdick portrayed the virgin birth as a scientific impossibility. He decried the idea of supernatural miracles that overrode the inviolable laws of nature as a fallacy, thus asserting that Jesus Christ was not the sinless Son of God, but rather a man like any other. All talk of a vicarious atonement and a future return was therefore entirely meaningless. Christians who believed it unnecessary to uphold the infallibility of the Scriptures and the virgin birth as irrefutable truths were to be met with tolerance. They were to have the freedom to believe or not to believe whatever they held to be truth, without any threat of denigration. The American pastor likened fundamentalists to the Pharisees. Conservatives were divided between two camps: on the one side were those willing to fight for what they believed to be the fundamentals of faith; on the other side were those who felt it unnecessary to disrupt church peace by defending what they considered to be insignificant theological differences. Only three years after the publication of Fosdick's sermon, the liberals had gained control of the largest and hitherto most theologically sound church in North America: the Presbyterian Church (U.S.A.). From there, Liberalism spread to other Protestant churches. Several years later, John D. Rockefeller, Jr., appointed Fosdick pastor of the most well-known Baptist church in New York City. Together, they ensured the wide acceptance of liberal theology among American Baptists.

Before the First World War, Fosdick was one of the most ardent advocates of the conflict. During the 1920s and 1930s, however, he became one of the most influential pacifists[264] – the central figure in America's peace movement. His change of opinion took place in 1917, when he travelled to Europe to encourage the Allied troops fighting in the trenches and to inform American citizens of the course of the war. After witnessing the awful effects of modern warfare, he began to revise publicly his positive attitude toward the barbaric slaughter on the battlefields.[265] His highest concern was the preservation of world peace.[266] Following the First World War, Fosdick insisted that social action and ethical education go hand in hand in order to find concrete

---

[263] Fosdick, "Shall the Fundamentalists Win?," 716-722.

[264] Harry Emerson Fosdick, "The Unknown Soldier," in Harry Emerson Fosdick, *Secrets of Victorious Living: Sermons of Christianity Today* (New York City, NY: Harper & Brothers, 1934) 88-98; https://archive.org/details/in.ernet.dli.2015.167149/page/n101

[265] Harry Emerson Fosdick, "An Interpretation of Pacifism," in ibid., 106; https://archive.org/details/in.ernet.dli.2015.167149/page/n119

[266] Harry Emerson Fosdick, "A Christian Conscience About War." A sermon delivered at the League of Nations Assembly Service at the Cathedral at Geneva September 13, 1925, 18-20; https://archive.org/details/christianconscie00fosd/page/n19

answers to the numerous problems in the modern world.[267] Repudiation of war could never be based on the decision of a lone individual, but had to be the constant standpoint of the nation as a whole. This could only happen if every individual strove for the good of the whole world, not the advantage of their own nation. The progressive theologian's pacifist convictions were based on the fact that he advocated global Interventionism (Internationalism) and therefore had no support for national Isolationism. He challenged every American to play their vital part in bringing about a new world order – a world federation.[268] The most important task was to foster an international mindset as widely as possible among the world's population. Since Protestantism was imbued with the spirit of modern Progressivism, there was good reason to be optimistic. Christians needed to do their utmost to support the establishment of a world government.

Although the U.S. Senate opposed America's membership of the League of Nations and refused to ratify the Treaty of Versailles, Internationalism could never again be banished to the background. Fosdick was certain of receiving the undivided support of the American Federal Council of Churches, which would work hard to promote a policy of collective security. Establishing himself as an advocate for the Protestant pacifists, he spent years calling for America to participate in the World Court.[269] However, he had no success. While anti-war sentiment continued unabated in the early 1930s, there was no reason for Fosdick to fear losing the majority support of the population. Over time, however, he observed a concerning change in general opinion on war policy. From 1935, Protestant churches which had previously been united in their support of Internationalism began to divide into different camps. Former pacifists spread the view that confronting dictators with armed force would be a worthier course of action than preserving peace.[270]

---

[267] Harry Emerson Fosdick, "The Church Must Go Beyond Modernism," in Ryan, *Harry Emerson Fosdick*, 109.

[268] Harry Emerson Fosdick, "What the War did to My Mind," *The Christian Century* (January 5, 1928), 43.

[269] Harry Emerson Fosdick, "The Cure of Disillusionment," in Fosdick, *Secrets of Victorious Living*, 23; https://archive.org/details/in.ernet.dli.2015.167149/page/n35; Harry Emerson Fosdick, "Unknown Soldier," in ibid., 97; https://archive.org/details/in.ernet.dli.2015.167149/page/n109; Harry Emerson Fosdick, "The Interpretation of Pacifism," in ibid., 101; https://archive.org/details/in.ernet.dli.2015.167149/page/n113; Harry Emerson Fosdick, "What are you standing for," in ibid., 223; https://archive.org/details/in.ernet.dli.2015.167149/page/n235; Harry Emerson Fosdick, "The Interpretation of Life," in ibid., 234; https://archive.org/details/in.ernet.dli.2015.167149/page/n247

[270] Robert Moats Miller, *American Protestantism and Social Issues 1919-1939* (Chapel Hill, NC: University of North Carolina Press, 1958) 342: "On the other hand, many of the peacemakers placed common sense above consistency and recognized that the triumph of dictators would be a fate worse than war. And increasingly as the decade deepened churchmen forsook pacifism for collective security. They accepted the revision of American neutrality legislation, urged sanctions against aggressor nations and aid to those attacked, and finally evidenced a willingness to risk war to prevent the victory of Germany and Japan." https://archive.org/details/americanprotesta0000mill/page/342

Fosdick, however, continued to speak out no less vehemently in favor of disarmament.

As the outbreak of another armed conflict in Europe became increasingly likely, the American pastor continued to support Roosevelt's Neutrality Acts but was unable to shake off the impression that the president was far from taking a strict pacifist stance. The beginning of the Second World War dealt a hard blow to his almost unshakeable confidence. The realization that his numerous efforts to preserve peace had been in vain was devastating.

13.5 Corruption among the war profiteers

In the 1930s, the American population was still deeply disillusioned by the course of the First World War. Sensational reports disclosed the warmongering behavior of American arms companies and banks in the months before Congress declared war on April 6, 1917. This led many Americans to advocate a policy of Isolationism, wanting to ensure that the United States adopted a neutral stance toward warring nations. The publication *Merchants of Death: A Study of the International Armament Industry*[271] was circulated widely among the American population from 1934.[272] Through its provocative title, its authors, Engelbrecht and Hanighen, indicated the controversial content of their exposé which revealed the corrupt schemes driven by war profiteers. The names of directors of arms companies and investment banks[273] show that they were often the same people. Only by cooperating with one another could they gain enormous mutual benefits.[274] Directors realized that their defense and finance companies only made substantial profits when working closely with the heads of state and parliamentarians who gave them access to the War Department and the Treasury.[275] The secret arrangements could not have been more effective.

A period of peace was also crucial. During quiet times, weapons technologies could be improved in order to bring new products onto the market which were often more costly than the older products. Banks also had other motives for welcoming a time of peace. Debt financing the complete

---

[271] H. C. Engelbrecht & F. C. Hanighen, *Merchants of Death: A Study of the International Armament Industry* (New York City, NY: Dodd, Mead and Co., 1934); https://archive.org/details/merchantsofdeath00enge/page/n5

[272] The topic of war profiteering is being discussed in the following books: Justus Doenecke, *Storm on the Horizon: The Challenge to American Intervention, 1939-1941* (Lanham, MD: Rowman and Littlefield, 2000); Wayne S. Cole, *Roosevelt and the Isolationists, 1934-1945* (Lincoln, NE: University of Nebraska Press, 1983); Wayne S. Cole, *Senator Gerald P. Nye and American Foreign Relations* (Minneapolis, MN: University of Minnesota Press, 1962).

[273] Engelbrecht & Hanighen, *Merchants of Death*, viii; https://archive.org/details/merchantsofdeath00enge/page/n11

[274] Ibid., 144-145; https://archive.org/details/merchantsofdeath00enge/page/144

[275] Ibid., 143; https://archive.org/details/merchantsofdeath00enge/page/142

reconstruction of war-damaged nations was a proverbial El Dorado: revenue received in this way greatly exceeded the war profits. Banks were celebrated as "helpers in time of need" and shamelessly exploited public support by raising mortgage interest rates. Despite the general practice of giving war materials to all nations that were considered financially strong customers, large arms manufacturers succeeded in portraying themselves as ardent patriots, as though they occupied one of the most important branches of industry in the national economy. Since managements consisted of directors of different nationalities, arms manufacturers were able to play their ace of feigned Patriotism to their maximum advantage. It was vital for them to have direct influence on the press in the countries with which arms companies conducted business. They consequently did all possible to persuade editors and journalists to take a certain line by means of generous advertisement spending and other financial contributions. Propaganda was one of the preferred means of steering the political opinion of a country in one direction or another. Arms manufacturers thus had the option to raise a sudden alarm of war when it lay in their own interests. All they had to do was encourage the press to convey more information about the thunderclouds gathering on the horizon of world politics. Sensational reports in the yellow press also resulted in a great increase in the circulation of newspapers.

The book *War is a Racket*[276], written by the dissident major general Smedley D. Butler (1881-1940) and published at the same time as *Merchants of Death*, caused a sensation. With no consideration for the damage to his own reputation, Butler criticized the imperialist schemes of bankers and U.S. politics.[277] War had been waged to the advantage of the few at the expense of the many.[278] Since the beginning of the First World War, the major American banks had sided with the Allied Forces, investing a fortune in Great Britain and France's government bonds while preventing the Central Powers from issuing debentures in the United States. They had worked skillfully and subtly to ensure a glorious end for the cause of the Entente. Operating in complete conjunction with the large banks, American industry had sided unreservedly with the Allies. The U.S. press naturally followed in the footsteps of industry as it led the way, being financially dependent on it. From 1915, the press spread virtually nothing but Allied propaganda. President Wilson was criticized incessantly in leading articles of principle newspapers such as the *New York Times* and the *Boston Globe* for his avowal of neutrality. In some cases, British secret agents took over the editorial management of American papers. Lord Northcliffe, an English media tycoon and director of propaganda,

---

[276] Smedley D. Butler, *War is a Racket* (New York City: NY: Round Table Press, 1935; Los Angeles, CA: Feral House, 2003); https://archive.org/details/warisaracketelectronicresource-theantiwarclassicbyam/page/n3

[277] Ibid., 10; https://archive.org/details/warisaracketelectronicresourcetheantiwarclassic-byam/page/n11

[278] Ibid. 23; https://archive.org/details/warisaracketelectronicresourcetheantiwarclassic-byam/page/n23

aimed his efforts at enemy countries and spent vast sums of money to guarantee complete control of the American media. The naval blockade set up by Great Britain in the Atlantic and the North Sea illegally prevented the transportation of American war materials to Germany. As a result, arms manufacturers and agricultural enterprises in the United States could only make significant profits by selling their products to Great Britain, France, Russia, and Italy. The Allied Forces could thus prolong the war until their opponents were bled dry and forced to their knees. Only victory against the Central Powers would enable the Allies to pay in full for government bonds and imported goods after the war.[279] Leading financial institutions in the United States therefore put great pressure on the Wilson administration to take America to war against the Central Powers.[280]

American bankers were on the brink of the abyss when the Allied Forces ran out of credit in late 1916. By the beginning of February 1917, not even the slightest chance remained for the U.S.A. to sell further government bonds to the countries of the Entente, all of which were bankrupt. A sense of desperation spread among Wall Street bankers. Their only hope of surviving this critical period was to shift the weight of financing the war from their own shoulders to the backs of the U.S. Treasury. This daring coup could only be realized if the United States abandoned its pretense of formal neutrality and entered the war. The German emperor's announcement of a reinitiation of submarine warfare on January 31, 1917, seemed like a godsend for the banks. They were now certain that the way would be opened for American intervention. When President T. Woodrow Wilson declared war on April 2, 1917, the mountain of debt owed by Great Britain to American banks had grown to almost 400 million U.S. dollars. The British Chancellor of the Exchequer admitted that the U.S. government's order for the entire sum to be credited to the account of J. P. Morgan & Co. had saved British public finances from collapse. Britain would otherwise inevitably have been the loser at the end of the world war. This eventuality would likewise have brought American banks to ruin. After the war, Americans realized that bankers had forced the United States' entry into the First World War for selfish reasons. Their main interest had been to maximize financial profit and to expand political power. Ethical considerations had played as small a role for the bankers as they had for arms manufacturers.

As a result of the shocking revelations of war profiteers' activities, various groups of anti-militarists publicly demanded a state investigation of the arms industry and banks. These investigations were carried out between 1934 and 1936, led by Senator Gerald P. Nye.[281] The published report exposed

---

[279] Robert W. Dunn, Adrian Richt, *American Foreign Investments* (New York City, NY: B. W. Huebsch and the Viking Press, 1926; New York City, NY: Arno Press, 1976) passim.; Grosvenor B. Clarkson, *Industrial America in the World War* (Boston, MA: Houghton Mifflin Co., 1923) passim.; https://archive.org/details/industrialameric00clar/page/n9

[280] John Kenneth Turner, *Shall It Be Again?* (New York City, NY: B. W. Huebsch, inc., 1922) chap. xxvii-xxxvii; https://archive.org/details/cu31924027862196/page/n267

[281] Cordell Hull, Andrew Henry, Thomas Berding, *The Memoirs of Cordell Hull* (London:

the grave corruption in the dealings of American arms manufacturers.[282] Many of these companies had indeed supplied weapons to a broad spectrum of customers – state governments of widely varying persuasions, often on both sides of the same war.[283] When the Nye Committee reached its peak popularity in the spring of 1935, Walter Millis's book *Road to War*[284] was published. It very quickly became the most widely read of all revisionist books to date. Charles Angoff, editor of the political magazine *Nation*, wrote an extremely positive review of this detailed study of America's entry into the war entitled "Road to National Insanity."[285]

The Nye Committee's meticulous study of the origins and course of the First World War paved the way for the publication of several new studies on the subject, written from the perspective of American Revisionism. No one imagined that the results of the research would ever again disappear from general knowledge. Nevertheless, in the two years preceding the events of December 7, 1941, the information revealed by the revisionists in answer to the key questions raised by the First World War came constantly under fire, resulting in what virtually no one had thought possible. The conventional beliefs concerning the background, course, and results of the First World War prevailed over statements to the contrary. The research results of Revisionism, which had far greater factual substantiation, disappeared almost entirely from public consciousness. Public opinion is largely a product of propaganda, which flows constantly into people's minds without offering them adequate protection.

However, the U.S. government was skeptical about whether it could maintain peace. In light of this fact, liberal journalists, reviewers, and commentators formed an unshakeable mutual opinion. The press agreed to work for nothing but a United States embroiled in another war, far worse than the former, in order to realize the yet unattained goal of establishing a world government. The philosopher and psychologist James Mark Baldwin's vision of a worldwide "federation of states" began to be realized more concretely. He had already articulated this vision clearly to the American public as much as half a century before.[286]

Hodder & Stoughton, 1948) vol. 1: 400; Robert Edwin Bowers, *The American Peace Movement, 1933-41* (Madison, WI: University of Wisconsin-Madison, 1947) 128ff.; Charles & Mary Charles A. Beard, Mary Ritter Beard, *America in Midpassage* (New York City, NY: The Macmillan Company, 1939) vol. 1: 401; https://archive.org/details/in.ernet.dli.2015.33972/page/n413

[282] "Report of the Nye Committee," or simply "Nye Report": U.S. Senate, Special Committee Investigating the Munitions Industry, 73rd Cong., 2nd sess., 1936.

[283] John E. Wiltz, *In Search of Peace: The Senate Munitions Inquiry, 1934-1936* (Baton Rouge, LA: Louisiana State University Press, 1965); https://archive.org/details/insearchofpeace0000unse

[284] Walter Millis, *Road to War: America, 1914-1917* (Boston, MA: Houghton Mifflin, 1935).

[285] *Nation* (May 8, 1935), 550-552.

[286] S. also: Chap. 9.6 Gradual formation of an idealized world federation; chap. 12.2 Complete rejection of a peace policy

14 The age of American global dominance

The term "Progressivism" can convey several different meanings. It can only be truly understood if examined more comprehensively against the historical background of America's Progressive Era, which lasted from around 1896 to 1921. A growing number of differing interpretations of the causes and effects of this ideology gave rise to divided opinions among historians. In order to establish a reputation, historians are required to promote the dominant ideology and evaluate the facts in a way that confirms the officially accepted view. Interpretations that draw on religious views must especially be excluded. This meticulous analysis of the changing conceptions of Progressivism not only enables better understanding of what lies behind them, but also provides insights into the intellectual trends of the twentieth and twenty-first centuries.

14.1 Pacifist spirit of Continental Americanism

Charles Austin Beard wrote numerous books, articles, and essays as history professor at Columbia University and as an independent scholar. [287] He received prestigious academic awards for his scientific achievements. His influence in American society increased year by year, even though some of his progressive views were deemed too controversial by the general public. The publication of his book[288] on the American Constitutional Convention in Philadelphia caused a sensation overnight. The American Constitution was adopted on September 17, 1787, and ratified in 1788. It laid down the nation's fundamental political and legal order and outlined a federal republic in the form of a presidential system. According to Beard, however, the Constitution provided the Founding Fathers with an effective means of becoming extremely rich. Beard's critics believed that he was a convinced Marxist; however, he claimed that his account of the economic interests behind the formulation of the Constitution had been inspired not by Karl Marx, but by James Madison[289]. In his works, Beard associated economic interests with specific social classes and emphasized the difference between the propertied and the dispossessed classes. By tracing the tradition of the Federalists and the Whigs, Beard presented the Constitution as an instrument through which the wealthy class protected itself from the dispossessed.

---

[287] Joseph R. Stromberg, "Charles Austin Beard: The Historian as American Nationalist," in *Old Cause* (Sunnyvale, CA: Antiwar.com, November 9, 1999) passim.

[288] Charles A. Beard, *An Economic Interpretation of the Constitution of the United States* (New York City, NY: MacMillan, 1913; New York City, NY: Simon and Schuster, 2012); https://archive.org/details/in.ernet.dli.2015.59388/page/n6

[289] Alexander Hamilton, James Madison & John Jay, *The Federalist* (New York City, NY: The Colonial Press, 1901); https://archive.org/details/federalist00hami/page/n14

This view of history must be clearly refuted: the idea of class interests is nonsensical. There are no homogeneous classes in society, only individual interests.[290] Of far greater importance is the fundamental distinction between "class" and "caste." Castes form where certain social groups are privileged or inhibited by the coercive power of the state and therefore stand in direct conflict with one another. Within the free market, the gain of one man is the gain of another; in contrast, government interventions produce favored and unfavored castes, so that the gain of one man or one caste is the loss of another. If textile manufacturers demand a protective tariff for their goods and are denied it by the state, they remain separate individuals competing against each other within the market; however, if the tariff is indeed granted by the state, they become a privileged caste with a common interest against other castes. Not only is Beard's assertion of a fight between the classes false, but his description of the individual classes is also incorrect. It is absurd to think that only peasants can be "debtors." Even in colonial times there were many wealthy debtors.

Despite these obvious defects in his historical analysis, Beard can nonetheless be recognized as having made a valuable contribution by publishing his books. He pointed out the financial motives behind a particular event which had largely been concealed. When people hold definite political views, they almost always state their idealistic motives and hide their personal interests. This is especially applicable to the historiography of the American Constitution, in which the real intentions of the Founding Fathers are clouded by a myth. Beard explained that the reason why wealthy bondholders (a specific caste) insisted on the establishment of a strong central government with the power to levy high taxes was that this meant an enormous increase in the value of the bonds. Land speculators in the West also wanted a strong government so that Indian tribes could be driven from their land, and so that the value of the land could increase as a result. The politically powerful union of army officers wanted a strong government that would have sufficient tax revenue to pay a large army. Beard certainly laid his finger on a sore point in early American history when he exposed the Founding Fathers' financial motives in drawing up a new constitution. The realization of personal economic interests is a continually strong motive in human actions.

Beard also showed how financial motives played a role in the U.S.A.'s decision to enter the First World War. He became increasingly convinced that Germany had not been solely responsible for the outbreak of the war, and that America's participation had not really served the country's national interests. From the mid-1920s, Beard was fully persuaded that the theory that the Allies (Russia, France and England) had been pure and noble in their

---

[290] Murray N. Rothbard, "Marxism and Charles Beard," in *Murray N. Rothbard, Strictly Confidential: The Private Volker Fund Memos of Murray N Rothbard*, ed. by David Gordon (Auburn, AL: Ludwig von Mises Institute, 2010) 69-74. Some of the following passages are based on information contained in this article.

intervention against the so-called villains (German and Austria) could not be sustained amid mounting evidence in the post-war period.[291]

Military clashes were, for Beard, the greatest catastrophe that could ever befall mankind, and imperialist conquests needed to be avoided at all costs. Beard's ideological position can be easily explained. For Beard, the basic prerequisite for an optimal economic system was a comprehensive state regulation of the economy; this was the only way to correct the numerous problems of a free market economy. He advocated an uncompromising introduction of State Monopoly Capitalism (Corporatism)[292] and emphasized that a comprehensive peace policy was a necessity for the progress of civilization.[293] He noted correctly that the Republican administrations of the 1920s had frequently intervened abroad despite claiming to practice a policy of isolation.[294] He showed that Franklin D. Roosevelt's call to increase military spending only made sense if the government had intended to take part in the next European war. Franklin D. Roosevelt's decisions, often made in secret, were what drove Beard to become a leading advocate of American neutrality. He believed that the country would have been spared conflict completely had Roosevelt genuinely pursued a foreign policy guided by the principle of non-intervention in other nations' affairs. Beard largely dedicated the final years of his life to showing that Roosevelt had deliberately strived for war, and that he had tried to maneuver the United States into the war since the vast majority of Americans were not in favor of their country's participation. For his militant strategy to succeed, the president had needed to ensure that the first shot was fired by Japan.[295]

Beard's concerns about the future course of American foreign policy motivated him to join forces with leading representatives of the "Old Right,"[296] a branch of American Conservatism. He presented and explained their political cause – a principled rejection of the New Deal – to his readers. This political reorientation was the decisive factor in the ideological reversion that makes his late works so interesting and important. Like many other Americans, Beard was dissatisfied with Franklin D. Roosevelt's shift to an aggressive foreign policy after the second phase of the New Deal in 1937

---

[291] Bernard C. Borning, *The Political and Social Thought of Charles A. Beard* (Seattle, WA: University of Washington Press, 1962) 106-112.

[292] Charles Austin Beard & George H. E. Smith, *The Open Door at Home: A trial Philosophy of national Interest* (New York City, NY: The Macmillan Company, 1934); Charles A. Beard, *The Idea of National Interest* (New York City, NY: Macmillan, 1934); https://archive.org/details/ideaofnationalin0000bear/page/n7

[293] Charles A. Beard, *Giddy Minds and Foreign Quarrels* (New York City, NY: The Macmillan Company, 1939); https://archive.org/details/giddymindsforeig00bear/page/n5

[294] Ibid., 26; https://archive.org/details/giddymindsforeig00bear/page/26

[295] Charles A. Beard, *President Roosevelt and the Coming of the War 1941* (New Haven, CT: Yale University Press, 1948) 517-569.

[296] Murray N. Rothbard, *The Betrayal of the American Right* (Auburn, AL: The Ludwig von Mises Institute, 2007); https://cdn.mises.org/The Betrayal of the American Right_2.pdf

plainly demonstrated the inadequacy of Corporatism to maintain an economic upturn caused by deficit financing. In his book *Giddy Minds and Foreign Quarrels*[297] (1939), Beard explored the beginnings of American Imperialism. In his analysis of the triggering factors, he placed particular emphasis on the economic conditions of America's foreign trade with China. Politicians referred to it euphemistically as the Open Door Policy. He concluded that the imperialist venture had generated immense costs for the whole nation, but had brought great profits to only a very number of individuals.

In *America in Midpassage,* vol. 1[298] (1939), a collaborative project with his wife Mary, Beard outlined his understanding of U.S. foreign policy and its alternatives. On the one hand was the unilateral Imperialism which Beard described somewhat confusingly as "imperial isolationism." This was President Franklin D. Roosevelt's Open Door Policy, which used its proponents to avoid unwanted alliances with other colonial powers. On the other hand was Wilson's program of "collective internationalism," an alliance of imperial powers which sought to maintain order and conduct military campaigns. The third variant, favored personally by Beard, was the school of "continental" or "American civilization," which restricted itself to defending the North American continent against all enemies while avoiding foreign conflicts.

In later years, Beard fell out of favor with progressive academics since he opposed Franklin D. Roosevelt's militant foreign policy before, during, and after the Second World War. Other scholars were either forced to give in to pressure from the government in Washington or yielded willingly to the state intelligence service's encouragement to support America's participation in the military conflict by drafting propaganda material. [299] Meanwhile, Beard largely remained an uncompromising critic of the deceitful foreign policy which the Roosevelt administration operated in order to plunge the country unnecessarily into war. Utterly powerless, he could only sit back and watch the United States become embroiled in a cutthroat military conflict. In light of America's true economic interests, the war in the Pacific could have been avoided. The propaganda claiming that free access to the Chinese sales market was of high national importance sounded plausible, but in retrospect proved to be a fallacy. The economic pressure on Japan enabled the Roosevelt administration to provoke a deliberate bombing raid on the Pacific Fleet in the port of Hawaii. The war in Asia served as a bridge for the American president and his war cabinet to intervene militarily in the European war. Beard feared that the great military conflict would result in tragic consequences

---

[297] Charles A. Beard, *Giddy Minds and Foreign Quarrels* (New York City, NY: The Macmillan Company, 1939).

[298] Charles A. Beard & Mary R. Beard, *America In Midpassagex* (New York City, NY: The Macmillan Company, 1939) vol. 1; https://archive.org/details/in.ernet.dli.2015.33972

[299] For example: 1) Military Intelligence Service; 2) Research and Analysis Branch of the Office of Strategic Services

through which not only his own country, but the entire world, would be subjected to a dictatorial future. His worst fears would be partially realized following agreements made by the Allies in Yalta and Potsdam.

The wide public acceptance of Beard's political position was suddenly reversed when he published his book *President Roosevelt and the Coming War*[300] in 1948. In this volume, he presented Franklin D. Roosevelt's declarations of neutrality in the years before America's entry into the Second World War as nothing but the lies of a president who wanted conflict. Beard's pacifist stance led him into tragic professional and personal difficulties. Their effects can still be felt in American historiography today by anyone aware of the bitter debate that took place between "court historians" and "revisionists" until the early 1960s. The historian Richard Hofstadter described Beard's subsequent loss of reputation among his colleagues as "an imposing ruin."[301] His strident opposition to the established historical interpretation of America's participation in the Second World War met with implacable hostility from the "court historians." The stakes were indeed extremely high. The entire post-war politics of the victorious powers rested on the official historiography of the outbreak and course of the Second World War, which was the only way to justify them. Anyone who questioned the official interpretation of these events could expect to be ignored at best or ostracized at worst. They were dealt an even harder blow when they were denounced as racists and Fascist sympathizers.[302] Beard came to the conclusion that America had strayed from the course of its traditional foreign policy since the beginning of the unjust, imperial war against Spain in 1898. He resolved to do everything possible to return the government to its former policy of non-intervention.[303]

The Second World War was a watershed for American Neoliberalism. Its proponents turned increasingly to an internationalist policy which they brought into accordance with their progressive standpoint. Beard, John T. Flynn, and others among the old guard grew increasingly concerned about the repercussions of participating in another world war for the country's institutions and constitutional government. Meanwhile, other neoliberals

---

[300] Charles A. Beard, *President Roosevelt and the Coming of the War, 1941* (New Haven, CT: Yale University Press, 1948).

[301] Richard Hofstadter, *The Progressive Historians: Turner, Beard, Parrington* (New York City, NY: Knopf Doubleday Publishing Group, [1968] 2012) 344; https://archive.org/details/progressivehisto0000hofs/page/344

[302] Ronald Radosh, *Prophets on the Right: Profiles of Conservative Critics of American Globalism* (New York City, NY: Simon and Schuster, 1975; New York City, NY: Free Life Editions, Inc., 1978) 58-60; s. also: Murray N. Rothbard & Jerome Tuccille, eds., *The Right Wing Individualist Tradition in America* (New York City, NY: Arno Press & The New York Times, 1972).

[303] George R. Leighton, "Beard and Foreign Policy," in Howard K. Beale, ed., *Charles A. Beard: An Appraisal*, (Lexington, KY: University of Kentucky Press, 1954) 162-164; https://archive.org/details/charlesabeardapp00beal/page/162; s. also: Ellen Nore, *Charles A. Beard: An Intellectual Biography* (Carbondale and Edwardsville, IL: Southern Illinois University Press, 1983) 184.

with a very different attitude saw the war as an opportunity to change society even more fundamentally than had been possible under the New Deal. The fears of Beard and others like him were eventually confirmed. Radical socialists, who considered themselves left-wing progressives, were sowing the seeds of an ideology that would later be known as Cultural Marxism.[304]

Before Beard became one of the administration's strongest critics, he had hoped to have at least a slight influence on the shaping of foreign policy. For a short time, it seemed as though he might actually be given the role of unofficial adviser to the president after attending a few dinners at the White House.[305] He was informed that Roosevelt had read his books *The Idea of the National Interest* and *The Open Door at Home*. However, his hopes of becoming at least an unofficial foreign policy adviser to Roosevelt were shattered during the president's first period in office. Furthermore, the administration was taking an increasingly aggressive stance against other countries while continuously building up its arsenal, especially through building warships. Beard therefore saw no alternative but to express his views publicly. Until the attack on Pearl Harbor, he pointed out repeatedly that Roosevelt's push for war stemmed from the failure of the New Deal to resolve America's economic crisis and to eliminate the social problems resulting from it. Military conflict in the Atlantic or the Pacific would, at least for a while, distract public attention from the internal problems. A compelling argument against the American government's jeopardization of its soldiers' lives and payment of immense sums for armaments was based on the fact that the Allied Forces, especially Great Britain, France, and the Soviet Union, had been the greatest imperial powers in the past. Germany or Japan would be no match for them, despite their own imperialist ambitions. It would be nonsensical to save other countries' colossal and declining empires. Such actions would contradict America's anti-imperialist tradition. Beard believed that the best service America could offer Europe was to stay out of the conflict. The United States had the resources to rebuild an utterly broken world once the war was over.[306]

Charles Beard was fully aware that his country's government had abandoned its traditional course in dealing with other nations half a century ago. Its march in the opposite direction had begun with its war with Spain and intervention in the First World War. Beard referred to his recommended foreign policy as "Continental Americanism." In his book *A Foreign Policy for America*[307], published in 1940, he explained his plan in detail. Continental Americanism was based on the traditional principle of non-intervention in

---

[304] Nore, *Charles A. Beard*, 182-183.

[305] Thomas C. Kennedy, *Charles A. Beard and American Foreign Policy* (Gainesville, FL: The University Press of Florida, 1975) 73; https://archive.org/details/charlesabeardame0000kenn/page/72

[306] Nore, *Charles A. Beard*, 185.

[307] Charles A. Beard, *A Foreign Policy for America* (New York City, NY: Alfred A. Knopf, 1940).

the wars of other nations. A further argument was built on the fact that America's geographical position is relatively isolated, thus largely precluding the danger of coming into conflict with other nations. The author took other matters into consideration, such as the necessity of maintaining international trade. Beard strongly recommended that America attend only to its own interests and pursue these alone in its foreign policy. Continental Americanism had been tried and tested over a century and was essentially the foreign policy promoted and practiced by the Founding Fathers.[308] To counter the criticism that his proposal was nothing more than Isolationism, Beard referred to George Washington and Thomas Jefferson's warning that the country needed to stay out of complex alliances. The Founding Fathers had not advocated a policy of Isolationism[309]; on the contrary, they had encouraged trade, cultural exchange, and relations with other countries and peoples.[310] In place of the derogatory term "Isolationism," Beard used the word "Non-Interventionism" in the internal affairs of other countries.[311]

In 1948, Beard published a book about Roosevelt's role in America's entry into the war. The historian's central thesis has since been confirmed many times: the Roosevelt administration, despite repeated public assurances that it was seeking to maintain peace and neutrality, subtly and secretly operated a campaign which made America's participation in the war imperative. Even Beard's accusation that Roosevelt had deliberately provoked Japan to fire the first shot at America had subsequently been proved true. One of the most significant results of the Allied victory was the rise of an American Empire that can be felt in every corner of the world. America has since been drawn into numerous wars caused by intranational power struggles, as well as by ethnic, border, and trade disputes. America's national security has never been at risk. Beard described such politics as a "perpetual war for perpetual peace."[312]

The effects of the war on American society were dramatic in every respect.[313] Restrictions to civil liberty became very evident to the public. Less visible were the immense burdens of the global empire which were imposed on taxpayers. However, these consequences were insignificant in comparison with the burdens laid on the defeated nations. The terms of surrender forced on Germany and Japan by the victorious Allies were not humane. People in

---

[308] Ibid., 12.

[309] Ibid., 23.

[310] Ibid., 34-35.

[311] Ibid.

[312] Harry Elmer Barnes, ed., *Perpetual War for Perpetual Peace: A Critical Examination of the Foreign Policy of Franklin Delano Roosevelt and its Aftermath* (Caxton Printers, Ltd., 1953; New York City, NY: Greenwood Press, Publishers, 1969) viii; https://archive.org/details/PerpetualWarForPerpetualPeace1953/page/n7

[313] Charles A. Beard & Mary R. Beard, *A Basic History of the United States* (Philadelphia, PA: The New Home Library, The Blakiston Company, 1944) 472-473; https://archive.org/details/in.ernet.dli.2015.169214/page/n487

the devastated cities of the Axis Powers could not expect to be treated civilly by the occupation troops. In the early post-war years, the Allies carried out numerous brutal atrocities against the defenseless German civilians and prisoners of war.[314] During the firebombing of Hamburg and Dresden in the final weeks and months of the war, awful crimes were already committed against countless women, children, and senior citizens. Before Dresden went up in flames in a mass dropping of detonation and incendiary bombs, the city had become overcrowded with refugees from the East.[315]

The Soviet Union profited most from Roosevelt's intervention in the war. The Communist dictator took advantage of Franklin D. Roosevelt's willing submission more than anyone else. The Allies carried out Stalin's territorial and political demands meticulously and without objection. Because Roosevelt pursued only one overriding goal, namely Germany's unconditional surrender, a power vacuum was created in central Europe which was filled immediately by the Stalinist Bolsheviks. The Morgenthau Plan is a sufficient example. The fact that War Minister Henry Stimson (ΦBK, Skull & Bones) partially prevented the worst of the Morgenthau Plan's deindustrialization of Germany just before it was carried out is unimportant. Enough books have since detailed Soviet agents' and Communist sympathizers' infiltration of the highest circles of the American government to argue who influenced Roosevelt when making his devastating decisions on the fate of the defeated enemies. For the countries of Eastern Europe and for the Soviet occupation zone in Central Germany, the Russian military's violent overthrow of Fascism and subsequent "liberation" proved in no way to be an advantage.[316] Although America celebrated as victor, it was soon brought back to harsh reality. The United States suddenly faced an enemy more powerful and more dangerous than the recently defeated Axis Powers. For those living behind the Iron Curtain, the following decades brought terrible hardship and deprivation as socialist collectives turned once thriving societies into "workers' paradises."[317] The Bolshevik leaders relied on the secret police to keep the population in check through harsh methods of suppression.[318]

---

[314] James Bacque, *Other Losses: An Investigation into the Mass Deaths of German Prisoners at the Hands of the French and Americans After World War II* (Toronto, Canada: Stoddard Publishing Co. Limited, 1989); s. also: James Bacque, *Crimes and Mercies: The Fate of German Civilians Under Allied Occupation 1944-1950* (Toronto, Canada: Little, Brown and Company [Canada] Limited, 1997); Ralph Franklin Keeling, *Gruesome Harvest: The Allies' Postwar: War Against the German People* (Chicago, IL: Institute of American Economics, 1947); https://archive.org/details/GruesomeHarvestTheAlliedAttemptToExterminateGermanyAfter1945

[315] Frederick J. P. Veale, *Advance to Barbarism: How the Reversion to Barbarism in Warfare and War-Trials Menaces Our Future* (Appleton, WI: C. C. Nelson Publishing Company, 1953); https://archive.org/details/VealeFJPAdvanceToBarbarism_201904

[316] Beard, *President Roosevelt and the Coming of the War, 1941*, 576-577.

[317] Ibid., 577.

[318] Stepháne Courtois et al., *The Black Book of Communism: Crimes, Terror, Repression*, trans.. by Jonathan Murphy & Mark Kramer (Cambridge, MA: Harvard University Press, 1999); https://archive.org/details/THEBLACKBOOKOFCOMMUNISM_201802/page/n2

America's enemy in the Pacific also suffered a terrible fate when firebombs reduced Tokyo to rubble and ashes, and when Hiroshima and Nagasaki were destroyed by nuclear bombs. Over the following years, Communism spread to an almost unimaginable extent throughout large areas of Asia and Europe – a development which was paradoxically welcomed and encouraged by American government circles and think tanks such as the Institute of Pacific Relations. The destruction of Japan meant that the Chinese Red Army could obtain urgently needed armaments from the Soviet Union during the civil war. Eight days before Japan's defeat, Stalin had declared war on the Far Eastern country and had taken away a huge number of armaments from the Japanese. A successful outcome to the Marxist revolution of China was thus only a matter of time.[319]

Although Beard's analysis of Roosevelt's foreign policy and predictions of post-war developments proved to be accurate[320], his advice on how to deal with the American economic crisis often missed the mark. His suggestions for remedying the financial misery were occasionally more radical and draconian than Roosevelt's. From time to time, he suggested that the economic crisis should be solved through a state-led planned economy and forced collectivization.[321] In the decades before the Great Depression, the economy was strictly regulated by the state. By the 1930s, the free market economy that had partially existed in America during the nineteenth century was no longer in place. State economic control through various regulations and taxation had escalated since America's entry into the First World War in 1917, especially within the critical area of the banking system. Progressive legislation rapidly destroyed possibilities for many entrepreneurs to establish their own businesses and run them according to best business practices, since the government indirectly controlled production processes and the distribution of consumer goods. The government introduced income tax and created numerous federal and state regulatory offices. Large banks encouraged and supported the establishment of a central banking system controlled in part by the government, since this eliminated the risk of a bank run. These banks could thus work undisturbed to create loans and banknotes "out of nothing," without fearing retaliation from those injured by the inflation that they initiated.

In the early 1920s, the central bank (Federal Reserve System) succeeded in gaining complete control of the money supply in circulation in America. This financial policy triggered an economic boom that lasted until the end of

---

[319] Radosh, *Prophets on the Right*, 62-63.

[320] S. also: Doris Kearns Goodwin, *No Ordinary Time: Franklin and Eleanor Roosevelt: The Home Front in World War II* (New York City, NY: Simon and Schuster, 1994; New York City, NY: First Touchstone Edition, 1995); https://archive.org/details/noordinarytimef000good/page/n5; Tom Brokaw, *The Greatest Generation* (New York City, NY: Random House, 1998); Tom Brokaw, *The Greatest Generation Speaks: Letters and Reflections* (New York City, NY: Random House, 1999).

[321] Beard & Beard, *The Open Door at Home*, 305-320.

the decade. The Fed had embarked on a perilous course that led to an enormous expansion of bank loans[322], which eventually made the collapse of the Wall Street stock market in October 1929 inevitable. The resulting financial panic spread to other branches of industry and caused the Great Depression. It can be shown that the recovery measures taken by Presidents Hoover and Roosevelt put a still greater strain on the economy and guaranteed its further decline.

Charles A. Beard, America First, and informal groups of anti-imperialists who opposed the United States' entry into the war failed to identify the underlying causes of the economic crisis. They were therefore unable to propose any workable measures to remedy the economic plight. Some historians see this as the primary reason why the social and war policies of the New Deal were able to persist despite their utter failure to resolve the economic depression. The consequence was participation in the Second World War. The free market economy favors a foreign policy that is limited to the defense of its own country alone. A political coalition seeking to live in peaceful coexistence with all nations and a minimalist state with few powers would likely have prevented the economic misery of the New Deal and the social and political upheaval of the era – including the Second World War.

14.2 Social Democratic character of Progressivism

(Changing understandings of Progressivism)
Progressivism was the prevalent ideology from around 1896 to 1921 and was interpreted in several different ways.[323] In the period following the Progressive Era, it was viewed in a positive light – as a protest movement that had opposed the excesses of Laissez Faire Capitalism. The state had wanted to create better living conditions for all people by submitting civil society to a fundamental social reform. Progressivism was thus seen as a movement for Social Democracy. However, as involvement in war demanded great sacrifices from the public and made the government dependent on industry, Progressivism met with increasing rejection.

After the Second World War, historians adopted a more critical attitude toward Progressivism.[324] They saw that politicians of the Progressive Era had

[322] G. Edward Griffin, *The Creature from Jekyll Island: A Second Look at the Federal Reserve*, 3 ed. (Westlake Village, CA: American Media, 1998); https://archive.org/details/TheCreatureFromJekyllIslandGriffin/page/n3

[323] Harold U. Faulkner, *The Quest for Social Justice, 1898-1914* (New York City, NY: The Macmillan Company, 1931); https://archive.org/details/in.ernet.dli.2015.544323; Charles A. & Mary R. Beard, *The Rise of American Civilization*, 2 vols. (New York City, NY: The Macmillan Company, [1927] 1930); https://archive.org/details/riseofamericanci0000bear; John D. Hicks, *The Populist Revolt: A History of the Farmers' Alliance and the People's Party* (Minneapolis, MN: University of Minnesota Press, 1931). https://archive.org/details/populistrevolthi00hick

[324] William E. Leuchtenburg, *The Perils of Prosperity: 1914-1932* (Chicago, IL: University of Chicago Press, 1958); https://archive.org/details/perilsofprosperi00leuc_0

been concerned primarily with power and status; they had stood up for the underprivileged only in order to win their votes. Social grievances had been redressed only superficially. Contrary to America's liberal tradition, progressives had taken part in the First World War for the sake of preserving Democracy and avoiding a further war. However, the fate of the war victims led to resentment of Progressivism. Rival camps began to form, and the movement began to decline.[325]

The phenomenal success enjoyed by progressives at the turn of the century contributed years later to the downfall of their movement. Having achieved their political goals, formerly influential supporters of Progressivism went into retirement like satisfied actors.[326]

Despite the general distrust of all ideologies in the 1950s, historians researched the intellectual origins of Progressivism.[327] They saw both Liberals and Conservatives as followers of the Enlightenment philosopher John Locke, concluding therefore that Progressivism had not been a revolutionary movement. They argued that progressive achievements had been minimal because the almost identical programs of the Liberal and Conservative Parties had posed no threat to the capitalist system. Historians who emphasize the unity and conformity of America's past are referred to as the Consensus School. During the Cold War period, they believed that politicians from both parties could find a common foreign policy. Progressivism had enabled Americans to increase their prosperity.

---

[325] David Burner, *The Politics of Provincialism: The Democratic Party in Transition, 1918-1932* (New York City, NY: Norton, [1968] 1975; Cambridge, MA: Harvard University Press, 1986); https://archive.org/details/politicsofprovin0000burn

[326] Richard Hofstadter, *The Age of Reform: From Bryan to F.D.R.* (New York City, NY: Vintage Books, 1955); https://archive.org/details/ageofreformfrom000hofs; Richard Hofstadter, *Anti-Intellectualism in American Life* (New York City, NY: Random House, 1963); https://archive.org/details/antiintellectual000187mbp/page/n7; Richard Hofstadter, *The Progressive Historians: Turner, Beard, and Parrington* (New York City, NY: Alfred A. Knopf, 1968); https://archive.org/details/progressivehisto0000hofs/page/n5; George Mowry, *The Era of Theodore Roosevelt and the Birth of Modern America, 1900-1912* (New York City, NY: Harper & Brothers, 1958); George Mowry, *Theodore Roosevelt and the Progressive Movement* (New York City, NY: Hill and Wang, [1946] 1960). https://archive.org/details/in.ernet.dli.2015.87002/page/n5

[327] Arthur S. Link, *Woodrow Wilson and the Progressive Era, 1910-1917* (New York City, NY: Harper & Brothers, 1954); https://archive.org/details/woodrowwilsonand007665mbp; C. Vann Woodward, *Origins of the New South, 1877-1913* (Baton Rouge LA: Louisiana State University Press, 1951); https://archive.org/details/originsofnewsout00wood; Russell B. Nye, *Midwestern Progressive Politics: A History of Its Origins and Development, 1870-1958* (East Lansing, MI: Michigan State University Press, 1959); https://archive.org/details/midwestern-progre0000nyer/page/n5; Arthur Mann, *Yankee Reformers in the Urban Age: Social Reform in Boston, 1880-1900* (New York City, NY: Harper & Row, [1954] 1966); https://archive.org/details/yankeereformersi0000mann/page/n5; Daniel Bell, *The End of Ideology: On the Exhaustion of Political Ideas in the Fifties*, with "The Resumption of History in the New Century" (New York City, NY: Collier Books, 1961; Cambridge, MA: Harvard University Press, 2001); https://archive.org/details/endofideologyone00bell_0/page/n5; Daniel J. Boorstin, *The Genius of American Politics* (Chicago, IL: University of Chicago Press, 1953); https://archive.org/details/americangovernme00bend/page/n5

Some historians viewed the Progressive Era as an intellectual revolution which had aimed to destroy the political status quo of the Gilded Age.[328] They believed that the decline of Progressivism in the 1920s was not the fault of external circumstances such as war and prosperity, but rather of the ideology's inherent contradictions. It had failed because of false prerequisites (advocacy of racism and anti-Semitism, for example) and unrealistic goals (the establishment of a utopian social order).[329]

14.3 Consolidation of State Monopoly Capitalism

(The economy harnesses the state for its interests)
In the late 1950s, Progressivism was reinterpreted in a way that viewed institutions and economic corporations in a positive light. The historian Samuel P. Hays notes that in the period from 1885 to 1914, the most predominant process in America[330] was neither exploitation, nor corruption, nor reform, but rather industrialization[331] – a process that affected all Americans. There was no ideological difference between rich and poor, for all were striving for wealth. Businessmen had been the first to learn how to survive in an industrial society because of their organization and consolidation. Working conditions had improved through better-balanced legislation.[332] The significance of the Progressive Era thus lay in its provision for the particular challenges of industrialization at that time. The historian Robert H. Wiebe observed that a new middle class had formed which defined behavioral norms for an industrial society[333]: all nineteenth-century values that had brought meaning and order had ceased to be valid. Individualism and Protestant ethics were replaced by predictability and efficiency. Economic processes were to be planned by a centralized government formed of experts

---

[328] Morton G. White, *Origin of Dewey's Instrumentalism* (New York City, NY: Columbia University Press, 1943); https://archive.org/details/in.ernet.dli.2015.504975/page/n5; Morton G. White, *Social Thought in America: The Revolt Against Formalism* (Boston, MA: Beacon Press, 1947; New York City, NY: Oxford University Press, 1985); https://archive.org/details/in.ernet.dli.2015.187202/page/n2; Eric Frederick Goldman, *Rendezvous with Destiny: A History of Modern American Reform* (New York City, NY: Knopf, 1952; Chicago, IL: Ivan R. Dee, 2001); https://archive.org/details/rendezvouswithde00goldrich; Daniel Aaron, *Men of Good Hope: A Story of American Progressives* (New York City, NY: Oxford University Press, 1951); https://archive.org/details/menofgoodhopeast009064mbp/page/n7

[329] Henry F. May, *The End of American Innocence: A Study of the First Years of Our Own Time, 1912-1917* (New York City, NY: Alfred A. Knopf, 1959); Chicago, IL: Quadrangle Books, inc., 1964); https://archive.org/details/endofamericaninn027203mbp/page/n7

[330] Samuel P. Hays, *The Response to Industrialism, 1885-1914* (Chicago, IL: University of Chicago Press, [1957] 1995); https://archive.org/details/responsetoindust00hays_0

[331] Ibid., 86-88; https://archive.org/details/responsetoindust00hays_0/page/86.

[332] Ibid., 87-90. https://archive.org/details/responsetoindust00hays_0/page/86

[333] Robert H. Wiebe, *The Search for Order, 1877-1920* (New York City, NY: Hill and Wang, 1967); https://archive.org/details/searchfororder1800wieb

(technocrats). Prerequisite to this government was a well-ordered, efficient, fair state authority. Progressivism originated with new technocratic ideas within the social sciences, and according to Wiebe, businessmen had played a leading role in the movement.[334] The fact that this interpretation of the Progressive Era differs so fundamentally from the "liberal" and "progressive" interpretations makes it clear that the older attempts at explanation were defective. According to Hays, progressive reformers were not politicians anxious for humanitarian social change, but self-confident, upper-class businesspeople. They bribed politicians, civil servants, and judges in order to gain greater social influence[335] and eliminate competition. The political system was corrupt from the inside out.[336] In the eyes of the convinced socialist John Chamberlain, Progressivism was a complete failure, since it never produced any real reforms and paved the way for American Fascism.[337]

During the Gilded Age, American politics was largely democratic. During the Progressive Era, in contrast, much of the population had to cede political power to technocratic experts who had taken control of government affairs and pretended to act in the public interest. The importance of Gabriel M. Kolko's historical revision cannot be rated too highly. His most important discovery regarding the course of American history can be summarized as follows: since 1789, the American Court of Justice and authorities within the federal government had seen it as their particular duty to promote the interests of industry in order to guarantee steady economic growth. Toward the end of the nineteenth century, key individuals in economics and politics had begun to see themselves as a type of central planning committee for American Capitalism. These efforts culminated in the economic and social reforms of the first Rooseveltian New Deal of 1933 to 1938. Most Americans adapted more or less willingly to the new, ever-changing economic system. The American War of Secession had shown that the government would not hold back from using force to achieve its goals of economic exploitation. According to Kolko, the conservative business program was the result of deliberate efforts to maintain the power and profits of large-scale industry. In this context, "conservative program" has a negative meaning: the preservation of the economic and political power gained by industrialists for the financial exploitation of the population.[338]

---

[334] Robert H. Wiebe, *Businessmen and Reform: A Study of the Progressive Movement* (Cambridge, MA: Harvard University Press, 1962); https://archive.org/details/businessmenrefor00wieb

[335] Stanley Buder, *Pullman: An Experiment in Industrial Order and Community Planning, 1880-1930* (New York City, NY: Oxford University Press, 1967).

[336] Samuel P. Hays, "The Politics of Reform in Municipal Government in the Progressive Era," *Pacific Northwest Quarterly*, LV (1964), 157-169.

[337] Joseph Chamberlain, *Farewell to Reform: The rise, life and decay of the progressive mind in America* (New York City, NY: The John Day Company, 1932; Chicago, IL: Quadrangle Books, inc., 1965); https://archive.org/details/farewelltoreform0000cham/page/n5

[338] David Kennedy, ed., *Progressivism: The Critical Issues* (Boston, MA: Little, Brown, 1971)

The historian William Appleman Williams (1921-1990) divided American history into three periods: 1) Mercantilism from 1740 to 1828 (the encouragement of foreign trade and industry in order to increase financial strength and government power), 2) Laissez-Nous Faire from 1819 to 1896 (free market economy), and 3) Corporatism from 1882 to the present day (the participation of social groups in political decision-making processes). In the early twentieth century, the industrial upper class tried to consolidate their economic dominance by forming corporations, doing so by bringing the government into play. Kolko notes that the men directing government railway regulations were neither populist farmers nor wage earners, but rather the directors of the railway companies themselves.[339] American political life in the nineteenth century was shaped by the fact that the initiative to impose state economic regulations was led by industry. Kolko argues that all capitalist systems that ever existed relied on generous funding from the state.[340] Politicians were all too willing to give large amounts of public resources to railroad companies in return for funding their election campaigns. The initial financing of the inland transport system clearly shows that the railroad companies were essentially either extreme overinvestments or misinvestments. Kolko also states that the new railroad industry caused both economic and social damage by imposing artificial economic conditions on a new nationwide market, with no concern for how its profit-oriented actions would affect local business. The railroad companies had encouraged the rise of corporations in other key industries; logically, therefore, the negative effects of State Monopoly Capitalism (Corporatism) also became apparent in other economic sectors. As indicated by the economist Michael Perelman, the railroad industry seemed immune to market forces.

The preferred method of implementing socialist concerns was political intervention in economic processes.[341] Large corporations had hoped that this would improve their own market dominance, or at least maintain the level of market penetration already achieved. The ultimate goal was to "stabilize" and "rationalize" the economy as a whole – a blunt way of expressing the need for a thorough elimination of economic competition. Industrialists wanted to monopolize every important branch of industry. Corresponding legislature was the only effective means of successfully controlling market forces and using them to full advantage. Kolko posed the daring but entirely reasonable theory that the reforms of the Progressive Era had been governed

1-5; https://archive.org/details/twentiethcentury00bern/page/n11

[339] Gabriel Morris Kolko, *Railroads and Regulation, 1877-1916* (Princeton, NJ: Princeton University Press, 1965; Westport, CT: Greenwood Press, 1976); https://archive.org/details/railroadsregulat0000unse/page/n5

[340] Joseph R. Stromberg, "Gabriel Kolko Revisited, Part 1: Kolko at Home," in *Future of Freedom* (Fairfax, VA: Future of Freedom, September 1, 2013) passim.

[341] Gabriel Morris Kolko, *The Triumph of Conservatism: A Reinterpretation of American History, 1900-1916* (New York City, NY: Quadrangle Books, 1963; New York City, NY: Free Press, 1977); https://archive.org/details/KolkoGabrielTheTriumphOfConservatism

by a conservative consensus. The primary concern of most Progressive Era politicians, regardless of which party they belonged to, had always been the profitable interests of industry and banking. The captains of industry had demanded and received a right of veto over the resolutions of the regulatory authorities. The higher prices of the merged companies' products were therefore no longer at risk of being undercut by competitors who could have sold their own products more cheaply through efficient manufacture methods and other means of saving. Corporatism emerged because of powerful individuals, such as Theodore Roosevelt, who legitimized large corporations by dividing them into good and bad cartels. The monopolization of the whole banking system effected the stability and continuity in the financial system that was needed to ensure tremendous growth in private fortunes.

Very few people were aware that T. Woodrow Wilson carried out a progressive program for the East Coast elite during the First World War. The Republican President Herbert C. Hoover (1874-1964) was mistakenly believed to uphold a classical-liberal policy; however, after the stock market crash of 1929, he practiced the same socialist economic principles that Franklin D. Roosevelt (1882-1945) later advanced on a large scale in his New Deal Policy.

14.4 The dilemma of escalating Militarism

The First World War was a catastrophe unprecedented in history. The enormous loss of life and substance drove European civilization to ruin.[342] Following the end of the war, once proud officers were degraded to a meagre existence on the margins of society: the spread of Socialism had completely destroyed the value placed on heroism by the former feudal society. The only people still given due respect were the technocrats. They alone understood the complex economic processes that optimized the production and sale of consumer goods, without which modern standards of living would be inconceivable.

History shows that the management of an existing empire always carries destructive potential. Land seized through military invasion is economically exploited as quickly as possible, and its people largely lose their freedom to decide what lies in favor of their own national interests. Resistance of colonial dictates by the native population results in a sharp rise in its death toll. Maintaining and expanding an empire requires constant military intervention. In addition to the senseless slaughter of human life, the hostility also destroys financial assets both at the center of the empire and in its colonies.

When the Allies began attacking the German defense line on the French Atlantic coast during the Second World War, the Americans decreasingly

---

[342] Gabriel Morris Kolko, *The Politics of War: The World and United States Foreign Policy, 1943-1945* (New York City, NY: Pantheon Books, [1968] 1990); https://archive.org/details/politicsofwarwor00kolkrichus

focused their strategy on forcing back the Wehrmacht[343]. To their horror, the Soviets' military success became a growing threat to America's geopolitical aims. In 1941, the peace plans of the State Department in Washington consisted of the following points: 1) the concrete realization of economic goals derived almost entirely from the international vision of T. Woodrow Wilson, and 2) a flexible approach to implementing economic goals aimed at transforming the world economy from the ground up.

The real drama between the rival power blocs began in the post-war period on the Italian peninsula, where the Anglo-American occupation policy set the course for later occupations. America wanted to keep Great Britain's continental influence as small as possible, while the government in London was equally intent on undermining its counterpart in Washington. The U.S.A. finally pushed Britain aside as the latter sought to impose its colonial policy on southern Europe. The crisis that arose from this clash of former comrades-in-arms did not benefit either party in any way as the Italians deftly evaded domination by either side. It therefore seemed advisable for Britain and America to work together to suppress the Italian government's attempts to gain independence. The actions required to contain the influence of the Italian rebels were clear to both parties: the irregular left-wing partisans needed to be disarmed, and the fascist bureaucrats needed to be reinforced as bulwarks against the Communism growing in the country. Despite many assurances of mutual support, a divided Europe was already in prospect by mid-1943, long before anyone dared think about a cold war.

According to the historian Gabriel M. Kolko (1932-2014), the American diplomatic corps saw their country's comprehensive trading policy as a panacea for all economic hardship around the world.[344] Central to their considerations was the need for the American government to dominate the regulation of all trade relations. The Americans referred to their strategy euphemistically as the Open Door Policy. The pragmatic interaction between the public and private sectors in the United States, which had lasted almost a century, provided key economic actors with a tried and tested precedent that could now be extended across the globe. The U.S. State Department gave American corporations permission to take raw materials from other nations at will and to force the opening of foreign markets. This concession must be seen as the key to American world politics since the end of the Second World War. The U.S. Secretary of State Cordell Hull and his successors offered seemingly plausible excuses whenever the aims of American foreign policy were questioned, one standard answer being the spread of Democracy. With time, even the somewhat obtuse might realize that America threw all idealistic goals overboard when it needed to pursue its economic aims consistently. Kolko even said that America's power elite could face a Soviet military

---

[343] Name of the armed forces of the Third Reich (1934-1945), founded in 1921 as Reichswehr

[344] Joseph R. Stromberg, "Gabriel Kolko Revisited, Part 2: Kolko Abroad," in *Future of Freedom* (Fairfax, VA: Future of Freedom, October 1, 2013) passim.

occupation of Eastern Europe with complete indifference as long as the fulfilment of their economic goals was secure. However, America's ruthless use of military power to open up "free markets" was in principle nothing new. Every colonial power throughout history has been known for its brutal subjugation of foreign peoples. What was actually new in this policy was the vast extent of its influence and its numerous negative consequences. The fact that an America-dominated world would come to economic stagnation was of no importance to the "peace" strategists in the State Department.

Great Britain and the United States had planned the radical destruction of Germany and Japan's urban populations long before the bombings of the Second World War were actually carried out. The war had brutalized America's military leaders to such an extent that they experienced no dilemma in burning countless men, women, and children with atom bombs in the spring of 1945. Violation of traditional legal and ethical standards through the arbitrary slaughter of civilians was one of the Allied Forces' distinguishing features.[345] During the Korean War (1950-1952), U.S. soldiers engaged still more consistently in barbaric warfare. The version of Internationalism that corresponded with America's ideas was the implementation of their own plan for world domination.

The founding fathers of the United Nations (henceforth "UN"), established in San Francisco in 1945, were aware of this fact and quietly accepted it. The 1944 Bretton Woods Agreement for global currency reform was designed to effect an enormous increase in global trade. The mass granting of loans to foreign debtors by private financial institutions and state offices in America served to subsidize the export of producer and consumer goods. In the post-war period, leading politicians in Washington spoke with an anti-colonialist rhetoric in public. When it emerged that they had agreed to the worldwide exploitation of raw materials, their reputation went largely unscathed. The leaders of the UN gave the idealistic impression that the international organization existed for the preservation of world peace and the good of all mankind. The declared goal of the New International Economic Order was the fair distribution of vital resources. However, reality was altogether otherwise. American corporations gained the lion's share of the raw materials available – peaceably where possible, and using destructive armed force where necessary. The disastrous result of all American interventions in Europe was the outbreak of the Cold War, initiated to keep defeated enemies (Germany and Japan) in check and to intimidate certain victors (Russia and Great Britain). All this was carried out under the pretext of seeking to contain the spread of Communism throughout the world.[346]

---

[345] Gabriel Morris Kolko, "Mechanistic Destruction: American Foreign Policy at Point Zero," *Antiwar.com* (August 10, 2007); https://original.antiwar.com/gabriel-kolko/2007/08/10/mechanistic-destruction-american-foreign-policy-at-point-zero/

[346] Gabriel M. & Joyce Kolko, *The Limits of Power: The world and United States foreign policy, 1945-1954* (New York City, NY: Harper & Row, 1972); https://archive.org/details/limitsofpowerwor00kolk/page/n7

Because of their positions in the upper class, the highest decision makers in American foreign policy were closely connected with the managers and directors of dominant industrial conglomerates. This engendered a political relationship that utilized the political power structure to promote the economic interests of American capitalists both at home and abroad. Kolko showed that British Mercantilism, advocated originally by Alexander Hamilton, was used to justify the worldwide spread and consolidation of American State Monopoly Capitalism (Corporatism).[347] This was the most significant result of the neoliberal economic reform in America. Robert McNamara's career as a technocratic Secretary of Defense proved that international banks had entrusted the task of global domination to the military establishment of the Johnson administration (1963-1969). The inability to realize this vision of global supremacy at the time was not due to lack of purpose, but rather to insufficient means of implementation.

According to Kolko, the U.S.A. needed to import enough raw materials throughout the twentieth century to maintain the industrial processes by which its commercial goods were produced. This explains why the United States intervened militarily in secondary and even tertiary markets, for example in Southeast Asia, during the time of its Open Door Policy – at great cost and with great loss of life. Progressivism was concerned only with steering the existing social order in the direction of Totalitarianism so that the principles of State Monopoly Capitalism (Corporatism) could be implemented consistently.[348] Decades later, the totalitarian approach of the ruling elite was evinced in the New Deal legislation that regulated the banking system: by taking political action, major banks were able to impose their (cartelizing) ideas on the national system at large.[349]

The U.S.A. continually extols the advantages of the free market, yet criticizes it when other industrialized nations sell their export goods for a greater profit. Since the key positions in the U.S. government, particularly in the State Department, are occupied by former heads of industry, banking, and leading law firms, it was only logical that politics would be subordinated to commercial interests. The upper class, which used politics in pure self-interest, acted in complete disregard of the affairs of the people they governed.

The Vietnam War (1955-1975) is a prime example of the tragic side of America's imperial expansion in the twentieth century.[350] The military intervention in Southeast Asia began on November 26, 1941, when Franklin D.

---

[347] Gabriel Morris Kolko, *The Roots of American Foreign Policy: An Analysis of Power and Purpose* (Boston, MA: Beacon Press, 1969); https://archive.org/details/rootsofamericanf-0000kolk_s3v2/page/n5

[348] Gabriel Morris Kolko, *Main Currents in Modern American History* (New York City, NY: Harper & Row, [1976] 1984); https://archive.org/details/maincurrentsinmo0000kolk/page/n3

[349] Ibid., 21.

[350] Gabriel Morris Kolko, *Anatomy of a War: Vietnam, the United States, and the Modern Historical Experience* (New York City, NY: Pantheon Books, 1985); https://archive.org/details/anatomyofwarviet00kolk

Roosevelt issued a humiliating ultimatum to the Japanese government demanding the complete withdrawal of their military forces from China and Indochina. The military goal pursued by the American president in the Pacific warzone was to drive the Japanese out of their Asian colonies and place the latter beneath his own control. The American army relied on its enormous firepower since this was the only type of warfare that the U.S. generals knew how to conduct. For this the people of Vietnam paid an enormous price. Through studying the perpetual wars of this era – the bloodiest in the history of mankind – Kolko concluded that leading politicians had unscrupulously sent millions of soldiers and civilians to their graves purely to protect their elevated status in society. Even at a time when the American government was relatively powerless to enforce its orders, it did not refrain from taking strong measures to bring American social conditions into conformity with progressive ideals. The guiding principle of this questionable "social engineering" was to do all possible to comply with the wealthy upper class.

It is easy to understand why industrialists went to such great lengths to maintain a close relationship with the state. In order to conceal their commitment to a total state, they had to act in such a way as to give the impression that they desired the very opposite. They accordingly encouraged a wide dissemination of the ideas of free market economy. Businessmen were encouraged to market themselves as enthusiastic proponents of a decentralized economy. The populist style of Margaret Thatcher and Ronald Reagan whitewashed the authoritative core of their politics without entirely concealing it. An intensely market-oriented rhetoric went hand in hand with a consistent strengthening of the state apparatus. During the 1980s, this policy was adhered to by many conservatives who did actually uphold the true ideals of minimalist government and were intent on a peace policy; however, this turned out to be extremely counterproductive. The implementation of classical-liberal economic principles in the wake of the "conservative revolution" thus never left the starting blocks, although this largely went unnoticed by the general population. Kolko's account of the progressive reforms carried out by every American president from the beginning of the twentieth century to the start of the Cold War, and continued thereafter in a much more concentrated form, repeatedly proved to be accurate in the period that followed.[351]

14.5 Tragic consequences of American diplomacy

The esteemed American historian William Appleman Williams (1921-1990) established the "Wisconsin School" of Revisionism at the University of

---

[351] Gabriel Morris Kolko, *Century of War: Politics, conflicts, and society since 1914* (New York City, NY: New Press; distributed by W.W. Norton, 1994); https://archive.org/details/centuryofwarpoli00kolk

Wisconsin between 1957 and 1968.[352] This school was characterized by meticulous analysis of primary sources and historical facts in order to re-examine and reinterpret conventional historiography. Arthur Meier Schlesinger, Jr. (1917-2007), an advocate of left-wing Neoliberalism during the Cold War, judged Williams unjustly as being sympathetic to totalitarian Communism.[353] The first edition of Williams's most influential book, *The Tragedy of American Diplomacy*[354] (published in 1959), articulated a clear and caustic polemic against America's imperial policy. Militarists in Washington, D.C., were shocked by his theories. They not only publicly expressed their disparaging views, but also underlined them with political harassment. Williams was forced to spend considerable amounts of time and money to defend himself against the false accusations of the government. As the tragedy of the Vietnam War became ever more apparent and questions were raised regarding the significance, justification, and implementation of the military conflict, Williams's ideas found an audience among the general public.[355]

Williams's academic work was quite conservative and patriotic in its ideological tone.[356] The New Left had left him deeply disappointed.[357] With respect to domestic policy, Williams divided U.S. history into successive periods of Mercantilism (1740-1828), Laissez-Nous Faire (an inconsistent form of free market economy) (1819-1896), and Corporate (Political) Capitalism (1882 onward). The third period was characterized by an alliance between the state and the business world which sought to consolidate existing relations between wealth and power. Meanwhile, the public's desire for relative financial security was only partially satisfied in order to keep them quiet. The primary goal was to protect the "stability" of the system by drastically reducing what was seen as chaotic and unprofitable competition.

---

[352] Joseph R. Stromberg, "William Appleman Williams: Premier New Left Revisionist," in *Old Cause* (Sunnyvale, CA: Antiwar.com, November 16, 1999) passim.

[353] Samuel Edward Konkin, "William Appleman Williams (1921-1990): Sire of Neo-Isolationism," *New Isolationist*, vol. 1, no. 1 (October, 1990) 6.

[354] William Appleman Williams, *The Tragedy of American Diplomacy* (Cleveland: World Publishing Company, 1959; New York City, NY: W.W. Norton & Company, 2009); https://archive.org/details/tragedyofameric100will/page/n3

[355] William Appleman Williams, *The Contours of American History* (New York City, NY: New Viewpoints, 1961); https://archive.org/details/contoursofameric007738mbp/page/n9; William Appleman Williams, *Shaping of American Diplomacy: Readings and Documents in American Foreign Relations, 1750-1955* (Chicago, Il: Rand McNally & Co., 1956); William Appleman Williams, *America Confronts a Revolutionary World* (New York City, NY: W. Morrow, 1976); William Appleman Williams, *Empire as a Way of Life: An essay on the causes and character of America's present predicament along with a few thoughts about an alternative* (Oxford: Oxford University Press, 1980).

[356] Williams, *The Contours of American History*, 357; https://archive.org/details/contoursofameric007738mbp/page/n367

[357] Andrew J. Bacevich, *American Empire: The Realities and Consequences of U.S. Diplomacy* (Cambridge, MA: Harvard University Press, 2002) 24; https://archive.org/details/americanempire00andr/page/24

Williams's particular focus was on United States foreign policy. Early in his career, he wrote a highly acclaimed essay entitled "The Frontier Thesis and American Foreign Policy." In this essay, he sought to explain how Americans' understanding of the role of the frontier in U.S. history had influenced foreign policy to the extent that elite politicians and industrial magnates felt the need to establish an empire overseas. This view was based on the famous "frontier thesis" of the historian Frederick Jackson Turner.[358] The existence of a frontier had afforded Americans a measure of comfortable prosperity and individual freedom for two centuries. However, when this lost its significance in the 1890s, it became necessary to explore new possibilities in order to avoid damage to the national economy. Williams began his account of America's political transformation from continental republic to global empire by indicating the success of American Capitalism, evidenced by the phenomenal growth of the economy after the War of Secession. American society repeatedly found itself in a precarious situation despite the remarkable economic upswing that took place in the northern states within a relatively short space of time, not least because of the southern states' economic reprisals and the omnipresent corruption in politics and society. In the late nineteenth century, the nation modernized its industry by making use of the numerous immigrants entering the country who were willing to work hard for little money. The pay gap between the privileged elite and the tirelessly laboring masses became increasingly wide until it could no longer be overlooked. Men like John D. Rockefeller, Sr., Andrew Carnegie, and Cornelius Vanderbilt – known as captains of industry – amassed enormous fortunes, while their factory laborers slaved away for sixty hours per week, often in dangerous conditions. The plight of many families was further aggravated by the fact that the expansion of urban infrastructure could not keep pace with the rapid growth of the population. Insufficient supplies of water and electricity and an inadequate wastewater disposal system were constant problems. Slums sprang up like mushrooms in the cities.[359]

The political and socioeconomic system was configured in a way that prevented people from advancing out of poverty. The history of economic and social development in the United States proves that the pay gap between rich and poor was institutionalized. In general, the wealthy upper class has assured protection against the rapid loss of their assets, whereas the virtually penniless lower class has no hope of escaping their predicament. This fact of economic circumstances contradicts the myth of the American dream, which leads the destitute to believe that with luck and hard work they can secure a higher standard of living. Even if there are occasional exceptions to the rule, most Americans are deeper in debt today than ever before and are thus in an

---

[358] William A. Williams, "The Frontier Thesis and American Foreign Policy," *Pacific Historical Review*, vol. 24, no. 4 (November, 1955), 379-395.

[359] John Blum, et al., *The National Experience: A History of the United State*, 6th ed. (San Diego, Harcourt Brace Jovanovich, 1984) 519; https://archive.org/details/historyofuniteds-00blum/page/518

extremely precarious situation where their finances are concerned. Social conditions in the early twenty-first century may appear to be steadily changing for the better as they did throughout much of the nineteenth and twentieth centuries – if the numerous economic crises of the last two hundred years are left out of the picture.

The social tensions between the privileged minority and the working majority could no longer be ignored. The American elite became deeply concerned when the most conservative sector of society – the farmers – called for an uprising which took place as the "Populist Revolt" of the late nineteenth century. Workers striking in the industrial centers had to contend with armed government troops or hired law enforcement officers, for example at the Homestead Steel Works in 1892. The unrest among the population increased dramatically in 1893 when the country fell into a prolonged economic depression. Panic in the New York stock markets fanned the flames of a fear of possible collapse in almost every area of the national economy. According to the diagnoses of financial experts, the problem was partly due to overproduction of industrial and consumer goods, especially in the agricultural sector, and to domestic underconsumption of these products. In 1898, members of the northeastern elite believed that the only suitable response to the economic crisis was a neo-mercantilist foreign policy that was constantly on the lookout for new markets overseas. Territorial expansion could only be guaranteed if the doors of all nations were open to America's goods, culture, social and political ideals, and even armies. The export of goods of all kinds needed to be maximized so that the increase in production could be boosted still further. In this way prosperity could be restored, industrial unrest reduced, and Capitalism saved. At the same time, the "American genius" of a modern attitude and lifestyle would be exported worldwide.[360] Virtually no one seemed to perceive the paradoxical contradiction between the glorified, unrealistic self-image and the unfortunate real-life situation. Williams pointed to Franklin D. Roosevelt as the only American president of the twentieth century who was aware of the great danger of taking such a daring approach to international relations, although he himself threw caution to the winds unlike anyone before or after him. Roosevelt's successor in the White House, Harry S. Truman, pursued objectives that made the Cold War inevitable. According to Williams, America's twentieth-century foreign policy was based on the Open Door Policy first pronounced by John Hay. Hay had been Lincoln's secretary, and in later years he was appointed Secretary of State by Presidents William McKinley and Theodore Roosevelt. Williams believed that the Open Door Policy had developed from a utopian idea into an ideology.[361]

How this foreign policy could actually be put into practice was a subject of great debate in the 1890s. Imperialists proposed the opening of foreign

---

[360] Williams, *The Tragedy of American Diplomacy*, 16-45; https://archive.org/details/trage-dyofameric100will/page/16

[361] Ibid., 239; https://archive.org/details/tragedyofameric100will/page/238

markets using the necessary aggression in a "just campaign of conquest." Theodore Roosevelt, who became president in 1901 after the assassination of William McKinley, sided with the military theorist Alfred Thayer Mahan and Senator Henry Cabot Lodge (ΦBK, Porcellian Club) in adhering to the "Large Policy." Two key elements of this policy were the recruitment of a large military contingent and the building of overseas supply bases – prerequisites for the global expansion of commercial and military interests. Critics argued that this violated important principles of the U.S. Constitution. Interestingly, neither the imperialists nor the so-called anti-imperialists opposed the global venture to open and dominate foreign markets. Both sides took this aim as a given. The discussion concerned only the nature of the means employed, not the specific purpose for which they were intended. The only main difference between the two sides was that the so-called anti-imperialists wanted to achieve this without resorting to violent and costly methods, as other world powers had done before them. After finally opting for a largely "informal" empire, the United States was able to use its overwhelming economic power to force the politics and economics of poorer, weaker, and underdeveloped countries into an American mold.

America's domestic and foreign policies were tightly coordinated. At the beginning of the twentieth century, the "Open Door Notes" of the former Secretary of State John Hay pointed to the possibility that America could use its growing economic power to dominate foreign markets even without military occupation. According to Williams, this policy is the key to almost the entire course of America's foreign policy during the twentieth century. The essence and ingenuity of American Imperialism was that the United States did not occupy underdeveloped nations in order to incorporate them into its own sphere of rule, as the European powers had done, but instead exercised control indirectly and discretely. High-minded moral sermons served as cunning camouflage. The citizens of foreign countries were able to see through the American politicians' hypocrisy relatively quickly. However, the situation was different among the American population, who seemed to take every moralizing word spoken by their politicians at face value. The United States was able to speak out against European-style Colonialism and still become the twentieth century's leading imperial power. Williams's socialist inclinations led him to make grave mistakes in his economic analysis as well as other errors in reasoning, but he nonetheless contributed many profound insights. He brilliantly refuted the generally accepted historical myth that the Republican administrations of the 1920s had kept out of world affairs and pursued a policy of Isolationism, as well as offering a well-informed account of the origins and events of the Cold War with the Soviet Union.

Williams related American history to the way that T. Woodrow Wilson thought and acted in the First World War. At the time, the president stated that America had taken part in the war reluctantly and had taken up arms largely on moral grounds – through a selfless desire to save Democracy, free the world from militaristic powers, and banish the scourge of war forever. However, Williams showed that Wilson's real motivation for sending hundreds of thousands of American soldiers to war and death on the battlefields of Europe was his realization of America's precarious economic situation. Wilson's political religion obliged him to do all that was humanly possible to extend the borders of Democracy in every direction, which was the only way for mankind to be saved. This statement of faith made it seemingly easy for him to integrate aggressive power politics, economic self-interests, and moral principles in an idealistic vision that determined America's foreign policy. Wilson initiated a legislation that enormously improved the competitive ability of American export corporations.

In seeking to implement their dollar diplomacy, strategists of the informal empire repeatedly ran into difficulties as they sought to implement their secret claims to power without being recognized as the true aggressors. Time after time they were forced to resort to direct military intervention in order to secure the "Open Door" in Central and South America. Between 1898 and 1933, the United States intervened at least thirty-five times in nine Latin American nations (Cuba, Haiti, the Dominican Republic, Costa Rica, Guatemala, Honduras, Panama, Mexico, and Nicaragua). When the Cold War began and dragged on for decades, the relationship of many Latin American states to America deteriorated visibly.

The main theses of Williams's books can be summarized as follows: 1) the American Open Door Policy for an informal empire was a brilliant move that led to a gradual expansion of America's economic and political power throughout the world, 2) America's growing economic power was able to cast the politics and economics of poorer, weaker nations into the mold of pro-American politics, 3) in their departure from traditional, militaristic Imperialism, advocates of the Open Door Policy clearly recognized that colonial campaigns of conquest were a colossal policy failure – and, most importantly, 4) if the Open Door Policy were not significantly improved or even fundamentally changed, it would sow the seeds of its own failure.

15 Postscript

Political, economic, and social developments are expressions of the prevailing philosophies of America's corresponding historical periods, arising ultimately from the theological climate. The teachings of Calvinism, Deism, Transcendentalism, and Social Darwinism were all reflected in social life. So it is with the idea of progress, which became the dominant social ideology and civil religion of American Progressivism. Over the almost five hundred years between the beginning of the fifteenth and end of the nineteenth centuries, Western civilization has cultivated an imperturbable and almost ubiquitous faith in progress.[362] In the late seventeenth century, the

---

[362] F. R. H. Du Boulay, *An Age of Ambition: English Society in the Late Middle Ages* (New

scientific and intellectual achievements of Sir Isaac Newton and John Locke contributed in particular to an optimistic, forward-thinking attitude which spread throughout the world during the eighteenth and nineteenth centuries. The American version of belief in progress combined themes of national self-expression in all its variations. Its ideological arsenal contained a large variety of components, the most significant being Puritan Postmillennialism, Enlightenment optimism, Hegelian dialectics, radical emancipation of slaves, Darwinian racism, and progressive Social Gospel Ecumenism. With respect to domestic policy, these components structured the nation's cultural and constitutional foundations to such an extent that a new system of government was established on the basis of Democratism, Egalitarianism, Universalism, efficiency, and centralization of power. In terms of foreign policy, they led to an imperialist politics. In a display of moral hubris, the American government has professed to apply the "gospel of social benefit" in many countries, while in reality it has provoked one catastrophic war after another.

15.1 Beginnings of a progressive society

Ideas often contribute to social change and are a good reflection of the cultural characteristics of any particular time period. This is especially true of the idea of progress, which can be defined concisely as follows: *A desirable future was, is, and will be the primary goal of civilization.* In contrast to ancient Paganism, which viewed history as a meaningless repetition of events that come and go in an endless cycle, the Christian faith sees history as a linear progression of time with a definite beginning and a definite end. Although the modern world still retains a teleological perspective in which events are seen as heading toward a goal, it has rejected belief in the judgment of God and the reality of heaven and hell.[363] Despite being derived from the biblical view of the future, the idea of progress has developed over the centuries into an anti-Christian ideology.[364] With the passage of time, humanity has allegedly become wiser, freer, happier, and better. Consumed with the idea that human nature will reach inevitable perfection, man can neither imagine having to come before the judgment seat of God to account for his life's deeds, nor see the need to be freed from his burden of debt through faith in the saving work of Jesus Christ. He instead believes that the laws of nature and history will lead to a glorious destination which will depend on neither his internal attitude nor his external actions. However, if the inevitable course of

---

York City, NY: Viking, 1970).

[363] Karl Löwith, *Meaning in History: The Theological Implications of the Philosophy of History* (Chicago, IL: University of Chicago Press, 1949) 197-198; https://archive.org/details/in.ernet. dli.2015.234312/page/n207

[364] Ibid., 84; https://archive.org/details/in.ernet.dli.2015.234312/page/n93; s. also: Frederick John Teggart, ed., *The Idea of Progress: A Collection of Readings*, rev. edition of G. H. Hildebrand (Berkeley, CA: University of California Press, 1949).

progress takes place as stated, the freedom that man claims for himself is a mere illusion.

The American idea of progress which prevailed in the early days of the American republic can be justifiably understood as the effect of the Enlightenment philosophy of eighteenth-century Europe. This quickly took on its own characteristics within the impressionable culture of the new nation. The experience gained through the establishment of the country's economic system motivated the dynamic realization of national ambitions.

The American revolutionaries Jefferson, Adams, Franklin, and Paine were inspired by the rationalist spirit and placed their faith in the glorious future described convincingly by Fontenelle, Condorcet, and Turgot among others.[365] The potential for scientific knowledge based entirely on human reason seemed limitless.[366] Even the austere and reticent Founding Fathers yielded to the temptation of overestimating the significance of their victory over English colonial domination.[367]

Ideas of a thousand-year reign had circulated in virtually every part of America since the seventeenth century. The most popular view was Postmillennialism, which promoted an optimistic view of the future and originated in the eschatological teachings of the Puritans. As an independent philosophy of history, Postmillennialism dates from the late eighteenth and early nineteenth centuries. During this period, Postmillennialism became more than a matter of setting a concrete date for the Second Coming of Christ. It promoted an understanding of history based on the idea that the world was gradually improving. Key to the formation of this perspective were the New England revivals of the eighteenth and nineteenth centuries. Outpourings of the Holy Spirit were originally understood as unexpected works of God; over time, however, they became so frequent that they were gradually taken to be a normal condition in church and society.[368] While many Protestants were still influenced by Calvinism, they saw these revivals as the blessing of God which they prayed for but could not bring about themselves. However, as the Calvinistic doctrines lost influence, the view of

---

[365] Robert A. Nisbet, *History of the Idea of Progress* (New York City, NY: Basic Books, 1980) 198-203.

[366] Albert H. Smyth, ed., *The Writings of Benjamin Franklin Writings* (New York City, NY: Macmillan, 1905-1907; New York City, NY: Haskell, 1970) vol. 8: 416; https://archive.org/details/writingsbenjami13frangoog/page/n440

[367] Ernest Lee Tuveson, *Redeemer Nation: The Idea of America's Millennial Role* (Chicago, IL: University of Chicago Press, 1968) 25; https://archive.org/details/redeemernation00erne/page/24; Forrest McDonald, *Novus Ordo Seclorum: The Intellectual Origins of the Constitution* (Lawrence, KS: University Press of Kansas, 1985) 6; https://archive.org/details/novusordo-secloru0000mcdo/page/6; Eric Voegelin, *From Enlightenment to Revolution*, ed. by John H. Hallowell (Durham, NC: Duke University Press, 1975) 181-182; https://archive.org/details/EricVoegelinFromEnlightenment/page/n187

[368] Calvin Colton, *History and Character of American Revivals of Religion* (London: Frederick Westley and A. H. Davis, 1832) 4, 6; https://archive.org/details/historycharacter00colt/page/6

what caused a revival underwent dramatic change. The growing opinion was that spiritual reform is an "object of systematic endeavor" or a "matter of human calculation." People filled with the Holy Spirit could supposedly start revivals at will. On the basis of this questionable assumption, it was claimed that God expected Christians to set in motion the mechanisms of spiritual awakening. This idea was responsible for the development of a new Protestantism which was characterized in particular by the innovative conversion methods introduced in Charles G. Finney's evangelization campaigns. Remaining faithful to his Pelagian position (that man is not corrupted by original sin and is able to save himself), Finney did not see revival as a supernatural event. Everything depended on the ability of man.[369] Mass influence techniques were used, and missionary societies sprang up everywhere. Widespread revivals were seen as an unmistakable sign of the appearance of a wonderful new age.[370]

In order to understand more deeply the cause and effect of this civil religion which guided political thought in Washington, it is important to examine the revival movement of the 1830s which was particularly influenced by Charles G. Finney. One of the prominent features of the form of Christianity propagated by Finney was a call for the church to concentrate first and foremost not on saving souls for eternity, but rather on attending to the social and material affairs of the whole of humanity in the here and now. The personal commitment and prayer of individual Christians was insufficient to meet this goal; rather the state needed to be brought into play with all its resources and means of power. Only American Christendom as a whole, driven by the highest ideals, would be able to establish the kingdom of heaven on earth. The concentrated power of the state was needed to eliminate sinful structures in society through coercive measures, so that the whole nation could enter a state of sanctification. Supporters of the revival movement particularly backed the Republican Party's initiatives to stop the consumption of alcohol, end the influence of Catholicism, and eradicate anarchist tendencies. They fought resolutely against "rum, Romanism, and rebellion."

---

[369] Whitney R. Cross, *The Burned-Over District: The Social and Intellectual History of Enthusiastic Religion in Western New York, 1800-1850* (New York City, NY: Harper Torchbooks, 1950) 182-184; https://archive.org/details/burnedoverdistri00cros/page/182

[370] Robert Baird, *Religion in America: or, an account of the origin, progress, relations to the state, and present condition of the evangelical churches in the United States; with notices of unevangelical denominations* (New York City, NY: Harper & Bros., [1844] 1856) 202; https://archive.org/details/cu31924029252032/page/n211; Charles Roy Keller, *The Second Great Awakening in Connecticut* (New Haven, CT: Yale University Press, 1942) 135-187; s. also: John D. Boles, *The Great Revival, 1787-1805: The Origins of the Southern Evangelical Mind* (Lexington, KY: The University Press of Kentucky, [1972] 2015) 184-186; William G. McLoughlin, Jr., *Modern Revivalism: Charles Grandison Finney to Billy Graham* (New York City, NY: Ronald Press Co., 1959) 3-121; https://archive.org/details/modernrevivalism00mclo; Charles I. Foster, *An Errand of Mercy: The Evangelical United Front, 1790-1837* (Chapel Hill, NC: University of North Carolina Press, 1960) 156-222; Donald G. Mathews, "The Second Great Awakening as an Organizing Process, 1780-1830: An Hypothesis," *American Quarterly*, 21 (Spring, 1969), 23-43.

Progressives did all they could to increase the centralization of political power in Washington, D.C.

Despite his enormous influence, it would be wrong to believe that Charles G. Finney initiated the disputes between Presbyterians of the Old and New Schools. Even before Finney's evangelization campaigns began in many frontier towns, the revival movement produced strange, aberrational spiritual phenomena such as senseless laughter, leaping, barking, speaking nonsense, and fainting.[371] In general, Finney showed great sympathy for the Methodist revivalists and a good deal of skepticism toward the Presbyterian preachers. The content of his preaching, which had a lasting influence on the great revival movement of the 1830s, can be summarized as follows: all people are responsible for their own salvation, which takes place at an emotional moment of rebirth. According to Finney, the door of heaven stands open to everyone, and every individual must therefore do their best to win as many souls as possible for the Gospel. The desire to work for others' salvation was motivated not only by the joy of seeing an increasing number of converts, but also by a profound fear of being unable to escape hell itself unless heart and soul was put into saving others. However, every Christian was confronted by his inability to ever do enough to save others from the temptations of sin. For this reason, it became generally accepted that only the state could ultimately fulfil the enormous task of eradicating sinful tendencies in society and build a New Jerusalem on earth. Since the preaching of the First Great Awakening (1739-1743) had Pietist undertones in style and content, it had conflicting results which completely destroyed the few remnants of the Calvinist social order in New England. The religious and political vacuum that followed was initially filled by Arminianism (which teaches that man has a free will and can make his own decision to be saved) and later by Unitarianism (a rejection of the doctrine of the Trinity and the divinity of Christ). The Second Great Awakening (1790-1850) was largely an Arminian revival movement and left a devasting legacy. Entire areas became known as "burned over districts" because their inhabitants suffered psychological damage from the emotionally charged revival campaigns and consequently turned their backs on the form of Christianity presented to them.[372]

The politicization of American Protestantism took place within a remarkably short period of time around 1830, and its momentous effects contributed significantly to the emergence and consolidation of the progressive welfare state. The new Protestantism of the early nineteenth century mainly spread through the northern Yankee areas. It was fundamentally different to the Christian religiosity of the South, which, unlike its northeastern counterpart, did not become known for aggressively spreading the teachings of Postmillennialism (that Christ will return to earth after a "thousand-year reign" of indefinite duration). In the Northeast, all

---

[371] Robert Baker, *Baptist Source Book* (Nashville, TN: Broadman, 1966) 46.

[372] Cross, *The Burned-Over District*; https://archive.org/details/burnedoverdistri00cros/page/n5

believers were understood to have a sacred duty to use everything at their disposal to establish the kingdom of God on earth. The new Protestantism defined sin in its own terms, condemning excessive alcohol consumption as the very worst form of sinful behavior.

Transcendentalism (based on German Idealism and the combined influences of English Romanticism, mystical ideas, and Indian philosophies) inspired the many reform movements that swept through America after 1830. The American Whigs and later the Republicans initially used Abolitionism (the elimination of slavery) as an instrument of cultural change. The dictatorial Republicans in the northern states made a far greater, and indeed unlimited, claim to power – not merely over the "rebellious" southern states, but eventually over the entire world. During the 1860s, free black people and other minorities in the northern states were forced to suffer all kinds of discrimination.

Since the founding of the United States, the North has viewed the government as a source of income. The Constitution was merely an instrument that could be manipulated to individual advantage. This unpleasant truth came to light through Alexander Hamilton's desire to establish a strong central government which could rely on the support of the wealthy upper class, since it offered them financial benefits. Obtaining the necessary financial resources required the increase of national debt, the manipulation of currency through a national bank, and the granting of various subsidies which were falsely claimed to be essential and beneficial to all Americans. Those who advocated a strong central government prevailed on the battlefields of the American War of Secession (1861-1865). Bankers in the northern states were the real beneficiaries of the conflict. The former commander of the Confederate Army, Robert E. Lee, believed that consolidating the once independent states into a united government system was a certain harbinger of ruin. With dark foreboding, he foresaw that American domestic policy and imperial foreign policy would be overtaken by Despotism.[373] In the period that followed, the negative impact of an all-powerful central state that was content with nothing less than political domination and economic exploitation of the entire world became increasingly evident. No one could oppose this military machinery with its enormous arsenal of conventional and nuclear weapons systems without running the risk of being attacked.

Throughout almost the entire nineteenth century, Postmillennialism was the generally accepted teaching among American Protestants. There were occasional visionaries who expected the world to end in 1843 or 1844, but other Millennialists put all their efforts into evangelistic preaching and social action, believing that this would hasten the dawn of the thousand-year kingdom on earth.[374] Following the example of charitable action, wealthy

---

[373] Robert E. Lee, "Letter to Lord Acton," December 15, 1866, in Rufus J. Fears, ed., *Selected Writings of Lord Acton*, vol. 1: *Essays in the History of Liberty* (Indianapolis, IN: Liberty Fund, 1986) 365.

[374] George M. Marsden, *Fundamentalism and American Culture: The Shaping of Twentieth*

benefactors committed themselves to a comprehensive and wide-reaching reform of the social welfare systems of their respective states. Although the combination of progress with symbols from the book of Revelation – such as the pouring out of the bowls of wrath, the raising of the dead, and the condemnation of the wicked – seemed extremely strange to people at the time, its widespread popularity indicated that Postmillennialism needed to be taken seriously. Although the contemporary theological currents and countercurrents were in conflict with each another for various reasons, they had one thing in common: the rejection of traditional Calvinism. The deliberate repudiation of the beliefs of the Reformation caused a fundamental change that fostered the rise of both Fundamentalism and Modernism.

Progressives replaced the Republicanism of the Constitution with a functional Social Democracy – known as Progressivism in the United States – which elevated the principle of the majority vote over that of the rule of law. Instead of the separation of powers into legislative, judicial, and executive, progressives wanted consensus and cooperation between different government departments and appealed to the alleged "public opinion." Instead of a confederation of states, they wanted a concentration of power in the federal government. The salient feature of the Progressive Era was a willing acceptance of centralized political power, which was no longer seen as the greatest threat to a life of freedom; however, over time it placed enormous restrictions on the liberty of the individual. Very few people realized that this restriction of freedom was accompanied by loss of prosperity. The willingness of progressives to increase the governing power of the state to such a great extent underlined the fact that loyalty to the constitutional republic had already been lost. Power would now be exercised by benevolent bureaucrats who were intent on achieving their utopian goals both at home and abroad. This monumental change took place among the educated Western elite within the period of one generation, from around 1890 to 1920.

Progressives turned more and more firmly to the Social Gospel. In matters of domestic policy, they followed the socialist principles of Democratism, Egalitarianism, and Universalism. In terms of foreign policy, they took a line based on the "gospel of social benefit" with the aim of building a global empire. As a wide movement of social and political change, Progressivism has influenced American history in numerous ways up to the present day. Historians generally classify the era as a period of reform, but it was a period of radical change in American society that left virtually nothing untouched, spanning the presidential terms of both Theodore Roosevelt and Woodrow Wilson. From the 1880s, politicians, businessmen, academics, and missionaries began to formulate a global manifesto of "Manifest Destiny": a declaration of the necessity and advantageousness of an American power politics that would be felt throughout the whole world. The United States, as

Century Evangelicalism, 1870-1925 (New York City, NY: Oxford University Press, 1980) 43-138; https://archive.org/details/fundamentalismam0000mars/page/42

"redeemer nation,"[375] was believed to be God's instrument for building the New Jerusalem on earth. During the twentieth and twenty-first centuries, this quest for salvation through the sacral mediation of a world state was concretized on the basis of Wilson's ideology, which called for a radical revolution that would supposedly establish perpetual peace in international relations. At the beginning of the twentieth century, supporters of the Social Gospel movement took up the cause of Progressivism.

15.2 Development of a progressive world order

Before the Progressive Era, the free market economy had precedence over any socialist economic system. However, the Progressive Era (1896-1921) saw the emergence of the American welfare state – of state intervention for the social, material and cultural wellbeing of its citizens. Very few of the reforms proposed by agitators were actually enforced in law. What actually brought decisive change was a fundamental shift in attitude among the population, one so profound that political and intellectual circles that advocated state intervention in the economy came to gain the upper hand in society. Progressives adopted the unwavering optimism displayed by the liberals, realizing that conveying a positive view of the future could enormously increase the spread and success of their own ideology. In all other respects, however, they stood in opposition to the principles of Classical Liberalism.

Just before the turn of the century, the liberals took a radical change of direction. New "liberals" were no longer content to rely on the laws of free market economy to bring about social progress, as they had done before, but instead wanted the state to intervene actively in economic processes. Progressives were able to harness state power for their purpose of ending traditional minimal government. Social scientists launched an ambitious program of social reform, turning to utopian socialists for inspiration. Those who supported the cause of the "Social Gospel" wanted the population to be subjected once more to state police power. Having gained dominance in politics and economics, progressives began referring to themselves as "liberals." In reality, however, they were socialists, pursuing a policy completely opposite to what had been held by the classical liberals.

The ideology of Progressivism can be traced back to the earliest days of the republic. However, it was in the late nineteenth century that it enveloped the United States. Direct conflict between state economic intervention and

---

[375] Ernest Lee Tuveson, *Redeemer Nation: The Idea of America's Millennial Role* (Chicago, IL: University of Chicago Press, 1968); https://archive.org/details/redeemernation00erne; James H. Moorhead, *American Apocalypse: Yankee Protestants and the Civil War, 1860-1869* (New Haven, CT: Yale University Press, 1978); https://archive.org/details/americanapocalyp-0000moor; s. also: Charles Royster, *The Destructive War: William Tecumseh Sherman, Stonewall Jackson, and the Americans* (New York City, NY: Alfred A. Knopf, 1991) chap. 6, "The Vicarious War".

the free market economy had commenced in 1884[376], and in the final years of the century, reformers and socialists such as Henry George, Edward Bellamy, and Henry Demarest Lloyd reached great numbers of people with their message of a state-initiated solution to social problems. The vast scale and steady growth of urban slums, largely caused by rapid industrialization, seemed to motivate the search for solutions that would be genuinely effective when put into practice. Social awareness took on new forms as Progressivism spread like wildfire through American Christianity and encouraged radical change. The primary problem that it sought to deal with was poverty. The wealthy believed that the poor were to blame for their own fate and felt morally superior to the socially weak.[377] Progressives of the old guard, such as the progressive pastor and Freemason Henry Ward Beecher, were unwilling to make even the slightest change to their arrogant behavior. In contrast, the new line-up of Social Gospel leaders displayed an attitude of compassion toward the poor. One of them, John A. Ryan, believed that social evils resulted from the grim living conditions endured by the working class.[378] Ryan was influenced by Richard T. Ely, who was exposed to Bismarck's ideology while studying economics at universities in Germany. The ultimate social objective of this ideology is the nationalist welfare state.[379] Ely's scientific work was steeped in the ideals of the Social Gospel. He had a great influence over his contemporaries: one of his students was T. Woodrow Wilson; another was Robert M. La Follette Sr. Follette became known in particular for developing the "Wisconsin idea," based on Ely's economic theories. Theodore Roosevelt paid tribute to Ely by indicating that he was the first person to have drawn his attention to radical economics.[380] As a leading advocate of the new political economy, Ely also influenced the most eloquent and self-confident spokesmen of progressive Liberalism: Herbert D. Croly, Walter Weyl, and Walter Lippmann – editor of the political magazine *The New Republic*.[381]

Economic efficiency began to be pursued with far greater intensity at the end of the nineteenth century. The frontier thesis and the Open Door Policy formed the two pillars of the entirety of American foreign policy from 1898 onward. This resulted in the sudden raging desire to take possession of distant colonies. With the beginning of the Spanish-American War in 1898, the government in Washington laid the first stone for a global empire.

---

[376] Sidney Fine, *Laissez Faire and the General-Welfare State* (Ann Arbor, MI: University of Michigan Press, 1956) 373.

[377] Carl Resek, ed., *The Progressives* (Indianapolis, IN: Bobbs-Merrill, 1967) xvi.

[378] Ibid., 125, 131-132.

[379] Fine, *Laissez Faire and the General-Welfare State*, 216.

[380] Ibid., 240.

[381] Richard Crockatt, "American Liberalism and the Atlantic World, 1916-1917," *Journal of American Studies*, II (April, 1977), 126-143; Charles Forcey, *The Crossroads of Liberalism* (New York City, NY: Oxford University Press, 1961).

For the United States, the temptation to build an overseas empire was very great. The domestic economic changes[382] that took place from 1865 following the War of Secession had virtually predestined America's quest for colonies. The landmass of the United States had expanded enormously in the early nineteenth century with the incorporation of southern and western territories. It might be assumed, therefore, that the ruling upper classes could have generated enough wealth for themselves and for their sympathizers through a domestic system of free trade. However, such a policy was not attractive enough for those in government circles. Many American politicians were sympathetic to the growing public protest against the established order. The minds of the American people accordingly became taken up with new ideologies and concrete programs of social and political reform.

Progressives rejected the American tradition of non-intervention and replaced it with an aggressive foreign policy. The utopian impulse behind Manifest Destiny (the idea that the U.S.A. had a divine mandate for expansion) and the Social Gospel's fundamental aim of social equality rejected the established way of dealing with other countries – namely with caution and reserve. During the 1890s, American export corporations complained about alleged overproduction and urged the government in Washington, D.C., to adopt a belligerent foreign policy. Popular, eloquent theorists spread the principles of Social Darwinism, believing that the Anglo-Saxon race – the Americans and the British – had a special qualification to dominate the whole world. They disguised their objectives by declaring an aim to help other races live in a more civilized manner. Another justification of America's expansionist policy, as it was soon termed, was based on a defective economic analysis – defective because it took only its own interests into account. The idea spread that the domestic economy was suffering from overproduction on the one hand and from underconsumption on the other. The only solution to the problem seemed to lie in the foreign market. The Washington government needed to put political and military pressure on other countries so that they would be forced to allow capital investments and the import of American goods in all available markets.

Republican statesmen – most of whom were Freemasons – pushed for an economic program based on the principles of Mercantilism (the strengthening of industry and foreign trade) for the sake of general prosperity. Other items on their agenda were subsidization of shipping, development of warships, the building of a canal in Nicaragua (more specifically in Panama), and economic penetration of markets, particularly in Asian countries. Foremost among the latter was China. This economic program became known as the "Large Policy." The United States' interest in overseas colonies was made particularly clear when President McKinley declared war on Spain in 1898. In a speech to the American people, he presented the war as a humanitarian crusade. However, the violent conflict revealed a completely

---

[382] Susan-Mary Grant, *North Over South: Northern Nationalism and American Identity in the Antebellum Era* (Lawrence, KS: University Press of Kansas, 2000).

different reality – one that began with the military occupation of Cuba, and that became far clearer still through the territorial occupation of Puerto Rico and the Philippines.

Progressive internationalists devised an aggressive foreign policy that culminated under the leadership of T. Woodrow Wilson. In 1916, contrary to the advice given by Washington in his farewell speech, Wilson rejected the policy of non-intervention in other countries' affairs. Emphasizing that destiny is determined by providence, he stated that "we are participants, whether we like it or not, in the life of the world."[383] When President Wilson delivered his war speech at a joint session of Congress in Washington, D.C., on April 2, 1917, he set out the fundamental pillars of a progressive foreign policy. A nation in service, he said, was willing to lay down its life for its friends.[384] The Founding Fathers had formed plans for the whole world, and America's entry into the First World War had only been the fruit of those plans. Like no other politician before or after him, Wilson disguised the harsh reality of a cutthroat campaign of conquest with a smooth, idealistic rhetoric of innocent humanitarianism.

Contemporary historians often speak of a short twentieth century spanning the years from 1914 to 1991, signifying an ideological era of intolerable outbreaks of violence that produced two world wars and the Cold War. The origins of these awful events are invariably attributed to the human, economic, social, and cultural devastation brought by the First World War, which destroyed the myth of progress at least for a time. The European balance of power had maintained world peace during the previous century; however, in 1914 it lost its equilibrium. This loss, according to the contemporary historical view, was the primary cause of the disasters that followed. The carnage of the First World War had thrown disoriented survivors into a moral vacuum, and totalitarian movements such as Communism, National Socialism, and Fascism had used this to their own advantage. With the added effects of the economic catastrophe that began with the Great Depression at the end of 1929 and which strengthened the power of dictatorships, the outbreak of the Second World War was only ever a matter of time. The escalation of violence revealed a bipolar world dominated

---

[383] Cit. in Walter A. McDougall, *Promised Land, Crusader State: The American Encounter with the World Since 1776* (Boston, MA: Houghton Mifflin, 1997) 122-123.

[384] T. Woodrow Wilson, "Address to a Joint Session of Congress," 2 April 1917, in Arthur S. Link, et al., ed., *The Papers of Woodrow Wilson* (Princeton, NJ: Princeton University Press, 1966-1993) vol. 41: 527; T. Woodrow Wilson, "Address to a Joint Session of Congress," 8 January 1918, ibid., vol. 45: 539; https://archive.org/details/papersofwoodroww0045wils/page/538: "It is the principle of justice to all peoples and nationalities, and their right to live on equal terms of liberty and safety with one another, whether they be strong or weak. Unless this principle be made its foundation no part of the structure of international justice can stand. The people of the United States could act upon no other principle; and to the vindication of this principle they are ready to devote their lives, their honor, and everything they possess. The moral climax of this the culminating and final war for human liberty has come, and they are ready to put their own strength, their own highest purpose, their own integrity and devotion to the test."

by rival power blocs, each intent on proving the validity of their own universal ideologies. The situation intensified still further when governments on both sides gained access to nuclear arms. But what if we are wrong in thinking that the origins of all these disastrous events lie in the year 1914? Could these successive misfortunes have actually resulted from the American government's foolish decision to enter the First World War in 1917?

In contrast to other periods of social change, such as those during Andrew Jackson and Franklin D. Roosevelt's terms of office, progressive goals were underpinned by a strong moral element. Historians even speak of a religious crusade. The idea of progress, which had long been a key factor in American civil religion, seemed to regain momentum when nationalistic ideals reappeared in social and political programs. Progressive reformers were particularly marked out by their almost religious veneration of the ideal of a democratic society. The drive for social change was directly linked with this ideal which had been shaped by the continual influence of past evangelical Protestantism. Protestant religiosity had a considerable influence on the social reform movements of 1880 to 1914, one of its most significant aspects being a version of Postmillennialism that was in keeping with the modern world. Many American Protestants eagerly anticipated the day on which the millennialist prophecy of the book of Revelation would be fulfilled, fully convinced that God would build his kingdom on earth as soon as the necessary preconditions were in place. They had no fears that this assumption might eventually prove false.

At the beginning of the twentieth century, a three-way relationship developed between leading politicians, wealthy industrialists and financiers, and influential intellectuals. Their common goal was to establish a privileged status in American society for each party involved. However, this could only be achieved if they had a strong influence on politics, economics, and culture. Progressivism thus became a movement that sought above all else to expand the government and its powers. As a result of the close cooperation between different groups of industrialists and financiers and an emerging group of progressive intellectuals, a technocratic program was formed that worked in the interests of these individuals alone. They conveyed their elitist views to the politicians that depended on them, who simultaneously relied on the support of financially powerful interest groups, most notably the investment bank J. P. Morgan & Co. This was the only way for them to gather enough campaign finances to enable their election to higher offices. Industrial magnates turned to the state to form cartels within the most important areas of the economy, to reduce competition, and to regulate production and prices.[385] Intellectuals turned to the government for help in limiting access to

[385] James Weinstein, *The Corporate Ideal in the Liberal State: 1900-1918* (Boston, MA: Beacon Press, 1968; Boston, MA: Beacon Paperback, 1969); Burton W. Folsom, Jr., *The Myth of the Robber Barons: A new look at the rise of big business in America*, 3 ed. (Herdon, VA.: Young America's Foundation, 1996); https://archive.org/details/mythofrobberbaro00fols; Gabriel Morris Kolko, *The Triumph of Conservatism: A Reinterpretation of American History, 1900-1916* (New York City, NY: The Free Press of Glencoe, 1963; Chicago, IL: Quadrangle

their professions and to gain lucrative government positions. Their primary task was to make the politics urged by the authorities seem plausible to the general public and to carry out the related administrative tasks.

Although popular interest groups seemed to present "fair competition" and "market stability" as desirable goals, the government committees and agencies of the time worked almost exclusively for the established industry. Their specific task was to place severe restrictions on any economic rivals to large-scale industry. Far from being a free market economy, the American economic system developed into State Monopoly Capitalism (Corporatism).[386] The state, being fundamentally reliant on this system, was even prepared to declare war on other countries in order to protect the financial interests of leading banks and corporations. By practicing a militaristic and imperialistic foreign policy, access to foreign markets could be enabled by force, and the sword of state could be used to protect foreign investment.

When the First World War broke out, the dream of the beginning of a thousand-year reign in America was brought to an abrupt end.[387] People had believed that progress would continue forever. However, the awful circumstances provoked by the war convinced many people that government power was not being used for the good of all. Technological achievements that had promised to advance civilization acted instead as instruments of regression. During the First World War, captains of industry used their influence to bring the economy under War Socialism with the help of the government. The upper class who supported them had invested much of their wealth in the arms industry, and made great profits from this economic monopoly which was based on pure exploitation. The system overtly favored the rich, who received generous dividends or large state subsidies for their various business enterprises. Although the plundering of taxpayers had a negative impact on the American economy, it nonetheless guaranteed political success for those with government power.[388]

When the Great Depression plunged the Western Hemisphere into great economic crisis during the 1930s, politicians took uncertain, untested actions which would never have been considered under normal circumstances. Until this point, it had been common practice to back the banknotes in circulation not only with gold, but also with foreign currencies that could be converted into gold. However, all Western governments rejected the gold exchange standard introduced during the inter-war period in favor of a fiat currency. At the same time, Keynesian economics (control of the demand for goods

---

Books, Inc., 1967); https://archive.org/details/KolkoGabrielTheTriumphOfConservatism/page/n3

[386] Ibid.

[387] Lewis Mumford, *Faith For Living* (London: Secker & Warburg, 1941) 168; https://archive.org/details/in.ernet.dli.2015.190139/page/n171

[388] H. C. Engelbrecht & F. C. Hanighen, *Merchants of Death: A Study of the International Armament Industry* (New York City, NY: Dodd, Mead and Co., 1934) 173; https://archive.org/details/merchantsofdeath00enge/page/172

and services and, if necessary, stimulation of the economy through increased public spending and inflationary monetary policy) were introduced in order to manipulate financial policy. The dissatisfaction felt among American and British politicians as stringent measures were avoided in global financial policy, which was controlled almost entirely by the United States and Great Britain, eventually led to the Second World War. The German Third Reich had negotiated economic agreements in the Balkans which had enabled direct exchange of goods without using the leading currencies of the time (the pound sterling and the U.S. dollar).[389] To say that Progressivism helped to destroy constitutional order rather than protect it is no exaggeration. Far from producing social peace, justice, and prosperity, the promises made by progressives came to nothing. By 1936, Progressivism had become almost wholly accepted as the preferred political worldview – as is sufficiently demonstrated by Fascism in Italy, National Socialism in Germany, and the New Deal in the United States.[390]

15.3 Realization of a progressive world order

Until around 1950, almost every American historian portrayed the Progressive Era as a transparent, optimistic period encompassing the first twenty years of the twentieth century, which could be considered the culmination of nineteenth-century historical developments. The Western Hemisphere had reached a point at which it could control its own fate and make even greater achievements. The spread and acceptance of Progressivism played a vital part in the formation of the political, economic, and ideological basis whereby most U.S. citizens gained their wealth. This is at least how devoted Americans perceived the myth of an indispensable nation, which came to be accepted as truth.

In his typical manner, Gabriel M. Kolko had serious doubts about this glorious vision of the future of American Progressivism. The historian researched and argued his theory that the Progressive Era had been an age of

---

[389] Murray N. Rothbard, *History of Money and Banking in the United States: The Colonial Era to World War II* (Auburn, Al: Ludwig von Mises Institute, 2002) 431: "As soon as England went off the gold standard, the pound fell by 30 percent. It is ironic that, after all the travail Britain had put the world through, the pound fell to a level, $3.40, that might have been viable if she had originally returned to gold at that rate. Twenty-five countries followed Britain off gold and onto floating, and devaluating, exchange rates. The era of the gold-exchange standard was over. The world was now plunged into a monetary chaos of fiat money, competing devaluation, exchange controls, and warring monetary and trade blocs, accompanied by a network of protectionist restrictions. These warring blocs played an important though neglected part in paving the way for World War II. This trend toward monetary and other economic nationalism was accentuated when the United States, the last bastion of the gold coin standard, devalued the dollar and went off that standard in 1933."

[390] James J. Martin, *Revisionist Viewpoints* (Colorado Springs, CO: Ralph Myles Press, 1971) 203, 205; s. also: John Maynard Keynes, *General Theory of Employment, Interest, and Money* (London: Macmillan and Co., 1936); https://archive.org/details/in.ernet.dli.2015.50092/page/n6

Conservatism lasting from around 1896 until the United States' entry into the First World War.[391] The Conservatism of the age was due to the concerted effort made to protect the fundamental social and economic relations vital to a capitalist society. According to Kolko, the roots of American Neoliberalism lay in the Progressive Era. By the early 1960s, Neoliberalism completely dominated America's ideological, economic, and political affairs. Widely read commentators assured the public that the magic formula for continual economic prosperity and political freedom had been discovered in the form of a capitalist system controlled by a powerful, centralized government.

At the end of the Second World War, after preliminary efforts to engage actively in world affairs, the United States once again assumed the position of an imperialist world power. What was peculiar about this situation was the ease and speed with which America came to dominate the world. The state issued anti-communist propaganda that presented the benefits of Capitalism as unquestionable. The military-industrial complex grew enormously during the Eisenhower administration (1953-1961), which, despite being barely noticed by the general public, had an immense influence on the country's economic development.[392] Following the Eisenhower era, the power of the Pentagon expanded more than the former American general could ever have imagined, along with many large and small arms companies, research centers at renowned universities, and the Washington administrative apparatus. Until this point, most Americans had supported Unilateralism (one-sided state action taken with no regard for other states) out of political tradition. Imperialists sought to deceive the public by criticizing anti-imperialists, accusing them of advocating a "policy of national isolation" which would prevent active cooperation with other nations. They warned that this poorly conceived policy would lead to the complete suspension of profitable foreign trade. However, this was untrue. Anti-imperialists were in favor of a free market economy at home and abroad, but were in firm opposition to violent conquest. They wanted to encourage peaceful trade with other nations – not destructive wars. Many Americans tragically confused anti-imperialists' commendable aims with imperialists' false accusations. Disguised as a noble cause, the brief military conflict with Spain from April 23 to August 12, 1898, became the first in an almost endless series of wars.[393] The United States was directly involved in 201 of the 242 wars fought around the world between 1945 and 2001[394] – and the Second Iran War and the conflicts in Afghanistan,

---

[391] Gabriel Morris Kolko, *Railroads and Regulation, 1877-1916* (Princeton, NJ: Princeton University Press, 1965; Westport, CT: Greenwood Press, 1976); Gabriel Morris Kolko, *The Triumph of Conservatism: A Reinterpretation of American History, 1900-1916* (New York City, NY: Quadrangle Books, 1963; New York City, NY: Free Press, 1977).

[392] Robert Alexander Nisbet, "Foreign Policy and the American Mind," *Studies in History and Philosophy*, No. 7 (Menlo Park, CA: Institute for Humane Studies, [1961] 1978), 14.

[393] Ibid., 14-15.

[394] William H. Wiist, et. al., "The Role of Public Health in the Prevention of War: Rationale and Competencies," *American Journal of Public Health*, vol. 104, no. 6 (June, 2014); https://

Libya, Syria, and Yemen are not yet included in these statistics. Most prominent Western newspapers state that America has only the best intentions in sending its soldiers abroad to establish Democracy in totalitarian countries. If the United States' goal of a united world government is a worthy cause, support must be raised to bring it to pass.

No matter the motives stated when America goes to war, the end result is always a call to a global crusade which usually draws on Wilson's former foreign policy: a global mission to conform the world to the image of the American "redeemer nation."[395] This evokes religious concepts that have underpinned America's progressive world view since the late nineteenth century. Such self-glorification of the state is not limited to the United States, but can be seen just as clearly in other countries such as Germany, England, and France. It can indeed be found wherever Hegelian philosophy and its derivative ideologies have shaped culture. A prime example is Jakob Böhme's Theosophy, which became widespread both on the continent and in England. Long before the rise of Hegelianism, European society had sought to reach its historical culmination through the circulation of religious utopias. The most obvious example is Marxism.

The statesmen who put the empire's ideology into practice[396] seek uncontested, militarily secure territorial supremacy over all nations. The Cold War militarists put forward a theoretically more comprehensive and ideologically more intensive justification for U.S. Interventionism that is unique for its systematic implementation. Advocates of imperialist ideology claim that America's great asset is its rejection of human traditions that are regarded as outdated practices from an uncivilized past. America is instead seen to be founded on abstract, universal principles, thus offering a new beginning for mankind. The nation has supposedly been entrusted with a great mission and must spread its principles throughout the world so that other nations may also have the opportunity to start afresh. The imperialist ideology challenges Americans' traditional fear of concentration of power:

---

ajph.aphapublications.org/doi/pdf/10.2105/AJPH.2013.301778 "Since the end of World War II, there have been 248 armed conflicts in 153 locations around the world. The United States launched 201 overseas military operations between the end of World War II and 2001, and since then, others, including Afghanistan and Iraq. During the 20th century, 190 million deaths could be directly and indirectly related to war – more than in the previous 4 centuries." S. also: Kathy Barker, "Academics and scientists on preventing war," May 15, 2014, Blog: Scientists As Citizens. Activism beyond the bench; http://scientistsascitizens.org/2014/05/15/academics-and-scientists-on-preventing-war/

[395] Ernest Lee Tuveson, *Redeemer Nation: The Idea of America's Millennial Role* (Chicago, IL: University of Chicago Press, 1968); https://archive.org/details/redeemernation00erne; James H. Moorhead, *American Apocalypse: Yankee Protestants and the Civil War, 1860-1869* (New Haven, CT: Yale University Press, 1978); https://archive.org/details/americanapocalyp-0000moor; s. also: Charles Royster, *The Destructive War: William Tecumseh Sherman, Stonewall Jackson, and the Americans* (New York City, NY: Alfred A. Knopf, 1991) chap. 6, "The Vicarious War".

[396] Andrew J. Bacevich, *The New American Militarism: How Americans are Seduced by War* (New York City, NY: Oxford University Press, 2005).

the nation's spirit of constitutional government in the form of Republican Democracy has more or less evaporated, if not completely disappeared. Two interest groups are continually at the fore in inciting an atmosphere of war among the American people: political neoconservatives and "Christian" postmillennialists. Representatives of both groups state strongly and repeatedly that the United States is called to bring about the golden age at which human history will supposedly arrive.[397] It is possible that the two groups secretly work together to achieve their aims. Among the most prominent neoconservatives are Elliot Abrams, William Bennett, Max Boot, Midge Decter, Douglas Feith, David Frum, Frank Gaffney, Robert Kagan, William Kristol, Michael Ledeen, Lewis "Scooter" Libby, Joshua Muravchik, Michael Novak, Richard Perle, Norman Podhoretz, James Woolsey, and Paul Wolfowitz. The late neoconservatives Irving Kristol and Charles Kraut-hammer were also key leaders of the movement during their lifetimes.

During the presidency of George W. Bush (Skull & Bones, 1968) from 2001 to 2009, the neoconservative ideology was adopted by many prominent politicians including Vice President Richard Cheney and Secretary of Defense Donald Rumsfeld. The ideology of the "moral" empire was supported by all of George W. Bush's advisers and speech writers without exception. They easily drove the president to take military action after the awful events of September 11, 2001, were declared an act of terrorism committed by Islamist militants. The terrorist attack was said to be the key motivation for the introduction of a highly ambitious foreign policy that was unprecedented in history. The aggression used to take imperialist control of major oil-producing countries in the Middle East was the very opposite of the policy presented to the American population in the presidential election campaign of 2000. America would not only lead a worldwide campaign against terrorism, but would also make pre-emptive strikes on any area that appeared to be a potential threat. In doing so, the American military would spread the greatest system of government in the world, its primary task being to realize the president's vision of a global democratic revolution. The American public was never told explicitly that this revolution would exemplify the spirit of Rousseau's democratic civil religion. During the Operation "Shock and Awe" of March 2003, in which air and land attacks were made on Baghdad and other strategic targets, George W. Bush declared in his "Bush Doctrine" that presidential powers take additional precedence over other government branches in times of national emergency. This statement is based on the totalitarian principle of unitary presidency. The mass media constantly reminded Americans that they were in a permanent state of emergency due to the pervading terror. Although President Bush seemed to be the most prominent advocate of this neoconservative ideology, he was by no means its initiator: it had already been propagated widely for decades. By the time Manhattan's Twin Towers collapsed, it had already been accepted by many

---

[397] Martin Erdmann, *Der Griff zur Macht: Dominionismus – der evangelikale Weg zu globalem Einfluss* (Augustdorf: Betanien Verlag, 2011).

leading politicians in both of America's national parties. Many of their most fervent supporters had originally been members of the Democratic Party before pledging allegiance to the other main party. Some of them had been ardent followers of Marxist Trotskyism in their youth (a variation of Communism represented by the Russian revolutionary and politician Leon Trotsky [Lev Davidovich Bronstein; 1879-1940] and his followers, which called for an immediate world revolution).

The neoconservative ideology was especially well-represented by the media in matters of foreign policy. The meaning of the term "Neoconservatism" is somewhat ambiguous. In contrast to traditional Conservatism, represented for example by the British statesman Edmund Burke (1729-1797), Neoconservatism has little interest in the cultural legacy of the past. Neoconservatives generally see traditions as outdated and obsolete. The new way of thinking consists of "Democracy" and "freedom," which will have a determining influence on the further course of human history. The neoconservative political scientist Allan Bloom said that the American project is uniquely applicable to all peoples of the earth, and that America is thus first and foremost an idea.[398] As the principles of freedom, equality, and the rights they engender are valid in America, so they are valid in all places on account of their rationality. Bloom and others ignored the fact that America's political tradition has deep roots in ancient Western civilizations that were primarily transmitted through British culture. This legacy from antiquity highlights the moral weaknesses of human nature, on which internal and external restrictions must be placed to prevent them from causing harm. The imperial ideology of Neoconservatism points in the opposite direction. It justifies and calls for the removal of restrictions, including the constitutional separation of powers, so that American supremacy can be established throughout the world. This ideology of Romantic Democracy speaks of a moral power which must be summoned for a glorious result.

There are notable similarities between the basic ideas of Neoconservatism and Rousseauism. Rousseau's philosophy undoubtedly gave rise to the founding of political clubs during the second half of the eighteenth century which spread across France and were subsequently responsible for the outbreak and development of the French Revolution. The French members of the Jacobin Club saw themselves as a great moral force in the world and referred to themselves as the Incorruptible. By advocating universal principles, they encouraged society to take on a radically different form from the one that had developed throughout history. Liberation of the general public from the yoke of aristocratic oppression was one goal that they pursued with great determination. Another was universal suffrage. They saw any obstacles to these principles as the embodiment of evil, requiring complete

---

[398] Allan Bloom, *The Closing of the American Mind: How higher education has failed democracy and impoverished the souls of today's students* (New York City, NY: Simon and Schuster, [1987] 2012); https://archive.org/details/closingofamerica00bloo

destruction. Maximilien Robespierre was greatly inspired by the ideal of Romantic Democracy as described by Rousseau in his book *The Social Contract, or Principles of Political Right*[399] (1762). In line with the idea that traditional religions and societies needed to be destroyed in order for man to be freed, the Jacobins sought to wipe out all representatives of the old order. Thousands of victims from the aristocracy, bourgeoisie, and working class came to a merciless end[400] under the guillotine.[401] Acting ruthlessly to bring in a new social order, the main conspirators on the Committee of General Security – Robespierre, St. Just, and Couthon – did far more than spread fear during the Reign of Terror. They sanctioned an assassination campaign[402] that led to the deaths of around 300,000 people.[403]

---

[399] Jean-Jacques Rousseau, *The Social Contract Or Principles Of Political Right* (London: George Allen And Unwin Limited, 1948); https://archive.org/details/in.ernet.dli.2015.203938/page/n7

[400] Nesta H. Webster, *World Revolution: The plot against civilization* (London: Constable and Company Ltd., 1921) 48; https://archive.org/details/worldrevolution00websgoog/page/n62: "Thus during the great Terror in Paris about 2800 victims perished, and out of these approximately 500 were of the aristocracy, 1000 of the bourgeoisie, and 1000 of the working-class."

[401] James H. Billington, *Fire in the Minds of Men: Origins of the Revolutionary Faith* (Piscataway, NJ: Transaction Publishers, 1980) 46-47; https://archive.org/details/jameshbillington-fireinthemindsofmen/page/n53

[402] Webster, *World Revolution*, 47; https://archive.org/details/worldrevolution00websgoog/page/n60: "'In the eyes of Maximilien Robespierre and his council,' says Babeuf, 'depopulation was indispensable because the calculation had been made that the French population was in excess of the resources of the soil and of the requirements of useful industry, that is to say, that with us men jostled each other too much for each to be able to live at ease; that hands were too numerous for the execution of all works of essential utility – and this is the horrible conclusion, that since the superabundant population could only amount to so much [...] a portion of sans-culottes must be sacrificed; that this rubbish could be cleared up to a certain quantity, and that means must be found for doing it.' The system of the Terror was thus the answer to the problem of unemployment – unemployment brought about on a vast scale by the destruction of the luxury trades."

[403] Nesta H. Webster, *The French Revolution* (London: Constable and Company Ltd., [1919] 1926) 424-429, 434, 439, 451, 454, 455; https://archive.org/details/in.ernet.dli.2015.16695/page/n447: "[...] a plan of systematic depopulation must be carried out all over France. [...] 'These men, in order to bring us to the happiness of Sparta, wish to annihilate twelve or fifteen millions of the French people [...] Another intime of Robespierre, the Marquis d'Antonelle, a member of the revolutionary tribunal, actually explained the whole scheme in print whilst the Terror was at its height. [...] 'He thought, like the great number of the revolutionary clubs, that, in order to institute the Republic on the ruins of the monarchy, it was necessary to exterminate all those who preferred the latter form of government, and that the former could only become democratic by the destruction of luxury and riches, which form the support of royalty; that equality would never be anything but a chimera as long as men did not all enjoy approximately equal properties; and finally that such an order of things could never be established until a third of the population had been suppressed; that was the general idea of the fanatics of the Revolution.' [...] Other leading revolutionaries considered, however, that far more drastic measures were necessary; thus Collot d'Herbois held that twelve to fifteen millions of the French must be destroyed. Carrier declared that the nation must be reduced to six millions. Guffroy in his journal expressed the opinion that only five million people should be allowed to survive, whilst Robespierre was reported to have said that a population of two millions would be more than enough. Ragè and Fantin Désondoards assert, however, that eight millions was

There are good grounds for referring to supporters of a "virtuous" world empire as the "new Jacobins."[404] Like the original Jacobins, those who champion American world domination seek to spread the general principles of Rousseau's social contract. The American government has used the euphemism "moral clarity" whenever it has claimed the right to intervene by force in any country's domestic affairs. It states that the "evil in the world" can only be destroyed if America leads a permanent campaign to introduce and implement "liberal Democracy" across the globe.

America's burgeoning arms industry produces weapons systems with an ever greater destructive potential. At the beginning of the twenty-first century, millions of so-called evangelical Christians in America backed an aggressive foreign policy and provided the crucial support for prolonged military operations in Afghanistan and Iraq. Many neoconservatives today are campaigning for war with Iran, Russian, and China, believing that success will remove unwanted figures such as the Chinese despot Xi Jinping and the Russian President Vladimir W. Putin.

The real father of Neoconservatism is the American James Burnham (1905-1987). Burnham was especially proud of his role as close confidante of the communist revolutionary Leon Trotsky. Through his work as an agitator, he learned first-hand the tactics and strategies of political infiltration and revolution used by those behind the Fourth International of 1938. During the 1940s, Burnham had a change of ideology and went from being an active member of the Fourth International to being an ardent supporter of right-wing Conservatism. His knowledge of communist conspiracy was a strong advantage in his new activism, through which he worked hard to spread anti-Stalinist propaganda. His book *The Managerial Revolution*[405], published in 1941, gained him much wealth and reputation. From that time onward, he acted as a key prophet of political development, predicting the emergence of an elite class of technocrats. He perceptively recognized the foundation of a modern totalitarian administrative state – an almost perfect realization of Jean-Jacques Rousseau's Romantic Democracy. When the Cold War began, Burnham easily manipulated popular opinion in America so that most citizens welcomed the political enthronement of power-hungry technocrats. As author of the book *The Machiavellians*[406], he succeeded in uniting America's left-wing Trotskyists and right-wing militarists into one group. This fateful union resulted in the seizure of state power by the neoconservatives from the time of George Herbert Walker Bush's vice presidency in the Reagan

---

the figure generally agreed on by the leaders."

[404] Claes G. Ryn, *America the Virtuous: The Crisis of Democracy and the Quest for Empire* (Piscataway, NJ: Transaction Publishers, 2003).

[405] James Burnham, *The Managerial Revolution: What Is Happening in the World* (New York City, NY: John Day Company, 1941; Bloomington, IN: Indiana University Press, 1973); https://archive.org/details/in.ernet.dli.2015.17923.

[406] James Burnham, *The Machiavellians: Defenders of Freedom* (London: Putnam and Company, Limited, 1943); https://archive.org/details/in.ernet.dli.2015.247666/page/n5

administration (1980-1988). Burnham's clear mission was to curb the Stalinism spreading through Western culture, economy, and politics. He saw the fall of democratic social order to be inevitable, and welcomed the impending rise of a power-hungry oligarchy (a state system in which political power is held by a small group) in Western countries. In his book *The Struggle for World Power*[407], published in 1947, he reiterated his already strong warning of the danger of another world war initiated by the Soviet Union. He advised the U.S. establishment to implement a permanent apocalyptic (destructive) policy of endless war against all threats.[408]

In 2016, President Barak Obama signed and ratified the Countering Disinformation and Propaganda Act, with many Americans completely unaware of its passing. This act authorized the establishment of a government department tasked with censoring information of all kinds. Similar characteristics are presented by the fictitious Ministry of Truth in George Orwell's novel *Nineteen Eighty-Four*[409]. President Trump's provocative order to fire fifty-nine Tomahawk missiles at Syrian airbases on April 7, 2017, backs the theory that America intends to start another war in the Middle East. Some commentators even believe that the Third World War has already begun. The neoconservative ideology of Imperialism has been, and is being spread avidly by editors of American news channels such as the *Wall Street Journal, Washington Post, New York Times, Time Magazine, Weekly Standard* (1995-2018), and *National Review*. The American Enterprise Institute has become the intellectual and political nerve center of Neoconservatism. Even if the neoconservative ideology of Imperialism is strongly criticized from time to time, its foreign policy agenda is often endorsed by the news programs of various radio stations, most television channels – especially Fox News – and many online platforms.

Figuratively speaking, neoconservative ideology is presented in the colors of the national flag and makes a great display of Patriotism. Millions of Americans are drawn to its apparently conservative message, unaware that it brings them ever closer to Jean-Jacques Rousseau's totalitarian vision of Romantic Democracy. Neoconservatives' mission to spread their particular form of Democracy throughout the world has unmistakable religious characteristics. The American philosopher Michael Novak said that the Christian tradition teaches the human race to make constant progress until the Creator's vision of a just, truthful, free, and creative civilization is fulfilled.[410] These ideas express the very opposite position to that held by true Christianity. The Bible declares unequivocally that man has a sinful nature which is in

---

[407] James Burnham, *The Struggle For The World* (London: Jonathan Cape, 1947); https://archive.org/details/BURNHAMJamesTheStruggleForTheWorld1947

[408] Burnham, *The Machiavellians: Defenders of Freedom*, 189ff.; https://archive.org/details/in.ernet.dli.2015.247666/page/n197

[409] George Orwell, *Nineteen Eighty-Four* (London: Secker & Warburg, 1949).

[410] Michael Novak, "Human Rights at Christmas," *Washington Times*, December 23, 1988.

constant opposition to the will of the Almighty. The natural order established by God stands in continual danger of distortion by human activity, and Christians are urgently warned not to place their hopes in man's capacity to create heavenly conditions on earth. The Latin Church Father Augustine (354-430) was among the first of many Christian thinkers to reject the idea that mankind is destined to make great progress in realizing a political utopia. Politics will never allow man to find perfect salvation in this world.[411] Although the Apostle Paul stated in his letter to the Romans that human governments should work to create circumstances conducive to social coexistence, he never suggested that a single system of rule could offer ideal living conditions for all people at all times. The Christian's hope is that God's thousand-year reign will commence with the visible return of Jesus Christ as King of kings and Lord of lords (Rev. 19:16) (Premillennialism, as based on Rev. 20:1-6[412]). Only then will near perfect conditions prevail on earth. Finally, after destroying the old creation, God will create new heavens and a new earth as prophesied by the Apostle Peter in the third chapter of his second letter:

7 But the heavens and the earth, which are now, by the same word are kept in store, reserved unto fire against the day of judgment and perdition of ungodly men. 8 But, beloved, be not ignorant of this one thing, that one day is with the Lord as a thousand years, and a thousand years as one day. 9 The Lord is not slack concerning his promise, as some men count slackness; but is longsuffering to us-ward, not willing that any should perish, but that all should come to repentance (i.e. to conversion). 10 But the day of the Lord will come as a thief in the night; in the which the heavens shall pass away with a great noise, and the elements shall melt with fervent heat, the earth also and the works that are therein shall be burned up. 11 Seeing then that all these things shall be dissolved (i.e. destroyed), what manner of persons ought ye to be in all holy conversation and godliness, 12 looking for and hasting unto the coming of the day of God, wherein the heavens being on fire shall be dissolved, and the elements shall melt with fervent heat? 13 Nevertheless we, according

---

[411] Augustinus, *Vom Gottesstaat* (München: dtv Verlagsgesellschaft, 2007; vollständige Ausgabe in einem Band. Buch 1-10, Buch 11-22).

[412] King James Version: 1 And I saw an angel come down from heaven, having the key of the bottomless pit and a great chain in his hand. 2 And he laid hold on the dragon, that old serpent, which is the Devil, and Satan, and bound him a thousand years, 3 and cast him into the bottomless pit, and shut him up, and set a seal upon him, that he should deceive the nations no more, till the thousand years should be fulfilled: and after that he must be loosed a little season. 4 And I saw thrones, and they sat upon them, and judgment was given unto them: and I saw the souls of them that were beheaded for the witness of Jesus, and for the word of God, and which had not worshipped the beast, neither his image, neither had received his mark upon their foreheads, or in their hands; and they lived and reigned with Christ a thousand years. 5 But the rest of the dead lived not again until the thousand years were finished. This is the first resurrection. 6 Blessed and holy is he that hath part in the first resurrection: on such the second death hath no power, but they shall be priests of God and of Christ, and shall reign with him a thousand years.

to his promise, look for new heavens and a new earth, wherein dwelleth righteousness.

A personal note to my readers

You may feel rather disillusioned after reading this book. Many Christians, while believing themselves to be building God's kingdom on earth, are won over to political ideologies which in reality seek power and supremacy. When placed under the burning glass of the Holy Scriptures, structures which thus far may have brought you security and stability prove to be false, ultimately enticing Christians away and leading to worldwide wars. Seemingly good intentions prove to be no more than means to an end. However, experiencing this disappointment is vital to preventing Christians from being drawn into aims that are in direct opposition to the Gospel.

I encourage you to hold fast to the Gospel as preached by the Reformers (Chapter 2). We are moving toward a time in which lies will be spread with ever greater force. Put on the armor of God (Eph. 6:10-18[413]). The best response to temptation by the promises of Progressivism is to study the Bible diligently, grow in the knowledge of God, and apply His Word.

Hold these Bible verses firmly in your hearts:

John 14:27 – Peace I leave with you, my peace I give unto you: not as the world giveth, give I unto you. Let not your heart be troubled, neither let it be afraid.

John 16:33 – These things I have spoken unto you, that in me ye might have peace. In the world ye shall have tribulation: but be of good cheer; I have overcome the world.

---

[413] King James Version: 10 Finally, my brethren, be strong in the Lord, and in the power of his might. 11 Put on the whole armour of God, that ye may be able to stand against the wiles of the devil. 12 For we wrestle not against flesh and blood, but against principalities, against powers, against the rulers of the darkness of this world, against spiritual wickedness in high places. 13 Wherefore take unto you the whole armour of God, that ye may be able to withstand in the evil day, and having done all, to stand. 14 Stand therefore, having your loins girt about with truth, and having on the breastplate of righteousness; 15 And your feet shod with the preparation of the gospel of peace; 16 Above all, taking the shield of faith, wherewith ye shall be able to quench all the fiery darts of the wicked. 17 And take the helmet of salvation, and the sword of the Spirit, which is the word of God: 18 Praying always with all prayer and supplication in the Spirit, and watching thereunto with all perseverance and supplication for all saints;

Bibliography

Books

A

Aaron, Daniel, *Men of Good Hope: A Story of American Progressives* (New York City, NY: Oxford University Press, 1951).

Abbott, Lyman, *The Evolution of Christianity* (Boston, MA: Houghton Mifflin, 1892).

Abbott, Lyman, *Reminiscence*, with an introduction by Ernest Hamlin Abbott (Boston, MA: Houghton Mifflin Co., [1915] 1923).

Abraham, Lyndy, *A Dictionary of Alchemical Imagery* (Cambridge: Cambridge University Press, 2001).

Adams, Charles Francis, ed., *The Works of John Adams: Second President of the United States* (Boston, MA: Little, Brown, 1851) vol. 1 (Life of the Author).

Adams, Henry, *Documents Relating to New England Federalism: 1800-1815* (Boston, MA: Little, Brown, 1877).

Adams, John Quincy, *An Address Delivered at the request of a Committee of Citizens of Washington: On the Occasion of the Reading of the Declaration of Independence, on the Fourth of July, 1821* (Washington, D.C.: Davis and Force, 1821).

Adams, Jr., Russell B., *The Boston Money Tree* (New York City, NY: Crowell, 1977).

Ahlstrom, Sydney Eckman, ed., *Theology in America: The Major Protestant Voices from Puritanism to Neo-Orthodoxy* (Indianapolis, IN: Bobbs-Merrill, 1967).

Ahlstrom, Sydney Eckman, *A Religious History of the American People* (New Haven, CT: Yale University Press, 1972; Garden City, NY: Image Books, 1975) vol. 1.

Alderfer, Everett Gordon, *The Ephrata Commune: An Early American Counterculture* (Pittsburgh, PA: University of Pittsburgh Press, 1985).

Allchin, Arthur M., *Participation in God: A Forgotten Strand in Anglican Tradition* (London: Darton, Longman and Todd, 1988).

Allen, Herbert, *John Hancock: Patriot in Purple* (New York City, NY: Macmillan, 1948; New York City, NY: The Beechhurst Press, 1953).

Alstedium, Johannem Henricum (Alsted, Johann Heinrich), *Scientiarum omnium encyclopædiæ*: tomus primus [...] (Lugduni: Sumptibus Ioannis Antonii Huguetan Filij, & Marci Antonii Ravaud, viâ Mercatoriâ ad insigne Sphæræ, 1649).

Alstedium, Johannem Henricum (Alsted, Johann Heinrich), *Diatribe De Mille Annis Apocalypticis, non illis Chiliastarum & Phantastarum, sed B. B. Danielis & Johannis* (Frankfurt am Main: Conradi Eifriti, [1627] 1630; Engl. translation, 1642).

Alsted, Johann Heinrich, *The Beloved City: or, the saints reign on earth a thousand yeares: asserted, and illustrated from LXV. places of Holy Scripture; besides the judgement of holy learned men, both at home and abroad; and also reason it selfe. Likewise XXXV. objections against this truth are here answered. Written in Latine by Ioan. Henr. Alstedius, professor of the University at Herborne. Faithfully Englished; with some occasionall notes; and the judgement herein not onely of Tycho Brahe, and Carolus Gallus; but also some of our owne famous divines* (London: [publisher not identified], 1643).

Althusius, Johannes, *Politica*, trans. by Frederick S. Carney (Indianapolis, IN: Liberty Fund, [1964] 1995).

Anderson, James, *The Constitutions of the Free-Masons* (London: William Hunter, for John Senex, and John Hooke, 1723).

Anderson, Dwight G., *Abraham Lincoln: The Quest for Immortality* (New York City, NY: Alfred A. Knopf, 1982).

Andreae, Johann Valentin, *Fama fraternitatis, oder, Entdeckung der Brüderschafft des löblichen Ordens dess Rosen Creutzes: beneben der Confession, oder, Bekantnus derselben Fraternitet, an alle Gelehrte und Häupter in Europa geschrieben: auch etlichen Responsionen von Haselmeyern und anderen gelehrten Leuten auff die Famam gestellet* (Dantzigk: Andream Hünefeldt, 1615).

Andreae, Johann Valentin, *Die Chymische Hochzeit des Christian Rosencreutz*, gedeutet und kommentiert von Bastiaan Baan (Strassburg: Lazari Zetzners s. Erben, 1616; Stuttgart: Verlag Urachhaus, 2001).

Ante-Nicene Fathers (Grand Rapids, MI: Eerdmans, 1990) vol. 2.

Archer, John, *The Personall Reigne of Christ Upon Earth: in a treatise wherein is fully and largely laid open and proved that Jesus Christ together with the saints shall visibly possesse a monarchiall state and kingdome in this world* [...] (London: Printed by Benjamin Allen, 1642).

Aristotle, *Politics*, trans. by Benjamin Jowett (Oxford: Oxford University Press, 1885).

Arnett, Alex Mathews, *Claude Kitchin and the Wilson War Policies* (Boston, MA: Little, Brown and Co., 1937; New York City, NY: Russell and Russell, 1971).

Augur, Helen, *The Secret War of Independence* (Boston, MA: Little, Brown, and Co., 1955).

Augustine, *The City of God*, transl. by William Babcock, notes by Boniface Ramsey (Hyde Park, NY: New City Press, 2012).

Auld, William, *The Free Masons pocket companion: containing the origin, progress and present state of that antient fraternity, the institution of the Grand Lodge of Scotland, lists of the Grand Masters and other officers of the Grand Lodges of Scotland and England, their customs, charges, constitutions, orders and regulations: for the instruction and conduct of the brethren: to which is added, by way of an appendix, act of the Associate Synod against the Free Masons, with an impartial examination of that act* [...] (Edinburgh: Printed by Ruddiman, Auld, and Company; and sold by William Auld [...], 1761).

B

Bacevich, Andrew J., *American Empire: The Realities and Consequences of U.S. Diplomacy* (Cambridge, MA: Harvard University Press, 2002).

Bacevich, Andrew J., *New American Militarism: How Americans are Seduced by War* (New York City, NY: Oxford University Press, 2005).

Bacon, Francis, *Advancement of Learning and The New Atlantis* (Oxford: Oxford University Press, 1913).

Bacon, Francis, *New Atlantis* (London: J. Crooke, 1627).

Bacon, Francis, *The Great Instauration* (1620), trans. by R. L. Ellis & J. Spedding, ed. by J. M. Robertson, *The Philosophical Works of Francis Bacon* (London: Routledge, 1905).

Bacque, James, *Other Losses: An Investigation into the Mass Deaths of German Prisoners at the Hands of the French and Americans After World War II* (Toronto, Canada: Stoddard Publishing Co. Limited, 1989).

Bacque, James, *Crimes and Mercies: The Fate of German Civilians Under Allied Occupation 1944-1950* (Toronto, Canada: Little, Brown and Company [Canada] Limited, 1997).

Baigent, Michael & Richard Leigh, *The Temple and the Lodge: The strange and fascinating history of the Knights Templar and the Freemasons* (New York City, NY: Arcade Publishers, 2011).

Baird, Robert, *Religion in America: or, an account of the origin, progress, relations to the state, and present condition of the evangelical churches in the United States; with notices of unevangelical denominations* (New York City, NY: Harper & Bros., [1844] 1856).

Baird, Samuel J., *A History of the New School: and of the questions involved in the disruption of the Presbyterian church in 1838* (Philadelphia, PA: Claxton, Remsen & Haffelfinger, 1868).

Baker, Robert, *Baptist Source Book* (Nashville, TN: Broadman, 1966).

Barratt, Norris S. & Julius F. Sachse, *Freemasonry in Pennsylvania, 1727-1907, as shown by records of Lodge No. 2. F. and A. M. of Philadelphia, from the year A.L. 5757, A.D. 1757*, 3 vols. (Philadelphia, PA: Grand Lodge F. & A.M. Penn., 1908-1910) vol. 2.

Barnes, Harry Elmer, *Social Institutions in an Era of World Upheaval* (New York City, NY: Prentice-Hall, 1942).

Barnes, Harry Elmer, *The New History and the Social Studies* (New York City, NY: The Century Co., 1925).

Barnes, Harry Elmer, *The Genesis of the World War: An Introduction to the Problem of War Guilt* (New York City, NY: Alfred A. Knopf, [1926] 1927).

Barnes, Harry Elmer, *Barnes against the Blackout* (Costa Mesa, CA: Institute for Historical Review, 1991).

Barnes, Harry Elmer, *Society in Transition* (New York City, NY: Prentice-Hall, 1952).

Barnes, Harry Elmer, ed., *Perpetual War for Perpetual Peace: A Critical Examination of the Foreign Policy of Franklin Delano Roosevelt and its*

Aftermath (Caxton Printers, Ltd., 1953; New York City, NY: Greenwood Press, Publishers, 1969).

Batten, Joseph Minton, *John Dury, Advocate of Christian Reunion* (Chicago, IL: Chicago University Press, 1944).

Batten, Samuel Zane, *The New World Order* (New York City, NY: American Baptist Publication Society, 1919).

Beard, Charles Austin, *An Economic Interpretation of the Constitution of the United States* (New York City, NY: MacMillan, 1913; New York City, NY: Simon and Schuster, 2012).

Beard, Charles Austin, *The Idea of National Interest* (New York City, NY: Macmillan, 1934).

Beard, Charles Austin, *President Roosevelt and the Coming of the War, 1941* (New Haven, CT: Yale University Press, 1948).

Beard, Charles Austin & Mary R., *The Rise of American Civilization*, 2 vols. (New York City, NY: The Macmillan Company, 1927).

Beard, Charles Austin & Mary R. Beard, *America In Midpassage* (New York City, NY: The Macmillan Company, 1939) vol. 1.

Beard, Charles A. & Mary R. Beard, *A Basic History of the United States* (Philadelphia, PA: The New Home Library, The Blakiston Company, 1944).

Beard, Charles Austin, *Giddy Minds and Foreign Quarrels* (New York City, NY: The Macmillan Company, 1939).

Beard, Charles Austin, *A Foreign Policy for America* (New York City, NY: Alfred A. Knopf, 1940).

Beard, Charles Austin & George Howard Edward Smith, *The Open Door at Home* (New York City, NY: Macmillan, 1934).

Becker, Carl Lotus, *How New Will the Better World Be?* (New York City, NY: Alfred A. Knopf, 1944).

Becker, Carl Lotus., *The Heavenly City of the Eighteenth-Century Philosophers* (New Haven, CT: Yale University Press, 1932).

Beissel, Conrad [Georg Konrad Beissel], *Das Büchlein vom Sabbath* (Philadelphia, PA: Bradford, 1728).

Bell, Daniel, *The End of Ideology: On the Exhaustion of Political Ideas in the Fifties*, with "The Resumption of History in the New Century" (New York City, NY: Collier Books, 1961; Cambridge, MA: Harvard University Press, 2001).

Bellamy, Edward, *Looking Backward: 2000-1887* (Boston, MA: Ticknor & Co., 1888; Boston, MA: Houghton Mifflin, 1889).

Benedikt, Heinrich Elijah, *Die Kabbala als jüdisch-christlicher Einweihungsweg* (Freiburg: Hermann Bauer, 1985; München: Ansata Verlag, 2004).

Benn, Alfred William, *History of English Rationalism in the Nineteenth Century* (New York City, NY: Longman, Green, and Co., 1906) vol. 1.

Bercovitch, Sacvan, *The American Jeremiad* (Madison, WI: University of Wisconsin Press, [1978] 1980).

Berk, Stephen E., *Calvinism Versus Democracy: Timothy Dwight and the origins of American evangelical orthodoxy* (New York City, NY: Archon Books, 1971).

Billington, James H., *Fire in the Minds of Men: Origins of the Revolutionary Faith* (Piscataway, NJ: Transaction Publishers, 1980).

Birmingham, Stephen, *America's Secret Aristocracy: The Families that Built the United State* (Boston, MA: Little, Brown and Company, 1987).

Blau, Joseph, *Men and Movements in American Philosophy* (New York City, NY: Prentice-Hall, 1952).

Blond, Georges & Germaine, *Histoire de la flibuste* (Paris: Stock, 1969; Geneve: Editions Famot, 1974).

Bloom, Allan, *The Closing of the American Mind: How higher education has failed democracy and impoverished the souls of today's students* (New York City, NY: Simon and Schuster, [1987] 2012).

Blum, John, et al., *The National Experience: A History of the United States*, 6th ed. (San Diego, CA: Harcourt Brace Jovanovich, 1984).

Bodin, Jean, *Methodus ad facilem historiarum cognitionem* (Paris: Martin Juven, 1566; Jaccobum Stoer, 1610).

Boles, John D., *The Great Revival, 1787-1805: The Origins of the Southern Evangelical Mind* (Lexington, KY: The University Press of Kentucky, [1972] 2015).

Boller, Jr., Paul F., *George Washington and Religion* (Dallas, TX: Southern Methodist University Press, 1963).

Boorstin, Daniel J., *The Genius of American Politics* (Chicago, Il: University of Chicago Press, 1953).

Borchard, Edwin & William Pooter Lage, *Neutrality for the United States* (New Haven, CT: Yale University Press, 1937).

Borning, Bernard C., *The Political and Social Thought of Charles A. Beard* (Seattle, WA: University of Washington Press, 1962).

Boydston, Jo Ann, et al., eds., *John Dewey: The Early Works, 1882-1989* (Carbondale, IL: Southern Illinois University Press, 1969-1971) vols. 2-4.

Bozeman, Theodore Dwight, *Protestants in an Age of Science: The Baconian ideal and antebellum American religious thought* (Chapel Hill, NC: University of North Carolina Press, 2012).

Brightman, Thomas, *A Revelation of the Revelation that is, The Revelation of St. John opened clearly with a logicall Resolution and Exposition. Wherein The Sence is cleared, out of the scripture, the euent also thinges foretold is Discussed out of the Church-Historyes* (Amsterdam: [publisher not identified], 1615; Amsterdam: Printed by Thomas Stafford, [1644] 1664).

Brisbane, Albert, *The Social Destiny of Man: or Association and reorganization of industry* (Philadelphia, PA: C. F. Stollmeyer, 1840).

Brokaw, Tom, *The Greatest Generation* (New York City, NY: Random House, 1998).

Brokaw, Tom, *The Greatest Generation Speaks: Letters and Reflections* (New York City, NY: Random House, 1999).

Brown, Ira V., *Lyman Abbott: Christian Evolutionist: A Study in Religious Liberalism* (Cambridge, MA: Harvard University Press, 1953).

Brown, Louise Fargo, *The Political Activities of the Baptists and the Fifth-Monarchy Men* (New York City, NY: B. Franklin, [1911] 1964).

Bryan, William Jennings & Mary Baird Bryan, *The Memoirs of William Jennings Bryan* (Chicago, IL: John C. Winston Co., 1925).

Buder, Stanley, *Pullman: An Experiment in Industrial Order and Community Planning, 1880-1930* (New York City, NY: Oxford University Press, 1967).

Bullock, Steven C., *The Ancient and Honorable Society: Freemasonry in America, 1730-1830* (Providence, RI: Brown University, 1986).

Burke, Peter, *Popular Culture in Early Modern Europe* (London: Temple Smith, 1978).

Burlingame, Roger, *Engines of Democracy: Inventions and Society in America* (New York City, NY: Charles Scribner's Sons, 1940; New York City, NY: Arno Press, 1976).

Burner, David, *The Politics of Provincialism: The Democratic Party in Transition, 1918-1932* (New York City, NY: Norton, [1968] 1975; Cambridge, MA: Harvard University Press, 1986).

Burnham, James, *The Managerial Revolution: What Is Happening in the World* (New York City, NY: John Day Company, 1941; Bloomington, IN: Indiana University Press, 1973).

Burnham, James, *The Machiavellians: Defenders of Freedom* (London: Putnam and Company, 1943).

Burnham, James, *The Struggle For The World* (London: Jonathan Cape, 1947).

Bury, John Bagnell, *A History of Freedom of Thought* (New York City, NY: H. Holt and company, 1913).

Bury, John Bagnell, *The Idea of Progress: An Inquiry into Its Origin and Growth* (London: Macmillan, 1920).

Butler, Jon, *Awash in a Sea of Faith: Christianizing the American People* (Cambridge, MA: Harvard University Press, 1990; Ann Arbor, MI: University of Michigan Library, Scholarly Publishing Office, 1992).

Butler, Smedley D., *War is a Racket* (New York City: NY: Round Table Press, 1935; Los Angeles, CA: Feral House, 2003).

C

Calvin, John, *Institutes of the Christian Religion: in two volumes*, transl. by Ford Lewis Battles (Philadelphia, PA: Westminster Press, [1559] 1960).

Campanella, Tommaso, *La città del Sole* (Roma: Newton & Compton [1995] 2018; edizione digitale).

Canis, Konrad, *Der Weg in den Abgrund: Deutsche Außenpolitik 1902-1914* (Paderborn: Verlag Ferdinand Schöningh [2011] 2013).

Capp, B. S., *The Fifth-Monarchy Men: A Study in Seventeenth-Century English Millennarianism* (London: Faber, 1972).

Carey, George W., *In Defense of the Constitution*, revised and expanded edition (Indianapolis, IN: Liberty Fund, 1995)

Chamberlain, Joseph, *Farewell to Reform: The rise, life and decay of the progressive mind in America* (Gloucester, MA: Peter Smith, 1958).

Chandler, David Leon, *The Jefferson Conspiracies* (New York City, NY: William Morrow and Company, 1994).

Cherry, Conrad, ed., *God's New Israel: Religious Interpretations of American Destiny* (Englewood Cliffs, NJ: Prentice-Hall, 1971).

Chevallier, Pierre, *Histoire de la Franc-Maconnerie Francaise: La Maconnerie: Ecole de L'Egalité, 1725-1799* (Paris: Fayard, [1974] 2002).

Chugerman, Samuel, *Lester Frank Ward: The American Aristotle* (Durham, NC: Duke University Press, 1939).

Clark, Christopher, *The Sleepwalkers: How Europe Went to War in 1914* (New York City, NY: HarperCollins, 2013).

Clark, Ronald W., *Benjamin Franklin: A Biography* (New York City, NY: Random House, 1983).

Clarkson, Grosvenor B., *Industrial America in the World War* (Boston, MA: Houghton Mifflin Co., 1923).

Clendenin, Daniel B., *Eastern Orthodox Christianity: A Western Perspective* (Carlisle, Cumbria, UK: Paternoster; Grand Rapids, MI: Baker, [1994] 2004).

Cole, Wayne S., *Senator Gerald P. Nye and American Foreign Relations* (Minneapolis, MN: University of Minnesota Press, 1962).

Coletta, Paolo E., *William Jennings Bryan: Political Evangelist, 1860-1908* (Lincoln, NE: University of Nebraska Press, 1964) vol. 1.

Colie, Rosalie, *Light and Enlightenment: A Study of the Cambridge Platonists and the Dutch Arminians* (New York City, NY: Cambridge University Press, 1957).

Colton, Calvin, *History and Character of American Revivals of Religion* (London: Frederick Westley and A. H. Davis, 1832).

Comenius, Jan Amos, *Janua Linguarum Reserata, cum Græca versione Theodori Simonii Holsati, innumeris in locis emendata à Stephano Curcellæo qui etiam Gallicam novam adjunxit* (Amsterdam: apud Danielem Elzevirium, [1631] 1665).

Comenius, Jan Amos, *A Reformation of Schools: Designed in two excellent treatises, the first whereof summarily sheweth, the great necessity of a generall reformation of common learning* (London: Printed for Michael Sparke, 1642).

Comenius, Jan Amos, *Via Lucis, vestigata et vestiganda* (London: 1641/42; first published 1668); English translation: John Amos Comenius, *The Way of Light*, trans. by E. T. Campagnac (London: The University Press of Liverpool; Hodder & Stoughton, 1938).

Comenius, Jan Amos, Robert Fitzgibbon Young, John N. Libbey *Comenius in England; the visit of Jan Amos Komenský (Comenius), the Czech philosopher and educationist, to London in 1641-1642; its bearing on the origins of the Royal society, on the development of the encyclopaedia, and on plans for the higher education of the Indians of New England and Virginia*, Robert Fitzgibbon Young, ed. (Oxford: Oxford University Press, 1932; New York City, NY: Arno Press, 1971).

Commons, John R., *Social Reform and the Church* (New York City, NY: Crowell, 1894).

Condorcet, Marie Jean Antoine Nicolas Caritat, Marquis de, *Esquisse d'un tableau historique des progrès de l'esprit humain* (chez Agasse, 1795); *Outlines of an historical view of the progress of the human mind, being a posthumous work of the late M. de Condorcet* (translated from the French) (Philadelphia, PA: M. Carey, 1796).

Coudert, Allison P., *Leibniz and the Kabbalah* (Dortrecht: Springer Science & Business Media, 1995).

Coulter, E. Merton, *The South During Reconstruction* (Baton Rouge, LA: Louisiana State University Press, 1947).

Courtois, Stepháne et al., *The Black Book of Communism: Crimes, Terror, Repression*, trans. by Jonathan Murphy & Mark Kramer (Cambridge, MA: Harvard University Press, 1999).

Cragg, Gerald R., *From Puritanism to the Age of Reason* (Cambridge: Cambridge University Press, [1950] 2008).

Cremin, Lawrence A., *The Transformation of the Schools: Progressivism in American Education, 1876-1957* (New York City, NY: Random House, 1961).

Croly, Herbert D., *The Promise of American Life* (New York City, NY: MacMillan, 1909).

Croly, Herbert D., *Progressive Democracy* (New York City, NY: MacMillan, 1914).

Cross, Whitney R., *The Burned-Over District: The Social and Intellectual History of Enthusiastic Religion in Western New York, 1800-1850* (New York City, NY: Harper Torchbooks, [1950] 1965).

Cubberley, Ellwood P., *Public Education in the United States* (Boston, MA: Houghton Mifflin, [1919] 1947).

Curti, Merle Eugene, *The Growth of American Thought* (New York City, NY: Harper & Brothers Publishers, [1943] 1951).

Curti, Merle Eugene, *The Roots of American Loyalty* (New York City, NY: Russell & Russell [1946] 1967).

D _____

Darley, Gillian, *John Evelyn: Living for ingenuity* (New Haven, CT: Yale University Press, 2006).

Davie, Maurice, *William Graham Sumner* (New York City, NY: Crowell, 1963).

Darwin, Erasmus, *The Temple of Nature, or, The Origin of Society* (London: Johnson, 1803; New York City, NY: Garland Pub., 1978).

Davidson, James W., *The Logic and Millennial Thought: Eighteenth Century New England* (New Haven, CT: Yale University Press, 1977).

Davis, Allen F., *Spearheads for Reform: The Social Settlements and the Progressive Movement* (New York City, NY: Oxford University Press, 1967).

De Jong, H. M. E., *Michael Maier's Atalanta Fugiens* (Lake Worth, FL: Nicolas-Hays, 1969).

Dennis, Lawrence, *Is Capitalism Doomed?* (New York City, NY: Harper & Brothers, 1932).

Dennis, Lawrence, *The Coming American Fascism* (New York City, NY: Harper & Brothers, 1936).

Devlin, Patrick, *Too Proud to Fight: Woodrow Wilson's Neutrality* (New York City, NY: Oxford University Press, 1975).

Dewey, Orville, *The Works of the Rev. Orville Dewey, D.D.* (London: Simms & McIntyre, 1844).

Dewey, Orville, *Works of Learned Benjamin Whichcote* (Aberdeen: Alexander Thomson, 1751).

DiLorenzo, Thomas, *Hamilton's Curse* (Danvers, MA: Crown Forum, 2009).

Dionysius the Areopagite, *The Complete Works* (New York City, NY: Paulist Press, 1987).

Dixon, William Hepworth, *Spiritual Wives* (London: Hurst & Blackett, 1868) vol. 1.

Dodd, William E., *Woodrow Wilson and His Work* (Garden City, NY: Doubleday Page, 1920).

Dobbs, Betty Jo Teeter, *The Janus Face of Genius* (Cambridge: Cambridge University Press, 1991).

Dodds, Eric Robertson, *The Ancient Concept of Progress and Other Essays on Greek Literature and Belief* (Oxford: Clarendon Press, [1973] 1974).

Doenecke, Justus, *Storm on the Horizon: The Challenge to American Intervention, 1939-1941* (Lanham, MD: Rowman and Littlefield, 2000).

Donnelly, Ignatius, *The Golden Bottle Or the Story of Ephraim Benezet of Kansas* (New York City, NY: Merrill, 1892).

Drummond, Robert Blackley, *Erasmus: His Life and Character as shown in his correspondence and works* (London: Smith, Elder & Co., 1873) vol. 1 & 2.

Du Boulay, F. R. H., *An Age of Ambition: English Society in the Late Middle Ages* (New York City, NY: Viking, 1970).

Duggan, Stephen P., ed., *The League of Nations: The Principle and Practice* (Boston, MA: Atlantic Monthly Press, 1919).

Dunn, Robert W., Adrian Richt, *American Foreign Investments* (New York City, NY: B. W. Huebsch and the Viking Press, 1926; New York City, NY: Arno Press, 1976).

Dunning, William Archibald, *Reconstruction: Political and Economic, 1865-1877* (New York City, NY: Harper & Brothers, 1907).

Dyer, Colin F. W., *William Preston and His Work* (Shepperton, Middlesex: Lewis Masonic, 1987).

E _____

Edelstein, Ludwig, *The Idea of Progress in Classical Antiquity* (Baltimore, MD: Johns Hopkins Press, 1967).

Edwards, Jonathan, *The Nature of True Virtue* (1749), in Paul Ramsey, ed., *Ethical Writings* (WJE Online vol. 8).

Ekirch, Jr., Arthur Alphonse, *Decline of American Liberalism* (Oakland, CA: Independent Institute, [1972] 2009).

Eliade, Mircea, *The Forge and the Crucible: The Origins and Structures of Alchemy* (New York City, NY: Harper & Row, [1956] 1971).

Ellis, Edward Robb, *The Epic of New York City* (New York City, NY: Kondansha, 1997).

Ely, Richard T., *The Social Aspects of Christianity and other Essays* (New York City, NY: Thomas Y. Crowell, 1889).

Ely, Richard T., *The Labor Movement in America* (New York City, NY: Thomas Y. Crowell & Co., 1886).

Ely, Richard T., *The Coming City* (New York City, NY: Thomas Y. Crowell, 1902).

Engelbrecht, H. C. & F. C. Hanighen, *Merchants of Death: A Study of the International Armament Industry* (New York City, NY: Dodd, Mead and Co., 1934).

Erasmus, Desiderius, *De libero arbitrio Diatribe sive collatio* (1524), in Desiderius Erasmus, *Ausgewählte Schriften von Erasmus von Rotterdam* (lateinisch-deutsch), ed. by Werner Welzig, vol. 4 (Darmstadt: WBG [Wissenschaftliche Buchgesellschaft], 2016; Basel: Ioannem Frobenium, 1524).

Erasmus, Desiderius, *Discourses on Free Will*, ed. and trans. by Ernest F. Winter, *Erasmus & Luther* (New York City, NY: Frederick Ungar, 1961).

Erdmann, Martin, *Ecumenical Quest for a World Federation: The Churches' Contribution to Marshal Public Support for World Order and Peace, 1919-1945* (Greenville, SC: Verax Vox Media, 2016).

Erdmann, Martin, *Der Griff zur Macht: Dominionismus – der evangelikale Weg zu globalem Einfluss* (Augustdorf: Betanien Verlag, 2011).

Everard, J., *The Divine Pymander of Hermes Mercurius Trismegistus* (London: G. Redway, 1884).

F

Fabricius, Johannes, *Alchemy: The Medieval Alchemists and Their Royal Art (Cockeysville, MD: Diamond Books, 1994).*

Fairchild, Hoxie Neale, *Religious Trends in English Poetry* (New York City, NY: Columbia University Press, [1942] 1964) vol. 2.

Fairchild, James Harris, *Reminiscences of Rev. Charles G. Finney: Speeches and Sketches at the Gathering of His Friends and Pupils, in Oberlin, July 28, 1876, Together With President Fairchild's Memorial Sermon, Delivered Before the Graduating Classes, July 30, 1876* (Oberlin, OH: E. J. Goodrich, 1876).

Faivre, Antoine, *Access to Western Esotericism* (Albany, NY: State University of New York Press, 1994).

Faivre, Antoine, *The Eternal Hermes* (Grand Rapids, MI: Phanes, 1995).

Faivre, Antoine & J. Needleman, eds., *Modern Esoteric Spirituality* (New York City, NY: Crossroad, 1992).

Faivre, Antoine & Rolf Christian Zimmermann, eds., *Epochen der Naturmystik: Hermetische Tradition im wissenschaftlichen Fortschritt* (Berlin: Erich Schmidt, 1979).

Farrar, Adam Storey, *A critical History of Free Thought in reference to the Christian Religion: Eight lectures preached before the University of Oxford, in the year M. DCCC. LXII* [...] (London: John Murray, 1862; New York City, NY: D. Appleton and Co., 1863).

Faulkner, Harold U., *The Quest for Social Justice, 1898-1914* (New York City, NY: The Macmillan Company, 1931).

Fay, Bernard, *Revolution and Freemasonry* (Boston, MA: Little, Brown & Co., 1935).

Fay, Bernard, *La franc maçonerie et la révolution intellectuelle du XVIIIe siècle* (Paris: Cluny, 1935).

Fay, Bernard, *Franklin: The Apostle of Modern Times* (Boston, MA: Little, Brown, and Co., 1929).

Fay, Peter Ward, *The Opium War 1840-1842* (Chapel Hill, NC: University of North Carolina Press, 1995).

Ferguson, Niall, *The Pity of War: 1914-1918* (London: Penguin Books, 1999).

Ferguson, Sinclair B. & David F. Wright & James I. Packer, eds., *New Dictionary of Theology* (Downers Grove, Il.: IVP Academic, 2008).

Fine, Sidney, *Laissez Faire Thought and the General-Welfare State: A Study of Conflict in American Thought, 1865-1901* (Ann Arbor, MI: University of Michigan Press, 1956).

Finney, Charles Grandison, *Lectures on Revival*, 2nd ed. (New York City, NY: Fleming H. Revell, [1835] 1868).

Finney, Charles Grandison, *Sermons on Important Subjects* (New York City, NY: John S. Taylor, 1836).

Finney, Charles Grandison, *Sermons on Gospel Themes* (Oberlin, OH: E. J. Goodrich; New York City, NY: Dodd, Mead, 1876).

Finney, Charles G., *Lectures on Systematic Theology, embracing ability (natural, moral and gracious) repentance, impenitence, faith and unbelief* […] (Oberlin, OH: James M. Fitch, 1847).

Finney, Charles Grandison, *Lectures on Systematic Theology, embracing ability (natural, moral and gracious) repentance, impenitence, faith and unbelief* […] (Boston, MA: Crocker and Brewster, 1847).

Finney, Charles Grandison, *Memoirs of Rev. Charles G. Finney* (New York City, NY: A. S. Barnes & Company, 1876).

Firth, Katherine R., *The Apocalyptic tradition in Reformation Britain, 1520-1645* (Oxford: Oxford University Press, [1978] 1979).

Fitzpatrick, John C., ed., *The Writings of George Washington*, 39 vols. (Washington, D.C., 1931-1844) vol. 29.

Fleming, Frank Denna, The Cold War and Its Origins, 1917-1960 (Garden City, NY: Doubleday, 1961).

Forcey, Charles, *The Crossroads of Liberalism: Croly, Weyl, Lippmann, and the Progressive Era, 1900-1925* (New York City, NY: Oxford University Press, 1961).

Fosdick, Harry Emerson, *Christianity and Progress* (New York City, NY: Fleming H. Revell Co., 1922).

Foster, Charles I., *An Errand of Mercy: The Evangelical United Front, 1790-1837* (Chapel Hill, NC: University of North Carolina Press, 1960).

Foster, Frank Hugh, *A Genetic History of New England Theology* (Chicago, IL: University of Chicago Press, 1907).

Freeman, Douglas Southall, *George Washington: A biography*, 7 vols. (New York City, NY: Charles Scribner's Sons, 1948) vol. 5.

Frothingham, Octavius Brooks, *George Ripley* (Boston, MA: Houghton, Mifflin and Company, 1883).

G

Gardner, Lloyd C., *Economic Aspects of New Deal Diplomacy* (Madison, WI: University of Wisconsin Press, 1964).

Ginger, Ray, *Age of Excess: The United States from 1877 to 1914* (Long Grove, IL: Waveland Press, 1965).

Ginger, Ray & Mike Davis, *The Bending Cross: A Biography of Eugene Victor Debs* (New Brunswick, NJ: Rutgers University Press, 1949).

Glad, Paul W., *The Trumpet Soundeth: William Jennings Bryan and His Democracy, 1896-1912* (Lincoln, NE: University of Nebraska Press, 1960).

Gladden, Washington, *Tools and the Man: Property and Industry under the Christian Law* (Boston, MA: Houghton Mifflin, 1893).

Gladden, Washington, *Applied Christianity: Moral Aspects of Social Questions* (Boston, MA: Houghton Mifflin, 1886).

Goldman, Eric Frederick, *Rendezvous with Destiny: A history of modern American reform* (New York City, NY: Knopf, 1952; Chicago, IL: Ivan R. Dee, 2001).

Goodwin, Doris Kearns, *No Ordinary Time: Franklin and Eleanor Roosevelt: The Home Front in World War II* (New York City, NY: Simon and Schuster, 1994; New York City, NY: First Touchstone Edition, 1995).

Graham, Jr., Otis L., *The Great Campaigns: Reform and War in America, 1900-1928* (Englewood Cliffs, NJ: Prentice-Hall, 1971; Malabar, FL: Robert E. Krieger, 1987).

Grand Lodge of Pennsylvania, *Proceedings of the right Worshipful Grand Lodge of* […] *Pennsylvania* […] *Bicentenary of the birth of* […] *Benjamin Franklin* […] (Philadelphia, PA: Grand Lodge F. & A.M. Penn., 1906).

Grant, Susan-Mary, *North Over South: Northern Nationalism and American Identity in the Antebellum Era* (Lawrence, KS: University Press of Kansas, 2000).

Green, Jack P., ed., *Colonies to Nation: A Documentary History of the American Revolution* (New York City, NY: W. W. Norton, 1975).

Gresham, John Leroy, *Charles G. Finney's Doctrine of the Baptism of the Holy Spirit* (Peabody, MA: Hendrickson, 1987).

Greschat, Martin, ed., *Zur Neueren Pietismusforschung* (Darmstadt: Wissenschaftliche Buchgesellschaft [Abt. Verl.], 1977).

Grey, Edward, Viscount Grey of Fallodon, *Twenty-Five Years, 1892-1916* (New York City, NY: Frederick A. Stokes, 1925).

Griffin, G. Edward, *The Creature from Jekyll Island: A Second Look at the Federal Reserve*, 3 ed. (Westlake Village, CA: American Media, 1998).

Grunberg, Paul, *Philip Jacob Spener*, 3 vols. (Göttingen: Vandenhoeck & Ruprecht 1893-1906; republication: Erich Beyreuther, ed., Hildesheim: Olms, 1988).

Guthrie, W. K. C., *In the Beginning: Some Greek views on the origins of life and the early state of man* (Ithaca, NY: Cornell University Press, [1957] 1965).

H
_____

Halévy, Elie, *A History of the English People in the Nineteenth Century: Epilogue, 1895-1905* (New York City, NY: Harcourt, Brace, 1926) vol. 2.

Halévy, Elie, *The Rule of Democracy: 1905-1914* (New York City, NY: Peter Smith, 1952) vol. 2.

Hall, G. Stanley, *Life and Confessions of a Psychologist* (New York City, NY: D. Appleton and Co., 1923).

Hamilton, Alexander & James Madison & John Jay, *The Federalist* (New York City, NY: The Colonial Press, 1901).

Handy, Robert T., *A Christian America: Protestant Hopes and Historical Realities* (New York City, NY: Oxford University Press, [1971] 1984).

Hardman, Keith J., *Charles Grandison Finney: Revivalist and Reformer* (Grand Rapids, MI: Baker and Syracuse University Press, 1987).

Hartlib, Samuel, ed., *A Designe for Plentie by an Universall Planting of Fruit-Trees: Tendred by Some Wel-Wishers to the Publick* (London: Printed for Richard Wodenothe, 1652).

Hartlib, Samuel, *The Reformed Commonwealth of Bees: Presented in Severall Letters and Observations to Samuel Hartlib* (London: Printed for Giles Calvert, 1655).

Hatch, Nathan O., *The Sacred Cause of Liberty. Republican Thought and the Millennium in Revolutionary New England* (New Haven, CT: Yale University Press, 1977).

Hatch, Nathan O., *The Democratization of American Christianity* (New Haven, CT: Yale University Press, 1989).

Hayek, Friedrich A., *The Counter-Revolution of Science: Studies in the Abuse of Reason* (Indianapolis, ID: Liberty Press, [1952] 1979).

Hays, Samuel P., *The Response to Industrialism, 1885-1914* (Chicago, IL: University of Chicago Press, [1957] 1995).

Heimert, Alan, *Religion and the American Mind from the Great Awakening to the Revolution* (Cambridge, MA: Harvard University, 1966).

Henrey, Blanche, *British Botanical and Horticultural Literature Before 1800*, 3 vols. (London: Oxford University Press, [1975] 1999) vol. 1.

Hershberger, Guy Franklin, *The Way of the Cross in Human Relations* (Scottdale, PA: Herald Press, 1958; Eugene, OR: Wipf and Stock Publishers, 2001).

Hicks, John D., *The Populist Revolt: A History of the Farmers' Alliance and the People's Party* (Minneapolis, MN: University of Minnesota Press, 1931).

Higgs, Robert, *Crisis and Leviathan: Critical Episodes in the Growth of American Government* (New York City, NY: Oxford University Press, 1987).

Hill, Christopher, *World Upside Down* (London: Temple Smith, 1972).

Hills, Aaron Merritt, *Life of Charles G. Finney* (Cincinnati, OH: God's Revivalist, 1902).

Hirst, Julie, *Jane Leade: Biography of a Seventeenth-Century Mystic* (Aldershot, Hampshire: Ashgate, 2006).

Hobbes, Thomas, *Leviathan, or The Matter, Forme, & Power, of a Common-Wealth Ecclesiasticall and Civill* (London: Printed for Andrew Crooke, 1651).

Hobbes, Thomas, *Leviathan*, ed. by J. C. A. Gaskin (Oxford: Oxford University Press, [1651] 2009).

Hobson, John Atkinson, *Imperialism: A Study* (London: James Nisbet & Co., 1902).

Hodgson, Godfrey, *Woodrow Wilson's Right Hand: The Life of Colonel Edward M. House* (New Haven, CT: Yale University Press, annotated edition, 2006).

Hofstadter, Richard, *Anti-Intellectualism in American Life* (New York City, NY: Alfred A. Knopf, [1962] 1966).

Hofstadter, Richard, *The Age of Reform: From Bryan to F.D.R.* (New York City, NY: Vintage Books, 1955).

Hofstadter, Richard, *The Progressive Historians: Turner, Beard, Parrington* (New York City, NY: Knopf Doubleday Publishing Group, [1968] 2012).

Holmes, Jr., Oliver Wendell, *The Common Law* (Boston, MA: Little, Brown and Company, [1881] 1923).

Holt, Michael Fitzgibbon, *The Rise and Fall of the American Whig Party* (Oxford: Oxford University Press, [1999] 2003).

Hopkins, James K., *Woman to deliver her People: Joanna Southcott and English Millenarianism in an Era of Revolution* (Austin, TX: University of Texas Press, 2010).

Hotson, Howard, *Johann Heinrich Alsted 1588-1638: Between Renaissance, Reformation, and Universal Reform* (New York City, NY: Clarendon Press, 2000).

Hotson, Howard, *Paradise postponed: Johann Heinrich Alsted and the birth of Calvinist millenarianism* (Dordrecht: Kluwer, 2000).

Hough, Joseph Howell & William Silas Whitehead, *Origins of Masonry in the State of New Jersey, and the Entire Proceedings of the Grand Lodge, from its First Organization, Trenton*, NJ: A.L. 5786 (Trenton, NJ: J. H. Hough, 1870).

Howard, Michael, *The Occult Conspiracy: Secret Societies, Their Influence and Power in World History* (Rochester, VT: Destiny Books, 1989).

Hull, Cordell & Andrew Henry & Thomas Berding, *The Memoirs of Cordell Hull* (London: Hodder & Stoughton, 1948) vol. 1.

Hurwitz, Samuel J., *State Intervention in Great Britain* (New York City, NY: Columbia University Press, 1949).

I _____

Inge, William Ralph, *The Philosophy of Plotinus*, 2 vols. (New York City, NY: Longmans, Green and Co., [1918] 1948) vol. 1 & 2.

Irenaeus, *Adversus haereses*, V. (Cantabrigiae: Typis academicis, 1857).

Irving, Washington, *Life of George Washington* (New York City, NY: Putnam, 1865).

J

Jacobs, Jane, *The Economy of Cities* (New York City, NY: Vintage, 1969).

Jacob, Margaret C., *The Radical Enlightenment: Pantheists, Freemasons and Republicans* (London: George Allen & Unwin, 1981).

Jacob, Margaret C., *Living the Enlightenment: Freemasonry and Politics in 18th Century Europe* (New York City, NY: Oxford University Press, 1991).

James, William, *Principles of Psychology* (New York City, NY: Henry Holt and Co., 1890).

Jenks, L. H., *Our Cuban Colony: A Study in Sugar* (New York City, NY: Vanguard Press, 1928).

Jue, Jeffrey K., *Heaven Upon Earth. Joseph Mede (1586-1638) and the Legacy of Millenarianism* (Dortrecht: Springer, 2006).

K

Kearney, Hugh J., *Science and Change: 1500-1700* (New York City, NY: McGraw-Hill, 1971).

Keeling, Ralph Franklin, *Gruesome Harvest: The Allies' Postwar: War Against the German People* (Chicago, IL: Institute of American Economics, 1947).

Keller, Charles Roy, *The Second Great Awakening in Connecticut* (New Haven, CT: Yale University Press, 1942).

Kennedy, David M., *Over Here: The First World War and American Society* (New York City, NY: Oxford University Press, 1980).

Kennedy, David M., ed., *Progressivism: The Critical Issues* (Boston, MA: Little, Brown, 1971).

Kennedy, Thomas C., *Charles A. Beard and American Foreign Policy* (Gainesville, FL: The University Press of Florida, 1975).

Keynes, John Maynard, *General Theory of Employment, Interest, and Money* (London: Macmillan and Co., 1936).

Khunrath, Henricus, *Amphitheatrum Sapientiae Aeternae, Solius, Verae, Christiano-Kabalisticum, Divino-Magicum, Physico-Chymicum,*

Tertriunum-Catholicon (Hamburg, 1595; Magdeburg 1608, 1609; Frankfurt 1653). German translation of *Amphitheatrum Sapientiae Aeternae*, ed. by Carlos Gilly, Anja Hallacker, Hanns-Peter Neumann and Wilhelm Schmidt-Biggemann (Stuttgart: Frommann-Holzboog, 2013).

Klein, Jürgen & Johannes Kramer, eds., *Johann Heinrich Alsted, Herborns calvinistische Theologie und Wissenschaft im Spiegel der englischen Kulturreform des frühen 17. Jahrhunderts. Studien zu englisch-deutschen Geistesbeziehungen der frühen Neuzeit* (Frankfurt am Main: Lang, 1988).

Knight, Melvin Moses, *The Americans in Santo Domingo* (New York City, NY: Vanguard Press, 1928).

Knightley, Phillip, *The First Casualty: The War Correspondent as Hero and Myth-Maker from the Crimea to Iraq*, 3 ed. (Baltimore, MD: John Hopkins University Press, 2004).

Knock, Thomas J., *To End All Wars: Woodrow Wilson and the Quest for a New World Order* (New York City, NY: Oxford University Press, 1992).

Knoop, Douglas & G. P. Jones, *The Genesis of Freemasonry* (Manchester: Manchester University Press, 1949).

Kolko, Gabriel Morris, *The Triumph of Conservatism: A Reinterpretation of American History, 1900-1916* (New York City, NY: Quadrangle Books, 1963; New York City, NY: Free Press, 1977).

Kolko, Gabriel Morris, *Railroads and Regulation, 1877-1916* (Princeton, NJ: Princeton University Press, 1965; Westport, CT: Greenwood Press, 1976).

Kolko, Gabriel Morris, *The Politics of War: The World and United States Foreign Policy, 1943-1945* (New York City, NY: Pantheon Books, [1968]1990).

Kolko, Gabriel Morris, *Main Currents in Modern American History* (New York City, NY: Harper & Row, 1976).

Kolko, Gabriel Morris, *The Roots of American Foreign Policy: An Analysis of Power and Purpose* (Boston, MA: Beacon Press, 1969).

Kolko, Gabriel Morris, *Anatomy of a War: Vietnam, the United States, and the Modern Historical Experience* (New York City, NY: Pantheon Books, 1985).

Kolko, Gabriel Morris, *Century of War: Politics, conflicts, and society since 1914* (New York City, NY: New Press; distributed by W.W. Norton, 1994).

Kolko, Gabriel M. & Joyce, *The Limits of Power: The world and United States foreign policy, 1945-1954* (New York City, NY: Harper & Row, 1972).

Krüger, G., *Die Rosenkreuzer: Ein Rückblick* (Berlin: Verlag von Alfred Unger, 1932).

Kvačala, Jan, *Johann Amos Comenius, sein Leben und seine Schriften* (Leipzig: J. Klinkhardt, 1892).

L _____

Langguth, A. J., *Patriots: The Men Who Started the American Revolution* (New York City, NY: Simon & Schuster, 1988).

Lansing, Robert, *War Memoirs* (Indianapolis, IN: Bobbs-Merrill, 1935).

Lasky, Melvin J., *Utopia and Revolution* (London: Macmillan and Company, 1977).

Lawrence, William B., *Sundays in New York: Pulpit Theology at the Crest of the Protestant Mainstream 1930-1955* (Lanham, MD: Scarecrow Press, Inc., 1996).

Leade, Jane Ward, *A Message to the Philadelphian Society, […] together with a call to the several gathered Churches among Protestants in this nation of England* (A further Manifestation, […] being a second message to the Philadelphian Society, etc. – The Messenger […] or a third message to the Philadelphian Society), vol. 2: *A Message to the Philadelphian Society, […] together with a call to the several gathered Churches among Protestants in this nation of England* (London: Printed for the Booksellers of London and Westminster, 1696).

Lennhoff, Eugen & Oskar Posner & Dieter A. Binder, eds., *Internationales Freimaurer-Lexikon* (Wien: Amalthea-Verlag; Graz: Akademische Druck- und Verlagsanstalt, 1965; München: Herbig, 2015).

Leuchtenburg, William E., *The Perils of Prosperity: 1914-1932* (Chicago, IL: University of Chicago Press, 1958).

Levine, Lawrence W., *Defender of the Faith, William Jennings Bryan: The Last Decade, 1915-1925* (Cambridge, MA: Harvard University Press, 1965).

Liggio, Leonard P., *Why the Futile Crusade?* (New York City, NY: Center for Libertarian Studies, 1978).

Linden, Stanton J., *Darke Hierogliphicks* (Lexington, KY: University Press of Kentucky, 2015).

Link, Arthur S., *Woodrow Wilson and the Progressive Era, 1910-1917* (New York City, NY: Harper & Brothers, 1954).

Link, Arthur S., ed., *The Papers of Woodrow Wilson* (Princeton, NJ: Princeton University Press, 1979) vols. 30, 41.

Lippmann, Walter, *A Preface to Politics* (New York City, NY: Mitchell Kennerley, 1913).

Lippert, Friedrich Adolf Max, *Johann Heinrich Alsteds Pädagogisch-Didaktische Reform: Bestrebungen und ihr Einfluss auf Johann Amos Comenius* (Meissen: C. E. Klinkicht & Sohn, 1898).

Lippmann, Walter, *Drift and Mastery: An attempt to diagnose the current unrest* (New York City, NY: Mitchell Kennerley, 1914).

Lohmann, Martin, *Die Bedeutung der deutschen Ansiedlungen in Pennsylvanien* (Stuttgart: Ausland & Heimat, 1923).

Löwith, Karl, *Meaning in History: The Theological Implications of the Philosophy of History* (Chicago, IL: University of Chicago Press, 1949).

Lucretius, *De Rerum Natura*, ed. by H. A. J. Munro (London: Novi Eboraci Apud Harperos fratres, 1883) book 5.

Luther, Martin, *The Bondage of the Will: A New Translation of De Servo Arbitrio (1525), Martin Luther's Reply to Erasmus of Rotterdam*, trans. by J. I. Packer and O. R. Johnston (Old Tappan, NJ: Fleming H. Revell Co., 1957).

Lynch, Frederick Henry, *The Challenge: The Church and the New World Order* (New York City, NY: Fleming H. Revell Company, 1916).

M

Mackey, Albert Gallatin, *History of Freemasonry in South Carolina: from its origin in the year 1736 to the present time; written at the request of the Grand Lodge of ancient Freemasons of South Carolina* (Columbia, SC: South Carolinian Steam Power Press, 1861).

Mackenzie, Norman, *Secret Societies* (London: Aldus Books, 1967).

Madden, Edward H., *Civil Disobedience and Moral Law in Nineteenth Century America* (Seattle, WA: University of Washington Press, 1968).

Madsen, Axel, *John Jacob Astor: America's First Millionaire* (New York City, NY: John Wiley, 2001).

Mahan, Asa, *Autobiography: Intellectual, Moral and Spiritual* (London: J. Woolner, 1882).

Maier, Johann, *Die Kabbalah. Einführung – Klassische Texte – Erläuterungen* (München: Verlag C.H. Beck, 1995).

Mann, Arthur, *Yankee Reformers in the Urban Age: Social Reform in Boston, 1880-1900* (New York City, NY: Harper & Row, [1954] 1966).

Marsden, George M., *Fundamentalism and American Culture: The Shaping of Twentieth Century Evangelicalism, 1870-1925* (New York City, NY: Oxford University Press, 1980).

Marsh, M. A., *The Bankers in Bolivia: A Study in American Foreign Investment* (New York City, NY: Vanguard Press, 1928).

Martin, Gaston, *La Franc-Maconnerie Francaise et La Preparation de la Revolution* (Paris: Les Presses universitaires de France, 1926; Paris: Champion, Slatkine, 1989).

Martin, James J., *Revisionist Viewpoints* (Colorado Springs, CO: Ralph Myles Press, 1971).

Marty, Martin E., *Righteous Empire: The Protestant Experience in American* (New York City, NY: Dial Press, 1970).

Mathews, Shailer, *The Faith of Modernism* (New York City, NY: AMS Press, [1924] 1969).

Mathews, Shailer, *The Gospel and the Modern Man* (New York City, NY: Macmillan, 1912).

Mathews, Shailer, *The Faith of Modernism* (New York City, NY: AMS Press, [1924] 1969).

Maurer, Wilhelm, *Aufklärung, Idealismus und Restauration*, 2 vols. (Gießen: A. Töpelmann, 1930) vol. 1.

May, Henry F., *The End of American Innocence: A Study of the First Years of Our Own Time, 1912-1917* (New York City, NY: Alfred A. Knopf, 1959).

McDonald, Forrest, *Novus Ordo Seclorum: The Intellectual Origins of the Constitution* (Lawrence, KS: University Press of Kansas, 1985).

McDougall, Walter A., *Promised Land, Crusader State: The American Encounter with the World since 1776* (Boston, MA: Houghton Mifflin, 1997).

McDowell, Paula, *The Women of Grub Street: Press, Politics, and Gender in the London Literary Marketplace 1678-1730* (Oxford: Clarendon P, 1998).

McKim, Randolph, *For God and Country: or, the Christian pulpit in wartime addresses* (New York City, NY: E.P. Dutton, 1918).

McLoughlin, William Gerald, *Modern Revivalism: Charles Grandison Finney to Billy Graham* (New Haven, CT: Yale University Press, [1984] 1994).

McLoughlin, William Gerald, *The American Evangelicals, 1800-1900* (New York City, NY: Harper Torchbooks, 1968).

McMeekin, Sean, *The Russian Origins of the First World War* (Cambridge, MA: Belknap Press of Harvard University Press, 2011).

Mead, Sidney E., *Nathaniel William Taylor, 1786-1858: A Connecticut Liberal* (Chicago, IL: University of Chicago Press, 1942).

Mead, Sidney E., *The Lively Experiment: The Shaping of Christianity in America* (New York City, NY: Harper & Row Publishers, [1963] 1987).

Mede, Joseph, *Clavis Apocalyptica [...] una cum commentario in Apocalypsin: quibus accessit hac tertia editione conjectura de Gogo et Magogo, ab eodem autore* (Cantabrigiae: R. Daniel, 1627); *The Key to Revelation, searched and demonstrated out of the Natural and proper Characters of the Vision*, trans. by Richard More (London: By J. L. for Phil. Stephens, 1643); R. Bransby Cooper, *A translation of Mede's Clavis apocalyptica* (London: Printed for J. G. & F. Rivington, 1833).

Mede, Joseph, *Apostacy of the Latter Times. In which, (according to Divine Prediction) the World Should Wonder After the Beast, the Mysterie of Iniquity Should So Far Prevaile Over the Mysterie of Godlinesse, Whorish Babylon Over the Virgin-Church of Christ, ... Revived in the Latter Times Amongst Christians, [...] &c. [...]* (London: Printed by L. N. for Samuel Man dwelling at the signe of the Swan in Pauls Church-yard, 1644).

Meister, Charles W., *The Founding Fathers* (Jefferson, NC: McFarland and Co., 1987).

Mencken, H. L., *A Mencken Chrestomathy* (New York City, NY: Alfred A. Knopf, 1949).

Meyer, Donald Harvey, *The Instructed Conscience: The shaping of the American national ethic* (Philadelphia, PA: University of Pennsylvania Press, [1972] 2016).

Meyer, Michael C. & William L. Sherman, *The Course of Mexican History,* 5th Edition (New York City, NY: Oxford University Press, 1995).

Miley, John, *The Atonement in Christ* (New York City, NY: Eaton & Mains; Cincinnati, OH: Jennings & Graham, [1879] 1907).

Miller, Perry, ed., *The Transcendentalists: An Anthology* (Cambridge, MA: Harvard University Press, [1950] 2001).

Miller, Perry, *The New England Mind: The Seventeenth Century* (Cambridge, MA: Harvard University Press, [1939] 1954).

Mills, C. Wright, *The New Men of Power* (New York City, NY: Harcourt, Brace, 1948).

Mills, C. Wright, *The Power Elite* (New York City, NY: Oxford University Press, 1956).

Mills, C. Wright, *The Sociological Imagination* (Oxford: Oxford University Press, [1959] 2001).

Miller, Perry, *The Life of the Mind in America: From the Revolution to the Civil War* (New York City, NY: Harcourt, Brace & World, 1965).

Miller, Robert Moats, *American Protestantism and Social Issues 1919-1939* (Chapel Hill, NC: University of North Carolina Press, 1958).

Miller, Robert Moats, *Harry Emerson Fosdick: Preacher, Pastor, Prophet* (New York City, NY: Oxford University Press, 1985).

Millis, Walter, *Road to War: America 1914-1917* (Boston, MA: Houghton Mifflin, 1935).

Moorhead, James H., *American Apocalypse: Yankee Protestants and the Civil War, 1860-1869* (New Haven, CT: Yale University, 1978).

More, Henry, *Enchiridion Ethicum* (London: Benjamin Tooke, 1666).

More, Henry, *Philosophia Teutonicae Censura* (London: 1679), in Henrici Mori, *Opera omnia, tum quae latine, tum quae anglice scripta sunt, nunc vero latinitate donata [...] impensis [...] Johannis Cockshuti, [...]* (Londini: Sumptibus J. Martyn et G. Kettilby, 1679) vol. 1.

More, Henry, *Enthusiasmus Triumphatus: or a Brief Discourse of the Nature, Causes, Kinds and Cures of Enthusiasm*, in Henry More, *A Collection of Several Philosophical Writings of Dr. Henry More* (London: Printed by James Flesher for William Morden Book-seller in Cambridge, 1662).

More, Paul Elmer, *Benjamin Franklin* (Boston, MA; New York City, NY: Houghton, Mifflin and Company, 1900).

Mosier, Richard, *The American Temper* (Berkeley, CA: University of California Press, 1952).

Mowry, George, *The Era of Theodore Roosevelt and the Birth of Modern America, 1900-1912* (New York City, NY: Harper & Brothers, 1958).

Mowry, George, *Theodore Roosevelt and the Progressive Movement* (New York City, NY: Hill and Wang, [1946] 1960).

Mumford, Lewis, *Faith For Living* (London: Secker & Warburg, 1941).

Mumford, Lewis, *The Condition of Man* (London: Secker & Warburg, 1944).

Murray, Iain H., *The Puritan Hope* (London: Banner of Truth, 1971).

Myers, Gustavus, *History of the Great American Fortunes*, 3 vols. (Chicago, IL: Charles H. Kerr & Company, 1907-1910) vols. 1 & 2.

N

Neumann, Franz, *Behemoth: The Structure and Practice of National Socialism* (London: Gollancz, 1942).

Nevins, Allan, *Grover Cleveland: A Study in Courage* (New York City, NY: Scribner's, 1932; Dodd, Mead, 1962).

Nicholl, Charles, *The Chemical Theatre* (London: Routledge & Kegan Paul, 1980; New York City, NY: Akadine Press, 1997).

Niebuhr, H. Richard, *The Kingdom of God in America* (New York City, NY: Harper & Row Publishers, [1938] 1980).

Niebuhr, Reinhold, *Nature and Destiny of Man* (New York City, NY: Charles Scribner's Sons, 1941) vol. 1.

Nisbet, Robert Alexander, *History of the Idea of Progress* (New York City, NY: Basic Books, 1980).

Nisbet, Robert Alexander, *The Social Philosophers: Community and Conflict in Western Thought* (New York City, NY: Washington Square Press, 1982).

Nisbet, Robert Alexander, *The Quest For Community: A Study in the Ethics of Order and Freedom* (New York City, NY: Oxford University Press, 1953; San Francisco, CA: Institute for Contemporary Studies, 1990).

Noble, David W., *The Eternal Adam and the New World Garden: The Central Myth in the American Novel Since 1830* (New York City, NY: George Braziller, 1968).

Noll, Mark, ed., *The Princeton Theology 1812-1921* (Grand Rapids, MI: Baker, 1983).

Nore, Ellen, *Charles A. Beard: An Intellectual Biography* (Carbondale and Edwardsville, IL: Southern Illinois University Press, 1983).

North, Gary, *Cross Fingers: How the Liberals captured the Presbyterian Church* (Tyler, TX: Institute for Christian Economics, 1996).

Nye, Russell B., *Midwestern Progressive Politics: A History of Its Origins and Development, 1870-1958* (East Lansing, MI: Michigan State University Press, 1959).

O

Oliver, George, *The golden Remains of the early masonic Writers* (London: Richard Spencer, 1847) vol. 1.

Orwell, George, *Nineteen Eighty-Four* (London: Secker & Warburg, 1949).

Ovason, David, *The Secret Architecture of Our Nation's Capital* (New York City, NY: Harper Collins, 1999).

P

Parker, Robert Allerton, *A Yankee Saint: John Humphrey Noyes and The Oneida Community* (New York City, NY: G. P. Putnam's sons, 1935).

Parrington, Vernon Louis, *Main Currents in American Thought: The Beginnings of Critical Realism in America, 1860-1920*, 3 vols. (New York City, NY: Harcourt, Brace & World, Inc., [1927] 1958).

Paterson, Thomas G., ed., *Major Problems in American Foreign Policy. Documents and Essays,* vol. 2: *Since 1914* (Lexington, MA: D. C. Heath, 1978).

Patrides, C. A. & Joseph Anthony Wittreich, eds., *The Apocalyse in English Renaissance Thought and Literature* (Manchester: Manchester University Press, 1984).

Patterson, Robert Leet, *The Philosophy of William Ellery Channing* (New York City, NY: Bookman Associates, 1952).

Peck, William F., *History of Rochester and Monroe County, New York* (New York City, NY: The Pioneer Publishing Company, 1908).

Peters, John Leland, *Christian Perfection and American Methodism* (Nashville, TN: Parthenon Press, 1956).

Peterson, Horace Cornelius, *Propaganda for War: The Campaign against American Neutrality, 1914-1917* (Norman, OK: University of Oklahoma Press, 1939).

Peterson, Horace Cornelius & Gilbert C. Fite, *Opponents of War, 1917-1918* (Seattle, WA: University of Washington Press, [1957] 1968).

Peuckert, Will-Erich, *Pansophie. Ein Versuch zur Geschichte der weißen und schwarzen Magie* (Stuttgart: Kohlhammer, 1936; three volume expanded edition: Berlin: E. Schmidt, 1956-1973).

Peuckert, Will-Erich, *Die Rosenkreutzer: Zur Geschichte einer Reformation* (Jena: E. Diederichs, 1928).

Pinchot, Gifford, *The Fight for Conservation* (New York City, NY: Doubleday, Page and Co., 1910).

Pollio, Marcus Vitruvius, *Zehn Bücher über Architektur;* translated and annotated by Jakob Prestel (Baden-Baden: Verlag Heitz GMBH, 1959).

Porter, Bruce, *War and the Rise of the State: The Military Foundations of Modern Politics* (New York City, NY: Free Press, [1994] 2002).

Powicke, Frederick J., *The Cambridge Platonists* (London: J. M. Dent and Sons, 1926).

Pringle, Henry Fowles, *Theodore Roosevelt: A Biography* (New York City, NY: Harcourt Brace, [1931] 1944; New York City, NY: Houghton Mifflin Harcourt, 2003).

Proceedings of a Conference of Governors (Washington, 1909), vol. 1.

Pruette, Lorine, *G. Stanley Hall* (New York City, NY: D. Appleton and Co., 1926).

Q

Quinn, D. Michael, *Early Mormonism and the Magic World View* (Salt Lake City, UT: Signature books, 1998).

R

Rader, Benjamin G., *The Academic Mind and Reform: The Influence of Richard T. Ely in American Life* (Lexington, KY: University of Kentucky Press, 1966).

Radosh, Ronald, *Prophets on the Right: Profiles of Conservative Critics of American Globalism* (New York City, NY: Simon and Schuster, 1975; New York: Free Life Editions, Inc., 1978).

Ratner, Joseph, ed., *Character and Events* (New York City, NY: Holt, 1929) vol. II, book 4.

Read, John & Frederick Henry Sawyer, *Prelude to Chemistry* (New York City, NY: The Macmillan Company, 1937).

Read, John Morgan, *Atrocity Propaganda, 1914-1919* (New Haven, CT: Yale University Press, 1941).

Reeves, Marjorie, *The Influence of Prophecy in the Later Middle Ages* (Oxford: Clarendon Press, [1969] 2000).

Reid, Thomas, *Essays on the Intellectual Powers of Man, to which are added, An essay on quantity, and An analysis of Aristotle's logic* (London: Thomas Tegg, 1827; Cambridge, MA: The M.I.T. Press, 1969).

Reinsch, Paul S., *World Politics: The End of the Nineteenth Century* (New York City, NY: Macmillan, [1900] 1908).

Resek, Carl, ed., *The Progressives* (Indianapolis, IN: Bobbs-Merrill, 1967).

Richey, Russell E. & Donald G. Jones, *American Civil Religion* (New York City, NY: Harper & Row Publishers, 1974).

Ringer, Fritz K., *The Decline of the German Mandarins: The German Academic Community, 1890-1933* (Cambridge, MA: Harvard University Press, 1969).

Ritchie, Robert C., *Captain Kidd and the War Against the Pirates* (Cambridge, MA: Harvard University Press, 1986).

Roberts, James D., *From Puritanism to Platonism in Seventeenth Century England* (Dordrecht: Springer Netherlands, 1968).

Roberts, John Morris, *The Mythology of Secret Societies* (London: Watkins Publishing, 2008).

Robinson, James H., *The New History: Essays Illustrating the Modern Historical Outlook* (New York City, NY: The Macmillan Company, 1912).

Rockwood, Raymond O., ed., *Carl Becker's Heavenly City revisited: Studies resulting from a symposium held at Colgate University, Hamilton, New York, October 13, 1956, as a phase of the sixth annual meeting of the New York State Association of European Historians* (Ithaca, NY: Cornell University Press: Ithaca, 1958; Hamden, CT: Archon Books, 1968)

Rosenberg, Nathan & L. E. Birdzell, Jr., *How the West Grew Rich* (New York City, NY: BasicBooks, 1986).

Ross, Dorothy, *G. Stanley Hall: The Psychologist as Prophet* (Chicago, IL: University of Chicago Press, 1972).

Rossiter, Clinton, *Seedtime of the Republic: The origin of the American tradition of political liberty* (New York City, NY: Harcourt, Brace, 1953).

Rossiter, Clinton I., *Alexander Hamilton and the Constitution* (New York City, NY: Harcourt, Brace & World, 1964).

Roth, Philip A., *Masonry in the Formation of Our Government (1761-1799)* (Milwaukee, WI: Masonic Service Bureau, 1917).

Roth, Philip A., *Freemasonry and the Causes That Led to the American Revolution* (Whitefish, MT: Kessinger Publishing, [1927] 2010).

Rothbard, Murray N., *The Betrayal of the American Right* (Auburn, AL: The Ludwig von Mises Institute, 2007).

Rothbard, Murray N., *Power and Market* (Auburn, AL: Ludwig Von Mises Institute, [1970] 2006).

Rothbard, Murray N. & Jerome Tuccille, eds., *The Right Wing Individualist Tradition in America* (New York City, NY: Arno Press & The New York Times, 1972).

Rothbard, Murray N., *Man, Economy and State* (Auburn, AL: Ludwig Von Mises Institute, [1962] 2004).

Rothbard, Murray N., *History of Money and Banking in the United States: The Colonial Era to World War II* (Auburn, Al: Ludwig von Mises Institute, 2002).

Rousseau, Jean-Jacques, *Discours sur l'origine et les fondements de l'inégalité parmi les hommes* (Amsterdam: Marc Michel Rey, 1755).

Rousseau, Jean-Jacques, *Du contrat social ou Principes du droit politique* (Amsterdam: Marc Michel Rey, 1762).

Rousseau, Jean-Jacques, *The Social Contract Or Principles Of Political Right* (London: George Allen And Unwin Limited, 1948; Harmondsworth: Penguin, 1968).

Royster, Charles, *The Destructive War: William Tecumseh Sherman, Stonewall Jackson, and the Americans* (New York City, NY: Alfred A. Knopf, 1991).

Ryan, Halford R., *Harry Emerson Fosdick: Persuasive Preacher* (New York, NY: Greenwood Press, 1989).

Ryn, Claes G., *America the Virtuous: The Crisis of Democracy and the Quest for Empire* (Piscataway, NJ: Transaction Publishers, 2003).

S

Sachse, Julius Friedrich, *Benjamin Franklin as a Freemason; compiled at the request of the right worshipful grand master of Pennsylvania and read at the bi-centenary of the birth of Benjamin Franklin before the right worshipful grand lodge of Pennsylvania, free and accepted masons, March seventh, nineteen hundred and six* (Philadelphia, PA: The New Era Printing Company, 1906).

Sachse, Julius Friedrich, *The German Pietists of Provincial Pennsylvania for the Chapter* (Philadephia, PA: Printed for the Author, 1895) vol. 1.

Sachse, Julius Friedrich, *The German Sectarians of Pennsylvania, 1708-1742 (1742-1800): A critical and legendary history of the Ephrata Cloister and the Dunkers*, 2 vols. (Philadelphia, PA: Printed for the author by P. C. Stockhausen, 1899-1900) vol. 1.

Sandeen, Ernest R., *The Roots of Fundamentalism: British and American Millenarianism, 1800-1930* (Chicago: University of Chicago Press, [1970] 2008).

Santillana, Giorgio de, ed., in Introduction to *The Age of Adventure* (Indianapolis, IN: Houghton Mifflin Company & New American Library of World Literature, Inc., 1956; New York City, NY: George Barzieller, 1957).

Scally, Robert J., *The Origins of the Lloyd George Coalition: The Politics of Social-Imperialism, 1900-1918* (Princeton, NJ: Princeton University Press, 1975).

Schaff, Philip, *Creeds of Christendom: with a history and critical notes*, 3 vols. (New York City, NY: Harper [1919] 1931) vol. 1.

Schick, H., *Das ältere Rosenkreuzertum* (Berlin: Nordland Verlag, 1942).

Schuchard, Marsha Keith, *Freemasonry, Secret Societies, and the Continuity of the Occult Traditions in English Literature* (Austin, TX: University of Texas, 1991).

Schultz, Edward Thomas, *History of Freemasonry in Maryland: of all the rites introduced into Maryland, from the earliest time [1783] to the present [...]*, 3 vols. (Baltimore, MD: J. H. Medairy, 1884-1887) vol. 2.

Secondat, Charles de, Baron de Montesquieu, *De l'esprit des loix* (Geneve: Chez Barrillot & Fils, 1748).

Seidensticker, Oswald, *Ephrata: Eine amerikanische Klostergeschichte* (Cincinnati, OH: Druck von Mecklenborg & Rosenthal, 1883).

Semmel, Bernard, *Imperalism and Social Reform: English Social-Imperial Thought, 1895-1914* (Cambridge, MA: Harvard University Press, 1960).

Seymour, Charles, *The Intimate Papers Of Colonel House*, 4 vols. (Boston, MA: The Houghton Mifflin Company, 1926) vols. 1 & 2.

Sharp, Alan, *The Versailles Settlement: Peacemaking in Paris, 1919* (New York City, NY: St. Martin's Press, 1991).

Shoham, Shlomo Giora, *Bridges to Nothingness: Gnosis, Kabala, Existentialism, and the Transcendental Predicament of Man* (London: Associated University Presses, 1994).

Simpson, Colin, *The Lusitania* (Upper Saddle River, NJ: Prentice Hall Press, 1972).

Singer, C. Gregg, *A theological Interpretation of American History* (Philadelphia, PA: Presbyterian and Reformed Publishing Co., 1964).

Smith, Adam, *An Inquiry into the Nature and Causes of the Wealth of Nations* (New York City, NY: Oxford University Press, 1976).

Smith, Gerald Birney, *Social Idealism and the Changing Theology* (New York City, NY: Macmillan, 1913).

Smith, Gerald Birney, ed., *Religious Thought in the Last Quarter-Century* (Chicago, IL: University of Chicago Press, 1927).

Smith, Ted A., *The New Measures: A Theological History of Democratic Practice* (Cambridge: Cambridge University Press, 2007).

Smith, Timothy L., *Revivalism and Social Reform: American Protestantism on the Eve of the Civil War* (Nashville, TN: Abingdon, 1957).

Smyth, Albert H., ed., *The Writings of Benjamin Franklin Writings* (New York City, NY: Macmillan, 1905-1907; New York City, NY: Haskell, 1970) vol. 8.

Snodgrass, Charles Albert, *The History of Freemasonry in Tennessee, 1789-1943: Its founders, its pioneer lodges and chapters, Grand lodge and Grand chapter, the Cryptic rite, the Templars, the Order of high priesthood and the ancient and accepted Scottish rite, with a foreword of its lineage and the ancient history and traditions* (Nashville, TN: Ambrose Printing Co., sold by Masonic History Agency, Chattanooga, TN, 1944).

Speer, Robert E., *The Christian Man, the Church and the War* (New York City, NY: Macmillan, 1918).

Spener, Philipp Jacob, *Pia Desideria*, in Kurt Aland, *Kleine Texte für Vorlesungen und Übungen*, vol. 170 (Berlin: A. Marcus und E. Weber's Verlag, 1940).

Spenser, Edmund, *The Complete Poetical Works: The Faerie Queene*, ed. by R. E. Neil Dodge (Boston & New York City, NY: Houghton Mifflin Co., [1590] 1908).

Sperle, Joanne, *God's Healing Angel: A Biography of Jane Ward Lead* (Ann Arbor, MI: University of Michigan Press, 1985).

Stoeffler, Fred Ernst, *The Rise of Evangelical Pietism* (Leiden, Boston, Köln: Brill, 1965).

Stokes, Anson Phelps, *Church and State in the United States*, 2 vols. (New York City, NY: Harper and Brothers, 1950) vol. 1.

Strong, Josiah, *Our Country: Its Possible Future and Its Present Crisis* (New York City, NY: Baker & Taylor, 1885; Cambridge, MA: Harvard University Press, 1963).

Strong, Josiah, *The New Era or the Coming Kingdom* (New York City, NY: Baker & Taylor, 1893).

Strong, Josiah, *The Twentieth Century City* (New York City, NY: Baker & Taylor, 1898).

Strong, Josiah, *Our World: The New World-Life* (New York City, NY: Doubleday, Page, 1913).

Struck, W., *Der Einfluss Jakob Boehmes auf die englische Literatur des 17. Jahrhunderts* (Berlin: Junker und Dünnhaupt, 1936).

Sumner, Charles, *The Works of Charles Sumner* (Boston, MA: Lee and Shepard, 1870) vol. 2.

Sumner, Charles & Edward Lillie Pierce, *Memoir and Letters of Charles Sumner* (Boston, MA: Roberts Brothers, 1877-1893) vol. 3.

Sumner, William Graham, *History of American Currency, with Chapters on the English Bank Restriction and Austrian Paper Money, to which is appended "The Bullion Report"* (New York City, NY: H. Holt, 1874).

Sumner, William Graham, *Lectures on the History of Protection in the United States: delivered before the International Free-Trade Alliance* (New York City, NY: Putnam's for the International Free Trade Alliance, 1877).

Sumner, William Graham, *Andrew Jackson as a public man: What he was, what chances he had, and what he did with them* (Boston, MA: Houghton, Mifflin, 1884).

Sumner, William Graham, *Andrew Jackson* (Boston, MA: Houghton, Mifflin, [1882] 1899).

Sumner, William Graham, *Alexander Hamilton* (New York City, NY: Dodd, Mead, and Company, 1890).

Sumner, William Graham, *The Financier and Finances of the American Revolution*, 2 vols. (New York City, NY: Dodd, Mead, and Company, 1891) vols. 1 & 2.

Sumner, William Graham, *Robert Morris* (New York City, NY: Dodd, Mead, and Company, 1892).

Sumner, William Graham, *A history of banking in all the leading nations; comprising the United States; Great Britain; Germany; Austro-Hungary; France; Italy; Belgium; Spain; Switzerland; Portugal; Roumania; Russia; Holland; the Scandinavian nations; Canada; China; Japan* (New York City, NY: The Journal of Commerce and Commercial Bulletin, 1896) vols. 1-4.

Sumner, William Graham, *What Social Classes Owe to Each Other* (New York City, NY: Harper & Brothers, [1883] 1920).

Sweeney, Douglas A., *Nathaniel Taylor, New Haven Theology, and the Legacy of Jonathan Edwards* (New York City, NY: Oxford University Press, 2003).

T

Tansill, Charles Callan, *America Goes to War* (Gloucester, MA: Peter Smith, [1938] 1963).

Tatsch, J. Hugo, *Freemasonry in the Thirteen Colonies* (New York City, NY: Macoy Publishing and Masonic Supply Company, 1929).

Taylor, Graham, *Religion in Social Action* (New York City, NY: Dodd, Mead, 1913).

Tcherkesoff, W., *Page of Socialist History* (New York City, NY: C. B. Cooper, 1902).

Teggart, Frederick John, ed., *The Idea of Progress: A Collection of Readings*, rev. edition of G. H. Hildebrand (Berkeley, CA: University of California Press, 1949).

Thomas, Keith, *Religion and the Decline of Magic: Studies in popular beliefs in sixteenth- and seventeenth-century* (London: Weidenfeld and Nicolson, 1971; London: Folio Society, 2012).

Thompson, Charles John Samuel, *The Lure and Romance of Alchemy* (London: G. G. Harrap, 1932; Detroit, MI: Gale Research Co., 1974).

Thune, Nils Brorson, *The Behmenists and the Philadelphians: A contribution to the study of English mysticism in the 17th and 18th centuries* (Uppsala: Almqvist & Wiksell, 1948).

Town, Salem, A *System of Speculative Masonry* (Salem, NY: H. Dodd and Co., 1822).

Tuchman, Barbara W., *The Proud Tower: A Portrait of the World Before the War, 1890-1914* (New York City, NY: Macmillan, 1966).

Tucker, Robert C., *Philosophy and Myth in Karl Marx* (Cambridge: Cambridge University Press, 1961).

Turgot, Anne Robert Jacques, baron de l'Aulne, Œuvres de Turgot et documents le concernant, Gustave Schelle, ed. (Paris: F. Alcan, 1913-1923) vol. 1 & 2.

Turnbull, George Henry, *Hartlib, Dury, and Comenius. Gleanings from Hartlib's Papers* (Liverpool: University Press of Liverpool & Hooder & Stoughton, 1947; London: Hodder and Stoughton, 1968).

Turner, John Kenneth, *Shall It Be Again?* (New York City, NY: B. W. Huebsch, inc., 1922).

Tuveson, Ernest Lee, *Redeemer Nation: The Idea of America's Millennial Role* (Chicago, IL: University of Chicago, 1968).

Twisse, William, *The doubting conscience resolved. In answer to a (pretended) perplexing question, &c. Wherein is evidently proved, that the holy Scriptures (not the pope) is the foundation whereupon the Church is built. Or, That a Christian may be infallibly certain of his faith and religion by Holy Scriptures* (London: Printed for Thomas Matthews at the sign of the Cock in St Pauls Church-yard, 1652).

Tyler, Alice Felt, *Freedom's Ferment: Phases of American Social History from the Colonial Period to the Outbreak of the Civil War* (Minneapolis, MN: University of Minnesota Press, 1944; New York City, NY: Harper & Row, 1962).

V

Van Doren, Carl, *Benjamin Franklin* (New York City, NY: The Viking Press, 1961).

Veale, F. J. P., *Advance to Barbarism: How the Reversion to Barbarism in Warfare and War-Trials Menaces Our Future* (Appleton, WI: C. C. Nelson Publishing Company, 1953).

Voegelin, Eric, *From Enlightenment to Revolution*, ed. by John H. Hallowell (Durham, NC: Duke University Press, 1975).

von Mises, Ludwig, *Bureaucracy* (New Haven, CT: Yale University Press, 1944; Grove City, PA: Libertarian Press, 1996).

W

Wade, Louise C., *Graham Taylor: Pioneer for Social Justice: 1851-1938* (Chicago, IL: University of Chicago Press, 1964).

Walker, Daniel Pickering, *Spiritual and Demonic Magic from Ficino to Campanella* (London: Warburg Institute, University of London, 1958).

Walker, Daniel Pickering, *The Decline of Hell: Seventeenth-Century Discussions of Eternal Torment* (Chicago, IL: University of Chicago Press, 1964).

Wallace, Henry A., *New Frontiers* (New York City, NY: Reynal and Hitchcock, 1934).

Wallman, Johannes, *Philip Jakob Spener und die Anfänge des Pietismus* (Tübingen: Mohr Siebeck, 1970).

Walzer, Martin, *The Revolution of the Saints: A Study in the Origins of Radical Politics* (New York City, NY: Atheneum Publishers, 1968).

Ward, Lester Frank, *Dynamic Sociology: Or Applied Social Science* (New York City, NY: D. Appleton, [1883] 1897) vols. 1 & 2.

Ward, Lester Frank, *The Psychic Factors of Civilization*, 2nd ed. (Boston, MA: Ginn & Company, [1893] 1906).

Ward, Lester Frank, *Pure Sociology* (New York City, NY: The Macmillan Company, 1903).

Ward, Lester Frank, *Glimpses of the Cosmos* (New York City, NY: G.P. Putnam's Sons, [1913] 1922) vol. 5.

Warfield, Benjamin B., *Selected Shorter Writings of Benjamin B. Warfield*, (Philipsburg, PA: Presbyterian and Reformed Publishing Co., [1970] 2011) vol. 1.

Warfield, Benjamin Breckinridge, *Perfectionism*, ed. by Ethelbert Dudley Warfield, 2 vols. (New York City, NY: Oxford University Press, 1931; Grand Rapids, MI: Baker, [1932] 2003).

Webb, Thomas Smith, *The Freemason's Monitor, or, Illustrations of Masonry* (Salem, MA: Flagg and Gould, Printers, 1818).

Webster, Nesta H., *World Revolution: The plot against civilization* (London: Constable and Company Ltd., 1921).

Webster, Nesta H., *The French Revolution* (London: Constable and Company Ltd., [1919] 1926).

Webster, Samuel, *A Winter-Evening's Conversation upon the Doctrine of Original Sin* (Boston, MA: Green and Russell, 1757).

Wecter, Dixon, *The Saga of American Society: A Record of Social Aspiration, 1607–1937* (New York City, NY: Charles Scribner's Sons, 1937).

Weddle, David C., *The Law as Gospel: Revival and Reform in the Theology of Charles G. Finney* (Metuchen, NJ: Scarecrow, 1985).

Weinberg, Albert K., *Manifest Destiny: A study of nationalist expansionism in American history* (Chicago, IL: Quadrangle, [1935] 1963).

Weingart, David, *Walter Lippmann: A study in personal journalism* (New Brunswick, NJ: Rutgers University Press, 1949).

Weinstein, James, *The Corporate Ideal in the Liberal State: 1900-1918* (Boston, MA: Beacon Press, 1968; Boston, MA: Beacon Paperback, 1969).

Weisberger, Richard William, *The Cultural and Organization Function of Speculative Freemasonry During the Enlightenment: A study of the craft in London, Paris, Prague, and Vienna* (Ann Arbor, MI: University Microfilms International, 1980).

Weiss, John, *Life and Correspondence of Theodore Parker, minister of the Twenty-eighth Congregational Society, Boston* (New York City, NY: D. Appleton, 1864) vol. 1.

Wells, Herbert George, *God The Invisible King* (London: Cassell & Co., Ltd., 1917).

Wesley, John, *A Plain Account of Christian Perfection* (London: J. Paramore, 1728) in *The Works of John Wesley*, vol. 11.

West, Robert Frederick, *Alexander Campbell and Natural Religion* (New Haven, CT: Yale University Press, 1948).

Weyl, Walter E., *The New Democracy* (New York City, NY: Macmillan, 1912).

Wheelan, Joseph, *Jefferson's War: America's first War on Terror 1801-1805* (New York City, NY: Carroll & Graf Publishers, 2003).

White, Michael, *Isaac Newton: The Last Sorcerer* (Reading, MA: Perseus Books, 1999).

White, Morton Gabriel, *Social Thought in America: The Revolt Against Formalism* (Boston, MA: Beacon Press, 1947; New York City, NY: Oxford University Press, 1985).

White, Morton Gabriel, *Origin of Dewey's Instrumentalism* (New York City, NY: Columbia University Press, 1943).

Wiebe, Robert H., *Businessmen and Reform: A Study of the Progressive Movement* (Cambridge, MA: Harvard University Press, 1962).

Wiebe, Robert H., *The Search for Order, 1877-1920* (New York City, NY: Hill and Wang, 1967).

Williams, William Appleman, *Shaping of American Diplomacy: Readings and Documents in American Foreign Relations, 1750-1955* (Chicago, Il: Rand McNally & Co., 1956).

Williams, William Appleman, *The Tragedy of American Diplomacy* (Cleveland: World Publishing Company, 1959; New York City, NY: W.W. Norton & Company, 2009).

Williams, William Appleman, *The Contours of American History* (New York City, NY: New Viewpoints, 1961).

Williams, William Appleman, *America Confronts a Revolutionary World* (New York City, NY: W. Morrow, 1976).

Williams, William Appleman, *Empire as a way of life: An essay on the causes and character of America's present predicament along with a few thoughts about an alternative* (Oxford: Oxford University Press, 1980).

Wilson, T. Woodrow, *Congressional Government: A Study in American Politics* (Gloucester, MA: Peter Smith, [1885] 1973).

Wilson, Major L., *Space, Time and Freedom: The Quest for Nationality and the Irrepressible Conflict, 1815-1861* (Westport, CN: Greenwood Press, 1974).

Wiltz, John E., *In Search of Peace: The Senate Munitions Inquiry, 1934-1936* (Baton Rouge, LA: Louisiana State University Press, 1965).

Woodward, C. Vann, *Origins of the New South, 1877-1913* (Baton Rouge, LA: Louisiana State University Press, 1951).

Wyatt-Brown, Bertram, *Lewis Tappan and the Evangelical War Against Slavery* (Cleveland, OH: Case Western Reserve University, 1969).

Y

Yates, Frances Amelia, *Giordano Bruno and the Hermetic Tradition* (London: Routledge, [1964] 2015).

Yates, Frances Amelia, *The Rosicrucian Enlightenment* (London: Routledge and Kegan Paul, 1972).

Yates, Frances Amelia, *The Occult Philosophy in the Elizabethan Age* (London: Routledge & Kegan Paul, 1979).

Z

Zinn, Howard, *Politics of History* (Boston, MA: Beacon Press, 1970; Urbana, IL: University of Illinois Press, 1990).

Articles, Book chapters & Speeches

A

"A New Step Forward: The Religious Citizenship League for Social Progress through Political Action," *The Gospel of the Kingdom* (January, 1914), 11-15.

Abrams, Ray H., "Harry Elmer Barnes as a Student of Social Problems," in Arthur Goddard, ed., *Harry Elmer Barnes, the learned Crusader: New History in Action* (Colorado Springs, CO: Ralph Myles, Publisher, 1968).

Adler, Cyrus & L. Hühner, "Leon, Edwin De," in Isidore Singer, et al., ed., *The Jewish Encyclopedia* (New York City, NY: Funk & Wagnalls, 1901-1906) vol. 8: 3.

Ahlstrom, Sydney Eckman, "Theology in America: A Historical Survey," in James W. Smith & A. Leland Jamison, eds., *Religion in American Life* (Princeton, NJ: Princeton University Press, 1961) vol. 1: 251-271.

Arndt, Karl, "George Rapp's Harmony Society," in Donald E. Pitzer, ed., *America's Communal Utopias* (Chapel Hill, NC: University of North Carolina Press, 1997), 57-88.

B

Barnes, Harry E., "Shall the United States Become the New Byzantine Empire?," (publisher not identified, 1947).

Barnes, Harry E., "The Responsibility of Education to Society," *Scientific Monthly*, LI (1940), 253.

Bates, J. L., "Fulfilling American Democracy: The Conservation Movement, 1907 to 1921," *Mississippi Valley Historical Review*, XLIV (June, 1957), 31.

Becker, Carl L., "Review of Barnes's *The New History and the Social Studies*," *Saturday Review of Literature*, II (August 15, 1925), 38.

Bellah, Robert M., "Civil Religion in America," *Daedalus* 96 (1967), 1-21.

Bethell, John T., "'A Splendid Little War'. Harvard and the commencement of the new world order," *Harvard Magazine* (November, 1998).

Beveridge, Albert J., "The March of the Flag," campaign speech on September 16, 1898 in Albert J. Beveridge, *The Meaning of the Times, and Other Speeches* (Indianapolis, IN: Bobbs-Merrill, 1908), 47-57.

Blewett, John, S. J., "Democracy as Religion: Unity in Human Relations," in John Blewett, ed., *John Dewey: His Thought and Influence* (New York City, NY: Fordham University Press, 1960), 33.

Boghardt, Thomas, "The Zimmermann Telegram: Diplomacy, Intelligence and the American Entry into World War I"; Working Paper No. 6-04 (Georgetown University, November 2003).

Bolton, Henry Carrington, "The Literature of Alchemy," republished in *The Pharmaceutical Review*, vol. XIX, nos. 4, 5 (1901).

Bowden, Henry Warner, "A Historian's Response to the Concept of American Civil Religion," *Journal of Church and State* 17 (1975), 495-505.

"Brightman, Thomas," in Sir Stephen Leslie, *Dictionary of National Biography* (London: Smith, Elder & Co. 1885-1900) vol. 6.

Butler, Jon, "Magic, Astrology, and the Early American Religious Heritage," *American Historian Review*, 84, no. 2 (April, 1979), 317-446.

C

Cavert, Samuel McCrea. "The Missionary Enterprise as the moral equivalent to War," *Biblical World* 50 (December, 1917), 351-352.

Celenza, Christopher S., "Marsilio Ficino," in Edward N. Zalta, ed., *The Stanford Encyclopedia of Philosophy*, Summer 2015 Edition (Stanford, CA: Stanford University Press, 2015).

Channig, William Henry, "Manifesto," *The Western Messenger*, VIII, 108, cit. in Perry Miller, *The American Transcendentalists, their Prose and Poetry* (Garden City, NY: Doubleday, 1957), 430.

Channig, William Henry, "Likeness to God. Discourse at the Ordination of Rev. F. A. Farley, Providence, Rhode Island, 1828," in *The Complete Works of W. E. Channing, D. D.* (London: George Routledge, 1870) vol. 4: 230-239.

Clendenin, Daniel B., "Partakers of Divinity: The Orthodox Doctrine of Theosis," *Journal of the Evangelical Theological Society* 37/3 (1994), 365-379.

Corduan, W., "A Hair's Breadth From Pantheism: Meister Eckhart's God-Centered Spirituality," *Journal of the Evangelical Theological Society* 37/2 (1994), 269-271.

Coudert, Allison P., "Leibniz, Locke, Newton and the Kabbalah," in Joseph Dan, ed., *The Christian Kabbalah* (Cambridge, MA: Houghton Library of the Harvard College Library, 1997), 149-179.

Coudert, Allison P., "A Quaker-Kabbalist Controversy: George Fox's Readton to Francis Mercury van Helmont," *Journal of the Warburg and Cortauld Institutes*, 39 (1976), 172-178.

Crockatt, Richard, "American Liberalism and the Atlantic World, 1916-1917," *Journal of American Studies*, II (April, 1977), 126-143.

Croly, Herbert D., "The Effect on American Institutions of a Powerful Military and Naval Establishment," *Annals of the American Academy of Political and Social Science*, vol. 66 (July, 1916), 157-172.

D

Davis, Allen F., "Welfare, Reform and World War I," *American Quarterly*, vol. 19 (Fall, 1967), 516-533.

DiLorenzo, Thomas J., "The Consolidation of State Power via Reconstruction, 1865-1890," *Journal of Libertarian Studies*, vol. 16, no. 2 (Spring, 2002), 139-161.

DiLorenzo, Thomas J., "The Culture of Violence in the American West: Myth versus Reality," *The Independent Review*, vol. 15, no. 2 (Fall, 2010), 227-239.

Dewey, John, "On Understanding the Mind of Germany," *Atlantic Monthly*, vol. 117 (February, 1916), 251-262.

Dewey, John, "Force and Coercion," *International Journal of Ethics*, vol. 26 (April, 1916), 364; "Force, Violence and Law," *The New Republic* (New York City), vol. 5 (January 22, 1916), 296; "The Future of Pacifism," vol. 11 (July 28, 1917), 359; "What America Will Fight For," vol. 12 (August 18, 1917), 69; "Conscription of Thought," vol. 12 (September 1, 1917), 128-130.

Dewey, John, "Reconstruction," *Monthly Bulletin of the Students' Christian Association of the University of Michigan*, 15 (June, 1894), 149-156.

Dwight, Timothy, "Sermon XXXII: Human Depravity; Derived from Adam," in *Theology: Explained and defended, in a series of sermons*, 4 vols. (New Haven, CT: S. Converse, 1825) vol. 1: 477-488.

E

Edwards, Jonathan, "Concerning the End for Which God Created the World," in Paul Ramsey, ed., *The Works of Jonathan Edwards*, Ethical Writings (New Haven, CT: Yale University Press, 1989) vol. 8.

Erdmann, Karl Dietrich, "War Guilt 1914 Reconsidered: A Balance of New Research," in H. W. Koch, ed., *The Origins of the First World War: Great Power Rivalries and German War Aims*, 2nd ed. (London: Macmillan, 1984), 342.

F

Finley, M. I., "Progress in Historiography," *Dædalus* (1977), 125-142.

Fosdick, Harry Emerson, "Shall the Fundamentalists Win?," *Christian Work* 102 (June 10, 1922), 716-722.

Fosdick, Harry Emerson, "The Unknown Soldier," in *Secrets of Victorious Living: Sermons of Christianity Today* (New York City, NY: Harper & Brothers, 1934), 88-98.

Fosdick, Harry Emerson, "An Interpretation of Pacifism," in Harry Emerson Fosdick, *Secrets of Victorious Living: Sermons of Christianity Today* (New York City, NY: Harper & Brothers, 1934), 106.

Fosdick, Harry Emerson, "The Cure of Disillusionment," in Harry Emerson Fosdick, *Secrets of Victorious Living: Sermons of Christianity Today* (New York City, NY: Harper & Brothers, 1934), 23.

Fosdick, Harry Emerson, "The Interpretation of Life," in Harry Emerson Fosdick, *Secrets of Victorious Living: Sermons of Christianity Today* (New York City, NY: Harper & Brothers, 1934), 234.

Fosdick, Harry Emerson, "The Church Must Go Beyond Modernism," in Halford R. Ryan, *Harry Emerson Fosdick: Persuasive Preacher* (New York, NY: Greenwood Press, 1989), 109.

Fosdick, Harry Emerson, "What the War did to My Mind," *The Christian Century* (January 5, 1928).

Fosdick, Harry Emerson, "A Christian Conscience About War." A sermon delivered at the League of Nations Assembly Service at the Cathedral at Geneva September 13, 1925, 18-20.

"Freemasonry," by William James Hughan, in *Encyclopaedia Britannica*, 11th edition, (Cambridge: Cambridge University Press, 1910–1911) vol. XI, 78-85.

G

Gerstner, John H., "Theological Boundaries: The Reformed Perspective," in David F. Wells, John Woodbridge, eds., *The Evangelicals: What They Believe, Who They are, Where They are Changing* (Grand Rapids, MI: Baker, 1977), 27.

Godfrey, W. Robert, "Haven't We Seen The 'Megashift' Before?," in *Modern Reformation* (January-February, 1993), 14-18.

Gunsaulus, Frank W., "The War and the America of Tomorrow," *Christian Century* 34, no. 43 (25 October 1917), 10-11.

H

Hannah, John, "The Doctrine of Original Sin in Postrevolutionary America," *Bibliotheca Sacra* 134 (July-September, 1977), 238-256.

Hays, Samuel P., "The Politics of Reform in Municipal Government in the Progressive Era," *Pacific Northwest Quarterly*, LV (1964), 157-169.

Hinson, E. Glenn, "Baptist Contributions to Liberalism," in *Baptist History and Heritage*, 35, no. 1 (Winter, 2000), 39-54.

Hodge, Charles, "Finney's Lectures on Theology," *Biblical Repertory and Princeton Review*, XIX (April, 1847), 237-277.

I

Iliffe, Rob, "'Making a Shew': Apocalyptic Hermeneutics and the Sociology of Christian Idolatry in the work of Isaac Newton and Henry More," in James E. Force & Richard H. Popkin, eds., *The Books of Nature and Scripture* (Berlin: Springer Science & Business Media, 1994).

J

Janicki, David A., "The British Blockade During World War I: The Weapon of Deprivation," *Inquiries* Journal, vol. 6, no. 8 (Boston, MA: Northeastern University, 2014), 1-5.

K

Kelpius, Johannes, "Brief an Heinrich Johann Deichmann [Engl. spelling: "Heinrich John Deichman"], 24. Februar 1697," in "The Diarium of Magister Johannes Kelpius," edited and trans. by Julius Friedrich Sachse, *Pennsylvania German Society, Proceedings and Addresses*, 30.

Kipling, Rudyard, "The White Man's Burden," in *McClure's Magazine* 12 (February, 1899).

Kolko, Gabriel Morris, "Mechanistic Destruction: American Foreign Policy at Point Zero," *Antiwar.com* (August 10, 2007).

Konkin, Samuel Edward, "William Appleman Williams (1921-1990): Sire of Neo-Isolationism," *New Isolationist*, vol. 1, no. 1 (October, 1990).

L

La Follette Sr., Robert M., "Speech on the Declaration of War against Germany," in Arthur A. Ekirch, Jr., ed., *Voices in Dissent: An Anthology of Individualist Thought in the United States* (New York City, NY: Citadel Press, 1964), 211-222.

LaFontaine, H. T. C. De, "Benjamin Franklin," *Ars Quatuor Coronatorum*, XLI (1929), 3-27.

Lee, Robert E., "Brief an Lord Acton," December 15, 1866, in Rufus J. Fears, ed., *Selected Writings of Lord Acton*, vol. 1: *Essays in the History of Liberty* (Indianapolis, IN: Liberty Fund, 1986), 365.

Leighton, George R., "Beard and Foreign Policy," in *Charles A. Beard: An Appraisal*, ed. by Howard K. Beale (Lexington, KY: University of Kentucky Press, 1954).

Leuchtenburg, William E., "Progressivism and Imperialism," *Mississippi Valley Historical Review*, vol. 39 (December, 1952), 483-504.

Levy, David W., "Herbert D. Croly," John Arthur Garraty, Mark Christopher Carnes, American Council of Learned Societies, *American National Biography* (New York City, NY: Oxford University Press, 1999) vol. 5: 757.

Levy, David W., "Weyl, Walter Edward" in *American National Biography Online* (2000).

Lindsay, A. D., "Individualism," in Edwin R. A. Seligman, ed., *Encylopaedia of the Social Sciences*, 8 vols. (New York City, NY: The Macmillian Co., 1932) vol. 7.

Loetscher, Lefferts A., "The Problem of Christian Unity in Early 19th Century America," *Church History* 32 (March, 1963), 3-16.

Lovejoy, Arthur O., "The Supposed Primitivism of Rousseau's 'Discourse on Inequality,'" *Modern Philology* 21, no. 2 (1923), 165-186; republished in Arthur O. Lovejoy, *Essays in the History of Ideas* (Baltimore, MD: Johns Hopkins Press, 1948), 14-37.

M

Maclear, James F., "The Republic and the Millennium," in Elwyn Allen Smith, ed., *The Religion of the Republic* (Philadelphia, PA: Fortress Press, 1971).

Mathews, Donald G., "The Second Great Awakening as an Organizing Process, 1780-1830: An Hypothesis," *American Quarterly*, 21 (Spring, 1969), 23-43.

McArthur Jr., J., "The Enigma of Kelpius' Cave," *Germantown Crier* 3 (Summer, 1983), 54-56.

McDowell, Paula, "Enlightenment Enthusiasms and the Spectacular Failure of the Philadelphian Society," *Eighteenth-Century Studies* 35.4 (2002), 516.

McGuire, J. E. & P. M. Rattansi, "Newton and the Pipes of Pan," *Notes and Records of the Royal Society of London*, XXI (1966), 108-143.

Mead, Sidney E., "The Nation with a Soul of a Church," *Church History* 36 (1967), 262-283.

Mills, C. Wright, "Mass Society and Liberal Education," in Irving Louis Horowitz, ed., *Power, Politics, and People: The Collected Essays of C. Wright Mills* (New York City, NY: 1963), 357-361.

Moorhead, James H., "The Millennium and the Media," in Leonard I. Sweet, ed., *Communication and Change in American Religious History* (Grand Rapids, MI: William B. Eerdmans, 1993) 216-221.

Moorhead, James H., "The American Israel: Protestant Tribalism and Universal Mission," in William R. Hutchinson & Hartmut Lehmann, eds., *Many Are Chosen: Divine Election and Western Nationalism* (Minneapolis, MN: Fortress Press, 1994), 145-166.

Mowry, George E., "The California Progressive and His Rationale," *Mississippi Valley Historical Review* (Cedar Rapids), XXXVI (September, 1949), 239-250.

Muller, Dorothea A., "Josiah Strong and the Social Gospel: A Christian's Response to the Challenge of the City," *Journal of the Presbyterian Historical Society*, 34 (September, 1961), 150-174.

N

Nation (May 8, 1935), 550-552.

Nisbet, Robert Alexander, "Foreign Policy and the American Mind," *Studies in History and Philosophy* No. 7 (Menlo Park, CA: Institute for Humane Studies, [1961] 1978), 14.

Novak, Michael, "Human Rights at Christmas," *Washington Times*, December 23, 1988.

O

Oakes, Walter J., "Toward a Permanent War Economy?," *Politics*, vol. I (February, 1944), 11-17.

P

Paine, Thomas, "Origins of Freemasonry," in Philip S. Foner, ed., *Complete Writings of Thomas Paine*, 2 vols. (New York City, NY: Citadel Press, 1945) vol. 2: 829-841.

Paine, Thomas, "The Rights of Man," in R. E. Roberts, ed., *Selected Writings of Thomas Paine* (New York City, NY: Everybody's Vacation Publishing Company, 1945), 328.

Perry, Matthew C., "Remarks of Commodore Perry upon the Expediency of Extending Further Encouragement to American Commerce in the East," *Narrative of the Expedition [...] to the Cian Seas and Japan* (House Ex. Doc. no. 97, 33 Cong., 2 Sess., II, 177-178).

Persons, Stow, "Christian Communitarianism in America," in Stow Persons & Donald Drew Egbert, eds., *Socialism and American Life* (Princeton, NJ: Princeton University Press, 1962) vol. 1: 127-151.

Platt, Frederick, "Christian Perfectionism," in James Hastings, ed., *Encyclopaedia, of Religion and Ethics* (New York City, NY: Charles Scribner's Son, 1908) vol. 9.

Pope, Alexander, "Essay on man," ed. by Mark Pattison (Oxford: The Clarendon Press, 1871) 58-59.

Priester, Claus, "Alchemie und Vernunft: Die rosenkreuzerische und hermetische Bewegung in der Zeit der Spätaufklärung," in Monika Neugebauer-Wölk, ed., *Aufklärung und Esoterik* (Hamburg: Felix Meiner Verlag, 2016), 305-334.

Proceedings of a Conference of Governors: In the White House, Washington, D.C., May 13-15, 1908 (Washington, D.C., Government Printing Office, 1909) vol. 1: 6ff.

R

Randall, John Herman, *Making of the Modern Mind* (Indianapolis, IN: Houghton Mifflin, 1940).

Rattansi, P. M., "Social Interpretation of Science in the Seventeenth Century," in Peter Mathias, ed., *Science and Society 1600-1900* (Cambridge: Cambridge University Press, 1972), 1-32.

Reichmann, F. & E. E. Doll, "Ephrata, as seen by contemporaries," in *Pennsylvanian German Folklore Society*, vol. 17 (Allentown, PA, 1953).

"Report of the Nye Committee," U.S. Senate, Special Committee Investigating the Munitions Industry, 73rd Cong., 2nd sess., 1936.

Robinson, James H., "The New History" (Proceedings of the American Philosophical Society, vol. 50, May 1st, 1911), 179-190.

Roosevelt, Theodore, "Expansion and Peace," *Independent*, vol. 51 (December 21, 1899), 3404, in William Harbaugh, ed., *Writings of Theodore Roosevelt* (Indianapolis, IN: Bobbs-Merrill, 1967).

Rothbard, Murray N., "Marxism and Charles Beard," in *Murray N. Rothbard, Strictly Confidential: The Private Volker Fund Memos of Murray N Rothbard*, ed. by David Gordon (Auburn, AL: Ludwig von Mises Institute, 2010), 69-74.

Rozbicki, Michal, "Between East-Central Europe and Britain: Reformation and Science as Vehicles of Intellectual Communication in the Mid-Seventeenth Century," *East European Quarterly*, XXX:4 (January, 1997), 401-416.

S

Sargent, Abel M., "The Halcyon Itinerary, and True Millennium Messenger" (Marietta, OH: S. Fairlamb; August, 1807), 9.

Seward, William Henry, *Cong. Globe, 33 Cong., 1 Sess., Senate (June 29, 1954)* (Washington, D.C.: U.S. Govt. Printing Office, 1954), 1566.

Shannon, William V., "Mr. Jefferson's Return," *New York Times* (Sunday, 17 October 1971), Section 4, 3.

Shaver, Muriel, "David Goodman Croly," in Allen Johnson, Dumas Malone & Harris E. Starr, eds., *Dictionary of American Biography*, 21 vols. (New York City: NY, Charles Scribner's Sons, 1943) vol. 4: 560.

Small, Albion W., "Christianity and Industry," *American Journal of Sociology*, 25 (May, 1920), 673-694.

Small, Albion W., "The Churches and City Problems," in John Henry Barrows, ed., *The World's Parliament of Religions* (Chicago, IL: Parliament Publishing, 1893) vol. 2: 1080-1082.

Smith, Robert Freeman, "American Foreign Relations, 1920-1942," in Barton J. Bernstein, ed., *Towards a New Past: Dissenting Essays in American History* (New York City, NY: Pantheon Books, 1968), 202-231.

Smylie, John E., "National Ethos and the Church," *Theology Today*, vol. XX, no. 3 (October 1, 1963), 314.

Sniegoski, Stephen J., "State Schools versus Parental Rights: The Legacy of Lester Frank Ward," *Journal of Social, Political and Economic Studies*, X (Summer, 1985), 215-227.

Speer, Robert E., "From World War to World Brotherhood," *Federal Council Bulletin* II (June, 1919), 103.

Stein, Stephen J., "A Notebook on the Apocalypse by Jonathan Edwards," *William and Mary Quarterly* (Ser. 3) 29 (1972), 623-634.

Stromberg, Joseph R., "William Appleman Williams: Premier New Left Revisionist," in *Old Cause* (Sunnyvale, CA: Antiwar.com, November 16, 1999).

Stromberg, Joseph R., "Charles Austin Beard: The Historian as American Nationalist," in *Old Cause* (Sunnyvale, CA: Antiwar.com, November 9, 1999).

Stromberg, Joseph R., "Harry Elmer Barnes, Progressive and Revisionist," in *Old Cause* (Sunnyvale, CA: Antiwar.com, February 7, 2000).

Stromberg, Joseph R., "Gabriel Kolko Revisited, Part 1: Kolko at Home," in *Future of Freedom* (Fairfax, VA: Future of Freedom, September 1, 2013).

Stromberg, Joseph R., "Gabriel Kolko Revisited, Part 2: Kolko Abroad," in *Future of Freedom* (Fairfax, VA: Future of Freedom, October 1, 2013).

Sumner, William Graham, "The Fallacy of Territorial Expansion" (1896), in William Graham Sumner, *War and Other Essays* (New Haven, CT: Yale University Press, 1911), 285-293.

Sumner, William Graham, "The Conquest of the United States by Spain" (1898), in William Graham Sumner, *War and Other Essays* (New Haven, CT: Yale University Press, 1911), 297-334.

Sumner, William Graham, "Theory and Practice of Elections, First Paper," in William Graham Sumner, *Essays of William Graham Sumner* (New Haven, CT: Yale University Press [1934] (1940) vol. 1: 263-285.

Sumner, William Graham, "Republican Government," in *Essays of William Graham Sumner* (New Haven, CT: Yale University Press, [1911] 1940) vol. 2: 195-212.

Swing, Albert Temple, *Bibliotheca Sacra*, LVII (190), 466-467.

T

Taylor, Nathaniel W., "Concio ad Clerum: A Sermon Delivered in the Chapel of Yale College, September 10, 1828."

"Theological Thinking in America," in Gerald Birney Smith, ed., *Religious Thought in the Last Quarter-Century* (Chicago, IL: University of Chicago Press, 1927).

Thomas, Keith, "An Anthropology of Religion and Magic, II," *Journal of Interdisciplinary History*, 6, no. 1 (Summer, 1975), 91-109.

Trevor-Roper, Hugh Redward, "Three Foreigners and the Philosophy of the English Revolution," *Encounter. Literature, Arts, Politics* 14 (1960), 3-20 in Hugh R. Trevor-Roper, *The Crisis of the Seventeenth Century: Religion, the Reformation and Social Change* (Indianapolis, IN: Liberty Fund, 2001), 219-272.

W

Wagner, Jürgen, "Amerikas Mission: Liberaler Imperialismus und US-Außenpolitik, in Wissenschaft und Frieden" (3/2003), 48-51.

Warfield, Benjamin B., *Princeton Theological Review*, XIX (January, 1921), 17-48.

Warfield, Benjamin B., *Princeton Theological Review*, XIX (July, 1921), 482.

Wiist, William H., et. al., "The Role of Public Health in the Prevention of War: Rationale and Competencies," *American Journal of Public Health*, vol. 104, no. 6 (June, 2014).

Wilkinson, Ronald Sterne, "The Alchemical Library of John Winthrop, Jr., 1606-1676," *Ambix* 11.1 (February, 1963), 33-51.

Wilkinson, Ronald Sterne, "The Hartlib Papers and Seventeenth-Century Chemistry," Part 1, *Ambix* 15.1 (February, 1968), 54-69.

Williams, William Appleman, "The Frontier Thesis and American Foreign Policy," *Pacific Historical Review* vol. 24, No. 4 (November, 1955), 379-395.

Wilson, Woodrow, "Address to a Joint Session of Congress," 2 April 1917, in Arthur S. Link, et al., eds., *The Papers of Woodrow Wilson* (Princeton, NJ: Princeton University Press, 1966-1993) vol. 41: 527.

Wilson, Woodrow, "Address to a Joint Session of Congress," 8 January 1918, in Arthur S. Link, et al., eds., *The Papers of Woodrow Wilson* (Princeton, NJ: Princeton University Press, 1966-1993) vol. 45: 539.

Worthington, John, "The Life of the Reverend and most learned Joseph Mede," in John Worthington, ed., *The Works of the Pious and Profoundly-Learned Joseph Mede, B.D., sometime fellow of Christ's Colledge in Cambridge* (London: Printed by James Flesher for Richard Royston, 1664).

Ph.D. Dissertation

H

Hollon, David L., "Love as Holiness: An Examination of Charles G. Finney's Theology of Sanctification, 1830-1860," (Ph.D. diss., Southern Baptist Theological Seminary, 1984).

Index

Abbott, Lyman	226-227, 353, 359
Adams, John Quincy (US President)	91, 181, 191, 257-258
administrative state	136, 215-219, 232, 349
alchemy	29-30, 32-33, 39, 44-47, 52, 55, 68, 70, 93, 365-366, 390, 395
alchemical speculations	31
alchemistic mythology	33
philosopher's stone (lapis philosophorum)	32-33, 46-47, 70, 172
Alsted, Johann Heinrich	47-48, 62, 354, 372, 374
American Democracy	135, 142, 249, 251, 395
American Party (Know-Nothings)	179
American System	119, 121, 184, 245
Ames, William	48
Technometria (1633)	48
Antichrist	61, 64, 74, 264
Apostle Paul	22-23, 44, 351
aristocracy	79-80, 84-85, 94, 101, 135, 148, 196, 256, 279, 348, 358
Aristotle	3, 11, 157, 235, 355, 361, 383
Arminius, Jacobus (Jakob Hermandzoon)	19-20, 22-23, 173

| Arminianism | 19-24, 104, 145, 154, 156, 170, 334 |

Arouet (Voltaire), François Marie | 105, 110, 128-129

Articles of Confederation | 122-123

Astor, John Jacob | 82-83, 377

astrology | 29, 39, 46, 61-62, 69-70, 396

autonomy | 8, 17, 94, 102, 124, 140, 150, 154, 242

Bacon, Francis | 5, 35-37, 45, 48-49, 65, 156, 355

Baconism | 157

New Atlantis (1627) | 35, 37, 65, 355

Baldwin, James Mark | 209, 214-215, 306

Bancroft, George | 135, 142

Barings Bank | 198

Barnes, Harry Elmer | 164, 171, 292-297, 313, 356, 368, 394-395, 404

The Genesis of the World War (1926) | 294, 356

Beard, Charles Austin | 123, 273-274, 292, 294, 306-307, 309-313, 316, 357, 359, 373, 381, 400, 404

A Foreign Policy for America (1940) | 312, 357

America in Midpassage, Vol. 1 (1939) | 306, 310, 357

Giddy Minds and Foreign Quarrels (1939) | 309-310, 357

Open Door at Home (1934) | 273, 309, 312, 315, 357

President Roosevelt and the Coming War (1948)	311
The Idea of the National Interest (1934)	312
Becker, Carl Lotus	104-107, 273-274, 292, 357, 384, 395
The Heavenly City of the Eighteenth-Century Philosophers (1932)	105-107, 357
Bellamy, Edward	201, 232, 338, 358
Bible (s. Holy Scriptures)	5, 13-15, 17, 39, 43, 49, 70, 99, 105, 108, 113, 119, 127, 146, 155, 160-161, 164-165, 168, 173-174, 206, 208, 211-212, 224-225, 227, 300-301, 350, 352
Daniel	30, 48, 53, 57, 62-65, 181-182, 233, 317-318, 353, 358-359, 361, 378, 391, 396
Epistle to the Galatians	23
Genesis	65, 93, 204, 224, 294, 356, 374
New Testament	7, 13-16, 23, 50, 62, 134
Old Testament	7, 34, 41-42, 60, 134, 211
Revelation	5, 34, 37, 49, 51-52, 61-65, 74, 101-102, 108, 111-113, 143, 150, 161-162, 211, 222-223, 228, 233, 336, 341, 359, 378
Bismarck-Schönhausen, Otto Eduard Leopold von (German Chancellor)	250, 285-287, 338
Bodin, Jean	4-5, 127, 358

Böhme, Jakob	31, 49, 51-52, 55, 59, 71, 73, 141, 172, 345
Boston Brahmins	83, 85, 181
British East India Company	83, 115-116
Brown, John	178, 186
Bruno, Giordano	29, 31, 47, 394
Bryan, William Jennings	233-234, 256, 272, 289-290, 317, 359, 361, 369, 372, 375
bureaucracy	12, 200, 217, 237-238, 391
Burnham, James	216-217, 349-350, 360
The Machiavellians (1943)	349-350, 360
The Managerial Revolution (1941)	197, 216-217, 349, 360
The Struggle for World Power, published (1947)	350
Bury, John Bagnell	2-5, 111, 190, 360
Bush, George H. W. (US President)	91
Bush, George W. (US President)	346
Bush Doctrine	346
Calvin, John	19, 21, 23, 26-28, 47, 91, 104, 150, 199, 226, 332, 360, 362
Institutes of the Christian Religion (1536)	21, 27-28, 69, 91, 360, 396
Cambridge Platonism	73, 138
More, Henry	49, 61-62, 64, 72-73, 139, 380, 399

Smith, John   73, 139, 190

Campanella, Tommaso   4, 30, 65, 361, 391

Capitalism   8, 82, 185, 199, 216-217, 227, 233,
                                     236, 238, 253, 262, 269-270, 273,
                                     276, 296, 309, 316, 318-320, 324,
                                     326-328, 342, 344, 364

central bank

    Bank of England   115

    Bank of the United States   87, 183

    Federal Reserve System   266, 315

China

    Canton (Guangzhou)   86, 89, 181, 198, 267

    opium trade   83, 86-89

Christianity   2, 16, 23-25, 30-31, 37, 39-40, 46,
                                     50, 53, 57-58, 65-66, 69, 72, 74, 92,
                                     95, 98-100, 102-103, 105, 108,
                                     111-112, 122, 131-133, 136-139,
                                     143-145, 148-150, 154, 158, 160-
                                     161, 163, 167, 169-170, 177, 186,
                                     202-209, 211, 217-218, 222, 224-
                                     229, 233-234, 264, 283, 298-301,
                                     333-334, 338, 350, 353, 361, 365,
                                     368-370, 378, 398, 404

    Evangelical Alliance   229

    liberal Christianity   205, 207, 299

    Pietism   23, 54-56, 169, 174, 201, 388

Christ, Jesus	13, 16, 19, 21, 23, 28, 32, 44, 49, 51, 57-59, 62-63, 65, 68, 102, 113, 126, 133, 136, 138, 141, 143, 145, 147, 154, 171, 194, 205, 211, 218-219, 225, 263-264, 300-301, 331, 351, 355
Church Fathers	3, 15, 56-59, 224, 351
Athanasius	57
Augustine	3-4, 18, 145, 174, 351, 355
Clement of Alexandria	50
Hilary of Poitiers	57
Irenaeus	56-57, 372
Origines	57
Churchill, Sir Winston Leonard Spencer (First Lord of the Admiralty, Prime Minister)	232, 288
civil liberty	134, 313
civil religion	12, 132, 149, 153, 161, 174, 189, 211, 226, 265, 330, 333, 341, 346, 384, 395
Clark University	230
Classical Liberalism	9, 103, 124, 199, 234, 238, 249, 252, 281, 337
Clay, Henry (US Secretary of State)	183-184, 190, 195
Cleveland, Grover (US President)	197, 241-242, 380
Cleveland administration	241, 243
Collectivism	130, 235, 252-254, 269

Colonialism	245, 248, 329
Columbia University	5, 88, 102, 286, 293, 307, 318, 366, 372, 393
Comenius (Komenský), Jan Amos	43, 47-50, 63, 65-66, 362, 375-376, 390
Pansophiae Prodromus (1639)	49
Commons, John R.	64, 176, 228-229, 362
Communism	103, 200, 216, 233, 270, 296, 314-315, 322-323, 326, 340, 347, 363
Comte, Auguste	7, 103, 201-202, 263
Condorcet, Marie Jean Antoine Nicolas Caritat (Marquis de Condorcet)	6, 105, 201, 332, 362
Conservatism	9, 185, 237, 309, 320, 341, 344, 347, 349, 374
Cosmopolitanism	114
Counter Reformation	39
Creator	11, 32-34, 44, 56, 74, 92, 95, 101-102, 134, 136, 139, 186, 191, 205, 213, 224-225, 350
Creel, George Edward	267, 292
Committee on Public Information	267, 292
Croly, Herbert D.	259-261, 263, 282, 338, 363, 368, 396, 400, 403
Cushing, Caleb	91, 179-183
Darwin, Charles	7, 202-203, 235

Descent of Man (1871)	202
evolution theory	7, 71, 194, 197, 201-203, 206-207, 209, 214-215, 224, 226-227, 230, 235, 260, 264, 353
The Origin of Species (1859)	201-203
Darwin, Erasmus	7, 202
Dee, John	34-35, 37, 48, 67, 184, 190, 192, 235, 318, 369
deification (s. Theosis)	32, 56-59, 142, 172, 227
Deism	23, 98, 102-104, 111-113, 126, 141-143, 150, 152, 163, 330
Delano, Jr., Warren	89, 181
Democracy	8, 78, 103, 113-114, 119, 124, 127, 129-137, 142, 144, 148, 150, 152, 154-155, 169, 174, 177, 185, 189, 214-219, 226, 228, 231, 233-234, 244, 249-251, 256, 259-261, 267, 270-271, 276, 278-280, 282, 286-287, 316-317, 322, 329-330, 336, 345-350, 358, 360, 363, 369-370, 385, 393, 395
Democratization	97, 145, 370
Modern Democracy	103, 133, 215, 217-219, 276
religion of Democracy	129, 261
Republican Democracy	132-133, 148, 152, 215, 217, 346
Romantic Democracy	129, 132-137, 148, 154-155, 174, 214-215, 217, 226, 347-350
Democratic Party	132, 196, 208, 233-234, 247, 254, 317, 347, 360
Descartes, René	5

Dewey, John	91, 228, 230-231, 261-262, 359, 395
Dulles, John Foster (US Secretary of State)	274, 297-298
Duraeus, Johannes (John Dury)	41, 63, 65-66, 357, 390
Dwight, Timothy	91, 150-151, 157, 229, 239-240, 354, 358-359, 397
economic cartel	86, 198-200, 237, 239, 251, 269, 321, 341
monopolization	195, 237, 254, 321
economic depression	8-9, 195-196, 198, 252, 316, 328
Edwards, Jonathan	74-75, 104, 151-152, 154, 157, 164, 189, 389, 397, 404
Egalitarianism	130, 331, 336
Ely, Richard T.	227-228, 338, 365, 383
Institute of Christian Sociology	227
Empiricism	48-49, 103-104
Enlightenment philosophy	9, 100-101, 104-107, 110, 113, 128, 152, 203, 332
Enlightenment religion	106
Ephrata Community	46, 52, 70-71
Epistemology	102, 143
Erasmus of Rotterdam	7, 14-18, 202, 363, 365-366, 376
On the Freedom of the Will (1524)	16-17
Esotericism	29-30, 33, 35, 40, 46, 48, 51, 96, 180, 366

ancient theology	29, 35-36
Occultism	45, 48, 197
Paracelsianism	45
Paracelsian Spagyric	51
prisca theologia	35, 37
Renaissance Neoplatonism	29, 47, 101
Theosophy	46, 49-53, 68, 70-71, 172, 345
Essex Junto	85, 178, 180-181, 183
Lowell, John	85-86, 180, 199
Evangelicalism	153-156, 163, 206, 336, 377
Fascism	270, 273, 295, 314, 319, 340, 343, 364
Fay, Sidney B.	88, 92, 108-109, 116, 293, 367
Federal Council of Churches	222, 234, 298, 302
Finney, Charles G.	75, 140, 145, 147, 151-176, 225-226, 333-334, 366-371, 378, 392, 399, 406
Lectures on Revival (1835)	154, 367
Fiore, Joachim de	4
theory of the three ages	7
Fletcher, Benjamin (Governor)	79-80
Flynn, John T.	199, 294, 311
Fontenelle, Bernard Le Bovier de	5, 332
Forbes, John Murray	86, 198

Fosdick, Harry Emerson	298-303, 368, 379, 385, 398
Founding Fathers	92, 107-109, 121-122, 129, 239-240, 247, 258, 268, 272, 288, 307-308, 313, 323, 332, 340, 379
Adams, John (US President)	109, 353
Adams, Samuel	118
Benjamin Franklin	71, 97, 107-110, 117-118, 332, 361, 369, 380, 385, 387, 390, 400
Hancock, John	115-116, 121, 354
Jefferson, Thomas (US President)	81-82, 85, 103, 108-109, 113-114, 121, 123-126, 134, 153, 198-199, 234, 247, 274, 313, 332, 361, 379, 393, 403
Livingston, Robert R.	81, 118
Madison, James (US President)	67, 108, 121, 123-124, 153, 213, 295, 306-307, 358, 368, 370
Monroe, James (US President)	81, 91, 121, 153, 162, 242, 257, 282, 382
Morris. Robert	94, 123-124, 237, 276, 320-321, 323-325, 341, 344, 374-375, 384, 389, 399
Paine, Thomas	108, 113, 152, 239, 332, 402
Washington, George (US President)	71, 80-81, 97, 107-108, 116-117, 119, 121, 124, 239, 241, 257, 268, 313, 359, 368, 372
Fourier, Charles	82, 146
Fourierism	146
Fourierist Society	146
Frederick V (Elector Palatine)	40

freedom	4, 8, 11-12, 16-17, 24, 60, 71, 75, 78, 90, 92, 97, 100-102, 104, 111, 115, 121, 127, 129-130, 134-136, 140, 142, 146, 148, 151-152, 155-156, 178, 186, 188, 193, 204, 209, 213-214, 218, 239-240, 248, 256-258, 263, 269, 271, 273, 278-279, 282, 297, 301, 320-322, 327, 332, 336, 344, 347, 349-350, 360, 381, 390, 394, 404
Freemasonry	35, 44, 48, 55-56, 79, 81, 85, 90, 92-99, 107-111, 113-114, 116, 119, 163, 179-180, 275, 356, 360, 367, 373-374, 376, 384, 386-387, 389, 392, 398, 402
Ancients	97
Anderson, James	95, 190, 239-240, 354
English Grand Lodge	96
Grand Lodge of Pennsylvania	97, 108-109, 369, 385
Grand Lodge of Tennessee	132
Grand Orient de France	111
Holland Lodge No. 8, F. & A. M.	81
Les Neuf Soeurs (The Nine Sisters)	110
Masonic lodges	67, 79, 84, 97, 114, 116-117
Masonic temple	79
Moderns	97
Scottish Rite of Freemasonry	96, 98, 179-180, 275, 387
The Saint Andrew Lodge	116

French Jacobins	239, 348-349
Jacobin Club	347
Robespierre, Maximilien	348
Fundamentalism	142, 147, 149, 176, 218, 225-226, 300, 335-336, 377, 386
Garrison, William Lloyd	178-183, 274
The Liberator (newspaper)	178, 180
George, David Lloyd (Prime Minister)	286, 294
German Empire	285-287, 289
German Idealism	127, 139, 141-142, 150, 222, 227, 335
Gilded Age	195, 200-201, 203, 318-319
Gladden, Washington	222, 226, 229, 369
Gnosticism	29, 40, 42, 50
Gnosis	33, 50-51, 58, 387
Gnostic thought	32
Golden Age	2, 5, 37, 51, 74, 78, 131, 210, 223, 346
Grant, Ulysses S. (US President)	194
Great Britain	58, 87, 114-115, 182, 228, 232, 241-242, 250, 267, 276, 284, 286-289, 304-305, 312, 322-323, 343, 372, 389
British Empire	34, 80, 84-87, 113, 116, 118, 120, 178, 180, 239, 241, 285
British Imperialism	37

Great Depression	315-316, 340, 342
Greek philosophy	18, 46, 73
Greenbacks / United States Notes	196
Grey, Lord Edward (Foreign Minister, 1st Viscount Grey of Fallodon)	286, 290
Grotius, Hugo	99, 166, 225
Habsburg Empire	34, 40, 284
Hall, G. Stanley	229-230, 383-384
Hamilton, Alexander (US Secretary of the Treasury)	79, 87, 106, 121, 123-124, 241, 258-259, 276, 307, 324, 335, 364, 370, 384, 389
Harrison, William Henry (US President)	181
Hartlib, Samuel	41-43, 49, 63, 66, 370
Hartlib Circle	41, 45, 49, 63
Harvard College	50, 73, 85-86, 90, 142, 144, 180-181, 396
Hays, Samuel Pfrimmer	318-319, 371, 399
Hegel, George Wilhelm Friedrich	141-142, 150, 236
Hegelian dialectics	271, 331
Hegelianism	142, 236, 345
Hell Fire Club	109, 117
Medmenham Abbey	117
Sir Francis Dashwood (11th Baron le Despencer)	109, 117

Hermeticism	29-31, 36-37, 39, 44, 64, 93-94
Corpus Hermeticum	37, 58
Eternal Restoration	7, 31
Hermes Trismegistus	29-30, 32
Tabula Smaragdina	32
Hesiod	2
Hobbes, Thomas	11-12, 24, 67, 72, 128, 132, 371
Holy Scriptures (s. Bible)	12-15, 17-18, 20, 24, 27, 49, 58, 63, 165, 169, 174, 203, 208, 211, 301, 352, 390
Holy Spirit	7, 9, 13, 19, 22, 25, 64, 104, 134, 156, 158, 165, 167-168, 210, 332-333, 369
Hong Kong	87
House, Edward Mandell (Colonel)	254-257, 386
Humanism	2, 15, 75, 95, 113, 138, 144, 167, 225-226
humanistic values	97-99
Humanitarianism	138, 340
human virtue	5, 94-95, 101, 104, 128-129, 134, 137, 144, 151, 174, 189, 263, 265, 295, 365
Huxley, Aldous	10
Brave New World (1932)	10
Idealism	10, 104, 127-128, 138-139, 141-142, 150, 153, 177, 222-223, 227, 261, 264, 335, 387

Imperialism	3, 37, 84, 177, 186, 221, 240, 245, 249, 251, 253, 255, 268, 273, 275-276, 280-283, 285-286, 292, 294, 310, 329-330, 350, 371, 400
American Imperialism	221, 245, 253, 282, 292, 294, 310, 329
British Empire	34, 80, 84-87, 113, 116, 118, 120, 178, 180, 239, 241, 285
Spanish Empire	175, 247-248, 268, 281
Indians	43, 66, 80, 82-83, 86, 116, 177, 189-192, 240, 362
Cherokees	190-191
genocide	190-192
Plains Indians	190-192
Individualism	55, 96, 101, 128-130, 174, 212, 216, 233, 238, 252, 259-260, 318, 400
industrialization	9, 194-195, 213, 260, 318, 338
Industrial Revolution	7, 208, 227, 250
Internationalism / Interventionism	187, 302, 310, 323, 345
Isolationism	241, 268, 302-303, 310, 313, 329
Jackson, Andrew (US President)	132-133, 136, 142, 145, 148, 151-152, 154, 243-244, 247, 272, 276, 278, 280, 327, 337, 341, 345, 385, 388
Jacksonian Democracy	133, 142, 145, 152, 174
Jacksonian era	133, 145, 174
James, William	92, 230, 398

J. P. Morgan & Co.	88, 197, 238, 243, 250, 259, 288, 305, 341
J. & T. H. Perkins Co.	86
Cushing, John Perkins	86, 180
Perkins, Thomas H.	86-87, 198
Judaism	33, 44, 46
Kabbalah	33-34, 37, 46, 48, 50, 53, 55, 69, 93, 362, 377, 396
"Christian" Kabbalah	34, 46, 48, 50, 396
Jewish Mysticism	33, 69
Kant, Immanuel	138, 141
Kelpius, Johannes	46, 68-69, 399, 401
Kelpius Society	69
Kolko. Gabriel Morris	237, 319-325, 341, 343-344, 374-375, 399, 404
La Follette Sr., Robert M. (US Senator, Governor of Wisconsin)	250, 258, 338, 400
Lane Theological Seminary	140
League of Nations	9, 262, 266, 271-272, 293, 297-298, 301-302, 365, 398
Leibnitz, Gottfried Wilhelm	5
Lester Frank Ward	231, 235-236, 253, 361, 404
Lieber, Francis	186-187
Lincoln, Abraham (US President)	184-189, 193, 233, 239-240, 258, 263, 295, 303, 328, 354, 361, 369
Lincoln cult	240

Lippmann, Walter	91, 259-260, 338, 368, 376, 392
Livingston, Robert	80-81
Lloyd, Henry Demarest	209, 213-215, 338
Locke, John	50, 100, 102-104, 112-113, 127, 130, 134, 203, 277, 317, 331, 396
Essay Concerning Human Understanding (1689)	104
Second Treatise on Government (1690)	100
Lodge, Henry Cabot	243, 250, 272, 329
Luther, Martin	13-19, 24-26, 38-39, 168, 366, 376
On the Bondage of the Will (1525)	17
Secular Authority: To what extent it should be obeyed (1523)	24-25
Machen, J. Gresham	226
magic	29-30, 33-34, 45-46, 69-70, 344, 383, 389, 391, 396, 405
Mahan, Asa	155-157
Managerialism	216
Manifest Destiny	9, 136, 177, 191, 210, 240, 245-247, 290, 336, 339, 392
Marx, Karl	82, 101-103, 131, 141, 201, 232, 236, 253, 307, 390
Massachusetts Bay Colony	45
Materialism	67, 72, 244
Mathews, Shailer	223-224, 258, 333, 355, 377, 401

McKinley, William (US President)	244-245, 247-249, 265, 328-329, 339
Mede, Joseph	62-64, 72, 373, 378, 406
Clavis Apocalyptica (1627)	62-64, 378
Mercantilism	85, 119-121, 123, 320, 324, 326, 339
mercantilist laws	120
mercantilist politics	188
mercantilist tax policy	120
mercantilist trade	120, 185
mercantilist trade restrictions	120
Neo-Mercantilism	270
Neo-Mercantilist economic regulation	200
Metaphysics	49, 143
Pantheistic Metaphysics	143
militarism	9, 221, 249, 270-271, 274-275, 280, 282-283, 285, 321, 345, 355
millennium	48-49, 59-65, 68-69, 74, 78, 142, 148, 153-154, 161-162, 201, 209-210, 228, 235, 370, 400-401, 403
Amillennialism	47, 60
Postmillennialism	1, 48, 60-62, 67, 74, 77-78, 138, 140, 147, 149, 157, 161, 186, 189, 201, 204, 210-211, 228, 271, 331-332, 334-336, 341
Premillennialism	60, 297, 351

thousand-year reign	6-7, 37, 48, 51, 59, 61-62, 64, 66, 74, 98, 127, 147-148, 161, 170, 189, 201, 210, 222, 263, 332, 334, 342, 351
Millis, Walter	306, 379
Road to War (1935)	306, 379
Mirandola, Giovanni Pico della	31, 48
Modernism	18, 224-225, 300, 302, 336, 377, 398
Money Trust	234
Monism	222
Monroe Doctrine	242, 257, 282
Mysticism	1, 30, 33, 39-40, 48, 51, 53, 55-56, 59, 69-70, 72-73, 95, 102, 139, 143, 390
national banking system	196, 280
Naturalism	7, 202, 205, 230
natural law	7, 102, 204, 212, 231, 252, 260
natural philosophy	29, 37, 42, 44, 202
Neoconservatism	347, 349-350
Burnham, James	216-217, 349-350, 360
new Jacobins	349
Neoplatonism	29, 44, 47, 49, 54, 72-73, 101, 138-139, 141
Neoplatonic Rationalism	104
Neoplatonic speculations	33
Plotinus	72, 372

New School Presbyterianism	98, 150-151, 153, 160, 163, 175, 185, 356
Newton, Isaac	4-5, 44-45, 50, 61-62, 67, 95, 112, 189, 203, 331, 361, 393, 396, 399, 401
new world order	34, 248, 264, 271-272, 298, 302, 357, 374, 376, 395
Nietzsche, Friedrich	9, 31
Nihilism	9, 104
Nisbet, Robert Alexander	2, 5, 11-12, 285, 332, 344, 371, 381, 401
Obama, Barak H. (US President)	350
Old School Presbyterianism	151, 163-164, 210, 225-226
Olney, Richard (US Secretary of State)	197, 241-243, 250
"Open Door" Imperialism / "Open Door" Policy	97, 250, 273, 309-310, 312, 315, 322, 324, 328-330, 338, 357
Orwell, George	10, 217, 350
Nineteen Eighty-Four (1949)	10, 217, 350, 381
Paganism	28, 58, 226, 331
Page, Walter Hines (US Ambassador to the United Kingdom)	290
Panentheism	74
Pansophism	41, 43, 46-48, 50, 66
universal language	43-44, 50, 66
Pantheism	29, 57, 144, 222, 396

paradise	1, 4, 7, 9, 28, 41-42, 47, 51, 53, 70, 105, 127, 147, 203, 229, 372
Paris Peace Conference	271-272, 297
Parker, Theodore	91, 173, 202, 381, 392
Paternalism	121, 134, 179, 208, 281
Patriotism	8, 132, 136, 147, 149, 153, 174, 248, 281, 304, 350
Pelagius	17, 145, 150
Pelagianism	151, 155, 164, 169, 226
Pelagian view	18
perfectionism	59, 140, 164, 169, 171, 173-175, 225, 392, 402
Christian Perfectionism	140, 173, 402
human perfection	9, 77, 126-127, 137
perfect society	10-11, 60-61, 67-68, 129, 131, 145, 170, 204, 208, 252, 265
Phi Beta Kappa Society (ΦΒΚ)	10, 81, 86, 88, 90-91, 138, 142, 144, 180-181, 190, 195, 198-199, 226, 228-230, 234, 242-243, 245, 259, 261, 274-275, 298-300, 314, 329
Philadelphia Society	52, 54, 59, 71
Leade, Jane Ward	52-54, 68, 71, 371, 375
Pordage, Dr. John	52
Philippines	248-249, 253, 255, 268, 281, 340
philosophy of equality	133
Pike, Albert	179-180

Pinchot, Gifford (Chief of the U.S. Division of Forestry, Governor of Pennsylvania)	252, 382
piracy	79-80, 86, 88, 114, 125-126
Kidd, William	79-80, 384
kingdom of Barataria (Louisiana)	81-82
kingdom of Libertalia (Madagascar)	78, 81
Tew, Thomas	79
Plato	3, 10-11, 35, 44, 56, 72, 128, 133
Theaetetus	56
Pluralism	149
Plutocracy	120, 184, 276, 280-282
Populism	234
Porcellian Club	89, 142, 243, 245, 329
Positivism	7, 202, 263
Comte, Auguste	7, 103, 201-202, 263
Pragmatism	9, 167, 205, 230
progress	2-12, 18, 65, 72, 78, 91-92, 94, 101, 105-107, 128-129, 131, 135-137, 142-143, 146-147, 153, 161, 177, 186-187, 189, 191, 195, 201-203, 205, 209-215, 217, 219, 223, 227, 229, 231, 235, 238, 244, 259-262, 270, 278, 299-300, 309, 330-333, 336-337, 340-342, 350-351, 355-356, 360, 362, 364-365, 368, 381, 389, 394, 397

belief in progress	9, 18, 106, 135, 161, 186, 212, 259, 261, 331
inevitability of progress	9
material progress	9, 244
Progressive Party	270, 282
Progressivism	2-3, 5, 7-9, 11, 18, 41, 77, 151-152, 160, 176-177, 201, 204, 207, 211, 214-215, 217-218, 221-224, 226, 228, 231, 233-236, 238, 249, 253, 259-261, 271-272, 281-283, 298-300, 302, 307, 316-319, 324, 330, 336-338, 341, 343, 352, 363, 373, 400
Progressive Era	133, 205-206, 232-233, 236, 251-252, 255, 259, 265, 275, 307, 316-321, 336-337, 343-344, 368, 376, 399
progressive movement	10, 223, 259, 270, 317, 319, 364, 380, 393
progressive Reformers	10, 319, 341
protective tariffs	114, 121, 183-185, 188, 198, 200, 208, 237, 245, 280
Protestant Liberalism	75, 142, 226
Puritanism	48, 71-72, 74, 102, 104, 107, 151, 154, 174, 234, 353, 363, 384
Pythagoreanism	30
Queen Elizabeth I	34, 37
Elizabethan England	34
Quietism	55-56
Radicalism	33, 49, 113, 188

railways

    Boston and Maine Railroad   197

    railroad companies   192, 194-195, 197-198, 207-208, 237, 320

    railway companies   197, 320

    Union Pacific Railroad   192

Rauschenbusch, Walter   209, 229, 299

Reconstruction   188, 193-194, 199, 228, 231, 241, 304, 362, 365, 397

Reformation   1, 12, 14-16, 20-21, 23-24, 26, 28, 33, 36-41, 43, 47, 54, 61-62, 65-66, 69, 71, 74, 93, 100-102, 127, 136, 140, 144-145, 158, 162-164, 168, 173, 210, 217-218, 225, 229, 232, 239, 300, 336, 362, 368, 372, 382, 398, 403, 405

Reform Darwinism   126, 235-237

Reid, Thomas   147, 155-157, 383

    Scottish Realism   155, 157

Renaissance   4, 7, 13, 29-31, 33-34, 47, 55, 61, 93, 95, 101, 138, 199, 372, 382

Republican Party   112, 142, 184, 187, 191-194, 196, 200, 208, 270, 289, 333

Republic of Texas   96, 136, 152, 182-183, 240, 254, 257, 372, 386

Revisionism   294-295, 306, 325

revivalism   151-152, 156-157, 171, 174-175, 333, 378, 387

    First Great Awakening   60, 74, 140, 151-152, 166, 171, 334

revival	8, 42, 153-163, 166, 169-170, 174, 206, 228, 332-334, 358, 362, 367, 392
revival campaigns	154, 157, 160, 162-163, 166, 169, 174, 334
revivalist movement	151, 153, 159, 161
Second Great Awakening	74-75, 140, 148, 153, 155, 169-170, 175, 333-334, 373, 401
revolution	4, 6-7, 11-12, 25-26, 33, 49, 53, 60, 63, 66, 68, 77-78, 92, 98-99, 103, 105, 108, 110-118, 124, 129, 141, 147-148, 152-153, 155, 167, 182, 193, 195, 197, 202, 205, 208, 216-217, 227, 231-232, 236, 242, 246-247, 250, 253, 261, 263, 271-272, 276, 291, 315, 318, 325, 332, 337, 346-349, 360, 367, 369, 371-372, 375, 377, 379, 384, 389, 391-392, 405
American Revolution (s. War of Independence)	60, 78, 99, 103, 110-118, 124, 152, 246, 263, 276, 369, 375, 384, 389
Bolshevik Revolution	291
English Civil War (s. English Revolution)	38, 66
English Revolution (s. English Civil War)	49, 63, 66, 405
French Revolution	6-7, 12, 33, 103, 110, 124, 236, 347-348, 392
Glorious Revolution	53
industrial revolution	7, 208, 227, 250
Robber barons	195, 341
Rockefeller, Jr, John D.	91, 300-301

Rockefeller, Sr, John D.	91, 199, 300-301, 327
Romanticism	102, 127, 139, 150, 222, 335
English Romanticism	102, 127, 139, 150, 222, 335
Romantic belief	9, 152
Romantic era	30, 128
Rome	3-4, 16-17, 271
Roosevelt, Franklin D. (US President)	89, 91, 199, 234, 252, 265, 271, 274, 294, 309-311, 314, 321, 324, 328, 341
New Deal Policy	199, 252, 269-271, 294-295, 309, 312, 316, 319, 321, 324, 343, 368
Rosicrucianism	35, 38, 51, 93-94, 96
Andreae, Johann Valentin	38-39, 51, 63, 65, 354
Chymical Wedding of Christian Rosenkreutz (1615)	38
Confessio Fraternitatis (1615)	38-39, 93
Fama Fraternitatis (1614)	38-39, 93, 354
legend of Christian Rosenkreutz	38
Rosicrucian Enlightenment	35, 37, 40, 93, 394
Rosicrucian fraternity	50-51
Rosicrucian movement	35
Rosicrucian Order	38, 93
Second Reformation	39-40

Rousseau, Jean-Jacques	11-12, 24, 100, 105, 127-134, 136, 146, 148, 154, 214-215, 217, 226, 346-350, 385, 400
general will (Fr. volonté Générale)	12, 127, 130-131, 133, 154
Social Contract (1762)	99-100, 103, 127, 131-132, 148, 215, 217, 348-349, 385
Royal Society	35-36, 39, 41, 43-44, 63, 66-67, 362, 401
Rudolf II (Holy Roman Emperor)	35, 40
Russell and Company	88-89
secularization	4, 36, 55, 108, 133, 222, 232
self-improvement	7, 23, 167, 202
Seneca	3, 11, 72
Shakespeare, William	31, 34-35
Sherman, William Tecumseh	91, 190, 192, 244, 247, 272, 337, 345, 385
Skull & Bones	88-90, 252, 276, 314, 346
Bush, George H. W. (US President)	91
Bush, George W. (US President)	346
Russell Trust Association	89
Russell, William Huntington	89-90
Sumner, William Graham	276-278, 281-283, 363, 404-405
Taft, Alfonso	89

slavery	60, 74, 84-85, 128, 138, 140, 143, 145, 147, 161-162, 170, 176, 178-179, 183, 185-189, 202, 247, 335, 394
abolition of slavery	10, 60, 84, 98, 134, 140, 161, 178, 180, 185-186, 188, 202, 216, 247, 261, 298, 335
slave dealers	114
slaves	84-86, 88, 117, 126-127, 140, 162, 175, 179, 186, 188, 192-193, 210, 295, 331
slave trade	84-87, 125, 187
Smith, Adam	100, 120
Wealth of Nations (1776)	100, 120, 387
social contract	99-100, 103, 127, 131-132, 148, 215, 217, 348-349, 385
Social Darwinism	9, 102, 126, 201, 203-205, 235, 245-246, 330, 339
social gospel	9, 151, 160, 194, 204, 206-211, 222-223, 228-229, 234, 243, 247, 263, 265, 298, 331, 336-339, 401
Socialism	128, 171-172, 207-209, 216, 227, 232-233, 238, 252-253, 261, 266, 269-270, 285, 321, 340, 342-343, 380, 402
social justice	129, 223, 227, 229, 233, 251, 262, 271, 277, 316, 367, 391
social welfare	134, 203, 238, 336
Socinianism	23
sociology	7, 61, 201, 209, 213, 227, 229, 231, 235-237, 294, 391, 399, 404

Speer, Robert Elliott	297, 387, 404
Spencer, Herbert	94, 201, 203, 235, 381
Spener, Philipp Jacob	51, 54-55, 370, 387, 391
Pia Desideria (1675)	54-55, 387
Spenser, Edmund	31, 387
spirituality	30, 39, 42, 56-57, 69, 71-73, 160, 169-170, 366, 396
State Monopoly Capitalism / Corporatism	185, 199, 236, 238, 269-270, 273, 309-310, 318, 320-321, 324, 342
Statism	228, 274
Strong, Josiah	222-223, 227, 229, 243-244, 401
Institute of Christian Sociology	227
Subjectivism	130, 143
Sumner, Charles (US Senator)	91, 388
Sumner, William Graham	276-278, 281-283, 363, 404-405
Taylor, Nathaniel W.	75, 151, 157, 164, 210, 225
technocracy	217, 270
technocratic society	232
technology	9, 37, 42, 45-46, 65, 130, 251, 275
The New Republic	149, 247, 258-259, 261-263, 338, 397
Croly, Herbert D.	259-261, 263, 282, 338, 363, 368, 396, 400, 403
Lippmann, Walter	91, 259-260, 338, 368, 376, 392

Theodore Roosevelt (US President)	243, 245-246, 250-251, 259, 270, 281-282, 317, 321, 328-329, 336, 338, 380, 383, 403
New Nationalism	251, 259
theology	5, 15-16, 20, 23-24, 26, 29, 35-36, 38, 43, 51, 54-60, 63-64, 69, 74-75, 96, 99, 104-105, 112, 126, 134, 136, 139, 141-142, 145, 149-153, 155-158, 163-168, 173-176, 189, 194, 202-207, 209-210, 222-226, 299-301, 353, 367-368, 375, 381, 387, 389, 392, 395, 397, 399, 404, 406
biblical prophecy	61, 112, 201, 263
Christian ethics	139, 209, 222, 236
Christian Theism	205
covenant theology	99
cross of Christ	17
doctrine of Creation	28, 30, 33, 37, 39, 42, 44, 53, 56, 74, 143, 166, 207, 224, 351
doctrine of divine goodness	113
doctrine of divine grace	18-19
doctrine of heaven	6, 13, 60, 63, 102, 105, 112, 122, 127, 135-136, 157, 160, 201, 263, 331, 333-334, 351, 373
doctrine of hell	16, 53-54, 109, 117, 160, 331, 334, 391
doctrine of holiness	18, 59, 140, 145, 154, 157, 170, 406
doctrine of justification by faith	14, 16, 18-24, 54, 102, 109, 145-146, 156, 168, 173, 209, 225, 228, 267, 281, 287, 295, 326, 339, 345

doctrine of man's depravity   103, 129, 137, 145, 150, 152, 168, 203, 205, 397

doctrine of original sin   18, 23, 36, 75, 114, 129, 138, 144-145, 150-151, 164, 168, 225, 301, 333, 392, 399

doctrine of predestination   104, 139, 154

doctrine of providence   5, 7, 9, 67, 97, 105, 113, 129, 137, 142-143, 177, 205, 222, 245, 340, 360, 396

doctrine of redemption   102, 168, 211, 225, 240, 246-247

doctrine of salvation   7, 11, 13-14, 16-24, 26, 30, 34, 36-37, 40, 44, 47, 54, 57-58, 60, 64, 75, 101, 113, 128, 136-137, 139-140, 145-146, 149-150, 152, 157, 159-160, 162, 164-170, 175-176, 202-207, 211-213, 218-219, 223, 225-229, 234, 240, 260, 264, 298-299, 301, 334, 337, 351-352

doctrine of sin   18-19, 21, 24, 150, 162, 165-166, 170, 174, 176, 301

doctrine of substitutionary atonement   14, 21-24, 145

doctrine of the Christian faith   9, 13-14, 16, 18-23, 25, 27-28, 31, 34, 37, 39-40, 44-45, 47, 53-54, 58, 63-64, 69, 78, 84, 98, 102, 105-106, 129, 132-133, 137, 140, 142, 144-145, 152, 159-160, 163-165, 173, 175, 177, 203-205, 207-208, 211, 214, 217, 219, 224-228, 233, 238, 252, 299-301, 330-332, 342, 348, 352, 358, 360, 367-368, 375, 377, 380, 390

doctrine of the cross of Christ   17

doctrine of the Trinity   13, 57, 59, 80, 100, 102, 113, 126, 138, 334

eschatology	48-49, 62
free will	17-18, 150, 153-156, 163, 167-169, 175, 207, 215, 334, 366
heavenly kingdom	19, 205
Higher Life Theology	176, 206
kingdom of Christ	25, 65
kingdom of God	60, 78, 129, 140, 148, 153, 161-162, 170-171, 176, 204, 206, 210-212, 223, 226-228, 232-233, 264, 298, 335, 380
Monergism	19
natural theology	20, 157
New Divinity (s. New Protestantism, New Haven Theology, Taylorism)	74-75, 149-152, 157, 161, 163-166, 210, 224-225
New England Theology	75, 145, 151, 163-165, 210, 368
New Haven Theology (s. New Divinity, New Protestantism, New Haven Theology)	150-151, 165, 225
New Haven Theology (s. New Divinity, New Protestantism, Taylorism)	150-151, 157, 210, 226, 389
New Protestantism (s. New Divinity, New Haven Theology, Taylorism)	148-150, 154-155, 157-158, 161, 169-170, 175, 225, 333-335
salvation history	11, 22, 60, 149
Synergism	19
Theosis (s. deification)	56-58, 396

Totalitarianism	10, 112, 124, 127-128, 268, 270, 274, 324
Tower of Babel	41-43
Transcendentalism	9, 87, 102, 127, 139, 141-146, 153, 172, 174, 194, 207, 236, 330, 335
Emerson, Ralph Waldo	86, 91, 137, 141, 144, 146
Ripley, George	91, 143-144, 368
Thoreau, Henry David	142, 144, 174
transformation	31-33, 38, 58, 71, 96, 99, 145-147, 211, 226, 229, 231, 247, 251-252, 254, 269, 327, 363
Treaty of Versailles	263, 272, 283, 293, 302
Triple Entente	286-290, 304-305
Trotsky, Leon (Lev Davidovich Bronstein)	347, 349
Turgot, Anne Robert Jacques (baron de l'Aulne)	6, 201, 332, 390
Twisse, Dr. William	63-64, 390
Union Theological Seminary	225
Unitarianism	9, 102, 104, 113, 127, 138-142, 151, 153, 334
universal law	133-134, 299
University of Chicago	53, 63, 68, 72, 74, 147, 149, 151, 157, 163, 165, 173, 185, 189, 223, 229, 231, 244, 247, 272, 316-318, 331-332, 337, 345, 359, 368, 371, 375-376, 378, 384, 386-387, 390-391, 405

US Constitution (1788)	71, 78, 85, 92-93, 95, 98, 101, 103, 121-124, 126, 150, 184, 188, 194, 230, 255, 279, 307-308, 329, 332, 335-336, 357, 361, 378, 384
utopia	4, 9-10, 65, 96, 105, 140, 146, 161, 171, 177, 201, 215, 265, 351, 375
Vanderbilt, Commodore	195
war	9-12, 38, 40-41, 43, 47, 53, 55, 60, 66, 73, 78, 80, 85-88, 98, 111, 114-121, 123, 125-126, 135, 138, 140, 147, 151, 153-154, 160, 167, 171, 176-178, 180, 182-193, 195-197, 200, 206, 208, 222, 228, 236-237, 239-240, 242-258, 261-276, 280-299, 301-306, 308-319, 321-331, 335, 337-346, 349-350, 355-357, 360-361, 367-369, 373-375, 378-379, 382, 384-385, 387, 389-390, 393-400, 402, 404-405
Allied Forces	288-289, 291, 299, 304-305, 312, 323
American Expeditionary Forces	291
American War of Secession	85, 138, 154, 160, 176, 183-185, 188, 190-191, 193, 196-197, 206, 208, 222, 237, 239-240, 247, 280, 295, 319, 327, 335, 339
Central Powers of Europe	256, 286, 289, 293, 295, 304-305
Cold War	200, 269, 274-275, 294, 296, 317, 322-323, 325-326, 328-330, 340, 345, 349, 368
First Opium War	87

First World War	9, 11, 228, 249, 253, 255-256, 258, 261, 263, 266, 268-270, 272, 275, 283-285, 287-288, 290, 293, 295, 297, 299, 301, 303-306, 308, 312, 315, 317, 321, 329, 340-342, 344, 373, 378, 397
Hussite Wars	40
Korean War	275, 323
Philippine-American War (Philippine Insurrection)	248
Second World War	12, 200, 236, 252, 266, 269-270, 273-274, 294-295, 303, 310-311, 316, 321-323, 340, 343-344
Spanish-American War	243, 248-249, 265, 281, 283, 338
Thirty Years' War	40-41, 43, 47, 55
Vietnam War	275, 324, 326
War of Independence (s. American Revolution)	60, 73, 78, 86, 98, 116-121, 123, 147, 355
Warfield, Benjamin Breckinridge	164, 167, 169, 174, 226, 391-392, 405
Wells, Herbert G.	232, 264-265, 300
Wesley, John	58-59, 173, 392
Whig Party	97, 117-119, 181, 184, 197, 204, 307, 335, 372
Wiebe, Robert Huddleston	318-319, 393
Wilhelm II (German Emperor / Kaiser)	9, 276, 285, 287, 289, 293, 305
Williams, William Appleman	58, 187, 293, 320, 325-330, 393, 399, 404, 406

Wilson, T. Woodrow (US President)	10, 91, 232, 239, 247, 254-258, 261-263, 265-272, 275, 282, 288-291, 293-294, 297, 304-305, 310, 317, 321-322, 329-330, 336-338, 340, 345, 355, 364, 371, 374, 376, 393-394, 406
New Freedom	256
Wilson administration	263, 288, 290, 305
Winthrop, John, Jr.	45-46, 244, 406
world domination	249, 251, 272, 323, 349
world federation	211, 285, 297-298, 302, 306, 366
world peace	9, 60, 146, 257, 263, 265, 292-293, 301, 323, 340
Yale College	73, 75, 89-90, 104, 140, 150-151, 405
Yankees	84, 160, 185, 239
"Young America" movement	177-180, 195, 341

More books by the same author

The Triumph of Progressivism

The idea of progress – the belief that humanity has been advancing constantly from past to present, and that this process will continue for the foreseeable future – is a worldview that has developed exclusively in the Western world. The idea has occupied a central position in the thinking of modern civilization from the late seventeenth-century Enlightenment to the present day. It is much more than a political theory. In its heyday, it permeated every area of social life. No one could avoid its pervasive influence; even those who took a negative view of abstract ideas succumbed to its irresistible charm. It came to constitute the predominant civil religion of Western civilization – a general religiosity in the political realm. Furthermore, it became part of the modern idea that every attempt to criticize amounts to an act of infidelity. It is time to realize that the ideology of continual social advance and human improvement essentially constitutes a religion in its own right, which, despite often bearing the name of Christianity, is in resolute opposition to biblical beliefs.

Verax Vox Media
780 Morning St. • Worthington, OH 43085 • USA
VeraxVoxMedia.com

Vol. 5: A Religious Quest for an Ideal Society
Paperback, 455 pages
Publication Date: January 2021
ISBN: 978-1-7347541-5-5

Hardcover, 455 pages
Publication Date: January 2021
ISBN: 978-1-7347541-7-9

Vol. 7: The Historic Pursuit of a World Federation

Paperback, 275 pages
Publication Date: July 2021
ISBN: 978-1-7347541-9-3

Siegeszug des Fortschrittsglaubens

Die Idee des Fortschrittes – der Glaube, dass sich die Menschheit in der Vergangenheit bis in die Gegenwart kontinuierlich weiterentwickelt habe und diesen fortschreitenden Prozess in der voraussehbaren Zukunft weiterführen wird – ist eine Weltsicht, die sich ausschließlich im Westen ausgebildet hat. Diese Idee nimmt seit der Aufklärung des späten 17. Jahrhunderts bis in unsere Zeit eine zentrale Stellung im Denken der modernen Zivilisation ein. Sie war weit mehr als eine philosophische Theorie. In ihrer Blütezeit hat sie das gesamte gesellschaftliche Leben durchdrungen. Niemand konnte sich ihrem penetranten Einfluss entziehen. Selbst diejenigen, die abstrakten Ideen negativ gegenüberstanden, erlagen ihrem unwiderstehlichen Charme. Aus ihr setzte sich die tonangebende Zivilreligion der westlichen Zivilisation – Phänomene einer allgemeinen Religiosität im politischen Bereich – zusammen. Sie wurde Teil des modernen Denkens, dass jeder Versuch der Kritik fast wie ein Akt der Treulosigkeit erschien.

Verax Vox Media
780 Morning St. • Worthington, OH 43085 • USA
VeraxVoxMedia.com

Bd. 1:Mystizismus als Nährboden des amerikanischen Postmillennialismus

Paperback, 469 Seiten
Erscheinungsdatum: März 2021
ISBN: 978-1-7347541-6-2

Bd. 2: Postmillennialismus als Inspiration des amerikanischen Progressivismus

Paperback, 734 Seiten
Erscheinungsdatum: November 2020
ISBN: 978-1-7347541-1-7

Bd. 3: Progressivismus als Triebfeder des amerikanischen Imperialismus

Paperback, 604 Seiten
Erscheinungsdatum: November 2020
ISBN: 978-1-7347541-2-4

Bd. 4: Progressivismus als Ausdruck der amerikanischen Zivilreligion

Paperback, 399 Seiten
Erscheinungsdatum: November 2020
ISBN: 978-1-7347541-4-8

Bd. 6: Weltföderation als Endziel des amerikanischen Imperialismus

Paperback, 636 Seiten
Erscheinungsdatum: Juli 2021
ISBN: 978-1-7347541-8-6

World Federation

The Ecumenical Agenda

In his book, World Federation, Dr. Erdmann deals primarily with John Foster Dulles' participation in the ecumenical movement from 1919 to 1945. Dulles' role in shaping the religious, economic and political policies of the Federal Council of Churches in its support of world order and peace, especially in his function as chairman of the Commission on a Just and Durable Peace, was crowned with success in the founding of the United Nations Organisation in 1945. His personal friends Philip Kerr (Lord Lothian) and Lionel Curtis, the principal leaders of the Round Table Group, come into the pictures at various times. By and large they pursued the same objectives as those of Dulles. The book shows the detailed influence of the Round Table Group and its affiliated organisations – such as the Royal Institute of International Affair (London) and the Council for Foreign Relations (New York City) – on the ecumenical movement, using it successfully for their purpose of creating an international community of nations.

Verax Vox Media
225 Barbours Lane • Greenville, SC 29607 • United States of America
VeraxVoxMedia.com

Paperback, 382 pages
Publication date: July 2021
ISBN: 978-1-7373483-0-6

Weltföderation

Die Ökumenische Agenda

Das 20. Jahrhundert war als ein Zeitalter durch eine andauernd expandierende Technokratie gekennzeichnet, eine Eigenschaft, die weder mit dem Ende des Jahrhunderts noch durch den Paradigmenwechsel der Moderne zur Postmoderne abgenommen hat. Vielmehr hat sich die Bewegung in Richtung einer Herrschaft von vermeintlich unvoreingenommenen Technokraten verstärkt, die sich nicht von Dogmen bestimmen lassen und angeblich frei von parteiischen Interessen sind, von denen sich die übrigen von uns bestimmen lassen. Auch war das religiöse Leben, das erklärtermaßen die Sphäre des Geistes und die persönliche Gemeinschaft mit Gott betrifft, frei von derlei Tendenzen und Interessen. Stattdessen erlebte das 20. Jahrhundert den Aufstieg der ökumenischen Bewegung; einem Versuch, die unterschiedlichen Kirchen auf globaler Ebene zu vereinen – eine Art kirchliches Gegenstück zum Völkerbund und später zu den Vereinten Nationen. Wie dieses Buch zeigt, spielte das kirchliche Drängen später tatsächlich auch eine Rolle bei der Geburt der United Nations Organization (UNO) selbst.

Verax Vox Media
225 Barbours Lane • Greenville, SC 29607 • United States of America
VeraxVoxMedia.com

Paperback
Erscheinungsdatum: Juli 2021
ISBN: 978-1-7373483-0-6

Spiritualisierung der Technologie

Die Suche des Menschen nach Vollkommenheit

Angesichts der rapiden technologischen Weiterentwicklung in der Informatik und der Nanotechnologie und der bereits hitzigen Debatte im Bereich der Gentechnologie wird in der Studie Spiritualisierung der Technologie eine geistesgeschichtliche Analyse des Strebens nach Vollkommenheit aus interdisziplinärer Perspektive vorgelegt. Deutlich erkennbar greifen die philosophischen Wurzeln des Perfektionismus weit zurück in die Zeit der griechischen Philosophie, der Hermetik, des Gnostizismus und des Neoplatonismus. Diese Gedankensysteme beanspruchen für sich, Erben der „prisca theologia", der altertümlichen Theologie, zu sein, die sich das Erlangen der „Göttlichkeit" des Menschen und damit die höchste Stufe der Vollkommenheit, zum höchsten Ziel setzte.

Es wird zum einen aufzuzeigen sein, dass die christliche Vorstellung der Ebenbildlichkeit Gottes im Menschen der bizarren Zukunftsvision einer transhumanistischen Posthumanität widerspricht, und zum anderen wird es wichtig sein, detailliert darzulegen, dass ein wirklicher wissenschaftlicher und technologischer Fortschritt, auch gerade im Bereich der Nanomedizin, auf Grundlage christlicher Ethik am besten realisiert werden kann.

Verax Vox Media
225 Barbours Lane • Greenville, SC 29607 • USA
VeraxVoxMedia.com

Paperback, 559 Seiten
Veröffentlichungsdatum: 1. November 2017
ISBN: 978-069267-898-5

Das Tausendjährige Reich

Frühkirchliche Kontroversen

Der Glaube an ein buchstäbliches Tausendjähriges Reich, wie es in Offenbarung 20, 1-10 beschrieben ist, war ein wichtiges Element in der christlichen Endzeitlehre in der Zeit vor dem Konzil von Nicäa im Jahr 325 n. Chr. Die meisten Kirchenväter leiteten ihre Überzeugungen nicht nur von dem Textabschnitt im Buch der Offenbarung ab, sondern auch von der jüdischen Vorstellung eines Goldenen Zeitalters, wie es die hebräischen Propheten beschrieben und die jüdischen Endzeitlehrer weiter ausführten.

Nachdem der christliche Glaube die Gunst des Kaisers Konstantin gewonnen hatte, änderte die Römische Kirche ihre Auffassung über das Tausendjährige Reich grundlegend. Die Hoffnung einer zukünftigen Herrschaft Christi auf Erden wich der Sicht eines Tausendjährigen Reichs, in dem die weltliche Macht dem Papsttum zugefallen ist und das sich vor den Augen der Menschen im Hier und Jetzt verwirklicht. Die Lehre eines buchstäblichen Tausendjährigen Reiches geriet über viele Jahrhunderte in Misskredit, weil einige ihre Befürworter sie falsch dargestellt und ihre Gegner sie absichtlich verdreht haben.

Das vorliegende Buch zeigt die Entwicklung der Entstehung der verschiedenen Sichtweisen auf, stellt die Stärken und Schwächen prägnant dar und plädiert für die ursprüngliche Auslegung von einem buchstäblichen Tausendjährigen Reich, das erst noch kommen wird.

Verax Vox Media
225 Barbours Lane • Greenville, SC 29607 • USA
VeraxVoxMedia.com

Paperback, 295 Seiten
Veröffentlichungsdatum: 7. Juni 2016
ISBN: 978-069273-561-9

Millennium

Historical & Exegetical Debate

The belief in a literal millennium was an important aspect in the Christian eschatology of the ante-Nicene age. Most of the Asiatic Church Fathers derived their chiliastic convictions not only from the millennial passage of Revelation, but also from the Jewish concept of a Golden Age, as described by the Hebrew Prophets and further developed by Jewish apocalyptic writers. The chiliastic doctrine was challenged, on exegetical and philosophical grounds, by the Alexandrian school of theology in the third century. The Church's elevation to imperial favour by Constantine was followed by a further shift in the understanding of the millennium. The chiliastic hope of a future earthly reign of Christ was substituted with the view of a realized millennium constituting the secular dominion of the Roman Church. The factor which most contributed to this change was Augustine's spiritualized interpretation of the first resurrection. He understood it to mean a resurrection of those dead in sin, raised to spiritual life. In his book, De civitate dei, he advanced the opinion that the kingdom of God was already set up at Christ's first coming and nothing remained to be accomplished before the final judgment except the brief reign of the Antichrist. Thus the teaching of a literal millennium became discredited because it was perverted by some of its friends and misrepresented by its opponents.

Verax Vox Media
225 Barbours Lane • Greenville, SC 29607 • USA
VeraxVoxMedia.com

Paperback, 264 pages
Publication Date: 20 January 2016
ISBN: 978-069262-643-6

Der Griff zur Macht

Dominionismus – der evangelikale Weg
zu globalem Einfluss

Die Evangelikalen suchen und gewinnen immer mehr Anerkennung und Einfluss in Gesellschaft und Politik. Doch zu welchem Preis? Entspricht dieser Weg dem biblischen Evangelium oder ist er ein Irrweg? Es ist Zeit, dass die Christen die wahren Beweggründe von „besucherfreundlichen Gottesdiensten", „Emerging Church", Rick Warrens Bestrebungen und der „Transformation" von Gemeinden und Gesellschaft erfahren. Dr. Martin Erdmann ist ein profunder Kenner der Zusammenhänge auf christlicher, politischer und wirtschaftlicher Ebene und verdeutlicht hier eine brisante und eklatante Notlage.

Betanien Verlag
Imkerweg 38 • 32832 Augustdorf • Deutschland
https://www.cbuch.de

Paperback, 287 Seiten
Veröffentlichungsdatum: 17. November 2011
ISBN: 978-393555-897-6

Made in the USA
Middletown, DE
01 August 2021